Disaster and Emergency Management Methods

Find the answers to disaster and emergency management research questions with *Disaster and Emergency Management Methods*. Written to engage students and provide a flexible foundation for instructors and practitioners, this interdisciplinary textbook provides a holistic understanding of disaster and emergency management research methods used in the field.

The disaster and emergency management contexts have a host of challenges that affect the research process that subsequently shape methodological approaches, data quality, analysis, and inferences. In this book, readers are presented with the considerations that must be made before engaging in the research process, in addition to a variety of qualitative and quantitative methodological approaches that are currently being used in the discipline. Current, relevant, and fascinating real-world applications provide a window into how each approach is being applied in the field.

Disaster and Emergency Management Methods serves as an effective way to empower readers to approach their own study of disaster and emergency management research methods with confidence.

Jason D. Rivera is an associate professor in the Department of Political Science and Public Administration at SUNY Buffalo State. He has completed research on all phases of disaster and emergency management using a broad range of methodological approaches and designs as a means of focusing on individual decision-making and behavior. Rivera is also interested in issues related to social equity, governance, organizational structures, and epistemology. Prior to his arrival at SUNY Buffalo State, Rivera earned his PhD at Rutgers University–Camden in public affairs and worked as a research associate at two different academic institutions: the William J. Hughes Center for Public Policy at Stockton University and the Liberal Arts and Science Institute for Research and Community Service at Rowan University.

"Each chapter in this edited volume offers novel insights into the pitfalls, promise, and possibilities of studying disasters. The authors, who write from many disciplinary perspectives, carefully consider a range of ethical and methodological approaches that advance the conduct and rigor of research in this area. This essential work is sure to become required reading for a generation of disaster and emergency management researchers."

Lori Peek, *Department of Sociology and Natural Hazards Center, University of Colorado Boulder*

"We have seen increased occurrences of disasters and crises during the last decade or so. Hurricanes, earthquakes, riots, terrorism, and COVID-19, of course, are some of the examples of these occurrences. As necessitated by this reality of our time, there is a substantial interest researching emergencies and crises, and identifying effective ways and means in dealing with them and building resilient communities. This volume provides perspectives for novice and experienced researchers alike from interdisciplinary perspectives."

Naim Kapucu, *Pegasus Professor, School of Public Administration, University of Central Florida (UCF)*

"Disaster and Emergency Management Methods, edited by Jason Rivera and featuring top researchers, is an important book that addresses a critical gap in the literature. Research should drive decision making. There are, however, few guides for conducting research in disaster scenarios. This book provides critical information to current and future researchers, guiding the conduct of effective data collection. Quality research will produce quality decisions. This book will help us to conduct quality research."

William Pelfrey, *Professor, program chair – homeland security and emergency preparedness, Virginia Commonwealth University*

"Dr. Rivera has drawn on his unique background and extensive research experience to put together a must-read methods primer for the field of study. This book offers a thoughtful approach to disaster research, written by experts in each dimension of the field. This book should be required reading in every emergency management program and would make a great addition to any applied policy methods course."

Warren S. Eller, *Associate Professor and Chair, Department of Public Management, John Jay College of Criminal Justice, CUNY*

Disaster and Emergency Management Methods

Social Science Approaches in Application

Edited by Jason D. Rivera

Routledge
Taylor & Francis Group

NEW YORK AND LONDON

First published 2022
by Routledge
605 Third Avenue, New York, NY 10158

and by Routledge
2 Park Square, Milton Park, Abingdon, Oxon, OX14 4RN

Routledge is an imprint of the Taylor & Francis Group, an informa business

Library of Congress Cataloging-in-Publication Data
Names: Rivera, Jason David, 1983– editor.
Title: Disaster and emergency management methods : social science approaches in application / edited by Jason Rivera.
Description: First Edition. | New York : Routledge, 2021. | Includes bibliographical references and index.
Identifiers: LCCN 2021005626 (print) | LCCN 2021005627 (ebook) | ISBN 9780367423988 (Hardback) | ISBN 9780367423964 (Paperback) | ISBN 9780367823948 (eBook) | ISBN 9781000411102 (Adobe PDF) | ISBN 9781000411164 (ePub)
Subjects: LCSH: Emergency management.
Classification: LCC HV551.2 .D49 2021 (print) | LCC HV551.2 (ebook) | DDC 363.34/8072—dc23
LC record available at https://lccn.loc.gov/2021005626
LC ebook record available at https://lccn.loc.gov/2021005627

ISBN: 978-0-367-42398-8 (hbk)
ISBN: 978-0-367-42396-4 (pbk)
ISBN: 978-0-367-82394-8 (ebk)

Typeset in Bembo STD and Helvetica Neue LT Pro
by Apex CoVantage, LLC

Contents

Boxes

Figures

Tables

Foreword

Disaster and Emergency Management Methods

I believe most disaster experts would agree that 2020 was truly an extraordinary year in terms of hazard events and their impacts on communities around the world. The record-breaking, raging wildfires on the West Coast of the United States, the most active Atlantic hurricane season on record, and the devastating COVID-19 global pandemic have had far-reaching health, social, economic, and political consequences. Further, most scientists agree that if 2020 does not become the warmest year on record globally, it will certainly be among the top five, potentially leading to even more severe hurricane seasons and wildfires.

Further, global demographic shifts taking place and the increasing proportion of population groups living in hazard-prone areas (e.g., coastal communities, floodplains), combined with the environmental consequences of climate change, mean that an ever-increasing proportion of the global population – especially highly vulnerable communities – will be at higher risk of adverse impacts from hazard events. On the public health side, COVID-19 has disproportionately affected highly vulnerable communities, especially communities of color in the United States. However, data documenting the impacts of COVID-19 on these communities has been fairly limited, and only now are we starting to see emerging research in this critical area.

This state of affairs also highlights the importance of studying these events from an interdisciplinary or transdisciplinary perspective. It also underscores the urgent need to collect qualitative and/or quantitative data that will allow us to understand the genesis, impact, and consequences of these emergencies and disasters, whether the product of natural hazard events (e.g., hurricanes, earthquakes, or floods) or a pandemic.

The kind of data we collect and the research methodology we use – whether qualitative, quantitative, or a combination thereof – may be determined by the event itself, including its duration, severity, and effects, as well as the research questions we seek to answer. However, one of the most pressing research concerns following hazard events is that some or much of the data is perishable. Consequently, if researchers do not respond quickly, these data may be lost forever, severely limiting our knowledge and access to "lessons learned" regarding these devastating events.

As highlighted by Brenda D. Phillips in this volume, "Researchers also worry that data may be perishable or lost if not secured during the response phase." Therefore, it is imperative that disaster scholars have a clear understanding of the types of data they need, what processes to follow, and the methodologies needed for data collection and analysis. Determining which is the most adequate methodology to answer our research questions is of critical importance. *Disaster and Emergency Management Methods* represents an important and significant effort to address these issues, and it does so quite successfully.

In his introduction, editor Jason D. Rivera indicates that social scientists in the disaster field have been "limited in their attention to exposing readers to *how* one might engage in research and/or data analysis, as opposed to educating the reader on what research designs are available to them." This edited volume aims to bridge this gap and provide disaster researchers, and others interested in this field, with the knowledge and tools to study disaster or emergency management topics using different methodological approaches, including quantitative and qualitative designs and techniques.

Disaster and Emergency Management Methods is an in-depth exploration into the research methodology that is available to researchers in the disaster or emergency management fields, with a concentrated focus on both qualitative and quantitative methodologies. Each chapter focuses on a different methodological approach with a focus on "how to" conduct research using the corresponding methodology, highlighting the challenges and opportunities provided by different methods, as well as the "dos" and the "don'ts" as we develop and implement our research design.

The goal of this edited volume is to help researchers enhance and expand their knowledge and expertise in developing and implementing research projects using different methodological approaches by discussing "lessons learned" through actual research; avoiding major pitfalls (i.e., ecological fallacy); taking into account ethical considerations; and navigating the research process. One of the strengths of this volume is that many of the authors create interconnections by cross-referencing and referring the reader to other relevant chapters. This helps alleviate the tendency of edited volumes to feel disjointed.

Part II concentrates on qualitative methodologies, ranging from focus groups to observation research, ethnographic methods, and content analysis, among others. Michèle Companion's discussion of site mapping as participatory action research is particularly compelling. She refers to "the identification and prioritization of resources that have cultural value, such as sacred sites, memorials, public and sacred art, and medicinal or sacred plants, or historical value, such as cemeteries, buildings, churches, sacred or cultural landscapes, and pilgrimage routes, that may be threatened" by a hazard event. This and other chapters throughout the volume allow researchers to explore important and innovative data collection strategies.

Part III is organized around quantitative methodologies, including using large secondary datasets, probability and non-probability samples, statistical modeling, multiple and logistic regression, social network analysis, and quasi-experimental research. Further, the use of geographic information systems (GIS) in mapping resilience, which has become an increasingly popular technique, is also covered in this volume. As with other chapters, the GIS discussion provides a general overview of the tools and techniques used and the types of research questions that can be addressed with GIS, as well as its application to actual hazards and disasters.

Quite appropriately, other chapters, such as the one by Barbara R. Russo, focus on mixed-methods research in disaster and emergency management. Russo argues that as "qualitative and quantitative mixed-methods research in disaster and emergency management continues to develop, it is only natural that these approaches have gained in popularity." Throughout her chapter, Russo highlights how the mixed-methods approach "brings the best of both quantitative and qualitative worlds to the table."

Further, in their chapter on sampling, Borie-Holtz and Koning argue that in survey methodology, there is not a "one-size-fits-all" study design. This also generally applies to the use of both qualitative and quantitative methodologies, and it is perhaps one of the major reasons why mixed-methods research in disaster and emergency management research studies is gaining in popularity, especially among new and emerging scholars.

While this volume includes the obligatory chapter on ethical challenges in research, one of the prevailing and unifying themes across many chapters is the ethical implications of studying populations impacted by disasters, especially highly vulnerable population groups. For example, the chapter by Rivera and Fothergill focuses on studying vulnerable populations in disasters, especially children and Native American communities, which is a much-needed consideration in the disaster and emergency management field.

Many of the chapters are further strengthened by the intersection of the methodologies being discussed with actual research studies on disasters and emergency management. Showing how these methods actually apply and can be implemented in disaster research, using specific disaster studies, is key, especially for researchers who want to utilize some of these methodologies in their own research work.

Another major strength of this volume is its interdisciplinary approach, with the integration of researchers from political science, public policy, emergency management, sociology, public affairs, public administration, urban studies, business administration, economics, and engineering. The volume includes both "traditional" and long-standing academic researchers but also includes some practitioners, who add a different and important approach and perspective to the study of disasters and emergency management.

This edited volume has a good mix of established scholars and researchers in the disaster research field, but also new and emerging scholars. It is very heartening to see a number of doctoral students as co-authors in some of the chapters. Training the next generation of disaster researchers and expanding the pipeline of the excellent research that will follow is particularly important, and this volume will play an important role in this regard.

The social science disaster research field is a growing and evolving field of study. Since the emergence of the Disaster Research Center (DRC) in 1963, the field has expanded in substance and in its methodological approaches. It has also become an increasingly interdisciplinary field of study, which brings with it a mix of new perspectives and methodological frameworks, as highlighted throughout these pages. Moreover, given the increasing complexity of disasters, as stated by Storr and Haeffele in their chapter, "disaster studies as a field must be multidisciplinary and multi-method." As discussed in their chapter, researchers must ask the poignant questions, and these questions should drive the methodology that we will use, not the other way around. Moreover, the heterogeneity and interdisciplinarity of the disaster and emergency management field will certainly generate issues and questions that require a multi-method approach. This volume is certainly an important step in the right direction.

Havidán Rodríguez

Acknowledgments

This volume benefited from the support and insights of many people.

First, I would like to thank my first mentor in disaster sciences and emergency management, Dr. DeMond S. Miller. Without Dr. Miller's tutelage and guidance, my career in this field would not have been possible.

Second, I would like to thank members of the American Society for Public Administration's (ASPA) Section on Emergency and Crisis Management (SECM) for their continued comments, suggestions, and support of this project.

Third, I would like to thank my family for their love and constant support.

Finally, I would like to thank the contributors of this volume, who worked through the COVID-19 pandemic in 2020 to make this project a reality. Your contributions and insights are more than appreciated and will enhance the study of disaster science and emergency management for years to come.

Contributors

Daniel P. Aldrich is Director of the Security and Resilience Studies Program and Professor in political science and public policy at Northeastern University in Boston. An award-winning author, he has published five books, including *Building Resilience* and *Black Wave*, and more than 55 peer-reviewed articles. He has written op-eds for the *New York Times, CNN, HuffPost*, and many other media outlets. He has spent more than 5 years in Japan carrying out fieldwork, and his work has been funded by the Fulbright Foundation, the National Science Foundation, the Abe Foundation, and the Japan Foundation.

DeeDee M. Bennett Gayle, PhD, is an associate professor at the University at Albany, State University of New York, in the College of Emergency Preparedness, Homeland Security, and Cybersecurity. Her research areas include emergency management, socially vulnerable populations during disasters, emergency communications, disaster policy, and mobile wireless communications. She received her PhD from Oklahoma State University in fire and emergency management. In addition to bringing expertise in emergency management, she has a unique academic background, having received both her MS in public policy and BS in electrical engineering from the Georgia Institute of Technology.

Debra Borie-Holtz is an associate professor of teaching at the Bloustein School at Rutgers University, where she also received her master's degree in public affairs and politics and her doctorate in planning and public policy. At the Eagleton Center for Public Interest Polling, she is the senior survey scholar and directs survey research projects for public, non-profit, and academic clients ranging from surveying populations in the aftermath of disasters and health outbreaks to national research on attitudes about climate change. She also specializes in polling issues from elections, legislative leadership, and social and economic behaviors. She is an expert on the intersection of politics and governing. Her scholarship and firsthand experience provide unique insights into the inner workings of party caucuses, legislative leadership, and gender. Before returning to Rutgers, she spent 20 years in senior government roles, including as chief of staff to the New Jersey majority leader, as the New Jersey assistant secretary of state, and as a presidential appointee in President Clinton's administration. She is also the co-author of *The Politics of Regulatory Reform*.

Monica Andrea Bustinza is a PhD candidate at Florida International University in the Department of Public Policy and Administration. Her research uses qualitative and quantitative approaches to examine the impact of local administrative actions on citizen participation within the United States. In doing so, she integrates ideas and concepts rooted in various disciplines to explain some of the connections between bureaucracy and democracy.

Michèle Companion is a professor of sociology at the University of Colorado–Colorado Springs. She is a food and livelihood security specialist, working in countries across the globe and in the United States with Native American Nations and international non-governmental organizations. Her work examines the link between cultural change and food access, including the expansion and development of market-based food security indicators to increase local sensitivity to food crisis triggers and on population displacement, migration, and resettlement. She also researches indigenous nutritional dynamics, including the impact of low-income diets on overall health outcomes and cultural survival. She has recently been examining Native American participation in the food sovereignty movements and cultural barriers to healthy eating among low-income urban Native American populations.

Stephen Danley is an associate professor and graduate director of the MS/PhD program in public affairs at Rutgers University–Camden. His research focuses on participation and protest, particularly in the context of segregation. He received a Marshall Scholarship and completed his DPhil at the University of Oxford, Nuffield College.

Frances L. Edwards is the Deputy Director of the National Transportation Security Center at the Mineta Transportation Institute and a professor and Director of the master of public administration program at San Jose State University. She is the past chair of the section on emergency and crisis management of the American Society for Public Administration. In her applied research, she focuses on community emergency management, including transportation issues and cultural competency. She is the editor or co-author of four books and numerous journal articles and book chapters. For 20 years she was an emergency management practitioner and is a certified emergency manager.

Alice Fothergill is Professor of sociology at the University of Vermont. She wrote the award-winning book, *Children of Katrina*, with co-researcher Lori Peek. She is an editor of *Social Vulnerability to Disasters* and the author of *Heads Above Water: Gender, Class, and Family in the Grand Forks Flood*. She studied volunteerism in the aftermath of the 9/11 terrorist attacks in New York City, and she was recently a Fulbright Fellow in New Zealand studying disaster preparedness for childcare centers. She is currently working on a study of children and older adults in the COVID-19 pandemic.

Timothy Fraser is a PhD candidate in political science at Northeastern University. His research had been funded by a 2020 Japan Foundation doctoral fellowship and 2016 Fulbright Fellowship. He has authored or co-authored 15 peer-reviewed studies and 6 working papers on disaster resilience and energy policy in the United States and Japan. His research highlights the role of social networks in communities' adaptation to climate change.

Nazife Emel Ganapati is an associate professor of public policy and administration and the Director of the Laboratory for Social Science Research, International Hurricane Research Center, Extreme Events Institute at Florida International University. She has served as the principal investigator (PI) or co-PI of several National Science Foundation (NSF) projects related to disaster recovery and resilience in the United States, Nepal, and Haiti. She currently serves as a member of FIU's Institutional Review Board for Social Sciences. She is a recipient of the Florida Education Fund's statewide 2018 William R. Jones Outstanding Mentor Award.

Jerry V. Graves is an environmental planning and emergency management consultant based in New Orleans, Louisiana. He is also an adjunct instructor at Tulane University and the University of New Orleans (UNO). He earned a doctorate in urban studies and master's degree in public administration from UNO. He also earned a bachelor's degree in political science from the University of Louisiana at Lafayette.

Stefanie Haeffele is a senior fellow for the F. A. Hayek Program for Advanced Study in Philosophy, Politics, and Economics at the Mercatus Center at George Mason University. She is the co-author of *Community Revival in the Wake of Disaster* (2015), along with Virgil Henry Storr and Laura E. Grube.

Kira Haensel is a PhD student in the business administration program at Florida International University's College of Business. She has a background in public administration. Her research interests are corporate sustainability and responsibility; in particular, the strategic management of environmental, social, and corporate governance activities of firms, their antecedents and consequences, and the management of crises.

Paul A. Jargowsky, PhD, is Professor of public policy at Rutgers University–Camden and Director of the Center for Urban Research and Education. His principal research interests are inequality, the geographic concentration of poverty, and residential segregation by race and class. He received a PhD in public policy in 1991 from Harvard University. He was a 2016–2017 Fellow at the Center for Advanced Study in the Behavioral Sciences (CASBS) at Stanford University. At Rutgers–Camden, he teaches courses on social policy and empirical methods in the PhD in public affairs program.

Claire Connolly Knox, PhD, an associate professor in the University of Central Florida's School of Public Administration, holds a joint appointment with the National Center for Integrated Coastal Research. She is an expert in environmental vulnerability, coastal resilience, and Habermas critical theory, and specializes in analyzing post-disaster plans and policies. Her analysis of Hurricanes Andrew, Katrina, Sandy, and Irma; the 2004 Florida hurricane season; the Boston Marathon bombing; and the 2016 Louisiana flood are in top-ranked journals. Routledge published her co-edited book, *Cultural Competency for Emergency and Crisis Management: Concepts, Theories and Case Studies*, in 2020. She serves as Chair of the ASPA's Section on Emergency and Crisis Management.

Ashley Koning is Director of the Eagleton Center for Public Interest Polling (ECPIP), the oldest statewide university-based survey research center in the country.

She runs and is the face of the Rutgers–Eagleton Poll, oversees all client projects, and manages a staff of undergraduate and graduate students to assist with day-to-day polling operations and studies. She has co-authored several book chapters and papers on public opinion. She was awarded the 2015 John Tarnai Memorial Scholarship by the Association of Academic Survey Research Organizations (AASRO) and was the recipient of the 2012 American Association for Public Opinion Research (AAPOR) Student Travel Award, the first-ever AAPOR Student Poster Award (2015), and the 2016 AAPOR Burns "Bud" Roper Fellow Award. She serves on the council of the Pennsylvania/New Jersey chapter of the AAPOR and on committees for AAPOR and AASRO at the national level.

Salimah LaForce is a research scientist at the Georgia Institute of Technology, and she serves as the senior policy analyst at Georgia Tech's Center for Advanced Communications Policy (CACP). She has 14 years' experience conducting research for CACP's emergency communications initiatives. She is a project director and co-investigator on several federally funded projects to build capacity for inclusive emergency response efforts, improve health outcomes for at-risk and underserved populations, increase accessibility and usability of wireless technologies, and improve employment outcomes for individuals with disabilities. She has co-authored more than 78 federal regulatory filings, papers, presentations, and journal articles.

Maureen Linden, MS, is a research engineer at the Georgia Institute of Technology's Center for Inclusive Design and Innovation. Her research identifies best practices in providing people with disabilities equitable access to participate in all aspects of society including education, employment, mobility, and access to new and emerging technologies. She has also managed programs in both medical and vocational rehabilitation models that deliver services to people with disabilities. She holds degrees in electrical and biomedical engineering from the University of Virginia. Presently, she is president of the Rehabilitation Engineering and Assistive Technology Society of North America (RESNA).

Jazmyne McNeese is a doctoral candidate at Rutgers University–Camden studying race, wealth, and business ownership. Originally from Los Angeles California, she obtained her BA in sociology with a minor in African American studies from the University of California, Irvine. her passion for advocacy reflects in her on- and off-campus experiences, where she developed an identity as a community organizer and researcher. Since relocating to New Jersey, she has worked with various organizations and state agencies, including New Jersey Policy Perspective, New Jersey Community Capital, and the Department of Community Affairs. She identifies as a researcher, unapologetic advocate, and a proud member of Delta Sigma Theta Sorority Incorporated.

Njoki Mwarumba is an assistant professor of emergency management and disaster science at the University of Nebraska, Omaha. Her PhD dissertation investigated global social vulnerability during the 2009 H1N1 pandemic. She reviewed commonly applied indicators for health, education, and economic indicators as well as some not typically integrated in investigating vulnerability to public health disasters, such as aviation patterns, corruption, governance, and human development – indicators she believes are pivotal in understanding vulnerability to public health disasters prior to leveraging resilience building. She also has research interests that highlight building social capacity in marginalized and indigenous communities and complex emergencies. She is a volunteer with the American Red Cross as a National Response Team member, with experience as a shelter support staff member and government operations liaison. During the COVID-19 pandemic, she has been engaged in various expert panel interviews, policy development, research, and community outreach in Kenya and the United States.

Mwarumba Mwavita is an associate professor in research, evaluation, measurement, and statistics and the Director of the Center for Educational Research and Evaluation at Oklahoma State University.

Courtney Page-Tan leverages her background in social capital, resilience, public policy, and GIS to explain how stakeholders can build resilience to unexpected shocks and disturbances by investing into online and offline social ties. She has consulted for UNDP–Paraguay, UNDP–Mexico, private sector technology firms, and local governments. Her research has been supported by outside grants and funding from diverse sources, such as federal government entities, local governments, private sector partners, and research institutions, including the Natural Hazards Center at the University of Colorado–Boulder and Northeastern University.

Sis. Anetha Perry is a PhD student in public affairs at Rutgers University–Camden. Sis. Perry was raised in Camden, New Jersey, with research interests including community development and empowerment. She was recognized as the Department of Public Policy and Administration's PhD Student of the Year in 2016.

Brenda D. Phillips, PhD, is the Dean of the College of Liberal Arts and Sciences and Professor of sociology at Indiana University South Bend. She is the lead author of *Introduction to Emergency Management and Business Continuity Planning* and the sole author of *Qualitative Disaster Research, Disaster Volunteers, Disaster Recovery* and *Mennonite Disaster Service*. She co-edited *Social Vulnerability to Disasters* and is the author of dozens of peer-reviewed publications, many funded by the National Science Foundation.

Lili Razi is currently pursuing a doctorate degree in public affairs with a focus on community development. Her research interests include urban sustainability, social and economic development strategies, civic engagement, and models of community participation in decision-making. Her experiences in architecture and urban planning engineering firms, and in adopting a participatory approach in non-governmental capacity development institutions, reinforced her decision to attain a post-graduate degree in development studies to elevate her future chances for shaping effective public policies.

Christa L. Remington is an assistant professor of public administration at the University of South Florida, where she teaches emergency management and non-profit leadership. She holds a master's degree in public administration and a PhD in public affairs from Florida International University in Miami. With a focus on cultural competence, training, and organizational policies, her research aims to improve the effectiveness of post-disaster response and recovery programs and reduce the negative impacts of the job on first responders and recovery workers.

Jason D. Rivera is an associate professor of political science and public administration, coordinator of the public administration track of the master of public administration (MPA) and the advanced certificate in disaster and emergency management program at SUNY Buffalo State. He is the co-author of *Hurricane Katrina and the Redefinition of Landscape* and a co-editor of several volumes dedicated to disaster and emergency management. He earned his PhD in public affairs at Rutgers University–Camden with a specialization in community development. He enjoys teaching courses in disaster and emergency management, public administration theory, organizational behavior, ethics, and epistemology.

Barbara R. Russo, PhD, CEM, currently serves as the Program Director and Assistant Professor for the Emergency Management and Homeland Security graduate program at Brevard College (NC). She has been involved in fire and emergency services for more than 20 years, serving as a career fire professional and emergency manager as well as an academic. Her research interests include gender and race in the fire and emergency services as well as emergency management policy.

Virgil Henry Storr is an associate professor of economics at George Mason University and the Don C. Lavoie Senior Fellow with the F. A. Hayek Program for Advanced Study in Philosophy, Politics, and Economics at the Mercatus Center at George Mason University. He is the co-author of *Community Revival in the Wake of Disaster* (2015) along with Stefanie Haeffele and Laura E. Grube.

Richard Sylves, PhD, is an emeritus professor of political science and international relations at the University of Delaware (1977–2010) and retired adjunct professor of the Department of Systems Management, Institute for Risk, Emergency and Crisis Management at The George Washington University (DC) (2010–2015). He has authored one university press book, has co-edited two books on emergency management, and is the author of *Disaster Policy and Politics* (2008, 2015, and 2020), now in its third edition. He is a recognized expert on presidential disaster declarations and has taught, lectured, and delivered speeches on U.S. disaster policy. He has served on a National Research Council panel on reducing the costs of natural disasters (1999–2000), and from 2002–2005 he was an appointed member of the National Academy of Science Board on Disasters. He won the Dr. Wayne Blanchard Award at FEMA for Excellence in Emergency Management Research.

Kaila Witkowski is a PhD candidate at Florida International University. Her research focuses on using mixed-method techniques to improve government action and policy outcomes responding to stigmatized health issues such as opioid abuse and HIV. Using methods such as network analysis, PhotoVoice, and plan quality assessment, she has recently completed projects on engaging long-term HIV survivors in the policy-making process and improving cross-sector collaborations focused on the opioid epidemic.

Introduction
Engaging in Research Within the Disaster and Emergency Management Context

Jason D. Rivera

Being a Student Interested in Disaster and Emergency Management

When should I go? How should I get there? Who should I speak to? What should I ask them? What shouldn't I ask them? How should I record the data? How should I analyze the data, and should I use software to help? Do I allow my participants to know what my results are before I publish them? What if I do not accurately reflect my participants' experiences? Will my research be meaningful?

These were some of the questions that went through my mind the first several times I attempted to approach research in the disaster and emergency management context on my own. Although I had been exposed to the disaster and emergency management field by the time I entered my doctoral program, I quickly learned that doing research on my own versus being mentored through it were very different things. Moreover, trying to bridge the academic disciplinary divide between my previous research experiences with sociologists and anthropologists to the fields of political science, public administration, and public policy was, for me, a bumpy road.

At the time, and to a certain extent now, I felt that these disciplines sometimes spoke different languages. They used unique jargon to explain social phenomena and placed different value on the events or variables that contributed to a particular event, policy, or behavior under study. Subsequently, as I internalized the materials presented in my methods courses and spoke to various researchers and practitioners at academic conferences and professional meetings, I learned that these disciplines were and are fundamentally interested in the same social phenomena related to disaster and emergency management. However, what was different were the research methods, designs, and theoretical orientations that each discipline and researcher favored to answer their questions about a particular phenomenon. Moreover, there were many methodological writings throughout the social sciences that emphasized the merit of quantitative research designs over qualitative, qualitative over quantitative, and even the use of mixed methods to combat the weaknesses of both quantitative and qualitative designs.

As a result, and still being a naïve doctoral student, I wanted to know what the "best" methodological approach to building knowledge was. Throughout my methods courses, at all levels of my formal education, I was exposed to examples of how to apply each of the broad methodological categories to one's research; however, in almost all circumstances, the examples that were provided within methods textbooks and journal articles, in addition to my respective professors, were situated in the traditional examples offered within various social science disciplines. I remember learning how survey methods were applied to the study of voting behavior, how to interview when studying neighborhood satisfaction, various statistical techniques to studying public housing policy, and focus group methods to understand public service professionals' views on program efficiency. The list goes on and on. But, what was missing were examples from the field I was most interested in – disaster and emergency management.

As many of my fellow MPA and doctoral students were able to directly apply what they learned in our methods courses to their own research interests, I struggled to make the connections and apply the same concepts and research practices to disaster science and emergency management. Moreover, there were issues related to research ethics, logistics, sampling, and personal risk indicative to completing field research in the disaster and emergency management context that were not discussed in any of my coursework. In all fairness, I should point out that I did not attend a school that contained anything similar to an emergency management program. All but a few professors I had the opportunity to learn from in a classroom setting had a research interest in the subject. So, in hindsight I should not have been surprised that there was little focus on applying methods to my field of interest. However, because of the lack of formal exposure to the application of research methods in the disaster and emergency management field, I relied on mentors, and mentors of those mentors, to understand how to complete research in this field. It is not an understatement to say that without them, I do not know where I would be.

Social Science Research and the Disaster and Emergency Management Context

Although the experiences I encountered and discuss above were my own, they have by no means been experienced only by me. Over the course of teaching across various institutions, interacting with students and professionals at all levels, in addition to speaking with fellow colleagues, I have come to understand my experiences were not isolated. More to the point, many students within various academic disciplines, interested in disaster and emergency management, continue to be under-served. When disaster and emergency management students are taught research methods, professors typically rely on texts from other academic disciplines, such as political science, public administration, sociology, and so forth. Although this reliance is practical, it is not necessarily efficient in exposing students to a broad range of methodological challenges indicative to the disaster and/or emergency management context.

The disaster and emergency management contexts have a host of challenges that can influence the research process and shape methodological approaches, data quality, analysis, and inferences. At times, some of these challenges are similar to those of other academic disciplines; however, at other times they are unique (Killian, 1956;

Stallings, 2002). Moreover, the reliance on discipline specific texts contributes to the potential of limiting interdisciplinary research and collaboration because they commonly place a preference on one "empirical" qualitative and/or quantitative method over another. This disciplinary valuing of one empirical approach over another can result in freshly degreed researchers who are skeptical of studies that engage in methodological approaches or even academic disciplines different from their own (Mahoney & Goetz, 2006). Mahoney and Goetz (2006) maintain that this methodological suspicion of the "other" is a by-product of different research goals and the use of different terms, as opposed to a true difference in data quality and rigor. Gerring (2001), also points out that "good scholarship" is that which talks to those in other social science fields, and not just to one's own.

To this end, King, Keohane, and Verba (1994, pp. 7–9) maintain that there are four characteristics that define all quality social science research: inference is the goal, procedures are public, conclusions are uncertain, and content is the method. The notion that procedures are public refers to a researcher's practice of explicitly detailing the method and logic of one's observations and inferences. Without explicitly detailing what was done in a study, there is no way to judge the scholarship's validity, the way observations were processed or recorded, or the logic by which conclusions were drawn. Moreover, "We cannot learn from their methods or replicate their results" (King et al., 1994, p. 8). Although King et al. speak generally of the social sciences, they maintain that researchers' practice of being methodologically transparent provides other scholars and students insight into the advantages and limitations of methods, which is critically important within the disaster and emergency management field. As such, the need to understand how methods are applied and the process through which a scholar employs respective approaches within the field of disaster and emergency management is a curricular need for enhancing scholarship.

But, despite the need and general increased interest in the field of disaster and emergency management, few extant books provide a holistic understanding of the application of social science research methods to the field. For example, Stallings (2002) provides a detailed discussion of the advantages and challenges of applying a variety of qualitative and quantitative designs to the disaster and emergency management context. The contributors to Stallings's volume provide students and researchers insight into the logistics of conducting research in the post-disaster setting, in addition to various ways in which data generated through primary research might be analyzed. Although Stallings's work is twenty years old, and various technological and methodological innovations have occurred since the work's publication, the volume continues to provide holistic examples of how and when to use a variety of research methods.

In addition to Stallings's work, Rodríguez, Quarantelli, and Dynes (2007) and Rodríguez, Donner, and Trainor (2018) are major contributions to the field of disaster and emergency management research methods. These two volumes provide students, practitioners, and academicians insight on the various research streams within disaster and emergency management literature. Specifically, the contributors of these two volumes discuss the trajectory of literature across a variety of academic disciplines on particular disaster and emergency management topics. Many of the contributions to each of these volumes discuss what methodological designs have been used in the context of collecting data germane to the disaster science and emergency management context. Similarly, Tierney (2019) discusses how researchers have approached the study of disasters using a variety of methodological approaches from a sociological perspective. She articulates various challenges and advantages associated with sociological approaches, which in turn fosters the development of new research questions among readers. However, despite the profound contributions these volumes make by helping readers generate their own research questions, they are limited in their attention to exposing readers to *how* one might engage in research and/or the analysis of data, as opposed to educating the reader on what research designs are available to them.

Along these lines, there are a few volumes that focus on *how* to conduct various types of research designs and analyses when studying disaster and/or emergency management topics. For example, Phillips (2014), provides instruction on how to go about conducting qualitative research designs in the context of disaster research. Her work provides students and researchers guidance on choosing an appropriate design, how to complete some qualitative data collection techniques, analyze data, write up results, and evaluate the work of others. Similarly, Upson and Notarianni (2012), provide guidance to students, professionals, and researchers in reference to completing quantitative research. Focusing on the context of fire and emergency medical services management, the authors guide the reader through the development of research questions, participant recruitment, and data collection and analysis. Finally, Norris, Galea, Friedman, and Watson (2006) provide insight into completing research on mental health within the disaster and emergency management field. Norris et al.'s volume provides not only background on the field of disaster research, similar to Rodríguez et al. (2007) and Rodríguez et al. (2018), but they also guide the reader through the development of research questions, in addition to sampling populations and collecting various types of data within a variety of organizational and community contexts.

Although each of these volumes provides rich information on various types of research designs that can be used within disaster and emergency management contexts, there are few that actually provide readers with the tools to complete research using these respective methods. Those that do provide some guidance are limited to specific types of data collection and/or analytic strategies. Additionally, many of these works are written with the experienced researcher or advanced student in mind, utilizing jargon and technical information and taking basic research method concepts for granted. In response, more junior-level students, professionals in the public and non-profit sectors, and individuals new to the field are limited in their access to the information contained within their pages.

Structure of This Volume

In response to this situation, this interdisciplinary edited volume exposes researchers, students, practitioners, and the generally interested reader to various research methods that are used to study topics related to disaster and emergency management. Throughout this entire volume, contributors draw on their own professional research experiences as they discuss various aspects of research, in addition to different methodological approaches and designs. Contributors not only provide technical information related to the advantages and challenges of a particular data collection and/or analytic approach, but they also provide insight into their own experiences attempting to utilize a respective technique. In this way, students, researchers, and the general reader become more aware of the realities of the research process when applying a particular strategy. Moreover, through the personalized examples provided by many of the contributors, the reader will become aware that challenges throughout the research process can, and typically do, occur no matter how experienced a researcher is.

To accomplish these goals, this book is organized into three sections. In Part I, the reader is exposed to various pre-research concepts that every researcher should think about before engaging in a study. As such, the section starts out with a discussion about research ethics and their application when dealing with human subjects. Although Chapter 1 is entirely dedicated to this concept, contributors throughout this entire volume revisit the notion of ethics within the application of various research designs. After discussing the profound importance of adhering to ethical standards, the rest of the section discusses some other general issues that should be considered before engaging in the research process. Specifically, Chapters 2 and 3 cover various sampling strategies and the use of various samples in disaster and emergency management research. The underlying theme of both these chapters is that variations in sampling strategy should be chosen based on what is most conducive to a researcher's questions and respective setting. Moreover, they also discuss how different samples influence a study's respective internal and external validity – in other words, the types of inferences one might draw from their analysis.

In addition to these preliminary considerations, Chapter 4 provides readers with a brief exposure to the theoretical underpinnings of qualitative, quantitative and mixed-methods research. Through the discussion of research paradigms, readers have the ability to consider what types of research designs are best suited to their respective studies, in addition to which theoretical orientation(s) they might personally subscribe to. Finally, in Chapter 5, the authors discuss the investigation of vulnerable populations in disaster and emergency management research. The authors of this chapter discuss what vulnerability is and revisit the discussion of ethical considerations when dealing with vulnerable populations. As opposed to just discussing how these communities have been studied in the past, this chapter highlights strategies that researchers should think about and can use to engage in research more successfully with vulnerable populations.

After discussing some topics that all researchers should consider before jumping into research, the book breaks into two separate sections. Part II focuses on some common qualitative research methods and designs used to conduct studies in the disaster and emergency management context. Contributors to this section discuss the advantages and challenges to generating primary data through the completion of interviews, focus groups, ethnography, and observational studies, in addition to applying theoretical frameworks such as language-based theories to the analysis of qualitative data. Moreover, in Chapter 12, the author provides guidance on how to access and analyze secondary qualitative data, which is typically the most accessible to new students and researchers. Throughout this section, and as a means of illustrating their points, the contributors often reminisce on their own personal research experiences in an attempt to connect with the reader.

Subsequent to discussing qualitative approaches, the book then transitions to discussing quantitative and policy designs in Part III. The section begins with a discussion on accessing large secondary datasets and the considerations that researchers should think about when using data generated by someone else. After discussing how one might acquire quantitative data, Chapter 14 provides a brief exposure to statistical modeling. This chapter provides an introduction to some statistical techniques and how to conduct these respective analyses using SPSS. This brief exposure to statistical analysis grounds even the most inexperienced researcher with a beginner's understanding of statistical analysis and the application of respective tools in the disaster and emergency management context. After this brief statistical introduction, most of the remaining chapters of this section discuss the use of various quantitative and policy approaches to studying social phenomena in the disaster and emergency management context. In addition to providing background information about a particular method or analytical approach, contributors provide instruction on how to complete respective analyses through the use of various computer software. Moreover, the section also highlights the use of quasi-experimental methods in disaster and emergency management research, which is often not used in social science studies.

Finally, the conclusion of this volume provides a discussion about the future of research methods within disaster and emergency management studies. The authors of this chapter argue that although qualitative and quantitative methods have their own unique advantages and challenges, developing more holistic answers to research questions requires the use of mixed method approaches. The authors call on researchers of all levels to be collaborative and cooperative as a means of enhancing the field and our understanding of social phenomena related to disaster and emergency management in the future.

Conclusion

Through the various discussions and personal author experiences provided throughout this book, readers will gain a better understanding of the research process specifically germane to the disaster and emergency management context. In addition to a more holistic understanding and appreciation of research processes, the varied depictions of qualitative and quantitative techniques provide guidance on how to enhance the reader's own research practices. After reading this book, new students, researchers, professionals, and the generally interested reader will be better able to apply general research method concepts and topics that are typically covered in mainstream academic discipline coursework to the context of disaster and emergency management. As such, this volume should be used alongside other course materials to provide the most effective educational experience.

It is my hope that after reading this book, some of the questions I asked myself early in my career, which I presented at the beginning of this introduction, are answered for the reader and their respective work. As Gerring (2001, p. xviii) maintains, "there is little point in studying methodology if the discoveries of this field are shared only among methodologists."

References

Gerring, J. (2001). *Social science methodology: A criterial framework*. Cambridge: Cambridge University Press.

Killian, L. (1956). *An introduction to methodological problems of field students in disasters*. National Research Council Publication No. 8. Washington, DC: National Academy of Sciences.

King, G., Keohane, R. O., & Verba, S. (1994). *Designing social inquiry: Scientific inference in qualitative research*. Princeton, NJ: Princeton University Press.

Mahoney, J., & Goetz, G. (2006). A tale of two cultures: Contrasting qualitative and quantitative research. *Political Analysis, 14*(3), 227–249.

Norris, F. H., Galea, S., Friedman, M. J., & Watson, P. J. (2006). *Methods for disaster mental health research*. New York: Guilford Press.

Phillips, B. (2014). *Qualitative disaster research: Understanding qualitative research*. Oxford: Oxford University Press.

Rodríguez, H., Donner, W., & Trainor, J. (Eds.). (2018). *Handbook of disaster research* (2nd ed.). Springer International.

Rodríguez, H., Quarantelli, E., & Dynes, R. (Eds.). (2007). *Handbook of disaster research*. Springer Science+Business Media, LLC.

Stallings, R. (Ed.). (2002). *Methods of disaster research*. International Research Committee on Disasters. Bloomington, IN: Xlibris Corporation.

Tierney, K. (2019). *Disasters: A sociological approach*. Medford, MA: Polity Press.

Upson, R., & Notarianni, K. A. (2012). *Quantitative evaluation of fire and EMS mobilization times*. Springer Science+Business Media, LLC.

Preliminary Considerations of Disaster and Emergency Management Research

1

Practical Considerations for Ethical Research in Post-disaster Communities

Frances L. Edwards

Introduction

Disaster field research design requires determining methodologies that will best collect and analyze data regarding the events and their impacts on human subjects and the natural environment. Research must consider the ethical standards that will impact the designs that are used and how they are implemented in the field. University institutional review boards (IRB)[1] enforce general norms of research in the behavioral sciences involving human subjects as articulated by the Nuremberg Code (NIH, 2016) and Belmont Report (HHS.gov, 2016). Ethical considerations for field research require the rigorous application of these norms.

Why Do Disaster Field Research?

Field research on disaster events has to be conducted as soon as possible after the event to capture the experiences of the survivors, responders, and observers while memories are fresh (Browne & Peek, 2014). Social science researchers have discovered that memories of disasters last only for a relatively brief time, no more than a decade (Economist, 2019). Yet, "collective memory is of more than just academic interest, precisely because resilience to future calamities is thought to depend on it" (Economist, 2019, p. 70). A field experiment by Fanta, Salek, and Sklenicka (2019) found that for over 1,000 years, people living in a flood prone area of Central Europe only remained away from the shoreline for one generation after a catastrophic flood, and then gradually moved back to the riverbank, only to relocate the community after the next catastrophic flood. They conclude that "living memory is apparently conditioned by the life span of the eye-witnesses. . . . However, once the eye-witnesses die out, the community forgets the consequences of such a disaster" (p. 6).

Fanta et al.'s (2019) findings validate the importance of rapid-response field research for influencing the resilience of future generations. Moreover, simple chronicles of the disaster will not impact community resilience decisions, as shown in their Central European river basin study (Economist, 2019). Rather, it must be a dynamic record of eyewitness experiences that is compelling and "not able to be downplayed"; "it is essential to keep reminding people of the extent of these events" (p. 6), a role played by effective field research reports.

As such, the goals of disaster field research are to:

- Improve the understanding of the impact of hazards on individuals, families, and communities;
- Bear witness to the event to influence people at risk in other areas, policymakers, and future generations to engage in prevention, protection, and mitigation activities; and
- Improve public policy regarding disaster preparedness and mitigation to prevent future disasters or lessen their impacts on the human community and environment for events that cannot be prevented.

Understanding Hazards

Hazards that lead to disasters can be categorized in a number of ways, but the most conventional is to describe them as natural hazards, technological hazards, or intentional human-caused hazards (FEMA, 2010). Table 1.1 lists the most common events in each category, although many other events might be viewed as hazards as well.

TABLE 1.1 Types of Hazards

Natural	Technological	Human-Caused
Rain/lightning/hail	Power outage	Medical emergency (e.g., heart attack)
Flood	Hazmat release	Industrial accident
■ Levee failure	Water system failure	Arson
Urban wildland/interface fire	Transportation accident (road, rail, air)	Urban fire/conflagration
Earthquake	Gas pipeline failure/explosion	Workplace violence
■ Shaking		Mass shooting
■ Landslides		Terrorist attack (guns)
■ Liquefaction		Terrorist attack (vehicles)
Tsunami/tidal surge		Terrorist attack (using chemicals)
Wind/tornado		Terrorist attack (using biological material)
Snow/ice/avalanche		Terrorist attack (using radiological materials)
Monsoons/hurricanes/storm surge		Terrorist attack (using explosives)
Heatwave		
Pandemic		

Source: Adapted from Edwards & Goodrich (2012).

Understanding human behavior during and in response to past disasters is critical for changing people's future behavior and building resilience (Fanta et al., 2019). Multiple factors make this knowledge increasingly important. For example, more people live in harm's way than ever before (NOAA, 2018). Moreover, 40% of the world's population lived within 100 kilometers of the coast a decade ago (Columbia University, 2006). Thus, sea level rise and cyclones (hurricanes, monsoons, and typhoons) will cause harm to more individuals and communities, increasing loss of life and economic damage.

Climate change and sea level rise make coastal living increasingly dangerous. A 2018 NASA study found that the sea level is likely to rise 26 feet by 2100 due to the expansion of warmer water and the melting of ice sheets in Greenland and the Antarctic (Weeman & Lynch, 2018), bringing the ocean's edge closer to the built environment. Sea level rise exacerbates storm surge, which caused $65 billion in damages from Hurricane Sandy in 2012. Other studies show that climate change is creating higher-intensity hurricanes, with a 2%–11% increase in wind speeds and a 20% increase in precipitation, which caused most of the damage during 2017's Hurricane Harvey (C2ES, n.d.).

Additionally, earthquake faults are found near many populous areas of the world. Scientists have determined that the Earth is made up of at least 12 tectonic plates that move against each other. "As the plates move, they may get stuck beneath the earth's surface. When the pressure has built up sufficiently, the subterranean rock breaks, causing an earthquake" (Edwards et al., 2015, p. 10). Many populous areas are affected by active tectonic plate movement, including most of the United States, western Canada, Mexico, Ecuador, El Salvador, Chile, the Caribbean, Turkey, Italy, Greece, Pakistan, India, Indonesia, the Philippines, Nepal, China, and Japan. Earthquakes are cyclical and generally predictable only within a framework of decades, or within a few seconds of initial rupture (Edwards et al., 2015).

Generally, hazardous events can be understood in a variety of ways. They may be predicted or cyclical emergencies, they may escalate in scale and impact, or they may become landscape-level catastrophes that cascade into additional impacts. A winter ice storm might begin as an emergency in a single community, but as the storm becomes regional it may be perceived as a disaster due to the number of people affected and the financial value of the damage to the natural and built environment. As it persists, it may become a catastrophe as regional power outages occur from ice on the lines, vehicle accidents are generated by ice on the roads, and water pipes freeze and break, which lead to increased human impacts, environmental damage, and escalating costs.

Disaster researchers see value in getting to the site of an event and doing research to understand how the disaster escalated, how technological systems fared, and how and why humans were impacted at such a scale. Researchers want to understand what mitigation measures had been taken for the infrastructure, what preparedness measures were taken by community members, and how first responders planned and exercised for such an event. Some questions they attempt to answer include "What plans and systems failed?"; "What elements of the response were inadequate?"; "Was the event unpredicted, or unpredictable, or was the magnitude unanticipated?"; "Did individuals, schools, hospitals, churches, non-governmental organizations, small businesses and other community members have emergency response plans for this event?"; and even "Did they implement the plans, and were they effective in mitigating losses?"

To answer these questions effectively, disaster field researchers must interview those who experienced the disaster to see how events unfolded, what the people involved perceived about the event, and how community leaders and responders understand their roles in the response and resolution. Framing and engaging in these conversations require researchers to apply ethical standards to the development of the interview, timing, sampling of respondents, the format and venues that will be used, and the questions themselves. Along these lines, the federal Common Rule (45 C.F.R. pt. 46) regulates the conduct of research using human subjects in the United States. It provides protections for participants in disaster field research, recognizing that they "contribute their time and assume risk to advance the research enterprise, which benefits society at large" (Federal Register, 2017, p. 7149). Publications such as SAMHSA's *Challenges and Considerations in Disaster Research* (2016) detail the purpose and application of disaster field research to a subset of activities, such as mental health services.[2] Moreover, Quarantelli (1997) lays out one of the earliest models and set of goals for disaster fieldwork in natural and technological events. Specifically, one goal is to understand the conditions, characteristics, consequences, and "careers" of disasters; however, "At another level, the goal was to further sociological understanding of emergent groups and organizational behavior" (Quarantelli, 1997, p. 5).

To achieve these goals, the disaster researcher must go to the impacted area soon after the event, while memories are fresh. Fieldwork in the post-disaster setting involves interviewing people "who have experienced severe loss and trauma" (Mukherji, Ganapati, & Rahill, 2014, p. 821). This also means that those memories will be painful for many interviewees, and the interview or focus group may cause the survivors to relive their traumas, creating some risk of psychological harm from post-traumatic stress disorder (Collogan, Tuma, Dolan-Sewell, Borja, & Fleishman, 2004), which is experienced by 22%–50% of disaster survivors (Canino, Bravo, Rubio-Stipec, & Woodbury, 1990; Richards, 2001). Thus, the application of the ethical standards of the Nuremberg Code and Belmont Report is crucial for all disaster field research with human subjects.

Regulatory Framework for Ethical Disaster Field Research

To ensure that all research is conducted ethically, researchers receiving federal support must submit plans for their work for review by other scholars through a governing body, known as the institutional review board (45 C.F.R. § 46.103). Disaster field researchers are generally required to take training on the concept of ethical research, which includes a review of the protocols and norms that guide research using human subjects. Additionally, they are required to complete a course and pass a test to demonstrate their understanding of the ethical structures in which they will work. To facilitate this regulation, the Collaborative Institutional Training Initiative (CITI) is one example of an organization that provides the mandatory training for scholars overseeing research (the principal investigator on a project) and researchers conducting any human subjects-based field research (CITI, n.d.).

The primary standard that provides ethical guidance for human subjects research is the Nuremberg Code of 1949 (NIH, 2016; see Box 1.1). Following the medical experiments that were conducted on prisoners during World War II and the Nuremberg trials that punished those who implemented the experimentation, the Nuremburg Code was established as an international norm for conducting experiments involving people. It requires that every participating subject must give informed consent to participate in the experiment. This means that the person must both be able to understand exactly what will be done with or to him or her, and also have the ability to decline to participate with no penalty. It also requires that the researcher must limit pain, fear, or other negative impacts to only that which is absolutely necessary to conduct the experiment. Further, the experimental design must demonstrate a clear benefit from its outcome, including the development of generalizable knowledge (NIH, 2016).

BOX 1.1 THE NUREMBERG CODE

1. The voluntary consent of the human subject is absolutely essential. This means that the person involved should have legal capacity to give consent; should be so situated as to be able to exercise free power of choice, without the intervention of any element of force, fraud, deceit, duress, over-reaching, or other ulterior form of constraint or coercion; and should have sufficient knowledge and comprehension of the elements of the subject matter involved, as to enable him to make an understanding and enlightened decision. This latter element requires that, before the acceptance of an affirmative decision by the experimental subject, there should be made known to him the nature, duration, and purpose of the experiment; the method and means by which it is to be conducted; all inconveniences and hazards reasonably to be expected; and the effects upon his health or person, which may possibly come from his participation in the experiment. The duty and responsibility for ascertaining the quality of the consent rests upon each individual who initiates, directs or engages in the experiment. It is a personal duty and responsibility which may not be delegated to another with impunity.

2. The experiment should be such as to yield fruitful results for the good of society, unprocurable by other methods or means of study, and not random and unnecessary in nature.

3. The experiment should be so designed and based on the results of animal experimentation and a knowledge of the natural history of the disease or other problem under study, that the anticipated results will justify the performance of the experiment.

4. The experiment should be so conducted as to avoid all unnecessary physical and mental suffering and injury.

5. No experiment should be conducted, where there is an a priori reason to believe that death or disabling injury will occur; except, perhaps, in those experiments where the experimental physicians also serve as subjects.

6. The degree of risk to be taken should never exceed that determined by the humanitarian importance of the problem to be solved by the experiment.

7. Proper preparations should be made and adequate facilities provided to protect the experimental subject against even remote possibilities of injury, disability, or death.

8. The experiment should be conducted only by scientifically qualified persons. The highest degree of skill and care should be required through all stages of the experiment of those who conduct or engage in the experiment.

9. During the course of the experiment, the human subject should be at liberty to bring the experiment to an end, if he has reached the physical or mental state, where continuation of the experiment seemed to him to be impossible.

10. During the course of the experiment, the scientist in charge must be prepared to terminate the experiment at any stage, if he has probable cause to believe, in the exercise of the good

faith, superior skill and careful judgement required of him, that a continuation of the experiment is likely to result in injury, disability, or death to the experimental subject.

Source: "Trials of War Criminals before the Nuremberg Military Tribunals under Control Council Law No. 10," Vol. 2, pp. 181–182. Washington, D.C.: U.S. Government Printing Office, 1949.

In addition to the atrocities of World War II, the United States had its own medical research tragedy, the Tuskegee Study, in which patients were allowed to die from syphilis so that researchers could study the progression of the disease (CDC, 2015). Many other research strategies that did not meet ethical norms included experiments on children with the promise of better care for them, and the use of elderly patients without their consent (Rothman, 1991). To ensure that such research strategies were never used on humans again, the National Research Act was passed by Congress and signed by President Richard M. Nixon in 1974. This created the National Commission for the Protection of Human Subjects of Biomedical and Behavioral Science Research. "The group identified basic principles of research conduct and suggested ways to ensure those principles were followed" (CDC, 2015, n.p.).

"In 1976, the Commission published the *Belmont Report*, which identifies basic ethical principles and guidelines that address ethical issues arising from the conduct of research with human subjects" (HHS, 2016). Doctors, lawyers, professors, ethicists, and religious scholars deliberated for two years, met for four days, and published the report as a statement of policy. It is based on three ethical principles: respect for persons, beneficence,[3] and justice. It requires informed consent, an assessment that balances the risks and benefits, and provides guidelines for the selection of subjects (HHS, 2016).

Federal regulations were then published to provide more specific direction for researchers. These regulations were first published by the Department of Health, Education and Welfare[4] in 1974, and amended through the years, most recently in 2018 (Federal Register, 2017). The Code of Federal Regulations provides details about which kinds of studies are covered by the regulations and defines covered research as the collection of data "through intervention or interaction with the individual. . . . Interaction includes communication or interpersonal contact between investigator and subject" (45 C.F.R. § 46.102(f)(1)–(2)). Subpart A is the Federal Policy for the Protection of Human Subjects, known as the "Common Rule," which guides the conduct of human subjects research in the United States by federal or federally funded entities. It also defines the work of the IRB and the oversight required for all research involving human subjects. Subparts of 45 C.F.R. pt. 46 provide information on extra protections for special populations, including pregnant women, prisoners, and children.

In 2018 new updates were published because of new circumstances, and with a new emphasis on behavioral and social science research.

The volume and landscape of research involving human subjects have changed considerably. Research with human subjects has grown in scale and become more diverse. Examples of developments include: an expansion in the number and types of . . . observational studies and cohort studies; a diversification of the types of social and behavioral research being used in human subjects research; . . . [T]he human subjects research oversight system . . . has remained largely unaltered over the past two decades.

(Federal Register, 2017, p. 7150)

The new (2018) rules strengthen the consent protocols for human subjects while adding a category of "exclusion" for research using data that has already been collected. Given the development of multiple methods of information sharing, it recognizes the possibility of "informational" harm that could result from the improper management of information and conclusions that result from the analysis of already collected data. This means that although new exempt categories have been created, there is a heightened concern for the management of personally identifiable information, even from secondary sources (Federal Register, 2017).

One significant change that impacts disaster field research is the addition of broad consent, "(i.e., seeking prospective consent to unspecified future research) from a subject for storage, maintenance, and secondary research use of identifiable private information" (Federal Register, 2017, p. 7150). This would allow field researchers to use focus group and interview information for the current identified project as well as for future analysis, synthesis, and publication, based on the one consent agreement obtained through the first contact with the human subject. For example, a focus group held following a community emergency was intended to determine what immediate relief was needed by the community. The consent form stated that the information would be used for "community needs evaluation." The comments from the focus group then became the basis for filing a Housing and Urban Development (HUD) grant proposal for new public housing as part of the long-term recovery process. Based on the totality of the focus group comments, it is likely that participants would have made specific suggestions about the kind of housing that they preferred, but the focus on immediate needs did not encourage detailed discussion of housing.

Another set of changes relates to the management of data. A new rule requires limited IRB review of exempt research based on its level of risk. The focus is "to ensure that there are adequate privacy safeguards for identifiable private information" (Federal Register, 2017, p. 7150). This could include the researcher's field notes, recordings, and photographs from observational research without intervention or interaction. Thus, personal field notes that identified the person being observed only for follow-up and clarification purposes to support a generalized discussion may now require IRB review of the method of storing the notes after the initial report is complete. Most researchers keep their private attributable notes for several years in case readers of the report raise questions about its validity. Under the new rule, these notes now have to be stored in a password-protected environment that is acceptable to the IRB.

The 2018 revisions to the Common Rule were caused by a recognition of the expansion of information gathering and processing capabilities:

Social scientists are developing techniques to integrate different types of data so they can be combined, mined, analyzed, and shared. The advent of sophisticated computer software programs, the Internet, and mobile technology has created new areas of research activity, particularly within the social and behavioral sciences. . . . The sheer volume of data that can be generated in research, the ease with which it can be shared, and the ways in which it can be used to identify individuals were simply not possible, or even imaginable, when the Common Rule was first adopted.

(Federal Register, 2017, p. 7151)

The Common Rule revisions further note that the kind of risk has changed from physical to informational. Many studies would now be exempt from the Common Rule because there is no intervention or interaction by the researcher, who is using stored or shared data. However, the importance of security of the original study subject's privacy is still critical.

Nonetheless those [informational] harms could be significant. . . . The fundamental principles in the *Belmont Report* that underlie the Common Rule – respect for persons, beneficence and justice – are applied . . . to the myriad new contexts in which U.S. research is conducted in the 21st century.

(Federal Register, 2017, p. 7151)

Guidance for Ethical Field Research

Ethical behavior is expected of people in their everyday relationships. Most of the world's religions espouse the goal of treating others as you would wish to be treated (Box 1.2). These precepts from many world religions demonstrate a common thread of respect for the "neighbor," or for the other person in a relationship. They all urge empathy, respect, justice, and caring. These same precepts resonate through the ethical standards of human subjects research across all professions.

BOX 1.2 ETHICAL PRECEPTS OF THE WORLD'S RELIGIONS

Bahá'í Faith

"If thou lookest for justice, choose thou for others what thou chooses for thyself."

Buddhism

"Hurt not others in ways that you yourself would find hurtful."

Christianity

"As ye would that men should do to you, do ye also to them likewise."

Confucianism

"Surely it is the maxim of loving-kindness: Do not unto others that you would not have them do unto you."

Gnosticism

"If you bring forth what is within you, what you bring forth will save you. If you do not bring forth what is within you, what you do not bring forth will destroy you."

Hinduism

"This is the sum of all true righteousness: deal with others as thou wouldst thyself be dealt by. Do nothing to thy neighbor, which thou wouldst not have him do to thee after."

Islam

"No one of you is a believer until he desires for his brother that which he desires for himself."

Jainism

"Indifferent to worldly objects, a man should wander about, treating all creatures in the world as he himself would be treated."

Judaism

"What is hateful to you do not to others. That is the entire Law, all the rest is commentary."

Native American

"The Universe is the Mirror of the People, and each person is a Mirror to every other person."

Shintoism

"Irrespective of their nationality, language, manners and culture, men should give mutual aid, and enjoy reciprocal, peaceful pleasure by showing in their conduct that they are brethren."

Sikhism

"As thou deemest thyself, so deem others; then shalt thou become a partner in Heaven."

Taoism

"The good man ought to pity the malignant tendencies of others; to rejoice over their excellence; to help them in their straits; to regard their gains as if they were his own, and their losses in the same way."

Wicca

"And ye harm none, do what ye will, lest in thy self-defense it be, ever mind the rule of three."

Zoroastrianism

"That nature only is good when it shall not do unto another whatever is not good for its own self."

Source: Henes (2012).

The earliest ethical guide for medical practitioners was the Greek Hippocratic Oath, which says, "I will benefit my patients according to my greatest ability and judgement, and I will do no harm or injustice to them" and "Whatever I see or hear in the lives of my patients, whether in connection with my professional practice or not, which ought not to be spoken of outside, I will keep secret, as considering all such things to be private" (U.S. National Library of Medicine, 2012). Recently, the Dalai Lama has encouraged people to see each other as deserving relationships in which one person does not create fear in another (The Dalai Lama, 2001). Because of their universal nature, these standards should be carefully applied to all field disaster research.

Ethics should guide the whole design and implementation of a research project, as every element of its execution can have a positive or negative impact on the survivor, the community, and even the researcher's own profession. Poorly designed and executed research poses a threat to validity. It can include the use of an inappropriate population for data collection and/or the collection of unresponsive or inaccurate data leading to unsupported inferences, which in turn can lead to misinformed public policy. As researchers collect data, they must be sure to measure the actual effects of an event rather than extraneous factors. Since gathering disaster survivors for focus groups inevitably includes some aspects of self-selection, true randomness of the results is lost, as only those still in the community may learn of the opportunity, skewing the perspective (Gooden & Berry-James, 2018). Therefore, field researchers should carefully apply the highest ethical standards and an unbiased perspective to all disaster field research design, execution, and analysis.

There are many methods used in disaster field research. "Data collection techniques used in social science disaster research [include] survey questionnaires, participant observation, in-depth interviews, and focus groups" (Pardee, Fothergill, Weber, & Peek, 2018, p. 673). Each has its own design challenges. Unfortunately, there are many ways that a failure to apply ethical standards and professional approaches can lead to a loss of internal and external validity (Gooden & Berry-James, 2018). The Nuremberg Code and the Belmont Report each offer lists of specific considerations for disaster field researchers to incorporate into their research designs and fieldwork to ensure that the outcomes of their work are ethical – respect for persons, beneficence, and justice (HHS, 2016).

Thinking About the Research Process and Ethical Considerations

Disaster field research places the scholar in the midst of individuals and a community that have been adversely impacted on many levels. These can include loss of home, possessions, livelihood, sense of place and community of neighbors, and the deaths of family and friends. At such times of increased vulnerability, the researcher must consider the need to do no harm, to be beneficent and just throughout the research, not simply at the inception when participant consent is obtained (Pardee et al., 2018). "Ethics in social research refers to the moral deliberation, choice and accountability on the part of researchers throughout the research process" (Pardee et al., 2018, p. 681). As such, ethical consideration should be made throughout various stages of the research process.

The Research Design Stage: Focus, Question Formation, and Subjects

An early ethical challenge for the researcher is the formation of the research focus and question. Careful selection of the focus area will consider avoiding embedding bias into the study. Along these lines, preconceived notions of a problem can lead to a slanted design. A good question provides enough structure for a complete research design, with a clear goal at the end of the research. Researchers often have a good idea of the kind of data that they want to collect and where they hope to find it, yet the research question must be an open inquiry. If researchers have already decided what the answer will be, they may design a question that will get them to that answer, and not generate data that might falsify their expected answer. As such, a "good" research question is one that truly questions social phenomena without a particular answer. The researcher may have his or her own hypotheses based on theory or experience, but the question should not be driven by what they "hope" to find.

Research Design and Researcher's Role

Multiple research designs are accepted in the social sciences, as the chapters in this book demonstrate. Selecting a design for research should be based on the goals of the research, which then form the basis for future ethical decisions involved with the development of the design. However, there are various viewpoints about what constitutes an ethical approach to research design implementation. Scholars have questioned whether ethical decisions "should be based on outcomes, justice, or rights, or from a feminist ethics perspective of care and responsibility" (Pardee et al., 2018, p. 681). However, regardless of what motivates them, the first decision that a researcher must make in the design of his or her study is the relationship that he or she will have with the community and/or respondents. To some extent, the method chosen will dictate the role of the researcher.

For example, an observational design will result in limited personal interactions with community members as the researcher travels through the disaster area and observes physical damage, location and types of services, the makeup of the population impacted (age, gender, race, and other observable characteristics), and public policy applications, such as the opening of assistance centers, distribution of aid, or infrastructure repairs. Such a design is based on the collection of largely anonymous data, but under what circumstances does an observer researcher intervene in the event? Is it legitimate to coach survivors on where assistance is available or to intervene on behalf of a disadvantaged survivor? What are the ethics of allowing harm to proceed in front of you and not intervene, as when a language barrier prevents a survivor from understanding how to access a shelter, or how to get needed documentation to file an aid application, and the researcher is bilingual? If approved research is purely observational, does it violate the IRB protocol by intervening in such circumstances? Is it reportable to the IRB as a formal protocol deviation (Browne & Peek, 2014)? Depending on the circumstances, and whether the intervention will change the outcome of the observation, the researcher will have to judge whether to intervene, remembering the caveat against doing harm. The decision to report the deviation to the IRB will depend on whether it effects the outcome of the observation.

BOX 1.3 CONFRONTING AN ETHICAL DILEMMA IN THE FIELD

The researcher was conducting a longitudinal study of the recovery of the residential housing stock of Ocean City, New Jersey, from the damage done by Hurricane Sandy in 2012 (Bergen, 2012). Each summer from 2013 through 2018, she collected photos of unrepaired residential structures, structures undergoing elevation, and vacant lots where houses once had been. She was measuring the speed and elevation of recovery of residential properties based only on observational data, which would be part of a larger study that included insurance rates. The project design did not include any interaction with human subjects.

In 2017, as she was biking around the island and photographing the addresses on her list, the researcher was verbally accosted by a woman who was unhappy about the photographing of the property, which displayed a large banner proclaiming it a historic restoration project. She spent several minutes telling the researcher that she was tired of "the government" trying to raise her taxes on her home, which was only partially habitable, and that she had waited years to finally get on the "historic" program. So she wanted the photographing to stop and the pictures destroyed. When she finally stopped yelling, the researcher offered her a university business card and explained that she was collecting photos of building recovery, and that she was not from any government agency.

At this time, the woman's two adult sons joined the discussion, and suggested that if the researcher did not get off their property (she was on the sidewalk) they would help her off. With that the woman said, "Oh, she's just some teacher from California. She don't mean no harm." And they all retreated to the house. So the researcher continued on her photography rounds in peace.

A research design that requires surveys, focus groups, or individual interviews to collect the facts about individual impacts will create a different relationship with disaster survivors and their community. Meeting with individuals and families in small groups and listening to their stories of impacts draws the researcher into the lives of those interviewed, and may even foster lasting relationships (Browne & Peek, 2014). In such relationships there may develop an emotional element to the researcher's connection to the event. Scholars have debated whether emotional involvement with the community and survivors is an important concern in research design. Some believe that "emotionality should be privileged in ethical decision-making and . . . researchers should build connected, empowering relationships with participants. Others assert, however, that this is not feasible, nor necessarily desirable" (Pardee et al., p. 681). Developing an emotional relationship with respondents may be the outcome of learning about their struggles and needs, but this may also taint researchers' ability to be objective in their analysis of the event. Furthermore, seeing the event through an emotionally informed perspective may make it difficult to treat a variety of viewpoints as equally valid.

Compensation of Research Subjects

The SAMHSA field guide (2016) notes the special difficulties of conducting post-disaster field research. "The primary dilemma faced by researchers is safely balancing the pursuit of answers to their questions with the serious and immediate needs of survivors" (p. 2). One of the first dilemmas to arise in the design of disaster field research is the question of compensation of research participants. When people have literally lost everything, what is the just approach to obtaining their participation in a focus group, survey, or interview? Their time is valuable, so it seems both beneficent and just to pay for that time, yet is "monetary compensation . . . appropriate or exploitive in a disaster aftermath" (Pardee et al., 2018, p. 681). When people are suffering "a crisis of basic needs" (Pardee et al., 2018, p. 681), does compensation change the nature of the communication between survivor and researcher? Small amounts of compensation may have a different impact on a survivor's decision to cooperate than higher-value gifts. Will people say what they think the researcher wants to hear to ensure that they are paid? Will the offering of compensation lead to a self-selection bias (SAMHSA, p. 7) based on the willingness to trade the revelation and probing of their pain for financial gain, or will some potential participants find that abhorrent? Is a donation to a community project less patronizing and paternalistic than direct compensation with a gift card, even when the interviewee lacks the basic necessities of life?

In sum, the decision on whether to compensate research participants, and in what form, will rest on the researcher's understanding of the act of gift giving (Browne, 2009). Is the researcher reciprocating the individual survivor for the gift of their time and information, or compensating the community for its overall cooperation with the research enterprise, or trying to make a survivor whole from the disaster when other sources have failed (Browne & Peek, 2014)? Browne and Peek recount the role of gift giving in helping children to recover from disaster but also its role in the development of jealousy among the recipients. Aristotle suggests that all such moral decisions require the use of "practical reason" to make the choice. McNaughton (2000) further suggests that "a given action may be right in itself, but other considerations have not yet determined whether, in this instance, it is in fact the right choice" (Browne & Peek, 2014, pp. 116–117).

Anonymous or Confidential?

Additionally, scholars debate the role of anonymity and confidentiality in research design. Anonymous data does not require strict sequestration during its use and analysis, but the lack of identifiers may interfere with the development of cross-tabulations that could have explanatory value. Some argue that confidentiality is essential to get honest responses. Others argue that confidentiality deprives the interviewee of credit for the contribution to the research (Pardee et al., 2018, p. 682). For example, surveys and data analysis designs can easily be anonymous, as illustrated in Box 1.4.

BOX 1.4 ANONYMITY

Hurricane Sandy was a landscape-level disaster, especially on the barrier islands of New Jersey. One such community is Ocean City, a summer resort with a permanent population of fewer than 12,000 people (Wittkowski, 2017). On October 29, 2012, when the hurricane struck Atlantic City, just 8 miles up the coast, Ocean City was spared the worst of the hurricane winds, but flooding was caused by the high tide and storm surge, causing beach erosion, dune displacement, and property damage. Most of the population had obeyed the governor's order to evacuate to the mainland (Bergen, 2012).

The researcher had designed a random anonymous survey to be administered on June 4, 2013, a few weeks before the tourist season began, which would swell the population to 150,000 (Wittkowski, 2017). The first 50 island residents, contacted by the researcher walking around the residential areas, who were willing to talk, would be interviewed about their evacuation experience and how it could have been improved. The day before, the researcher had interviewed the New Jersey State Police to get data on the evacuation and the police agency's view of the evacuation's success.

People were outdoors painting the woodwork and repairing landscape damage from Sandy. The researcher greeted the residents, commented on the projects underway, and inquired whether she could ask the person a few questions. Most people were happy to describe their pre-storm experiences with evacuation, the drive up the crowded Garden State Parkway to the Atlantic City Expressway, the blocked exits that funneled them to Philadelphia's New Jersey suburbs for shelter. Most reported staying with family and friends until it was safe to return home. Almost all of the people were retired or working in post-retirement part-time jobs during the tourist season, so few had suffered loss of income. The researcher left a business card with each interviewee, and welcomed them to send any additional information that they wanted to share. At Christmas she got an email from an unfamiliar person. The message read, "Thanks for letting me share my evacuation story. No one ever asked me about my adventures." Attached was a picture of the beautiful restored beach covered with a light dusting of snow.

However, despite one's views on anonymity or confidentiality, ensuring that studies remain anonymous can be accomplished in several ways. For example, stripping identifying information from school records, medical records, or returned surveys is simple when using computer-based materials. In small sample studies, even demographic data, if included, may easily reveal the source, such as when there are a small number of participants from one ethnicity and age group. Alternatively, in large-n studies, it may be possible to retain some key demographic or otherwise identifying information without risking a breach of anonymity. For example, when there are hundreds of families in each ethnic group, it becomes less obvious which family is responding.

Confidentiality is possible in one-on-one interviews, with the burden falling on the researcher to collect and store the research in a way that protects the identity of the survivor — thus the focus of the new Common Rule on information management. Typically, data has to be retained on password-protected computers accessed only by the researcher. However, it is difficult to obtain confidentiality in other settings. Focus groups or group interviews have multiple participants, and while all are asked to undertake a commitment to confidentiality, interpersonal relationships outside of the interview may drive the survivor's decision on whether to respect the commitment. Peek and Fothergill (2009) recount instances of information disclosed during confidential group interviews becoming the basis for family dissention. Therefore, even when a researcher is engaging in ethical behavior, there is always a concern that all respondents might not behave in similar ways.

Managing Survivor Re-traumatization

Studies have shown that over half of the American population has experienced trauma, with natural disaster the second most common triggering event (SAMHSA, 2017). Researchers have noted that post–disaster research has social value, as it allows for evaluation and improvement of disaster response systems (Ferreira, Buttell, & Ferreira, 2015). Yet the interviews and focus groups may lead to the vivid recall of the disaster and its impacts, leading to re-traumatization of the survivor participant, which is highlighted in several chapters of this book. Since researchers have no way of estimating the level of distress that a participant may experience from discussing the disaster or hearing others discuss the disaster, they should be prepared to provide immediate supportive intervention and referrals to community mental health resources (SAMHSA, 2016). Handout materials like the SAMHSA publication "Tips for Survivors of a Disaster or Other Traumatic Event: Coping with Retraumatization" (2017) should be available for immediate distribution in the group or to the interviewee. Trauma management educational materials should be available in all the relevant community languages before interviews begin, as required in 45 C.F.R. pt. 46.

First Responders as Sources of Data

Disaster field researchers may view first responders as the best source of unbiased and comprehensive disaster information. They may interview first responders to get a detailed view of the community impacts. Firefighters, search and rescue teams, law enforcement members and emergency medical service workers will have been dispatched to the disaster in its early stages and will have useful insights into how the disaster unfolded. Non-traditional first responders like engineers and heavy-equipment operators may be included in first responder teams. However, the likelihood of re-traumatization of first responders also needs to be considered when designing field research with them. For example, a number of researchers (Fullerton, McCarroll, Ursano, & Wright, 1992; Fullerton, Ursano, & Wang, 2004; North et al., 2002) have focused on the adverse impact of disasters on disaster response workers. Perrin et al. (2007) found that over 12.4% of the first responders at the World Trade Center disaster in 2001 suffered from post-traumatic stress disorder (PTSD). However, while only 6.4% of law enforcement officers reported PTSD, 22% of engineers and heavy-equipment operators had PTSD. Moreover, they found that workers with the least previous exposure to death and injury, and with the longest exposure to the disaster, were the most likely to be adversely affected.

One way of reducing adverse psychological risks to first responder participants is to consider a design that does not require intervention with first responders. Observation of their work and interaction with the community might be sufficient. Review of published after action reports (AARs) might provide adequate details for the event background. The researcher should consider what valuable information will be garnered from first responder interviews and what the cost will be to those being interviewed. The Belmont Report requirement for beneficence might militate against interviews

However, in the event that using first respondents as participants is unavoidable, many public safety agencies have relied on Critical Incident Stress Debriefing (CISD) to mitigate the trauma of an emergency event (Mitchell, 1988). The system, which features a structured recounting of the event and its impacts, has been used by first responder agencies to limit long-term psychological damage to their members (Hiley-Young & Gerrity, 1994). However, some recent research studies have failed to find a high correlation between CISD and successful management of PTSD (Litz, Williams, Wang, Bryant, & Engel, 2004; Bisson, Shepherd, Joy, Probert, & Newcombe, 2004; McNally, Bryant, & Ehlers, 2003; Watson et al., 2003). As such, psychological first aid is now becoming the preferred approach for assisting first responders to process disaster impacts (Benedek, Fullerton, & Ursano, 2007). It was recommended in the 2008 edition of the National Response Framework (U.S. Department of Homeland Security, 2008; Uhernik & Hussan, 2009). This is an early intervention model that facilitates triage, psychosocial support, and referral to definitive care (Benedek et al., 2007). Researchers designing interviews, focus group, or close observation methods should include access to psychological first aid resources before beginning interaction with first responders.

Self-selection Bias and False Findings

The design of research must also take into account the likelihood of self-selection bias among the people who volunteer to be interviewed about a disaster. For example, in a post–disaster environment, it will be difficult to recruit focus group participants (Browne & Peek, 2014). A valid study requires a random sample, but this may be difficult.

> In the disaster context, using random samples not only is impractical but perhaps irrelevant for the goals of disaster research. . . . If a representative sample is not used, inferences cannot be made about the population from which the study participants were selected. . . . researchers should strive to avoid selection biases (e.g., self-selection bias).
>
> (Pfefferbaum et al., 2013, p. 291)

Self-selection is likely to lead to a distorted representation of the true population (Heckman, 1990), creating a threat to validity of the conclusion. Consider the likelihood of the desired population volunteering to be part of the research.

For example, in 1978 Pacific Southwest Airlines Flight 182 crashed on approach to Lindbergh Field in San Diego, California, killing everyone aboard and people on the ground. A police cadet class was brought to the scene to assist with recovery of the remains, which were then placed in the St. Augustine High School gymnasium, which became the morgue for the event (Rowe, 2018). Researchers postulated that this experience must have impacted the cadets, so 2 years later they went to the San Diego Police Department and asked to interview the cadets who had been part of the rescue. The department circulated the request for interviews among all their current members, since there was no accurate list of everyone who had assisted at the crash scene. After several weeks no one had responded to the request for an interview, so the researchers concluded that none of the cadets was a San Diego police officer any longer. For many years, training for emergency managers used this as an example of the importance of providing post-disaster psychological care to first responders following disasters. Thirty years later, an emergency manager was attending a social event when the subject of the air crash came up. He mentioned that all the cadets had left law enforcement, and one of the other attendees said that was not true. This person had been in charge of the cadets that day, and she was still in touch with many of them as their careers and hers had progressed. When the emergency manager asked why she and the cadets did not respond to the interview request, she said, "Why would any of us want to do that?"

This cautionary tale demonstrates a practical experience of self-selection in field research. None of the desired population wished to discuss the event. The result was an inaccurate conclusion – all the cadets had left law enforcement – which was then taught for 30 years in emergency management courses. In research design, consider who is likely to volunteer to participate, what more would have to be done to attract reluctant participants, and how to ensure that those who participate are not inventing information to qualify for the compensation.

Survivors as a Hidden Population

A final challenge to consider when attempting to use survivor participants in research projects is that the survivors may behave like a hidden population, which is also discussed within several chapters of this book. However, for now, in the discussion of ethics, a hidden population is defined by the medical community as "when there is no sampling frame within a certain group or the group is concerned that making its population public would bring social stigma" (Jung, 2015, p. 4677). Within the medical community, cancer survivors are a hidden population, for example (Jung, 2015). Populations also may be hidden because they are hard to find (Ellard-Gray, Jeffrey, Choubak, & Crann, 2015), as was the case with the Hurricane Katrina survivors who were dispersed throughout a number of cities for disaster sheltering. Being disenfranchised, discriminated against, or subject to stigma are other factors that would prevent people from volunteering to be identified with a specific group or event (Ellard-Gray et al., 2015).

Hidden populations may have the only data about a phenomenon within the disaster. For example, the people who worked in nursing homes in the New Orleans area before Hurricane Katrina would have been a useful disaster survivor cohort, who could have described their conflicting responsibilities as they faced the decision on whether to go home to help their families, or whether to stay with their dependent nursing home residents. Most chose to go home to their families, a fact revealed by surviving residents who had been abandoned in the nursing homes. The perspective of those nursing home employees is mostly missing from the Katrina literature because of the stigma of being someone who abandoned patients, even though most of the nursing home employees were not licensed professionals and probably had no legal obligation to stay, although the argument could be made that they had a moral and ethical responsibility.

Conclusion

Disaster field research poses many intricate problems for the research designer that may not be covered in the standard methodology text. Additionally, Browne and Peek (2014) urge the use of a framework to "think through ethical dilemmas as they arise" (p. 82). Ethical practice should be the guiding principle in the research design framework, which is echoed throughout the entirety of this book. The guiding principles of that framework would be the following tenets: (1) do no harm; (2) respect the privacy of all research participants; and (3) respect the person, act with beneficence, and be just. These tenets may not resolve all field research design challenges, and other chapters in this book provide some solutions, work-arounds, and better designs. But, under all circumstances, ethical practice should be the basis of every disaster field research project.

Notes

1. Subpart A of 45 C.F.R. pt. 46 defines the composition and role of IRBs nationwide.
2. SAMHSA is the U.S. Substance Abuse and Mental Health Services Administration.
3. Beneficence means "doing or producing good" (*Merriam-Webster Collegiate Dictionary*, 11th ed., 2019).
4. This department was subsequently divided into the Department of Health and Human Services and the Department of Education.

Further Readings

Buscher, M., Easton, C., Kuhnert, M., Wietfeld, C., Ahlsen, M., Pottebaum, J., & Van Veelen, B. (2014). Cloud ethics for disaster response. In S.R. Hiltz, M.S. Pfaff, L. Plotnick, & P.C. Shih (Eds.), *Proceedings of the 11th International ISCRAM Conference*. University Park, PA.

Gardner, H. (2005). Compromised work. *Daedalus, 134*(3), 42–51.

Hunt, M., Tansey, C.M., Anderson, J., Boulanger, R.F., Eckenwiler, L., Pringle, J., & Schwartz, L. (2016). The challenge of timely, responsive and rigorous ethics: Review of disaster research. *PLOS One*. doi.org/10.1371/journal.pone.0157142

Larkin, G.L. (2010, June) Unwitting partners in death: The ethics of teamwork in disaster management. *Virtual Mentor: American Medical Association Journal of Ethics, 12*(6), 495–501.

Lavarias, R. (2013). The role of ethical behavior in emergency management. *P.A. Times*. Retrieved from https://patimes.org/role-ethical-behavior-emergency-management/

Mezinska, S., Kakuk, P., Mijaljica, G., Waligóra, M., & O'Mathúna, D. (2016). Research in disaster settings: A systematic qualitative review of ethical guidelines. *BMC Medical Ethics, 17*(62). https://doi.org/10.1186/s12910-016-0148-7

Quill, L. (2014). Should a communitarian ethic be taught? *Society, 51*(4), 389–392.

References

Benedek, D.M., Fullerton, C., & Ursano, R.J. (2007). First responders: Mental health consequences of natural and human-made disasters for public health and public safety workers. *Annual Review of Public Health, 28*, 55–68.

Bergen, D. (2012, October 31). Record storm leaves residents stranded and island devastated. *Patch*. Retrieved from https://patch.com/new-jersey/oceancity/record-storm-leaves-residents-stranded-and-island-devastated

Bisson, J.I., Shepherd, J.P., Joy, D., Probert, R., & Newcombe, R.G. (2004). Early cognitive-behavioral therapy for post-traumatic stress symptoms after physical injury: Randomized controlled trial. *British Journal of Psychiatry, 184*, 63–69.

Browne, K.E. (2009). Economics and morality: Introduction. In K.E. Browne & L. Milgrim (Eds.), *Economics and morality: Anthropological approaches*. Lanham, MD: AltaMira Press.

Browne, K.E., & Peek, L. (2014, March). Beyond the IRB: An ethical toolkit for long-term disaster research. *International Journal of Mass Emergencies and Disasters, 32*(1), 82–120.

C2ES (formerly Pew Center on Global Climate Change). (n.d.). *Hurricanes and climate change*. http://www.c2es.org/content/hurricanes-and-climate-change/

Canino, G., Bravo, M., Rubio-Stipec, M., & Woodbury, M. (1990). The impact of disaster on mental health: Prospective and retrospective analyses. *International Journal of Mental Health, 19*(1), 51–69.

Centers for Disease Control and Prevention (CDC). (2015, December 14). *U.S. Public Health Service syphilis study at Tuskegee: Research implications. How Tuskegee Changed Research Practices*. http://www.cdc.gov/tuskegee/after.htm

CITI. (n.d.). *Research ethics and compliance training*. https://about.citiprogram.org/en/homepage/

Code of Federal Regulations (CFR). (2018). *45 CFR part 46 – Protection of Human Subjects*. http://www.ecfr.gov/cgi-bin/retrieveECFR?gp=&SID=83cd09e1c0f5c6937cd9d7513160fc3f&pitd=20180719&n=pt45.1.46&r=PART&ty=HTML

Collogan, L.K., Tuma, F., Dolan-Sewell, R., Borja, S., & Fleischman, A.R. (2004). Ethical issues pertaining to research in the aftermath of disaster. *Journal of Traumatic Stress, 17*(5), 363–372.

Columbia University. (2006). *Coastal population indicator: Data and methodology page*. Center for International Earth Science Information Network (CIESIN). http://sedac.ciesin.columbia.edu/es/csdcoastal.html

The Dalai Lama. (2001). *Ethics for the new millennium*. New York: Riverhead Books.

Economist. (2019, April 20). When will they ever learn? pp. 70–71.

Edwards, F. L., & Goodrich, D. C. (2012). *Introduction to transportation security.* Boca Raton, FL: CRC Press.

Edwards, F. L., Goodrich, D. C., Hellweg, M., Strauss, J., Eskijian, M., & Jaradat, O. (2015). *Great East Japan Earthquake, JR East mitigation successes, and lessons for California high-speed rail.* San Jose, CA: MTI. https://transweb.sjsu.edu/sites/default/files/1225-great-east-japan-earthquake-lessons-for-California-HSR.pdf

Ellard-Gray, A., Jeffrey, N. K., Choubak, M., & Crann, S. E. (2015). Finding the hidden participant: Solutions for recruiting hidden, hard-to-reach, and vulnerable populations. *International Journal of Qualitative Methods,* 1–10. https://doi.org/10.1177/1609406915621420

Fanta, V., Salek, M., & Sklenicka, P. (2019). How long do floods throughout the millennium remain in the collective memory? *Nature Communications.* https://doi.org/10.1038/s41467-019-09102-3.

Federal Emergency Management Agency. (2010, November). *Developing and maintaining emergency operations plans: Comprehensive preparedness guide 101.* Washington, DC: FEMA. http://www.fema.gov/media-library-data/20130726-1828-25045-0014/cpg_101_comprehensive_preparedness_guide_developing_and_maintaining_emergency_operations_plans_2010.pdf

Federal Register. (2017, January 19). Federal policy for the protection of human subjects. *Executive Summary, 82*(12), 7149–7273.

Ferreira, R., Buttell, F., & Ferreira, S. (2015). Ethical considerations for conducting disaster research with vulnerable populations. *Journal of Social Work Values and Ethics, 12*(1), 29–40.

Fullerton, C. S., McCarroll, J. E., Ursano, R. J., & Wright, K. M. (1992). Psychological responses of rescue workers: Fire fighters and trauma. *American Journal of Orthopsychiatry, 62*(3), 371–378.

Fullerton, C. S., Ursano, R. J., & Wang, L. (2004). Acute stress disorder, post-traumatic stress disorder, and depression in disaster or rescue workers. *American Journal of Psychiatry, 161,* 1370–1376.

Gooden, S. T., & Berry-James, R. M. (2018). *Why research matters: Essential skills for decision making.* Melvin & Leigh.

Heckman, J. J. (1990). Selection bias and self-selection. In J. Eatwell, M. Milgate, & P. Newman (Eds.), *Econometrics.* London: New Palgrave and Palgrave Macmillan.

Henes, M. D. (2012, October 23). The universal golden rule. *Huffington Post.* http://www.huffpost.com/entry/golden-rule_n_2002245

HHS.gov. (2016, March 15). *The Belmont Report.* Office for Human Research Protections. http://www.hhs.gov/ohrp/regulations-and-policy/belmont-report/index.html

Hiley-Young, B., & Gerrity, E. T. (1994, Spring). Critical incident stress debriefing (CISD): Value and limitations in disaster response. *NCP Clinical Quarterly, 4*(2).

Jung, M. (2015). Probability sampling methods for a hidden populations using respondent driven sampling: Simulation for cancer survivors. *Asian Pacific Journal of Cancer Prevention, 16*(11), 4677–4683.

Litz, B. T., Williams, L., Wang, J., Bryant, R., & Engel, C. C. (2004). A therapist-assisted Internet self-help program for traumatic stress. *Professional Psychology: Research and Practice, 35,* 628–634.

McNally, R., Bryant, R., & Ehlers, A. (2003). Does early psychological intervention promote recovery from posttraumatic stress? *Psychological Science in the Public Interest, 4,* 45–79.

McNaughton, D. (2000). Intuitionism. In H. LaFollette (Ed.). *The Blackwell guide to ethical theory* (pp. 268–286). Malden, MA: Blackwell Publishing.

Merriam-Webster. (2019). *Dictionary: Beneficence.* http://www.merriam-webster.com/dictionary/beneficence

Mitchell, J. T. (1988). The history, status and future of critical incident stress debriefings. *Journal of Emergency Medical Services, JEMS, 11,* 47–52.

Mukherji, A., Ganapati, N. E., & Rahill, G. (2014). Expecting the unexpected: Field research in post-disaster settings. *Natural Hazards, 73,* 805–828. https://doi.org/10.1007/s11069-014-1105-8

National Institutes of Health (NIH). (2016, February 19). *The Nuremberg Code.* Office for Human Research Protections. https://history.nih.gov/research/downloads/nuremberg.pdf

NOAA. (2018, June 25). *What percentage of the American population lives near the coast?* National Ocean Service. https://oceanservice.noaa.gov/facts/population.html

North, C.S., Tivis, L., McMillen, J.C., et al. (2002). Coping, functioning, and adjustment of rescue workers after the Oklahoma City bombing. *Journal of Trauma Stress, 15,* 171–175.

Pardee, J., Fothergill, A., Weber, L., & Peek, L. (2018). The collective method: Collaborative social science research and scholarly accountability. *Qualitative Research, 18*(6), 671–688. https://doi.org/10.1177/1468794117743461

Peek, L., & Fothergill, A. (2009). Using focus groups: Lessons from studying daycare centers, 9/11, and Hurricane Katrina. *Quantitative Research, 9*(1), 31–59. https://doi.org/10.1177/146879 4108098029

Perrin, M.A., Digrande, L., Wheeler, K., Thorpe, L., Farfel, M., & Brackbill, R. (2007). Differences in post-traumatic stress prevalence and associated risk factors among world trade center disaster rescue and recovery workers. *American Journal of Psychiatry, 164*(9), 1385(10).

Pfefferbaum, B., Weems, C.F., Scott, B.G., Nitiema, P., Noffsinger, M.A., Pfefferbaum, R.L., Varma, V., & Chakraburtty, A. (2013). Research methods in child disaster studies: A review of studies generated by the September 11, 2001, terrorist attacks; the 2004 Indian Ocean Tsunami; and Hurricane Katrina. *Child Youth Care Forum, 42*(4), 285–337. https://doi.org/10.1007/s10566-013-9211-4

Quarantelli, E.L. (1997). *The Disaster Research Center (DRC) field studies of organized behavior in the crisis time period of disasters.* Paper # 254. Disaster Research Center, University of Delaware. http://udspace.udel.edu/bitstream/handle/19716/198/PP254-DRC?sequence=1

Richards, D. (2001). A field study of critical incident stress debriefing versus critical incident stress management. *Journal of Mental Health, 10*(3), 351–362. https://doi.org/10.1080/09638230 124190

Rothman, D.J. (1991). *Strangers at the bedside: A history of how law and bioethics transformed medical decision making.* New York: Basic Books.

Rowe, P. (2018, September 23). PSA crash at 40: A page of San Diego history "written in blood." *San Diego Union Tribune.* http://www.sandiegouniontribune.com/news/sd-me-psa-crash-20180914-story.html

SAMHSA. (2016, January). *Challenges and considerations in disaster research.* Disaster Technical Assistance Center Supplemental Research Bulletin. http://www.samhsa.gov/sites/default/files/dtac/supplemental-research-bulletin-jan-2016.pdf

SAMHSA. (2017). *Tips for survivors of a disaster or other traumatic event: Coping with retraumatization.* https://store.samhsa.gov/product/Tips-for-Survivors-of-a-Disaster-or-Other-Traumatic-Event-/sma17-5047

Uhernik, J.A., & Hussan, M.A. (2009). Psychological first aid: An evidence-informed approach for acute disaster behavioral health response. In G.R. Walz, J.C. Bleuer, & R.K. Yep (Eds.), *Compelling counseling intervention VISTAS 2009* (pp. 271–280). Alexandria, VA: American Counseling Association.

U.S. Department of Homeland Security. (2008). *National response framework.* (now obsolete).

U.S. National Library of Medicine. (2012). *Hippocratic Oath.* National Institutes of Health, Department of Health and Human Services. http://www.nlm.nih.gov/hmd/greek/greek_oath.html

Watson, P.J., Friedman, M.J., Gibson, L.E., Ruzek, J.I., Norris, F.H., & Ritchie, E.C. (2003). Early intervention for trauma-related problems. *Review of Psychiatry, 22,* 97–124.

Weeman, K., & Lynch, P. (2018, February 13). *New study finds sea level rise accelerating.* NASA, Global Climate Change: Vital Signs of the Planet. https://climate.nasa.gov/news/2680/new-study-finds-sea-level-rise-accelerating/

Wittkowski, D. (2017, September 5). As tourists leave, ocean city residents eagerly await "local summer." *OCNJ Daily.* https://ocnjdaily.com/as-tourists-leave-ocean-city-residents-eagerly-await-local-summer/

2

Sampling in Disaster and Emergency Management Research

Debra Borie-Holtz and Ashley Koning

Introduction

Summer felt like it had returned along the New Jersey and New York coasts as weekend beachgoers frolicked along the sandy shoreline. Temperatures rose to 66 degrees on that sunny Monday in October. There were no hints of clouds, or of the catastrophic threat posed by the tropical wave developing in the western Caribbean Sea. In just 8 days, the intensifying storm would travel 900 miles and wreak havoc along its trajectory. Making landfall as a Category 2 hurricane in the bi-state region, Hurricane Sandy would demolish large swaths of boardwalk and beachfront properties; overflow berms to flood cities, forcing massive evacuations; and swamp transportation tunnels and arteries. Disguised as a lower-rated hurricane, Sandy's devastating punch was made worse by a low-pressure system that fueled tropical-force winds and drenching rains, resulting in prolonged power outages and fires left smoldering due to trapped emergency response equipment. As the hurricane spread westward to states without any sea borders, Sandy continued along its coastal track, fundamentally changing the footprint of many communities. Some neighborhoods would never recover in the aftermath, as abandoned homes remained vacant when storm victims choose not to rebuild.

Dubbed by the media as "Superstorm Sandy," the rebuilding and recovery price tag topped $70 billion and caused the highest human death toll along the Eastern Seaboard until Hurricanes Harvey and Maria ravaged the Atlantic in 2017. These immense restoration costs, coupled with the milieu of climate studies that predict an increased likelihood in the incidence of weather-related disasters, have spawned interest in research studies centered on populations that live in the path of nature's greatest threats. Among these investigations, survey research is an optimal approach, as it is highly efficient, versatile, and generalizable when probability sampling is utilized.

Yet in survey methodology, there is no "one-size-fits all" study design. "Part of the task of a survey methodologist is making a large set of decisions about thousands of individual features of a survey in order to improve it" (Groves et al., 2009, p. 33), as described by experts including Robert Groves, a sociologist who headed the U.S.

Census Bureau from 2009 to 2012. "Each of these decisions has the potential to affect the quality of estimates that emerge from a survey" (p. 33). These decisions, made more difficult when surveying disaster victims, require identifying and locating a displaced population among a fractured community following a natural or emergency management event. Surveying participants who have experienced trauma also raises concerns about the risks versus the benefits of asking them emotionally provoking and sensitive questions, in addition to recognizing the potential barriers to gaining their participation.

Inherently, one of the first challenges researchers confront is to determine who they want to survey, the modes by which they contact the target population, and how to foster a social exchange with the defined target population to encourage their participation. In effect, the Tailored Design method focuses attention on every aspect of survey design that influences a respondent while recognizing the design must be adapted to the dynamics and nuances of the research objectives (Dillman, Smyth, & Christian, 2009). In this chapter, we use these challenges to steer our discussion of the strategies available to researchers who want to survey disaster survivors. We also review the strengths and limitations of these approaches, which include an evaluation of probability and non-probability sampling methods.

More specifically, this chapter first discusses survey research that relies on probability sampling to collect observations from a random sample of a population in order to have confidence that the generalizations made reflect the attitudes, beliefs, and behaviors of the whole population. For random probability surveys, the focus on high-quality data and high response rates is the aim of the Tailored Design method (Dillman et al., 2009), to which we subscribe. Informed by this theoretical frame, we focus on techniques to accurately define the geographic parameters of the disaster-impacted target population to reduce threats to validity. We recommend tools to estimate the population parameters within these boundaries that often share little in common with chartered geographical borders. We then review non-probability sampling strategies that offer approaches to reach populations when constructing a sample frame is not feasible due to time or cost constraints. We intersperse two case studies throughout the chapter to contextualize both the challenges and strategies that informed our design decisions when we fielded surveys of two disparate communities impacted by Hurricane Sandy.

The Gold Standard: Probability Surveys

Random probability surveys are highly efficient and versatile, and enable researchers to generalize their findings to the population under study. Probability surveys are considered the gold standard in the field as there is no systematic bias – the selection of a participant in the survey is determined by chance, and one's likelihood of selection is known and never equal to zero (Chambliss & Schutt, 2019). With an eye towards attaining reliable and valid data, one of the tenets of Tailored Design is to reduce "total survey error," which serves as the framework that guides survey design and informs survey quality for probability surveys (Groves, 1989). Unlike some survey studies, which only account for sampling error, "total survey error" focuses on reducing coverage, non-response, and measurement error, along with sampling error. Giving prominence to only one kind of survey error risks putting faith in results that are just plain wrong. This risk exponentially increases when exogenous events, such as natural disasters, limit the ability to obtain a sampling frame of the target population. To understand the effect "total survey error" has on ensuring measurement validity, we examine *errors of observation* and *errors of non-observation* (Groves et al., 2009). We begin with measurement error.

Measurement Error

Measurement error results from errors of observation that occur when we fail to measure what we want to measure (Groves et al., 2009). This results when poorly worded survey questions fail to accurately measure data or when the data collected varies from the actual concept we want to learn about. Question wording, question order, framing, the presentation of written questions, possible "interviewer effect" during oral interviews, and whether to craft an open-ended or closed-ended question are some of the numerous details that need to be carefully considered when crafting a survey instrument (Dillman et al., 2009).

Measurement error occurs when respondents give us incorrect information or even tell us what they think we want to hear. They may alter their responses, or they may opt to skip socially sensitive questions based on the perceived race, ethnicity, or gender of the interviewer. For example, a respondent may conceal his true feelings about immigration policy if he senses the interviewer is Hispanic. Similarly, he may voice support for pay equity mandates if the interviewer is female. Scholars refer to this error as "interviewer effect," which is more likely to occur in telephone surveys. Alternatively, social desirability bias, which is a desire to be viewed favorably by others, will vary depending on the mode in which the survey is conducted. Among disaster victims, establishing a social contract that researchers rely upon to gain the participation of those sampled is also at risk. In our personal experiences, we have interviewed respondents who resist or even resent being surveyed in the aftermath of an exogenous event. As expressed by one victim who refused to participate in our survey, she was weary of answering questions to "help researchers" study the aftereffects of the hurricane when she felt so helpless and still had not recovered from the disaster herself.

Sampling Error

Errors of non-observation are also widely recognized across the multidisciplinary fields that employ survey methodology. Non-observational errors are "the deviations of a statistic estimated on a sample from that on the full population," which includes sampling, coverage, non-response, and post-survey adjustment errors (Groves et al., 2009, p. 40). Sampling error occurs when researchers use a random sample of the target population that deliberately omits some persons from the sample. One of the largest determinants of simple sampling error is the number of randomly recruited respondents who complete the survey (N size). The larger the number of respondents, the smaller the sampling error. Although sampling error is a reliable indicator that reflects upon the quality of the data collected, it is not a cure-all for eliminating threats of bias. In our own research, we typically calculate both "simple sampling error" and "adjusted sampling error" to improve the precision of our estimates.

Because it is rarely feasible to conduct a census of a population, researchers draw a random sample of persons from a population. Simply put, a random sample allows researchers to make inferences about those not observed in the population with a level of confidence. Known as "simple sampling error," we calculate the expected probable difference between interviewing everyone in a population versus a scientific sampling drawn from that population ($N = 750$). As a result, our simple sampling error of ± 3.6 percentage points means if 50% of adults favored a particular position, one would be 95% sure that the true figure is between 46.4% and 53.6% (50 ± 3.6) if all adults were interviewed, rather than just a random sample ($N = 750$).

Non-response Error

While random sampling error, or the error that occurs by random chance, is the non–observational gap between the sampling frame and the sample (Groves et al., 2009), it does not measure bias. Even large probability samples are not free from potential threats of bias. We must also consider the bias that comes from non-response error when some folks who are randomly recruited refuse to talk to pollsters. Overall, we expect to find mismatches when surveying populations, particularly with phone-only surveys versus mix-mode designs. Recent response rates for telephone-fielded surveys have dropped to below 10% (Kennedy & Hartig, 2019). Mismatches also occur with higher levels of ethnically and racially diverse populations, as well as those from lower socioeconomic rungs and hard-to-reach persons. Physical displacement may occur following a disaster, resulting in short- and long-term relocations, which increases the potential for non-response error among subgroups. Additionally, poorly drafted survey instruments may lead to skipped items or higher respondent dropout rates before interview completion, contributing further to non-response error.

Coverage Error

When the respondents in a sampling frame are different from the target population, coverage error results (Groves et al., 2009). Coverage error "exists before the sample is drawn," and it exists whether researchers are relying on a sample of the target population or conducting a census of the target population (Groves et al., 2009, p. 55). Once you decide who you want to survey, you must create or obtain a list of all eligible members of the target population. Recall that a probability survey relies on drawing a random sample in which all members of the population have an equal chance of selection and their chance of selection is known and not equal to zero (Chambliss & Schutt, 2019).

If, for example, you are a member of a population to be surveyed by phone, but you have no phone, you will be omitted or missed in the sample frame. In effect, you have zero chance of selection. By comparison, disaster survivors who have relocated to another city or town will be missed, resulting in under-coverage. Similarly, residents who move into the impacted neighborhood after the event will be included in the sample frame, resulting in over-coverage since they are ineligible participants who did not experience the disaster. The impact of over- or underestimating the target population can result in biased inferences. Of course, survey screener questions can aid in weeding out ineligible members; however, screening significantly increases the costs of fielding, and screener questions may not always produce a reliable measure. One mechanism to guard against missing eligible members is to utilize enhanced tools to create the sample frame essentially from scratch. This approach is illustrated in the electoral polling scenario that follows and is applied more broadly in our case study of a disaster population, as its application is relevant for both.

Electoral polling in the United States provides an example of the perfect storm for surveyors. During the 2018 midterm election cycle, the challenge for pollsters was to determine who would be voting, since the first step in research design is to decide who researchers want to interview, specifically defining the target population. Drawing a sample from all registered voters might miss those who recently registered to vote (under-coverage), while including all registered voters would select among those who routinely do not cast ballots during every election cycle (over-coverage). Historically, the target population for a "likely voter" midterm election delineates less frequent voters than those who cast ballots during the presidential cycle.

Defining this target population was elusive in 2018. As it turned out, a historic number of votes were cast across the country. As an example, nearly 1 million voters cast ballots in Nevada, a state we polled, by the time the polls closed on Tuesday evening. That record was just shy of the 2016 presidential election turnout. Although our random survey of adults screened first for registered voters, and second for likely voters, we could not rely that the sample we surveyed looked like the target population of previous cycles. The only way to ensure our sample was representative of the expected target population was to make inferences about the demographics of the likely surge voter before we started fielding.

We estimated Nevada's surge voters would be more diverse, younger, and less frequent participants than either the expected midterm or presidential voter. By more accurately delineating the target population, we were able to minimize coverage error. Minimizing coverage error also served to minimize the design effect, which requires an adjustment to the basic sample error calculation due to weighting.

Weighting

When fielding is complete, one of the first post-analysis tasks for researchers is to determine whether a mismatch between the sample and population parameters exists. When the sample demographic parameters are different from the target population parameters, weighting is employed to correct for any imbalances. When a weight is applied to data, it has the effect of increasing or decreasing a survey item's relative importance in the aggregate findings to help ensure the weighted data is representative of the population from which the sample is drawn.

Simply stated, weighting data helps ensure the estimates of the findings are representative of the population. Yet, the process of weighting data creates a design effect which increases the basic margin of sampling error and lowers the precision of the estimates. If there is a large design effect, it should raise concerns about potential validity threats that may have resulted from coverage and non-response error. We recommend that sampling error should be adjusted to recognize the effect of weighting data to better match the population, which is called the "adjusted margin of error."

This math illustration highlights the differences between "simple sampling error" and "adjusted sampling error." In a random probability survey of 2,100 (N) adults, the simple sampling error is ±2.1 percentage points at a 95% confidence interval. Thus if 50% of adults surveyed favor a particular position, we would be 95% sure that the true figure is between 47.9% and 52.1% (50 ± 2.1) if all adults in the population had been interviewed, rather than just a sample. Here, simple sampling error is small due to the large number of respondents ($N = 2,100$) randomly surveyed.

Let us now factor in the design effect of weighting. In the study described above, the all-adult sample weighting design effect was 2.82, making the adjusted margin of error ±3.6 percentage points for the adult sample, using trimmed weights at 5% and 95%. Thus if 50% of adults favor a particular position, we would be 95% sure that the true figure is between 46.4% and 53.6% (50 ± 3.6) if all adults in the population had been interviewed, rather than just a sample. Note, the simple sampling error (±2.1) is lower than the adjusted sampling error (±3.6). The design effect varies between surveys and should always be reported by researchers.

Life on the Coast: Meeting the Challenges of Surveying in the Aftermath of a Disaster

In the aftermath of Hurricane Sandy, the landscape was so damaged and scarred that it was commonplace for someone taking a neighborhood stroll to meander past new construction sites sandwiched between vacant lots and condemned homes still awaiting their fate. In fact, when we were asked to interview Sandy survivors during the fall of 2015, only about a quarter of families had recovered from the hurricane in New York City, where federal and state disaster funds were augmented by a city program called Build It Back. It was not until the summer of 2016 that approximately half of all Build It Back recipients received their full funding awards (Sandy Funding Tracker, 2020). Given the slow restoration following the hurricane, the time was ripe to measure the effects of those residents whose lives had been changed by the storm and the prolonged recovery. Fear and apprehension loomed long after the storm, and uncertainty threatened optimism toward the restoration among vulnerable residents. To encourage rebuilding of sustainable neighborhoods, property owners whose dwellings were substantially damaged had to agree to elevate their homes and structures in order to receive building funds from the Build It Back program. State and federal funds were also available in the bi-state region for those areas hit hardest by the storm. In the end, homeowners would make decisions about whether to rebuild or relocate to a new area – in effect, abandoning their roots. While some homeowners chose to rebuild in the neighborhoods where their families had dwelled for decades, others, temporarily displaced, opted for the buyout funds from New York City. Aside from the local economic impact on businesses, the social network of these communities had been transformed. It was in this context and with this focus that researchers at the State University of New York asked us to help them measure *Life on the Coast: Before and After Hurricane Sandy* from late 2015 through early spring in 2016.

Customized Sample Frame

The first question facing all research teams is to define who they want to survey. Most often this is a straightforward task for general population studies, which include all adults in a heterogeneous populace. Following the aftermath of a disaster or emergency event, this task is more complex given the physical dislocations that accompany these events. Recall that we need to acquire or build a list of everyone in the target population; we do not want to miss anyone or include ineligible persons, whether we are drawing a random sample or conducting a census of the target population (Groves et al., 2009). When there is uncertainty about the units (or persons) within a target population, customizing the sample frame yields many advantages, including the ability to conduct a probability survey or census.

To start, we had to draw our own boundaries around the Sandy disaster–impacted target population because there were no predefined geographic parameters for the target population as defined by our client. The budget also constrained our approach, as we estimated that approximately 2,000 residents could be targeted in a mix-mode design. With this number as the maximum N size for eligible participants, the client prioritized the areas that were hardest hit by Hurricane Sandy. The theoretical target population included 11 areas within New York City, New York State (outside NYC), and New Jersey. The areas lay within jurisdictions heavily damaged, but they were also areas eligible to receive federal, state, or local disaster funds. Because the chartered boundaries did not align with a census tract or legal municipal designation, as displayed in Table 2.1, the challenge was to develop a strategy to identify those residents and only those residents who lived within the target population.

We asked the client to provide a description of the heaviest damaged neighborhoods and to identify the streets that bounded the northern, eastern, southern, and western parameters of each neighborhood. Using this visual sketch, we created digital maps of the area and then overlaid street maps to identify all the streets in each area. We then asked the client to confirm the physical properties of the delineated target population they wanted to interview. We then treated each of the targeted neighborhoods as a stratified area within the non-contiguous parameters of the target population. After layering tax data for each neighborhood onto the digital maps, we had an estimate of the number and type of housing units that lie within the target population. We imported the block and lot numbers of the parcels for all property owners listed within the digitized boundaries to ensure our sample frame was in proportion to the target population. In the sample frame, 2,001 parcel lot owners formed the panel, establishing a census of the target population. Relying on the property tax records to create the sample frame was a strategic decision we made at the start of the design. An immediate

TABLE 2.1 Sample Area Displays the Communities in the Wake of Hurricane Sandy Along the New York/New Jersey Coastline in 2015

Neighborhood/Town Area	County	State	%
Broad Channel	Queens	NY	21
Crescent Beach	Richmond	NY	8
Gerritsen Beach	Kings	NY	7
Graham Beach	Richmond	NY	5
Howard Beach	Queens	NY	12
Lindenhurst	Suffolk	NY	5
Lower Tottenville	Richmond	NY	12
Oakwood Beach	Richmond	NY	14
Ocean Breeze	Richmond	NY	6
South Beach	Richmond	NY	8
Woodbridge	Middlesex	NJ	4
Total Sample Area	Bi-state region		100

TABLE 2.2 Parcel Types by Number and Percentage (Coded Value)

Type	N	%
One-family residential (1)	1,134	57
Three-family residential (3)	191	10
Two-family residential (2)	183	9
Residential (4)	164	8
Single condo unit (5)	72	4
Vacant land (6)	207	10
Other* (7)	50	3
Total property parcels	2,001	100

* Two multi-condo units not included in Table 2.2.

challenge we had to address, once we defined the target population, was to assess the storm's aftereffects on *only* those residents who were Sandy survivors. This meant, we had to narrow the parameters of those we interviewed to include *only* those panel participants who lived in the area at the time Hurricane Sandy occurred on October 29, 2012. In addition to only surveying these eligible residents, we also needed to interview those who had relocated after receiving New York State funding to purchase their properties. Table 2.2 displays the parcel types of the current owners at the time the panel was constructed. Eighty-seven percent of parcel lots were residential. In the panel, 313 properties were listed as being owned by the New York State Housing Trust Fund Corporation, reflecting the fact that the former property owners had taken advantage of the state buyout program and had relocated. Despite their relocation, these impacted Sandy residents were part of the target population.

Mix-mode Design

Guided by the Tailored Design paradigm, which advocates approaches to address the four cornerstones of quality surveys by minimizing the four elements of total survey error (Dillman, Smyth, & Christian, 2014), our design strategy next anticipated concerns about non-response given the physical displacement that occurred, coupled with the emotional stress this portended for potential participants. Non-response error does not occur simply when a low number of participants agree to participate, but it also occurs when the responders are different from the non-responders (Dillman et al., 2014). By customizing the sample frame, we gained confidence that our sample frame accurately reflected the target population, so we did not have to allocate resources to screening for eligible participants. Non-response error can also result when you attempt to contact participants in a limited way through only one modality or when you do not present the survey in a format that encourages participation (Dillman et al., 2014). As such, we shifted our resources to designing a mix-mode instrument which fielded the survey in three modes: by mail, over the phone, and through email. We designed the mail mode as the first wave of recruitment.

Finding the eligible participants of a target population presents the second challenge for surveyors. Overall, address-based samples (ABS) consistently yield high response rates, and the ABS frame covers 95% or more of U.S. households (Iannacchione, 2001). As discussed, we customized an ABS for the target population, recognizing two hurdles: an ABS sample obtained from the U.S. Postal Service would not filter out those who did not live in the area at the time of the storm, and forwarding addresses had expired for approximately 16% of the panel who had relocated.

Access to public tax records aided us in overcoming the first hurdle. The tax rolls yielded the names and addresses of all current property owners, the date of acquisition, and the record for property owners dating back through October 29, 2012. Among the 2,001 records found, we removed duplicate property owners from the sample frame, reducing the N to 1,876 panelists. Since the unit of analysis was individuals, we did not want to bias the results by allowing some property owners with multiple holdings an increased likelihood of selection. To address the second hurdle, we cross-referenced our property lists to publicly available records of recipients who received state buyout funds from the New York State Housing Trust Fund Corporation. We used these secondary records to update our mail contact information for these panelists. Using three data sources, we identified addresses for 1,876 panelists. Overall, less than 3% of mailed surveys were returned as having insufficient addresses.

In total, the mail response rate represented more than half of the completed surveys we fielded (55%), resulting in a 7% response rate, which was comparable to telephone surveys during this period (9%) and higher than today's rate (6%; Kennedy & Hartig, 2019). If more budget resources had been available, we would have recommended beginning with a pre-notification to the panel, offering a financial incentive to establish the social contract, sending a reminder postcard appealing for their help, and forwarding a follow-up mail survey within 1 month of the initial mailing. No doubt this would have increased the overall mail response rate among an extremely hard-to-reach target population.

Within the available resources, we fielded two subsequent waves of the survey by landline phone and emails. We utilized a social network aggregator database (Spokeo.com) to augment our property records with landline phone numbers and emails. Among the 1,876 panelists, we collected landline numbers for 1,096 records and 631 valid emails. Responses by phone represented 29% of all completions; online responses represented the remaining 16% of completions.

Statistical Analysis Strengthens Inferences

When surveying a census of a small population, as in our case study, calculating the sampling area is not applicable. An alternative approach to determining how representative the sample of the population was, as compared to the full panel of property owners, tests whether differences exist between those who responded and the non-responders. For this analysis, we conducted the chi-square test for association to observe whether the difference observed was statistically significant among the distinct buyout group studied. Overall, we did not find differences that provided the client with a degree of confidence in making inferences about the findings within these buyout neighborhoods.

Tools of the Trade

Constructing a customized sample frame can prove to be a daunting challenge for researchers; however, the benefits add value by minimizing total survey error, promoting enhancements through mix-mode designs, and lowering fielding costs by improving the quality of the sample frame. Additionally, because our sample frame had to include and exclude participants within specific time parameters, and recruitment was conducted in disparate geographies, customizing the sample frame proved the only way to survey the target population while minimizing threats to validity. Without a customized sample frame, a quantitative research approach may not have been possible.

To customize a sample frame, reference librarians in county and state libraries, and at major colleges and universities, are valuable resources. Numerous guides exist to research public records and to determine what is available and how to find records, including those guides published by government entities and non-profit organizations. Of note, some states have laws that prohibit the dissemination of records to individuals other than to the individual or a family member, but a librarian would have knowledge of these restrictions.

An example of two subgroups that can be identified through address lists in public record searches are senior citizens and veterans. In states like New Jersey, these individuals are eligible for one or more forms of tax rebates and credits. These benefits, reimbursed to local towns and cities through the state, are recorded on tax records and accessible through open public record requests. Such lists may be of importance to researchers surveying disaster or emergency survivors assessing the impact on vulnerable subgroups within a population, measuring recovery benefits targeted to at-risk subgroups that vary from the general population, or appending existing sample frames to enhance coverage of the target population.

Many libraries also have access to databases that provide access to lists of individuals and organizations with indicators ranging from an entity's location, type of business, size, and revenue. Another frame in which to identify and build a sample frame of individuals and businesses is the North American Industry Classification System (NAICS), which is the federal government's mechanism for collecting and reporting statistical data related to economic sectors. These classifications may be useful for researchers studying the impact of a disaster event on the local economy by surveying business owners and managers in both for profit and not-for-profit operations. Knowing how to categorize individuals and organizations by their area of specialization is directly linked to knowing how they are regulated or licensed.

For other studies, in which the population is delineated by geographic regions, an address-based sample is recommended to provide the household frame even when mail mode is not the planned field modality. Today, address-based lists are considered the gold standard for surveying national U.S. households (Harter et al., 2016). In addition to offering the ability to delineate address-based lists by street addresses and zip codes within geographic regions, the lists can also be aligned with census tracts. The benefits of this approach are highlighted in our second case study. Marketing companies and sample vendors that provide address-based samples typically have their lists updated monthly or even more frequently, so be sure to inquire as to when the list was last updated when requesting a quote.

The most recent innovations in the field now provide ways to append household names and telephone numbers to address-based samples. When you begin with a household frame, many vendors offer value-added data services that overlay information ranging from household names, phone numbers, and demographics about the household. These data enhanced household frames extend design options by providing researchers with a mix-mode field strategy.

Texting, as a design mode, is made possible through listed samples provided by sample vendors. Products such as "smart cell samples" now provide a comprehensive list of cellular phone records with "targetable geographic and demographic variables" (SSI). Demographic targets include age, gender, ethnicity, income, occupation, and education. While some indicators are more reliable than others, it provides a way to randomly target those hard-to-reach populations if you determine respondents are not representative of the target population while you are still in the field, which has the effect of minimizing design effects. For example, increasing the incidence rate of finding a known Hispanic population living within a disaster area serves to decrease non-response error and reduce fielding time and effort, resulting in lower costs.

Finally, surveying online provides researchers with the lowest acquisition costs and the shortest fielding time, which is why it is preferred by so many. However, this mode is only available when email lists or cell phone numbers are available. When a general population study is the target, we recommend that you contract with a vendor who has experience providing or appending address-based lists with demographic and contact information, including emails. Reliable vendors can tell you in advance, before you incur any fees, what the likely match of emails to your data file is. Further, only use vendors who regularly scrub their list. This cleaning process ensures email and cell number verification, active landline verification, and regular updates match to national change of address databases, along with Social Security Death Index matching. This latter provision is extremely important when you are surveying a population that has been severely impacted and may have experienced high fatality rates.

Hardest Hit Survivors: One Mile From the Water's Edge

Just 20 months after Hurricane Sandy transformed coastal communities, we were asked to collaborate with researchers at Rutgers, The State University of New Jersey to assess the information infrastructure in New York City on behalf of Internews. This phase of the client's research centered on the information ecosystem of city residents in two distinct geographic areas that likely did not share the same sources of local information. In the context of this research, the client defined information ecosystems as "complex adaptive systems that include information infrastructure, tools, media, producers, consumers, curators and sharers . . . through which information moves and transforms in flows" (Information Ecosystems in Action: New York, 2014). Unlike our first case study, eligible participants for this study did not have to reside in the area at the time of the hurricane. Instead, the target population included current residents living within 1 mile of the water's edge in the boroughs of Staten Island and Brooklyn. Without any residency constraint, the target population included 80% of respondents who reported living in the area at the time of the storm, while 20% reported moving in after Sandy hit the area.

For this research, the survey instrument we designed measured how information needs changed over time, particularly in the aftermath of a substantive and disruptive event. An information assessment of New York City posed unique challenges, since the city is densely populated and lies within the largest media market in the United States including multilingual media outlets. Within these parameters, the survey instrument measured trust in information, identified neighborhood influencers, and explored the relationship of local information sources to information related to post–Hurricane Sandy recovery (Information Ecosystems in Action: New York, 2014).

Defining the target population was an important consideration in the design phase given the diversity and geographic expanse of New York City. According to the Centers for Disease Control and Prevention (CDC), most of the hurricane-related deaths that occurred in the bi-state region resulted from drowning (as cited in Information Ecosystems in Action: New York, 2014). According to the report's findings (2014):

> Tragically, approximately half of the drowning deaths occurred in flooded homes located in areas under mandatory evacuation. A better understanding of how communities' information ecosystems function can shed light on whether and how people received information to evacuate, how they evaluate it, and what led them to act on it (or not).

Thus, this is the reason our client defined the target population as those residences that lie within the storm's most heavily impacted areas within the city.

Within this definition, the immediate problem facing our research team was how to find those residents who experienced the worst flooding conditions and loss of electricity and related communication failures during the storm. Since the study was designed as a random digit dialing (RDD) phone survey, our challenge was to minimize coverage error that was likely to include ineligible units outside the target population. Although mail-fielded surveys can target geographically bounded targets with more precision, phone number sample frames are less accurate even when the area codes, prefixes, and associated identifiers are available. At the time, smart cell products, with a higher incidence of geographic indicator, were not available.

Adding screener questions to the instrument for phone-based surveys do serve to filter those participants that do not meet the criteria of the target population. Although an effective tool, screener questions that are used to recruit a smaller proportion of an eligible target population from a large and diverse population increase the length of the survey, which may increase respondent acquisition costs by one-third.

For Staten Island residents, the geographic parameter was defined as the entire borough. Staten Island is bounded by water on all sides and is the smallest of the City's five boroughs, with a population of approximately 470,000, according to the 2010 Census. Our task proved more daunting in constructing the sample frame for residents living in Brooklyn along the water's edge; specifically, those residents living within 1 mile of the waterfront, anywhere in the borough. Brooklyn is the most populated of the City's boroughs (2,505,000) and has five times more residents as compared with Staten Island, according to the 2010 Census.

We began with the premise that most residences do not know the distance to the water's edge unless they reside immediately adjacent to the water. To narrow eligible participants within the targeted land area, we utilized digitized geographic information to draw a buffer within 1 mile of water in Brooklyn. We then overlaid the census tracts on the digital map to identify those tracts or portions thereof contained within this area. We imported data that displayed the streets and block numbers of the residences in this area. Within these defined parameters, we ordered a dual sample frame list of landlines and cells in proportion to the known demographics of the bounded area from our sample vendor. We estimated that one-fifth of Brooklyn residents lived within the eligible target population.

With more confidence in the coverage of our sample frame, we were still interested in ensuring that the households randomly dialed were eligible to participate. Now, starting with a more precise coverage parameter for the target population, the use of screener questions was an effective, low-cost means to recruit eligible participants. In Brooklyn only, we relied upon a series of screener questions to assist respondents in estimating their proximity to the water's edge. We asked respondents for their home zip code, but we also asked participants to tell us if they lived about one mile from the water in Brooklyn. For those unsure, we probed further and asked how many blocks away from the water they estimated they lived. Our acceptance threshold was set at 10 blocks or closer, based upon our digital analysis.

Finally, given our utilization of the census information and digitized mapping, we knew the population parameters of the target population before we began fielding. Within this area, Staten Island and the water's edge in Brooklyn made up approximately 50% each of the target population. This allowed us to stratify the sample before fielding and establish respondent quotas in proportion, given our N size of 750 respondents. Another advantage a probability sample provides is that we can estimate sampling error, with design effects, to better measure the precision of our estimates. Finally, we were able to weight the data during the post–analysis phase to the general population parameters on gender and age within each stratified region of the sample.

Overall, weighting would not have been as accurate, if recommended at all, if we had to weight the sample parameters for the Brooklyn portion to the demographic parameters of the target population for the whole of the borough. Knowing the target population parameters is essential in minimizing total survey error and fielding costs. Further, advanced tools and modes available in 2020 permits fielding to be conducting in waves which allows survey methodologists to refresh samples based on specific parameters for subgroups within the target population that are harder to find or reach. Such strategies employed throughout the fielding process served to lower the design effect on sampling error, which ensured that the generalized inferences were higher in validity.

When All Else Fails: Benefits of Non-probability Samples

Methodologically speaking, a random probability survey of a population is the gold standard for generalizing the findings from a sample to the target population. Simply stated, a smaller probability sample is more generalizable than a large non-probability sample (Remler & Van Ryzin, 2014). Still, there are real-world challenges to conducting a probability sample. Pragmatism, including time and funding limitations, often limits the decision and design options for researchers (Rivera, 2018). Recognizing what researchers trade away in terms of minimizing total survey error, reducing threats to validity, and generalizing to the population, there are strengths to employing non-probability samples to survey populations (Groves et al., 2009).

All research begins with a literature review, which should include a discussion of the content area as well as recommended methodologies, including both probability studies and qualitative approaches such as non-probability surveys. Our client, Internews, conducted robust qualitative studies before initiating phase two of their probability survey research with us, which explored how information ecosystems had changed in New York City. This research included a review of the theoretical literature, case studies, and primary research employed and guided the question wording and question order of the instrument we fielded. The literature review also provided a comparative analysis revealing similarities between the information ecosystem of New York and Internews' international focus in locations such as Jakarta (Internews Center for Innovation and Learning, May 2015). In effect, understanding how communities utilize and access information, and how this varies during major disruptions, can help researchers make decisions about when and how to employ non-probability surveys to collect data. With this guidance in mind, researchers may alternatively choose to generalize their findings to theory (Remler & Van Ryzin, 2014). Non-probability surveys are also subject to selection bias; therefore, researchers should fully discuss the limitations and the rationale for the non-probability sampling method selected; namely, convenience or availability, quota, snowball, and purposive sampling.

Convenience or Availability Sampling

Convenience describes this sampling method aptly; it is a useful strategy to employ in preliminary or exploratory studies asking questions about the "how" and "why." When a sample frame of the target population is unknown or unavailable, availability sampling provides a haphazard, accidental, or convenient way to recruit participants for a survey (Chambliss & Schutt, 2019). An example of this sampling method is akin to collecting person-on-the-street interviews. Researchers collect data from the most readily available participants (Remler & Van Ryzin, 2014). The risk to this approach is selection bias, such that only those who are available and willing to participate are included in the sample, ruling out the possibility that everyone in the target population has an equal chance of selection. However, replicating convenience sampling in various settings improves the observations rendered in non-random studies (Remler & Van Ryzin, 2014).

Quota Sampling

To minimize the weaknesses of convenience sampling, researchers can set quotas (Chambliss & Schutt, 2019). Quotas are employed in probability surveys to recruit representative samples of eligible participants. Similarly, quota sampling is a valuable tool for non-probability samples that allow participants to draw and limit selections from specific subgroups of a known population. When researchers know the demographics of the population parameters, quotas should be established in non-probability survey studies. Setting proportional quotas based on a wide array of demographics strains toward validity, particularly when the quotas align with census parameters. Census data also sheds light on the primary languages spoken in an area. This will help guide the language in which interviews need to be fielded.

Snowball Sampling

The Tailored Design paradigm emphasizes the importance of establishing a relationship between the interviewer and likely participants. This approach begins with establishing a social contract between the parties; the most successful relationships are forged when trust is established among potential participants. When surveying hard-to-find participants, who are often the most socially and economically disadvantaged, snowball sampling offers an important approach. Snowball sampling relies on multiple and successive informants, with the interviewee serving as the primary informant or recruiter. Snowball referrals are especially valuable when surveying vulnerable populations such as disabled veterans, HIV drug users, women who have experienced domestic abuse, or disaster survivors who lost their income and/or homes after a major traumatic event.

In the latter case, if a researcher wants to interview those who have been displaced by events occurring more than 12 months earlier, after U.S. Postal Service forwarding orders have expired, snowball sampling may be the only way to locate those who moved away. In the absence of a government program that required forwarding addresses for grant recipients, neighbors often serve as the best and only resource for contacting former residents. Snowball sampling relies on the premise that the last question asked of an interviewee is "Who else do you recommend I interview, and what am I missing?" In this case, snowball sampling continues until saturation is reached, meaning subsequent informants do not provide any "new" information as compared to those already interviewed (Chambliss & Schutt, 2019).

Purposive Sampling

Another strong example of a non-probability sample appropriate to a specific target audience is purposive sampling (Chambliss & Schutt, 2019). Here the participants are selected for a purpose; namely, they meet specific criteria or conditions, or they possess unique characteristics to qualify as an eligible participant. These kinds of individuals range from hospital administrators, municipal managers, and non-profit directors to public health officials. Each participant has a unique asset or is in a discrete role that makes them of interest to the researchers. When surveying potential participants about disaster or emergency management events, these individuals play a valuable role prior to, during, and after a disaster. Consider physicians and medical personnel on the front line during an emergency event. As elite participants, it is difficult and more expensive to recruit these individuals through a probability sample of the general population. Alternatively, a purposive sample recruits elites at events where their attendance is expected, such as a public health forum or an American Medical Association convention. The key to conducting purposive sampling relies on finding out when and where events open to the public are held or scheduled. Identifying stakeholders, influencers, and opinion leaders in a community often means going to places with purpose, where these elites are expected to be found in large numbers.

When Hurricane Sandy made landfall on the Eastern Seaboard, she disrupted the population and the normal cadence of life, forcing the cancellation of major events, including an annual convention of publicly elected and non-elected individuals and business leaders in New Jersey. We were asked to help the sponsoring organization survey whether to reschedule the event. We relied upon a list of previous attendees and exhibit sponsors to measure both interest and scheduling availability. Surveying potential participants was different from surveying regular attendees; in effect, we conducted a purposive survey of confirmed participants. While our findings were not generalizable, we categorized participants by known characteristics including large and small entities, across the state's geographic parameters, to make assessments that the survey results likely represented the preferences of attendees.

Targeted Non-probability Sampling

Non-probability sampling is applicable to research that is more exploratory rather than hypothesis driven. Surveys utilizing non-probability sampling are also better suited to reflexive research designs that occur in naturalized settings, as when the researcher needs to immerse himself or herself in the experiences of disaster victims. The leverage-saliency theory argues that survey respondents are motivated to respond to surveys for varying reasons (Groves, Singer, & Corning, 2000). Social exchange theory (Dillman, 1978) focuses on appealing to respondents in a variety of ways.

Yet, in a generalized probability sample, asking for help from an individual respondent is effective when the interviewer or researcher conveys there is a social return that is greater than the cost to the respondent. The conventional ways to increase participation and to decrease the costs of participation may not be applicable to disaster survivors. The costs of participation are generally higher for disaster survivors who may be asked to recall significant losses, sometimes permanent in nature. In sum, many of the tools of probability surveys can be employed using non-probability samples; however, exercise caution when reporting the findings.

Non-probability studies are also optimal when researchers do not have the time or budget resources needed to construct a sample frame of a potentially scattered target population, yet they need to explore the impact of a disaster or emergency event on a population. In these instances, researchers should limit their generalizations to theory. Additionally, researchers should employ sampling strategies that allow them to mitigate against threats to bias, which are likely to occur when participants are not randomly selected. For instance, employ quotas to ensure respondents are representative of key subgroups of the target population. In this way, researchers may mute some criticism about threats to validity by providing a profile of the sample demographics as compared to the population benchmarks.

Further Readings

Callegaro, M., Villar, A., Yeager, D.S., & Krosnick, J.A. (2014). A critical review of studies investigating the quality of data obtained with online panels based on probability and nonprobability samples. In M. Callegaro, R. Baker, J. Bethlehem, A. Goritz, J. Krosnick, & P. Lavrakas (Eds.), *Online panel research: A data quality perspective* (pp. 23–53). Chichester: Wiley.

MacInnis, B., Krosnick, J.A., Ho, A.S., & Cho, M.J. (2018). The accuracy of measurements with probability and nonprobability survey samples: Replication and extension. *Public Opinion Quarterly, 82*(4), 707–744.

Toninelli, D., & Revilla, M.A. (2016). Smartphones vs PCs: Does the device affect the web survey experience and the measurement error for sensitive topics? A replication of the Mavletova & Couper's 2013 experiment. *Survey Research Methods, 10*(2), 153–169.

Yeager, D.S., Krosnick, J.A., Chang, L., Javitz, H.S., Levendusky, M.S., Simpser, A., & Wang, R. (2011). Comparing the accuracy of RDD telephone surveys and internet surveys conducted with probability and non-probability samples. *Public Opinion Quarterly, 75*(4), 709–747.

References

Chambliss, D. F., & Schutt, R. K (2019). *Making sense of the social world methods of investigation* (6th ed.). Thousand Oaks, CA: Sage.

Dillman, D.A. (1978). *Mail and telephone surveys: The total design method.* New York: Wiley.

Dillman, D. A., Smyth, J. D., & Christian, L. M. (2009). *Internet, mail, and mixed-mode surveys: The tailored design method* (3rd ed.). New York: Wiley.

Dillman, D. A., Smyth, J. D., & Christian, L. M. (2014). *Internet, mail, and mixed-mode surveys: The tailored design method* (4th ed.). New York: Wiley.

Groves, R. M. (1989). *Survey errors and survey costs.* New York: Wiley.

Groves, R. M., Fowler, F. J., Jr., Couper, M. P., Lepkowski, J. M., Singer, E., & Tourangeau, R. (2009). *Survey methodology* (2nd ed.). Hoboken, NJ: Wiley.

Groves, R. M., Singer, E., & Corning, A. (2000). Leverage-saliency theory of survey participation: Description and an illustration. *Public Opinion Quarterly, 64*(3), 299–308.

Harter, R., Battaglia, M. P., Buskirk, T. D., Dillman, D. A., English, N., Fahimi, M., . . ., & Zukerberg, A. L. (2016). *Address-based sampling.* Report prepared for the AAPOR Council by the Task Force on Address-based Sampling. https://www.aapor.org/AAPOR_Main/media/MainSiteFiles/AAPOR_Report_1_7_16_CLEAN-COPY-FINAL.pdf

Iannacchione, V. G. (2011, Fall). The changing role of address-based sampling in survey research. *Public Opinion Quarterly, 75*(3), 556–575. https://doi.org/10.1093/poq/nfr017

Information Ecosystems in Action: New York. (2014, November). *A companion to mapping information ecosystems to support resilience: A decision support framework.* https://internews.org/sites/default/files/resources/Internews_Information_Ecosystems_in_Action-NewYork.pdf

Kennedy, C., & Hartig, H. (2019). Response rates in telephone surveys have resumed their decline. *Pew Research Center.* https://www.pewresearch.org/fact-tank/2019/02/27/response-rates-in-telephone-surveys-have-resumed-their-decline/

Remler, D. K., & Van Ryzin, G. G. (2014). *Research methods in practice: Strategies for description and causation.* Los Angeles: Sage.

Rivera, J. D. (2018). When attaining the best sample is out of reach: Nonprobability alternatives when engaging in public administration research. *Journal of Public Affairs Education, 25*(3), 314–342.

Sandy Funding Tracker. (2020). https://www1.nyc.gov/content/sandytracker/pages/

3

Disastrous Inferences? The Ecological Fallacy in Disaster and Emergency Management Research

Paul A. Jargowsky

Introduction

In research on disaster and emergency management, the limited available data is often summarized at higher levels of aggregation, particularly summaries for geographic areas – sometimes referred to as "ecological data." Measures of social vulnerability and disaster post-mortems based on such data purporting to measure or explain individual-level phenomena have been criticized as committing an "ecological fallacy" (Duneier, 2006; Gall, 2007; Rivera, 2019). In fact, estimates of causal effects from aggregate data can be wrong both in magnitude and direction (Robinson, 1950). This chapter examines the factors that contribute to incorrect inferences that can arise from the analysis of aggregate data and provides guidance to disaster and emergency management researchers to help them avoid committing ecological fallacies.

Stated briefly, *one commits an ecological fallacy if one assumes that relationships observed at an aggregated level imply that the same relationships exist at the individual level.* For example, observing that the mortality rate from a disaster and the percent living alone are correlated at the level of neighborhoods does not necessarily imply that individuals living alone are more likely to die than otherwise similar people who live with others. Indeed, it is possible that the correlation of two variables at the aggregate level can have the opposite sign as the correlation at the individual level. As a result, it can be risky to infer individual-level relationships from aggregated cross-sectional data, an issue known as the problem of ecological inference.

In the context of disaster research, individual-level data on the consequences of weather events, industrial calamities, and terrorist attacks are rarely available. Instead, researchers rely on aggregate figures on casualities and losses, as well as population covariates, summarized at various geographic levels – typically neighborhoods, cities, counties, states, or even nations. Kamel and Loukaitou-Sideris (2004), for example, used zip code data after the earthquake in Northridge, California, to show that "areas with high concentrations of persons of Hispanic origin, low-income and immigrants" were disadvantaged in the distribution of federal assistance. However, they moved from the ecological level to the individual level in attributing this finding to "structural constraints embedded in federal programmes that, to a great extent, excluded very low-income households from the major sources of assistance" (557). The assumption that low-income *individuals* received less aid based on the fact that low-income *areas* received less aid is an example of an ecological inference. As we shall see below, despite seeming plausible and reasonable, such inferences may well be false. Thus, there is ample potential for research in disaster and emergency management to reach potentially faulty conclusions about individual-level causal relationships by generalizing from data collected and analyzed at aggregate levels.

A further complication is that variables can have subtle variations in meaning when measured at different levels of aggregation. Social capital, for example, can be measured at a macro level as a characteristic of a community (e.g., the density of civic organizations), or it can be measured at the micro level as the number of connections a given individual has. Kyne and Aldrich discuss the importance of social capital in contributing to disaster resilience, defined as "community members' capacity to utilize local and extra-local resources to deal with shocks and crises" (2020, pp. 63–64). However, the social capital indicators they define are based on county-level aggregate data. The role that social capital plays in helping a community recover from disaster is a conceptually distinct question from the role it plays in helping individuals or families recover: using data from one level to draw conclusions about the other risks committing an ecological fallacy (Rivera, 2019).

When thinking about disaster planning and mitigation strategies, those reasoning from aggregate data can also fall prey to ecological fallacies. For example, the climate change debate involves deciding whether to take potentially costly measures today to offset future harms. Yet people in the future are likely to be richer on average than people today due to economic growth, leading some to ask whether it is reasonable to impose huge costs on today's population to benefit tomorrow's presumably far richer population (Lomborg, 2010; Schelling, 1995). However, treating "people today" and "people in the future" as aggregates commits an ecological fallacy (Rendall, 2019). The costs of taking action today could be imposed on today's rich through progressive taxation and the benefits may be felt by the future's poor persons living in low-lying areas such as Bangladesh and Jakarta. The aggregate differences between today's and tomorrow's populations do not necessarily tell you about the distribution of costs and benefits at the individual level.

These few examples make it clear that disaster and emergency management researchers need to give careful consideration to the ecological inference problem. In this chapter, I will examine two cases in which the charge of ecological fallacy has been brought to bear against research in the field. The first is Eric Klinenberg's analysis of the deadly Chicago heat wave of 1995 in his award-winning book, *Heat Wave: A Social Autopsy of Disaster in Chicago*. Among other findings, Klinenberg argued that some neighborhoods experienced higher death rates than others due to a higher degree of social isolation: elderly African-American Chicagoans "died alone" in disproportionate numbers "because they lived in social environments that . . . created obstacles to social protection" (Klinenberg, 2015, p. 127). Duneier (2006), noting that Klinenberg "presents no data on specific individuals who passed away," challenged the finding as an ecological fallacy, based on data he collected about individuals who died in the heat wave, showing that few of them lived alone and they were not especially isolated. The second case is the burgeoning field of developing indices to measures social vulnerability and resiliency. For example, the Disaster Risk Index (DRI) and other social vulnerability indices often rely on data for nations but are sometimes used to draw conclusions about smaller areas and demographic subgroups (Gall, 2007). Before addressing those cases, however, I will discuss the history of the concept of ecological fallacy and illustrate, graphically and mathematically, how the use of aggregate data can lead to wrong and misleading results.

Understanding the Problem

Although not the first to draw attention to the problems of ecological inference, Robinson (1950) had the most dramatic impact. He cited a number of famous studies from several disciplines that were based on what he called "ecological correlations" (pp. 351–352). That is, the cited studies relied on ordinary Pearsonian correlation coefficients between two variables calculated from the *averages* of those variables for spatially defined groups of individuals, such as neighborhoods, cities, states, or regions. These studies had assumed, often implicitly, that the implications that could be drawn from the sign, magnitude, and significance of the ecological correlations applied equally to the relationship between the two variables at the level of individuals, which in almost all cases was the primary objective of the research.

Robinson's Critique of Ecological Inference

Robinson contrasted individual and ecological correlations in cases where data were available at both levels. He showed that the individual-level correlation between race and illiteracy in the United States in 1930 was 0.203, but the correlation between percent black and percent illiterate at the state level was far higher, 0.773. Robinson showed that not even the sign of ecological correlations could be trusted. The correlation between having been born abroad and being illiterate was 0.118 at the individual level (again using 1930 data for the United States), probably reflecting the lower educational standards of the immigrants' countries of origin. However, the correlation at the state level between the corresponding ecological aggregates (percent foreign born and percent illiterate) was a counterintuitive -0.526 – the opposite direction of the individual correlation! Robinson concluded that "there need be no correspondence between the individual correlation and the ecological correlation" (1950, p. 354). Moreover, he said he provided "a definite answer as to whether ecological correlations can validly be used as substitutes for individual correlations." His answer: "They cannot" (p. 357).

The impact of Robinson's condemnation of ecological inference was profound. Indeed, inferences about individual relationships from aggregate data came to be regarded not just as problematic but – though Robinson's seminal article did not use this word – as a fallacy (Selvin, 1958, p. 615). And while Robinson's critique was stated in terms of simple bivariate correlation coefficients, his argument is a challenge to regression analyses based on aggregate data as well. All slope coefficients in bivariate and multiple regressions can be expressed as functions of either simple or partial correlation coefficients, respectively, scaled by the standard deviations of the dependent and independent variables. Because standard deviations are always positive, the sign of any regression coefficient reflects the sign of the correlation coefficient on which it is based. Thus, regression analysis on aggregated data – a common practice in several disciplines – runs the risk of committing the ecological fallacy as well.

The Limitations of Robinson's Critique

Seen in retrospect, Robinson's analysis seems to ignore the presence of confounding variables. For example, in Robinson's second example, immigrants tended to flock to industrial states in search of jobs; these states were wealthier and had higher literacy rates than poor (jobless) Southern states that failed to attract as many immigrants. To a modern reader, Robinson's analysis seems to lack appropriate controls for socioeconomic status, regional dummy variables, or a fixed-effects model to isolate the effect of illiteracy from other covariates. Indeed, Hanushek et al. revisited Robinson's data and showed that the sign of his correlation was a reflection of left-out variable bias (1974, pp. 90–95); in other words, his model was underspecified.

If the anomalous results attributed to the ecological fallacy actually result from model mis-specification, then "the ecological fallacy itself is a near fallacy" (Firebaugh, 1978, p. 570; see also Schwartz, 1994). On the other hand, if the divergence between individual- and aggregate-level estimates are more subtle and intractable, then ecological inference is dangerous business. The following section illustrates the demographic underpinnings and mathematical structure of the ecological fallacy, which in turn gives some guidance as to how it can be avoided.

Illustration of the Ecological Fallacy

We begin by considering a few hypothetical scenarios using scatter plots and line graphs, following the example of Gove and Hughes (1980). Keeping with the theme of *Heat Wave*, assume we have data on the mortality rate for neighborhoods involved in some sort of catastrophe and the percentage of neighborhood residents who live alone. We are interested in the hypothesis that living alone is associated with higher mortality during the heat wave, but we lack data on individuals. Thus, we do not separately observe the death rate for those living alone and the death rate for those living with others. What we do observe is that the death rate increases steadily as the neighborhood percentage of persons living alone increases from zero to 100%. Figure 3.1 shows a scatter plot of the observed data and an upward-sloping bivariate regression line capturing the relationship of mortality and living alone at the aggregate (neighborhood) level.

Figure 3.2 shows how ecological inference is supposed to work. Hypothetical sets of death rates for those living alone and those living with others, which the researcher does not observe due to data limitations, are shown as dashed lines. Of course, there would be random variation at the neighborhood level, but the important thing is the trend. In this figure, those living alone have a higher death rate than those living with others regardless of neighborhood composition. The observed death rate at the neighborhood level increases steadily because the composition of the neighborhood changes along the x-axis. The death rate increases by 0.02 for each percentage point increase in living alone at the neighborhood level. An inference that the death rate for individuals living alone was 2.0 points higher than for individuals living in groups would, in this case, be correct.

The problem is that the same observed aggregate pattern can be generated by many different sets of underlying death rates for the two groups. In Figure 3.3, those living alone are more likely to die than those living with others, regardless of neighborhood composition; the difference is about 1.0. However, the mortality rate of both groups rises as percent living alone in the neighborhood rises, perhaps because percent living alone in the neighborhood is correlated with some other variable, such as family

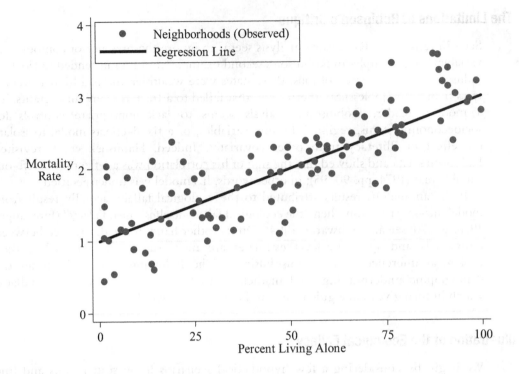

FIGURE 3.1 Mortality and Percent Living Alone: The Observed Data

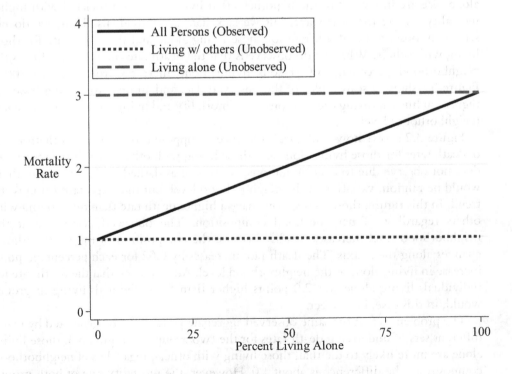

FIGURE 3.2 Scenario With Correct Inference From Ecological Data

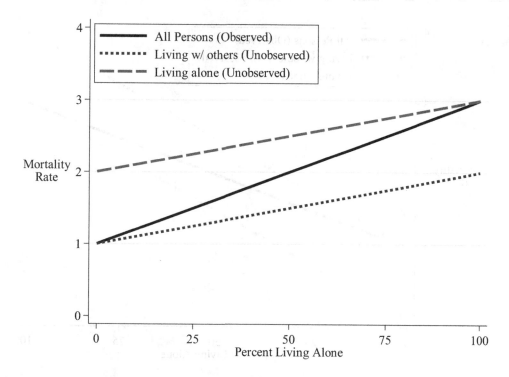

FIGURE 3.3 Aggregate Relationship Overestimates Individual Effect

income, which independently affects mortality. The aggregate relationship based on the observed data confounds these two different effects. Only half of the total effect (1.0 out of 2.0) at the aggregate level is due to individual level differences; the other half is associated with aggregation.

In fact, as shown in Figure 3.4, inference from ecological data can give entirely misleading results. In this case, those living with others have a *higher* mortality rate than those living alone, regardless of neighborhood composition. The ecological regression coefficient will still have the same slope as in the previous figures, but in this case it is driven by the fact that the overall mortality rises sharply as the percent living alone rises. In this case, the ecological regression would correctly report that mortality is positively associated with percent living alone at the neighborhood level, but the inference that individuals living alone are more likely to die than others would be wrong. They are not more likely to die, either in any given neighborhood or in the area as a whole.

This is an example of what is known as Simpson's Paradox. While it may seem far-fetched, it is actually not that uncommon. For example, a state-level regression of share voting Democratic on average household income would show a positive relationship; richer states are more likely to vote Democratic. Yet looking within any state, you will find that the probability of voting Democratic declines as a function of household income (Gelman & Hill, 2006).

Other scenarios are possible. Suppose the mortality rates are exactly the same within each neighborhood regardless of living arrangements, but the rates for both groups rise as the percent living alone rises. A figure for this scenario is omitted,

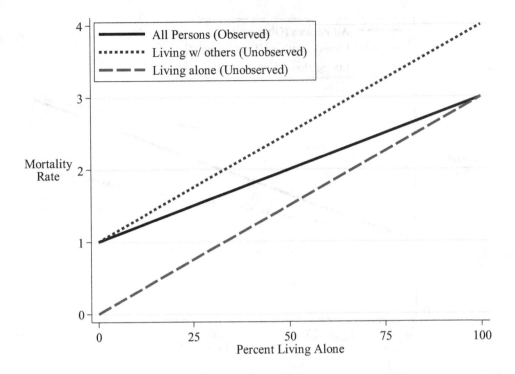

FIGURE 3.4 Incorrect Inference Leading to Wrong Sign

because all three lines would simply lie on top of each other. At the neighborhood level, the observed mortality rate would slope upwards, even though there is no effect operating at the level of individuals of living alone versus living with others once neighborhood composition is taken into account.

Figure 3.5 shows a case where the mortality rate rises as the percent living alone rises because of an *interaction* between mortality and the neighborhood composition that varies by whether the individual is living alone or not. In neighborhoods with relatively few single-person households, those living alone actually have a lower death rate, but as the neighborhood percentage of that group increases, the death rate for those living alone crosses over and is higher in those neighborhoods where they are concentrated.

The underlying group mortality rates in Figures 3.2–3.5 were constructed to produce exactly the same aggregate (observed) relationship between mortality and living arrangements. In Figure 3.2, the aggregate pattern was a good guide to the underlying trend. In Figure 3.3, those living with others were more likely to die conditional on neighborhood than those living alone, but the aggregate trend overestimated the individual effect by 100%. In Figure 3.4, the trend at the aggregate level had the opposite sign as the relationship at the individual level. In Figure 3.5, the group with the highest death rate conditional on neighborhood depended on the composition of the neighborhood. Observationally, these scenarios are equivalent and produce the same aggregate relationship between mortality and living alone, but with vastly different underlying individual relationships.

By itself, therefore, the aggregate relationship is not a good guide to individual relationship, at least without a more robust analysis as discussed below. In general, the observed aggregate relationship is a combination of the individual relationship and

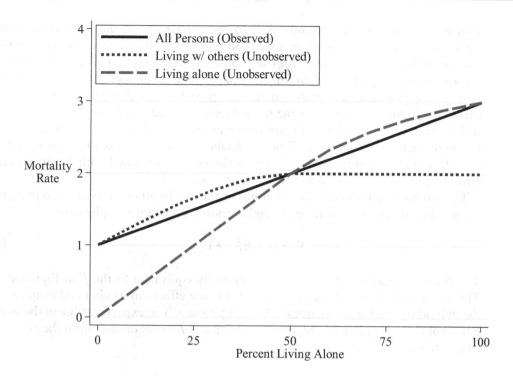

FIGURE 3.5 Incorrect Inference Due to Missing Interaction

correlation that arises via the grouping process. The latter may reflect confounding variables correlated with one of the two variables at the neighborhood level or effects of concentration of one group or the other independent of the individual-level effect. It may also reflect sorting pressures that generate selection bias. Care must be taken to disentangle these factors to avoid incorrect inferences.

The Mathematics Underlying the Ecological Fallacy

The problem described above can be restated as a form of aggregation bias (Freedman, 2001; Irwin & Lichtman, 1976; Jargowsky, 2005; Stoker, 1993; Theil, 1954). Assume we have data on an outcome variable Y and a causal variable X for individuals who are scattered across a set of geographic entities (e.g., neighborhoods). We can obtain an estimate of the effect of X on Y by applying ordinary least squares (OLS) to the following population regression equation:

$$Y_{ij} = \alpha + \beta X_{ij} + u_{ij} \tag{1}$$

in which j indexes neighborhoods and i indexes individuals within neighborhood j, and u_{ij} is the disturbance term. The OLS estimator of the slope, $\hat{\beta}$, has the following expected value:

$$E\left[\hat{\beta}\right] = \beta + E\left[\frac{\sum_j \sum_i X_{ij} u_{ij}}{\sum_j \sum_i \left(X_{ij} - \bar{X}\right)^2}\right] \tag{2}$$

This result is mathematically equivalent to the standard proof that OLS coefficients are unbiased, which is found in any econometrics textbook (e.g., Greene, 2000; Gujarati & Porter, 2008), except for the double summation sign. However, in view of the associative property of addition, the double summation sign does not affect the sums or the conclusion. For the coefficient $\hat{\beta}$ to be an unbiased estimator of the parameter β, the expectation of the second term in Equation 2 must be zero, which will occur if and only if X and u are uncorrelated. The disturbance term, however, implicitly includes the effect of all other variables as well as random influences. If the net effect of these omitted variables and influences is correlated with X, the second term does not reduce to zero and the estimator is biased.

By summing up individual observations to the neighborhood level and dividing by the number of observations in each neighborhood, Equation 1 implies that

$$\bar{Y}_j = \alpha + \beta \bar{X}_j + \bar{u}_j \qquad [3]$$

The β that appears in Equation 3 is algebraically equivalent to the β in Equation 1. Thus, in principle, an unbiased estimate of the true effect can be obtained from either the individual-level or the aggregate-level regressions. The expected value of the slope estimator from the aggregate regression, denoted as $\hat{\beta}$ to distinguish from the estimate based on individual-level data, is

$$E\left[\hat{\beta}|X\right] = \beta + E\left[\frac{\sum_j \bar{X}_j \bar{u}_j}{\sum_j \left(\bar{X}_j - \bar{X}\right)^2}\right] \qquad [4]$$

At the aggregate level, therefore, the condition for unbiasedness is that there is no correlation between the neighborhood means of the disturbance term and the independent variable. It is quite possible that, in any given set of data, the criteria for unbiasedness is met at the individual level but violated at the aggregate level. For example, a correlation could arise if the grouping process is related to some variable Z, not included in the regression, which is correlated with the outcome variable (Freedman, 2001). Thus, the ecological fallacy can arise as a particular kind of left-out variable bias, one that is introduced or exacerbated because of the aggregation process. In addition, a correlation between X and u at the aggregate level could arise if the grouping process is based on the values of the dependent variable, Y; in that case, either extreme values of X or extreme values of u would produce extreme values of Y that would tend to be grouped together, inducing a correlation between X and u.

Although I have explicated these ideas in the context of a bivariate regression, they apply equally well in the multiple regression context. In fact, in the world of social phenomena, where there are always correlations among explanatory variables, it is highly unlikely to be the case that a bivariate regression would be correctly specified at either the individual or the aggregate level. In the multivariate context, however, one additional problem arises. An outcome variable for an individual may be affected by both the individual's value of X *and* by a contextual variable that is a function of the aggregated values of X, such as the mean of X (Firebaugh, 2015). A common example is that a child's educational achievement can be affected by the family's poverty and also by the average poverty level of the school or neighborhood (Jargowsky & El Komi, 2011; Lauen & Gaddis, 2013; Summers & Wolfe, 1977).

When the individual data are aggregated, the individual and contextual values of X may not be separately identified.

The first implication of the foregoing discussion is that if both the individual and ecological regressions are correctly specified, both types of analyses will provide equally unbiased estimates of the true slope parameter:

$$E[\beta] = E[\beta *] = \beta \qquad [5]$$

Thus, an ecological regression is not necessarily wrong, though the aggregation process increases the potential for mis-specification.

The second implication is that both regressions can be mis-specified. Indeed, there is no guarantee that the individual regression is the better of the two. Grunfeld and Griliches (1960), referring to individual regressions as micro equations and ecological regressions as macro equations, argue that ecological regressions may be better in certain circumstances:

> In practice we do not know enough about micro behavior to be able to specify micro equations perfectly. . . . Aggregation of economic variables can, and in fact frequently does, reduce these specification errors. Hence, aggregation does not only produce aggregation error, but may also produce an aggregation gain.
>
> (p. 1)

It is not hard to think of examples where aggregation could reduce correlation between the disturbance term and a given independent variable. For example, persons may choose their neighborhoods based on unobserved characteristics that also affect their wages. In that case, neighborhood characteristics will be correlated with the disturbance term in a wage regression, resulting in biased estimates of the neighborhood effect on wage. Aggregating to the metropolitan level would sharply reduce this source of bias by subsuming all neighborhood-to-neighborhood selection into the metropolitan averages.

The third implication is that it is possible to think about the conditions under which the bias term in Equation 4 has an expectation that differs from zero. Assume that we can write down a well-specified individual model based on individual-level variables, as in Equation 1, but only lack the data to estimate it. If the same equation estimated at the aggregate level produces biased estimates, then there must be something about the grouping process that leads to correlation between the relevant X variables and the disturbance term. In other words, it matters how the data were aggregated (Jargowsky, 2005). It is useful to consider the following possibilities and their implications:

1. Random grouping is not very likely to arise in practice, but it is instructive to consider the possibility. If the data are aggregated randomly and the model was correctly specified at the individual level, there will be no aggregation bias. The expected value of mean X and mean u for all groups will be the grand mean of X and u, respectively, and they will not be correlated.

2. If the grouping is based on the X (or multiple Xs), there will also be no aggregation bias. This follows because the conditional mean of the disturbance term is zero for all values of X if the individual model is correctly specified.

3. If the grouping is based on Y, aggregation bias is very likely. For example, if Y and X are positively related, in the groups with higher levels of Y one would find both high values of X and larger than average disturbance terms, and at lower levels of Y, the opposite would occur. Thus, the aggregate levels of X and u will be correlated and the ecological regression is mis-specified.

4. Grouping based on geography, the most common method, is the most difficult to evaluate because neighborhood selection may be based on a complex set of factors operating at different levels. However, if the dependent variable is something like income, the danger exists that neighborhood aggregation is more like case 3. If the dependent variable is less likely to be involved in the residential choice function, then sorting by neighborhood will be more like case 1 or 2.

Consequently, when data are provided in an aggregate form, the researcher must understand and evaluate how the groups were formed. Then, the researcher must try to ascertain whether the procedure is likely to introduce aggregation biases or aggregation gains in view of the specific dependent variable and explanatory models under consideration.

Group-level Effects

Equation 1 does not take into account the possibility of group-level effects on individuals. That is, the individual-level equation only includes individual-level variables. But it is possible, indeed likely, that the mean value of X in a neighborhood could have an independent effect on Y even after controlling for the individual's own level of X. Firebaugh (1980) describes several possibilities. An intelligent student may well learn more in the presence of other intelligent students (Manski, 1993, 2000). On the other hand, a mediocre student might be discouraged in such an environment and do better if he were "a big fish in a small pond" (Firebaugh, 1980). Group effects include neighborhood effects, peer group effects, and social network effects.

In general, we can characterize these models as including some measure of a group-level variable in the individual-level model in addition to the variable measured at the individual level:

$$Y_{ij} = \beta_1 + \beta_2 X_{ij} + \beta_3 \bar{X}_j + u_{ij} \tag{6}$$

At the aggregate level, this model becomes:

$$\begin{aligned} \bar{Y}_j &= \beta_1 + \beta_2 \bar{X}_j + \beta_3 \bar{X}_j + \bar{u}_j \\ &= \beta_1 + (\beta_2 + \beta_3) \bar{X}_j + \bar{u}_j \end{aligned} \tag{7}$$

Clearly, even if there is no bias of the type discussed in the previous section, the individual and group effects are not separately identified, only their sum. In the absence of individual data or outside information on the magnitude of one or the other of the two effects, the lack of identification in the aggregate models poses a formidable obstacle.

Fortunately, in certain cases, the sum of the two effects may itself be of interest. For example, suppose the dependent variable is a measure of children's health, and X is a measure of insurance coverage through a public program. One might expect a direct impact of the child's own coverage status as well as an effect of the level of coverage in his or her area, through reduction of contagious diseases and increased availability of medical service providers (a supply response). Both effects are real benefits of the program and both are included in the coefficient from the ecological regression (Schwartz, 1994). To borrow a cheeky phrase from software development, "it's not a bug, it's a feature." When group-level effects of this type are suspected, researchers should apply appropriate methods for variables measured at multiple levels, including multilevel models and hierarchical linear models (Gelman, Park, Ansolabehere, Price, & Minnite, 2001; Gelman & Hill, 2006; Piguet, 2010; Raudenbush & Bryk, 2001). Such models, however, require at least some of the variables to be measured at the individual level, so they are not magic bullets to avoid the ecological fallacy when a researcher has access only to aggregated data.

The Ecological Fallacy and Disaster Research

Disasters and emergencies, by their very nature, strike geographic areas. It is easy to imagine that the results of such events for individuals will be influenced both by their own characteristics and those of the people and institutions around them. Add to that limitations on individual data and the conditions are ripe for ecological inference problems. Having seen the mechanisms through which bias can emerge in analyses of aggregate data, I discuss a few examples from the disaster and emergency management literature where research has been criticized for suffering from ecological inference problems.

The Heat Wave Controversy

Eric Klinenberg's 2002 book, *Heat Wave: A Social Autopsy of Disaster in Chicago*, won widespread acclaim for its analysis of the factors that led to the deaths of over 700 Chicagoans in a single week of 100-degree days in July 1995. Elderly, low-income African Americans were particularly hard-hit. A team of researchers from the Centers for Disease Control and Prevention (CDC) identified many factors that exacerbated a person's risk of death, including not owning an air conditioner, having a medical condition, living alone, not leaving one's house or apartment daily, and not having social contacts nearby (Semenza et al., 1996). For his part, Klinenberg sought to "move beyond the population risk factors to identify the social environmental conditions that elevate or reduce the probability that residents would survive the heat" (2015, p. 80).

In seeking to understand why African Americans had the highest death rate, Klinenberg contrasted neighborhoods with roughly similar demographic risk factors yet markedly different death rates, particularly North Lawndale and South Lawndale. With 19 deaths, North Lawndale's death rate was 40 per 100,000 residents, far higher than the overall Chicago rate of 7 per 100,000, whereas South Lawndale had only 3 deaths for a below-average mortality rate of 4 deaths per 100,000 residents. While both neighborhoods were poorer than the city as a whole and had roughly similar percentages of elderly persons living alone, the former was largely African American and had experienced abandonment and social isolation, whereas the latter was largely Hispanic and maintained a greater degree of community cohesion. Klinenberg conducted 6 months of fieldwork primarily in these two neighborhoods. Drawing on his fieldwork and published empirical work, he noted that African Americans in Chicago lived in highly segregated neighborhoods characterized by population decline, vacant residential buildings, empty trash-strewn lots, boarded-up store fronts, and poorly maintained parks, streets, and sidewalks. Many North Lawndale residents Klinenberg interviewed related how these conditions made them fearful to venture out from their houses or apartments. In addition, "Violent crime and active street-level drug markets, which are facilitated by these ecological conditions, exacerbate the difficulties of using public space and organizing effective support networks in such areas" (Klinenberg, 2015, p. 127). These conditions contrasted sharply with the Hispanic neighborhood of South Lawndale, where population had been increasing and the streets were humming with pedestrians, street vendors, and active shopping districts. These differences in social climate, Klinenberg concluded, were "a key reason that African Americans had the highest death rates in the Chicago heat wave" (Klinenberg, 2015, p. 127).

Mitchell Duneier (2006) criticized *Heat Wave* because, he argued, "Klinenberg's book provides no data on the individuals who died" (679). Using death records and news accounts, Duneier tracked down people who were relatives or acquaintances of 16 of the known 19 North Lawndale victims and 2 of the 3 South Lawndale victims. In contrast to Klinenberg's emphasis on social isolation and dying alone, information from Duneier's informants suggested that only 2 of the decedents in North Lawndale were living alone at the time of their deaths; three-fourths were living with family members or were in domestic relationships; 14 of 16 were said to have left their house or apartment regularly. He argued that if a researcher wants to know how people died, "*it is best to try to study individual-level morbidity and mortality* before making general claims about how deaths fit into a broader social and political landscape." In particular, he continued, ethnographers more than most researchers have a "special opportunity to show the people" and that by doing so "*they can avoid the perils of the ecological fallacy*, allowing social theories to be firmly anchored in social facts (Duneier, 2006, p. 687, emphasis added; see also Chapter 10).

Duneier's argument is that Klinenberg used contrasts between *neighborhoods*, such as North and South Lawndale, to draw conclusions about factors that led some *individuals* to die while others survived. In contrast to social isolation, Duneier noted that his informants described 8 of the 16 North Lawndale victims as "alcoholics, heavy drinkers, and/or drug users" (683). Fifteen of the 16 lived on the top floor, which is both the hottest part of most buildings and requires the greatest effort to venture outside, particularly for those with limited mobility. Duneier finds "knowledge of how individuals actually live and die" more persuasive than "easy generalizations about whole neighborhoods and cultural environments" (687). He acknowledges that "ecological inference is necessary when individual level data are not available," but argues that in the case of the Chicago heat wave, "as I demonstrate here, the individual-level data were still possible to collect almost 10 years later" (687).

In response, Klinenberg noted that his argument in *Heat Wave* did not rely on differences between neighborhoods to explain why individuals die, but instead rested on the findings of the CDC study (Semenza et al., 1996). This case control study, conducted immediately after the heat wave, identified 339 pairs of heat wave–related decedents and survivors. For each decedent, the researchers attempted to identify a neighbor of approximately the same age at an immediately neighboring residence. They collected information through interviews with the matched controls and surrogates for the respondents, such as "family members, friends, or neighbors." This information was supplemented by data from death certificates, police reports, and phone calls to the case subject's next of kin, as well as inspection of the residences by CDC staff (Semenza et al., 1996, p. 85).

The CDC team used the matched pairs to calculate odds ratios for each hypothesized risk factor. Importantly, the use of age-matched pairs from neighboring housing units implicitly controls for neighborhood factors and neighborhood-age interactions. Their analysis found that the risk of death was more than double for those living alone, 4.7 times greater for those living on the top floor, 6.7 times greater for those who did not leave home, and 70% lower for those who had friends in Chicago (Semenza et al., 1996, p. 87, table 2). This study, which is not only based on individual-level data but which took pains to control for neighborhood and community characteristics, "shows – more powerfully than any research Duneier or I have done – that not having an air conditioner, lacking social contacts, and not leaving home were the key risks for death" (Klinenberg, 2006, p. 692).

The CDC analysis estimated the effect of individual risk factors on the individual odds of death, but what it could not do is explain "why neighborhood mortality varied so dramatically . . . nor why African American communities were disproportionately affected." Klinenberg continues, "My research strategy was to cite the CDC's individual-level findings and advance knowledge by focusing on the neighborhood level" (Klinenberg, 2006, p. 692). *Heat Wave* provides voluminous quantitative and qualitative evidence that residents of North Lawndale felt increasingly unsafe in their community and that they were hesitant to leave home given its deserted streets, vacant buildings, and rising crime and violence. South Lawndale, in contrast, was growing in population fueled by Hispanic immigration. Though poor, it had vibrant street life and low crime rates. *Heat Wave* looks beyond North and South Lawndale, comparing the neighborhoods throughout the city with the highest and lowest mortality rates during the crisis. The lowest, regardless of ethnic and racial composition, "did not suffer greatly from ecological depletion, the collapse of local infrastructure and commerce, population decline and high levels of violent crime," while the highest were characterized by social disorganization, population decline, and disinvestment (Klinenberg, 2015, pp. 126–127). Klinenberg argues that Duneier's approach, by focusing on individualistic explanations only, gives short shrift to structural conditions and public policies that leave some people and places more vulnerable than others. He invokes Amartya Sen, "who famously established that people die in famines because of political economic institutions that limit the distribution of food" (Klinenberg, 2006, p. 697). While the proximate cause of death in famines is a lack of food, Sen's point is that the structural cause is that which prevents the food from reaching those in need of it.

Ultimately, Duneier's claim that Klinenberg was guilty of committing an ecological fallacy falls flat. Not being a clinician or public health researcher, Klinenberg did not seek to determine the cause of death of individuals. As a sociologist, his interest was in social structures at the level of neighborhood, community, and society and the institutions and public policies that shape the interactions between individuals and the social world. His hypotheses about neighborhoods were inspired by empirical findings about individuals as reported by the CDC's study of individuals. But Klinenberg addressed his questions about neighborhoods with evidence about neighborhoods, which is entirely appropriate. Despite that, Duneier's critique was taken seriously enough to be published in the *American Sociological Review*, indicating just how difficult it can be to sort out different levels of evidence and analysis. Klinenberg's response is a good reminder that an exclusive focus on individual explanations can ignore some of the most interesting and important questions social scientists need to address. To protect oneself from the accusation of ecological fallacy, it is important to carefully articulate the level of the question under consideration and to justify the appropriateness of the evidence to address that question.

Social Vulnerability Indices

Anyone in the position of analyzing the factors contributing to deaths, losses, survival, and resilience in the aftermath of a disaster may well come face-to-face with similar issues and critiques. After a disaster has occurred, the dead are not available to answer your questions (Gove & Hughes, 1980). Paper records, if any, are often destroyed. Networks of family and friends may be dispersed, as after Hurricane Katrina, for example. Researchers using aggregate figures to reconstruct vulnerabilities and explain disaster outcomes may, like Klinenberg, find themselves subject to criticism on the grounds they are committing an ecological fallacy.

A key topic in disaster and emergency management research is understanding the factors that contribute to a community's vulnerability in the face of adverse circumstances, its capacity to cope with such situations, and the degree of resilience a community may exhibit in recovery. To study these issues, one needs first to measure them. A great deal of research has therefore gone into developing composite indices of social vulnerability, capacity, and resilience (Beccari, 2016). Such indices are necessary both to operationalize these conceptual variables and to rank places and identify areas where interventions are needed to reduce vulnerability, increase administrative capacity, and develop resiliency (Mendes, 2009). Examples include the Social Vulnerability Index, the Disaster Risk Index (DRI), and Prevalent Vulnerability Index (Cutter, Boruff, & Shirley, 2003; Flanagan, Gregory, Hallisey, Heitgerd, & Lewis, 2011; Peduzzi, Dao, Herold, & Mouton, 2009). An attempt to catalogue the indices proposed or in use in 2008 found 178 indices "that rank or benchmark countries according to economic, political, social, or environmental measures" (Beccari, 2016).

With so many indices available, much work needs to be done to benchmark them and compare their performance in various uses. As always, a key challenge to constructing composite indicators is the availability of well-measured indicators with data at the appropriate level of aggregation (Birkmann, 2007; Fekete, 2012; Piguet, 2010). In an analysis of the accuracy and validity of selected social vulnerability indices, Gall (2007) criticized the Disaster Risk Index's use of national level data to measure social vulnerability. On the one hand, Gall notes, physical exposure to disaster risk "is meticulously delineated and modeled at the local level to determine populations at risk." Yet, in contrast, social vulnerability is measured through "the use of canned and widely available social vulnerability indicators at the country level." Gall concludes that "the DRI is contestable due to its implicit acceptance of ecological fallacy . . . since it neglects the socioeconomic characteristics of its population at risk in the demarcated exposure zones" (pp. 109–110).

Beccari (2016) notes that indices are developed at different geographic levels to serve different purposes. Subnational indices outnumber national indices by 4 to 1, although disproportionate attention is devoted to the latter. Yet virtually all indices, whether national or subnational, are built upon data for well-defined administrative units. This is hardly surprising, given the way data are collected and disseminated

(Meentemeyer, 1989; Piguet, 2010). "This suggests," Beccari concludes, "that most authors are attempting to tailor their approach to a particular level and at least in this sense are not in danger of committing the ecological fallacy."

Perhaps this sentiment is valid when indices are used for ranking and planning purposes. Yet if the purpose is truly understand the determinants of vulnerability, capacity, and resilience, failure to distinguish between forces that operate at the individual and aggregate levels is a real loss (Piguet, 2010; Rivera, 2019). In interpreting empirical results derived from aggregated data, Piguet cautions that "any consideration regarding the mechanisms at stake should be done at the level of the area and not at that of individuals" (2010, p. 519). Moreover, when indices are published and disseminated, many users will fail to make such fine distinctions, resulting in stereotyping of individuals from different ethnic and minority groups based on findings derived from aggregate data (Fekete, 2012; Robinson, 1950).

Conclusion

Anselin put it best: "There is no solution to the ecological inference problem" (2000, p. 589). There are only estimates based on assumptions, but this is also true about regressions on individual-level data. In the absence of data about individuals, one can derive estimates about individual relations only by carefully specifying a model, and these assumptions must be guided by theory, experience, and consistency with observable relations. When social scientists attempt to analyze aggregate data, the best course of action is to parameterize the variables relevant to the grouping process as well as possible. As noted previously, Hanushek, Jackson, and Kain (1974) were able to show that the real problem with Robinson's data was an underspecified model, not aggregation. For example, it would be particularly important to control for race and income if the data are neighborhood aggregates, given the degree of segregation that is common on those dimensions (Darden, 1986; Jargowsky, 1996; Massey, 1990). If there are contextual effects, these need to be modeled as well, perhaps using multilevel models (Brown & Saks, 1980; Daoud, Halleröd, & Guha-Sapir, 2016; Firebaugh, 1978, p. 570).

One can be misled by ecological correlations or by regressions on aggregate data, but one can be equally misled by simple correlations or regressions based on individual data, and for some of the same reasons: left out variables, model mis-specification, and false assumptions about the process under study. Robinson's (1950) article has generated seven decades of productive debate over the ecological fallacy and related topics such as ecological inference, aggregation bias, and contextual effects. With multivariate analysis, advanced modeling techniques, and an understanding of the aggregation process, researchers can mostly avoid falling victim to the ecological fallacy.

Indeed, in certain specific situations, aggregate data may be better than individual data for testing hypotheses, even if those hypotheses are about individual behavior. Piguet notes that "analyses strictly centered on individual data are symmetrically subject to the so-called atomistic fallacy of missing the context in which behavior takes place" (Piguet, 2010, p. 519). Thus, the advice to disaster and emergency management researchers is not to avoid aggregate data altogether or to never use such data to study individual risks and outcomes. Rather, the point is be crystal clear about the unit of analysis (whether explicit or implicit) of your hypotheses, to think carefully about the relevance of data measured at different levels to address those hypotheses, and to be aware of the potential for bias in any analysis that crosses between individual and ecological levels.

Further Readings

Idrovo, A. J. (2011). Three criteria for ecological fallacy. *Environmental Health Perspectives*, *119*(8), a332–a332. https://doi.org/10.1289/ehp.1103768

King, G. (1997). *A solution to the ecological inference problem: Reconstructing individual behavior from aggregate data*. Princeton, NJ: Princeton University Press.

Piantadosi, S., Byar, D.P., & Green, S.B. (1988). The ecological fallacy. *American Journal of Epidemiology*, *127*(5), 893–904.

Schuessler, A.A. (1999). Ecological inference. *Proceedings of the National Academy of Sciences*, *96*(19), 10578–10581. https://doi.org/10.1073/pnas.96.19.10578

Tranmer, M., & Steel, D.G. (1998). Using census data to investigate the causes of the ecological fallacy. *Environment and Planning A: Economy and Space*, *30*(5), 817–831. https://doi.org/10.1068/a300817

Wakefield, J., & Shaddick, G. (2006). Health-exposure modeling and the ecological fallacy. *Biostatistics*, *7*(3), 438–455. https://doi.org/10.1093/biostatistics/kxj017

References

Anselin, L. (2000). The alchemy of statistics, or creating data where no data exist. *Annals of the Association of American Geographers*, *90*, 586–592.

Beccari, B. (2016). A comparative analysis of disaster risk, vulnerability and resilience composite indicators. *PLOS Currents*, *8*. https://doi.org/10.1371/currents.dis.453df025e34b682e9737f95070f9b970

Birkmann, J. (2007). Risk and vulnerability indicators at different scales: Applicability, usefulness and policy implications. *Environmental Hazards*, *7*(1), 20–31. *International Journal of Digital Earth*, *25*.

Brown, B.W., & Saks, D.H. (1980). *Economic grouping and data disaggregation issues in aggregation* (Vol. 6). Jossey-Bass.

Cutter, S.L., Boruff, B.J., & Shirley, W.L. (2003). Social vulnerability to environmental hazards★. *Social Science Quarterly*, *84*(2), 242–261. https://doi.org/10.1111/1540-6237.8402002

Daoud, A., Halleröd, B., & Guha-Sapir, D. (2016). What is the association between absolute child poverty, poor governance, and natural disasters? A global comparison of some of the realities of climate change. *PLOS One*, *11*(4), e0153296. https://doi.org/10.1371/journal.pone.0153296

Darden, J.T. (1986). The significance of race and class in residential segregation. *Journal of Urban Affairs*, *8*(1), 49–56.

Duneier, M. (2006). Ethnography, the ecological fallacy, and the 1995 Chicago heat wave. *American Sociological Review*, *71*(4), 679–688.

Fekete, A. (2012). Spatial disaster vulnerability and risk assessments: Challenges in their quality and acceptance. *Natural Hazards*, *61*(3), 1161–1178. https://doi.org/10.1007/s11069-011-9973-7

Firebaugh, G. (1978). A rule for inferring individual-level relationships from aggregate data. *American Sociological Review*, *43*, 557–572.

Firebaugh, G. (1980). *Groups as contexts and frog ponds: Issues in aggregation* (Vol. 6). Jossey-Bass.

Firebaugh, G. (2015). Ecological fallacy, statistics of. In *International encyclopedia of the social & behavioral sciences* (pp. 865–867). Elsevier. https://doi.org/10.1016/B978-0-08-097086-8.44017-1

Flanagan, B.E., Gregory, E.W., Hallisey, E.J., Heitgerd, J.L., & Lewis, B. (2011). A social vulnerability index for disaster management. *Journal of Homeland Security and Emergency Management, 8*(1). https://doi.org/10.2202/1547-7355.1792

Freedman, D.A. (2001). Ecological inference. In N.J. Smelser & P.B. Baltes (Eds.), *International encyclopedia of the social and behavioral sciences* (pp. 4027–4030). Elsevier.

Gall, M. (2007). Indices of social vulnerability to natural hazards: A comparative evaluation. *University of South Carolina, 231.*

Gelman, A., & Hill, J. (2006). *Data analysis using regression and multilevel/hierarchical models.* Cambridge: Cambridge University Press.

Gelman, A., Park, D.K., Ansolabehere, S., Price, P.N., & Minnite, L.C. (2001). Models, assumptions and model checking in ecological regressions. *Journal of the Royal Statistical Society. Series A (Statistics in Society), 164*(1), 101–118.

Gove, W.R., & Hughes, M. (1980). Reexamining the ecological fallacy: A study in which aggregate data are critical in investigating the pathological effects of living alone. *Social Forces, 58*, 1157–1177.

Greene, W.H. (2000). *Econometric analysis.* Prentice Hall.

Grunfeld, Y., & Griliches, Z. (1960). Is aggregation necessarily bad? *Review of Economics and Statistics, 42*, 1–13.

Gujarati, D.N., & Porter, D.C. (2008). *Basic econometrics* (5th ed.). McGraw-Hill Education.

Hanushek, E.A., Jackson, J.E., & Kain, J.F. (1974). Model specification, use of aggregate data, and the ecological correlation fallacy. *Political Methodology, 1*(1), 89–107. JSTOR.

Irwin, L., & Lichtman, A.J. (1976). Across the great divide: Inferring individual level behavior from aggregate data. *Political Methodology, 3*, 411–439.

Jargowsky, P.A. (1996). Take the money and run: Economic segregation in US metropolitan areas. *American Sociological Review, 61*(6), 984–998.

Jargowsky, P.A. (2005). The ecological fallacy. In K. Kempf-Leonard (Ed.), *The encyclopedia of social measurement* (Vol. 1, pp. 715–722). Elsevier.

Jargowsky, P.A., & El Komi, M. (2011). Before or after the bell? School context and neighborhood effects on student achievement. In H.B. Newburger, E.L. Birch, & S.M. Wachter (Eds.), *Neighborhood and life chances: How place matters in modern America* (pp. 50–72). Philadelphia: University of Pennsylvania Press.

Kamel, N.M.O., & Loukaitou-Sideris, A. (2004). Residential assistance and recovery following the Northridge earthquake. *Urban Studies, 41*(3), 533–562. https://doi.org/10.1080/0042098042000178672

Klinenberg, E. (2006). Blaming the victims: Hearsay, labeling, and the hazards of quick-hit disaster ethnography. *American Sociological Review, 71*(4), 689–698.

Klinenberg, E. (2015). *Heat wave: A social autopsy of disaster in Chicago* (2nd ed.). Chicago: University of Chicago Press.

Kyne, D., & Aldrich, D.P. (2020). Capturing bonding, bridging, and linking social capital through publicly available data. *Risk, Hazards and Crisis in Public Policy, 11*(1), 61–86. https://doi.org/10.1002/rhc3.12183

Lauen, D.L., & Gaddis, S.M. (2013). Exposure to classroom poverty and test score achievement: Contextual effects or selection? *American Journal of Sociology, 118*(4), 943–979. https://doi.org/10.1086/668408

Lomborg, B. (2010). *Cool It: The skeptical environmentalist's guide to global warming.* Vintage Books.

Manski, C.F. (1993). Identification of endogenous social effects: The reflection problem. *The Review of Economic Studies, 60*(3), 531–542. https://doi.org/10.2307/2298123

Manski, C.F. (2000). Economic analysis of social interactions. *Journal of Economic Perspectives, 14*(3), 115–136.

Massey, D.S. (1990). American apartheid: Segregation and the making of the underclass. *American Journal of Sociology, 96*(2), 329–357.

Meentemeyer, V. (1989). Geographical perspectives of space, time, and scale. *Landscape Ecology, 3*(3), 163–173. https://doi.org/10.1007/BF00131535

Mendes, J. M. de O. (2009). Social vulnerability indexes as planning tools: Beyond the preparedness paradigm. *Journal of Risk Research, 12*(1), 43–58. https://doi.org/10.1080/13669870802447962

Peduzzi, P., Dao, H., Herold, C., & Mouton, F. (2009). Assessing global exposure and vulnerability towards natural hazards: The disaster risk index. *Natural Hazards and Earth System Sciences, 9*, 1149–1159.

Piguet, E. (2010). Linking climate change, environmental degradation, and migration: A methodological overview. *Wiley Interdisciplinary Reviews: Climate Change, 1*(4), 517–524. https://doi.org/10.1002/wcc.54

Raudenbush, S. W., & Bryk, A. S. (2001). *Hierarchical linear models: Applications and data analysis methods* (2nd ed.). Sage.

Rendall, M. (2019). Discounting, climate change, and the ecological fallacy. *Ethics, 129*(3), 441–463. https://doi.org/10.1086/701481

Rivera, J. D. (2019). Returning to normalcy in the short-term: A preliminary investigation of the recovery from Hurricane Harvey among individuals with home damage. *Disasters.* https://doi.org/10.1111/disa.12387

Robinson, W. S. (1950). Ecological correlations and the behavior of individuals. *American Sociological Review, 15*, 351–357.

Schelling, T. C. (1995). Intergenerational discounting. *Energy Policy, 23*(4), 395–401. https://doi.org/10.1016/0301-4215(95)90164-3

Schwartz, S. (1994). The fallacy of the ecological fallacy: The potential misuse of a concept and the consequences. *American Journal of Public Health, 84*(5), 819–824.

Selvin, H. C. (1958). Durkheim's suicide and problems of empirical research. *American Journal of Sociology, 63*(6), 607–619. https://doi.org/10.1086/222356

Semenza, J. C., Rubin, C. H., Falter, K. H., Selanikio, J. D., Flanders, W. D., Howe, H. L., & Wilhelm, J. L. (1996). Heat-related deaths during the July 1995 heat wave in Chicago. *New England Journal of Medicine, 335*(2), 84–90. https://doi.org/10.1056/NEJM199607113350203

Stoker, T. M. (1993). Empirical approaches to the problem of aggregation over individuals. *Journal of Economic Literature, 31*, 1827–1874.

Summers, A. A., & Wolfe, B. L. (1977). Do schools make a difference? *American Economic Review, 67*(4), 639–652.

Theil, H. (1954). *Linear aggregation of economic relations.* North-Holland.

Mixed-methods Research in Disaster and Emergency Management

Barbara R. Russo

Introduction

Traditional disaster scholars have long believed that qualitative and quantitative research methods cannot or should not be combined because each method stands for a different type of reasoning – deductive or inductive – and they are essentially mutually exclusive (Smith, 1983). The main challenge is combining the two paradigms into one throughout all phases of the research design to result in an effective mixed-methods project. As the value of qualitative and quantitative mixed-methods research in disaster and emergency management continues to develop, it is only natural that these approaches have gained in popularity.

This chapter highlights the merits of selecting mixed-methods design for disaster and emergency management research so that researchers might consider them as appropriate avenues for research. Mixed-methods research will be compared and contrasted with qualitative and quantitative methods, and the advantages and challenges of using mixed-methods research in the disaster and emergency management context will be discussed. Finally, examples of mixed-methods applications in the disaster and emergency management setting will be provided.

Paradigms

A paradigm is merely a lens through which a person views the world. In science, paradigms include the rules under which researchers operate as they undertake their approaches to scientific inquiry. Thomas Kuhn (1970), a philosopher of science, expressed: "the study of paradigms . . . is what mainly prepares the student for membership in the particular scientific community with which he will later practice" (p. 10). In other words, paradigms provide researchers with specific approaches to scientific inquiry that are consistent with prior practices in the field. Paradigms are key drivers in directing research along the correct path (Babbie, 2007). According to Payne and Payne (2004), a paradigm outlines the conceptual and philosophical assumptions that will justify the researchers' use of a particular research method. Some of the earliest disaster research, such as Samuel Prince's study of the Halifax explosion, have helped expose some of the challenges posed by the nature of the discipline. Drabek (1986) suggests Prince derived his theory of catastrophe and social change from the use of grounded theory in his research (p. 2). However, Prince noted that it must be realized that the "data of greatest value is left sometimes unrecorded and fades rapidly from special memory. Investigation is needed immediately after the event" (Prince, 1920, p. 22).

In some of the earliest disaster research, such as the studies conducted by Fritz and Marks (1954), the researchers were quick to note the serious difficulties in obtaining valid and reliable information (p. 26), which has already been highlighted in Chapters 2 and 3 of this volume. In Fritz and Marks's (1954) groundbreaking work, they concluded that experimentation is extremely limited in that the extreme stresses of disaster situations cannot be replicated in a laboratory under controlled conditions. While frightening and even traumatic experiences could reasonably be reproduced in a laboratory setting, they would possibly cause harm to the subjects and would therefore not be permissible as described in Chapter 1. As a result of these limitations, Fritz and Marks made every attempt to utilize sound scientific procedures, yet they recognized the need to add to other existing data in an attempt to gather overwhelming support for their findings. Their research ultimately took the form of a mixed-methods approach (p. 27).

Through the years, many prominent researchers have outlined various paradigms that form the basis of current social scientific inquiry. Along these lines, Creswell (2014) classifies four classifications that he labels post-positivist, advocacy/participatory, constructivist, and pragmatic. The majority of disaster and emergency management research today stems from the pragmatist view. Pragmatists argue that the most important determinant of research philosophy stems from the research problem itself, not the methods used (Saunders, Lewis, & Thornhill, 2007; Creswell, 2009a). As a result, pragmatists may use many approaches to understanding the problem and demonstrate that one approach may be more appropriate than another for answering particular questions (Saunders et al., 2007). Along these lines, mixed methods become possible within a single study (Creswell, 2009a). The major elements of Creswell's (2014) paradigms are highlighted in Table 4.1.

TABLE 4.1 Creswell's Paradigms

Post-Positivism	**Social Constructivism**
■ Determination	■ Understanding
■ Reductionism	■ Multiple participant meanings
■ Empirical observation and measurement	■ Social and historical construction
■ Theory verification	■ Theory generation
Advocacy/Participatory	**Pragmatism**
■ Political	■ Consequences of actions
■ Empowerment issue oriented	■ Problem centered
■ Collaborative	■ Pluralistic
■ Change oriented	■ Real-world practice oriented

Source: Creswell (2014, p. 6).

In contrast, post-positivists believe that causes most likely determine the effects or outcomes of a particular phenomenon. They believe that *the* absolute truth can never be found because scientists and researchers alike are inherently biased by their own cultural experiences (see Goddard, 1973; Harding, 1977). Post-positivists believe we cannot observe the world we are a part of objectively; however, they do believe in a possible objective reality. As such, post-positivists believe we should approximate that reality as best we can while realizing our own subjectivity is shaping that reality. As a result, rather than finding the truth, the post-positivist will simply try and represent reality the best he or she can (Rorty, 1991; Muisj, 2004). They feel that all measurement is fallible, which is why they insist on multiple observations and measurements that may introduce different types of errors, thus posing the need for triangulation of the data (Erzberger & Prein, 1997). Creswell (2014) argues that data, evidence, and rational considerations shape knowledge, and being objective is essential for competent inquiry where researchers must examine methods and conclusions for bias.

In response to the notion of bias, Guba (1990) argues that post-positivists use methods that strive to be as unbiased as possible; however, they also actively attempt to be aware of any of their own values that may compromise neutrality. Thomas Kuhn (1970), who became known for his post-positivist views, argued that through the use of the paradigm (i.e., theories, formal methods, tacit practices, and exemplary problems) one could come to some understanding of the Aristotelian approach. "Though his understanding did not make him a proponent of the Aristotelian approach, he could recognize the merits of both the Aristotelian approach and the approach of modern physics" (Guba, 1990, p. 201).

Creswell's (2014) third category of paradigms is social constructionism. Social constructivists look for complex views rather than narrow ones. They believe that human beings construct meanings from the world they are interpreting and that they make sense of it based on historical and social perspectives (Andrews, 2012; Creswell, 2014; Burr, 2015). As a result, generalizations beyond the sample are often inadvisable without strong evidence from other studies which many research see as a disadvantage. The earliest emergence of social constructivism appeared in the famous book *The Social Construction of Reality* (Berger & Luckman, 1967), in which the authors placed emphasis on people developing meanings for their activities together. Another early social constructionist researcher in the field was Elfreda Chatman (1991, 1992), whose work focused on the information-seeking behavior of such groups as prisoners or older women living alone in a retirement village. Later, Tuominen and Savolainen (1997) point out the advantages of social constructivism in which they favored discourse analysis due to the "processual negotiation of meanings" (p. 82). Generally, discourse analysis is a research method for studying written or spoken language in relation to its social context (Johnstone, 2018). As such, one might focus on the purposes and effects of different types of languages or dialects, which are influenced by people's experiences and respective cultures and ideologies. In this way, social constructionists might make sense of the world and social phenomena that may be both objective and subject at the same time, depending on the source of particular data.

Researchers subscribing to the advocacy/participatory paradigm believe that research inquiry needs to be intertwined with politics and a political agenda. Much social justice research rests in this paradigm as it seeks to bring about changes to practices and help groups and organizations rather than just the individual (Steinberg, 1996; Haviland, Frye, & Rajah, 2008; Creswell, 2014). Moreover, participatory research is a means of putting research capabilities in the hands of disenfranchised people so they can identify themselves as knowing actors, define their reality, name their history, and transform their own lives (Humphries & Truman, 1994). Participatory research views knowledge production as a dynamic process of "engagement, education, communication, action and reflection" (Finn, 1994, p. 27). According to McTaggart (1994), it is a form of

> self-reflective inquiry undertaken by participants in social situations in order to improve the rationality, justice, coherence and satisfactoriness of (a) their own social practices, (b) their understanding of these practices, and (c) the institutions, programs and ultimately the society in which these practices are carried out.

The advocacy/participatory view requires the researcher to remain an outsider yet empower their participants to transform their own lives through knowledge and the research process. Participants in action research programs expect to be treated not as objects or even subjects but as co-researchers engaged in "empowering participation" and in "co-generative dialogue" between "insiders and outsiders" (Dickens & Watkins, 1999), as illustrated in Chapter 8 of this book.

Finally, pragmatists are not committed to any one system of philosophy and reality. They look to the "what" and "how" to research, and they agree that research always occurs in social, historical, political, and other contexts (Shields, 2003; Hildebrand, 2005). What pragmatism does most is open the door for the mixed-methods researchers to utilize "multiple methods, different worldviews, and different assumptions, as well as different forms of data collection and analysis" (Creswell, 2014, p. 11) as a means of attempting to explore societal and/or organizational phenomena. As such, pragmatism emphasizes that all aspects of research inherently involve decisions about which goals are most meaningful and which methods are most appropriate (Morgan, 2014). Pragmatism as a paradigm for social research is not an entirely new concept (see Patton, 1988; Gage, 1989) and has been frequently linked with mixed-methods research (Hall, 2013; Johnson & Onwuegbuzie, 2004; Pearce, 2012; Tashakkori & Teddlie, 2010).

A Brief History of Mixed-methods Research

For more than a century, advocates of qualitative and quantitative research have engaged in a long-lasting dispute. According to Johnson and Onwuegbuzie (2004), two sides emerged from these philosophical debates – quantitative purists, such as Thompson (1992), Maxwell and Delaney (2004), and Popper (1959), to name a few – and qualitative purists including Lincoln and Guba (1985), Denzin and Lincoln (2018), and Spradley (2016). Quantitative purists believe that social science observations are objective, much like the way physical scientists treat their experiments. Their assumptions are based on positivist philosophy, the phrase initially coined by Auguste Comte (Schmaus, 2008), arguing that the real causes of social scientific outcomes can be determined by both reliability and validity. Individuals subscribing to this philosophy believe that in the social sciences, implied facts are not significantly encumbered by context. Rather, explanatory variables have the same effect on a social phenomenon regardless of the context in which they are present. As such, understanding the context of facts is not a prime consideration, and in some cases it is altogether arbitrary. However, because researchers considered themselves "discoverers," they did not completely abandon contextual considerations. Because positivists view explanatory variables as devoid of contextual means, they are able to remain emotionally detached from their subjects, eliminate possible biases, and test or empirically prove or disprove their stated hypotheses – essentially embracing a deductive scientific method. These types of researchers typically call for rhetorical neutrality, write using the impersonal passive voice, and use technical terminology (Tashakkori & Teddlie, 1998).

Alternatively, qualitative purists rejected positivism and embraced the concepts of constructivism, humanism, idealism, and sometimes even postmodernism, among others (Smith, 1983). Unlike their quantitative counterparts, they believe that it is impossible to fully differentiate causes and effects, that logic flows from specific to general (e.g., explanations are inductively drawn from the data), and that the knower and known are intertwined and cannot be separated because the subjective knower is the only source of reality (Guba, 1990). Constructivism seeks to undertake research in natural settings, as seen extensively through the works of Guba and Lincoln. The influence of constructivism is clearly seen in an increasing number of disaster research studies as well (Miller, Fernando, & Berger, 2009; Teasley & Moore, 2010; Powell & Bui, 2016). Researchers are given an opportunity to examine the human experience while people live and interact within their own social worlds. This allows for the understanding of the variety of constructs people possess while trying to achieve some meaning, yet always being alert to new explanations with the benefit of experience and increased information that is provided (Guba & Lincoln, 1994).

Similarly, humanistic researchers are interested in complex and dynamic wholes: experiences, places, and lives. Humanism interpreted in this way generates an approach or attitude rather than a set of specific and unique people-centered methods. The emphasis is on holism, participation, empathy, explication, induction, authentication and trust – all characteristics one might expect necessary in the disaster context. Therefore, humanists have adopted a number of existing methodologies, notably

> participant observation, in-depth interviewing, and group-based approaches – and supplemented them with the interpretive reading of texts, images and cultural practices and critical reflection on their own involvement in the research process itself as a "participant" in the world being studied.
>
> (Aitkin & Valentine, 2006, pp. 263–264)

Moreover, idealists believe that the social world consists of ideas, that it exists only because we think it exists, and we reproduce it on that basis. The means of that reproduction is considered to be language, and therefore to know a culture, one must come to know the language of that culture (Habermas, 1974; Lewis-Beck, Bryman, & Futing Liao, 2004; Forchtner, 2010).

As a result of these separate views, both sides of purists advocate that their paradigm is the ideal form of research design. Moreover, these same purists implicitly and/or explicitly argue that the two are incompatible – meaning these two methods *cannot* and *should not* be mixed (Mahoney & Goertz, 2006). This has often been referred to as the incompatibility thesis (Howe, 1988). Purists maintain that quantitative and qualitative methods stem from different epistemological, ontological, and axiological assumptions about the nature of research (Tashakkori & Teddlie, 1998). Additionally, for purists, the assumptions associated with both paradigms are incompatible about how the world is viewed and what is important to know. As a result, purists argue for single-method studies (Onwuegbuzie & Leech, 2003). However, not all researchers agreed with the incompatibility thesis and sought to combine the two perspectives. According to Johnson, Onwuegbuzie, and Turner (2007), mixed-methods research has become the third major research approach behind the qualitative and quantitative approaches.

The primary philosophy today of mixed research is pragmatism. Sechrest and Sidani (1995) have noted a growth in the pragmatic researcher movement has the potential to reduce some of the problems associated with singular methods. The growth of pragmatism allows researchers to incorporate the strengths of both paradigms and respective methodologies. Along these lines, pragmatists are more likely to be cognizant of the many available research techniques and to select methods with respect to their value for addressing the underlying research questions, rather than with regard to some preconceived biases about which paradigm is the best fit (Onwuegbuzie & Leech, 2003). Pragmatists take an approach toward knowledge (theory and practice) that attempts to account for multiple perspectives, viewpoints, standpoints, and positions. Disaster and emergency management researchers benefit greatly from subscribing to the pragmatist view because they are not committed to one system of philosophy and reality. They also believe that research occurs in social, historical, political, and a whole host of other contexts/landscapes that have various effects on a phenomenon (see Miller & Rivera, 2008). Therefore, for the mixed-methods researcher, pragmatism opens the door to multiple methods, different assumptions, and different forms of data collection and analysis (Creswell, 2009b) because methodological approaches are chosen based on what is more appropriate for answering a particular research question.

More specifically, disaster and emergency management research are deeply rooted in the history of the social and behavioral sciences. As such, it should be no surprise that mixed research, as it was originally known, began with researchers and methodologists who believed both quantitative and qualitative methodologies complemented each other as they addressed their research questions. Some of the very first mixed research work appeared in studies conducted by early anthropologists and sociologists (e.g., Hollingshead, 1949). Because of the varied disciplinary use, leading researchers in the field of mixed research use varying definitions of the term, as shown in Box 4.1.

BOX 4.1 LEADERS IN THE FIELD DEFINING MIXED-METHODS RESEARCH

John Creswell:

"Mixed methods research is a research design (or methodology) in which the researcher collects, analyzes, and mixes (integrates or connects) both quantitative and qualitative data in a single study or a multiphase program of inquiry."

Burke Johnson and Anthony Onwuegbuzie:

"Mixed methods research is the class of research where the researcher mixes or combines quantitative and qualitative research techniques, methods, approaches, concepts or language into a single study or set of related studies."

> **Abbas Tashakkori and Charles Teddie:**
>
> "Mixed methods research is a type of research design in which QUAL and QUAN approaches are used in type of questions, research methods, data collection and analysis procedures, or in inferences."
>
> *Source*: Johnson et al. (2007, pp. 119–123).

However, despite the difference in terminology, the more common term "mixed methods" has emerged through the work completed by Campbell and Fiske (1959), in which they formally introduced the concept of triangulation, referring to "multiple operationalism" where more than one method is used as a validation process of observations.

Ultimately it was Webb, Campbell, Schwartz, and Sechrest (1966) who gained credit for coining the term *triangulation*. Based on the notion of triangulation, social scientists have argued for its application within research designs as a means of assessing the validity of social science research results. Others argue that triangulation is a "dialectical" process in which researchers seek a more in-depth and nuanced understanding of research findings – clarifying disparate results by placing them in dialogue with one another (Mertens & Hesse-Biber, 2012). However, it was ultimately Denzin (1978) who provided a detailed discussion of *how* to actually triangulate. In doing so, he outlined three particularly useful types of triangulation that can be applied in the disaster research context: (1) data triangulation including time, space, and person; (2) investigator triangulation; and (3) methodological triangulation (pp. 294–307).

Data Triangulation

Data triangulation is nothing more than using several data sources to investigate the same phenomenon. One example might be including more than one person as a source of data. However, under Denzin's theory of data triangulation, the inclusion of time and space must also be considered based on the assumption that understanding a social phenomenon requires one to examine it under a number of different conditions. For example, think of it more simply as a situation faced by a lost hiker. If the hiker has no cell phone, compass, or GPS, how can she find her way back to the campsite? By determining the direction of the sun (knowing it rises in the east and sets in the west), looking for past landmarks, trees, or large boulders that may have been passed along the way, or even following a stream knowing that it will ultimately lead back to the trailhead (because that is where the campsite sits) are all means of using various types of data that include time and space.

Another example of triangulation conducted in the disaster research context is a study completed by Powell and Bui (2016) that included a yearlong study of the impact of a school-based psychosocial curriculum titled the Journey of Hope (JoH). It was an eight-session intervention that attempted to reduce the psychosocial impacts of the 2013 tornado disaster in Moore, Oklahoma, by enhancing protective factors such as social support, coping and psycho-education. Their study was conducted 1 year after the tornado struck Moore, killing 24 people, a number of whom were schoolchildren. The study employed both quantitative and qualitative measures to examine the impact of the JoH intervention. Powell and Bui used quantitative measures to examine coping, general self-efficacy, prosocial behaviors, and overall stress, in addition to qualitative data that was obtained through structured interviews with students in an attempt to determine what the children learned, liked, and felt was beneficial from taking part in the JoH program (Powell & Bui, 2016, p. 106). Previous studies on JoH revealed it was effective in enhancing peer relationships and prosocial behaviors following a disaster; however, no mixed-methods studies had examined whether findings were reinforced on the outcomes of prosocial behavior or peer support. As a result, their study indicated that prosocial support is a core component of the Journey of Hope. However, more importantly, they found support that healthy peer relationships are a protective factor in post-trauma recovery (Powell & Bui, 2016), which was only possible by analyzing both the qualitative and quantitative data.

Investigator Triangulation

Investigator triangulation involves having more than one investigator playing an active role in the investigation process. On most occasions this may already be built into the research project, since most studies, especially larger ones such as those following a disaster, require more than just one researcher to gather data. The most difficult decisions to be made include the roles each of the investigators will play in the process in terms of data collection and analysis. Denzin (2009) points out that this does not include coders, graduate students/assistants, or data analysts. Rather, the persons with the best skills should be closest to the data. Bias is mitigated by different investigators observing the same data who may not agree on its interpretation. The application of investigator triangulation is revised in Chapter 9, in Knox's detailing of the use of language-based theories in disaster and emergency management research.

Methodological Triangulation

Finally, methodological triangulation includes the use of multiple methods to examine a social phenomenon. In Denzin's (1978) work, he outlined four different types of triangulation including data triangulation (e.g., a variety of sources in a study); investigator triangulation (e.g., the use of several researchers); theory triangulation (e.g., the use of multiple theories and perspectives to interpret the results of a study); and methodological triangulation (e.g., use of multiple methods to study a research problem; Johnson et al., 2007). A recent mixed-methods example with the application of triangulation practices can be found in Islam and Hasan's (2016) case study of Cyclone Aila in the southwest coastal region of Bangladesh. The researchers employed a number of methods to collect data including a household survey and semi-structured interviews. Moreover, the authors used focus group discussions, participant observation, and in-depth case studies to acquire additional data. The mix of methods allowed for the triangulation of data on key questions, providing both qualitative and quantitative insights into individual household experiences (Islam & Hasan, 2016).

However, Denzin (1978) made certain to point out that methodological triangulation can occur within method or between methods. The generally accepted method is to triangulate the multiple sources of data from one design. For example, triangulating data from multiple data collection methods all used within the same study, such as through interviews, focus groups, and/or observations, is considered *within-method triangulation*. *Between-method triangulation* entails triangulating data from a combination of quantitative and qualitative techniques; for example, between closed-ended survey data and semi-structured interviews. However, this may prove challenging, since potential flaws within one method (i.e., the use of within-method triangulation) may impact the quality of data and subsequent inferences drawn through this type of triangulation. As a result, Denzin (2009) believes that *between-method triangulation* is ideal as it can account for the flaws and deficiencies: it takes the best of both to overcome the weaknesses of each. It is the in-depth understanding of the phenomenon, which is the goal, though the validity is not always enhanced (Fusch et al., 2018, p. 23).

One example of between-method triangulation can be found in Thomas et al.'s (2016) study, *Media Coverage of the 2014 West Virginia Elk River Chemical Spill: A Mixed-Methods Study Examining News Coverage of a Public Health Disaster*. The study provides a look at how the media frame human-initiated industrial disasters and the media's role in mediating messages and influencing disaster-related policy outcomes. This is also one of only a few framing studies to conduct a content analysis of media (quantitative) in conjunction with in-depth interviews (qualitative) of community members. Their results revealed that interview and content analysis findings were largely consistent, with both quantitative and qualitative data suggesting that media may have played an important role in shaping policy-related outcomes of the investigated chemical spill.

Finally, Figure 4.1 depicts a visual diagram of the triangulation process. Quantitative and qualitative methods are depicted in capital letters. Along the lines of the notation system for mixed-methods strategies maintained by Morse (2003), capitalization means the priority is equal between the two approaches (Atif, Richards, & Bilgin, 2013).

Researchers will often use this method of triangulation (Creswell & Plano Clark, 2007; Johnson & Onwuegbuzie, 2004), as it can answer a broader and more complete range of research questions because integrating qualitative and quantitative approaches can overcome the weaknesses and utilize the strengths of each approach. Moreover, and according to Atif et al. (2013), applying the mixed-methods approach can improve insights into and understanding of the data that might be overlooked when using a single approach, can provide stronger evidence for conclusions, and when triangulation is used, can increase the validity of results and inferences.

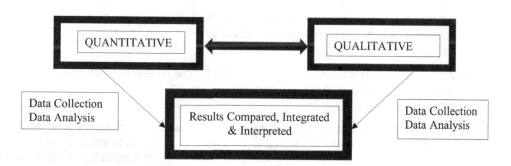

FIGURE 4.1 A Visual Diagram of Mixed-Methods Concurrent Triangulation Strategy
Source: Atif et al. (2013).

Strengths and Challenges of Mixed-methods Research

According to Stallings (2002), "What makes disaster research unique is the *circumstances* in which otherwise conventional methods are employed. Put differently, it is the *context* of research not the methods of research that makes disaster research unique" (p. 21). Much of disaster and emergency management research today is people centered. We tend to look at how disasters impact people throughout the four phases of disaster and, more recently (as explained in Chapter 5), attention is being given to marginalized and vulnerable persons in society based on such statuses as race, gender, ethnicity, disability, sexual orientation, religion, and immigration status. As a result, there is a heightened interest and desire to empower these populations, and mixed-methods research can be employed to determine best practices that might be used to assist these populations during times of a disaster or emergency. However, before one can engage in these types of research designs, they should be cognizant of the various benefits and costs associated with mixed-methods approaches.

As with any research methodology, strengths and challenges will be some of the many deciding factors when selecting a method to apply to any research project. Table 4.2 highlights some of the most commonly acknowledged strengths and challenges associated with the use of mixed-method designs. Although the strengths of this type of research design have profound implications on the potential quality of data and inferences that can be made in a study, the challenges that are associated with these designs are important for consideration. As such, researchers seeking to engage

TABLE 4.2 Strengths and Challenges Associated With Mixed Methods

Strengths	Challenges
■ Words, pictures, and narrative can be used to add meaning to numbers.	■ Can be difficult for a single researcher to carry out both quantitative and qualitative research, especially if used concurrently; may require a research team.
■ Can provide both qualitative and quantitative strengths.	■ Researcher has to learn multiple methods and approaches and understand how to mix them appropriately.
■ Researcher can generate and test a grounded theory.	■ Methodological purists contend that one should always work with either a qualitative or a quantitative paradigm.
■ Can answer a broader and more complete range of research questions because the researcher is not locked into a single method or approach.	■ Can be more expensive.
■ A researcher can use the strengths of an additional method to overcome the weaknesses in another method by using both in a research study.	■ More time-consuming.
■ Can provide stronger evidence for a conclusion through convergence and corroboration of findings.	■ Some of the details of mixed research remain to be worked out fully by methodologists (e.g., problems of paradigm mixing, how to qualitatively analyze quantitative data, how to interpret conflicting results).

Strengths	Challenges
■ Can add insights and understanding that might be missed when only a single method is used.	
■ Can be used to increase the generalizability of the results.	
■ Quantitative and qualitative research used together produce more complete knowledge necessary to inform theory and practice.	

Source: Johnson and Onwuegbuzie (2004, p. 2).

in mixed-method designs in the disaster and emergency management context should use the following discussion as a means of helping to decide whether a mixed-methods approach to answering a research question is appropriate or – possibly just as importantly – practical.

In reference to associated strengths, mixed-methods approaches allow for the use of language, pictures, and/or narratives to enhance the meaning of numbers or codings (Johnson & Onwuegbuzie, 2004). Quantitative data in and of itself is simply numerical, and it does not display any imagery. Moreover, it situates itself within a positivist paradigm in which context does not matter and individuals have the same perceptions of fact as one another. However, as previously indicated, this perspective on data has not been fully accepted. In response, and through the use of other types of data such as pictures, researchers can compensate for the lack of rationality between individuals and contexts (Gephart, 1999). You have heard the saying often: "A picture is worth a thousand words." Think how impactful photos of disaster damage and victims have been in the media and how invaluable they might be to a research project. People are more than just a statistical number.

Mixed-methods approaches also bring the best of both quantitative and qualitative worlds to the table. In many cases, qualitative data can be viewed as an enhancer to quantitative data. Additionally, the research also gets the opportunity to generate and test a grounded theory. For example, Glaser and Strauss (1967) were the first to maintain that some common methods used in grounded theory, such as participant observation, interviews, and the collection of artifacts and texts, could be combined within a single study to answer a broader range of research questions. In many cases, a selected method used on its own may be weaker at answering a particular research question; however, by adding an additional data collection method, a researcher is able to potentially reduce the weaknesses of one method and capitalize on the combined strengths of each data collection strategy. Subsequently, a researcher is able to enhance their data's internal validity in addition to enhancing a study's replicability.

Using mixed methods also allows the researcher to determine if findings actually converge or corroborate, which provides for stronger evidence when making inferences. Along these lines, data from various collection strategies can add insight and understanding that may be missed when just one single method is used; this is especially true if quantitative is the only method chosen. Moreover, the use of mixed methods often can lead to greater generalizability of the results (Hesse-Biber, 2010). Finally, quantitative and qualitative research, used together, produce more holistic knowledge that is necessary to inform theory and practice.

Despite all of these strengths, challenges do exist; however, they are minimal. First, it is often difficult for a single researcher to carry out mixed methods, especially if the research project is relatively large. This may be remedied by bringing in a team of researchers if the methods must be used concurrently (Johnson & Onwuegbuzie, 2004). Second, the researcher must also be adept and confident in the use of the various employed methods, not just one or the other, as well as how they should be combined. Purists are still making the argument that the two should never be mixed (Creswell & Plano Clark, 2007). However, one cannot dispute that mixed methods are much more time-consuming due to things such as interview transcription and coding, and they can also be costly when having to allocate funds toward interviewers, travel, and so forth (Ivankova, Creswell, & Slick, 2006). Third, there is still no complete agreement from scholars as to exactly how to mix these paradigms and how to deal with conflicting results that often arise (Creswell & Plano Clark, 2007).

As a means of exemplifying the use of mixed methods, Box 4.2 highlights some of the methodological challenges and decisions made in one of my own research projects. You may be wondering why the deductive-inductive mode of inquiry I chose to follow was so significant. Hesse-Biber (2015) found through her teaching of mixed-methods courses to her students that one of the biggest challenges faced involves moving students from either a *deductive* mode of research inquiry to an *inductive* one or vice versa. In doing so, the transition in knowledge building requires one to discuss the paradigmatic viewpoints discussed earlier in this chapter, which are linked to research questions that are then linked to the research methods selected. In doing so, students proceed to transition to other ways of knowing and find themselves asking philosophical questions that may start to upend their former ways of thinking about research inquiry (p. 467). Often this is how students (and researchers) come to select a mixed-methods approach for their project.

BOX 4.2 DECIDING TO USE A MIXED-METHODS APPROACH

In my work, *Women Firefighters' Strategies for Advancement in the Fire Service: Breaking Down Barriers in Gender-Based Occupations* (Russo, 2013), I was interested in identifying the obstacles women face in order to advance through the ranks of the fire service as well as the strategies used to overcome them. In order to do so, I sampled 224 female firefighters and used both qualitative and quantitative data collection methods. The project was based on a balance of inductive and deductive reasoning. All of the exigent research focused on the barriers women faced when entering the fire service. However, no research had been completed to understand why women either left the fire service within a short time period or failed to be promoted similarly to their male counterparts. Generally, there were simply many unanswered questions that I wanted to address as a means of increasing the number of women throughout various levels of the fire service.

I used inductive research largely because there was no theory to test and there was little to no existing literature to draw upon. As a result, I had to rely on research within the context of other public safety and paramilitary organizations, in addition to the military, to frame my initial research. Then, with what little fire service literature was available, I was able to formulate a few hypotheses based on some of the existing theories, such as high incidences of sexual harassment on the job. From there, I developed my research questions and designed my mixed-methods research project.

The decision to take a mixed-methods approach did not emerge fully until after I had firmed up my research questions, which were:

1. What obstacles do women perceive in establishing a long-term career in the fire service?
2. What strategies do women follow to adapt to and succeed within a historically segregated occupation, namely the fire service?

At first glance, even novice researchers would agree that these questions could easily be answered through a quantitative analysis of data from a closed-ended survey. However, the data would only provide half of the story. To fully understand the experiences of these women, who are often too afraid to come forward with their experiences for fear of retaliation in the profession by their male counterparts, a qualitative component had to be considered as a complement to the quantitative portion of the data collection. After careful consideration, additional open-ended questions were added, as well as an option for respondents to participate in one-on-one interviews following the online surveys.

To analyze the quantitative data, crosstabs, chi-square tests of association, Spearman correlations, and multiple linear regressions were used to determine the relationships between female firefighters' upward mobility through the ranks and a variety of variables. While the quantitative method certainly answered the research questions, the qualitative data identified and narrowed down the problem, and in many cases in the women's very own words, which were very powerful. As a result, the qualitative data collected from open-ended survey questions and interviews from the respondents were invaluable. The use of mixed methods in this research allowed for a much more robust evaluation and understanding of why women do not advance at the same rates as their male counterparts or remain in the service as long as men.

My mixed-methods study not only unveiled the obstacles that women perceived were preventing their advancement through the ranks in the fire service, and strategies for overcoming those obstacles, but it also uncovered the existence of a glass ceiling for promotion at the rank of captain for most women, which had not previously been discovered. Overall, the findings presented contributed to our further understanding of women in the fire service, the obstacles they perceive, and some of the strategies they use to overcome them. However, the limitations of quantitative research demonstrate the need to take this study further with additional qualitative study shifting toward a true mixed-methods approach.

Although the project highlighted in Box 4.2 had organizational and human resource applications, it was also a personal interest of mine since I had been a division chief in the fire service. As a result, questions of potential bias, especially when the researcher is also a member of the population pool being studied (Chenail, 2011) arose in the qualitative data collection phase of the project. It is simply impossible to remove all bias because we are all human beings. But just like risk and risk mitigation, we must mitigate bias as best as we can (Amerson, 2011). By employing an interview protocol, member checking, data saturation, and mitigating the use of just one personal lens during the data collection process (I had two additional interviewers assisting with interviews), I feel that bias was eliminated as best as possible and I am confident in the fact that the data gathered was both rich (in terms of quality) and thick (as in terms of quantity).

Conclusion

While most disasters are sudden and unexpected, what is not so unexpected are the typically slow funding processes that follow, which may pose a problem for disaster researchers. An example of a comprehensive disaster study that unveiled significant findings about low-income populations and disasters was part of the Resilience in Survivors of Katrina (RISK) project, which produced several notable publications. The Lowe, Green, and Rhodes (2012) study contained three components: mixed methods, interdisciplinary collaboration, and pre-disaster data. Though methodological issues will continue to plague disaster research, mixed-methods projects are a way to remedy some of these issues. For example, early research on social inequalities and disasters primarily used qualitative methods. However, over the past two decades, more scholars have approached social vulnerability issues using quantitative methods (Cutter, 1996; Phillips, Thomas, Fothergill, & Blinn-Pike, 2010). The next natural step for disaster researchers is to continue to combine these techniques and work toward more rigorous and comprehensive mixed-methods research projects, such as RISK. As more comprehensively discussed in the concluding chapter of this book, disaster research needs both the deep, rich context that qualitative research can provide and the statistically generalizable information that quantitative data captures.

It is evident through the literature that mixed-methods research is here to stay (Hesse-Biber, 2015; Giddings & Grant, 2006). For instructors of mixed methods to be successful, it is crucial for them to possess extensive training in both *theory* and *method*. In addition, they should also have actual experience conducting their own mixed-methods research projects so that they may address the same issues and questions students will be bringing into their classrooms. Instructors who teach mixed methods who have only one type of training and skill set are often unable to teach such a course successfully. Through her experiences in teaching mixed methods, Hesse-Biber (2015) has learned the significance of taking a hands-on approach – providing students with in-class exercises addressing some of the thornier issues of using mixed methods. Peer group learning has been observed to also be effective with small-group class discussions and getting feedback from students early and often, as the mixed-methods course proceeds will help deal with many of the gray areas of learning about mixed-methods research (Levine et al., n.d.).

Perhaps Creswell stated it best in his 2009 editorial, in which he wrote:

> We will look back in several years and see that it was the graduate students who promoted mixed methods research and who taught their faculty the importance of this approach to inquiry and the value of not adhering strictly to either quantitative or qualitative approaches. The students will be more interested in how best to address their research problems than the politics of methodology.
>
> (p. 106)

Additionally, mixed-methods techniques will continue to be refined and expanded with more models to choose from, and at last, mixed methods will no longer be seen as a "new approach" in any academic discipline.

Further Readings

Creswell, J. W., & Plano Clark, V. L. (2007). *Designing and conducting mixed methods research.* Thousand Oaks, CA: Sage.

Miller, K., Fernando, G., & Berger, D. (2009). Daily stressors in the lives of Sri Lankan youth: A mixed methods approach to assessment in a context of war and natural disaster. *Intervention,* 7(3), 187–203.

Roosli, R., & O'Keefe, P. (2016). *A Malaysian study of mixed methods: An example of integrating quantitative and qualitative methods.* Newcastle Upon Tyne: Cambridge Scholars.

Tashakkori, A., & Teddlie, C. (Eds.). (2003). *Handbook of mixed methods in the social & behavioral sciences.* Thousand Oaks, CA: Sage.

Teasley, M., & Moore, J. (2010). A mixed methods study of disaster case managers on issues related to diversity in practice with Hurricane Katrina victims. *Journal of Indigenous Voices in Social Work, 1*(1), 1–18.

Teddlie, C., & Yu, F. (2007). Mixed methods sampling: A typology with examples. *Journal of Mixed Methods Research, 1*(1), 77–100.

References

Aitkin, S., & Valentine, G. (2006). *Approaches to human geography.* Thousand Oaks, CA: Sage.

Amerson, R. (2011). Making a case for the case study method. *Journal of Nursing Education, 50,* 427–428.

Andrews, T. (2012). What is social constructionism? *Grounded Theory Review, 11*(1), 39–46.

Atif, A., Richards, D., & Bilgin, A. (2013). *A student retention model: Empirical, theoretical and pragmatic considerations.* Proceedings of the 24th Australasian Conference on Information Systems. December 4–6, Melbourne, Australia.

Babbie, E. (2007). *The practice of social research* (11th ed.). Belmont: Thomson Higher Education.

Berger, P., & Luckman, T. (1967). *The social construction of reality: A treatise in the sociology of knowledge.* New York: Anchor Press.

Burr, V. (2015). *Social constructionism* (3rd ed.). New York: Routledge.

Campbell, D. T., & Fiske, D. W. (1959). Convergent and discriminant validation by the multitrait-multimethod matrix. *Psychological Bulletin, 56*(2), 81.

Chatman, E. (1991). Channels to a larger social world: Older women staying in touch with the great society. *Library and Information Science Research, 42*(6), 438–499.

Chatman, E. (1992). *The information world of retired women.* Westport, CT: Greenwood Press.

Chenail, R. (2011). Interviewing the investigator: Strategies for addressing instrumentation and researcher bias concerns in qualitative research. *Qualitative Report, 16,* 255–262.

Creswell, J. (2009a). *Research design: Qualitative, quantitative, and mixed methods approaches* (3rd ed.). Thousand Oaks, CA: Sage.

Creswell, J. (2009b). Mapping the field of mixed methods research – Editorial. *Journal of Mixed Methods Research, 3*(2), 95–108.

Creswell, J. (2014). *A concise introduction to mixed methods research.* Los Angeles: Sage.

Creswell, J., & Plano Clark, V. (2007). *Designing and conducting mixed methods research.* Thousand Oaks, CA: Sage.

Cutter, S. (1996). Societal vulnerability to environmental hazards. *International Social Science Journal, 47,* 525–536.

Denzin, N. (1978). *The research act: A theoretical introduction to sociological methods.* New York: McGraw-Hill.

Denzin, N. (2009). *The research act: A theoretical introduction to sociological methods* (3rd ed.). Englewood Cliffs, NJ: Prentice Hall.

Denzin, N., & Lincoln, Y. (2018). *The SAGE handbook of qualitative research* (5th ed.). Thousand Oaks, CA: Sage.

Dickens, L., & Watkins, K. (1999). Action research: Rethinking Lewin. *Management Learning, 30*(2), 127–140.

Drabek, T. (1986). *Human system responses to disaster: An inventory of sociological findings.* New York: Springer-Verlag.

Erzberger, C., & Prein, G. (1997). Triangulation: Validity and empirically-based hypothesis construction. *Quality and Quantity, 31*(2), 141–154.

Finn, J. L. (1994). The promise of participatory research. *Journal of Progressive Human Services, 5*(2), 25–42.

Forchtner, B. (2010). Jürgen Habermas' language-philosophy and the critical study of language. *Critical Approaches to Discourse Analysis Across the Disciplines, 4*(1), 18–37.

Fritz, C., & Marks, E. (1954). The NORC studies of human behavior in disaster. *Journal of Social Issues, 10*(3), 26–41.

Fusch, P., Fusch, G., & Ness, L. (2018). Denzin's Paradigm shift: Revisiting triangulation in qualitative research. *Journal of Social Change, 10*(1), 19–32.

Gage, N.L. (1989). The paradigm wars and their aftermath: A "historical" sketch of research and teaching since 1989. *Educational Researcher, 18*, 4–10.

Gephart, R. (1999). Paradigms and research methods. *Academy of Management Research Methods Forum, 4*, 1–12.

Giddings, L., & Grant, B. (2006). Mixed methods research for the novice researcher. *Contemporary Nurse, 23*, 3–11.

Glaser, B., & Strauss, A. (1967). *The discovery of grounded theory: Strategies for Qualitative research.* Chicago: Aldine.

Goddard, D. (1973). Max Weber and the objectivity of science. *History and Theory, 12*(1), 1–22.

Guba, E. (1990). The alternative paradigm dialogue. In E.G. Guba (Ed.), *The paradigm dialog* (pp. 17–27). Newbury Park, VA: Sage.

Guba, E., & Lincoln, Y. (1994). Competing paradigms in qualitative research. In N.K. Denzin & Y.S. Lincoln (Eds.), *Handbook of qualitative research* (pp. 105–117). Thousand Oaks, CA: Sage.

Habermas, J. (1974). Reflections on communicative pathology. In J. Habermas (Ed.), *On the pragmatics of social interaction: Preliminary studies in the theory or communicative action* (pp. 131–170). Cambridge: Polity Press.

Hall, J. (2013). Pragmatism, evidence, and mixed methods evaluation (Special Issue: Mixed methods and credibility of evidence in evaluation). *New Directions for Evaluation, 2013*(138), 15–26.

Harding, S.G. (1977). Does objectivity in social science require neutrality? *Soundings: An Interdisciplinary Journal, 60*(4), 351–366.

Haviland, M., Frye, V., & Rajah, V. (2008). Harnessing the power of advocacy – Research collaborations: Lessons from the field. *Feminist Criminology, 3*(4), 247–275.

Hesse-Biber, S. (2010). Qualitative approaches to mixed methods practice. *Qualitative Inquiry, 16*(6), 455–468.

Hesse-Biber, S. (2015). The problems and prospects in the teachings of mixed methods research. *International Journal of Social Research Methodology, 18*(5), 463–477.

Hildebrand, D.L. (2005). Pragmatism, neopragmatism, and public administration. *Administration & Society, 37*(3), 345–359.

Hollingshead, A. B. (1949). Class and Kinship in a Middle Western Community. *American Sociological Review, 14*(4), 469–475.

Howe, K. (1988). Against the quantitative-qualitative incompatibility thesis, or Dogmas die hard. *Educational Researcher, 17*(8), 10–16.

Humphries, B., & Truman, C. (1994). *Rethinking social research: Anti-discriminatory approaches in research methods.* New York: Routledge.

Islam, M., & Hasan, M. (2016). Climate-induced human displacement: A case study of Cyclone Aila in the south-west coastal region of Bangladesh. *Natural Hazards, 81*, 1051–1071.

Ivankova, N., Creswell, J., & Slick, S. (2006). Using mixed-methods sequential explanatory design: From theory to practice. *Field Methods, 18*, 3–20.

Johnson, B., & Onwuegbuzie, A. (2004). Mixed methods research: A research paradigm whose time has come. *Educational Researcher, 33*(7), 14–26.

Johnson, B., Onwuegbuzie, A., & Turner, L. (2007). Toward a definition of mixed methods research. *Journal of Mixed Methods Research, 1*(2), 112–133.

Johnstone, B. (2018). *Discourse analysis* (3rd ed.). Hoboken, NJ: Wiley.

Kuhn, T. (1970). *The structure of scientific revolutions* (2nd ed.). Chicago: University of Chicago Press.

Levine, A., Nicolau, B., & Pluye, P. (n.d.). *Challenges in teaching mixed methods.* Poster presentations. McGill University, Montreal, Canada.

Lewis-Beck, M., Bryman, A., & Futing Liao, T. (2004). *The SAGE encyclopedia of social science research methods* (Vols. 1–0). Thousand Oaks, CA: Sage.

Lincoln, Y., & Guba, E. (1985). *Naturalistic inquiry.* Beverly Hills, CA: Sage.

Lowe, S., Green, G., & Rhodes, J. (2012). What can multi-wave studies teach us about disaster research? An analysis of low-income Hurricane Katrina survivors. *Journal of Traumatic Stress, 25,* 299–306.

Mahoney, J., & Goertz, G. (2006). A tale of two cultures: Contrasting quantitative and qualitative research. *Political Analysis, 14*(3), 227–249.

Maxwell, S., & Delaney, H. (2004). *Designing experiments and analyzing data.* Mahwah, NJ: Lawrence Erlbaum.

McTaggart, R. (1994). Participatory action research: Issues in theory and practice. *Educational Action Research, 2*(3), 313–337.

Mertens, D., & Hesse-Biber, S. (2012). Triangulation and mixed methods research: Provocative positions. *Journal of Mixed Methods Research, 6*(2), 75–79.

Miller, D.M., & Rivera, J.D. (2008). *Hurricane Katrina and the redefinition of landscape.* Lanham, MD: Rowman & Littlefield.

Miller, K, Fernando, G., & Berger, D. (2009). Daily stressors in the lives of Sri Lankan youth: A mixed methods approach to assessment in a context of war and natural disaster. *Intervention, 7*(3), 187–203.

Morgan, D. L. (2014). Pragmatism as a paradigm for social research. *Qualitative Inquiry, 20*(8), 1045–1053.

Morse, J. (2003). Principles of mixed-methods and multi-method research. In A. Tashakkori & C. Teddlie (Eds.), *Handbook of mixed-methods in social and behavioral research* (pp. 189–208). Thousand, Oaks, CA: Sage.

Muisj, D. (2004). *Doing quantitative research in education with SPSS.* Thousand Oaks, CA: Sage.

Onwuegbuzie, A., & Leech, N. (2003). *On becoming a pragmatic researcher: The importance of combining quantitative and qualitative research methodologies.* Paper presented at the Annual Meeting of the Mid-South Educational Research Association. Biloxi, MS, November 5–7, 2003.

Patton, M. (1988). Paradigms and pragmatism. In D. Fetterman (Ed.), *Qualitative approaches to evaluation in educational research* (pp. 116–137). Thousand Oaks, CA: Sage.

Payne, G., & Payne, J. (2004). *Key concepts in social research.* London: Sage.

Pearce, D. (2012). Mixed methods inquiry in sociology. *American Behavioral Scientist, 56,* 829–848.

Phillips, B., Thomas, D., Fothergill, A., & Blinn-Pike, L. (2010). *Social vulnerability to disasters.* Boca Raton, FL: CRC Press.

Popper, K. (1959). *The logic of scientific discovery.* New York: Routledge.

Powell, T., & Bui, T. (2016). Supporting social and emotional skills after a disaster: Findings from a mixed methods study. *School Mental Health, 8*(1), 106–119.

Prince, S. (1920). *Catastrophe and social change.* New York: Columbia University.

Rorty, R. (1991). *Objectivity, realism, and truth: Philosophical papers.* Cambridge: Cambridge University Press.

Russo, B. (2013, December). *Women firefighters' strategies for advancement in the fire service: Breaking down barriers in gender-based occupations* (Dissertation), Oklahoma State University.

Saunders, M., Lewis, P., & Thornhill, A. (2007). *Research methods for business students* (4th ed.). Pearson.

Schmaus, W. (2008). Review: Rescuing Auguste Comte from the philosophy of history. *History & Theory, 47*(2), 291–301.

Sechrest, L., & Sidani, S. (1995). Quantitative and qualitative methods: Is there an alternative? *Evaluation and Program Planning, 18*(1), 77–87.

Shields, P.M. (2003). The community of inquiry: Classical pragmatism and public administration. *Administration & Society, 35*(5), 510–538.

Smith, J. K. (1983). Quantitative versus qualitative research: An attempt to clarify the issue. *Educational Researcher, 12*(3), 6–13.

Spradley, J. (2016). *The ethnographic interview.* Long Grove, IL: Waveland Press.

Stallings, R. (2002). *Methods of disaster research.* LaVerne, TN: Xlibris.

Steinberg, R.J. (1996). Advocacy research for feminist policy objectives: Experiences with comparable worth. In H. Gottfried (Ed.). *Feminism and social change: Bridging theory and practice* (pp. 225–255). Urbana: University of Illinois Press.

Tashakkori, A., & Teddlie, C. (1998). *Mixed methodology: Combining qualitative and quantitative approaches.* Applied Social Research Methods Series (Vol. 46). Thousand Oaks, CA: Sage.

Tashakkori, A., & Teddlie, C. (2010). Overview of contemporary issues in mixed methods research. In A. Tashakkori & C. Teddlie (Eds.), *Handbook of mixed methods research for the social & behavioral sciences* (2nd ed., pp. 1–44). Thousand Oaks, CA: Sage.

Teasley, M., & Moore, J. (2010). A mixed methods study of case managers on issues related to diversity in practice with Hurricane Katrina victims. *Journal of Indigenous Voices in Social Work, 1*(1), 1–18.

Thomas, T.L., Kannaley, K., Friedman, D.B., Tanner, A.H., Brandt, H.M., & Spencer, S.M. (2016). Media coverage of the 2014 west Virginia Elk River chemical spill: A mixed-methods study examining news coverage of a public health disaster. *Science Communication, 38*(5), 574–600.

Thompson, B. (1992). Misuse of ANCOVA and related "statistical control" procedures. *Reading Psychology: An International Quarterly*, 13, iii–xvii.

Tuominen, K., & Savolainen, R. (1997). A social constructionist approach to the study of information use as discursive action. In P. Vakkari, R. Savolainen, & B. Dervin (Eds.), *Information Seeking in Context: Proceedings of an International Conference on Information Needs, Seeking and Use in Different Contexts*, 14–16 August 1996, Tampere, Finland (pp. 81–96). London: Taylor Graham.

Webb, E.J., Campbell, D.T., Schwartz, R.D., & Sechrest, L. (1999). *Unobtrusive measures* (Vol. 2). Thousand Oaks: Sage Publications.

5

Studying Vulnerable Populations in Disasters

Jason D. Rivera and Alice Fothergill

Introduction

A major focus in the literature over the last 30 years has been to understand the contexts and experiences of individuals who are part of so-called vulnerable populations. According to Cannon (1994) and Wisner, Blaikie, Cannon, and Davis (2003), vulnerability refers to the characteristics of a person or group and their situation that influences their ability to prepare, cope, respond, and recover from a disaster. The reason for the focus on these populations is partly because they are less likely to have access to resources that have the potential to enhance their chances of preparing for and recovering from a disaster event, and in some cases they never recover (Giddens, 1994; Yoon, 2012). The situations in which these groups are contextualized are typically the by-products of historically perpetuated social forces. For example, historical patterns of segregation have divided people based on race and class into locations with relatively fewer resources (Cutter, Boruff, & Shirley, 2003) that can be used to enhance recovery practices. Moreover, given the physical locations in which these groups sometimes find themselves as a by-product of historical segregation, specific populations have been placed in high-hazard areas (Miller & Rivera, 2008).

Vulnerability is not an innate characteristic, but rather a societal creation (Wisner et al. 2003). Vulnerability increases due to a social structure that has historically privileged some characteristics over others, such as policies and practices around the globe that have discriminated against women and people of color. Thus, some disaster studies have tended to focus on demographic factors such as age, race, ethnicity, gender, and socioeconomic status to understand vulnerability (Phillips & Morrow, 2007). In addition, there are other characteristics, such as disability, health status, language, and other contextual stressors, that can make a population vulnerable (Ferreira, Buttell, & Ferreira, 2015; Thomas, Phillips, Lovekamp, & Fothergill, 2013). According to Phillips and Morrow (2007), the understanding of how society creates their vulnerability is limited because studies tend to treat characteristics, such as social class or ethnicity, in isolation as opposed to viewing the intersectionality in their lived experience. As a result, it becomes ever more important for the development of effective policies and programs that relate to reducing disaster vulnerability to understand these intersectional dynamics.

The notion of vulnerability has become elastic in its application, often overused, and increasingly abstract (Satori, 1984). Indeed, the abstraction of the concept of vulnerability has produced confusion within the research community with reference to how vulnerable populations who experience disasters are different from other potentially vulnerable populations (Levine, 2004). Despite this confusion and abstraction of the concept within disaster and emergency management literature, vulnerability is still a profoundly important issue to consider, and many studies still seek to understand the experiences of vulnerable populations and the root causes of the vulnerability. Indeed, there is a responsibility to study those who are considered potentially vulnerable in a disaster context. According to Packenham et al. (2017), disaster research on members of protected or vulnerable groups should be "encouraged [as] valuable, informative research data may be lost if studies do not include these populations in disaster studies," and we should develop "new strategies to overcome the perceived barriers" to research with these populations (p. 3).

As a result of the need and importance of this research, this chapter explores the methodological issues and challenges related to studying vulnerable populations in disasters. Along these lines, we explore ethical considerations mentioned in Chapter 1 in addition to issues of power and status in data collection and accessibility to vulnerable populations. Although vulnerable populations could include a large variety of groups, in this chapter we focus on three contexts: research with vulnerable groups in general, children, and Native Americans. To this end, we provide examples from the extant literature and our own individual research experiences to highlight how the methodological issues we encountered when working with these populations might play out in other situations. Finally, we provide various recommendations and highlight best practices for researchers who seek to engage in research with vulnerable populations, to improve the research experience for both the researcher and the research participants, and to increase researchers' data quality and validity.

Ethical Considerations When Studying Vulnerable Populations

In Chapter 1 of this volume, Edwards describes the historical evolution of ethical considerations and the importance of institutional review boards (IRBs) in disaster and emergency management research. However, because there is increasing concern and research interest in the experiences of those who are considered to be members of vulnerable populations, we will build on Edwards's discussion and focus on ethical issues specifically related to vulnerability. In the context of ethical considerations, vulnerability not only can refer to the social and/or physical exposure of individuals or groups to disasters, but also to the likelihood and/or historical experiences related to being misled, mistreated, or taken advantage of as participants in research (Levine, 2004). According to Levine (2004), the notion of vulnerability also refers to populations who have insufficient agency over their own interests, which can subsequently result in them being treated in ways that degrade their dignity. As such, the Federal Policy for the Protection of Human Subjects (45 C.F.R. pt. 46, 1991) has created specific categories of "protected" groups that have the potential for being adversely taken advantage of in research. Specifically, these groups include children, prisoners, pregnant women, and fetuses (45 C.F.R. § 46.201, 1991; 45 C.F.R. § 46.301, 1991). Moreover, and in many circumstances more germane to social science studies that take place in the aftermath of disasters, the regulations also cover individuals who are cognitively impaired and those who suffer from educational or economic disadvantage (45 C.F.R. § 46.111, 1991). As such, prior to beginning a study, researchers should consider whether there might be any adverse effects to particular vulnerable groups participating in research studies as a by-product of their social, physical, and/or economic status. Along these lines, researchers should consider the benefits and risks associated with vulnerable groups' participation. Some advocate for the use of an "ethical toolkit" when doing disaster research, which would involve building awareness of moral obligations and reviewing the ethics of the project throughout the research process, not just during the pre-research IRB process (Browne & Peek, 2014).

According to Collogan, Tuma, Dolan-Sewell, Borja, and Fleischman (2004), there are a number of potential benefits to respondents who participate in research within the post-disaster context. Benefits include enhanced insights into the experiences of others, positive attention from investigators and/or the media, the development of kinship with others, empowerment, and an enhanced understanding about the availability of disaster recovery–related material resources and medical health services (Newman, Walker, & Gefland, 1999). Moreover, Newman et al. (1999) maintain that the level of benefit taken from participation in studies is related to the methodological design of the study itself. Specifically, they observed that disaster-affected individuals who participated in interview-based research designs experienced greater benefits than those who were respondents in survey-based designs. Despite the potential for benefits stemming from the research process itself, there is currently a lack of research on what kinds of participants are more likely than others to benefit. Along these lines, anecdotal observations from the field have provided some guidance, indicating that individuals belonging to socioeconomically disadvantaged groups, women, and/or racial and ethnic minorities express having benefited from disaster-related research processes more consistently than others (Ganapati, 2013; Thomas et al., 2013; North et al., 2013; Phillips, 2014; Rivera, 2016).

Despite the potential advantages that research in the aftermath of disasters can have on vulnerable groups, there is a great deal of concern for the risks associated with their participation (Packenham et al., 2017). Some of these risks include (but are not limited to) inconvenience, legal action, economic hardship, psychological discomfort, loss of dignity, violations of confidentiality, and unwelcome media attention (Collogan et al., 2004). Although all disaster victims who choose to participate have the potential of experiencing these risks, Newman and Kaloupek (2004) maintain that they have a higher likelihood of occurring among participants who are either relatively young or old, have relatively higher levels of social vulnerability in times of normalcy, have a history of exposure to traumatic events, are physically injured, or have pre-existing mental illness. Moreover, Collogan et al. (2004) maintain that continual participation in disaster research has the potential to increase risks among these groups of people.

BOX 5.1 RESEARCH AS A THERAPEUTIC PROCESS

Focus group processes have been observed to have therapeutic effects on some participants, which became clear in the midst of my doctoral investigation of disaster recovery from Hurricane Sandy in New Jersey. During one focus group, individuals were asked to comment on how the extended loss of electricity affected their lives. When most people discussed the loss of fresh food and use of appliances, one elderly man began to cry. After several others had noticed, I asked him if he was OK. With tears running down his cheek, he said, "I'm sorry I can't help it. My wife was using a respirator when the electric stopped. By the time it had come back . . . she had passed." Immediately the mood of the group became somber and melancholy. After a few seconds, another participant spoke out across the room: "My daughter also passed away when the electricity went out. She was on a dialysis machine."

People began to bow their heads and sit in silence. Some women in the group walked over to the two individuals who had expressed their losses to place their hands on their shoulders or backs to comfort them. Others quietly mouthed to one another, "I'm sorry." After about two minutes of group members comforting each other, the man who had mentioned his late wife said, "I'm sorry, but thank you. I haven't spoke about my wife's passing with others outside my family. It's sorta good to know I'm not alone in my loss. I feel like a weight is lifted."

Source: Rivera (2016).

However, despite the potential occurrence of strong emotional reactions by respondents in the research process, many scholars have observed that participants do not necessarily regret their research experience (Kassam-Adams & Newman, 2005; Ruzek & Zatzick, 2000), and in many cases, participants perceive the strength of their emotional responses as personally therapeutic (North et al., 2013; Phillips, 2014; Rivera, 2016). Women-identified survivors of the Grand Forks Flood of 1997, for example, found participating in post-disaster research to be a positive experience (Fothergill, 2004), and children who expressed themselves and their concerns in research found it therapeutic (Ferreira, Buttell, & Cannon, 2018). Rivera (2016) observed a supportive episode when he investigated people's recovery from Hurricane Sandy in New Jersey, which is illustrated in Box 5.1. As a result, the careful weighing of risks and benefits to disaster research participants, especially those from populations considered vulnerable, is paramount.

Ethical Considerations With Children

In studies involving children, it is recommended that researchers see children as "social actors in their own right and adapt and refine their methods to better fit their lives" (Corsaro, 2018, p. 48). Methods for studies with children and youth should be careful, appropriate, and ethical. In a disaster setting, there may be particular ethical concerns when studying children and youth that should be considered. The federal government requires that research on individuals under the age of 18 classifies them as a protected status for IRB consideration, and thus there are special regulatory requirements that provide additional protection for the children involved in the research. Since children are not old enough to give consent, researchers must obtain the permission of their parents or guardians, and then obtain the assent – which is the agreement but not legal consent – of the children. Some specific concerns are children's vulnerability to exploitation by adults, the differential power relationships between adult researcher and child participant, and the role of adult gatekeepers in mediating access to children.

In the last several decades, social science research on children and youth in disasters has grown substantially, with an enormous increase after 2010 (Peek, Abramson, Cox,

Fothergill, & Tobin, 2018). These studies have provided important data that help us understand children's experiences in a disaster context, and they have shed light on children's vulnerabilities, as well as their capacities, in preparedness and recovery (Mort, Rodriguez Giralt, & Delicado, 2020). Some children have lost loved ones and peers, become orphaned, been left homeless or separated from family, lost valuable school time, and experienced displacement and disorientation for months or even years after a disaster event. Moreover, disasters and their aftermaths can be profoundly frightening and distressing to children, perhaps even more so than for adults (Norris et al., 2002). Anderson (2005) argued that it is imperative that social scientists include children in their research, as they have valuable insights into the disaster experience, and their experiences are distinct from the experiences of adults.

The risks to children to disasters around the globe are high and getting higher, as children are exposed to disasters related to the climate crisis such as droughts, floods, and heat waves. In a pandemic such as COVID-19, they are at risk of a loss of schooling and increased food insecurity. Thus, including children's perspective is imperative, and research on them in disasters can be ethical with the appropriate methodology and sensitivities. Researchers in Australia explored the question of whether to involve children in post-bushfire research by consulting with experts internationally (Gibbs, MacDougall, & Harden, 2013). The study found that this potential research with children was appropriate, important, and ethical if the methodology was "sensitive and allowed children to provide informed consent and to have a sense of control over the issues being discussed" (p. 119). They advocated for a carefully staged process of participation and consent, so the children determined how often and how deeply they participated in the research, and the researchers considered the children's right to be safe and supported in the research process.

Ethical Considerations for "Research" With Native Americans

Within disaster science, there has been an appreciation of and interest in the experiences of Native Americans in the aftermath of disasters. However, conducting research with these groups within American society has its own ethical and procedural intricacies that move beyond those that must be observed in studies with other vulnerable populations as participants. Along these lines, relatively few non–Native researchers have an awareness or understanding of Native American cultures, belief systems, or the effects that American colonialism has had on Native people's ability to operate in times of normalcy, let alone in the aftermath of disasters (Rivera, 2010; Durham & Miller, 2010; Smith, 2012). Kelley, Belcourt-Dittloff, Belcourt, and Belcourt (2013) maintain that in order to engage in ethical research with these vulnerable groups, researchers must be aware of and appreciate the extent to which federal government organizations, affiliated agencies, and even academic institutions have historically oppressed, discriminated against, and engaged in culturally biased practices predominantly for their own benefit as opposed to the benefit of indigenous communities.

As a result of this history, many Native American communities are hesitant to participate in research proposed by outside researchers, even if there is a potential for communal benefits (Harding et al., 2012). One reason for this stems from their historical role in the research process. For example, Sobeck, Chapleski, and Fisher (2003) maintain that Native Americans and other indigenous communities throughout the world have only had the opportunity to participate in research studies as subjects. According to Trimble (1977), these communities volunteer their time to contribute to a researcher's respective agenda but have not been able to participate in the development of the research's design and instruments, and sometimes they have not even been informed about the results. Additionally, tribal needs are not typically bound by researchers' timelines, which are often relatively short (one-time federally funded projects) or too long (when research is oriented toward publication as opposed to remedies for the community itself) (Harding et al., 2012). As such, Native American tribes and other overseeing bodies have had to develop their own ethical policies that guide research (Sobeck et al., 2003).

Although not new, since 2013 there have been no fewer than 28 IRBs that have been created to exclusively serve tribal Nations throughout the United States and are registered with the Office of Human Research Protection. Although these IRBs conform to the typical federal standards, they also provide additional protections to the indigenous communities they serve through provisions that address community-level protections, protocol reviews by cultural committees or elders, publication and dissemination agreements, agreements related to monetary benefits, and tribal considerations of the meaning of research questions (Sahota, 2007). Moreover, even the notion of "research" itself is subject to consideration and interpretation among tribes. Kelley et al. (2013; see also Freeman & Romero, 2002; Alderte, 1996) maintain that through the development of polices and oversight boards, tribes define what research is, not researchers. As such, each individual tribe may have a different notion of what constitutes research, which may or may not be synonymous with definitions from a federal agency or an academic institution. For example, federal definitions of research sometimes do not protect Native American communities from some forms of ethnographic research and are therefore not considered research; however, when activities involve community histories, intellectual property, or simply the participation of community members, tribes consider these behaviors as part of research (Kelley et al., 2013). Therefore, even prior to attempting to develop study questions or instruments, ethical procedures dictate that individuals interested in pursuing some manner of research in the aftermath of disasters with Native American communities need to develop relationships first, as opposed to the other way around (Wilson, 2008; Keene, 2018).

Specifically, Smith-Morris (2007) reminds us that when working or attempting to engage in research with Native American communities, a great deal is predicated on the researcher's ability to build trust, develop and maintain clear lines of communication with community decision-making bodies and potential participants, and be responsive to the tribe's expressed needs (Kaufert, 1999). Along these lines, individuals interested in engaging in studies centered on indigenous peoples must first engage in the *coproduction* of research questions as a means of developing tribally relevant research agendas and community benefits. Piquemal (2001) maintains that this process calls for negotiation, renegotiation, and confirmation if one is to legitimize their study and gain acceptance from indigenous groups of interest. Although specifically discussing consent, Hudson and Tylor-Henley (2001) provide four overarching guidelines to the process of research coproduction with indigenous communities:

1. Elder input is accepted and utilized throughout the entire research process;

2. The traditional language of the respective community is used whenever possible;

3. Research should have some immediate benefit to the community; and

4. The Nation/community controls the research.

Although the first three guidelines are typically understood as methodological and ethical standards shared by most social science researchers, the fourth is typically less common. For Hudson and Tylor-Henley (2001), in order to overcome the legacy of colonialism, Native American communities must be involved and steer the entire research process. This not only results in the coproduction of what constitutes research and what questions should and will be answered, but also allows the community to avoid the historical practice of being taken advantage of or profited from as a by-product of the research. However, from a more pragmatic perspective, following these procedural ethics can result in more community buy-in to projects, which has the potential to enhance internal validity.

Issues of Power in Data Collection for Vulnerable Populations

In most research, there is assumed to be an asymmetrical power balance between researchers and their participants. Typically, this is viewed from the perspective that the researcher has control over what is discussed in an interview or questioned in a survey, in addition to the interpretation of the participants' responses to queries (Kvale, 2006; Anyan, 2013). Although this can occur in all research interactions that are not guided in ways that attempt to mitigate power imbalances, the potential for the effect of power to manifest has an increased probability in situations that include vulnerable populations. Specifically, Anyan (2013; see also Fairclough, 1989; Merriam et al., 2001; Thornborrow, 2002; Johnson-Bailey, 1999) maintains that power imbalances can detrimentally affect the generation of data, in addition to its interpretation, when study participants differ in their socioeconomic status, educational, gender, professional background, or ethnicity with relation to the researcher.

Generally speaking, the asymmetric power distributions that are typically of concern arise in the prescribed roles of interaction between interviewer and interviewee. In these situations, whether in a qualitative interview or in a closed-ended survey, the interviewer is viewed to have power over the interviewee because they control the environment, frame questions, and control the script of discussion that can occur (Brinkmann & Kvale, 2005). Along these lines, once an interviewee provides a sufficient response to the researcher's question, the interaction progresses to the next series of questions. However, the notion of what constitutes a "sufficient" response is typically socially constructed by the researcher based on their own communal and/or professional positions. As such, the responses gathered by researchers have the potential to be subject to measurement error based on what the researcher has previously conceived as a possible response to their question. Subsequently, this provides the researcher with another element of power in the research process: the ability to construct a story and meaning to the responses of participants.

Researchers have the ability to interpret and report what participants meant by their responses. In the best of circumstances, the researcher uses their power of interpretation to reflect the actual reality and meaning of participants' responses. But Kvale (2006) argues that what can occur is that the researcher uses their power of interpretation when working with vulnerable communities to report on the points of interest to their research. Moreover, what participants meant by their responses is often interpreted and applied within the sociocultural context of the researcher without the input of participants (Karnieli-Miller, Strier, & Pessach, 2009). As such, when power dynamics such as these arise, vulnerable populations' experiences in a disaster are further marginalized because individuals' true experiences and sentiment are abstracted to fit researchers' meanings and needs.

In response, and as a means of mitigating this possibility, IRBs have taken various steps to help protect vulnerable populations from research power dynamics that are detrimental to participants and their communities. Adding to the discussions on power in Chapter 1 of this volume and earlier in this chapter, we will now highlight some of the issues of power in research with children and Native American participant populations.

Issues of Power in Data Collection for Children

The principles of the United Nations 1989 Convention on the Rights of the Child ensure that the human dignity of children is honored and their rights and well-being are respected in all arenas, including when they are part of the research process. Furthermore, Article 12 of that document gives children the right to have their voices heard in matters that concern them. Research helps us hear the voices of children, understand their lives, and meet their needs, and we must also understand how to make sure they are respected and not exploited in the research process. They have the right to participate in the research and to receive its benefits, but also to be protected in the process.

Social scientists have discussed the power differential in researching children for many years and have tried to address this power imbalance between researchers and the research participants under 18 years of age. Child sociologist William Corsaro states this power imbalance is heightened because of the age, authority, and size of the adult. According to Corsaro (2018, p. 54), "gaining acceptance into children's worlds is especially challenging given that adults are physically larger than children, are more powerful, and are often seen as having control over children's behavior." The power imbalance can be reduced with certain kinds of methods, such as collecting data through "research conversations" with children (Mayall, 2008) or by carefully entering the children's space, sitting down, and waiting for them to react to the researcher, which may take some time (Corsaro, 2018).

Disaster scholars have also been addressing the issues of power and status in disaster research conducted with children. Focus groups after disaster help to lessen the power imbalance, as there is one adult researcher and numerous children, so they have some power from their greater numbers (Peek & Fothergill, 2009). Some have employed participatory methods as one way to democratically engage children and youth in the research process (Peek et al., 2016; Mort et al., 2020). Non-traditional methods, such as drawings and other child-centered techniques, which are recommended in general for research on children, also work well in disaster settings (Fothergill & Peek, 2015). These methods might help give children some control in a research setting, as described by Fothergill in Box 5.2.

BOX 5.2 ZACHARY

Zachary and I walked out the door together onto the small wood deck at the back of his home. We sat down on the bowed wood stairs to talk. Zach, 13 years old, was not a big talker. In fact, over the years we gotten used to a lot of the children we met to answer any questions with "yes" or "no" or "uh-huh." This was the fifth time I'd met with Zach (the first time was when he was

7), so he knew me and was familiar with the project. But this time I had something new. I took out a small stack of six laminated cards, a little bigger than playing cards, and I handed them to him. He was intrigued. Each card had a colorful drawing of something relevant to his life – they represented the spheres of children's lives – and included a house, a group of friends, a school, a family, a church, scenes of recreation. After I explained that he could decide which card to address and for how long, he started to shuffle the cards, then he laid them all out in front of him on the wood plank. Then he picked them up, examined them, held them as if in a card game, and then laid them down again. Then he rearranged them, then again. I liked how he was taking his time, contemplating the images. It was warm afternoon but we were in the shade, and we had plenty of time. I remember thinking at that moment: "I absolutely love these cards." The cards put the control of the interview in the hands of the children; they determined the pace and the topic order. Zach decided to start with the friend card. He picked it up and held it. "Okay," he said. "Well, first, my best friend moved back to New Orleans last week." He looked at me, then looked back at the card. "And I'm so happy he's back."

Source: Fothergill (original for this chapter).

It is also important to consider the way that age intersects with other characteristics, such as socioeconomic status, race and ethnicity, ability status, and gender, and how that affects power and status in the research process. Children, in other words, do not all experience the same level of vulnerability (see, e.g., Ducy & Stough, 2011). Some children have more power and status than others in a disaster context, and some are able to be shielded from some of the detrimental aspects of a disaster. Children in families with resources, for example, may be able to evacuate early from a dangerous situation and not witness or experience the intensity of the hazard threat. Furthermore, some children may receive more support during recovery and more assistance with their coping, and may have families in social classes that can navigate the bureaucracies of middle-class institutions (Fothergill & Peek, 2015). Thus, disaster researchers should be cognizant of the fact that children come to the research process from different backgrounds, levels of privilege, and a range of disaster experiences.

Issues of Power in Data Collection for Native Americans

Gaining acceptance into Native American worlds is as equally important in the devolution of power imbalances throughout the disaster research process as it is in other marginalized and vulnerable communities. According to Smith-Morris (2007), a researcher's ability to reduce power imbalances begins with their ability to establish and build trust, develop clear lines of communication with and between individuals and indigenous decision-makers or bodies, and be responsive to their needs. This is particularly important in Native communities because of the mistreatment, abuse, experimentation, and sporadic "drive-by" research projects that have detrimentally affected these groups throughout history (Lawrence, 2000; Smith, 2006). As such, engaging in research that is beneficial for Native American communities in the aftermath of disasters requires the researcher to acknowledge traditional power dynamics in research, such as who has access to data and who interprets the results of an analysis (Collins, 1998; Mihesuah & Wilson, 2004). Therefore, indigenous communities or their decision-makers must be involved not only in providing consent for participation in research but also in projects' data interpretation. Within the realm of disaster and emergency management research, these practices help to place the needs of the Native community at the center of research at the same time as providing participants power within the process. By not engaging in these types of research practices, disaster and emergency management researchers are participating in acts of colonialism themselves (Jacob, 2006).

Mihesuah and Wilson (2004) and Swisher (1998) maintain that Native people must be included in all aspects of research in which they are participating, from inception to writing up results, as a means of avoiding deliberate or unconscious effects of cultural misinterpretation and abuses of power on the behalf of the researcher. In addition to reducing abuses, inclusionary research practices also aid in reducing the perception of power from the perspective of participants. For example, Jacob (2006) highlights that while engaging in research with Native communities, potential participants perceived there to be others within the research process who held more power than the researcher:

> I was asked, "Who is this research for?" I occasionally was asked if my professors had sent me out to collect data, signaling that they thought I was perhaps being used, as Medicine (2001) has noted, as a "tool" of "real" White male anthropologists (p. 5). And oftentimes, I was asked if the government was involved in the collection or ownership of the data.
>
> (Jacob, 2006, p. 455)

As Jacob (2006) highlights, even when research processes are inclusionary and transparent, indigenous participants may continue to harbor notions of asymmetries of power within the research relationship because of their historical collective experiences. Moreover, the apprehension of abuses of power within the research process is so strong that various tribes have developed principles that outline their general expectations:

1. Do not plan about us without us;

2. All tribal systems will be respected and honored, emphasizing policy building and bridging;

3. Policies will not bypass tribal government review and approval before implementation; and

4. Tribal specific data will not be published without tribal authorization (Walters et al., 2009).

As a result, these principles help to ensure that power and authority within the research process are settled within the community or tribal entity.

These principles protect the participants, and they also enhance the quality of research more generally. They require that the researchers adhere to an orientation that focuses on relationships between themselves and their community partners that are built upon co-learning, mutual benefit, and long-term commitment (Wallerstein & Duran, 2006). Along these lines, the reduction of true and perceived power within the research process can be reduced through adherence to community-based participatory research (CBPR) ideals (Minkler, 2004; Walters et al., 2009). According to Israel, Schultz, Parker, and Becker (2001), research relationships that are created and sustained through CBPR have the ability to generate a more holistic understanding of a phenomenon in which knowledge is gained with actions that benefit the communities involved. As such, adherence to research orientations such as these allow researchers to engage in scientifically rigorous projects without compromising Native communities' self-determination in the process (Smith-Morris, 2006, 2007).

Gaining Access to Vulnerable Populations

It has often been said that disasters provide valuable opportunities for researchers, as they have advantages that are not there in non-disaster times. In times of normalcy, various groups within society are difficult to access through traditional sampling methods because of the groups' social or physical location or vulnerability (Ellard-Gray, Jeffrey, Choubak, & Crann, 2015). These "hard to reach" populations are difficult to access because of their physical isolation in remote geographic areas or because of their vulnerability (Shaghaghi, Bhopal, & Sheikh, 2011; Sydor, 2013). Accessing vulnerable populations requires an appreciation and understanding of their disenfranchisement and stigmatization by larger social groups within a society (Stone, 2003; Liamputtong, 2007).

In many situations, disasters may bring "normally private behavior under public observation" and social processes become more visible (Fritz, 1961, p. 654). It may be that those with the fewest resources, and often the most vulnerable, are more prominently under public observation. Low-income individuals, for example, are more likely to use mass shelters or find temporary shelter in FEMA trailers, and are thus exposed to the eyes of researchers, journalists, and government representatives (Mileti, Sorensen, & O'Brien, 1992; Brodie, Weltzien, Altman, Blendon, & Benson, 2006). So, on the one hand, it may seem that there is increased "access" to vulnerable populations; however, on the other hand, this perceived increased access has the potential to reduce access as well. For example, Stallings (2007) warns that when vulnerable populations become more visible in the aftermath of disasters, researchers tend to converge on the places in which they are located. This convergence of researchers (Fritz & Mathewson, 1957) has the potential to overload potential respondents with requests to participate in studies. As a result, respondents from vulnerable populations may provide "canned" or rehearsed responses to all interested researchers, or they may even decide to not participate in any research (see Chapters 6 and 10 for examples).

To access participants, Stallings (2007) argues that timing is key, as the first researchers on the scene have a competitive advantage. Not only does getting on the scene first provide better access to respondents, but it also reduces the likelihood that respondents who fit the study's inclusion criteria will have left the disaster setting. Uekusa (2019) and Marlowe (2015) maintain that the longer a researcher takes to appear in the field, the more likely it is that key informants will have moved away, which is even more pronounced with some vulnerable groups such as immigrants and refugees. However, Uekusa (2019) also warns that rushing into the field does not guarantee access to vulnerable populations. Typically, there is a discrepancy between when researchers want to interview or collect data from respondents and when the disaster victims are cognitively willing to talk (WHO, 2001). In some cases, the notion of timing and when it is most appropriate to collect data from individuals belonging to vulnerable groups is a methodological and ethical gray area that requires augmentation and reassessment on the behalf of the investigator.

However, even if one has access to a population that is willing and ready to participate in research, an investigator should pause and consider the ethical issues of the research indicative to the specific population of interest. As has already been pointed out in this chapter, some populations, such as children and Native Americans, may have increased protections, and a goal may be to actually control or decrease access to researchers from taking advantage of them, especially to those researchers who may be responding to a disaster in a "gold rush" fashion (Gaillard & Gomez, 2015).

Accessing Children

Because children are a protected group under the rules for human subjects, there are some built-in issues around accessibility. IRBs, themselves, play a significant role in whether researchers have access to children for research, and under what conditions, even when the IRB members have insufficient knowledge about the research context. Indeed, IRBs are an influential and overlooked "gatekeeper" in research on children (Harger & Quintela, 2017). Sometimes IRB members rely on their perceptions and own personal experiences, requesting changes to studies with children and sometimes even preventing the research entirely. They may also put up roadblocks to protect vulnerable children and view youth as unable to make their own decisions (Harger & Quintela, 2017).

In addition to the IRB, there are other gatekeepers who must grant permission to study children in disasters, including parents, guardians, school principals, childcare center directors, and other personnel overseeing children's well-being. Some researchers study children's experiences in a disaster by having adults (such as teachers), not the children, as the research participants who have firsthand knowledge about the children (see, e.g., Ducy & Stough, 2011). For direct access to children in schools, researchers have to carefully consider how to gain permission from school administrators and individual teachers. In general, there are growing concerns that more schools are asking parents for active consent, instead of asking them to "opt out" of research.

In the disaster context, there may be additional factors as schools often close or are used as shelters in disasters, children are displaced to new schools, and teachers and parents may be new to each other and do not have established trusting relationships (Fothergill & Peek, 2015). These issues make access more challenging. For children and families who do not speak or read the dominant language, issues of access are also problematic. Translators may not be available in a disaster aftermath, and if they are, there are issues around confidentiality and privacy, especially if the community is particularly small and the participants and the translators know each other (Jacobson & Landau, 2003). In addition, it is possible that gatekeepers may disagree about research access to children. For example, challenges may arise if parents, teachers, and school administrators are not in agreement about access, or they disagree about what research methods would be acceptable.

Accessing Native American Communities

Similar to gaining access to other vulnerable populations, working with Native American populations has various obstacles to overcome. In addition to these communities' relative concentration in various geographic locations, their historical relationship with government and academic organizations has led to distrust and resistance to participating in research. This is especially the case when researchers have not established a relationship with community members or leaders in the past, and when the research does not directly benefit the population (Lawrence, 2000; Smith, 2006). Despite these previous interactions, outside researchers are able to gain access to indigenous populations if they are respectful, inclusive, and give up a measure of control over the research process (Mihesuah & Wilson, 2004).

Specifically, researchers working with indigenous populations on disaster research typically benefit from a history of individual interaction with the community. Moreover, following the guidelines established by Hudson and Tylor-Henley (2001) that were previously outlined in this chapter can help provide a researcher with the necessary rapport to engage in research with Native American peoples. However, adhering to these guidelines requires a great deal of investment of time and social capital on the behalf of the researcher, especially when it comes to getting buy-in from community elders, using traditional languages, adhering to cultural nuances, and allowing the community to control the research process. Minimally, it requires a level of cultural competence that is not necessarily learned or characteristic of every researcher.[1] As such, gaining access and engaging in research with these populations is a long-term endeavor (Poupart, Baker, & Red Horse, 2009; Dwyer & Buckle, 2009; Mail, Conner, & Conner, 2009), which is discussed in Chapter 8 of this volume.

Conclusion

Research on vulnerable populations in disasters is extremely valuable, and those considered vulnerable have the right to participate in disaster research and the right to the benefits of the research. While there may be added challenges, such as receiving extra permissions and mitigating additional risks, this does not mean that the research should not be carried out; indeed it is imperative that vulnerable populations be studied (Packenham et al., 2017). It is also important to remember that everyone in a disaster is not considered vulnerable, even though it is acknowledged that they have had a disaster experience.

When considering vulnerability, one important consideration is that not everyone in a "vulnerable group" has the same circumstances or shares the same social location. Bodstein, Lima, and Barros (2014) make the case about the vulnerability of older adults in Brazil in disasters:

> The elderly do not represent a homogenous group, given that an array of specific conditions – financial resources, cultural differences, access to education, to leisure, to basic sanitation and healthcare services, for example – impact on their quality of life and influence their ageing process. Therefore, due to the specificities that distinguish them from each other, not all senior citizens have equal or similar needs, and this aspect also needs to be taken into account by public policies, including those on protection in disasters.
>
> (p. 182)

Similar arguments could be made for other groups seen as potentially vulnerable, such as racial minority groups, children, and women – groups that are also heterogeneous.

While all research needs to consider if the risks associated with the research are greater than the benefits, it is especially important to emphasize this with vulnerable populations in disaster settings. Research fatigue is a real concern, too, as some groups, such as poor communities, racially marginalized communities, people with HIV, and those with disabilities get over-researched in non-disaster times. In high-profile disasters there can be a mass of researchers descending on the disaster scene (Gaillard & Gomez, 2015). Research fatigue is a growing concern in the COVID-19 global pandemic atmosphere, and one reason for research fatigue is a feeling of being devalued by the researchers, not getting the results, or not even being thanked for participating (Patel, Webster, Greenberg, Weston, & Brooks, 2020).

As discussed in this chapter, there are some best practices suggested by researchers for those who will conduct research with vulnerable populations. Understanding historical circumstances, past and current exploitation, and experiences of discrimination and oppression is imperative. Careful, deliberate, thoughtful attention to research methods makes a difference. When methods are respectful, research can have a therapeutic or positive effect on participants. Best practices also include recognizing the needs of communities, being mindful of the timing of post-disaster fieldwork, developing relationships before starting the research, and delivering findings back to the community.

Overall, situations in disasters are constantly shifting, and researchers need to be prepared for the dynamic nature of recovery and shifting vulnerability. A disaster event may create vulnerability in different ways for different populations. In the COVID-19 pandemic, for example, many older adults were vulnerable due to the increased health risk to the virus, while children were vulnerable to the risks associated with the disruption of education and the potential threats of neglect and abuse at home during quarantine. Finally, groups labeled as vulnerable also have capacities and strengths, and it is critical that vulnerability not be equated with weakness or a lack of agency.

Note

1. For more information on cultural competence in emergency and disaster management, see Knox and Haupt (2020).

Further Readings

Brockie, T.N., Dana-Sacco, G., Lopez, M.M., & Wetsit, L. (2017). Essentials of research engagement with Native American tribes: Data collection reflections of a tribal research team. *Progress in Community Health Partnerships: Research, Education, and Action, 11*(3), 301–307.
Fothergill, A., & Peek, L. (2015). *Children of Katrina*. Austin: University of Texas Press.
Liamputtong, P. (Ed.). (2008). *Doing cross-cultural research: Ethical and methodological perspectives*. Springer Science+Business Media B.V.

References

Anderson, W. (2005). Bringing children into focus on the social science disaster research agenda. *International Journal of Mass Emergencies and Disasters, 23*, 159–175.

Anyan, F. (2013). The influence of power shifts in data collection and analysis stages: A focus on qualitative research interview. *Qualitative Report, 18*(36), Article, 1–9.

Alderte, E. (1996). The formulation of a health research agenda by and for indigenous peoples: Contesting the Western scientific paradigm. *Journal of Alternative and Complementary Medicine, 2*(3), 377–385.

Bodstein, A., Lima, V. V., & Barros, A. M. (2014). The vulnerability of the elderly in disasters: The need for an effective resilience policy. *Ambiente y Sociedade, 17*(2), 157–174.

Brinkmann, S., &. Kvale, S. (2005). Confronting the ethics of qualitative research. *Journal of Constructivist Psychology, 18*(2), 157–181.

Brodie, M., Weltzien, E., Altman, D., Blendon, R. J., & Benson, J. M. (2006). Experiences of Hurricane Katrina evacuees in Houston Shelters: Implications for future planning. *American Journal of Public Health, 96*, 1402–1408.

Browne, K. E., & Peek, L. (2014). Beyond the IRB: An ethical toolkit for long-term disaster research. *International Journal of Mass Emergencies and Disasters, 32*(1), 82–120.

Cannon, T. (1994). Vulnerability analysis and the explanation of "natural" disasters. In A. Varley (Ed.), *Disasters, development and environment* (pp. 13–30). Hoboken, NJ: Wiley.

Collins, P. H. (1998). *Fighting words.* Minneapolis: University of Minnesota Press.

Collogan, L. K., Tuma, F., Dolan-Sewell, R., Borja, S., & Fleischman, A. R. (2004). Ethical issues pertaining to research in the aftermath of disaster. *Journal of Traumatic Stress, 17*(5), 363–372.

Corsaro, W. A. (2018). *The sociology of childhood* (5th ed.). Thousand Oaks, CA: Sage.

Cutter, S. L., Boruff, B. J., & Shirley, W. L. (2003). Social vulnerability to environmental hazards. *Social Science Quarterly, 84*(2), 242–261.

Ducy, E. M., & Stough, L. M. (2011). Exploring the support role of special education teachers after Hurricane Ike: Children with significant disabilities, *Journal of Family Issues 32*(10), 1325.

Durham, C., & Miller, D. S. (2010). Native Americans, disasters, and the U.S. government: Where responsibility lies. In J. D. Rivera & D. S. Miller (Eds.), *How ethnically marginalized Americans cope with catastrophic disasters: Studies in suffering and resiliency* (pp. 17–36). Lewiston, NY: Edwin Mellen Press.

Dwyer, S. C., & Buckle, J. L. (2009). The space between: On being an insider-outsider in qualitative research. *International Journal of Qualitative Methods, 8*(1), 54–63.

Ellard-Gray, A., Jeffrey, N. L., Choubak, M., & Crann, S. E. (2015). Finding the hidden participant: Solutions for recruiting hidden, hard-to-reach, and vulnerable populations. *International Journal of Qualitative Methods, 14*(5), 1–10.

Fairclough, N. (1989). *Language and power.* London: Longman.

Ferreira, R. J., Buttell, F., & Cannon, C. (2018). Ethical issues in conducting research with children and families affected by disasters. *Current Psychiatry Reports, 20*(42).

Ferreira, R. J., Buttell, F., & Ferreira, S. B. (2015). Ethical considerations for conducting disaster research with vulnerable populations. *Journal of Social Work Values and Ethics, 12*(1), 29–40.

Fothergill, A. (2004). *Heads above water: Gender, class, and family in the Grand Forks Flood.* Albany, NY: State University of New York (SUNY) Press.

Fothergill, A., & Peek, L. (2015). *Children of Katrina.* Austin: University of Texas Press.

Freeman, W. L., & Romero, F. C. (2002). Community consultation to evaluate group risk. In R. Amdur & E. Bankert (Eds.), *Institutional review board: Management and function* (pp. 160–164). Sudbury, MA: Jones & Bartlett.

Fritz, C. E. (1961). Disaster. In R. K. Merton & R. A. Nisbet (Eds.), *Contemporary social problems* (pp. 651–694). New York: Harcourt, Brace and World.

Fritz, C. E., & Mathewson, J. H. (1957). *Convergence behavior in disasters: A problem in social control.* Washington, DC: National Academy of Sciences, National Research Council.

Gaillard, J. C., & Gomez, C. (2015). Post-disaster research: Is there gold worth the rush? *Jàmbá: Journal of Disaster Risk Studies, 7*(1), Art. #120,

Ganapati, N. E. (2013). Measuring the processes and outcomes of post-disaster housing recovery: Lessons from Gölcük, Turkey. *Natural Hazards, 65*(3), 1783–1799.

Gibbs, L., MacDougall, C., & Harden, J. (2013). Development of an ethical methodology for post-bushfire research with children. *Health Sociology Review, 22*(2), 114–123.

Giddens, A. (1994). *Beyond right and left: The future of radical politics*. Cambridge: Polity Press.

Harding, A., Harper, B., Stone, D., O'Neill, C., Berger, P., Harris, S., & Donatuto, J. (2012). Conducting research with tribal communities: Sovereignty, ethics and data-sharing issues. *Environmental Health Perspectives, 120*(1), 6–10.

Harger, B., & Quintela, M. (2017). The IRB as gatekeeper: Effects on research with children and youth. In S. Castro & B. Harger (Eds.), *Researching children and youth: Methodological issues, strategies, and innovations*. Bingley: Emerald Group.

Hudson, P., & Tylor-Henley, S. (2001). Beyond the rhetoric: Implementing a culturally appropriate research project in First Nations communities. *American Indian Culture and Research Journal, 25*(2), 93–105.

Israel, B.A., Schultz, A.J., Parker, E.A., & Becker, A.B. (2001). Community-based participatory research: Policy recommendations for promoting a partnership approach in health research. *Education and Health, 14*(2), 182–197.

Jacob, M.M. (2006). When a native "goes researcher": Notes from the North American indigenous games. *American Behavioral Scientist, 50*(4), 450–461.

Jacobson, K., & Landau, L. (2003). The dual imperative in refugee research: Some methodological and ethical considerations in social science research on forced migration. *Disasters, 27*(3), 185–206.

Johnson-Bailey, J. (1999). The ties that bind and the shackles that separate: Race, gender, class and color in a research process. *International Journal of Qualitative Studies in Education, 12*(6), 659–670.

Karnieli-Miller, O., Strier, R., & Pessach, L. (2009). Power relations in qualitative research. *Journal of Qualitative Health Research, 19*(2), 279–289.

Kassam-Adams, N., & Newman, E. (2005). Child and parent reactions to participation in clinical research. *General Hospital Psychiatry, 27*(1), 29–35.

Kaufert, J. (1999). *Looking for solutions: Recognizing communities in research ethics review*. Ottawa: National Council on Ethics in Human Research.

Kelley, A., Belcourt-Dittloff, A., Belcourt, C., & Belcourt, G. (2013). Research ethics and indigenous communities. *American Journal of Public Health, 103*(12), 2146–2152.

Keene, A. (2018). Understanding relationships in the college process: Indigenous methodologies, reciprocity, and College Horizons students. In R.S. Minthorn & B.M.J. Brayboy (Eds.), *Reclaiming indigenous research in higher education* (pp. 47–63). New Brunswick, NJ: Rutgers University Press.

Knox, C.C., & Haupt, B. (2020). *Cultural competency for emergency and crisis management: Concepts, theories and case studies*. New York: Routledge.

Kvale, S. (2006). Dominance through interviews and dialogues. *Journal of Qualitative Inquiry, 12*(3), 480–500.

Lawrence, J. (2000). The Indian health service and the sterilization of Native American women. *American Indian Quarterly, 24*(3), 400–419.

Levine, C. (2004). The concept of vulnerability in disaster research. *Journal of Traumatic Stress, 17*(5), 395–402.

Liamputtong, P. (2007). *Researching the vulnerable: A guide to sensitive research methods*. London: Sage.

Mail, P.D., Conner, J., & Conner, C.N. (2009). New collaborations with Native Americans in the conduct of community research. *Health Education & Behavior, 33*(2), 148–153.

Mayall, B. (2008). Conversations with children: Working with generational issues. In P. Christensen & A. James (Eds.), *Research with children: Perspectives and practices* (2nd ed.), pp. 109–124. New York, NY: Routledge.

Marlowe, J. (2015). Belonging and disaster recovery: Refugee-background communities and the Canterbury earthquakes. *British Journal of Social Work, 45*(1), i.188–i.204.

Medicine, B. (2001). *Learning to be an anthropologist and remaining "Native."* Urbana: University of Illinois Press.

Merriam, S.B., Johnson-Bailey, J., Lee, M., Kee, Y., Ntseane, G., & Muhamad, M. (2001). Power and positionality: Negotiating insider/outsider status within and across cultures. *International Journal of Lifelong Education, 20*(5), 405–416.

Mihesuah, D.A., & Wilson, A.C. (2004). Introduction. In D. Mihesuah & A.C. Wilson (Eds.), *Indigenizing the academy: Transforming scholarship and empowering communities* (pp. 1–15). Lincoln: University of Nebraska Press.

Mileti, D. S., Sorensen, J. H., & O'Brien, P. W. (1992). Toward an explanation of mass care shelter use in evacuations. *International Journal of Mass Emergencies and Disasters, 10*, 24–42.

Miller, D. S., & Rivera, J. D. (2008). *Hurricane Katrina and the redefinition of landscape.* Lanham, MD: Rowman & Littlefield.

Minkler, M. (2004). Ethical challenges for the "outside" researcher in community-based participatory research. *Health Education & Behavior, 31*(6), 684–697.

Mort, M., Rodriguez Giralt, I., & Delicado, A. (2020). *Children and young people's participation in disaster risk reduction: Agency and resilience.* Bristol: Bristol University Press.

Newman, E., & Kaloupek, D. (2004). The risks and benefits of participation in trauma-focused research studies. *Journal of Traumatic Stress, 17*(5), 383–394.

Newman, E., Walker, E. A., & Gefland, A. (1999). Assessing the ethical costs and benefits of trauma-focused research. *Annals of General Hospital Psychiatry, 21*(3), 187–196.

Norris, F. H., Friedman, M. J., Watson, P. J., Byrne, C. M., Diaz, E., & Kaniasty, K. (2002). 60,000 disaster victims speak: Part I. An empirical review of the empirical literature, 1981–2001. *Psychiatry, 65*(3), 207–239.

North, C. S., Pfefferbaum, B., Hong, B. A., Gordon, M. R., Kim, Y., Lind, L., & Pollio, D. E. (2013). Workplace response of companies exposed to the 9/11 World Trade Center attack: A focus group study. *Disasters, 37*(1), 101–118.

Packenham, J. P., Rosselli, R, T., Ramsey, S. K., Taylor, H. A., Fothergill, A., Slutsman, J., & Miller, A. (2017). Conducting science in disasters: Recommendations from the NIEHS working group for special IRB considerations in the review of disaster related research. *Environmental Health Perspectives, 125*(9), 094503.

Patel, S. S., Webster, R. K., Greenberg, N., Weston, D., & Brooks, S. K. (2020). Research fatigue in COVID-19 pandemic and post-disaster research: Causes, consequences and recommendations. *Disaster Prevention and Management, 29*(4), 445–455.

Peek, L., Abramson, D. M., Cox, R. S., Fothergill, A., & Tobin, J. (2018). Children and disasters. In H. Rodriguez, J. Trainor, & W. Donner (Eds.), *Handbook of disaster research* (2nd ed.) (pp. 243–262). New York: Springer.

Peek, L., & Fothergill, A. (2009). Using focus groups: Lessons from studying daycare centers, 9/11, and Hurricane Katrina. *Qualitative Research, 9*(1), 31–59.

Peek, L., Tobin-Gurley, J., Cox, R. S., Scannell, L., Fletcher, S., & Heykoop, C. (2016). Engaging youth in post-disaster research: Lessons learned from a creative methods approach. *Gateways: International Journal of Community Research and Engagement, 9*(1), 89–112.

Phillips, B. (2014). *Qualitative disaster research: Understanding qualitative research.* Oxford: Oxford University Press.

Phillips, B., & Morrow, B. H. (2007). Social science research needs: Focus on vulnerable populations, forecasting and warnings. *Natural Hazards Review, 8*(3), 61–68.

Piquemal, N. (2001). Free and informed consent in research involving Native American communities. *American Indian Culture and Research Journal, 25*(1), 65–79.

Poupart, J., Baker, L., & Red Horse, J. (2009). Research with American Indian communities: The value of authentic partnerships. *Children and Youth Services Review, 31*(11), 1180–1186.

Rivera, J. D. (2010). Native American experiences with disaster. In J. D. Rivera & D. S. Miller (Eds.), *How ethnically marginalized Americans cope with catastrophic disasters: Studies in suffering and resiliency* (pp. 13–16). Lewiston, NY: Edwin Mellen Press.

Rivera, J. D. (2016). *Acquiring federal disaster assistance: Investigating equitable resource distribution within FEMA's home assistance program.* Doctoral dissertation, Rutgers, The State University of New Jersey.

Ruzek, J. I., & Zatzick, D. F. (2000). Ethical considerations in research participation among acutely injured trauma survivors: An empirical investigation. *Annals of General Hospital Psychiatry, 22*(1), 27–36.

Sahota, P. C. (2007). *Research regulation in American Indian/Alaskan Native communities: Policy and practice considerations.* Washington, DC: National Congress of American Indians Policy Research Center. Retrieved November 25, 2019, from http://depts.washington.edu/ccph/pdf_files/Research%20Regulation%20in%20AI%20AN%20Communities%20-%20Policy%20and%20Practice.pdf

Satori, G. (1984). *Social science concepts: A systematic analysis.* Sage.

Shaghaghi, A., Bhopal, R.S., & Sheikh, A. (2011). Approaches to recruiting "hard to reach" populations into research: A review of the literature. *Health Promotion Perspectives*, *1*(2), 86–94.

Smith, A. (2006). *Conquest*. Cambridge, MA: South End Press.

Smith, L.T. (2012). *Decolonizing methodologies: Research and indigenous peoples*. London: Zed Books.

Smith-Morris, C. (2006). Community participation in tribal diabetes programming. *American Indian Culture and Research Journal*, *30*(2), 85–110.

Smith-Morris, C. (2007). Autonomous individuals or self-determined communities? The changing ethics of research among Native Americans. *Human Organization*, *66*(3), 327–336.

Sobeck, J.L., Chapleski, E.E., & Fisher, C. (2003). Conducting research with American Indians. *Journal of Ethnic and Cultural Diversity in Social Work*, *12*(1), 69–84.

Stallings, R.A. (2007). Methodological issues. In H. Rodríguez, E. L Quarantelli, & R.R. Dynes (Eds.), *Handbook of disaster research* (pp. 55–82). New York: Springer Science + Business Media, LLC.

Stone, T.H. (2003). The invisible vulnerable: The economically and educationally disadvantaged subjects of clinical research. *Journal of Law, Medicine, and Ethics*, *31*(1), 149–153.

Swisher, K.G. (1998). Why Indian people should be the ones to write about Indian education. In D.A. Mihesuah (Ed.), *Natives and academics: Researching and writing about American Indians* (pp. 190–199). Lincoln: University of Nebraska Press.

Sydor, A. (2013). Conducting research into hidden or hard-to-reach populations. *Nurse Researcher*, *20*(3), 33–37.

Thomas, D.S., Phillips, B.D., Lovekamp, W.E., & Fothergill, A. (2013). *Social vulnerability to disasters* (2nd ed.). Boca Raton, FL: CRC Press.

Thornborrow, J. (2002). *Power talk: Language and interaction in institutional discourse*. Harlow: Longman.

Trimble, J.E. (1977). The sojourner in the American Indian community: Methodological issues and concerns. *Journal of Social Issues*, *33*(4), 159–174.

Uekusa, S. (2019). Methodological challenges in social vulnerability and resilience research: Reflections on studies in the Canterbury and Tohoku disasters. *Social Science Quarterly*, *100*(4), 1404–1419.

Wallerstein, N.B., & Duran, B. (2006). Using community-based participatory research to address health disparities. *Health Promotion Practice*, *7*(3), 312–323.

Walters, K.L., Stately, A., Evans-Campbell, T., Simoni, J.M., Duran, B., Schultz, K., . . . Guerrero, D. (2009). "Indigenist" collaborative research efforts in Native American communities. In A.R. Stiffman (Ed.), *The field research survival guide* (pp. 146–173). Oxford: Oxford University Press.

Wilson, S. (2008). *Research is a ceremony: Indigenous research methods*. Winnipeg: Fernwood.

Wisner, B., Blaikie, P., Cannon, T., & Davis, I. (2003). *At risk: Natural hazards, people's vulnerability and disasters* (2nd ed.). London: Routledge.

World Health Organization (WHO). (2001). *Putting women first: Ethical and safety recommendations for research on domestic violence against women*. Geneva, Switzerland: World Health Organization.

Yoon, D.K. (2012). Assessment of social vulnerability to natural disasters: A comparative study. *Natural Hazards*, *63*(2), 823–843.

Qualitative and Interpretivist Approaches to Studying Disaster and Emergency Management

6

Interviewing in a Disaster Context

Brenda D. Phillips

Introduction

Qualitative interviewing follows traditions that first require and respect a carefully negotiated and ethical set of interactions between interviewers and interviewees, as discussed in Chapter 1. Such an ethical stance remains particularly important when conducting research in a disaster context. To start, the principle "do no harm" applies to disaster context interviewing (Bolton & Tang, 2004). That context, which varies considerably across the life cycle of disasters (i.e., preparedness and planning, response, recovery, mitigation) means that interviewers will need to appropriately consider and manage the circumstances under which interviewees will be living and working, as indicated in Chapter 5. For example, the preparedness phase for an emergency manager or a family likely means engaging in basic, easily accomplished tasks like amassing resources over a long period of time (e.g., extra water or food, winter weather car kit, or pet supplies). In comparison, consider the response time circumstances when emergency managers support search and rescue efforts and shelters, organize debris removal, and launch recovery amid long days and nights with little sleep. Or, think about the circumstances for the family that awaits rescue or has become separated en route to shelters. What would it be like to be asked for an interview?

The disaster context affects the interviewer as well. During the preparedness phase, an interviewer can easily find both professionals and families to talk to about how they get ready for a disaster. Interviews can be set up, informed consent can be obtained, recording devices can be used, and time exists to process interviews, write up notes, and analyze data. But in a response period, interviewing professionals working in emergency operating centers or survivors who have temporarily (or permanently) relocated may be impossible. Disasters impact interviewing sites as well, with noise and interruptions overtaking a recording device and interrupting the highly desirable rapport that produces useful information during an interview. Researchers may not be able to reach a site or gain access to interviewees as well. Overall, conditions may be quite challenging.

However, do not give up! Disaster science needs dedicated researchers willing to embrace these challenges to produce science useful to practitioners, policymakers, agencies, voluntary organizations, and families. This chapter helps readers understand and manage the challenges associated with interviewing in a disaster context. To do so, I address how to gain access, establish rapport, respect human subjects, identify research participants, conduct an interview in a range of settings, insure quality data collection, manage qualitative interview data, and conduct preliminary analyses. Both domestic and international case examples will illustrate how successful researchers have navigated varying cultural, economic, and political contexts that also infuse the disaster setting (Lehnert, Craft, Singh, & Park, 2016).

The Purposes of Qualitative Interviewing

Qualitative interviewing should lead researchers to elicit culturally "thick, rich" description far different from a news report or social media post (Geertz, 1973). The purpose is to share useful information about the context (time, place, and circumstances) so that readers can determine if the findings hold transferable and actionable information for their local setting (Weiss, 1995). Housing recovery, for example, varies significantly across socioeconomic classes, geographic locations, and political systems, with people and places regaining permanent homes at varying paces – and sometimes not at all (Comerio, 1998). The body of data that researchers amass by studying housing recovery enables emergency managers, long-term recovery groups, and elected officials to craft better solutions, create more effective programs, and get people back home. Rich bodies of data can also push forward the lines of literature that inform theory and practice and lead us into even more promising research agendas. Deeply developed interview data also enable researchers to hear and respect the voices of people who share their time and experiences in order to help other disaster victims in the future (Rubin & Rubin, 2012). Securing a rich body of data requires dedicated effort and intentional listening in order to surface the best questions that interviewees will want to answer in depth. This disaster insider viewpoint represents the valuable core of thick, rich description emanating from the perspectives of those who survived or managed the disaster that can offer hard-earned insights.

Access in the Disaster Context

Each disaster is different, presenting new challenges each time. In the early 1980s, the Disaster Research Center (DRC; then at Ohio State University, now at the University of Delaware) engaged in a study of emergent citizen groups (e.g., Stallings & Quarantelli, 1985). To conduct the study, graduate students traveled to a disaster site, with some of the events (tornadoes, floods) having happened years before, others yet to unfold (a nuclear plant that concerned locals), and one that just had just occurred (an earthquake). The DRC's graduate students learned quickly that the phase of the disaster mattered, because it influenced who would be available and how much time they would have. Given the time frame, they also enjoyed relatively easy access to disaster sites and could gain entrée to emergency operating centers, recovery meetings, and shelters. Today, gaining access has become far more difficult, particularly during the response phase of a disaster when barricades go up around those disaster sites and related settings. Researchers may experience difficulty reaching the site, finding people to interview, and implementing their methodology. Doing so is not impossible, however, as the disaster response period tends to represent the phase that has yielded more research studies than other times.

Researchers also worry that data may be perishable or lost if not secured during the response phase (Michaels, 2003). Quarantelli (1995) identified four phases of housing recovery, with the emergency sheltering phase occurring first and often ending quickly when people abandon tents, cars, lawns, and overpasses for better shelter. Researchers traveling to a site to study emergency sheltering may not arrive in time before shelter evacuees relocate, losing the chance to secure important information on how people make choices to protect themselves in the first few hours to days. For example, although people survived longer on rooftops and overpasses after Katrina in 2005, the flooded city of New Orleans was impossible to get into while emergency officials were understandably trying to get people out. Additionally, the long-term tent cities after the 2010 Haiti earthquake presented a large population, but getting there was expensive or impossible, coupled with a question of whether researchers should be there at all.

Non-response phases may be easier to manage, and they represent ripe opportunities for students to collect useful data. Access to interviewees involved in preparedness and planning efforts tends to be easier as people do not feel as pressed or stressed in a non-disaster environment. The mitigation phase occurs over longer periods of time, like in mitigation planning or building a levee. Recovery often falls into short-term (days, weeks, months) to long-term (months to years) time periods. Though it might seem easier to do recovery research, the displacement that people and places experience can make it challenging – though not impossible. Thus, researchers should not feel discouraged about disaster reviewing but should prepare themselves to acknowledge, prepare for, and meet the challenges embedded in disaster science. Because our research goals bear direct relevance for the well-being of people, places, and animals, we should invest ourselves in meeting those challenges.

Disaster Interviewing

In a non-response context, which could occur during the preparedness, planning, and mitigation phases, some traditional steps usually suffice for conducting qualitative interviewing. Once a research problem has been identified and qualitative interviewing is deemed methodologically appropriate and ethically situated, researchers set about finding people to interview.

Identifying Research Participants

The process starts with identifying the kinds of people who would be best able to provide useful information, often with a snowball sampling approach generated by researchers or key informants (Peek & Fothergill, 2009). This kind of non-probability sampling approach identifies interviewees holding information appropriate for the research question. A random probability sampling of city officials could completely miss the city's emergency manager, fire chief, or public works director – all of whom may be critical to interview (Stallings, 2006). Tornadoes are unpredictable, and a random sampling of a neighborhood could miss many who lost their homes. Alternatively, a non-probability quota sampling might be more useful, as it allows an interviewer to settle participants into groups with minimal, major, and complete loss/damage levels.

A good start is to amass an initial set of potential interviewees that can offer productive insights on the research question. To use a snowball example for a mitigation planning effort, an interview list might start with the emergency manager and public works director. They might direct an interviewer to the local champion for disaster mitigation who has lobbied officials, written grant proposals, gathered signatures, and led a planning committee. At that point, a decision can be made to move to another form of sampling. Quota non-probability sampling, for example, can ensure that researcher includes the perspectives of city officials, agencies, volunteers, residents, and outsiders who helped to create and then benefit from a disaster mitigation planning effort. The rich, thick descriptive data yielded by the interviews will enable readers to determine its use value and transferability to their context.

Do qualitative interviewers conduct probability sampling? Though less common, it does happen in disaster research. In our study of post-Katrina shelters, we amassed a list of shelters in nearly 1,000 locations across multiple states and then sorted the sites into types of shelters (e.g., formal, emergent, first responder, animal). A random sampling process then pinpointed as many shelters as the team could viably reach before they closed and until research funds ran out. Shelter managers at 82 shelters were interviewed across four states. When we discovered that a shelter had already closed, we selected the next shelter on the list in order to continue creating a generalizable sample (Phillips, Wikle, Head Hakim, & Pike, 2012).

However, shelters represent only one kind of disaster setting. Interviews typically take place where interviewees want them to occur in a comfortable and familiar location. When they take place in someone's office or home, a more localized context can appear to enrich the interview further. People's offices often include pictures, awards, or symbols that tell researchers about their work and accomplishments. In a disaster setting, additional items can help triangulate the research, such as a daily tasks board that concurs with what an interviewee said about their typical day (see Figure 6.1). Interviewees may also find it easier to share information they have on hand, such as the copy of a mitigation plan, data on the number and kinds of people in a shelter, the guidelines for worksite safety procedures, or a mutual aid agreement. People's homes also tell researchers a lot about what they value. In one of my post-Katrina studies, people had decorated their newly rebuilt homes with photos of volunteers and placed post-disaster house blessing items (quilts, crosses, plaques) in prominent locations (see Figure 6.2; Phillips, 2014a). From a social science perspective, such a display says more than "these people were here" and can lead to a deeper and richer discussion of what the volunteers meant to the homeowners who traveled through the housing recovery process.

Post-Katrina, an important set of studies were completed following displaced residents who had evacuated across the entire nation, with interviewees found in Colorado, Texas, and South Carolina, among other sites (Weber & Peek, 2012; Fothergill & Peek, 2015). Similarly, University of Texas social work faculty interviewed people adapting to a new culture, finding jobs to support themselves, and searching for housing (Bell, 2008). By conducting studies close to a researcher's location, which may be fortuitous, researchers also follow a time-worn "start where you are" tradition that began with the Chicago School field studies in the 1920s (see, e.g., Deegan, 1988).

Traveling to a study site, and particularly to a different nation, will also require extraordinary care to respect scientific ethics, cultural dynamics, language differences, and appropriateness. After the 2004 tsunami, our team studied a very difficult topic of mass fatalities within India. To be sure we behaved in an ethical manner, we first

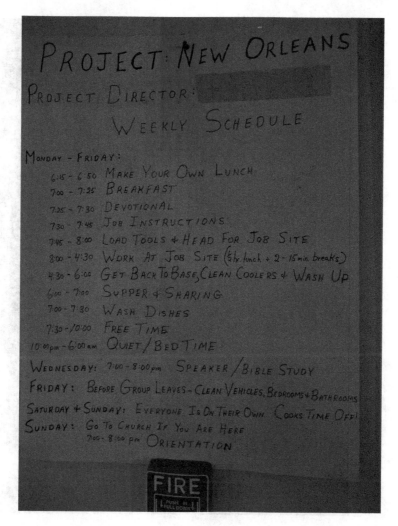

FIGURE 6.1 Daily Task Board

involved our own graduate students from the nation and affected region. They helped us to understand the difficult impacts on the people and create informed consent procedures in multiple languages and in a manner appropriate to the political structure of the affected locations (Phillips, Neal, Wikle, Subanthore, & Hyrapiet, 2008). We also asked the graduate students to train the team in culturally appropriate behaviors and incorporated visits to cultural and historic sites once in the nation. That work paid off when everyone understood the seal of Tamil Nadu connected so closely to the sea, thus helping the team to understand not only the loss of lives but of livelihoods and people's feelings of personal safety within a previously familiar – and now frightening – physical landscape.

Gaining Access

Be ready for qualitative disaster interviewing, because to finally reach an interviewee, you may need to navigate the kind of disaster as well as the setting's gatekeepers,

FIGURE 6.2 A Personal Memorial

security barriers, safety issues, and more. Wise interviewers will make informed choices and trade-offs will likely occur as interviewers find themselves blocked from the people they need to talk to. Again, the disaster context matters in various ways. First, the kind of disaster may influence access. In the case of a technological disaster like an oil spill, involved corporations will likely close their doors to researchers due to pending litigation or criminal investigation. For a terror attack or active shooter, key interviewees may not be available because it is a crime scene likely involving arrests, trials, and lawsuits.

Second, to gain access, researchers will have to move past gatekeepers, the people who will not let you gain access to an important interviewee, like an administrative assistant or the security team. For example, after one hurricane, I went to the shelter that our team had preselected to be included in the sample. A volunteer assistant shelter manager met me at the door and I went through an explanation of why we were there, showed her the informed consent procedures along with my university credentials, and offered evidence that the study had been funded by the National

Science Foundation. In a very loud voice that many could hear, she said "I have no reason to believe you about any of this, there's nothing to keep you from giving that information to CNN!!!." Stunned and chagrined, I explained that doing so would be unethical and cost everyone their jobs; she yelled at me again and told me, "Get out!" Fortunately, this was the only such event in nearly 40 years of disaster interviewing. At another shelter not too far away, I drove up to the security booth staffed by a soldier. I went through the same procedures and he waved me through with a smile, saying "Go Cowboys!" in deference to my university affiliation and his home state. The warm welcome buoyed me greatly and the interviews went incredibly well. But our entire team was stonewalled repeatedly when trying to conduct an analysis of mass fatalities after Hurricane Katrina, when the government locked up the temporary morgue site for investigations tied to potential crimes surrounding some of the deaths. It did not matter that funding for the study had come from another governmental agency, the National Science Foundation. In short, sometimes gaining access can go well and sometimes not at all, so have a backup place.

Third, gaining access will also vary by phase, with the easier access likely during preparedness and mitigation phases and less so during response. After the 1989 Loma Prieta earthquake, the City of Santa Cruz, California, erected a barricade around the entire downtown out of concern over aftershocks and potential injuries from damaged buildings. Seeing the damage required securing a pass from the emergency operations center (EOC) and being placed on a tour. Obtaining this access turned out to be the first step my team needed to observe and interview within that EOC. The recovery phase can also be challenging because survivors may be found in tent cities, shelters, motels, cruise ships, trailer parks, open parks, congregate care facilities, apartment buildings, rental homes, and sites where pre-disaster homeless gather. Similarly, a researcher looking at infrastructure reconstruction, for example, may require interviews among multiple offices, agencies, and consultants, who will move into and out of an area as the work slowly unfolds over years.

Fourth, when considering access, the researcher should also include a review of personal safety. In more than 35 years of conducting disaster interviews around the world, I have never had any problems with personal safety nor have any members of my team, although my car once went airborne from an earthquake-buckled highway. Disasters also disrupt normal routes, take away signage and stoplights, and generate hazards for researchers to avoid in the field, with downed power lines, widely dispersed glass, splintered wood, snakes and fire ants, and hazardous materials, to name just a few concerns. When team members are in the field, they should be prepared for the site, including personal stamina that can withstand heat, humidity, and long days. Sturdy boots can also prevent injuries, as can sunscreen, insect repellant, hydration bottles, and personal fitness. Depending on the location, additional immunizations or medications may be required to reduce the possibility of serious illnesses. And, even though crime rates drop in a disaster (e.g., Tierney, Bevc, & Kuligowski, 2006), interviewers should also be alert to the possibility of personal theft or other crimes that may occur while in the field. While in North Carolina, for example, someone stole our center's identification magnet from a vehicle.

However, trust works both ways. People may be reluctant to grant an interview given the specifics of the disaster context. After 9/11, Muslim Americans suffered losses among the fatalities and also significant backlash including harassment, verbal and non-verbal threats, and hate crimes. Would you be willing to trust an unknown interviewer to share your experience? To gain access, one researcher connected with student groups through a key informant who enabled access and helped to build trust with an outsider. In this instance, focus groups also helped interviewees feel more comfortable (Peek, 2011; Peek & Fothergill, 2009).

Finally, access problems can mean that even incredibly important research questions may have to go unstudied – a potentially terrible loss for science, practice, policy, and the people likely to be involved in a future, similar event. Nonetheless, disaster interviewers should not give up. Some strategies for managing access include the following:

■ Choose a phase in the disaster life cycle that permits better access to interviewees. These phases remain understudied and research can make a significant contribution. Such an option may be particularly useful for those facing a tenure clock.

■ Pre-establish an agreement with agencies and areas likely to be impacted and/or involved in non-response time activities like planning, exercising, organizing, crafting mutual aid agreements, and more.

■ Develop an arrangement with specific agencies to gain access to settings when a disaster occurs, like shelters (human and animal), EOCs, and key meetings.

■ Create a longitudinal plan of research for a topic of interest and follow it through the life cycle of disaster. For example, follow a state voluntary organization active in disaster (VOAD, or its community counterpart, COAD) as it evolves during preparedness to acquire and train members. Then, continue to study the unit as it deploys in response and recovery to understand volunteer management, inter-organizational collaboration and coordination, deployment practices, and on-site integration into a new disaster site. By selecting units likely to be involved in high-hazard areas (e.g., locales prone to hurricanes, tornadoes, or wildfires), the chances of gaining access across time increase.

■ Partner with local researchers. Universities and colleges in the affected area will likely be able to gain access more readily than outsiders and potentially add more theoretical sensitivity to your work (Marks, 2015; see also Kroll-Smith, Baxter, & Jenkins, 2015).

■ Partner with local agencies and organizations, who may be involved in the various phases of disasters. A local volunteer management effort, for example, may want to know how they did and what they can do better. A partnered effort can yield useful information for the effort's leadership and fruitful data for a researcher who needs to publish.

■ Wait. Disasters take time to unfold, and access will likely be easier after the response period. Recovery can take years, and by waiting, interviewers will be able to gain access to recovery leaders, involved agencies, and survivors more easily. Because recovery remains significantly understudied, important advances can be made even if waiting is involved.

Your abilities to gain access will improve with experience and practice. Be reassured that gaining such a skill is part of your educational process. Access is one of many such skills you will need to develop when interacting with people. One key next step is the ability to connect with those you want to learn from: your interviewees.

Establish Rapport

A highly desirable quality of the interviewer-interviewee relationship is often called "rapport," which can be described as an authentic connection that spans the customary divide between a researcher and a "subject." Such a connection often relies on what are often called "people skills," which are not something everyone inherently possesses (but one can learn it, as with other skills; see Clark & Sousa, 2017; Phillips, 2002, 2014b, 2014c). Given that those involved in this research relationship probably did not know each other much in advance before the interview, making a sincere connection – which helps produce useful information – will need to be carefully and ethically developed. Rapport should never be forced or faked from the researcher's side. Doing so exploits the interviewee solely for the purpose of data collection and undermines the respect that interviewees deserve and that disciplinary ethics demand (see Chapter 1).

People skills include the ability to connect with others in a sincere manner and to truly care about the other person's experiences, viewpoints, and perspectives. Interviewers should listen carefully to what the interviewee is saying, both verbally and non-verbally, and about all aspects of the interview from the initial request to the interview location, informed consent procedures, and interview content. An ability to read non-verbal behavior may be particularly important, because it can alert an interviewer to someone being uncomfortable with a question or line of inquiry. Skilled interviewers can navigate an interviewee through that discomfort or know when to offer a different question to provide some relief. Listening also means being much more interested in what the interviewee has to say than one's own words.

But how does one establish rapport in a disaster context? Again, the phase may influence how this unfolds. Within non-response phases, researchers can take the time to get to know interviewees with advance phone calls, emails, and both video and in-person meetings. Taking your time with an interviewee can help to build the understanding and trust that leads to rapport (Marks, 2015; Wolgemuth et al., 2015). But taking time is not always possible, especially when interviewees have minimal time for an interview. Busy agency heads may schedule an interview for 30 minutes, or an interviewer may find themselves standing in a field next to a unit commander who has to leave in 15 minutes. Evacuees may be getting ready to leave a shelter or go to school or work, and time to develop rapport may be short.

Additionally, interviewees often want to know if they will be heard, if their replies will matter, if their time will be used well, and the ways in which their data will be used. The informed consent protocol required by most nations and institutions can help with some of this, since it includes the interviewers' institutional affiliation that may provide credibility. But more is required, because rapport relies on exhibiting a sincere interest in the person, their situation, and their insights. Rapport also relies on empathy, an ability to put yourself into their situation and see the situation from their point of view.

If you feel uncertain about your people skills, bear in mind that disasters provide highly compelling reasons for people to want to share their insights. What prospective interviewees have experienced or learned can yield valuable information to help other communities impacted by disasters. This reason alone – to be helpful to others by sharing their own experiences – can inspire a connection. Disaster science also draws in people who want to help others through research and its implications for practice and policy. When interviewees learn that what they offer could be made useful through scientific research and, by application, in classrooms, agencies, and organizations, they tend to feel a stronger interest in helping. Finally, what many interviewers also know is that just by asking the right opening question and leaning in to listen with sincere intent, the door to rapport often opens easily.

Respect Human Subjects

Beginning interviewers should not worry as they start their research careers, because mentors will help you and you will develop your abilities over time. I remember well the very first interview I ever did, which I thought would derail my research career. I met with an emergency responder who had handled a situation involving a significant number of mass fatalities. I did everything by the book and as my mentor Dr. E. L. Quarantelli (co-founder of the Disaster Research Center) had taught me to do. Yet, despite my best efforts, the respondent answered in terse, short replies and seemed to be clearly upset. I could not determine what I had done or said to cause this. After about a half hour, I concluded the interview and turned off the recorder, certain that Dr. Quarantelli would soon fire me. The interviewee then turned to me and said, "I'm not crazy and I want you to know that." Confused, I assured him that I did not think he was crazy; this led to him telling me about a prior interviewer who had conducted a research study on the mental health of those who had responded to the tragedy. He had left that experience deeply offended by a presumed assumption about his mental health and remained upset over a year later when I spoke to him. Something had gone wrong in that first interview he experienced and it spilled over into my interview with him. I have never forgotten him, or how important it is to treat people with respect and consideration for the impact of our research efforts on people and on future researchers. Dr. Quarantelli listened to the interview and asked me what happened. He then gave me another chance and assured me the next interview would go better. It did, and I am grateful to him for my career spanning nearly 40 years as a disaster researcher. Your mentors can do the same for you.

The core of what happened in that first interview stemmed from the interviewee's experience of the nature of the mental health research, which should be spelled out clearly in the informed consent protocols. Those protocols should clearly explain the purposes of the study and in a way that leaves a participant feeling comfortable about the content and process and with the right to refuse the interview or to stop it at any time. Still, not much has been written on ethical standards for human subjects – *people* – in a disaster context.

Recently, researchers have called for high standards in the conduct of disaster research, including interviewing (Gaillard & Peek, 2019). One concern emanates from the manner in which researchers have descended on places that are impacted in what can sometimes be a significant convergence of interviewers. One reason for this convergence is that funding agencies tend to support research on major events, which enables such inquiry. Another reason is that people new to disaster research seek to conduct a study out of interest based on their discipline. In reply, several impacted sites have curtailed access. After the Oklahoma City bombing in 1995, for example, the state set up a review board to determine which projects would merit access to potentially highly traumatized survivors and responders (Pfefferbaum, Call, & Sconzo, 1999; North et al., 2002). New Zealand also limited access after the 2011 Christchurch earthquake (Gaillard & Peek, 2019). In a related vein, researchers should engage in learning how to respectfully invite people who may be traumatized and grieving while also recognizing their rights to negotiate, continue, or end that interview (Rosenblatt, 1995; Fu et al., 2018). Care should also be taken in a disaster context that may alter survivors' previous beliefs and how they view themselves, their surroundings, their faith, and more (O'Grady et al., 2018). In general, though, some believe that disaster interviewing does not unduly impact survivors and may actually prove therapeutic (Collogan, Tuma, Dolan-Sewell, Orja, & Fleischman, 2004).

Another ethical concern arises out of the use value of disaster research, with researchers taking information but not returning it to benefit locals, a disparate outcome that magnifies inequities between privileged researchers and marginalized people and places (Gaillard & Peek, 2019). Qualitative interviewers tend to be more sensitive to such inequities and try to rectify the imbalances in the researcher-researched relationship. Doing so starts from a solid commitment to ethical research practices. The first step for disaster interviewers should be to determine if the study should be done at all. What is the value to science of the proposed project? What is the value to practice and policy? How will the study impact local people?

Calls for joint efforts with local researchers and people are being increasingly recommended (Gaillard & Peek, 2019). Locals can help outsiders to understand the context, including the ways in which local communities are structured, how people interact and communicate, which local expressions or social structures may influence interviews, and when is the right time to conduct an interview, because the phase of a disaster can influence availability, perspectives, interest, and fatigue. Working in a coordinated effort can reduce impacts on locals affected by the disaster and the arriving researchers.

The consent form, in a disaster context, can also be an issue. As indicated in Chapter 1, review boards want extensively developed forms that lay out benefits, risks, and protocols. Doing so is imperative, but it also presents challenges in presenting these legal-looking documents to people who have never seen anything like them. In my experience, two reactions tend to occur. One is that an interviewee flips the form over and signs it without reading it, which then prompts me to verbally walk through the benefits, risks, and procedures as due diligence. Another response is to ask questions that an interviewer should work through carefully. On a few occasions, interviewees have asked me to come back after their legal unit review the forms (I did), and only once has someone declined to join the study because of the forms. Non-response phases make the process easier because sufficient time typically exists to work through the complexity of the protocols. During a response phase, though, the forms may be cumbersome to manage given the time availability of an interviewee. You may have to come back at a later date, which can be challenging based on time availability and funding.

Traveling out of one's country, culture, or language can present additional challenges with informed consent. The first step is to determine what research rules and regulations are required by a country one plans to visit, followed by consultation with people from and/or in that nation. Determining that nation's standards will influence the content of the forms and if that nation requires additional review, which is in part why locals should be involved in research. Locals can also help researchers understand how culture influences personal interactions and communications so that outsiders do not make missteps in crafting and conducting an interview. Language also matters because, as the foundation of culture, people use verbal and non-verbal language to convey meanings, intent, perspectives, innuendo, and the heart of who they are as a people.

For example, as an outsider to the Louisiana context, our team benefited greatly from how faculty members at the University of New Orleans Center for Hazards Assessment, Research, and Technology (CHART) enabled understanding of the region and its unique mix of ethnic groups, languages, and customs. We met with community and faith leaders before trying to launch a local project and enjoyed seeing the area outside of the tourist sector, which for many characterizes New Orleans. Our hosts – our teachers – showed us the unique neighborhoods of New Orleans and the bayou communities. They explained the history of canal development and its impact on flooding, loss of livelihoods, and threats to entire ways of life. From their efforts, we worked with a local community to secure National Science Foundation funding for a participatory action research project prior to Katrina, a storm that leveled the community and derailed our project. But the relationships flourished, with one researcher continuing to work closely with the community as it faced not only Katrina but also the 2010 BP oil spill that invaded their bayou, and another convincing a voluntary organization to help rebuild homes.

Disaster interviewers shoulder an ethical responsibility to not just take information but to return useful information to the area and its people, as discussed in Chapter 5. Along these lines, Stokes (1997) refers to this as "use-inspired research," an approach that fits nicely in the disaster researcher's wheelhouse. Several strategies can be leveraged:

- Participatory research involves local people, not just local researchers or practitioners, in the study. Their viewpoints can be particularly helpful in surfacing key questions and in situating the research in the local context. Some disaster projects have been trending in this direction, although funded projects may take considerable time to develop. A carefully cultivated team will be needed to ensure that the participatory process stays on track and truly involves local stakeholders at a high level of influence and interaction.

- Team research can also help produce more useful research, especially if it includes area practitioners, policymakers, and researchers. Their roles can vary from consultation to highly interactive.

- Researchers can also offer workshops on their findings or products in an effort to return information to the communities affected.

- Websites can be developed to disseminate the results, and social media platforms can be leveraged to share information.

- Apps can be created to provide useful decision-making tools and to offer information to a device-savvy public.

Ethical stances and actions should always drive any interview-based project because people live at the heart of that study. Their time and perspectives should always be valued in every aspect of interviewing a fellow human being.

Conducting an Interview

Now that the interviewees have been identified, the interviewer has gained access and established rapport, and the informed consent protocols have been secured, it is time to actually conduct the interview. A key part of this is managing the physical environment in which the interview is to take place. Researchers will likely want to record an interview in order to be as accurate as possible, but noise is often a part of the disaster context. Even interviewing someone in an office during a non-response phase may mean that an interviewee's radios, phones, or other devices may need to be on, with the interviewee potentially distracted while monitoring for alerts or messages. In a home, a parent may have to manage children or pets. I remember trying to interview the high-ranking military officer in charge of a tent city. He provided valuable information willingly, but constantly arriving helicopters meant that none of the content could be recorded. I juggled the recording device anyway, while jotting down his words and jogging to keep up as he moved rapidly from location to location. As soon as the interview ended, I found a quiet place and transitioned the jotted notes to full field notes, but I lost any chance at attaining a complete transcription from a recording. I regret losing the data given the unusual degree of access, but sometimes you have to do the best you can. In another setting, my team used the bathrooms in a large meeting hall, full of recovery organizations, to update notes and coordinate next steps.

In addition to the setting, the recording device itself can be intrusive. Regardless of whether researchers are using a notebook, a digital pen or recorder, phone, tablet, or something as obtrusive as a video camera on a tripod, interviewees will likely notice the recording tool. Such devices also fail routinely, such as in the noisy environment just mentioned or when a disaster-related power outage prevents a researcher from recharging a device. Ideally, have a second person manage the note-taking or recording while a primary interviewer leads the interviewee through the conversation. When an interviewee feels they have to slow down so that their comments can be recorded accurately, rapport may be compromised and an interview can fail to achieve the desired outcomes. Recording people who have been through a traumatic experience should also be a concern, particularly when interacting with survivors of terror attacks including active shooters. A particularly skilled research team should take on this kind of interview in order to monitor the potential impacts of resurfacing traumatic events. One alternative is to put control of the interview into the hands of the interviewee, as discussed in the previous chapter. One study did this by giving cameras to shelter evacuees to take pictures of their life and then invited them to title and discuss the images (Pike, Phillips, & Reeves, 2006).

Managing Qualitative Interview Data in the Field

Much of our interviewing takes place in the field, and managing field data can present a number of challenges. For most of my team's research, we had access to reasonable accommodations, although at times we had to drive significant distances to find them when a disaster happened. We stayed in hotels most of the time, but also on the couches of colleagues and in the homes of friends of friends. Sometimes we secured places where we could all stay, and at other times team members conducted research at a significant distance. We have relied on internet access from hotel rooms, fast-food franchises, coffee shops, and airports. Those settings influenced some key steps necessary for managing interview data, which include the following:

- Transcribe interviews as fully and as soon as possible, alongside notes about verbal inflections, non-verbal behaviors, and the context in which the interview occurred —even if it is handwritten because of a power outage. Doing so represents a highly time-consuming effort. Transcribing programs can help in the field but can also take time for verification. While in the field, one strategy is to write up a summary of the interview from notes, and then to verify its accuracy at a later date from a recording.

- Upload key documents to a secure server while taking care not to include confidential data that could be compromised.

- Make backups of the data to keep within the team, and always carry your data with you on the way home to ensure security and to safeguard interviewees' rights per the IRB protocol.

- Launch preliminary data analysis while still in the field or still conducting interviews.

Why Do Preliminary Analysis in the Field?

Because qualitative research embraces an inductive approach, data analysis should begin with the first interview. Field-based analysis provides dividends when interviewers can focus their questioning more appropriately by reflecting on if they asked a good question. Did the participants answer fully or not? What might improve the questions to elicit better information? Preliminary data analysis also allows interviewers to monitor and improve the sample and to pursue a more reflexive stance (Marks, 2015; Pessoa, Harper, Santos, & Carvalho da Silva Gracino, 2019). Did a participant recommend someone else who might provide rich, deep information? (Malterud, Siersma, & Guassora, 2016). Did the participant turn out to be not as helpful as hoped? Did the interview uncover a promising new direction and set of people to talk to, such as an emergent citizen group engaged in what was thought to be professional search and rescue? Preliminary work also allows the research team to communicate better, because their collective eyes and minds on the data can enable them to redirect and leverage their energies, efficiently saving time and money (Horsley, 2012).

Typically, such an effort begins by listening to the interview again or by reviewing the interview notes. As a classic approach, grounded theorists employ a procedure called "open coding" to start their preliminary analysis (Glaser & Strauss, 1967; Tausch et al., 2011; Marks, 2015). Grounded theory involves looking at segments of the data (interview notes, transcripts, recordings) and assigning codes to them. For example, consider the coding you see in Table 6.1. In this study, I worked with a volunteer disaster organization to do an assessment of their Katrina work, with the requirement that the research be conducted in a scientific manner suitable for a scholarly publication. The organization asked for several questions to be raised, which appear in italics in Table 6.1. At the end of each bulleted item, you can see a number that represents the size of the file after open coding had been completed using NVivo, a qualitative data analysis software package. For the italicized items, the coded data indicated that people talked the most about financial stewardship, or how the organization took care of their insurance money and federal grants to rebuild their homes.

But interviewers need to remain open to what else they hear, which is called "theoretical sensitivity," an ability to what people are saying at deeper levels. In this instance, interviewees often said, "Yes, yes, the house is fine," and then went right into a detailed, unprompted discussion of the volunteers, as indicated by the size of the file on "building relationships" and "character of the volunteers." Note that the open codes (non-italicized) represent what *else* the interviewees wanted to talk about. In short, their experience was not about the house; it was about feeling made whole again by volunteer effort. In Box 6.1, readers can see how Bogdan and Biklen's (2016) strategy enables a deeper look at "perspectives held by subjects," where interviewees revealed they thought of the volunteers "like family," which was easily the most frequently appearing word in the data.

TABLE 6.1 Open Coding

■ Building relationships 69	■ Hurricane Rita 15
■ *Challenges* 30	■ Impact on local community 25
■ Character of the volunteers 57	■ Katrina 20
■ Client appreciation 19	■ Leadership 25
■ *Client problems* 21	■ *Mission* 22
■ *Client selection* 35	■ *Nature of partnership* 30
■ Clients pay it forward 13	■ Oil spill 17
■ Collaboration 21	■ *Organizational partners* 19
■ *Communication* 13	■ Prior presence 14
■ Computers 13	■ *Recommendations*
■ *Decision-making* 37	■ *Reputation (safety, elevations, utilities)* 42
■ *Did they build the best house for you?* 25	■ *Return preference* 17
■ Faith 26	■ Special populations 25
■ *Financial stewardship* 52	■ Students 15
■ Healing 19	■ *Successes* 27
■ *Homeowner contributions* 23	■ Transitions 18
■ *House dedications* 29	■ *Type of work* 23
■ Housing issues 12	■ Volunteer abilities (gender, age) 19
■ Hurricane Ike 19	

Source: Phillips (2014a).

BOX 6.1 HOW DID THEY TREAT YOU?

■ "They were great workers, very friendly. They became like family to us in just a week."

■ "Very good people, very nice. They became part of our family."

■ "We all became a family, we still talk and stay in touch. Some of them have come for a visit."

■ "They were wonderful. They were real nice, they worked hard. We were full up with volunteers, it was like a family reunion when they came back."

■ They treated me like family and I treated them like family. [He begins to cry.] It was a very rewarding experience. I have grandchildren they can visit now."

■ "They were like family. People with big hearts. They took their vacation and family time. I prayed for them and thanked God for them every day. They have a spirit in their heart to come here and do work on the coast."

Source: Bogdan and Biklen (2016); results in Phillips (2014a).

Another preliminary way to think through the data is the C-model used historically by the DRC (Quarantelli, 1987, 2002). Although the Cs have changed over the years, they represent parts of what could become a descriptive case study. Career represents the history of an event, effort, or agency. Imagine, for example, interviewing meteorologists on the steps they took in warning an area of an impending event. Their stepwise efforts could be laid out chronologically to see the time frame in which people might have received and acted on a warning. Characteristics could include a description of the people involved in writing and disseminating the warning, as well as the demographics of the people living in the warned area. Conditions describe what factors may have influenced the warning and response. For example, was the warning issued in English where there is a large Spanish-speaking population? Did Spanish-language stations or messaging systems exist? Or, could the message have been mistranslated, as happened in Saragosa, Texas, when nearly 30 people died as a result of the 1987 tornado? (Aguirre, 1991). Such deaths would represent the Consequences or outcomes of an event. The C-model allows researchers to step back and make an initial assessment of their data: What is missing? Who do I still need to talk to? Have I covered all angles that should be considered? Preliminary data analysis in the field must be done to enrich the study and make the best use of the interviewer's and the interviewee's time.

Conclusion

You can do it. You can face the challenges, develop your skills, and become a qualitative interviewer and disaster researcher. Take the time now to learn the process, to read multiple books and studies that provide guidance and examples. Find a mentor who will put in the time to develop your skill set. Volunteer to help a faculty member or an experienced researcher with their project. Observe, listen, and learn. Practice your skills with fellow students and then shadow a researcher in the field. Start with an easier interview, with a person who willingly wants to share their time and experiences with you (social service agencies and voluntary organizations are a good place for a student to start honing their interview skills). Dedicate yourself to the highest ethical practices in the field and remember that researchers are always privileged to be let into the lives of those who face disasters, willingly as professionals or not so willingly as survivors. Honor their experiences and voices, and carefully work through the analytical work required to produce a piece of scholarly work with integrity.

Further Readings

Fothergill, A., & Peek, L. (2015). *Children of Katrina*. Austin: University of Texas Press.

Kroll-Smith, S., Baxter, V., & Jenkins, P. (2015). *Left to chance: Hurricane Katrina and the story of two New Orleans neighborhoods*. Austin: University of Texas Press.

Lois, Jennifer. (2003). *Heroic efforts: The emotional culture of search and rescue volunteers*. New York: New York University.

Peek, L. (2011). *Beyond the backlash: Muslim Americans after 9/11*. Philadelphia: Temple University Press.

Rubin, H. J., & Rubin, I. S. (2012). *Qualitative interviewing: The art of hearing data*. Newbury Park, CA: Sage.

Spradley, J. P. (2016). *Ethnographic interviewing*. Long Grove, IL: Waveland Press.

References

Aguirre, B. (1991). *Saragosa, Texas tornado of May 22, 1987: An evaluation of the warning system*. Washington, DC: National Academies.

Bell, H. (2008). Case management with displaced survivors of Hurricane Katrina: A case study of one host community. *Journal of Social Service Research, 34*(3), 15–27.

Bogdan, R. C., & Biklen, S. K. (2016). *Qualitative research for education: An introduction to theories and methods*. Uttar Pradesh: Pearson.

Bolton, P., & Tang, A. (2004). Using ethnographic methods in the selection of post-disaster, mental-health interventions. *Prehospital and Disaster Medicine, 19*(1), 97–101.

Clark, A., & Sousa, B. (2017). The five neglected skills all qualitative researchers need. *International Journal of Qualitative Methods, 16*, 1–3.

Collogan, L., Tuma, F., Dolan-Sewell, R., Orja, S. B., & Fleischman, A. (2004). Ethical issues pertaining to research in the aftermath of disaster. *Journal of Traumatic Stress, 17*(5), 363–372.

Comerio, M. (1998). *Disaster hits home*. Berkeley: University of California Press.

Deegan, M. J. (1988). *Jane Addams and the men of the Chicago school, 1892–1918*. New York: Taylor & Francis.

Fothergill, A., & Peek, L. (2015). *Children of Katrina*. Austin: University of Texas Press.

Fu, F., Chen, L., Sha, W., Chan, C., Chow, A., & Lou, V. (2018). Mothers' grief experiences of losing their only child in the 2008 Sichuan earthquake: A qualitative longitudinal study. *OMEGA – Journal of Death and Dying*, 1–15.

Gaillard, J. C., & Peek, L. (2019). Disaster-zone research needs a code of conduct. *Nature, 535*, 440–442.

Geertz, C. (1973). *The interpretation of cultures*. New York: Basic Books.

Glaser, B., & Strauss, A. (1967). *The discovery of grounded theory*. New York: Aldine.

Horsley, J. (2012). Planning for spontaneity: The challenges of disaster communication fieldwork. *International Journal of Qualitative Methods, 11*(3), 180–194.

Kroll-Smith, S., Baxter, V., & Jenkins, P. (2015). *Left to chance: Hurricane Katrina and the story of two New Orleans neighborhoods*. Austin: University of Texas Press.

Lehnert, K., Craft, J., Singh, N., & Park, Y.-H. (2016). The human experience of ethics: A review of a qualitative ethical decision-making research. *Business Ethics, 25*(4), 498–537.

Malterud, K., Siersma, V., & Guassora, A. (2016). Sample size in qualitative interview studies: Guided by information power. *Qualitative Health Research, 26*(13), 1753–1760.

Marks, L. (2015). A pragmatic, step-by-step guide for qualitative methods: Capturing the disaster and long-term recovery stories of Katrina and Rita. *Current Psychology, 34*, 494–505.

Michaels, S. (2003). Perishable information, enduring insights? Understanding quick response research. In J. Monday (Ed.), *Beyond September 11th: An account of post-disaster research* (pp. 15–48). Boulder, CO: Natural Hazards Research and Applications Information Center.

North, C. S., Tivis, L., McMillen, J. C., Pfefferbaum, B., Cox, J., Spitznagel, E. L., . . . Smith, E. M. (2002). Coping, functioning, and adjustment of rescue workers after the Oklahoma City bombing. *Journal of Traumatic Stress, 15*(3), 171–175.

O'Grady, K., Orton, J., Stewart, C., Flythe, W., Snyder, N., & Desius, J. (2018). Resilience in the wake of disasters: A two-wave qualitative study of survivors of the 2010 Haiti earthquake. *Journal of Psychology and Christianity, 37*(1), 43–56.

Peek, L. A. (2011). *Beyond the backlash: Muslim Americans after 9/11*. Philadelphia: Temple University Press.

Peek, L. A., & Fothergill, A. (2009). Using focus groups: Lessons from studying daycare centers, 9/11, and Hurricane Katrina. *Qualitative Research, 9*(1), 31–59.

Pessoa, A., Harper, E., Santos, I., & Carvalho da Silva Gracino, M. (2019). Using reflexive interviewing to foster deep understanding of research participants' perspectives. *International Journal of Qualitative Methods, 18*, 1–9.

Pfefferbaum, B., Call, J., & Sconzo, G. (1999). Mental health services for children in the first two years after the 1995 Oklahoma City terrorist bombing. *Psychiatric Services, 50*(7), 956–958.

Phillips, B. D. (2002). Qualitative methods of disaster research. In R. A. Stallings (Ed.), *Methods of disaster research* (pp. 194–211). Philadelphia, PA: Xlibris/International Research Committee on Disasters.

Phillips, B. D. (2014a). *Mennonite disaster service: Building a therapeutic community after the Gulf Coast Storms*. Lanham, MD: Lexington Books.

Phillips, B. D. (2014b). *Qualitative disaster research*. Oxford: Oxford University Press.

Phillips, B.D. (2014c). Qualitative disaster research methods. In P. Leavy (Ed.), *The Oxford handbook of qualitative research methods* (pp. 553–556). Oxford: Oxford University Press.

Phillips, B.D., Neal, D., Wikle, T., Subanthore, A., & Hyrapiet, S. (2008). Mass fatality management after the Indian Ocean tsunami. *Disaster Prevention and Management, 17*(5), 681–697.

Phillips, B.D., Wikle, T., Head Hakim, A., & Pike, L. (2012). Establishing and operating shelters after Hurricane Katrina. *International Journal of Emergency Management, 8*(2), 153–167.

Pike, L., Phillips, B.D., & Reeves, P. (2006). Shelter life after Katrina: A visual analysis of evacuee perspectives. *International Journal of Mass Emergencies and Disasters, 24*(3), 303–330.

Quarantelli, E.L. (1987). *Research in the disaster area: What is being done and what should be done?* Preliminary Paper #118. University of Delaware: Disaster Research Center.

Quarantelli, E.L. (1995). Patterns of sheltering and housing in U.S. disasters. *Disaster Prevention and Management, 4*(3), 43–53.

Quarantelli, E.L. (2002). The Disaster Research Center (DRC) field studies of organized behavior in the crisis time period of disasters. In R.A. Stallings (Ed.), *Methods of disaster research* (pp. 94–126). Philadelphia, PA: Xlibris/International Research Committee on Disasters.

Rosenblatt, P. (1995). Ethics of qualitative interviewing with grieving families. *Death Studies, 19*(2), 139–155.

Rubin, H.J., & Rubin, I.S. (2012). *Qualitative interviewing: The art of hearing data.* Newbury Park, CA: Sage.

Stallings, R. (2006). Methodological issues. In H. Rodríguez, E.L. Quarantelli, & R. Dynes (Eds.), *Handbook of disaster research* (pp. 55–82). New York: Springer Verlag.

Stallings, R., & Quarantelli, E.L. (1985). Emergent citizen groups and emergency management. *Public Administration Review, 45*, 93–100.

Stokes, D. (1997). *Pasteur's quadrant: Basic science and technological innovation.* Washington, DC: Brookings.

Tausch, C., Marks, L., Brown, J., Cherry, K., Frias, T., McWilliams, Z., . . . Sasser, D. (2011). Religion and coping with trauma: Qualitative examples from Hurricanes Katrina and Rita. *Journal of Religion, Spirituality and Aging, 23*(3), 236–253.

Tierney, K., Bevc, C., & Kuligowski, E. (2006). Metaphors matter: Disaster myths, media frames and their consequences in Hurricane Katrina. *Annals AAPSS, 604*, 57–81.

Weber, L., & Peek, L. (2012). *Displaced: Life in the Katrina diaspora.* Austin: University of Texas Press.

Weiss, R. (1995). *Learning from strangers: The art and method of qualitative interviewing.* New York: Free Press.

Wolgemuth, J., Erdil-Moofy, Z., Opsal, T., Cross, J., Kaanta, T., Dickmann, E., & Colomer, S. (2015). Participants' experiences of the qualitative interview: Considering the importance of research paradigms. *Qualitative Research, 15*(3), 351–372.

7

Focus Group Research in Disaster and Emergency Management

Kaila Witkowski, Christa L. Remington,

and Nazife Emel Ganapati

Introduction

> This meeting, I was particularly surprised. For some reason, I had made the assumption that racial prejudices were not going to be extremely prevalent or at least not outrightly expressed. One of the participants had said something along the lines of "that happened in the Dominican [Republic]?" Another participant stepped up and called this participant out for her prejudices. That was a dynamic and interaction I had not expected.[1]

This quote embodies both the purpose and the challenge of focus groups: group interaction. Focus groups are often described as small-group interviews or discussions designed to elicit perceptions or experiences about a particular topic (Krueger, 1994; Morgan, 1997). While group members often vary along demographic criteria, their connection to the topic draws cohesion and a sense of group purpose. It is within this interaction between and among group members that researchers unearth unique and often untold truths about a phenomenon. As identified in the quote above, group members can support, challenge, encourage, and validate others' opinions and feelings regarding the topic. This is what makes focus groups distinct from other qualitative methods like interviews that were discussed in the last chapter; the unit of analysis may well be the interaction among group members (Lune & Berg, 2016).

Focus groups have gained popularity as a data collection method in emergency management and have been used in such diverse fields as public administration (Miles & Chang, 2006; Pyles, 2007), geography (Tobin & Whiteford, 2002), sociology (Peek, 2005), social work (Rahill, Ganapati, Clérismé, & Mukherji, 2014) and urban planning (Ganapati & Ganapati, 2008). To assist students and researchers interested in using this method, we outline the goals of this chapter: (1) to identify the benefits and challenges of using focus groups as a method in emergency management; (2) to provide examples of using focus groups as a data collection method in emergency contexts; and (3) to offer guidance to researchers on refining and expanding their focus group–based research.

The chapter is based on a review of example focus group applications that were published within the last 15 years and were chosen to showcase the method's range of possible applications. Based on the review, we argue that, in part due to their academic and applied nature, focus groups have been used extensively in the interdisciplinary field of emergency management across all four disaster phases and across disciplines. Despite new and innovative developments in the field, the emergency management literature has yet to take full advantage of the focus group method or address the method's limitations. While emergency management research collects both textual and non-textual data from focus group discussions, it tends to overlook the optimum size of focus group participants, confidentiality and privacy concerns, and the method's strengths in terms of analyzing data at the individual, group, and interaction levels. Furthermore, emergency studies published in academic journals provide minimal data on the method itself (e.g., sample size) and the context within which the focus group research (e.g., place) was conducted.

The chapter is structured around eight sections. The next section focuses on why there is a need for focus group research in the emergency management field. The third section provides details on the method's challenges in terms of logistics, discussion, confidentiality and privacy, cultural norms, and disaster-affected populations' everyday challenges. The fourth section deals with analyzing focus group data, a major challenge of the method, highlighting the importance of examining data at the individual, interaction, and group levels and of checking the consistency of findings within a given focus group and across a number of focus groups. The following sections provide examples from the literature on applications of this method in the emergency management field across different disaster phases, outline our critical observations about this literature, and introduce new methodological focus group trends. These trends include virtual focus groups that have become increasingly relevant in the context of pandemics and community-based participatory research (e.g., PhotoVoice). The chapter concludes with a discussion on how to enhance the method in the field and introduces new directions for research.

Why Conduct Focus Group Research?

As with any research instrument, the focus group method has multiple strengths and challenges. Being aware of these can help the researcher decide whether or not focus groups are an appropriate means of data collection and help them skillfully navigate the nuances of this method in a complex emergency management setting. Along these lines, focus groups offer several advantages to emergency management researchers. First, they are a way to increase the sample size in a relatively inexpensive and time-efficient manner, especially if time at the location is limited (Peek & Fothergill, 2009; Rahill et al., 2014). Second, they have the potential to increase the number of willing individuals who meet the study criteria for interviews (Peek, 2005; Rahill et al., 2014). Third, the focus group's fluid nature and ability to be customized to cultural and social norms can help bring out human experiences and emotions (Kieffer et al., 2005; Liamputtong, 2011). Fourth, focus groups can empower study participants, encourage individuals to share about sensitive topics, and mimic the social support provided in a support group setting (Kitzinger, 1994; Johnson, 1996; Kieffer et al., 2005; Peek, 2005). Fifth, focus group participants often represent various socioeconomic, ethnic, racial, or cultural backgrounds. While the collective nature of focus groups can help draw attention to these differences in disaster contexts, it can also pull together common experiences and opinions, leading to a more comprehensive understanding of the disaster experience and of each other. Sixth, focus groups can help marginalized groups feel more comfortable putting their thoughts into words (Liamputtong, 2011). This quality makes focus groups especially important for understanding the experiences of racial and religious minorities (Peek, 2005), low-income groups (Kieffer et al., 2005), and those who have difficulty communicating, as pointed out in Chapter 5.

Challenges of Conducting Focus Groups

Because the group environment is an essential component of the focus group, researchers utilizing this research design need to be prepared to address the complexities of human interaction. A well-thought-out research design will take these group processes into consideration while also considering the challenges that are unique to the contexts of disasters. As research has shown, challenges of focus groups in non-disaster contexts can be further exacerbated by the physical, emotional, and logistical challenges associated with disaster contexts, as detailed through the five themes below.

Making Logistical Arrangements

Organizing focus groups require the research team to contact and coordinate meetings for several participants (5–8 individuals). Managing schedules, transportation challenges, and organizing meeting times and locations can be burdensome. There can also be additional challenges in post-disaster contexts, such as lack of power, heat, or air-conditioning in the meeting location or participants not feeling safe in focus group venues. When we were conducting focus groups at a church site with those who were displaced by the 2010 Haiti earthquake (Rahill et al., 2014; Mukherji, Ganapati, & Rahill, 2014), for instance, our participants started to feel uneasy after about an hour of discussion. They were wary of staying inside a concrete structure for a long time due to their recent earthquake experience. Hence, careful thought should be given to the meeting location, as it needs to be not only easily accessible and comfortable but also quiet, private, and safe enough for in-depth discussions to occur.

Running the Discussion

Bringing together a group of unrelated individuals to discuss a common topic (Barbour, 2005) can help explore research questions from different angles and include diverse experiences and perspectives in data collection (Morgan & Krueger, 1993). It can also create disagreements between members if the topic is a sensitive one. Too many streams of thought can be disruptive and hinder themes from forming. Hence, moderators not only need to be skilled in eliciting thoughts and feelings from participants (Stewart, Shamdasani, & Rook, 2006) but also in controlling group dynamics. This would include managing dominating voices, encouraging unheard participants to speak (Powell & Single, 1996; Wibeck, Dahlgren, & Oberg, 2007), or asking participants to take turns answering questions (Rahill et al., 2014).

Protecting Participants' Confidentiality and Privacy

Unlike interviews in which the researcher has relative control over participant data, the interactive nature of focus groups poses a greater risk to the disclosure of personal, and perhaps confidential, information by other participants (Powell & Single, 1996; Wilkinson, 1998). To limit this risk, scholars suggest that moderators set ground rules, verbally or in writing, similar to those established in support groups – "the information shared in the group, stays in the group" (Powell & Single, 1996; Wilkinson, 1998). Researchers can also ask if participants would like to use pseudonyms during the meetings, although our experience shows that this could make note-taking challenging.

Taking Participants' Cultural Norms Into Account

In many cultures, both males and females, those of different socioeconomic levels, and those who do not conform to traditional societal norms may feel marginalized and be unwilling to share their beliefs, impressions, and concerns freely in the presence of others due to inherent power differences (Pollack, 2003; Mezinska, Kakuk, Mijaljica, Waligóra, & O'Mathúna, 2016). For example, in Peek's (2003) study on the experiences of Muslim Americans post-9/11, some female students preferred mixed-gendered groups while others felt reluctant to speak freely in such settings (see Peek & Fothergill, 2009). Therefore, the researchers should give serious thought to the composition of the focus group and take into account the cultural norms that may impact the comfort level and involvement of the participants as well as the nuances of data collection.

Understanding Participants' Everyday Struggles

Emergency management researchers should be aware of the everyday struggles that participants may experience following a disaster. Focus group members may have lost loved ones, homes, or possessions, or they may have experienced psychological trauma. Although participants rarely regret their involvement in post-disaster research studies (Newman & Kaloupek, 2004), asking them to discuss their experiences in a group setting may risk re-traumatization (Mukherji et a., 2014). Hence, the researchers need to consider whether it is a burden or opportunity for participants to share experiences in a group setting (Peek, 2005; Mukherji et al., 2014). As discussed in Chapters 1 and 5, institutional review boards (IRB) play an important role in this context, as they help researchers reflect on these challenges and ensure that research participants are protected from undue stress and burden. To limit potential risks to study participants, scholars can also (1) train the research team about how they can handle unintended emotions and other challenges that may be faced during the focus group (Mukherji et al., 2014; Mezinska et al., 2016); (2) outline the potential benefits and risks to participants during informed consent procedures; and (3) connect them with local resources (e.g., social workers, non-governmental organizations) for additional support (Mezinska et al., 2016).

Challenges of Analyzing Focus Group Data

Another challenge inherent to the focus group method is analyzing data, as analysis can occur at many different levels. The first and most widely used level of analysis is the individual level. This occurs by looking at the thoughts, opinions, and language of members within a focus group, similar to what would occur during an in-depth interview (Wilkinson, 1998; Wibeck et al., 2007), as discussed in Chapter 6. This approach, however, limits the breadth and depth of analysis. Because the identifying feature of a focus group is the interaction *between* participants, a level of group interaction should also be present between individual members or between naturally occurring sub-groups (Stevens, 1996). Finally, the group as a whole can be the unit of analysis, with a focus on consensus and shared experiences that emerge from the focus group (Morgan, 1995, 1997). To assist in analyzing focus group data at multiple levels, researchers should follow systematic data collection, analysis, and reporting criteria, all of which are discussed below.

Preparing Data for Analysis

Systematic data collection procedures are essential for focus groups, because how the data is collected will determine the quality of the analysis. There is general consensus that some form of audio or video recordings should be used within focus groups to create verbatim transcripts for analysis (Krueger, 1997). However, some participants (e.g., immigrants) may not feel comfortable having aspects of their identity recorded. When dealing with sensitive topics, researchers can include procedures in which the audio recordings will be destroyed directly after transcription (Worthington, Piper, Galea, & Rosenthal, 2006) or use field notes as the primary data collection technique to capture comprehensive details in order to provide enough data to be analyzed (though this is not ideal for analysis). For field notes, researchers can use a structured note-taking guide and depict elements such as the basic discussion themes from the instrument (Krueger, 1997), general impressions, notations on body language, facial expressions (Barbour & Kitzinger, 1998), where participants are seated (Cameron, 2005), interactions before or after the focus group, details on where the focus group took place, or the overall "energy" of the discussion (Krueger, 1997). Post-discussion debriefing sessions between the researchers can also serve as an opportunity to collect data and check opinions regarding themes and topics (Krueger, 1997). Use of a computer-assisted analysis program (e.g., NVivo) can also strengthen the analyses of focus group data from the transcriptions and field notes.

Coding Data and Identifying Themes

As in other forms of qualitative research, coding focus group data involves researchers taking the data and categorizing parts of the text into topics. These topics are informed by the research design, interview guide, research questions, and the existing literature (Krueger, 1997; Morgan, 1997) or by the themes emerging directly from the data (Charmaz, 2001). The difference is that the focus group analyses need to contain elements of the interaction among and between participants. However, there are limited methods for analyzing group interactions within focus groups (Kitzinger, 1994; Wilkinson, 1998; Wibeck et al., 2007). Some authors suggest a mix of moving between the different levels of analysis, which can capture both individual narratives and group interactions (Morgan, 1997; Wibeck et al., 2007; Peek & Fothergill, 2009). Others suggest looking at shared knowledge and experiences by examining the questions raised by group members (Wibeck et al., 2007). Others (Stevens, 1996, p. 172) have developed a set of questions that help examine consensus, conflict, and shared meanings to guide analysis:

- Which situations produced conflict?
- How was conflict addressed?

- Which experiences elicited consensus or silenced opinions?
- What subgroups were formed?
- How did shared experiences build or shift the discussion?

Reporting Data

A common pitfall to avoid when analyzing and reporting focus group data is only capturing the group consensus. This can lead to inaccurate results and curability issues. Triangulating focus group data with other qualitative or quantitative data collection methods, similar to those discussed in Chapter 4, can ensure that results are credible and accurately represent what the participants intended (Marshall & Rossman, 2016). An example of triangulation is pairing focus groups with interviews, which can add comprehensive individual narratives to analysis. Secondary resources (e.g., photographs, news pieces) and surveys are another way to contextualize focus group themes within a greater population.

Example Applications of the Focus Group Method in Emergency Management Research

Our goal in this section is to provide examples of how the focus group method can be applied in emergency and disaster management rather than to provide a systematic review of the literature per se (see Rivera (2019) for such a review). Along these lines, we present example studies under each disaster phase below.

Preparedness

A number of studies have relied on focus groups to identify the problems and capabilities of different communities, demographic groups, sectors, and organizations as they prepare for the next disaster. Asfaw, Nation, McGee, and Christianson (2019), for instance, conducted a focus group in conjunction with interviews to identify the challenges of emergency evacuation in an indigenous community. McGee and Gordon (2012) sent emergency alerts to the cell phones of undergraduate students via text and used focus groups to gauge their readiness for emergencies. Based on a focus group and an online survey, Horney et al. (2017) evaluated the impact of health departments' contextual factors on public health preparedness. Javor, Pearce, Thompson, and Moran (2014) combined simulation exercises with focus groups and interviews to understand the decision-making process at emergency operations centers (EOCs).

Response

Research done on the response phase of a disaster has utilized focus groups to uncover the effectiveness of response efforts or the lived experiences of different groups (e.g., survivors, responders) in the aftermath of a disaster. Examples to the former include Paul, Acharya, and Ghimire's (2017) study that examines the effectiveness of relief efforts after the 2015 Nepal earthquakes, and Binder and Baker's (2017) study focusing on the effectiveness of a local versus an external response following the 2009 earthquake and tsunami in American Samoa. Examples of the latter include studies conducted on the lived experiences and trauma of children after Hurricane Katrina

(Peek & Fothergill, 2006) and the characteristics and traits of effective first responders and emergency nurses (Cone & Murray, 2002; Remington & Ganapati, 2017; Berastegui, Jaspar, & Nyssen, 2018).

Recovery

Studies done on the recovery phase have examined issues ranging from recovery trajectories and factors that affect recovery to impacts of disasters on different groups during recovery. Epstein et al. (2018), for instance, looked at the diverse household and community recovery trajectories after the 2015 Nepal earthquakes. Regarding factors affecting recovery, studies have examined, among others, the role of government and institutions (Ganapati & Ganapati, 2008; Pathak & Ahmad, 2018), social capital (Ganapati, 2012, 2013; Masud-All-Kamal & Hassan, 2018; Rahill et al., 2014), work (Galanti & Cortini, 2019), and women (Alam & Rahman, 2019). As for examples of group impacts, studies have focused on the impact of 9/11 on Muslim students (Peek, 2003); the impact of displacement, relocation and resettlement on disaster survivors (Nikuze, Sliuzas, Flacke, & van Maarseveen, 2019); and the psychosocial impacts of disasters on response and recovery workers (Kroll, Remington, Awasthi, & Ganapati, 2020). While most recovery studies utilizing focus groups are undertaken within the first few years after a disaster, some studies (e.g., Sword-Daniels, Twigg, & Loughlin, 2015) adopt a long-term perspective to recovery, as the recovery process can spread over decades.

Mitigation

Mitigation studies utilizing focus groups typically deal with disaster risk reduction strategies or the role of different factors in mitigation efforts. Tanwattana (2018), for instance, investigates the emergence of community-based organizations in flood-prone urban communities in Thailand. Nyahunda and Tirivangasi (2019) examine challenges faced by rural residents while mitigating climate change effects in Zimbabwe's communal lands. Kontar et al. (2018) compare flood risk reduction strategies in the rural Arctic in the United States and Russia. Additional studies take a closer look at the role of factors such as ecological knowledge (Barua & Rahman, 2018) and remittances (Pairama & Le Dé, 2018) in disaster risk management. A unique mitigation study is Yamori (2012), which utilizes focus groups to derive the scenarios for group learning games in Japan for disaster prevention purposes (e.g., tsunami) based on experiences of the 1995 Kobe earthquake, as well as to have each game-playing group discuss the results of their game. See Table 7.1 for selected works that have used focus group discussions in their research.

Assessment of the Focus Group Method in Emergency Management Research

Our close reading of selected emergency management studies indicates an important need for researchers to provide details on the method itself, take full advantage of the focus group method, and address the method's limitations in their research. We elaborate on our assessment of the literature below and provide a checklist in Table 7.2 to address the existing limitations in the literature.

TABLE 7.1 Sample Research by Disaster Phase Relevance

Authors	First Author's Discipline or Affiliation Unit	City/Country	Disaster	Disaster Phase Relevance	Focus Group Composition	Topic of Research	Other Data Collection Methods
Carter, Weston, Betts, Wilkinson, & Amlôt (2018)	Emergency response	United Kingdom	N/A	Response	2 × 2 × 3 mixed design ($n = 62$)	Examining public perceptions of different interventions for emergency decontamination	Pre- and post-disaster focus group questionnaire survey (one immediately afterward and the other after 3 months)
Chandra, Dargusch, McNamara, Caspe, and Dalabajan (2017)	Earth and environmental sciences	Minando region of the Philippines	N/A	Mitigation	13 focus groups ($n = 77+$)	Identifying the challenges to implementing new technologies and management techniques to addressing climate risks in smallholder agriculture	Interviews; field observations
DeJoy, Smith and Dyal (2017)	Public health	Metropolitan fire departments in the United States	N/A	All	10 focus groups ($n = 86$)	Developing a safety climate model for the fire services	None (focus groups only)
Hamidazada, Cruz, and Yokomatsu (2019)	Disaster prevention research	Sayad village, Afghanistan	N/A	All	3 focus groups ($n = 26$)	Identifying vulnerability factors of Afghan women to disasters	Interviews
Khan et al. (2018)	Public health	Canada	N/A	Preparedness	6 focus groups (utilizing the Structured Interview Matrix facilitation technique) ($n = 160$)	Identifying the necessary elements of a resilient public health emergency system	Review of secondary sources
McGee and Gow (2012)	Earth and atmospheric sciences	University of Alberta in Edmonton, Canada	N/A	Response	4 focus groups ($n = 22$)	Understanding how students may respond to a university emergency alert	None (focus groups only)

Study	Discipline	Location	Event	Disaster phase	Focus group details	Research aim	Other methods
Peek (2005)	Sociology	Muslim university students in Colorado and New York	Post-9/11	Response and recovery	23 focus groups ($n = 68$)	Understanding the reactions and response of Muslim students to 9/11	Interviews; review of secondary sources
Misra, Goswami, Mondal, and Jana (2017)	Rural development and management	West Bengal	Tropical Cyclone Aila (2009)	Response and recovery	4 focus groups (n not specified)	Generating and mapping social network data with a post-disaster focus	Review of secondary sources (e.g., maps)
O'Sullivan, Kuziemsky, Toal-Sullivan, and Corneil (2013)	Health sciences	Canada		Preparedness	9 focus groups (utilizing the Structured Interview Matrix facilitation technique) ($n = 143$)	Identifying levers for action to promote population health and resilience among high-risk populations	None (focus groups only)
Pairama and Le Dé (2018)	Public health and psychosocial studies	Pacific Island migrants in New Zealand	N/A	Preparedness and mitigation	1 focus group (with participatory tools including carousel, scoring, and the matrix with proportional piling technique) ($n = 25$)	Examining the role of remittances for assisting communities' disaster risk management	Interviews
Rahill et al. (2014)	Social work	Haiti	Haitian earthquake (2010)	Recovery	12 focus groups (conducted in two rounds, 6 months apart) ($n = 63$)	Determining the role of social capital in shelter recovery	Interviews; field observation; review of secondary sources
Saha (2015)	Sociology	West Bengal	Tropical Cyclone Aila (2009)	Preparedness and mitigation	14 focus groups (including a component where participants were asked to assign a score from 1 to 10 for each vulnerability factor) ($n = 116$)	Assessing vulnerability to disaster risks	Field observations

(Continued)

TABLE 7.1 (Continued)

Authors	First Author's Discipline or Affiliation Unit	City/Country	Disaster	Disaster Phase Relevance	Focus Group Composition	Topic of Research	Other Data Collection Methods
Sword-Daniels et al. (2015)	Civil, environmental and geomatic engineering	Montserrat, West Indies	Soufrière Hills Volcano (1995–2012)	Recovery	4 focus groups (utilizing an inductive timeline tool to understand long-term recovery changes) ($n = 28$)	Documenting the post-disaster changes in health care system over two decades	Review of secondary sources; interviews
Zimmerman et al. (2010)	Public service	N/A	Hypothetical disasters	Preparedness	4 focus groups ($n = 24$)	Understanding risk communication for catastrophic events (e.g., chemical and biological attacks)	None (focus groups only)

TABLE 7.2 Checklist for Conducting and Reporting on Focus Group Data

Item 1. Identify methodological details including:

- The purpose and justification for using focus groups
- Sequencing of focus groups in relation to other data collection methods (e.g., before or after interviews)
- The sampling strategies, size, and characteristics of the sample
- The venue and time of discussion
- The duration of the focus group
- How the data was recorded, translated (if not in English), transcribed, coded, and analyzed
- The characteristics and number of moderators and researchers in attendance
- The format of the discussion and the instrument (including question sequence)
- How the limitations and challenges of conducting focus groups were addressed

Examples. Studies with exceptional detail:

- Peek (2003); Zimmerman et al. (2010); McGee and Gow (2012); O'Sullivan et al. (2013); Rahill et al. (2014); Saha (2015); Sword-Daniels et al., (2015); DeJoy, Smith, and Dyal, (2017); Misra et al. (2017); Carter et al. (2018); Khan et al. (2018)

Item 2. Consider adjusting the number of participants:

- Keep the size of focus groups between 5 and 8 (the ideal is 7; Krueger, 1994)
- If larger, implement strategies to address larger groups, such as using the Structured Interview Matrix (SIM) facilitation technique (see Khan et al. 2018)

Caution. It is difficult to manage larger groups:

- It can hinder less vocal participants (Breakwell, Hammond, Fife-Schaw, & Smith, 2006)
- It often requires a skilled moderator to sustain a balanced discussion (Tower et al., 2016)

Item 3. Consider including non-text data:

- Try implementing a questionnaire to collect demographic data before or after the focus group
- Consider adding a word-frequency analysis
- Try collecting network data

Examples:

- Questionnaires (Rahill et al., 2014; Pathak & Emah, 2017; Carter et al., 2018)
- Content analysis (Galanti & Cortini, 2019)
- Network analysis (Misra et al., 2017)

Item 4. Analyze data at multiple levels:

- Refer back to Stevens's (1996) analysis questions

Examples:

- Rahill et al. (2014); Pairama and Le Dé (2018)

Item 5. Take steps to ensure the confidentiality of participants:

- IRB approval prior to beginning research
- Receive IRB approval from U.S. institutions and the visiting country's IRB system
- Remove personal identifiers, if necessary

Examples:

- Curnin, Owen, and Trist (2014); Rahill et al. (2014); Farra and Smith (2019)

First, while there are many studies that use focus groups, we find the emergency management literature to be lacking in detail about the focus group method. This is especially true for articles that use focus groups in combination with other qualitative and/or quantitative data collection methods, such as interviews, observation, review of secondary sources, and surveys. Commonly ignored details are included in Table 7.2, Item 1. All of these details are important for evaluating the quality of research published, guiding future researchers who are planning to utilize focus groups, and understanding the applicability of this method within emergency management contexts.

Second, there are significant variations in terms of the size of each focus group conducted in emergency management research, ranging from 3 or 4 participants (e.g., Peek, 2005; McGee & Gow, 2012) to 45 participants (e.g., McNaught, Warrick, & Cooper, 2014). While some of the studies with a large number of participants acknowledge the challenges associated with the size of the focus group (Tower et al., 2016), others make no mention of the challenges they faced and how they addressed these challenges.

Third, most emergency management studies produce qualitative textual data from focus groups. There are very few studies that supplement qualitative textual focus group data with non-textual quantitative data collected from focus groups participants before, during, or after the discussion (e.g., via questionnaires) or generated from further analysis of focus group data (e.g., word frequency tables, network data), which can add rich details to the study.

Fourth, we found very few studies that analyzed focus group data at the individual, group, and interaction levels, despite scholars emphasizing the importance of conducting such analyses. Many studies do, indeed, acknowledge the strength of focus groups in capturing group-level dynamics. Yet, in the respective "findings" sections, they typically do not mention what they have observed in terms of group dynamics or group consensus.

Fifth, one of the challenges researchers face while conducting focus groups relates to ethics specifically ensuring confidentiality by focus group participants. Although many studies mention aspects of the IRB process (e.g., approval, removal of participants' identifiers), most emergency management studies do not address the issue of what researchers can do to ensure the confidentiality of discussions by focus group participants. They also do not mention obtaining approval from international IRBs for studies conducted in other countries. See Table 7.2 for a checklist on how to design focus groups and analyze focus group data to overcome these limitations and for examples.

New and Interesting Trends

Based on our review of studies that utilized focus groups, there are several relatively newer trends that are useful for focus group research in emergency and disaster management, which we will discuss in the following section.

Virtual Focus Groups

The growth of the digital era and pandemics such as COVID-19 have generated heightened attention to virtual and online focus groups. Attempting to utilize convenience and accessibility of online forums, several scholars have adapted the in-person focus group method to the virtual arena (Adler & Zarchin, 2002; Turney & Pocknee, 2005). There are generally two types of virtual focus groups: synchronous and asynchronous studies (Stewart & Williams, 2005). Synchronous focus groups use online video conferencing technology (e.g., Skype, Zoom) to allow participants to speak to each other in real time or to interact with each other through their avatars in a virtual environment, like Second Life (Stewart & Williams, 2005). Asynchronous focus groups use online technology such as online forums and email, which allow participants to respond on their own time. Generally, synchronous focus groups are preferred because asynchronous groups limit the depth of data collection.

While there are many concerns with using virtual focus groups (e.g., verifying identity and inclusion criteria), scholars such as Turney and Pocknee (2005) found virtual focus groups to be as valid as in-person groups when rigorous methodological criteria are followed. Currently, virtual focus groups are primarily used within studies about healthcare issues and within settings that limit face-to-face interactions (e.g., women on bedrest; Adler & Zarchin, 2002). However, virtual focus groups hold promise for researchers studying emergency situations. Virtual focus groups can allow researchers to recruit hard-to-engage populations (Turney & Pocknee, 2005; Biedermann, 2018) and connect populations that are geographically dispersed (Stewart & Williams, 2005) – both common barriers to post-disaster research. A notable example in emergency management is Lin, Margolin, and Wen's (2017) online focus group method called "Computational Focus Groups," which used Twitter data to track and analyze individual distress of social media users who were near the Paris terrorist attacks on November 13, 2015.

Participatory Research

Community-based participatory research (CBPR) is another method that encourages stakeholders to take an active role in bettering their community by becoming members of the research team (Wang & Burris, 1997). This requires researchers to recruit and solicit participant views before developing the purpose of the research project. A developing trend in CBPR research is PhotoVoice. PhotoVoice is a method that encourages participants to critically reflect and analyze community strengths and weaknesses through participant-taken photographs (Wang, 1999). Participants meet in focus groups for several months to learn the PhotoVoice method and engage in facilitated discussion to determine the purpose of the project, analyze photographs as a group, and plan an exhibition launch to influence community leaders and policymakers.

PhotoVoice has been used in many different disaster contexts, including a chlorine gas spill in South Carolina (Annang et al., 2016), the earthquake and tsunami in Japan in 2011 (Yoshihama & Yunomae, 2018), and to examine disaster preparedness of Native Hawaiians (Torris-Hedlund, 2019). Similar to virtual focus groups, PhotoVoice is a useful method for engaging difficult-to-reach populations (Hennessy et al., 2010; Padilla, Matiz-Reyes, Colón-Burgos, Varas-Díaz, & Vertovec, 2019). It can also provide the researcher entrée into how participants normally interact and talk to others regarding topics, concerns, and experiences.

Schumann, Binder, and Greer (2019) argue that PhotoVoice has an "unseen potential" in hazard and disaster science due to its potential for "capturing understandings of hazards and disasters and for providing rich theoretical insights related to extreme events, which are intrinsically geographical and place-based" (p. 273). They also note the method's value in terms of offering "policymakers a valuable window into the public's understanding of issues related to extreme events" and empowering "individuals to consider their own capabilities to reduce risk in their communities and contribute to broader resilience building efforts" (p. 273).

Conclusion: Future Directions for Research

In this chapter, we shed light on the focus group method in emergency management literature, highlighted the need for using this method as a data collection tool, and addressed its strengths and challenges. We provided examples of its use in current literature from across disaster phases and shared our opinion on what this literature is missing. We highlighted the literature's failure to (1) build on the method's strengths to capture data at the individual, group, and interaction levels and to capture both textual and non-textual data; and (2) address its limitations in terms of manageable discussions (e.g., small group size) and human subjects' confidentiality and privacy concerns.

Based on our reading of the sample literature, we can confidently say that the literature can greatly benefit from addressing the strengths and limitations of this method, which have already been established in the qualitative methods literature in general and in the emergency and disaster management literature specifically. It is also important for researchers to provide a thorough explanation of the "Who, What, When, Where, How, and Why" in their method sections, as highlighted by Annesley (2010, p. 897). In this way, researchers can directly educate others in reference to enhancing the practice of focus group methods in the future. As such, we invite researchers who have not had the opportunity to practice focus groups to open up their horizons and add this methodological design strategy to their repertoire.

As Schumann et al. (2019, p. 273) note, "Disaster science is surprisingly methodologically stagnant, often relying solely on traditional surveys, interviews, and focus groups to gather qualitative data." They go on to state that social science fields in general, which often contribute to emergency management literature, have begun to expand their methods into more alternative and participatory methodological forms. Sharing these researchers' sentiments, we invite focus group researchers to open up their horizons and add their own variations to focus group design, as in the case of Yamori (2012), or to adopt some of the new, emerging, and exciting techniques, including PhotoVoice (Schumann et al., 2019), the Structured Interview Matrix (O'Sullivan et al., 2013; Khan et al., 2018), the inductive timeline tool for retrospective studies (e.g., Sword-Daniels et al., 2015), or the World Café format (Koch, Franco, O'Sullivan, DeFino, & Ahmed, 2017). Such designs can enrich the focus group discussion experience even more. There certainly is so much more to explore!

Note

1. An excerpt from student field notes on a project titled "Mi Vida con VIH / My Life with HIV" conducted at Florida International University under the direction of Dr. Mark Padilla and Dr. Armando Matiz Reyes, in partnership with Pridelines, Inc. and funded by the Kimberly Green Latin American and Caribbean Center (LACC).

Further Readings

Morgan, D. L. (1996). Focus groups. *Annual Review of Sociology, 22*(1), 129–152.

Onwuegbuzie, A.J., Dickinson, W.B., Leech, N.L., & Zoran, A.G. (2009). A qualitative framework for collecting and analyzing data in focus group research. *International Journal of Qualitative Methods, 8*(3), 1–21.

Peek, L., & Fothergill, A. (2009). Using focus groups: Lessons from studying daycare centers, 9/11, and Hurricane Katrina. *Qualitative Research, 9*(1), 31–59.

Rivera, J. D. (2019). Focus group administration in disaster research: Methodological transparency when dealing with challenges. *International Journal of Mass Emergencies and Disasters, 37*(3), 241–263.

References

Adler, C. L., & Zarchin, Y. R. (2002). The "virtual focus group": Using the Internet to reach pregnant women on home bed rest. *Journal of Obstetric, Gynecologic, and Neonatal Nursing, 31*(4), 418–427.

Alam, K., & Rahman, M. H. (2019). Post-disaster recovery in the Cyclone Aila affected coastline of Bangladesh: Women's role, challenges and opportunities. *Natural Hazards, 96*(3), 1067–1090.

Annang, L., Wilson, S., Tinago, C., Wright Sanders, L., Bevington, T., Carlos, B., . . . Svendsen, E. (2016). Photovoice: Assessing the long-term impact of a disaster on a community's quality of life. *Qualitative Health Research, 26*(2), 241–251.

Annesley, T. M. (2010). Who, what, when, where, how, and why: The ingredients in the recipe for a successful methods section. *Clinical Chemistry, 56*(6), 897–901.

Asfaw, H. W., Nation, S. L. F., McGee, T. K., & Christianson, A. C. (2019). Evacuation preparedness and the challenges of emergency evacuation in Indigenous communities in Canada: The case of Sandy Lake First Nation, Northern Ontario. *International Journal of Disaster Risk Reduction, 34*, 55–63.

Barbour, R. S. (2005). Making sense of focus groups. *Medical Education, 39*(7), 742–750.

Barbour, R. S., & Kitzinger, J. (Eds.). (1998). *Developing focus group research: Politics, theory and practice*. London: Sage.

Barua, P., & Rahman, S. H. (2018). The role of traditional ecological knowledge of southeastern island communities of Bangladesh in disaster risk management strategies. *IUP Journal of Knowledge Management, 16*(1), 19–43.

Berastegui, P., Jaspar, M., Ghuysen, A., & Nyssen, A.-S. (2018). Fatigue-related risk management in the emergency department: A focus-group study. *Internal and Emergency Medicine, 13*(8), 1273–1281.

Biedermann, N. (2018). The use of Facebook for virtual asynchronous focus groups in qualitative research. *Contemporary Nurse, 54*(1), 26–34.

Binder, S. B., & Baker, C. K. (2017). Culture, local capacity, and outside aid: A community perspective on disaster response after the 2009 tsunami in American Samoa. *Disasters, 41*(2), 282–305.

Breakwell, G. M., Hammond, S., Fife-Schaw, C., & Smith, J. A. (2006). *Research methods in psychology* (3rd ed.). Thousand Oaks, CA: Sage.

Cameron, J. (2005). Focusing on the focus group. *Qualitative Research Methods in Human Geography, 2*(8), 116–132.

Carter, H., Weston, D., Betts, N., Wilkinson, S., & Amlôt, R. (2018). Public perceptions of emergency decontamination: Effects of intervention type and responder management strategy during a focus group study. *PLOS One, 13*(4), e0195922.

Chandra, A., Dargusch, P., McNamara, K. E., Caspe, A. M., & Dalabajan, D. (2017). A study of climate-smart farming practices and climate-resiliency field schools in Mindanao, the Philippines. *World Development, 98*, 214–230.

Charmaz, K. (2001). Grounded theory. In R.M. Emerson (Ed.), *Contemporary field research: Perspectives and formulations* (2nd ed., pp. 335–352). Prospect Heights, IL: Waveland Press.

Cone, K.J., & Murray, R. (2002). Characteristics, insights, decision making, and preparation of ED triage nurses. *Journal of Emergency Nursing, 28*(5), 401–478.

Curnin, S., Owen, C., & Trist, C. (2014). Managing the constraints of boundary spanning in emergency management. *Cognition, Technology and Work, 16*(4), 549–563.

DeJoy, D.M., Smith, T.D., & Dyal, M.A. (2017). Safety climate and firefighting: Focus group results. *Journal of Safety Research, 62*, 107–116.

Epstein, K., DiCarlo, J., Marsh, R., Adhikari, B., Paudel, D., Ray, I., & Måren, I.E. (2018). Recovery and adaptation after the 2015 Nepal earthquakes. *Ecology and Society, 23*(1).

Farra, S.L., & Smith, S.J. (2019). Anxiety and stress in live disaster exercises. *Journal of Emergency Nursing, 45*(4), 366–373.

Galanti, T., & Cortini, M. (2019). Work as a recovery factor after earthquake: A mixed-method study on female workers. *Disaster Prevention and Management: An International Journal, 28*(4), 487–500.

Ganapati, N. E. (2012). In good company: Why social capital matters for women during disaster recovery. *Public Administration Review, 72*(3), 419–427.

Ganapati, N. E. (2013). Downsides of social capital for women during disaster recovery: Toward a more critical approach. *Administration & Society, 45*(1), 72–96.

Ganapati, N.E., & Ganapati, S. (2008). Enabling participatory planning after disasters: A case study of the World Bank's housing reconstruction in Turkey. *Journal of the American Planning Association, 75*(1), 41–59.

Hamidazada, M., Cruz, A.M., & Yokomatsu, M. (2019). Vulnerability factors of Afghan rural women to disasters. *International Journal of Disaster Risk Science, 10*(4), 573–590.

Hennessy, E., Kraak, V.I., Hyatt, R.R., Bloom, J., Fenton, M., Wagoner, C., & Economos, C.D. (2010). Active living for rural children: Community perspectives using photo voice. *American Journal of Preventive Medicine, 39*(6), 537–545.

Horney, J.A., Carbone, E.G., Lynch, M., Wang, Z.J., Jones, T., & Rose, D.A. (2017). How health department contextual factors affect public health preparedness (PHP) and perceptions of the 15 PHP capabilities. *American Journal of Public Health, 107*(S2), S153–S160.

Javor, A.J., Pearce, L., Thompson, A.J., & Moran, C.B. (2014). Modeling psychosocial decision making in emergency operations centres. *International Journal of Mass Emergencies and Disasters, 32*(3), 484–507.

Johnson, A. (1996). "It's good to talk": The focus group and the sociological imagination. *Sociological Review, 44*(3), 517–538.

Khan, Y., O'Sullivan, T., Brown, A., et al. (2018). Public health emergency preparedness: A framework to promote resilience. *BMC Public Health, 18*(1), 1344.

Kieffer, E.C., Salabarria-Pena, Y., Odoms-Young, A.M., Willis, S.K., Baber, K.E., & Guzman, J.R. (2005). The application of focus group methodologies to community-based participatory research. In B.A. Israel, E. Eng, A.J. Schulz, & E.A. Parker (Eds.), *Methods for community-based participatory research for health* (pp. 249–276). San Francisco: Wiley.

Kitzinger, J. (1994). The methodology of focus groups: The importance of interaction between research participants. *Sociology of Health and Illness, 16*(1), 103–121.

Koch, H., Franco, Z.E., O'Sullivan, T., DeFino, M.C., & Ahmed, S. (2017). Community views of the federal emergency management agency's "whole community" strategy in a complex US city: Re-envisioning societal resilience. *Technological Forecasting and Social Change, 121*, 31–38.

Kontar, Y.Y., Eichelberger, J.C., Gavrilyeva, T.N., Filippova, V.V., Savvinova, A.N., Tananaev, N.I., & Trainor, S.F. (2018). Springtime flood risk reduction in rural Arctic: A comparative study of interior Alaska, United States and Central Yakutia, Russia. *Geosciences, 8*(3), 90.

Kroll, A., Remington, C.L., Awasthi, P., & Ganapati, N.E. (2020). Mitigating the negative effects of emotional labor: A study of disaster response and recovery workers after the 2010 Haiti earthquake. *Governance.* https://doi.org/10.1111/gove.12476.

Krueger, R.A. (1994). *Focus groups: A practical guide for applied research* (2nd ed.). Thousand Oaks, CA: Sage.

Krueger, R.A. (1997). *Analyzing and reporting focus group results* (Vol. 6). Thousand Oaks, CA: Sage.

Liamputtong, P. (2011). Focus group methodology: Introduction and history. In P. Liamputtong (Ed.), *Focus group methodology: Principles and practice* (pp. 1–14). London: Sage.

Lin, Y.R., Margolin, D., & Wen, X. (2017). Tracking and analyzing individual distress following terrorist attacks using social media streams. *Risk Analysis, 37*(8), 1580–1605.

Lune, H., & Berg, B.L. (2016). *Qualitative research methods for the social sciences.* Boston: Pearson.

Nyahunda, L., & Tirivangasi, H.M. (2019). Challenges faced by rural people in mitigating the effects of climate change in the Mazungunye communal lands, Zimbabwe. *Jàmbá: Journal of Disaster Risk Studies, 11*(1), 1–9.

Marshall, C., & Rossman, G. (2016). *Designing qualitative research* (6th ed.). Thousand Oaks, CA: Sage.

Masud-All-Kamal, M., & Hassan, S.M. (2018). The link between social capital and disaster recovery: Evidence from coastal communities in Bangladesh. *Natural Hazards, 93*(3), 1547–1564.

McGee, T.K., & Gow, G.A. (2012). Potential responses by on-campus university students to a university emergency alert. *Journal of Risk Research, 15*(6) 693–710.

McNaught, R., Warrick, O., & Cooper, A. (2014). Communicating climate change for adaptation in rural communities: A pacific study. *Regional Environmental Change, 14*(4), 1491–1503.

Mezinska, S., Kakuk, P., Mijaljica, G., Waligóra, M., & O'Mathúna, D.P. (2016). Research in disaster settings: A systematic qualitative review of ethical guidelines. *BMC Medical Ethics, 17*(1), 62.

Miles, S., & Chang, S. (2006). Modeling community recovery from earthquakes. *Earthquake Spectra, 22*(2), 439–458.

Misra, S., Goswami, R., Mondal, T., & Jana, R. (2017). Social networks in the context of community response to disaster: Study of a cyclone-affected community in Coastal West Bengal, India. *International Journal of Disaster Risk Reduction, 22*, 281–296.

Morgan, D.L. (1995). Why things (sometimes) go wrong in focus groups. *Qualitative Health Research, 5*(4), 516–523.

Morgan, D.L. (1997). *Focus groups as qualitative research* (2nd ed.). Thousand Oaks, CA: Sage.

Morgan, D.L., & Krueger, R.A. (1993). When to use focus groups and why. In D. Morgan. (Ed.), *Successful focus groups: Advancing the state of the art* (pp. 3–19). Newbury Park, CA: Sage.

Mukherji, A., Ganapati, N.E., & Rahill, G. (2014). Expecting the unexpected: Field research in post-disaster settings. *Natural Hazards, 73*(2), 805–828.

Newman, E., & Kaloupek, D.G. (2004). The risks and benefits of participating in trauma-focused research studies. *Journal of Traumatic Stress: Official Publication of the International Society for Traumatic Stress Studies, 17*(5), 383–394.

Nikuze, A., Sliuzas, R., Flacke, J., & van Maarseveen, M. (2019). Livelihood impacts of displacement and resettlement on informal households-A case study from Kigali, Rwanda. *Habitat International, 86*, 38–47.

O'Sullivan, T.L., Kuziemsky, C.E., Toal-Sullivan, D., & Corneil, W. (2013). Unraveling the complexities of disaster management: A framework for critical social infrastructure to promote population health and resilience. *Social Science & Medicine, 93*, 238–246.

Padilla, M., Matiz-Reyes, A., Colón-Burgos, J.F., Varas-Díaz, N., & Vertovec, J. (2019). Adaptation of photo voice methodology to promote policy dialog among street-based drug users in Santo Domingo, Dominican Republic. *Arts & Health, 11*(2), 147–162.

Pairama, J., & Le Dé, L. (2018). Remittances for disaster risk management: Perspectives from Pacific Island migrants living in New Zealand. *International Journal of Disaster Risk Science, 9*(3), 331–343.

Pathak, S., & Ahmad, M.M. (2018). Role of government in flood disaster recovery for SMEs in Pathumthani province, Thailand. *Natural Hazards, 93*(2), 957–966.

Pathak, S., & Emah, I.E. (2017). Gendered approach towards disaster recovery: Experiences from 2011 floods in Pathumthani province, Thailand. *International Journal of Disaster Risk Reduction, 24*, 129–134.

Paul, B.K., Acharya, B., & Ghimire, K. (2017). Effectiveness of earthquakes relief efforts in Nepal: Opinions of the survivors. *Natural Hazards*, *85*(2), 1169–1188.

Peek, L. (2003). Reactions and response: Muslim students' experiences on New York City campuses post 9/11. *Journal of Muslim Minority Affairs*, *23*(2), 273–285.

Peek, L. (2005). Becoming Muslim: The development of a religious identity. *Sociology of Religion*, *66*(3), 215–242.

Peek, L., & Fothergill, A. (2006). *Reconstructing childhood: An exploratory study of children in Hurricane Katrina*. Quick Response Report #186. Boulder, CO: Natural Hazards Research and Applications Information Center, University of Colorado.

Peek, L., & Fothergill, A. (2009). Using focus groups: Lessons from studying daycare centers, 9/11, and Hurricane Katrina. *Qualitative Research*, *9*(1), 31–59.

Pollack, S. (2003). Focus-group methodology in research with incarcerated women: Race, power, and collective experience. *Affiliate*, *18*(4), 461–472.

Powell, R.A., & Single, H.M. (1996). Focus groups. *International Journal for Quality in Health Care*, *8*(5), 499–504.

Pyles, L. (2007). Community organizing for post-disaster social development: Social work. *International Social Work*, *50*(3), 321–333.

Rahill, G.J., Ganapati, N.E., Clérismé, J.C., & Mukherji, A. (2014). Shelter recovery in urban Haiti after the earthquake: The dual role of social capital. *Disasters*, *38*(s1), S73–S93.

Remington, C.L., & Ganapati, N.E. (2017). Recovery worker skills in post-earthquake Haiti: The disconnect between employer and employee perspectives. *Natural Hazards*, *87*(3), 1673–1690.

Saha, C.K. (2015). Dynamics of disaster-induced risk in southwestern coastal Bangladesh: An analysis on Tropical Cyclone Aila 2009. *Natural Hazards*, *75*(1), 727–754.

Schumann, R.L., Binder, S.B., & Greer, A. (2019). Unseen potential: Photovoice methods in hazard and disaster science. *Geo Journal*, *84*(1), 273–289.

Stevens, P.E. (1996). Focus groups: Collecting aggregate-level data to understand community health phenomena. *Public Health Nursing*, *13*(3), 170–176.

Stewart, D.W., Shamdasani, P.M., & Rook, D.W. (2006). *Focus groups: Theory and practice* (2nd ed.). Thousand Oaks, CA: Sage.

Stewart, K., & Williams, M. (2005). Researching online populations: The use of online focus groups for social research. *Qualitative Research*, *5*(4), 395–416.

Sword-Daniels, V.L., Twigg, J., & Loughlin, S.C. (2015). Time for change? Applying an inductive timeline tool for a retrospective study of disaster recovery in Montserrat, West Indies. *International Journal of Disaster Risk Reduction*, *12*, 125–133.

Tanwattana, P. (2018). Systematizing community-based disaster risk management (CBDRM): Case of urban flood-prone community in Thailand upstream area. *International Journal of Disaster Risk Reduction*, *28*, 798–812.

Tobin, G., & Whiteford, L. (2002). Economic ramifications of disaster: Experiences of displaced persons on the slopes of Mount Tungurahua, Ecuador. In *Papers and proceedings of applied geography conferences* (Vol. 25, pp. 316–324). Tampa: University of South Florida.

Torris-Hedlund, M.A. (2019). Examining the use of photovoice to explore disaster risk perception among Native Hawaiians living on Oʻahu: A feasibility study. *Hawaiʻi Journal of Health & Social Welfare*, *78*(9), 287–292.

Tower, C., Altman, B.A., Strauss-Riggs, K., Iversen, A., Garrity, S., Thompson, C.B., . . . Barnett, D.J. (2016). Qualitative assessment of a novel efficacy-focused training intervention for public health workers in disaster recovery. *Disaster Medicine and Public Health Preparedness*, *10*(4), 615–622.

Turney, L., & Pocknee, C. (2005). Virtual focus groups: New frontiers in research. *International Journal of Qualitative Methods*, *4*(2), 32–43.

Wang, C.C. (1999). Photo voice: A participatory action research strategy applied to women's health. *Journal of Women's Health*, *8*(2), 185–192.

Wang, C.C., & Burris, M.A. (1997). Photo voice: Concept, methodology, and use for participatory needs assessment. *Health Education & Behavior*, *24*(3), 369–387.

Wibeck, V., Dahlgren, M.A., & Oberg, G. (2007). Learning in focus groups: An analytical dimension for enhancing focus group research. *Qualitative Research, 7*(2), 249–267.

Wilkinson, S. (1998). Focus group methodology: A review. *International Journal of Social Research Methodology, 1*(3), 181–203.

Worthington, N., Piper, T.M., Galea, S., & Rosenthal, D. (2006). Opiate users' knowledge about overdose prevention and naloxone in New York City: A focus group study. *Harm Reduction Journal, 3*(1), 19.

Yamori, K. (2012). Using games in community disaster prevention exercises. *Group Decision and Negotiation, 21*(4), 571–583.

Yoshihama, M., & Yunomae, T. (2018). Participatory investigation of the Great East Japan Disaster: Photo voice from women affected by the calamity. *Social Work, 63*(3), 234–243.

Zimmerman, R., Restrepo, C.E., Culpen, A., Remington, W.E., Kling, A., Portelli, I., & Foltin, G.L. (2010). Risk communication for catastrophic events: Results from focus groups. *Journal of Risk Research, 13*(7), 913–935.

8

Site Mapping as Participatory Action

A Methodology for Practitioners, Academics, Students, and the Community

Michèle Companion

Site mapping is an important disaster methodology. It can be used to identify high-risk geographic areas, resources, and at-risk populations. Because it is both participatory and action oriented, this methodology can help to bridge local organizations with disaster agencies and with broader local populations, identify opportunities for collaboration, build social networks and social capital, facilitate data gathering, and improve analytical insights into specific problems and possible resolutions. This methodology is viable at the local neighborhood or community levels as well as at the broader institutional and more macro levels. Site mapping can also be used in institutional analysis to identify gaps in service coverage. This is beneficial for emergency planners, policymakers, and responding agencies or organizations. Disaster mitigation, response, and recovery requires the active participation of all levels of agencies, communities, and households to contribute to effectively understand community needs and engage in action-oriented planning to effectively address them. This chapter will provide a discussion of methodological strategies and provide an example of an effective application in the field.

Introduction

Site mapping is a critical component in the disaster mitigation, risk reduction, response, and rebuilding toolkit. It is a participatory activity that can incorporate multiple voices to create action-oriented outcomes, such as evacuation drills, real-time threat monitoring and reporting mechanisms to improve survival chances, and resource protection strategies. Site mapping allows for professionals of various types, stakeholders, and local community members to identify areas of high risk, such as low-lying roads that are prone to flooding or slopes that are susceptible to landslides. It enables the identification and prioritization of resources that have cultural value, such as sacred sites, memorials, public and sacred art, and medicinal or sacred plants, or historical value, such as cemeteries, buildings, churches, sacred or cultural landscapes, and pilgrimage routes, that may be threatened. It also facilitates the identification of segments of the community that are particularly vulnerable to the impacts of disasters. Proper identification of vulnerable populations, areas, structural and other tangible resources, and community resources can improve the development and implementation of emergency response policies and operations and facilitate recovery. Morrow (1999) notes that this process must begin by compiling a community vulnerability inventory, which is a process of identifying vulnerable groups, individuals, and resources and where they are. Site mapping is an essential strategy for this process.

As indicated in Chapter 5, disaster vulnerability is socially constructed. Those who experience the greatest impacts and have repeated exposure to disaster events tend to be geographically marginalized, living in hazard prone areas, economically marginalized, living in poorly built and inadequately maintained housing without adequate access to resources to aid in evacuation or mitigation, politically marginalized (lacking voice, representation, and power to impact policy creation and enforcement), and socially marginalized due to racism, sexism, ethnocentrism, and limited educational, skills-based, and linguistic proficiency (Companion, 2015; Mercer, Kelman, Lloyd, & Suchet-Pearson, 2008; Morrow, 1999). It is well documented that certain demographic groups (see Companion & Chaiken, 2017; Enarson & Morrow, 1998; Gaillard et al., 2017; Morrow, 1999) are consistently more vulnerable to disaster risks, including both the elderly and areas that have large numbers of young children. Also at higher risk are the poor, renters, households headed by women, those with mental and physical disabilities, recent migrants and immigrants, tourists, the homeless, and groups that experience other forms of marginalization, including linguistic and colonicalistic oppression.

Site mapping can counteract marginalizing forces by empowering local communities to improve capacities among demographic groups that have been labeled as both vulnerable and disempowered. Studies have shown that young people can not only influence local disaster risk reduction policy and practices, but they can also become active participants in disaster response efforts (Haynes & Tanner, 2015; Marchezini & Trajber, 2017; Trajber et al., 2019). Indigenous communities and women's groups have also utilized this technique with tremendous results (Henderson et al., 2017; Lambert, 2015). Larger site mapping projects, as will be discussed below, can build bridges between agencies, organizations, community groups, and policymakers to identify and reduce gaps in disaster planning coverage and improve response and recovery initiatives. Morrow (1999) argues that developing vulnerability maps is an essential step in compiling a community hazard and risk assessment or access profiles (p. 10). Site mapping is an effective methodology for developing these types of maps and for facilitating community resource prioritization.

This chapter argues for the viability of site mapping as a disaster risk reduction strategy to help build capacity and response by and on behalf of a demographic group that has been labeled as marginalized, which includes indigenous populations, youth, students, the elderly, and low-income individuals. Site mapping will first be situated into a larger tradition of participatory action research. This will be followed by a methodological discussion and a detailed example of a project that effectively utilized site mapping as a community and capacity building exercise, a disaster resource prioritization strategy, and a bridge to local, state, and federal organizations.

Participatory Action Research

Participatory action research (PAR) comes out of a longer history of advocating for bottom-up, localized participation in rapid rural appraisals, participatory rural appraisals, and rapid food security assessments during and after crises. It later expanded in scope to facilitate community involvement with local and international stakeholders to develop disaster mitigation strategies and risk reduction plans. Robert Chambers (1994), Michael Cernea (1985), and others advocated for research that was driven by local participants to allow them to produce detailed accounts, maps, and tangible products using their own local frameworks of understanding and references in their own words. Organizations such as Oxfam, the World Bank, and the UN Food and Agricultural Organization (FAO) compiled training manuals and toolboxes that advocated for greater local participation in non-government organization (NGO) mitigation and recovery projects (e.g., FAO, 1999). These toolboxes and training resources include site mapping as an essential strategy to build community capacity and to identify opportunities and vulnerabilities within and near the communities.

As Mercer et al. (2008) note, PAR is an evolving bundle of research techniques "that include, but are not limited to, participant observer (PO), participatory rural appraisal (PRA), participatory action research (PAR), and participatory innovative development (PID) and are often collectively summarized as participatory approaches (PA) and participatory learning and action (PLA)" (p. 174). Pelling (2007) includes participatory disaster risk assessment (PDRA) in the evolving list of acronyms. All variations have taken on a strong social justice emphasis, arguing that the process of engagement should be empowering to participants. FAO (1999) states that PAR "places emphasis on empowering local people to assume an active role in analyzing their own living conditions, problems, and potentials in order to seek for a change in their situation." Site mapping is central to this framework, because it allows local individuals and working groups to identify resources and vulnerabilities that are deemed critical from their point of view, such as places where medicinal plants grow.

Contextual Advantages of PAR

PAR should be capacity building, which requires a human rights–based approach (Gibson & Wisner, 2016; Ofreneo & Hega, 2016; Pyles, 2015; Scheib & Lykes, 2013). Pyles (2015) notes, "one of the primary objectives of PAR practice is to confront the subtleties of power" (p. 637). Ofreneo and Hega (2016) argue that "PAR is built on an understanding of the particular history, culture, local context, and social relationships embedded in each case" (p. 173); therefore, it needs to have a gender responsive lens. Studies have employed this lens to look at gender minorities, to whom a man-woman binary construct does not apply (Gaillard et al., 2017) and girl-centered community resilience building in South Africa (Forber-Genade & van Niekerk, 2019).

Scholars (Cadag & Gaillard, 2012; Johnson, Needelman, & Paolisso, 2017; Maldonado et al., 2017) find that this form of research can improve collaboration between stakeholders, including local communities, government authorities, NGOs, tribal or indigenous leadership and collaboratives, faith-based organizations and groups, scientists (practitioners and academics), advocacy groups, and schools. Cadag and Gaillard (2012) state that "local knowledge is invaluable for understanding historical hazard events" (p. 100). They employ a 3D mapping project, using colored pushpins, yarns, and other materials, which is housed at the center of the community for all to access. It is easily updated and usable by those with a range of literacy levels. This broadens opportunities for participation, contributions, and utilization.

Mercer et al. (2008) note that "use of participatory techniques increased the space for indigenous communities to express and control the knowledge identified" (p. 175). As a result, there has been a strong movement to recognize traditional ecological knowledge (TEK) and actively include it and value it as part of participatory action research, especially within disaster and climate change studies (Finn, Herne, & Castille, 2017; Laska et al., 2015; Maldonado, Naquin, Dardar, Parfait-Dardar, & Bagwell, 2015; Maldonado et al., 2017; Mercer, Kelman, Taranis, & Suchet-Pearson, 2010). TEK refers to a specific subset of indigenous knowledge that elucidates the strong interconnection of humans and the environment. This knowledge is preserved and transmitted through oral tradition in the form of songs, jokes, stories, folklore, and cautionary tales. It is also conveyed through material cultural expressions, such as arts and crafts, and non-material forms, including ceremonies, rituals, and dance. The cultivation, collection, and preparation of traditional foods and medicines are intimately intertwined with oral tradition and material and non-material cultural expression. TEK and site mapping have been combined to engage in the invigoration of harvesting and use and preservation of medicinal, traditional, and ceremonial plant resources, as will be discussed below.

Limitations and Critiques of PAR

As wonderfully inclusive and empowering as it sounds, PAR is not without significant criticism and limitations. Cadag and Gaillard (2012) note that

> many scientists and government officials often underestimate – if not dismiss – the value of local knowledge and community activities. . . . Such a gap between stakeholders . . . is considered a major obstacle for reducing the risk of disasters in a sustainable manner and on a large scale.
>
> (p. 100)

Pelling (2007) finds that a lack of common definitions and frameworks "opens this field of work to misplaced or exaggerated claims of participation, inclusiveness or . . . empowerment" (p. 375). Mercer et al. (2010, p. 218) argue that

> indigenous knowledge is oppressed in a number of ways as a result of marginalization, exploitation, powerlessness, cultural imperialism, violence and denial of existing knowledge . . . in a society where the scientific culture is dominant . . . indigenous knowledge is hidden and dismissed by the tendency of scientific knowledge to deny the importance of the other.

Thus, as Mercer et al. (2008) note, what is most important is not the technique that is applied, but rather the level of engagement of the participants with the project and with the practitioners involved (p. 174).

Pyles (2015) generates a nuanced hierarchy of project participation to elucidate this problem. At the bottom of the scale is manipulative participation, in which participation is a pretense and participants and community members have no real power (p. 634). Gibson, Hendricks, and Wells (2019) refer to this as tokenism, which includes various levels of placation, consultation with limited input from the community (passive participation), and information gathering, an extractive process whereby community members provide external agents with information.

Emergency managers, policy planners, and agency representatives, including the Army Corps of Engineers, have often been accused of engaging in manipulative participation or tokenism by scholars and community activists. This can be related to a failure to recognize their own positions of privilege and power and/or a lack of political will to truly engage with communities, because it may enhance program complexity and extend project timelines. This reluctance to properly implement PAR can be reinforced as a result of being imbedded in organizational cultures that distance themselves from community-based knowledge, because it is not related to credentialing mechanisms and is therefore deemed as invalid. This reflects Pyles's (2015) critique about agency failures to confront the subtleties of power. Cadag and Gaillard (2012) note that a lack of political will on the part of officials and non-community located stakeholders inhibits the mainstreaming of good practices, such as properly conducted PAR. They note that there are insufficient frameworks and tools that provide space for stakeholders to collaborate (p. 100).

Site mapping can help to redress this problem. Federal agencies or other stakeholders can begin the process by turning to census data to generate a broad understanding of the general demographic characteristics of the overall community, recognizing that these data exclude significant population segments. They can research meso-level or bridging agencies or organizations such as Boys and Girls Clubs, NAACP chapters, Indian Centers, social welfare organizations, churches, and other local NGOs. Reaching out to these organizations begins the process of identifying various components of the target area. Local organizations can broker ties to key community leaders to help further identify important sub-populations. For example, as part of the creation of their five-year emergency management plan, emergency managers in a large county in Florida connected to a small, local Haitian radio station to begin the process of identifying key connections to a community that was not as inclined to interact with government officials. This outreach allowed them to map major population, structural, and resource vulnerabilities and identify trusted community sources through which they could disseminate relevant emergency alerts, updates, and resources. A similar technique was used in Los Angeles. It is important to note that it takes time to properly identify and establish connections to all relevant community stakeholders and partners to ensure more comprehensive participation.

At the top end of the inclusion scale, Pyles (2015) places interactive participation, "where people participate in joint analysis and development of action plan; participation is a right" (p. 634), and self-mobilization, where "local people take initiatives independently of external institutions though they may use external resources; retain control over how resources are used" (p. 634). The site mapping project discussed below exemplifies both interactive participation and self-mobilization.[1]

Community Context and Description

The project discussed here evolved over a two-year period and has been ongoing for over five years. The community that generated the project is a population subset within a medium sized Midwestern city. Because of the relatively small size of the Native American community, a more specific description would render the community as identifiable. As a consequence, it would also be possible to identify the specific individuals that make up this group. This would violate their privacy and professional ethical standards. Thus, from this point forward, in order to speak plainly about the challenges faced and to protect individuals' privacy, the town will be referred to as "City" and the group that generated and engaged in the project as "Community."

City faces numerous challenges from a disaster perspective – it is experiencing rapid population growth in a drought-prone region. Pushed by this growth, building has expanded onto slope areas and into grasslands. Areas that had been able to absorb heavy precipitation have been converted into large housing tracts to accommodate the influx of families. As a result, water channels are being created, altered, or diverted to improve runoff from concrete surfaces, altering historical flood and absorption patterns. Development has also shifted public or traditionally accessed land into private land, eliminating access to resources by destruction, fencing, or blocking rights of way or pilgrimage routes.

Climate change has altered summer and winter precipitation patterns. Summers are hotter and longer, with increasingly erratic to non-existent rainfall, leading to prolonged and more widespread and intense drought patterns. Winters are also warmer, with progressively sporadic snowfall totals. As a result, the area has experienced several large wildfire events, escalating flash flood and debris flow risks in previously unimpacted areas. Changing weather patterns have also brought several destructive summer storms, generating tornadoes and baseball-sized hail. These storms damaged fragile plants and some sacred landscapes and sites. Hail choked waterways and drains, resulting in flooding in numerous areas simultaneously, including urban zones. Linked to these environmental changes, local plant species have died off and been replaced by non-native and invasive species. This too impacts the vulnerability of areas to fires and floods.

Community, which generated the site mapping project, comprises Native Americans and Alaska Natives from around the United States, but it is not dominated by any one tribal group. City has a significant military presence. As a result, service members retired to the area to take advantage of base amenities and medical and GI benefits. In addition, City is only about two hours from a large metropolitan area that was designated as part of the Bureau of Indian Affairs' Termination and Relocation Program in the 1950s, increasing the diversity of tribal affiliations represented locally. It is six to seven hours from other major metropolitan areas that participated in that program. Finally, City is within a day's drive of several large reservations and tribal groups. Many of City's Native Americans fall near or below the poverty line. Education levels range from doctorates to high school dropouts.

Community can best be described as being fraught with dynamic internal divisions. Power relations revolve around length of time residing in City, squabbles between families, participation in certain activities or connections or affiliations with local organizations, government agencies, or individuals, disagreement over what defines "Indianness", tribal affiliations, and clashes over belief systems, including gendered roles, along with a host of other issues. Despite the tremendous heterogeneity of Community, there is a strong willingness to continually reaffirm a pan-indigenous/community identity, especially in the face of threats from outsiders or external circumstances. To counteract divisive forces, Community was consistently seeking opportunities to (re)build social relationships amongst themselves. The site mapping project was prompted by population and climatic pressures, combined with increased hazard exposure on City, the surrounding area, and the local resources.

During conversations at a gathering about traditional foods and their links to cultural and physical survival, individuals noted that many traditional foods that they would gather with family and friends were becoming scarcer. Some resources were impacted by climate/drought. Other growing areas were diminished or eradicated by construction, fire, or changes in runoff patterns and flood zones. Still others were privatized and removed from public access. This was having a significant impact on Community, because some were reliant on gathered resources to supplement limited incomes.

For all, loss of traditional plants or sites represents a palpable threat to cultural survival and physical and spiritual well-being. Youth must be the receptors of traditional knowledge. It cannot be passed down if the resources are not present to be incorporated into oral tradition, ritual, and all aspects of daily life. Loss of connection to tribal identity and culture can leave the young adrift, without the grounding, pride, and sense of belonging that traditions can provide. Community was battling high rates of addiction and suicide. There was widespread belief that engaging youth and elders into identity and cohesion-building activities would help to combat these trends.

As it happens, I was the guest speaker at this event and participated in the discussion. I was asked if I would be willing to act as a neutral facilitator of the discussion and to help with training and implementation of the projects that were eventually agreed upon. I agreed to 2–5 years of engagement in the process, which meant commuting to City at least once a month for 3 days at a time and innumerable phone conversations.

Those present at the event decided to generate a pan-Indian agricultural calendar, which would serve two purposes. The first would be to identify existing traditional food, ceremonial, and medicinal resources, along with spiritual sites when appropriate, using site mapping techniques. Mapping activities would also incorporate ethnographic interviews of elders, family members, and other members of Community to catalog positions of lost resource sites and to add additional resources to the search list. This mapping process would allow for the classification of threats to remaining identified resources and to prioritize action items, such as digging up certain plants and moving them to greenhouses for preservation and replication, where possible.

The second was to build interpersonal ties and capacities by developing harvesting, production, and feasting events around the agricultural calendar. Participants viewed the site mapping and agricultural calendar project as a way to learn about how other tribes and families used certain resources. The primary aspirational goal was to learn about commonalities to foster stronger interpersonal ties and reduce infighting. The secondary aspirational goal was to learn new things about other cultures and families by engaging in cultural and educational exchanges. The tertiary goal was to improve integration of elders and establish stronger ties between youth and elders.

Methodological Approach and Project Evolution

The project had many phases, one of which was site mapping. As noted above, PAR includes a variety of research methodologies and applied techniques. The genesis of the project began at a unique event (an invited guest speaker on a topic of local interest and importance) combined with a feast, so Community attendance was three times that of a normal monthly event. Community had its own regular meeting space. Special events were held periodically, including performances, holiday events, emergency gatherings due to a death or crisis, or themed feasts, through which the author was recruited into this project. Potluck dinners/Community meetings were held once a month. Potlucks are important regular events in many Native communities, providing opportunities for socializing, meeting new people, and reinforcing coherence. The act of bringing even a small amount of food to share allows for greater inclusion of those with the most limited resources and provides a leveling of social and economic differences, as does sitting at large, shared round tables. It also facilitates educational exchanges, as many will bring traditional foods in their families or from their cultures. In Community, dinners were combined with meetings to provide a regularized space to discuss challenges, opportunities, make announcements, and share good or bad news.

Events were advertised on websites, Facebook, in the Community newsletter (mailed and emailed), and in the local newspaper. In addition, phone trees, email lists, and personal contact chains were used to contact individuals to promote attendance at such events to improve the number of voices and perspectives represented in discussions. Volunteers coordinated transportation for individuals who needed assistance to improve participation of the elderly, disabled, and those who were severely poor and would not have otherwise had the resources to attend.

Phase I – Developing a Project Together

Consistent with PAR ideals, this project was community generated through open forum discussions about threats to cultural and spiritual resources as a result of local disasters and climate change. In this initial meeting, Community, with the prompting of the author, identified local stakeholders who could contribute resources (e.g., physical maps, books of local plants, notebooks, compasses) and skills (e.g., ethnographic methodology, how to identify GPS coordinates, how to plot them on Google maps) to the project. Connections were generated to local educational institutions, urban planning and emergency management administrations, federal and state agency personnel (e.g., forest rangers, Bureau of Land Management [BLM] and National Oceanic and Atmospheric Administration [NOAA] personnel, and permitting agents), organizations (e.g., master gardeners' organizations, philanthropic organizations, social justice NGOs), and local clubs (e.g., geocaching, hiking, botany). Community then identified the priorities for this project, the ideal goals of the project, and specific tangible outcomes. This mirrors Mercer et al.'s (2010) stated framework for integrating indigenous and scientific knowledge.

A second community meeting and potluck was organized for the following month. As noted above, the potlucks were regularly scheduled events that were always followed by discussions, so it was easy for the project to piggyback on regularized participation and to forgo the time and resource burden and participation defection that might be associated with scheduling a separate meeting. After the meal, participants were broken down into tables. Each table was provided with calendars. Storytelling techniques, prompted by the author/facilitator, were used to generate a discussion of what local resources were being harvested and actively used by those at the table. Tables presented their findings to the room to generate discussion and prompt other ideas. All table calendars were compiled in the week that followed to start creating a master calendar and initial list of resources.

Site mapping was the next step. Site mapping is a technique that allows individuals and teams to generate a product that can be evaluated by all interested parties to ensure that it is representative of the desired project objectives. It can be modified with new information and continually updated. From a PAR perspective, site mapping allows for not only the creation of the map but also for the creation of action items in the next phase. Cadag and Gaillard's study (2012) demonstrates this effectiveness. Their study community generated a map of hazard prone areas, which was then overlaid with existing scientific data and information from local officials to enhance overall understanding of local vulnerability. Based on that map, the community designed specific activities focused on preparedness, warning, and evacuation. For example, different activities would be triggered based on changes in water level in the local river (p. 106). Community followed a similar procedure with their project.

Concurrent with site mapping activities were ethnographic interviews of elders, family members, and other members of Community. The author worked with Community to start creating prompting questions to get conversations started and to ensure that specific data points were addressed. Using snowball sampling and a variety of networks, Community youth and others were dispatched with maps and books of plants as prompts to interview long-time area residents and elders, which contributes to the fulfillment of the community connection and integration goal. Data gathered from these interviews were added into the agricultural calendar and to the list of species to be mapped. Through formal and informal Community-based networks, hikers, fishermen, hunters, those making targeted trips to gather these resources, and others started to compile their own maps. Physical maps, drawings, photos, story-based descriptions, and GPS location data and mapping software were used to note resources. The multiple forms of data collection and presentation allowed Community members to present and interpret data from their own personal and tribal cultural perspectives. This improved project participation and retention rates and fostered the incorporation of a broader range of perspectives.

At each monthly potluck, participants would submit their data. After the meal, storytelling formats were used to discuss what was found, not found/destroyed, or threatened and where. Multiple accounts over time were used to verify resource locations and proper identification of plants. Students working with local teachers and faculty compiled the monthly submissions into booklets of maps, pictures, and descriptions and online maps for those wishing to utilize different technologies. These resources were to be distributed at the annual year-end holiday celebration and by drop-off to those who could not attend. The process was to be repeated annually to ensure that results were corroborated, new resources incorporated, and losses and threats were recorded. At the time of this writing, 4 years of data has been compiled and distributed and a fifth was underway.

Map coordinators, local faculty, and designated Community leaders met with local emergency managers, urban planners, geographers, and state and federal agents multiple times over the course of the first 2 years, and periodically thereafter. These experts provided insights into vulnerable areas, based on previous events and computer predictions about various impacts that might result from building and other housing expansion plans, a new and catastrophic fire event, and other changes. These maps were combined to create a disaster threat assessment of local cultural, physical, and spiritual resources. Community spent months, while the aforementioned activities were ongoing, engaging in a form of cultural triage. They were working to come to consensus about which resources were deemed most threatened and most vital and to develop action plans to prepare for disaster scenarios, which included prolonged drought, fire, landslides, flash flooding with debris flow particularly near the burn scars, flooding, tornadoes, damaging hail, and urban development/privatization.

Phase II – Converting Site Maps Into Action Items and Institutional Bridges

Site mapping and overlaying scientific hazard risk assessment maps and urban planning projections onto master maps were ongoing projects. While these activities were occurring, the next step was for Community to implement the action items identified in the first months of the project. These include plans for moving certain vulnerable plants to less vulnerable locations for preservation, access, and replication. To achieve this, partnerships with master gardeners, local schools and campuses via the Title VII (Indian, Native Hawaiian, and Alaska Native Education) Program,[2] and gardening clubs had to be established to identify accessible and safer spaces to move plants, strategies for ensuring that they thrived, and advice on replication and generation of resources needed to accomplish the program.

The presentation of site maps with hazard overlays provided local experts and other stakeholders with tangible evidence of threats to resources, facilitating bridging efforts. Organizations were more willing to have meetings and engage in productive dialogue when told they would be presented with scientifically validated data. One result of bridging activities was the creation of greenhouse gardens at three schools across several school districts. Teachers worked with representatives from Title VII, volunteer master gardeners, a botanist, a geographer, and a sociologist (me) to find creative ways to incorporate the gardens and their contents into curriculum for all students. The traditional plant gardens were incorporated into English, art, biology/science, geography, history, nutritional/health, and social studies classes in culturally sensitive and affirming ways. Gardens were also created on college campuses. Students and faculty members of Community worked together to link the campus gardens to broader networks of student clubs and into classroom curriculum across multiple disciplines and programs.

This phase also involved partnering with city, state, and federal officials to identify ownership of land on which the most vulnerable resources were located and obtaining permission to remove plants or to create disaster plans to protect certain resources. Again, the site maps with hazards overlays provided a strong incentive for officials to engage in dialogue. They provided scientific validity for claims of threats, combined with a rationale of community need. For resources that could not be moved, such as sacred sites, landscapes, or trees, Community had to decide how much information would be shared with non-Native people, a frequently contentious process without complete resolution. Those resources that could be agreed upon were presented to the relevant authorities/agencies to initiate hazard mitigation plans (Phase III).

The second action item for Phase II was to create specific events to bring Community together and foster the better integration of youth and elders. Site maps and the agricultural calendar were used to identify opportunities for a traditional harvest. A large stand of greenthread (*Thelesperma megapotamicum*) was selected as the object of the first Community harvest. Greenthread is also known as Indian tea, Hopi tea, and Navajo tea. It has medicinal properties and is a traditional-use plant for numerous tribes. It has recently become a popular staple in the natural wellness movement. However, processed and packaged (and pricey) variations are sold at harder-to-reach specialty stores, such as Whole Foods Markets and Natural Grocers. Culturally and spiritually, there are concerns about relying on store-bought resources, because the appropriate harvesting and handling practices, including rituals and songs, are not likely to have occurred. This renders the final product potentially more spiritually and culturally harmful than physically helpful.

Elders were brought in to do the blessings. Youth did much of the labor, given the physical limitations of many of the elders. Community members were taught how to properly and respectfully harvest and bundle the greenthread. Through a bridging opportunity with the Department of Corrections, incarcerated Native American youth who were participating in a cultural treatment/rehabilitation program were bused in to participate as well, to improve their engagement with cultural practices and other Native American people in the area. Gathered and bundled resources were distributed to elders and other members of Community who were not able to participate. Over 50 people participated in this event (excluding Department of Corrections officers) and over 100 received resources from the harvest. Based on this success, harvests for each season of the agricultural calendar were carried out over the next year.

Lessons Learned and Future Plans

The site mapping project was a community generated and implemented project, fulfilling the premise and promise of participatory action research. It integrated TEK and cultural traditions with data provided by the local scientific community, providing a strong voice from a traditionally marginalized group. The data generated a list of vulnerable resources that are at high risk of damage or destruction from an array of hazards. This enabled Community to approach local emergency managers, disaster policymakers, and urban planners with scientifically validated findings, increasing the likelihood of meetings and improving the receptiveness of typically technocratic personalities to the issues being raised. Through these meetings, Community was able to point out gaps in disaster strategies and initiatives, such as not incorporating the specific needs of Native people into local disaster risk reduction and response plans, and concerns with development proposals.

The process of establishing the hazard map provided the opportunity for Community members to utilize their networks to create bridges to important institutions, organizations, and key figures in the broader local population. Through engagement in this project, Community also generated a social map (Gibson et al., 2019), which increased access to key local figures. Community felt that this increased their presence and voice in local politics, noting that they were invited to participate in certain City Council planning meetings and to provide comments at disaster policy forums, from which they had previously been excluded. Community perceived these invitations as evidence of a more respected standing in the region that they hoped would grow into greater opportunities for inclusion and partnerships. While these invitations have not yet resulted in specific plans to protect sites or resources within emergency planning and disaster response documents (ideal Phase III), Community is hopeful that continued pressure to enact such changes will eventually garner results.

With each step of the process and each new iteration of the site maps, Community members generated tangible products that are collectively owned and incorporate an array of voices and priorities. Beyond the maps and agricultural calendars, there are now seven established gardens. Schools are working with Title VII coordinators and local affiliates to continue to create curriculum and events around the gardens that bring students, educators, Community, and local residents together in cultural and educational exchanges.

Community strategized an ideal Phase III: the establishment of a Native American Center for Sustainability and Education to be housed on a local campus. Collaborating with local faculty affiliates from a variety of disciplines, elders and selected members of Community developed a project plan, mission statement, resource inventory based on the social maps, and an impact statement. Community is actively searching for sites for this center, which would integrate elder knowledge, facilitate cultural knowledge transmission, and have its own garden.

Conclusion

Despite formal inclusion in disaster policies and response strategies not having materialized yet, Community is hopeful that it will. Community members feel empowered and mobilized to participate in City Council meetings. Information from those meetings are reported at the potlucks, invigorating discussion and additional strategizing. New action items are generated from these potlucks, and continued pressure is placed on organizations, agencies, and key individuals to incorporate Native American priorities into disaster mitigation and response plans.

While the results have not been perfect, this case study demonstrates the potential for greater inclusion of traditionally marginalized groups in participatory action research. Community and the amount of progress they have achieved exemplifies Pyles's (2015) ideal levels of participation – interactive participation and self-mobilization.

This project provides an additional validation of site mapping as a viable, powerful, inclusive methodology. Iterations of mapping, discussion, and validation created a vehicle for the integration of TEK, local resources knowledge, and scientific hazard data. The marriage of these data streams has provided agency officials with incentives to engage with Community, because they perceive the data presented as properly corroborated. The product of this integration is continuing to evolve as new data emerges and are incorporated, compelling Community advocates to continue to engage emergency management and other local officials.

Notes

1. The newest form of projects labeled as PAR is "citizen science" research. This research, while able to generate large data sets, does not fit with FAO's (1999) definition of PAR, because it does not emphasize representation of all community sectors. Grace-McCaskey, Iatarola, Manda, and Etheridge (2019) note that, in the United States, many of the citizen scientists are white, older, retired, affluent, and well educated (p. 1125). Their research highlights the fact that, contrary to the social justice aims of participatory action research, "socioeconomic barriers and lack of access to transportation affect the diversity of participants" (p. 1133). Despite this critique, Gibson, Hendricks, and Wells (2019) were able to successfully mobilize lower income, African American communities to engage in a heritage resource/site mapping project to identify local resources and how they were used and perceived (cultural, social, and historical importance).
2. The No Child Left Behind Act of 2001 (Public Law 107–110), Title VII – Indian, Native Hawaiian, and Alaska Native Education, Parts A, B, and C, to "support the efforts of local

educational agencies, Indian tribes and organizations . . . to meet the unique educational and culturally related academic needs of American Indian and Alaska Native students."

Further Readings

Chari, R., Sayers, E. L. P., Amiri, S., Leinhos, M., Kotzias, V., Madrigano, J., . . . Uscher-Pines, L. (2019). Enhancing community preparedness: An inventory and analysis of disaster citizen science activities. *BMC Public Health, 19*, 1356.

Laska, S., & Companion, M. (2021). The social justice issues of the climate change conditions that "never happened before." In A. Jerolleman & W. A. Waugh (Eds.), *Justice, equity and emergency management, community, environment and disaster risk management* series (Vol. 23). Bingley: Emerald Group.

Maldonado, J. (2016). Considering culture in disaster practice. *Annals of Anthropological Practice, 40*(1), 52–60.

Shaw, R. (2014). Typhoon, flood, and landslide related disasters in Japan: Role of communities. In, R. Shaw (Ed.), *Community practices for disaster risk reduction in Japan* (pp. 33–47). New York: Springer.

Strasser, B.J., Baudry, J., Mahr, D., Sanchez, G., & Tancoigne, E. (2019). "Citizen science?" Rethinking science and public participation. *Science and Technology, 32*(2), 52–76.

References

Cadag, J. R. D., & J. Gaillard, C. (2012). Integrating knowledge and actions in disaster risk reduction: The contribution of participatory mapping. *Area, 44*(1), 100–109.

Cernea, M. (1985). *Putting people first: Sociological variables in rural development.* Oxford: Oxford University Press.

Chambers, R. (1994). The origins and practice of participatory rural appraisal. *World Development, 22*, 953–969.

Companion, M. (2015). *Disaster's impact on livelihood and cultural survival: Losses, opportunities, and mitigation.* Boca Raton, FL: CRC Press.

Companion, M., & Chaiken, M.S. (2016). *Responses to disasters and climate change: Understanding vulnerability and fostering resilience.* Boca Raton, FL: CRC Press.

Enarson, E.P., & Morrow, B.H. (1998). *The gendered terrain of disaster: Through women's eyes.* Westport. CT: Praeger.

FAO (Food and Agricultural Organization of the United Nations). (1999). *Conducting a PRA training and modifying PRA tools to your needs: An example from a participatory household food security and nutrition project in Ethiopia.* Addis Ababa, Ethiopia: Food and Agricultural Organization of the United Nations, Economic and Social Development Department.

Finn, S., Herne, M., & Castille, D. (2017, August 20). The value of traditional ecological knowledge for the environmental health sciences and biomedical research. *Environmental Health Perspectives, 125*(8), 085006.

Forber-Genade, K., & van Niekerk, D. (2019). GIRRL power! Participatory action research for building girl-led community resilience in South Africa. *Action Research, 17*(2), 237–257.

Gaillard, J.C., Sanz, K., Blagos, B.C., Dalisay, S. N. M., Gorman-Murray, A., Smith, F., & Toelupe, V. (2017). Beyond men and women: A critical perspective on gender and disaster. *Disasters, 41*(3), 429–447.

Gibson, J., Hendricks, M.D., & Wells, J.C. (2019). From engagement to empowerment: How heritage professionals can incorporate participatory methods in disaster recovery to better serve socially vulnerable groups. *International Journal of Heritage Studies, 25*(6), 596–610.

Gibson, T., & Wisner, B. (2016). "Let's talk about you . . ." Opening space for local experience, action and learning in disaster risk reduction. *Disaster Prevention and Management, 25*(5), 664–684.

Grace-McCaskey, C. A., Iatarola, B., Manda, A. K., & Etheridge, J. R. (2019). Eco-ethnography and citizen science: Lessons from within. *Society and Natural Resources, 32*(10), 1123–1138.

Haynes, K., & Tanner, T. M. (2015). Empowering young people and strengthening resilience: Youth-centered participatory video as a tool for climate change adaptation and disaster reduction. *Children's Geographies, 13*(3), 357–371.

Henderson, T. L., Shigeto, A., Ponzetti, J. J., Jr., Edwards, A. B., Stanley, J., & Story, C. (2017). A cultural-variant approach to community-based participatory research: New ideas for family professionals. *Family Relations, 66,* 629–643.

Johnson, K. J., Needelman, B. A., & Paolisso, M. (2017). Vulnerability and resilience to climate change in a rural coastal community. In M. Companion & M. S. Chaiken (Eds.), *Responses to disasters and climate change: Understanding vulnerability and fostering resilience* (pp. 4–14). Boca Raton, FL: CRC Press.

Lambert, S. (2015). Indigenous communities and disaster research: Maori and the Christchurch earthquakes of 2010–2011. *Third Sector Review, 21*(2), 31–48.

Laska, S., Peterson, K., Rodrigue, C. L., Cosse', T., Phillipe, R., Burchette, O., & Krajeski, R. L. (2015). Layering of natural and human-caused disasters in the context of sea level rise: Coastal Louisiana communities at the edge. In M. Companion (Ed.), *Disaster's impact on livelihood and cultural survival: Losses, opportunities, and mitigation* (pp. 225–238). Boca Raton, FL: CRC Press.

Maldonado, J. K., Lazrus, H., Bennett, S. K., Chief, K., Dhillon, C. M., Gough, B., . . . Whyte, K. P. (2017). The story of rising voices: Facilitating collaboration between Indigenous and Western ways of knowing. In M. Companion & M. S. Chaiken (Eds.), *Responses to disasters and climate change: Understanding vulnerability and fostering resilience* (pp. 15–25). Boca Raton, FL: CRC Press.

Maldonado, J. K., Naquin, A. P., Dardar, T., Parfait-Dardar, S., & B. Bagwell. (2015). Above the rising tide: Tribes in coastal Louisiana apply local strategies and knowledge to adapt to rapid environmental change. In M. Companion (Ed.), *Disaster's impact on livelihood and cultural survival: Losses, opportunities, and mitigation* (pp. 239–253). Boca Raton, FL: CRC Press.

Marchezini, V., & Trajber, R. (2017). Youth-based leaning in disaster risk reduction education: Barriers and bridges to promote resilience. In M. Companion & M. S. Chaiken (Eds.), *Responses to disasters and climate change: Understanding vulnerability and fostering resilience* (pp. 27–36). Boca Raton, FL: CRC Press.

Mercer, J., Kelman, I., Lloyd, K., & Suchet-Pearson, S. (2008). Reflections on use of participatory research disaster risk reduction. *Area, 40*(2), 172–183.

Mercer, J., Kelman, I., Taranis, L., & Suchet-Pearson, S. (2010). Framework for integrating indigenous and scientific knowledge for disaster risk reduction. *Disasters, 34*(1), 214–239.

Morrow, B. H. (1999). Identifying and mapping community vulnerability. *Disasters, 23*(1), 1–18.

Ofreneo, R. P., & Hega, M. D. (2016). Women's solidarity economy initiatives to strengthen food security in response to disasters: Insights from two Philippine case studies. *Disaster Prevention and Management, 25*(2), 168–182.

Pelling, M. (2007). Learning from others: The scope and challenges for participatory disaster risk assessment. *Disasters, 31*(4), 373–385.

Pyles, L. (2015). Participation and other ethical considerations in participatory action research in post-earthquake Haiti. *International Social Work, 58*(5), 628–645.

Scheib, H. A., & Lykes, M. B. (2013). African American and Latina community health workers engage PhotoPar as a resource in a post-disaster context: Katrina at 5 years. *Journal of Health Psychology, 18*(8), 1069–1084.

Trajber, R., Walker, C., Marchezini, V., Kraftl, P., Olicato, D., Hadfield-Hill, S., Zara, C., & Montiero, S. F. (2019). Promoting climate change transformation with young people in Brazil: Participatory action research through a looping approach. *Action Research, 17*(1), 87–107.

9

Language-based Theories and Methods in Emergency and Disaster Management

Claire Connolly Knox

Introduction

A search of language-based or narrative theory and emergency management results in fewer scholarly articles compared to public administration, planning, and policy. This is not surprising, considering the emergency and disaster management discipline is relatively new and derives its interdisciplinary foundation from related disciplines including (but not limited to) public administration, sociology, policy, political science, business management, communications, and public health. For the purposes of this chapter, I will focus the discussion to those theories derived from the public administration, planning, and policy disciplines.

Many researchers have argued for an alternative, interpretive approach to policy analysis (Fischer, 1990; Schneider & Ingram, 1997; Stone, 2002; Yanow, 1993, 1996). Building from Weber's critique, this approach "challenges the presumed objectivity of the policy sciences" and shifts the analysis focus to the "meanings that different persons bring to the policy process, the arguments used to legitimate policies, and the hidden assumptions or implications of the policy" (Schneider & Ingram, 1997, p. 37). Studying the policy process with an interpretative approach, especially in an emergency or crisis context, is "critical to understanding which proposed solution reach[es] the agenda and with what effect" (Birkland, 1997, p. 15). An interpretive analysis is important to identify narratives, gaps, and trends, and to provide alternative explanations for policy change and implementation outcomes.

These theories and frameworks are primarily from the post-positivist perspective. As discussed in Chapter 4, post-positivists value the inclusion of narratives while analyzing policies, plans, and institutions (i.e., Fischer, 2003; Knox, 2013). Unique to this group of theories is how they have embraced Lasswell's (1951) normative approach to policy studies or a voice for democracy in the policy sciences. While there are language-based theoretical frameworks in the positivist perspective (e.g., Narrative Policy Framework [Jones & McBeth, 2010; Shanahan, Jones, & McBeth, 2011]), this chapter will focus on the post-positivist approaches using qualitative methods. Commonly used language-based theoretical frameworks, scholars, and perspectives in public administration and policy are provided in Table 9.1.

TABLE 9.1 Language-Based Theories and Frameworks

Theory/Theoretical Framework	Scholar(s)
Social construction framework	Schneider and Ingram (1997); Stone (2002)
Critical theory	Habermas (1975); Marcus (1964)
Critical race theory	Ladson-Billings (1998); Tate (1997); Winant (2000)
Post-structuralism/postmodernism	Foucault (1983); Derrida (1972)

This chapter highlights two of these theories – social construction and critical theory – which are concerned with the discourse, rhetoric, and story lines in the policy-making and implementation processes. The social construction framework builds upon Karl Mannheim's idea that there is "no 'single' view of reality, that social science has to be an 'interpretative' science to be useful and insightful" (Ingram, Schneider, & deLeon, 2007, p. 94). Theorists in this framework view policy issues as both symbolic and substantive, and presume that they can be constructed in different ways. Some constructions are in competition with each other to convey a story or myth about why it is a problem to begin with, who is advantaged or disadvantaged by the problem, who is at fault, and how the problem can be solved (Birkland, 1997; Schneider & Ingram, 1993; Stone, 2002; Yanow, 1992, 1996). For example, is an individual directly impacted by a disaster or crisis a "victim" or a "survivor"? Why does this matter? Research from a social constructionist framework concludes that how the individual's story is framed in the news media can impact response efforts, institutional and policy decisions, and access to recovery programs (Davis & French, 2008). It can also impact the dominant discourse used by elected officials and decision makers to justify which group of individuals is or is not deserving of public assistance and resources (Blessett, 2015).

Critical theorists (e.g., Adorno, Horkheimer, Marcuse, Habermas, and Offe) have roots in the Frankfurt School and provide a traditional, German ideological critique of contemporary society. These critiques of ideas or theories were not conducted using previously conceived values or conceptions but on their own accord, thereby bringing to light the underlying untruths. Their critiques were some of the first to cross disciplinary boundaries and provide new perspectives on religion, morality, reason, science, and rationality. By blending the disciplines, these theorists went against the increasingly popular specialized academic domains approach (Finlayson, 2005). These theorists were heavily influenced by the events of World War II, the rise and fall of Nazism, the writings of Marx, the failure of the communist movement in Germany, and the American "cultural industry" (Finlayson, 2005; Alvesson & Deetz, 1999). Central to critical theory is the Weberian notion of rationalizing the processes of modern society. The goal was "not just to determine what was wrong with contemporary society at present, but, by identifying progressive aspects and tendencies within it, to help transform society for the better" (Finlayson, 2005, p. 4). Human emancipation is a central theme for critical theorists, and they draw on Weber's notion of not only transforming society but also doing so with empowered individuals. Like the social construction framework, Habermas (1975) believes that political actors use various symbols, ideologies, and language to engage the public.

Regardless of the theoretical framework, analyzing language includes several methodological approaches: quantitative, qualitative, and mixed methods. From a qualitative approach, a researcher can select from more than 20 methods (Brower,

Abolafia, & Carr, 2000). Some of these include in-depth interviews (e.g., structured, semi-structured, non-structured; see Chapter 6), focus groups (see Chapter 7), observations (see Chapter 11), and content analysis (see Chapter 12). This chapter focuses on qualitative methods, primarily the coding of documents including plans, policies, reports, and interviews. Before providing examples of coding analysis, we will discuss multiple advantages and challenges of applying a qualitative methodological approach to language-based data below.

Advantages of Language-based Theory

Advantages of applying a language-based theory allows the researcher to better understand the policy problem, administrative dilemma, competing rhetoric, and social context (Fischer, 2003). This analysis is important to identify narratives, gaps, and trends, as well as to provide alternative explanations for policy change and implementation outcomes. Theorists, especially critical theorists, question the epistemological notion of instrumental rationality and offer communicative rationality as the alternative (Eriksen & Weigård, 2003). They also assume that government and its public policies are part of the problem because they are included in the "institutional structures of society that have created and maintained systems of privilege, domination, and quiescence among those who are the most oppressed . . . rather than as a potentially positive means for reducing domination and oppression" (Schneider & Ingram, 1997, p. 53).

As discussed earlier, qualitative methods provide the context behind the numbers/data in quantitative analysis. It allows the researcher to ask the "how" and "why" questions often missing from data. Additionally, positivist scholars and quantitative scholars overlook outliers or anomalies – important points of data that fall either before or after the normative curve – which blind them to important nuisances of government activities. These include communication blockages, contradictions between speech and action, legitimation and motivation problems, and rationality failures (Knox, 2010). These disregarded data points often provide the qualitative researcher with alternative explanations, variations of a theory, or alternate research questions that should be explored further (Corbin & Strauss, 2015).

Advantages of applying this methodological approach are that the data – policies, after action reports, newspaper articles, and so forth – are available for free and usually easily accessible via an organization's website. The vast majority are available under the Freedom of Information Act (FOIA) or a state's sunshine law (e.g., Florida) request. As such, if the research is only using public records and documents, they do not need to apply for approval from the institutional review board (IRB; see Chapter 1).

Finally, specific to plan evaluation and analysis, this methodology provides a systematic and valid approach to coding and analyzing emergency management plans and reports within and across jurisdictions and disasters. Davies and colleagues (2018) systematically reviewed 24 articles and reports published between 2000 and 2015 in which scholars were analyzing after action reports; they found variation in the qualitative methods, which calls into question the validity of the studies. Therefore, this methodological approach has been validated by the urban and regional planning literature and is a better option for emergency and crisis management researchers.

Challenges of Language-based Theories

Challenges of applying language-based theories primarily stem from engaging with individuals for research, such as interviews and focus groups. Depending on the university, the IRB process can be lengthy with delays. This is problematic for disaster researchers who need to interview individuals quickly – whether it be community members, first responders, response personnel, or others. If this is the case, contact your organization's IRB representative regarding a request for a quick or expedited review to enter the field.

Another challenge is the lack of documents to analyze. For example, after action reports are required following any exercise as per the Homeland Security Exercise and Evaluation Program (HSEEP). However, they are not required following an emergency or disaster. Across the United States and throughout the world, many local jurisdictions do not have the capacity to facilitate or contract with an external organization to complete a "hot wash," which forms the basis of an after action report. In fact, some jurisdictions do not have the capacity to respond to the event/incident. Therefore, the lack of details following a disaster, especially at the local jurisdiction level, can be a limitation to the research.

Another challenge is potential bias indicative to qualitative methods more generally. Qualitative researchers recognize themselves in the analysis because of their interaction with the interviewees and view subjectivity in the social sciences as unavoidable. Alternatively, quantitative researchers attempt to remain objective and "detached from their research participants to avoid having the participants react to their presence" (Brower et al., 2000, p. 366). Therefore, it is important to include inductive and deductive coding techniques when completing an analysis because qualitative researchers acknowledge that relationships and concepts are data driven. Specifically, the researcher's bias can distort the meaning of the analysis (Corbin & Strauss, 2015). As discussed in the following section, the use of coding techniques is a marked difference between qualitative and quantitative researchers.[1]

Despite the general criticisms of qualitative methods, regardless of which method a scholar uses, there will be limitations. As such, it is crucial that any manuscript, report, or policy white paper stemming from research includes a limitations section (ideally at the end of the document or within the methods section).

Reducing Bias and Increasing Credibility

Of the ways to reduce bias and increase credibility (often viewed as validity by positivists), this chapter focuses on three commonly used approaches: triangulation, member checking, and testing for intercoder reliability. First, as discussed in Chapter 4, triangulation is one of the few approaches approved and used by positivist and post-positivist methodologists (Yanow & Schwartz-Shea, 2006). With this technique, the researcher blends at least three types or sources of data for analysis (e.g., observations, interviews, survey questions, documents, archival records, quantitative data, multiple coders or field team members) to confirm a concept in the analysis. For example, when coding transcripts from interviews about Everglades restoration plans, a theme from multiple interviews was "usual suspects," which evolved to "dominant versus minor coalitions of stakeholders." To confirm, I reviewed every related local and state committee meeting roster (for this policy as well as previously related policy meetings), speaker cards from local public meetings, recoded previous interviews for discussion of stakeholders, and asked a related follow-up question of each interviewee. The power struggle between the coalition groups played an important role in the passage of the legislation in question and led me (as a non-native Floridian) to adequately capture the coalitions and power dynamics. An interesting by-product of this triangulation process was the ability to document the evolution of these coalitions in the Everglades policy arena (Knox, 2013).

The second is to have one or more experts in the field review and provide feedback on the analysis and findings. This is called member/informant checking. It is an important tool for the researcher to help identify any interpretive or observational errors, especially since "data" and "facts" are contextual and socially embedded (Loftland, Snow, Anderson, & Loftland, 2006). This can be helpful when the researcher is studying or analyzing an incident after the fact, which can often happen in emergency and crisis research. The researcher needs to place observations and/or interviews with disaster survivors in the situational context that they did not personally experience.

For another example, if a researcher is originally from one state, region, or country and they are studying a phenomenon in a different location, then they have the potential to not understand local customs. Therefore, they run the risk of biasing the analysis. The researcher could have one or more local experts review the analysis for any bias or credibility issues. A specific example is a researcher from Florida analyzing the response to a hurricane in Louisiana. It is safe to assume that they will know what to anticipate regarding preparing and responding to a hurricane, since both states experience them on a frequent basis, and that they will know federal policies that apply to all states. However, there are cultural, social, legal, and political differences that the researcher needs to account for when completing an analysis of observations, interviews, after action reports, newspaper articles, and so forth. These can include (but are not limited to) parishes instead of counties, Napoleonic law, not requiring local jurisdictions to have a comprehensive emergency management plan or designated emergency manager, the role of religion, and so forth. These might seem like minor differences, but they can have large implications to the results of an analysis. It is these contextual nuances that provide the rich details in a qualitative analysis and set it apart from quantitative analysis.

Finally, have at least one other trained person code the materials with the researcher. It is important the researcher trains the coders in coding methodology. As discussed later in this chapter, memoing is an important component to the coding process. These memos allow the team to discuss sections of the text that were difficult to code, address conflicting codes, request clarification of a code, and so forth.

Once the coders are trained, the researcher has two choices: (1) have each coder independently code all of the plans or reports (known as double coding) or (2) have one coder code half of the plans while the other coder completes the second half. The latter option is beneficial when there are many plans, policies, or other documents to code in a short amount of time. For example, in Jacques and Knox's (2016) analysis of climate change denial narratives during Hurricane Sandy, we split the 360 tweets between two coders after they reached the intercoder reliability threshold. Either way, the researcher needs to complete a quality check in which the team members independently code 10% of the text and test for intercoder reliability (discussed later in this chapter). Once the coding analysis has met the threshold (generally 80%), the research can select which option the team will take. Additionally, the research team needs to meet regularly to review coding and memoing issues.

Coding Analysis

Coding analysis is one type of qualitative analysis frequently completed on interview transcripts, plans, policies, reports, newspaper articles, historical documents, and other documents. While on the surface, the reduction of language into categories and codes seems like a quantification of the "data," it is the process by which the researcher creates the categories, codes, code book, and memos that makes this process qualitative (Yanow & Schwartz–Shea, 2006). This section breaks down the steps required for completing a code analysis, including creating and updating a code book, memoing, coding, testing for intercoder reliability, and reporting the results and research limitations.

The Code Book

An essential component of coding for qualitative analysis is creating a detailed code book. This is where inductive and deductive approaches come into play. After extensively reviewing the literature related to the phenomenon the researcher is studying, they will create a code book. This becomes even more important when using another coder or team of coders for consistency; they need to have the same definition for the terms/concepts found in the documents. As seen in the example below, the code book not only includes the definition but also related words to the concept (see Table 9.2). This is important because individuals or organizations in different communities may refer to a concept differently. The researcher or research team does not want to miss that concept in the community's documents.

As previously discussed, member checking is an important tool when finalizing the code book. Therefore, in the research exemplified in Table 9.2, it is invaluable that the city and county's planning and emergency management staff reviewed the indicators and provide feedback unique to that jurisdiction prior to the research team starting to code the documents.

To be clear, the code book is a living document that is reviewed and updated throughout the coding process. The content evolves as the research team codes the documents, which is why memoing, discussed below, is crucial. New indicators

TABLE 9.2 Example Code Book

Factual Basis Component Indicators	Factual Basis Component Details
Coastal zone boundary and maps	Location-based disaster risk information, GIS maps
Disaster vulnerable areas	Risk or hazard information/details specific to their county pre- and post-disaster
Identification of vulnerable populations	Elderly (65 and older), unregistered/undocumented individuals, low socioeconomic status, minorities, medically assisted individuals, prisoners, children
Critical facilities and services	Hospitals, fire stations, city hall/government buildings, police stations, emergency operations center
Critical infrastructure	Wastewater treatment system, power grid, water purification system, roads, levees, dikes, seawalls, 911 system, communications system

derived from the coded documents are added to the code book (i.e., inductive approach). Once the code book is updated, the research team will need to recode the impacted section(s) of the document.

Memoing

An essential element to coding, especially when there are multiple coders, is to memo. Three common types of memos are code memos, theoretical memos, and operational/ procedural memos (Corbin & Strauss, 2015). First, code memos help the research team to refine the code book and clarify codes, especially those that are abstract, repetitive, and ambiguous (Loftland et al., 2006). For example, in my analysis of Louisiana's Coastal Master Plan, a review of the appendices included a fuller discussion of the physical measures of the program which allowed me to refine and clarify the code book (Knox, 2017).

Second, theoretical memos allow the researcher to build upon their theoretical understanding of the phenomenon and concepts being studied (Loftland et al., 2006). In the example shown in Box 9.1, I am memoing while coding a semi-structured interview. I wrote most of the memos while coding the transcribed interviews, but I wrote the first memo during the interview as the interviewee's demeaner changed and was worth noting. It became an important piece of my understanding of "Everglades restoration" during the coding process.

BOX 9.1 EXAMPLE OF CODING AND MEMOING

"If the Everglades restoration program continues on the track it has for the last 10 years then I really do not see it producing major results in the next 10 years. You probably sense my *frustration* with the process."

Memo: Interviewee lowers his voice, looks down, and shakes his head when he makes this statement. Researcher senses frustration and sadness in his body language.

Memo: States they are frustrated with the process. Add new category: Frustrated.

Memo: Stresses "major results" versus minor results. Interviewee is possibly looking at the larger picture of the Everglades restoration program.

Memo: States "last 10 years" and "next 10 years." Interviewee has been around this program for a number of years. Although frustrated with the restoration process, he mentions "next 10 years." This leads the researcher to believe that he is dedicated to continue working in this program.

Source: Knox (2013, p. 6).

Finally, operational or procedural memos can be for the individual or for the research team to consider, such as expanding the coding scale, adding more interviews or focus group sessions, recommending other data sources for triangulation, or re-engaging interviewees with follow-up questions (Loftland et al., 2006). For example, in the analysis of Louisiana's comprehensive land-use and emergency management plans, one of my memos focused on expanding a list of potential focus group members for the next stage of analysis (Knox, 2017). It stated: "Recommend we contact XX at Tulane University, XY with University of New Orleans Center for Hazards Assessment, Response and Technology, YY and YX with the National Sea Grant Program, and ZX with the Louisiana State University's Coastal Sustainability Studio for additional interviews."[2]

Coding Example

Once the documents are collected, the code book is finished (again, it is a living document), and the coders are trained, the research team independently codes the documents and meets regularly. In this section, I provide an example of a coding methodology from the urban and regional planning literature. For this project, the researcher was tasked with measuring various elements of resiliency within and across three plans: the city's comprehensive master plan, the county's comprehensive land use plan, and the county's comprehensive emergency management plan.

Since 1994, urban and regional planning scholars have created and tested a methodology to systematically analyze the content and quality of various plans. For this chapter, we are specifically using a plan assessment process developed by Dr. Samuel Brody at Texas A&M University. Researchers have used this method to analyze emergency management related plans including disaster recovery (Berke, Cooper, Aminto, Grabich, & Horney, 2014), coastal hazards (Deyle & Smith, 1998), natural hazard mitigation (Berke, Smith, & Lyles, 2012; Lyles, Berke, & Smith, 2016), and climate change (Baynham & Stevens, 2014; Stone, Vargo, & Habeeb, 2012).

The assessment is comprised of five core components: Factual Basis; Goals and Objectives; Policies, Tools, and Strategies; Inter-organizational Coordination; and Implementation and Monitoring (see Table 9.3 for description). The research team derived the indicators from the literature (deductive approach) and the plans (inductive approach), and organized them into one of these five components.

TABLE 9.3 Description of Core Components

Component	Description
Factual Basis	Quality is dependent upon maps, videos, tables, checklists, and detailed plans and is critical in setting the direction for well-informed goals and policies.
Goals and Objectives	Specify ways to create a vision and evaluate its components in terms of thoroughness, clarity, long-term mindset, consistency, implementation strategies, and adoption protocols. Must value population safety, property, and the environment.
Policies, Tools, and Strategies	Incorporates the actual means to realizing the goals and objectives. May include development regulations, land and property acquisition, information dissemination, and building standards.
Inter-organizational Coordination	Incorporate steps to ensure cooperation among specified levels of government, neighboring jurisdictions, and applicable agencies and organizations.
Implementation and Monitoring	Indicators include clarity of schedule, allocation of resources, and frameworks for program and process evaluation.

Source: Brody (2003).

For the coding portion of the analysis, the two trained coders apply a three-point coding system (0, 1, 2) generated from previous planning evaluation research to measure depth and breadth of the indicators (see Table 9.4).

Once the team completes the coding, the researcher further analyzes the data utilizing IBM SPSS software to measure the depth and breadth of the data. More specifically, the plan components and total plan quality are calculated using these equations:

$$PC_j = \frac{10}{2m} \sum_{i=1}^{mj} Ii \qquad [1]$$

$$TPQ = 5 \sum_{j=1}^{5} PCj \qquad [2]$$

In Equation 1, PCj is the quality of the jth plan component (with a range of 1–10); mj is the number of indicators within the jth plan component; and Ii is the ith plan indicator score (with a range of 0–2). In Equation 2, TPQ is the total score of the plan (with a range of 0–50; Tang et al., 2008).

Table 9.5 illustrates a breakdown of this analysis using a spreadsheet. The first column contains the factors within the Goals and Objectives category. The next two columns are the independent coding results from coder 1 and 2. To calculate the depth score, create a column after the final coder. Now, calculate the average code between the coders. For the first factor, the average code is 2 (2 + 2 = 4/2). To calculate the total score for this component, sum all the depth scores for the total raw score. In this example, it is 13. Since each component has a different number of factors, the raw score is skewed. Therefore, the researcher needs to weight the raw score. To do this, divide the raw score by the highest score that could be obtained in this category. For this example, there are eight factors that could have scored a 2, so the highest score for this category is 16 (8 × 2). Then multiply this number by 10. For the score of 8.13, the equation is 13/16 × 10, for a weighted score of 8.13. This process will be repeated for all five categories.

The breadth score is calculated differently. The score is 1 or 0; either the factor is present (1) (regardless of whether it is a 1 or 2) or not (0). This is later reported as being included, but the depth score 0, 1, or 2 will indicate to what level the factor was discussed in the plan.

TABLE 9.4 Indicator Measurement

Types	Score of 0	Score of 1	Score of 2
Factual-related indicators (described/classified/ visualized)	■ Not described ■ Not classified ■ Not visualized or mapped	■ Vague description ■ No specific description ■ Vague classification	■ Full identification ■ Clear statement ■ Classification/catalog
Goal-related indicators	■ Not identified	■ Vague identification ■ No specific objectives	■ Clear identification ■ Measurable objectives
Policy coordination/ implementation indicators	■ Not identified/adopted	■ Non-mandatory words: may/prefer/encourage ■ Suggest/should/intend ■ Consider to adopt	■ Mandatory words: mandate/must/will/shall ■ Already adopted

Source: Tang, Lindell, Prater, and Brody (2008).

TABLE 9.5 Example of Coding Spreadsheet

Goals and Objectives	Coder 1	Coder 2	Depth	Breadth
Protect and restore significant coastal resources	2	2	2	1
Prevent and reduce polluted runoff to coastal waters	1	1	1	1
Protect life and property in hazardous areas	1	1	1	1
Build disaster-resistant, healthy, safe community	1	1	1	1
Promote sustainable growth in coastal communities	2	2	2	1
Provide for priority water-dependent uses	2	2	2	1
Improve public shoreline access	2	2	2	1
Improve government coordination and decision-making	2	2	2	1
Total (raw score)			13	
Total (weighted score; maximum of 10)			8.13	

Intercoder Reliability Test

Throughout the coding process, the researcher tests for intercoder reliability. There are multiple tests available including percent agreement, Holsti's method, Cohen's kappa, Scott's pi, and Krippendorff's alpha. In the planning literature, Stevens, Lyles, and Berke (2014, p. 81), as well as other scholars, have debated these multiple tests against five criteria:

1. Assess the agreement between two or more coders working independently of one another;

2. Do not be confounded by the number of scoring options made available for coding the items;

3. Be interpretable relative to a numerical scale, with at least two points on the scale (i.e., an upper point and a lower point) having meaningful reliability interpretations;

4. Adjust for the possibility that some level of agreement across coders may be likely to occur solely as a result of chance; and

5. Be usable with data measured at different levels of measurement (e.g., nominal or ordinal).

Along these lines, the most reliable test for intercoder reliability that meets the five criteria is Krippendorff's alpha (Lyles & Stevens, 2014; Stevens et al., 2014). However, it has a limitation: it is unable to measure when there is a lack of variation. For example, if coders agree on a set of factors but the code is 0 for each one, then the test will produce an error message. In this situation, it is recommended to run a second test using Cronbach's alpha, which does not have this limitation but is not as powerful for testing intercoder reliability.

The following figures contain samples of the results when the researcher runs an intercoder reliability test for 39 indicators on one of the five components. The first set of results is from Cronbach's alpha (Figure 9.1), while the second set is from

Case Processing Summary

		N	%
Cases	Valid	39	100.0
	Excluded[a]	0	0.0
	Total	39	100.0

[a] Listwise deletion based on all variables in the procedure.

Reliability Statistics

Cronbach's α	N of Items
.967	2

FIGURE 9.1 Cronbach's Alpha Reliability Estimate Results

	α	LL (95% CI)	UL (95% CI)	Units	Observers	Pairs
Ordinal	.9401	.8243	1.0000	39.0000	2.0000	39.0000

FIGURE 9.2 Krippendorff's Alpha Reliability Estimate Results

Krippendorff's alpha (Figure 9.2). For the two intercoder reliability tests, the coders are 96.7% in agreement (Cronbach's alpha) and 94% in agreement (Krippendorff's alpha) across the 39 factors. This is above the recommended 80% threshold.

Finally, the important but often overlooked part of this coding process is the detailed memos each coder keeps. These notes provide the crucial context behind the numbers in the spreadsheet above. It is the "So what?" behind a 0, 1, or 2. Each coder will individually memo within and across the plans. The memos can be specific to the indicator being coded, while others can include questions for the team, general observations, and comparison notes with other coded plans or indicators (see Corbin and Strauss [2015] for additional memo strategies). Then, the lead researcher will combine the memos to review and open code the memo notes. This analysis will not only provide context to the data but will also compare aspects of the reports or plans not captured in the coding analysis. It is important for the researcher to review the memos throughout the coding process, as these notes could lead to critical changes to the code book. Again, this is part of the inductive approach to coding.

For example, when coding the city's and county's plans, the research team met weekly to discuss any questions from the memos. One question raised by both coders was the definition of "vulnerable," as the coders were having difficulty locating the "identification of vulnerable populations" in the different plans. We needed to expand the code book for this indicator, and we searched academic and practitioner documents to guide us. Once we expanded the code book, the coders recoded all the plans and noted that this indicator remained rarely included in any of the plans. This led to connections with other plans and sections of the plans. Finally, not only were we able to state the low score, but also we could bring in recent history (i.e., disproportionate impacts of the recent hurricane season on socially vulnerable residents) and provide a detailed recommendation to the city and county staff. This additional information is in the next section of this chapter.

Reporting the Results

The following is an example of how a researcher reports the results of a city's comprehensive master plan quality analysis.

Plan Quality Results

With a maximum score of 50, the city's comprehensive master plan scored 38.1, indicating a sufficiently good job overall. Of the five components, Goals and Objectives received the highest score of 8.33 (on a 10-point scale), meaning the city demonstrates a very good job of goals and objectives in its comprehensive master plan (see Table 9.6). Compared to land-use plan analysis in the United States, this is an above-average score and stronger than most other plans. The second highest score of 8.33 is Implementation and Monitoring, indicating a moderately good effort. Coming in a close third and fourth are Factual Basis at 7.67 and Inter-organizational Coordination at 7.71. The weakest category is Policy, Tools, and Strategies at 6.25. While scoring above the mean, this result is not surprising, as this category tends to be the weakest one in comprehensive land-use plan analysis across the United States. When looking for areas to increase the city's resiliency, this category would be the first to consider, as it would have the greatest long-term impact on community resilience.

Indicator Results

Results highlight a strength among 54% (n = 46) of the 85 resiliency indicators used in the analysis of the city's comprehensive master plan. Of the remaining indicators, 33% (n = 28) are included, but not thoroughly or in great detail. These are the factors the research team recommends the city focus on to build resiliency, as they are included in the current comprehensive master plan but are lacking details and/or mandatory words. Finally, 13% (n = 11) of the indicators are rarely or not discussed in the city's plan. While many of them are included in the county's comprehensive emergency management plan, this plan does not have legal standing like a comprehensive master plan. Therefore, the research team recommended increasing the city's resiliency by incorporating these factors into the comprehensive master plan. Research concludes that integrating a comprehensive master plan with a comprehensive emergency management plan increases a community's resilience (Burby, 2006; Evans-Cowley & Gough, 2008).

TABLE 9.6 City's CMP Component and Total Plan Scores

Component	Score	Out of
Factual Basis	7.67	10
Goals and Objectives	8.13	10
Policies, Tools, and Strategies	6.25	10
Inter-organizational Coordination	7.71	10
Implementation and Monitoring	8.33	10
Total Plan Quality	38.1	50

TABLE 9.7 Indicators Discussed, but Not in Great Detail

Category	Indicator
Factual Basis	▪ Coastal zone boundary and maps
	▪ Identification of vulnerable populations
	▪ Critical facilities and services
	▪ Global warming, climate change, sea level rise
	▪ Coastal construction control line
Goals and Objectives	▪ Protect life and property in hazardous areas
	▪ Build disaster-resistant, healthy, safe community
Policies, Tools, and Strategies	▪ Affordable housing
	▪ Performance zoning
	▪ Hazard setback ordinances
	▪ Limitation of shoreline development
	▪ Restrictions on dredging/filling
	▪ Coastal vegetation protection regulations
	▪ Land acquisition
	▪ Density bonuses
	▪ Requirements for locating public facilities and infrastructure
	▪ Using urban service areas to limit development
	▪ Lower tax rates for preservation
	▪ Special tax assessment districts
	▪ Public-private partnerships
	▪ Suitable building sites in hazard prone areas
	▪ Special building techniques for hazard prone areas
	▪ Identify stakeholders and their interests
Inter-organizational Coordination	▪ Coordination with state agencies
	▪ Coordination with private organizations
	▪ Coordination with non-profit organizations
Implementation and Monitoring	▪ Necessary technical assistance
	▪ Regular monitoring, review, and updating

The example illustrated in Table 9.7 includes indicators that were included (breadth score of 1), but not thoroughly or in great detail (depth score of 1). Table 9.7 includes the 33% ($n = 28$) of indicators discussed in the comprehensive master plan, but not in depth. The majority are in the Policies, Tools, and Strategies component, which is consistent with analysis of other city/county master plans. These indicators would be considered the easiest to improve upon, as they are discussed in the plan; however, each one needs to be more detailed, include measurable objectives, and include mandatory words (e.g., mandate, must, will, shall, adopt/ed).

Indicator Discussion

As discussed previously, the data is only part of the story. The coders' memos are essential to expand upon these indicators within and, more importantly, across plans. While the final report to the city and county officials included a breakdown of these indicators, this chapter will highlight one: "Identification of vulnerable populations".

This indicator, within the Factual Basis component, scored a 1 because these populations were only included in reference to populations located in the Hurricane Vulnerability Zone. In fact, while "vulnerability" is mentioned throughout the plan's section discussing the Hazard Vulnerability Zone, "vulnerable" is only included twice in the entire plan. However, as highlighted in Chapter 5, communities have different types of vulnerable populations that city and county comprehensive master plans and comprehensive emergency management plans should consider. Adequately identifying these groups in the plans can allow for fuller integration of them in all phases of emergency management and the planning process (Cutter, Burton, & Emrich, 2010).

For example, one vulnerable population group is individuals living at or below the poverty level, which aligns with "Affordable housing," which also scored a 1 because the plan's language did not include mandatory or committal words. Alternatively, the plan states "encourages" in the Future Land Use Element. As such, there were no inclusion of mandatory words for affordable housing in the county's comprehensive emergency management plan. After Hurricanes Irma and Maria in 2017, transitioning individuals from short-term to long-term housing was an issue with the lack of affordable housing in Central Florida (Emrich, Alvarez, Knox, Sadiq, & Zhou, 2020).

It also aligns with "Coordination with non-profit organizations" and "Coordination with faith-based organizations," which were rarely or not mentioned in the comprehensive master plan. Research highlights that most vulnerable populations trust and rely on non-profit and faith-based organizations in their personal networks (which ties into their social capital). These networks can reduce a population's vulnerability and increase a community's resilience (Rivera & Nickels, 2014). Not including these organizations in the plans assumes they are not engaged in the planning process for the comprehensive master plan.

While this analysis is limited to three plans within one county, the fact that vulnerable populations are not defined (outside the hurricane zone) calls into question the county's efforts for resilience and the whole community approach. The lack of inclusion in these plans leads the researcher to see a narrative of disregard or lack of concern for these individuals. From a critical theory perspective, this could lead to one of four crises for public administrators (Habermas, 1975). Most notably, a legitimation crisis can occur when the public questions the actions or inactions of public administrations, including planners and emergency managers. To avoid a legitimation crisis, government officials should encourage citizen participation in the planning process to help legitimize its administrative decisions (Edgar, 2005; Habermas, 1975). Further, the results of these participation activities are then reflected in the county plans. Future research should analyze if other county documents and plans account for these groups.

Limitations

Every methodology has limitations. A main limitation to coding these types of plans or reports is that city and county emergency management and planning staff use standard language across the plans. This can make it difficult to discern individual or unique narratives if standard language is being used. This is most evident when a consultant group is hired by many local jurisdictions within a state or region. As coders we write a memo to this effect. One way to overcome this challenge is to code and analyze other department documents or interview staff members and decision makers. This will allow for additional context to the data analysis.

While some states have sunshine legislation, which makes public documents easily available, such as a comprehensive master or emergency management plan, not all local jurisdictions comply fully. Instead, they will provide the plan but not the appendices, or they will provide a public-facing document. These public-facing documents are more streamlined and have specific organizational information removed, which is a common occurrence among first-responder agencies. For example, if a researcher wants to code and analyze an agency's continuity of operations plan, they will not receive the appendices that include the call-down list with personal information, location of essential equipment, or alternative location details. The researcher will need to go through their organization's IRB process, and there is no guarantee the jurisdiction or organization will comply.

Another limitation, especially when analyzing plans from multiple jurisdictions, is that each plan is written or updated at different times. Some plans are updated annually, while others are on 5- or 10-year rotations. Therefore, it is important for the research team to consider the plan date when memoing, as recent lessons learned are not included in older plans. For example, when coding comprehensive land use plans in coastal Louisiana, many of the older plans scored very low for global warming and climate change–related indictors (Knox, 2017). Tang (2008) and other scholars confirm that this phenomenon is common in older plans. Yet, considering Louisiana's political climate during the study period, it was worth mentioning the lack of climate change indicators in most of the more recently approved plans. This was one of many related memos the research team made throughout the coding process.

Conclusion

When used appropriately, the application of language-based theories to emergency and disaster management research has the potential to provide deep and rich information and understanding to data. As I have documented in this chapter, the process of applying language-based theories is not a straightforward endeavor and requires continual revisiting since it is organic. However, with practice and training, more researchers can be in a better position to utilize these types of research designs within the context of disaster and emergency management research.

Notes

1. See Marshall and Rossman (1999) for additional information.
2. Individuals' names were removed from this chapter for reasons related to anonymity.

Further Readings

Crenshaw, K., Gotanda, N., Peller, G., & Thomas, K. (1995). *Critical race theory: The key writings that formed the movement.* New York: New Press.

Eriksen, E.O., & Weigård, J. (2003). *Understanding Habermas: Communicative action and deliberative democracy.* London: Continuum.

Habermas, J. (1996). *Between facts and norms: Contributions to a discourse theory of law and democracy.* Cambridge, MA: MIT Press.

Knox, C.C. (2016). Unearthing steering activities in Everglades policy development: A Habermas critical theory analysis. *Critical Issues in Justice and Politics, 9*(1), 1–35.

Marcuse, H. (2001). *Towards a critical theory of society: Collected papers of Herbert Marcuse* (Vol. 2). Routledge.

References

Alvesson, M., & Deetz, S. (1999). Critical theory and postmodernism: Approaches to organizational studies. In S.R. Clegg & C. Hardy (Eds.), *Studying organization: Theory and method* (pp. 185–211). London: Sage.

Baynham, M., & Stevens, M. (2014). Are we planning effectively for climate change? An evaluation of official community plans in British Columbia. *Journal of Environmental Planning and Management, 57*(4), 557–587.

Berke, P., Cooper, J., Aminto, M., Grabich, S., & Horney, J. (2014). Adaptive planning for disaster recovery and resiliency: An evaluation of 87 local recovery plans in eight states. *Journal of the American Planning Association, 80*(4), 310–323.

Berke, P., Smith, G., & Lyles, W. (2012). Planning for resiliency: Evaluation of state hazard mitigation plans under the Disaster Mitigation Act. *Natural Hazards Review, 13*(2), 139–149.

Birkland, T.A. (1997). *After disaster: Agenda setting, public policy, and focusing events.* Washington, DC: Georgetown University Press.

Blessett, B. (2015). Disenfranchisement: Historical underpinnings and contemporary manifestations. *Public Administration Quarterly, 39*(1), 3–50.

Brody, S.D. (2003). Implementing the principles of ecosystem management through local land use planning. *Population and Environment, 24*(6), 511–540.

Brower, R.S., Abolafia, M.Y., & Carr, J.B. (2000). On improving qualitative methods in public administration research. *Administration & Society, 32*(4), 363–397.

Burby, R.J. (2006). Hurricane Katrina and the paradoxes of government disaster policy: Bringing about wise governmental decisions for hazardous areas. *Annals of the American Academy of Political and Social Science, 604*(1), 171–191.

Corbin, J., & Strauss, A. (2015). *Basics of qualitative research: Techniques and procedures for developing grounded theory* (4th ed.). Sage.

Cutter, S.L., Burton, C.G., & Emrich, C.T. (2010). Disaster resilience indicators for benchmarking baseline conditions. *Journal of Homeland Security and Emergency Management, 7*(1).

Davies, R., Vaughan, E., Fraser, G., Cook, R., Ciotti, M., & Suk, J. E. (2018). Enhancing reporting of after action reviews of public health emergencies to strengthen preparedness: a literature review and methodology appraisal. *Disaster Medicine and Public Health Preparedness*, 1–8.

Davis, J. M., & French, N. T. (2008). Blaming victims and survivors: An analysis of post-Katrina print news coverage. *Southern Communication Journal*, *73*(3), 243–257.

Derrida, J. (1972). Discussion: Structure, sign and play in the discourse of the human sciences. In R. Macksey & E. Donato (Eds.), *The structuralist controversy* (pp. 247–272). Baltimore: Johns Hopkins University Press.

Deyle, R. E., & Smith, R. A. (1998). Local government compliance with state planning mandates: The effects of state implementation in Florida. *Journal of the American Planning Association*, *64*(4), 457–469.

Edgar, A. (2005). *The philosophy of Habermas*. Montreal: McGill-Queen's University Press.

Emrich, C., Alvarez, S., Knox, C. C., Sadiq, A. A., & Zhou, Y. (2020). Hurricane Irma and cascading impacts. In C. Rubin & S. Cutter (Eds.), *U.S. Emergency management in the 21st century: From disaster to catastrophe* (pp. 123–154). New York: Routledge.

Eriksen, E. O., & Weigård, J. (2003). *Understanding Habermas: Communicative action and deliberative democracy*. London: Continuum.

Evans-Cowley, J. S., & Gough, M. Z. (2008). Evaluating environmental protection in post-Hurricane Katrina plans in Mississippi. *Journal of Environmental Planning and Management*, *51*(3), 399–419.

Finlayson, J. G. (2005). *Habermas: A very short introduction*. Oxford: Oxford University Press.

Fischer, F. (1990). *Technocracy and the politics of expertise*. Newbury Park, CA: Sage.

Fischer, F. (2003). *Reframing public policy: Discursive politics and deliberative practices*. Oxford: Oxford University Press.

Foucault, M. (1983). Structuralism and post-structuralism. *Telos*, 55, 195–211.

Habermas, J. (1975). *Legitimation crisis*. Boston: Beacon Press.

Ingram, H., Schneider, A. L., & deLeon, P. (2007). Social construction and policy design. In P. Sabatier (Ed.), *Theories of the policy process* (2nd ed., pp. 93–126). Boulder, CO: Westview Press.

Jacques, P., & Knox, C. C. (2016). Hurricanes and hegemony: A qualitative analysis of micro-level climate denial discourses. *Environmental Politics*, *25*(5), 831–852.

Jones, M. D., & McBeth, M. K. (2010). A narrative policy framework: Clear enough to be wrong? *Policy Studies Journal*, *38*(2), 329–353.

Knox, C. C. (2010). *Competing paradigms for analyzing policy development in Everglades restoration: Case study using advocacy coalition framework and Habermas's critical theory*. (Dissertation), Florida State University.

Knox, C. C. (2013). Distorted communication in the Florida Everglades: A critical theory analysis of "Everglades restoration." *Journal of Environmental Policy and Planning*, *15*(2), 269–284.

Knox, C. C. (2017). A football field lost every 45 minutes: Evaluating local capacity to implement Louisiana's coastal master plan. *Coastal Management Journal*, *45*(3), 233–252.

Ladson-Billings, G. (1998). Just what is critical race theory and what's it doing in a nice field like education? *International Journal of Qualitative Studies in Education*, *11*(1), 7–24.

Lasswell, H. D. (1951). The policy orientation. In D. Lerner & H. D. Lasswell (Eds.), *The policy science: Recent developments in scope and methods*. Stanford, CA: Stanford University Press.

Lofland, J., Snow, D., Anderson, L., & Lofland, L. H. (2006). *Analyzing social settings: A guide to qualitative observation and analysis* (4th ed.). Belmont, CA: Thomson and Wadsworth.

Lyles, W., Berke, P., & Smith, G. (2016). Local plan implementation: Assessing conformance and influence of local plans in the United States. *Environment and Planning B: Planning and Design*, *43*(2), 381–400.

Lyles, W., & Stevens, M. (2014). Plan quality evaluation 1994–2012: Growth and contributions, limitations, and new directions. *Journal of Planning Education and Research*, *34*(4), 433–450.

Marcuse, H. (1964). *One-dimensional man: Studies in the ideology of advanced industrial society*. Boston: Beacon Press.

Marshall, C., & Rossman, G. B. (1999). *Designing qualitative research* (3rd ed.). London: Sage.

Rivera, J.D., & Nickels, A.E. (2014). Social capital, community resilience, and faith-based organizations in disaster recovery: A case study of Mary Queen of Vietnam Catholic Church. *Risk, Hazards and Crisis in Public Policy, 5*(2), 178–211.

Schneider, A.L., & Ingram, H. (1993). Social construction of target populations: Implications for politics and policy. *American Political Science Review, 87*(2), 334–347.

Schneider, A.L., & Ingram, H. (1997). *Policy design for democracy.* Lawrence: University Press of Kansas.

Shanahan, E.A., Jones, M.D., & McBeth, M.K. (2011). Policy narratives and policy processes. *Policy Studies Journal, 39*(3), 535–561.

Stevens, M.R., Lyles, W., & Berke, P.R. (2014). Measuring and reporting intercoder reliability in plan quality evaluation research. *Journal of Planning Education and Research, 34*(1), 77–93.

Stone, B., Vargo, J., & Habeeb, D. (2012). Managing climate change in cities: Will climate action plans work? *Landscape and Urban Planning, 107*(3), 263–271.

Stone, D. (2002). *Policy paradox: The art of policy decision making* (Rev. ed.). New York: Norton.

Tang, Z. (2008). Integrating the principles of strategic environmental assessment into local comprehensive land use planning. *Journal of Environmental Assessment Policy and Management, 10*(2), 143–171.

Tang, Z., Lindell, M.K., Prater, C.S., & Brody, S.D. (2008). Measuring tsunami planning capacity on US Pacific coast. *Natural Hazards Review, 9*(2), 91–100.

Tate IV, W.F. (1997). Chapter 4: Critical race theory and education: History, theory, and implications. *Review of Research in Education, 22*(1), 195–247.

Winant, H. (2000). Race and race theory. *Annual Review of Sociology, 26*(1), 169–185.

Yanow, D. (1992). Silences in public policy discourse: Organizational and policy myths. *Journal of Public Administration Research and Theory, 2*(4), 399–423.

Yanow, D. (1993). The communication of policy meanings: Implementation as interpretation and text. *Policy Sciences, 26*(1), 41–61.

Yanow, D. (1996). *How does a policy mean? Interpretive policy and organizational actions.* Washington, DC: Georgetown University Press.

Yanow, D., & Schwartz-Shea, P. (Eds.). (2006). *Interpretation and method: Empirical research methods and the interpretive turn.* Armonk, NY: M.E. Sharpe.

Ethnography Without Experimentation

Ethnographic Methods in Post-disaster Contexts

Stephen Danley, Sis. Anetha Perry,
Jazmyne McNeese, and Lili Razi

You never want a serious crisis to go to waste.

– Rahm Emmanuel

Introduction

Rahm Emmanuel's quip about the financial crisis captures the ethos of many in post-disaster contexts. Klein and Peet (2008) call this *disaster capitalism*. In New Orleans, it was called the *blank slate*. For policymakers, such disasters can be opportunities for dramatically remaking institutions and systems. For researchers, disasters can be *natural experiments* that help build knowledge about these new policies. But, such policy changes (and, by extension, research) often directly contradict the desire of communities to rebuild in the image of the pre-storm community (Haas, Kates, & Bowden, 1977).

The desire of many residents for a community to return to the pre-disaster state is a serious challenge for research on multiple levels. The first is logistical. Communities are often skeptical of researchers who they see as part of a wider system that is remaking policy, or simply exploiting community, without community input. That makes it harder to collect data and hurts the quality of research. More importantly, critics argue research in post-disaster contexts is extractive, can damage a community, and takes time and resources from a community with little of either to spare. Our chapter examines these challenges by laying out the foundation of the critiques of experimentation upon post-disaster communities, and positing ethnography as a methodology that both addresses those challenges and should be informed by them. In doing so, we draw on examples from a multi-year ethnographic study of neighborhood activism in post-Katrina New Orleans to elucidate both the challenges and possibilities of such study (see Box 10.1).

BOX 10.1 NEW ORLEANS

In post-Katrina New Orleans, frustration with what residents called *helicopter research* and with policy experimentation was often a subtext for interactions with communities about our research, except on the days when they became pretext. On one such day, a member of our team walked into the Community Book Center – New Orleans' oldest Black-owned bookstore – and was told, "you're the problem with this city." Over the next hour, the bookstore patron explained how young, white, highly educated newcomers to the city had largely replaced teachers of color in the public school district after all the teachers (over 7,000) were fired. Our team member argued that as a researcher, he was not a part of the organizations such as Teach for America replacing the teacher force. In response, the patron asked, "*Why can't a resident do the research you're doing?*"

Source: Danley (2018a).

During our time in the field, we were often asked by neighborhood leaders to prove the worth of our project for the New Orleans community. The conversation in Box 10.1 was perhaps the most explicit interaction expressing skepticism of researchers, but the general sentiment was present in a never-ending series of similar exchanges. In response, we developed a series of approaches to such challenges. In this chapter, we attempt to theorize that skepticism in light of the dramatic changes to community and institutions in post-disaster contexts, specifically by highlighting the tension between policy experimentation/New Localism (Katz & Nowak, 2017) and the sentiment of residents that they want the return of their community as it was pre-storm (Haas et al., 1977). We argue that the skepticism of policy experimentation in post-disaster communities of color is deeply rooted in the history of experimentation to the detriment of these communities, most famously with the Tuskegee Experiment, but also with a broader history of medical experiments upon slaves (Washington, 2006) and beyond. We argue that this history informs and frames the skepticism and rhetoric of residents toward both policy experimentation and research in post-disaster contexts. Given these challenges, we posit ethnography as a way to reframe research in post-disaster contexts, arguing that ethnography's propensity for centering listening to vulnerable communities provides those communities an opportunity to reframe such research around the issues that would have impact and import to residents, and that doing so is an ethical necessity. We also argue that, in order for ethnography to fulfill that promise, it must take into account the specific critiques around experimentation and incorporate those critiques into the practice of the method.

Defining Ethnography

We argue that ethnography should be informed by critiques of experimentation upon vulnerable post-disaster communities, but when conducted correctly, can also be an appropriate methodological response to such critiques. That argument requires a discussion of the practice of ethnography itself. Ethnography, as a methodology, has a rich history that has emerged from social anthropology, urban sociology, and geography (e.g., Hannerz, 1980; Burgess, 1982; Hammersley & Atkinson, 1983; Ellen, 1984; see also Ryan, 2017 and Brewer, 2000). Though formal definitions of ethnography are contested (see Hymes, 1978), Creswell and Poth (2007, p. 68) describe it as when "the researcher describes and interprets the shared and learned patterns of values, behaviors, beliefs, and language of a culture-sharing group." They go on to say that

> ethnography is a way of studying a culture-sharing group, as well as the final, written product of that research. As a process, ethnography involves extended observations of the group, most often through participant observation, in which the researcher is immersed in the day-to-day lives of the people.

Moreover, according to Agar (1980), ethnography is both process and product. As a process, ethnography is how a researcher attempts to learn about or understand some human group, and the name of the action is fieldwork (Boyle, 1994).

Based on this general definition, various scholars with anthropological backgrounds have used ethnographic methods to study how populations, social groups, and cultures interact, react, and evolve as a by-product of natural and man-made disasters (Oliver-Smith, 1986; Hoffman, 2002; Hoffman & Oliver-Smith, 2002; Haynes, 2017). Along these lines and over the past 50 years, much of this work has focused on humanitarian interventions following disasters and their respective impacts on communities (Oliver-Smith, 1986), social reaction to evacuation and displacement from disaster areas (Hansen & Oliver-Smith, 1982; Weber & Peek, 2012; Alaniz, 2017), and the local consequences of reconstruction (Kroll-Smith, 2018). Moreover, due to the ever-evolving nature of long-term recovery, ethnographic methods have been continually used to understand community recovery trajectories that one-time interviews, focus groups, or other quantitative methods (described later in this book) struggle to capture.

Along these lines, the focus of ethnography on groups and cultural positions is ideal for post-disaster research in communities that are insisting on community voice and are skeptical of the unintended consequences of policy experiments. Communities critique research that has a focus on narrow evaluations of "What works." Different approaches to ethnography are constructed to turn the focus of research back onto community and culture. For example, urban ethnography is meant "to convey the inner life and texture of the diverse social enclaves and personal circumstances of urban societies" (Jackson, 1985, p. 157). Focusing on culture, social enclaves, and personal circumstances is likely to result in dramatically different findings than studies that narrowly define policy success and consider such factors complications to be randomized. In ethnography, community is present because the starting place is immersion in culture. As we discuss below, this approach stands in sharp contrast to the experience post-disaster communities often face of being the policy experiment or blank slate for others' policy ideas.

Ethnography has historically considered (and problematized) the different impacts researchers have had on research, which puts it in a strong position to do so in specific post-disaster circumstances. Ethnography has built theory around how to ethically and rigorously conduct research in vulnerable communities (Pacheco-Vega & Parizeau, 2018). Pacheco-Vega and Parizeau (2018) build upon McGranahan's (2014) and Warren's (2014) work describing doubly engaged ethnography as an opportunity to understand social phenomena in geographical sites where highly vulnerable individuals reside, balancing ethical approaches with rigor. Pacheco-Vega and Parizeau (2018) lay out a three-pronged approach to ethnography in vulnerable populations, focusing on (1) representation, (2) positionality, and (3) engagement versus exploitation. That framework shows both the strengths of ethnography for specifically addressing research challenges in post-disaster contexts and also how ethnography needs to intentionally consider the dangers of experimentation within its approach.

Pacheco-Vega and Parizeau (2018) focus on representation and positionality as key ways to address the challenges of ethnography with vulnerable populations. By representation and positionality, Pacheco-Vega and Parizeau (2018) refer to both their own status as insider or outsider (Sultana, 2007), as well as what voices are heard within the context of their research. These issues have long been key points of debate in ethnography. Danley (2018b) argues:

> Identity itself has often been criticized while in the field. Gold (1958) famously wrote that researchers may "go native" while conducting fieldwork, becoming too close to research subjects and undermining the research. But Kanuha (2000) argues that the issue is more complex and that being a part of a community is actually a benefit in conducting research.

In post-disaster contexts such as New Orleans, it is critical to have researchers from a community who both understand the context of such actions and have roots in a community that allow them to gain access to community perspectives. Community representation on research teams builds on the principles of standpoint theory (see Collins, 2002; Creedon & Cramer, 2007; Walker, Geertsema, & Barnett, 2009), which argues that research should intentionally incorporate voices from marginalized communities, particularly communities of color (Fuery & Mansfield, 2000; Collins, 2002).

Other corners of the ethnographic universe have already incorporated many of these principles into theory and practice. For example, analytic autoethnography (Anderson, 2006) centers the experience of the ethnographer as worthy of study, in contrast to much participant observation, which is focused outward on a community. Anderson writes that the challenge is to avoid a "turn towards blurred genres of writing, a heightened self-reflexivity in ethnographic research, an increased focus on emotion of sciences, and the postmodern skepticism regarding generalization of knowledge claims" (Anderson, 2006, p 373), while acknowledging the analytic value of studying one's own experiences. Such approaches allow for the possibility of rigorous social science research that is bettered by its ability to incorporate and capture community voice and perspective.

Our own research in New Orleans faced the challenge of a community deeply skeptical of helicopter researchers. But, it also was informed by a long history of considering this challenge within the ethnographic tradition. Below, we use vignettes from that fieldwork to make visible the community argument against experimentation, and we address the ways we used ethnography to ethically respond to these concerns.

Laboratories of Democracy and the "Blank Slate"

The phrase in the air, as New Orleans turned from disaster response to the longer, more arduous task of recovery, was the *blank slate*. For policymakers both in New Orleans and across the world, the post-Katrina context in New Orleans was an opportunity to test new ideas. Most famously, the school system transitioned to the first 100% charter school district in the nation with entirely open enrollment.[1] But the city took the opportunity to remake (or try to remake) a variety of policies, from health care to transportation and from public housing to city planning. In doing so, policymakers imagined that the post-disaster context was a blank slate, where circumstances (and funding) provided a rare opportunity to dramatically remake systems. They turned New Orleans into a laboratory of democracy (Mock, 2015).

Laboratories of democracy traditionally refer to the U.S. system of federalism. In a system of checks and balances, getting national legislation passed can be extremely difficult. But states sometimes provide opportunities to *experiment* with policies that can be adopted by the whole country, should the policy be effective (Goossens, 2014). As states have become more bifurcated between city and rural communities, cities have increasingly become the location of such laboratories. Katz and Nowak (2017) argue that a "New Localism" is emerging because of the rapid changes in cities due to technological advances that put traditional slow legislative processes at odds. This language of New Localism is deeply rooted in British understandings of top-down versus bottom-up governance. John Stuart Mill (1871, as in Clarke, 2009, pp. 498–499) said in *Considerations on Representative Government*:

> Local political institutions are closer to the people than their national counterparts; local institutions provide public goods that reflect the preferences of people under their jurisdiction; local institutions hold other levels of government open to a plurality of territorial and functional interests; and local institutions act as laboratories or training grounds for the government in general.

The formal concept of Localism has roots in the British Labour Party's response to Margaret Thatcher and the Conservative Party in the 1980s, a response echoed in the governance and sociopolitical dynamics of the EU (Hildreth, 2011). Traditionally, Localism has focused on scale and small-scale democracy (Davoudi & Madanipour, 2015), although Purcell (2006) calls this the "local trap" and argues that local scales are not necessarily more democratic than other scales. In this way, Localism has been a debate between arguments supporting the traditional state systems versus decentralization.

New Localism, particularly as it is understood in the United States, pivots from a frame of top down versus bottom up and toward a frame of innovation. Katz and Nowak (2017) argue that the government ought not to dominate localities, but rather foster institutional problem solving at the local scale – the district, city, county, and metropolitan levels. In their view, local policy can incubate scalable solutions. This concept broadly applies to a host of different ideological policy experiments. For example, the $15 minimum wage was largely trialed at the municipal level prior to its viability at the state or national scale. This type of experimentation is often possible at the city level because of polarization: cities are often much more progressive than their wider states. Thus, progressive policies are more accessible at the city level, as seen in Philadelphia, where the city started an eviction support fund (McCabe, 2019). Yet, much of the New Localism literature centers on preemption (see, e.g., Goho, 2012), which does not focus on progressive experimentation but on neoliberal policies that innovate through the use of market mechanisms (Sakakeeny, 2012), such as school choice to address inequality.

BOX 10.2 EXCERPT FROM *A NEIGHBORHOOD POLITICS OF LAST RESORT*

"After Hurricane Katrina, New Orleans became the heart of a pushback against a technocratic approach to public policy. Policy experts inundated the city (recruited in part by then Lt.

Governor Mitch Landrieu, who would later become mayor), eager to try the newest, most modern, and highest-impact policy ideas. Planners attempted to remake the city to eliminate residential housing and even commercial development in areas more likely to flood. Health care clinics proliferated through the city in an attempt to bring health care closer to residents' lives. The school system was reimagined without boundaries, so that any child could attend any of the multitude of charter schools cropping up throughout the city. And New Orleanians protested all of it. They protested not just the policy changes, but the way they were enacted and in particular, the exclusion of residents in the planning and development of policy changes. A fierce localism became central to city politics."

Source: Danley (2018a, p. 4).

Sakakeeny (2012) makes an explicit link between New Localism and the New Orleans post-Katrina context. In post-Katrina New Orleans, the trends that make New Localism are supported and furthered by the post-disaster context. The destruction of vast amounts of public infrastructure such as schools, hospitals, roads, and housing, and the subsequent influx of dollars to rebuild those systems, created a "blank slate" (we will critique this idea below). The remade systems were often highly influenced by market mechanisms, whether by neoliberal approaches such as choice in the school system or the wider influence of disaster capitalism as laid out by Klein and Peet (2008). For the years after Hurricane Katrina, New Orleans became one of the most acute examples of a type of New Localism: it was the site of policy innovation. It became a municipal laboratory of democracy. However, despite these oft-lauded policy changes in New Orleans, many city residents bucked at the idea of the city as a blank slate for such reforms (Mock, 2015; see Box 10.2).

The Experience of Being an Experiment

If declaring cities to be laboratories of democracy held great promise for policymakers, it held a different meaning for Black communities. Mock (2015) addresses fears of experimentation in terms of the wider New Orleans community. Those questions are even more salient for Black communities that have faced a distinct history of abuse by experimentation (Washington, 2006). We argue that just as medical experiments stripped Black communities of their rights and health, policy experiments in cities are often harmful in similar ways. They fail to inform, involve, and empower communities to have ownership over decision-making.

Within the context of New Localism, the language of experimentation and laboratories is closely associated with progress and innovation. But for the most vulnerable, such language is often a sign that they will be left out of these new systems. For example, James Reiss (chairman of the Regional Transit Authority in New Orleans) stated after Hurricane Katrina that "those who want to see this city rebuilt want to see it done in a completely different way: demographically, geographically and politically" (Mock, 2015, n.p.). This quote drove the perception that existing Black residents would be left out of the recovered city – a fear that became reality when public housing was closed and then demolished in Black neighborhoods. These fears of gentrification and exclusion of the Black community in post-Katrina New

Orleans are rooted in a history of bearing the brunt of risk associated with management of the flood system. Moreover, they are also rooted in a history of abusive experimentation in Black communities (Washington, 2006).

Black communities have a history of being chosen as the test subjects of experimentation at the expense of their health, agency, and consent. Perhaps most infamously, the Tuskegee Experiment misled Black men for decades about having syphilis. Participants were told they had "Bad Blood" when they were asked to join experimental trials (Jones, 1993). In the experiments, 399 Black men in the final stages of the illness and 201 Black men without the illness were used to evaluate the progression of the disease without their consent (Jones, 1993). The study offered a small stipend and long-term care, enticing Black men already struggling with poverty and racial discrimination to participate in exploitative research (Jones, 1993). It was evident that the government would protect its citizens; it just didn't include poor Black people (Jones, 1993). Using an individual's financial struggles, illiteracy, and hunger for security against them for financial gain or the *greater good* has been practiced time and time again in Black communities (Jones, 1993).

The Tuskegee Experiment is just the highest-profile example of what was a pattern of using Black bodies for medical experimentation. That history encompasses the use of elderly slaves for medical experiments (Washington, 2006) and the eugenics movement (Black, 2003). Eugenics idolized a racial preference for white people (blond hair and blue eyes) and that they were superior to Black people. It called for a removal of the Black and poor from human existence as the fundamental idea of the movement (Black, 2003). Using sterilization and segregation, the practice of eugenics classified certain groups as "unfit," and generated programs that would kill bloodlines (Black, 2003).

The story of Henrietta Lacks vividly illustrates a story of experimentation for the sake of progress. Henrietta Lacks was a patient in the 1950s whose cancer tumor and cells were harvested without her permission (Skloot, 2017). Her cells were given to doctors who used her samples to cure polio, send Americans to the moon, and create blood-pressure medicines – and these are just *some* examples (Skloot, 2017). Her cells, now known as HELA, have been distributed to doctors all over the world, who have profited from her flesh (Skloot, 2017). Her family was never compensated and is still paying the price of these harms. Her daughter writes:

> I always have thought it as strange, if our mother cells done so much for medicine, how come her family can't afford to see no doctors? . . . I used to get so mad about that to where it made me sick and I had to take pills. But I don't have it in me no more to fight.
>
> (Skloot, 2017, p. 9)

Henrietta's story is a story of past experimental harms affecting the livelihoods of future generations of Black families (Skloot, 2017). It is a story that provides an example of how ignoring social vulnerabilities in experimentation can easily perpetuate exploitation in ways that are often unseen (Skloot, 2017).

All of this may seem far from the types of policy experimentation we saw in New Orleans, and even further from the ethics and effectiveness of research in post-disaster contexts that is detailed in Chapter 1, but politicians, activists, and residents often hearken to this language to point out similar challenges to policy change and to research. Many scholars have examined the role that experimentation has played in urban communities (Hutton, 2009; Bach, 2010; Super, 2008; Berk, Boruch, Chambers, Rossi, & Witte, 1985). Ras Baraka, mayor of the city of Newark, also acknowledged these policy experiments when he said that the city has become "a laboratory for experiments in top-down reforms" (Cowen, 2014). Shahyd Sumpter, a mother and community member of a non-profit network, echoes this concern when she stated, "we're not experimenting with rich people or well-to-do white people" (Mock, 2015). The common thread is that "democratic" decisions for the betterment of society are constantly imposed on Black communities without their input.

Cruikshank (1999, p. 3) notes that most "social service programs, philanthropy, and political associations" focus on groups whose voices go unheard. Cruikshank's work exemplifies how policies of experimentation tend to prey on the most vulnerable, similar to spatial policies that focus on issues of gentrification, urban renewal, or economic development (Atkinson, 2000; Fullilove, 2016; Newman, Velez, & Pearson-Merkowitz, 2016). The pattern being that current communities, often of color, are in fear of being pushed out, removed, or priced out of their homes, or simply made unwelcome in their own communities, for the good of those to come (Danley & Weaver, 2018). The same pattern emerges in the policy sphere, when we look at policies like Temporary Assistance for Needy Families (TANF), the Crime Bill of 1994, or No Child Left Behind (Kasich, 1996; Chung, Pearl, & Hunter, 2019; Gill, Zimmer, Christman, & Blanc, 2007). Allowing Black bodies to suffer through policies that mismeasure systemic inequalities and consequently disenfranchise whole communities is problematic. TANF was created to decrease out-of-wedlock births, but it actually made it harder for Black families to get access to welfare, as out-of-wedlock births continued to increase (Kasich, 1996). Politicians frame the issue as a fault of Black motherhood, when in fact white families use the program the most (Kasich, 1996). The Crime Bill of 1994 was created to combat violent crime; however, it actually put more cops on the street and gave way for the phenomenon of mass incarceration, incriminating Black poor households regardless of trends in crime (Chung et al., 2019).

In New Orleans, many of the policy experiments after Hurricane Katrina shared apparent similarities with these wider policy experiments and with the medical experiments, particularly the lack of consent by the communities affected, as exemplified in Box 10.3.

BOX 10.3 A LACK OF CONSENT IN POLICY

On August 27th, 2009 – just after the 4th anniversary of Hurricane Katrina – the Secretary of Housing and Urban Development (HUD) Shaun Donovan visited New Orleans for the groundbreaking of the Lafitte Public Housing complex. A member of our research team attended the groundbreaking and the protest afterwards. At the groundbreaking, proponents of the project cried to see the long-delayed project finally moving forward. But for its opponents – a mix of public housing advocates and preservationists – the tears were of anger and frustration. At the protest that evening – where it was rumored that Secretary Donavan would show, though he never did – our team member had a chance to ask about that frustration. Activists cited a variety of complaints, from complains that people had been excluded from their community for 4 years (with no end in sight) despite the Lafitte buildings getting less than two feet of flooding, to concerns that the new development would result in fewer units (previous demolitions in the city had resulted in far fewer units being built, though in Lafitte the developer had promised 1–1 replacements), to concerns about gentrification, and finally, to concerns about lost culture as the Hope VI–style housing would lead to less density and a more dispersed community even if each unit was ultimately replaced.

Source: Unpublished field notes from Danley (2018a).

Public housing captures both the promise of New Localism in post-Katrina New Orleans and the ways it was weaponized against Black communities. For many, the demolition and rebuilding of these projects represented progress: a shift from traditional high-rise projects, which were largely seen to be a failed model, to Hope VI models with lower density and a lower concentration of poverty. In Lafitte, the project was even more progressive, addressing concerns of past Hope VI projects that resulted in less housing by guaranteeing a one-to-one replacement of units. The storm presented a rare opportunity to radically upgrade the facilities.

But that was not the whole story. The *New York Times* captured the other side of the public housing discussion (Saulny, 2006, n.p.):

> Some officials have made remarkably unveiled comments suggesting that the storm did the city a favor in terms of sweeping away the poor.
>
> Representative Richard H. Baker, a Republican from Baton Rouge, said just after the hurricane: "We finally cleaned up public housing in New Orleans. We couldn't do it. But God did."

This quote captures the experience of being an experiment. The policies may represent new innovation or progress, but they often intersect with those who weaponize that progress and do harm directly to a community. Rarely does the community being affected have input or control over that harm. The pattern repeated itself over and over in New Orleans. It is possible to quibble about whether the shift to health clinics or charter schools or Hope VI–style public housing was a prudent policy choice, but they all happened at a time when residents were displaced and had little say over their government. To borrow a term from research ethics, they happened without consent.

But What About Research?

This may seem distant from the world of research, but throughout our fieldwork it rarely was. There was consistent skepticism about researchers that was tied to policy experimentation. That skepticism was linked to the ways that researchers saw these policy changes as opportunities to test policy experiments. Many residents did not distinguish between the policy community and the research community. In the post-disaster context, that made sense; researchers and policymakers were in New Orleans for the same reason. They wanted to test and understand a new policy. That struck residents as sharply different, and often in conflict with, residents' own attempts to rebuild their city. The activists we spoke to often emphasized the need for humility and listening as the start of such projects; rather than begin from the frame of testing a policy experiment, they asked that we be allies in understanding the perspectives of community members rather than allies of disaster capitalism (Klein & Peet, 2008) that sought to benefit from the post–disaster context.

BOX 10.4 THE IMPORTANCE OF LISTENING

During one of our interviews with a neighborhood association leader – which took place in her living room – the leader insisted that researchers were missing what was really happening in post-Katrina New Orleans by insisting on focusing on policy. Instead, she insisted, the story was one of deep dysfunction and neighborhood leaders trying to fill that gap despite not being prepared for it. She pulled out a small poster that was essentially an organizational chart showing how New Orleans city government worked. She said that this was the heart of her work – that much of what her organization had done after the storm was to try to figure out who in government should be doing what, then be watchdogs to make sure government did it. At a time when school choice advocates were championing deregulation and decentralization, and libertarians (largely from George Mason University) were championing the potential of neighborhood organizations to replace government functions, hers was a deeply contrarian take. Years later, when our publication included findings such as neighborhood leaders resisting taking on more responsibility to provide social services, and the ways neighborhood leaders faced burnout, she got on Facebook and publicly thanked her interviewer. Of all the researchers that came to New Orleans after the storm, she said, he was the one that listened.

Source: Unpublished field notes from Danley (2018a).

From the ground, this distinction did not always feel sharp – many of those pushing for policy experiments were doing so because they truly believed they would help New Orleans – but the culture of these movements was distinct. Few advocates for policy change were deeply rooted in New Orleans itself; most were considered outsiders. We took this critique of research seriously in our work, so much so that we conducted what we would later call *presearch* or *pre-research* – which consisted of trips to New Orleans to connect with community members about the scope of the project prior to its formal design or execution. Community members later cited that approach in a discussion of our work, as highlighted in Box 10.4. However, despite our approach, skepticism was a typical challenge in the field. Residents had research fatigue. Just as we were often asking for their cooperation to collect data, they would often respond with what we came to think of as a *localness test* in which their participation in the study was predicated on us showing that we had local knowledge, and had considered residents' perspective while designing our study.

Ethnography Without Experimentation

Upon reflection, the use of ethnography played a central role in our ability to respond to community skepticism. We saw ethnography as a means to an ethical response that centers community voices and community experiences in research. Also, we used ethnography as a way to meet these research challenges that came from both lack of buy-in and lack of community perspective, which improved the quality of research. It was also something community members specifically called on us to consider, as indicated in Box 10.5.

BOX 10.5 COMMUNITY-CENTERED RESEARCH

During our first research trip to New Orleans, we were advised to talk to folks in the Community Book Center – New Orleans' oldest Black-owned bookstore. When a member of our team first entered the bookstore, he was asked "what are you here for?" The manager of the bookstore rightly sized up that our team was there for a research purpose, rather than to buy a book. Years later, the bookstore manager explained that interaction was the start of a series of questions she would always ask non-profit leaders or researchers who made their way to the bookstore. She would always ask four questions: (1) What are you here for? (2) What are you asking from the community? (3) What are you going to get out of it? (4) What is the community going to get from it?

Source: Unpublished field notes from Danley (2018a).

Many of the strategies we employed in New Orleans were only possible through the use of ethnography as a research approach that intentionally built upon these themes of engaging with the community.

We also found the literature on ethnography addressed ethically researching vulnerable populations to be the foundation for doing that work. As suggested by Pacheco-Vega and Parizeau (2018), we often took time to address our positionality and approached our *outsider* status with humility. Ethnography's inductive nature helped with that process: it allowed us to pivot in response to what we heard from residents and activists. Similarly, while our research group was not representative (Pacheco-Vega and Parizeau, 2018), "native" (Kanuha, 2000), or autoethnographic (Anderson, 2006), we used standpoint theory (see Collins, 2002; Creedon & Cramer, 2007; Walker, Geertsema, & Barnett, 2009) as a starting point to ensure that our research did not privilege voices of authority or traditional expertise over community voices.

Our use of ethnography as our primary method of study allowed us to directly orient our research around community voices, interpretations, and understanding. It centered a community vision of what was important in the post-disaster context – in sharp contrast with much other research that centered whether policy experiments *worked*. Our research is one of many ethnographies that demonstrate that ethnography has the potential to ethically address vulnerable communities – in this case, a post-disaster community – but that doing so must pay particular attention to being inclusive and listening to community voice.

We found that work *necessary* because so much research in post-disaster contexts is exploitative. The more typical approach of conceptualizing New Orleans as a *blank slate* or a post-disaster context as a *laboratory of democracy* has vastly different contextual meanings for vulnerable communities, and specifically for the Black community. These critiques help us to codify the ways ethical and rigorous research in post-disaster contexts can be conducted. Such research must prioritize listening to and representing the community. It must center community experiences rather than centering evaluations of policy or innovation. And it *must* have a direct impact on the community it serves.

Conclusion

As we have laid out, ethnography is a powerful method with existing theory designed to address these critiques. Doubly engaged ethnography and autoethnography draw from traditions that specifically consider vulnerable populations or underrepresented communities. Similarly, ethnography's focus on shared culture makes it more likely to capture harm to community, or alternate community perspectives, than more narrow policy evaluation that focuses on predetermined outcome variables.

But ethnography also needs to be informed by these critiques. Just because it is well-positioned to be more representative, to include community voices, or to focus beyond the scope of narrow variables, does not mean it always does so. And ethnography, as a method, still needs to more directly address concerns that it is extractive. Ethnography, and particularly ethnography in post-disaster contexts, needs to consider how to fulfill the promise of marrying theoretical gains with community benefit.

Note

1. Charter schools are privately operated (non-profit or for-profit) schools that receive public dollars to educate children for free.

Further Readings

Duncan, G. A. (2002). Critical race theory and method: Rendering race in urban ethnographic research. *Qualitative Inquiry, 8*(1), 85–104. https://doi.org/10.1177/107780040200800106

Ellis, C., & Bochner, A. P. (2000). Autoethnography, personal narrative, reflexivity: Researcher as subject. In N. K. Denzin & Y. S. Lincoln (Eds.), *Handbook of qualitative research* (2nd ed., pp. 733–768). London: Sage. https://scholarcommons.usf.edu/spe_facpub/91

Narayan, K. (2012). *Alive in the writing: Crafting ethnography in the company of Chekhov.* Chicago: University of Chicago Press.

Wacquant, L. (2002). Scrutinizing the street: Poverty, morality, and the pitfalls of urban ethnography. *American Journal of Sociology, 107*(6), 1468–1532. http://www.journals. uchicago.edu/doi/pdf/10.1086/340461

References

Agar, M. (1980). Stories, background knowledge and themes: Problems in the analysis of life history narrative. *American Ethnologist, 7*(2), 223–239. https://doi.org/10.1525/ae.1980.7.2. 02a00010

Alaniz, R. (2017). *From strangers to neighbors: Post-disaster resettlement and community building in Honduras.* Austin: University of Texas Press.

Anderson, L. (2006). Analytic autoethnography. *Journal of Contemporary Ethnography, 35*(4), 373–395. https://doi.org/10.1177/0891241605280449

Atkinson, R. (2000). Measuring gentrification and displacement in greater London. *Urban Studies, 37*(1), 149–165. https://doi.org/10.1080/0042098002339

Bach, W. A. (2010). Governance, accountability, and the new poverty agenda. *Wisconsin Law Review,* 239–296. Retrieved from https://heinonline.org/HOL/LandingPage?handle=hein. journals/wlr2010&div=12&id=&page=

Berk, R.A., Boruch, R.F., Chambers, D.L., Rossi, P.H., & Witte, A.D. (1985). Social policy experimentation: A position paper. *Evaluation Review, 9*(4) 387–429. https://doi.org/10.1177/0193841X8500900401

Black, E. (2003). The horrifying American roots of Nazi eugenics. *History News Network.* http://hnn.us/articles/1796.html

Boyle, J.S. (1994). Styles of ethnography. In J.M. Morse (Ed.), *Critical issues in qualitative research methods* (pp. 159–185). London: Sage.

Brewer, J.D. (2000). *Ethnography.* Buckingham: Open University Press.

Burgess, R.G. (1982). *Field research: A sourcebook and field manual.* London: Taylor & Francis. https://doi.org/10.4324/9780203379998

Chung, E., Pearl, B., & Hunter, L. (2019). The 1994 crime bill continues to undercut justice reform – here's how to stop it. *Center for American Progress.* http://www.americanprogress.org/issues/criminal-justice/reports/2019/03/26/467486/1994-crime-bill-continues-undercut-justice-reform-heres-stop/

Cowen, S., (2014). The New Orleans experiment in school reform: Lessons learned. *Huffington Post.* http://www.huffingtonpost.com/scott-cowen/the-new-orleans-experimen_b_5702778.html

Clarke, N. (2009). In what sense "spaces of neoliberalism"? The new localism, the new politics of scale, and town twinning. *Political Geography, 28*(8), 496–507. https://doi.org/10.1016/j.polgeo.2009.12.001

Collins, P.H. (2002). *Black feminist thought: Knowledge, consciousness, and the politics of empowerment.* London: Routledge.

Creedon, P.J., & Cramer, J. (Eds.). (2007). *Women in mass communication.* Thousand Oaks, CA: Sage.

Creswell, J.W., & Poth, C.N. (2007). *Qualitative inquiry and research design: Choosing among five approaches.* Thousand Oaks, CA: Sage.

Cruikshank, B. (1999). *The will to empower: Democratic citizens and other subjects.* Ithaca, NY: Cornell University Press.

Danley, S. (2018a). *A neighborhood politics of last resort: Post-Katrina New Orleans and the right to the city.* Montreal: McGill-Queen University Press.

Danley, S. (2018b). An activist in the field: Social media, ethnography, and community. *Journal of Urban Affairs*, 1–17. https://doi.org/10.1080/07352166.2018.1511797

Danley, S., & Weaver, R. (2018). "They're not building it for us": Displacement pressure, unwelcomeness, and protesting neighborhood investment. *Societies, 8*(3), 74. MDPI AG. https://doi.org/10.3390/soc8030074

Davoudi, S., & Madanipour, A. (2015). Localism and the "post-social" governmentality. In S. Davoudi & A. Madanipour (Eds.), *Reconsidering localism* (pp. 77–102). London: Routledge.

Ellen, R.F. (1984). *Ethnographic research: A guide to general conduct.* London: Academic Press.

Fullilove, M.T. (2016). *Root shock: How tearing up city neighborhoods hurts America, and what we can do about it.* New York: New Village Press.

Fuery, P., & Mansfield, N. (2000). *Cultural studies and critical theory.* Oxford: Oxford University Press.

Gill, B., Zimmer, R., Christman, J., & Blanc, S. (2007). Student achievement in privately managed and district-managed schools in Philadelphia since the state takeover. Research Brief. *RAND Corporation.* http://www.rand.org/pubs/research_briefs/RB9239.html.

Goho, S.A. (2012). Municipalities and hydraulic fracturing: Trends in state preemption. *Planning & Environmental Law, 64*(7), 3–9. https://doi.org/10.1080/15480755.2012.699757

Gold, R.L. (1958). Roles in sociological field observations. *Social Forces, 36*, 217–223. https://doi.org/10.2307/2573808

Goossens, J. (2014, July 18). Direct democracy and constitutional change: Institutional learning from state laboratories in the USA. *Icon – International Journal of Constitutional Law.* https://biblio.ugent.be/publication/5746208

Haas, J.E., Kates, R.W., & Bowden, M.J. (1977). Reconstruction following disaster. In *Reconstruction following disaster.* Cambridge, MA: MIT Press.

Hammersley, M., & Atkinson, P. (1983). *Ethnography principles in practice*. London: Tavistock.

Hannerz, U. (1980). *Exploring the city: Inquiries toward an urban anthropology*. Cambridge, MA: Columbia University Press.

Hansen, A., & Oliver-Smith, A. (1982). *Involuntary migration and resettlement: The problems and responses of dislocated peoples*. Boulder, CO: Westview Press.

Haynes, D. (2017). *Every day we live is the future: Surviving in a city of disasters*. Austin: University of Texas Press.

Hildreth, P. (2011). What is localism, and what implications do different models have for managing the local economy? *Local Economy: The Journal of the Local Economy Policy Unit, 26*(8), 702–714. https://doi.org/10.1177/0269094211422215

Hoffman, S. (2002). The monster and the mother: The symbolism of disaster. In S. Hoffman & A. Oliver-Smith (Eds.), *Catastrophe and culture: The anthropology of disaster* (pp. 113–141). Santa Fe, NM: School of American Research Press.

Hoffman, S., & Oliver-Smith, A. (2002). *Catastrophe and culture: The anthropology of disaster*. Santa Fe, NM: School of American Research Press.

Hutton, T. A. (2009). Trajectories of the new economy: Regeneration and dislocation in the inner city. *Urban Studies, 46*(5–6), 987–1001. https://doi.org/10.1177/0042098009103852

Hymes, D. H. (1978). *What is ethnography?* Sociolinguistics Working Paper# 45. Indiana University: Southwest Education Laboratory. https://eric.ed.gov/?id=ED159234

Jackson, P. (1985). Urban ethnography. *Progress in Geography, 9*(2), 157–176. https://doi.org/10.1177/030913258500900201

Jones, J. H. (1993). *Bad blood*. New York: Simon & Schuster and Free Press.

Kanuha, V. K. (2000). "Being" native versus "going native": Conducting social work research as an insider. *Social Work, 45*(5), 439–447. https://doi.org/10.1093/sw/45.5.439

Kasich, J.R.H.R.3734–104th Congress. (1995–1996). Personal Responsibility and Work Opportunity Reconciliation Act of 1996 | congress.gov | library of congress 06/27/1996 [cited 10/19/2016 2016]. Retrieved from Kasich, J.R.H.R.3734–104th Congress (1995–1996).

Katz, B., & Nowak, J. (2017). *The new localism: How cities can thrive in the age of populism*. Washington, DC: Brookings.

Kroll-Smith, S. (2018). *Recovering inequality: Hurricane Katrina, the San Francisco earthquake of 1906, and the aftermath of disaster*. Austin: University of Texas Press.

Klein, N., & Peet, R. (2008). The shock doctrine: The rise of disaster capitalism. *Human Geography, 1*(2), 130–133. https://doi.org/10.1177/194277860800100215

McCabe, C. (2019). Philly bill moves forward to provide free legal counsel for low-income tenants facing eviction. *Philadelphia Inquirer*. http://www.inquirer.com/real-estate/housing/city-council-right-to-counsel-bill-helen-gym-philadelphia-eviction-landlord-tenant-committee-20191029.html

McGranahan, C. (2014). What is ethnography? Teaching ethnographic sensibilities without fieldwork. *Teaching Anthropology, 4*, 23–36. https://doi.org/10.22582/ta.v4i1.421

Mock, B. (2015). New Orleans, the reluctant "city laboratory." *CITYLAB*. http://www.citylab.com/design/2015/08/new-orleans-the-reluctant-city-laboratory/401144/

Newman, B. J., Velez, Y., & Pearson-Merkowitz, S. (2016). Diversity of a different kind: Gentrification and its impact on social capital and political participation in Black communities. *Journal of Race, Ethnicity and Politics, 1*(2), 316–347. https://doi.org/10.1017/rep.2016.8

Oliver-Smith, A. (1986). *The martyred city. Death and rebirth in the Andes*. Albuquerque: University of New Mexico Press.

Pacheco-Vega, R., & Parizeau, K. (2018). Doubly engaged ethnography: Opportunities and challenges when working with vulnerable communities. *International Journal of Qualitative Methods, 17*(1–13). https://doi.org/10.1177/1609406918790653

Purcell, M. (2006). Urban democracy and the local trap. *Urban Studies, 43*(11), 1921–1941. https://doi.org/10.1080/00420980600897826

Ryan, G. S. (2017). An introduction to the origins, history and principles of ethnography. *Nurse Researcher, 24*(4), 15–21. https://doi.org/10.7748/nr.2017.e1470

Sakakeeny, M. (2012). New Orleans exceptionalism in "the neoliberal deluge" and "treme." *Perspectives on Politics, 10*(3), 723–726.

Saulny, S. (2006). Clamoring to come home to New Orleans projects. *New York Times*. http://www.nytimes.com/2006/06/06/us/nationalspecial/06housing.html

Skloot, R. (2017). *The immortal life of Henrietta Lacks*. Portland, OR: Broadway Books.

Sultana, F. (2007). Reflexivity, positionality and participatory ethics: Negotiating fieldwork dilemmas in international research. *Acme, 6,* 374–385. https://doi.org/10.1016/j.ijedudev.2008.02.004

Super, D. A. (2008). Laboratories of destitution: Democratic experimentalism and the failure of anti-poverty law. *University of Pennsylvania Law Review, 157,* 541–616. https://heinonline.org/HOL/LandingPage?handle=hein.journals/pnlr157&div=13&id=&page=

Walker, D. L., Geertsema, M., & Barnett, B. (2009). Inverting the inverted pyramid: A conversation about the use of feminist theories to teach journalism. *Feminist Teacher, 19*(3), 177–194. http://www.jstor.org/stable/40546099

Warren, S. (2014). "I want this place to thrive": Volunteering, coproduction and creative labour. *Area, 46,* 278–284. https://doi.org/10.1111/area.12112

Washington, H. A. (2006). *Medical apartheid: The dark history of medical experimentation on Black Americans from colonial times to the present*. New York: Doubleday Books.

Weber, L., & Peek, L. (2012). *Displaced: Life in the Katrina diaspora*. Austin: University of Texas Press.

11

Observation Research in Emergency and Disaster Management

Monica Andrea Bustinza, Kira Haensel,
and Nazife Emel Ganapati

> Go and sit in the lounges of the luxury hotels and on the doorsteps of the flophouses; sit on the Gold Coast settees and on the slum shakedowns; sit in the Orchestra Hall and in the Star and Garter Burlesk. In short, gentlemen, [*sic*] go get the seats of your pants dirty in real research. [McKinney, 1966, p. 71]
> —An unpublished quote by Robert Park (1920s), recorded by Howard Becker

Introduction

Robert Park's quote highlights the essence of the observation method: the researcher carefully watching people, "usually in a natural setting (that is, not one you have created or manipulated), over a period of time in order to learn about their patterns of interaction and behavior" (Gordon, 2019, p. 62). Observation allows the researcher not only to produce a direct account of the venue and the experience of its participants but also to make the research audience feel like they were "there."

In this chapter, we explore the use of the observation method in emergency management. In this field, observation is used across the social science disciplines, including sociology (e.g., Peek, 2003), anthropology (e.g., McLean et al., 2018), social work (e.g., Rahill, Ganapati, Clérismé, & Mukherji, 2014), medicine (e.g., Kaji & Lewis, 2008), urban planning (e.g., Ganapati & Ganapati, 2008), geography (Grove, 2014), and environmental sciences (Chandra, Dargusch, McNamara, Caspe, & Dalabajan, 2017). Our review of the literature is not meant to be systematic. Instead, it is meant to provide examples of the method's use in the field and to share our reflections on the method's current and potential use.

Our critical review of the interdisciplinary emergency management literature suggests that researchers find uniquely creative and context-specific ways of accessing the field and its participants (e.g., by giving participants footbaths in Japan). Yet, the observation method remains under-explained in the literature, in most cases with missing details on the nature of observation (e.g., structured vs. unstructured). It is also under-utilized in preparedness and response research. We urge researchers to tap more into the observation method's potential for (1) theory and model building; (2) collecting numerical data through structured observation; and (3) exploring the promise of the virtual world to collect data (e.g., using Avatars in Second Life) in emergency contexts.

In the next section, we briefly introduce the observation method (the *what* of the method) and its strengths (the *why* of the method), followed by a discussion about its challenges. We then summarize the sampled disaster literature utilizing this method and share our reflections on its use. The chapter concludes with new directions for conducting observational research in the field.

The *What* of the Observation Method

While observing, the researcher can engage their senses simultaneously and collect rich data (Stoller, 1989). Such data could be qualitative or quantitative derived from verbal or non-verbal exchanges. *Verbal exchanges* include conversational interactions. *Non-verbal exchanges* can include body movements, facial expressions, or tone of voice (Marshall & Rossman, 2014). Along these lines, observation can be either *unstructured* or *structured*. In unstructured observation, the researcher immerses oneself in the observation venue without clearly defining the elements to be observed before the study. Alternatively, in structured observation, the researcher has predetermined boundaries for verbal and/or non-verbal exchanges to be observed and can develop a checklist (e.g., how many people and how many times). The researcher may also put together a schedule before data collection and use time or event sampling to determine time periods or pre-specified events for when the observation will take place (see Gordon, 2019, for sampling in observation). Although structured observations enable "relatively uniform comparisons" across different observation venues (Friedman, 2012, p. 56), it may lead to the loss of potentially valuable data that does not get recorded because it does not fit some predetermined criteria. However, structured and unstructured approaches are not mutually exclusive (Friedman, 2012) and can be quite fluid. For example, researchers can start their research in an unstructured manner and structure it as research themes evolve (O'Leary, 2020).

Whether the researcher decides to conduct a *structured* or *unstructured* observation, she can adopt different levels of participation and roles (Gold, 1957). Observations can be non-participatory or participatory. The former does not allow the researcher to engage with people and take an active role in the observation's venue. The latter involves the researcher fully immersing oneself as a participant in an interactive observation experience. While non-participant observation is non-invasive for study participants, it may hinder the researcher's ability to have an in-depth and intimate understanding of the setting that may be developed through participant observation (Bonner & Tolhurst, 2002). At the same time, the participant researcher may sympathize with the observed, which may affect data reliability. As such, the researcher must decide what level of participation is appropriate given the context, research goals, and questions (Laurier, 2010).

The observation method has common elements with ethnographic research as described in Chapter 10. Both require the researcher to understand the context in greater depth by watching and taking detailed notes about the people, their interactions, and the natural setting, as well as collecting qualitative or quantitative data. Furthermore, both need to be based on trust, so that the participants are "comfortable enough" with the researcher that "they are willing to behave in their usual ways while" the researcher is observing (Gordon, 2019, p. 66). However, the two have three notable differences. First, observers may be detached and conduct observation only from time to time (e.g., observing five public meetings), while ethnographers are deeply immersed in the culture and become part of research subjects' everyday lives for months or even years. In the words of Gordon (2019), "not all observation researchers do their research from afar – many do integrate themselves into the group; ethnographers, however, *always* do" (p. 64). Second, observers mainly watch and listen to the venue. Ethnographers collect other types of data (e.g., diaries) and conduct data informally (e.g., asking informal and clarifying questions to people as they mingle with them) in their fieldwork. Third, observers are sometimes involved in applied research; yet, this is very rare in the case of ethnographers (Gordon et al., 2006).

In emergency management, observation has typically been utilized at events or organizations (e.g., the emergency operations centers [EOCs]) while most ethnographic work has been conducted by researchers embedded in communities. Our chapter's focus is on observation research. However, we make references to ethnographic work periodically and we do indicate if the method is an ethnographic one.

The *Why* of the Observation Method

The observation method offers seven unique advantages in emergency management research. First, it allows for a more authentic and holistic understanding than other methods, as data is often collected using multiple senses. Moreover, since data collection occurs in a natural setting, researchers have the potential to understand not only the setting but also its components, interactions that take place in a particular location, indicative processes, and developments that might not be otherwise possible in a synthetic environment (Homan, 1980). This is unlike interviews and focus groups with often guided discussions and access to only parts of such data (Ritchie, Lewis, Nicholls, & Ormston, 2013).

Second, it enables the researcher to capture data on verbal and non-verbal exchanges among different stakeholders. This can be extremely informative, as emergency and disaster management encompass numerous actors including elected officials, emergency responders, and affected populations. The method can inform researchers, for instance, on how elected officials make decisions and manage their emotions at the EOCs or how emergency responders handle affected populations.

Third, observation can help understand the differences between what people say and what they actually do. With other methods, the researcher relies on the information provided by the participant, whereas in observation the researcher can directly experience the actions and interactions of participants in their natural setting, uncovering information that may not be revealed in an interview or focus group. As noted by Quarantelli (1997), "field workers who do good participant observations can "see" things that cannot or will not be reported on in a later interview" (p. 12).

Fourth, observation is a relatively less invasive method that typically does not disrupt study participants' routines – especially non-participant observations. Interviews or focus groups require dedicated time and the willingness to participate, which can be a lot to ask for under already stressful post-disaster conditions. For instance, researchers studying EOCs will not be able to interview emergency management officials at the time of a full-scale activation but can conduct observation at the EOCs without burdening these officials. They can also supplement their observation data with subsequent interviews or focus group data for a deeper understanding of their observation-based authentic data.

Fifth, observation allows capturing of data as events unfold, changes in the venue occur, and behaviors take place right then and there and as people navigate through these changes (Morrison, Haley, Sheehan, & Taylor, 2011; Mulhall, 2003). This has implications for disaster research, as the method provides a more accurate understanding of the disaster context and of how people, households, organizations, and communities prepare for, respond to, and recover from disasters.

Sixth, the method's potential for collecting data on the physical setting (Mulhall, 2003) is important for disaster researchers. Disaster researchers can collect data, for example, on neighborhoods' physical vulnerabilities, disaster impacts on housing and infrastructure, and how neighborhoods recover physically. When they publish their observation findings, through "thick description" (Geertz, 1973), researchers can assist their readers with visualizing the disaster setting.

Seventh, observation is suitable for gathering information about behaviors that are "complex, difficult, or embarrassing for participants to recall or describe" (Mair, Whitford, & Mackellar, 2013, p. 60). In disaster contexts, affected populations may be experiencing confusion, loss, and frustration (Oliver-Smith, 1996), or may be suffering from the stigma of aid (Fothergill, 2003; Ganapati, 2013b). The method can help people understand such behaviors without directly asking or offending them.

Challenges of Conducting Observations

Although there are a variety of advantages to conducting observational studies, there are some challenges a researcher must be aware of. Along these lines, below we discuss some of the challenges that are unique to disaster contexts. Moreover, we broadly categorize these challenges as either ethical or logistical challenges. Potential ethical challenges relate to informed consent, the Hawthorne Effect, and researcher misrepresentations and/or burdens. Logistic challenges are associated with accessing and exiting the field and recording and managing data collected.

Ethical Challenges

Informed Consent

There are two complications concerning the expectation of receiving consent. First, as observation is not as well-known as other data collection methods (e.g., interviews), people can have difficulties understanding the research process and purpose of observations (Mulhall, 2003). Second, depending on the scene, it can be challenging to inform and seek consent from everyone who enters into the observation setting. This applies especially to venues where people continuously enter and exit the field (e.g., offices, parks, or plazas). In cases where some people provide consent while others do not, researchers may not collect or utilize data involving the exchanges of those without consent, and only include those with consent (see Gordon, 2019, p. 72). As a result, the research might be forced to disregard valuable data if consent cannot be acquired.

Researcher's Involvement and the Hawthorne Effect

The decision to conduct a *covert* or *overt* study, where the researcher disguises or discloses her identity as an observer (Walliman, 2017), has important ethical implications. In a covert study, the decision may affect the relationships between the researcher and the observed if the researcher's identity is revealed later in the process – unless the venue is a public place (e.g., park). In an overt study, the decision may threaten data validity as people might be aware that they are being observed and may change their behavior while being observed (Turnock & Gibson, 2001), often described as the *Hawthorne Effect* (Mayo, 1949). However, some research has indicated that people being observed may become used to the researcher over time and less inclined to change their behavior in the researcher's presence (Palinkas, 2006).

Researcher's Misrepresentation of or Burdens on the Observed

Disaster contexts are characterized by relatively high levels of vulnerability and uncertainty. Hence, the researcher needs to verify that she not only does not misrepresent the study participants but also ensures that her research does not further harm disaster survivors or place any additional burden on those who are there to aid the survivors. To address these concerns, the researcher can (1) invite study participants to check the observation findings; (2) triangulate the findings with interviews, focus groups, surveys, and/or document analyses (Creswell & Miller, 2000); (3) conduct participatory observation to view the events from the participants' eyes; (4) have the data coded by an independent researcher (Creswell & Miller, 2000); and/or (5) explicitly acknowledge in publications that "the physical vantage point from which they [researchers] make the observation also makes a difference" (Gordon, 2019, p. 66) and elaborate on how researcher biases may have affected data and its interpretation.

Logistical Challenges

Accessing and Exiting the Field

Gaining access to the observation setting or group can require significant amounts of "time, effort, patience, and diplomacy" (Baker, 2006, p. 180), unless the researcher is already part of the setting or group. In a disaster context, this process can be especially difficult, as people already find themselves in stressful situations. Government officials, for instance, might not grant researchers access to a hurricane-impacted area before evacuated residents return to the area for security and safety purposes. Exiting the field might also be a challenge for researchers. Phillips (2014) recommends the researcher to stay in the field until no novel behavior is observed, which can be especially challenging in disaster situations as patterns of behavior in a highly dynamic and complex environment may be difficult to grasp. Some strategies to address this include working in teams to cover multiple angles and collecting and analyzing observation data concurrently in the field so that the researcher can change the observation's focus if required (Gordon, 2019). Another issue relates to *how* to leave the field (Baker, 2006): abruptly (e.g., upon the termination of a funded study) or gradually (when no novel behavior can be observed, as described by Phillips, 2014). In contexts where the disaster researcher is highly immersed in the setting, as in ethnographic research, exiting the field can be emotionally challenging (Mukherji, Ganapati, & Rahill, 2014) as well as procedurally difficult.

Recording and Managing Data

Researchers typically record verbal or non-verbal exchanges in observation settings through field notes, photography, video and audio recordings, and/or illustrations, a combination of which offer benefits for a singular study (Paterson, Bottorff, & Hewat, 2003). Creating categories for such observation data may be challenging for researchers. The same is true for recording observation data. Researchers typically take quick, brief notes about the highlights of behaviors, actions, and events of the observed setting in the field, often referred to as *jottings* (Emerson, Fretz, & Shaw, 2001), since (1) they do not have much time to take long notes about everything they see; and (2) taking long notes may affect the behavior of the observed. While jotting down notes, researchers may "often experience deep ambivalence about whether, when, where, and how to write" them (Emerson et al., 2001, p. 357). Moreover, researchers need to elaborate on the jottings outside the field through their *field notes* (Delamont, 1975). These notes should be thorough, detailed, and concrete descriptions of what has been observed and include the researcher's interpretations of those data (Marshall & Rossman, 2014). Procedurally, they should be written immediately after leaving the observed setting – ideally the same day (see Emerson et al., 2001; Emerson, Fretz, & Shaw, 2011; Mulhall, 2003; see Phillippi & Lauderdale, 2018 for more on-field notes). Alternatively, video and audio recordings may be intimidating and stressful for the subjects being recorded (Mack, Woodsong, MacQueen, Guest, & Namey, 2005). Finally, receiving institutional review board approvals for observation research might be demanding due to the method's potential to cause personal harm to the participants (e.g., through revealing of their identity) or the researchers (e.g., in covert research).

Examples From the Emergency and Disaster Management Literature

Since we have explained some of the advantages and challenges associated with completing observation studies, we will now provide information on a sampling of how the observation method has been utilized in emergency management literature. As displayed in Table 11.1, this method has been applied to disasters across disciplines and in a variety of settings ranging from public meetings, parks, plazas, and community events (e.g., festivals, weddings, funerals) to private gatherings (e.g., dinners). Below is a summary of this interdisciplinary literature, structured around disaster phases similar to the examples from the literature presented in Chapter 7. Moreover, our goal in this section is to provide examples of how the observation method can be applied in emergency and disaster management rather than to provide a systematic review of the literature.

TABLE 11.1 Selected Research Utilizing Observation Method by Author (Alphabetical Order)

Author(s)	First Author's Discipline or Affiliation Unit	Disaster Phase Relevance	Research Context	Duration in the Field	Nature of Observation (P: Participant, N: Non-Participant, S: Structured, U: Unstructured, if Indicated)	Purpose of Study (S)/ Observation (O)	Other Data Collection Methods
Aros and Gibbons (2018)	Business and public policy	Response	United States	Multiday (10 days)	Observation of response-focused national disaster exercises facilitated by FEMA (e.g., related to response coordination and defense logistics)	S: Assessing the effects of different types of communication media on response. O: Building agent-based simulation model of inter-organizational communications during response coordination	Informal interviews; review of secondary sources
Atsumi and Goltz (2014)	Human sciences	Preparedness, response and recovery	Japan	15 years	Ethnographic methods involving disaster volunteers (P)	S: Understanding the evolution of a volunteer organization	Review of secondary sources; interviews
Chandra et al. (2017)	Earth and environmental sciences	Mitigation	Philippines	February–August 2015 (7 months)	Attending school sessions and taking transect walks by smallholder farms	S: Identifying the challenges in implementing new technologies and management techniques to addressing climate risks in smallholder agriculture	Interviews; focus groups

(Continued)

TABLE 11.1 (Continued)

Author(s)	First Author's Discipline or Affiliation Unit	Disaster Phase Relevance	Research Context	Duration in the Field	Nature of Observation (P: Participant, N: Non-Participant, S: Structured, U: Unstructured, if Indicated)	Purpose of Study (S)/ Observation (O)	Other Data Collection Methods
Epstein et al. (2018)	Earth sciences	Recovery	Nepal	—	Attending public meetings, training workshops and community events (e.g., festivals, wedding, funeral)	S: Tracking diverse recovery trajectories at the household and community levels	Focus groups; interviews; surveys
Ganapati (2013b)	Public administration	Recovery	Turkey	6.5 months	Attending events held by the government (e.g., public meetings) and by the community (e.g., street protests, campaigns, fundraising events, training sessions of search and rescue teams, and annual commemoration events (P)	S: Identifying the downsides of social capital; O: Seeing events in context, understanding daily routines and everyday lives of affected populations and policymakers	Interviews; focus group; review of secondary sources
Grove (2014)	Geography and earth sciences	Preparedness, mitigation and recovery	Jamaica	7 months	Institutional ethnography with the national-level disaster management agency, including transect walks (P)	S: Conducting a critical analysis of participatory disaster resilience programs in the country	Interviews; focus groups

Study	Discipline	Phase	Country	Duration	Observation	Aim	Methods
Javor et al. (2014)	Justice	Preparedness and response	Canada	—	Observing an emergency simulation exercise on a severe winter storm scenario (researcher-driven) at EOCs (N)	S: Understanding decision-making processes at EOCs	Interviews; focus groups
Kontar et al. (2018)	Law and diplomacy	Mitigation and recovery	United States and Russia	Several visits October 2015–September 2016 (e.g., 12 months)	Observing interactions between the residents and the physical environment and between the residents and local officials as well as flood sites	S: Examining key components of flood risk and existing practices in flood risk reduction	Archival data; surveys; focus group discussions
Lorenz, Schulze, and Voss (2018)	Disaster research	Preparedness and response	Germany	7 hours	Observing a full-scale training exercise on a severe weather scenario (S)	S: Understanding factors hindering collaboration of unaffiliated and professional rescue team members	Survey; interviews; review of secondary sources
Peek (2003)	Sociology	Response and preparedness	United States	6 weeks	Observing the lives of Muslim students in New York and Colorado (e.g., by attending prayers, weddings, and dinners and traveling with them)	S: Exploring responses and reactions toward Muslim students following the events of 9/11 O: Verifying findings from focus groups and interviews (P)	Focus groups; interviews

(Continued)

TABLE 11.1 (Continued)

Author(s)	First Author's Discipline or Affiliation Unit	Disaster Phase Relevance	Research Context	Duration in the Field	Nature of Observation (P: Participant, N: Non-Participant, S: Structured, U: Unstructured, if Indicated)	Purpose of Study (S)/ Observation (O)	Other Data Collection Methods
Rahill et al. (2014)	Social work	Recovery	Haiti	Visits over 1 year	Observing camps, church meetings, cluster meetings, and community meetings (e.g., voodoo ceremonies) (P)	S: Determining the role of social capital in shelter recovery O: Reinforcing trust, getting referrals, seeing events in contexts, understanding daily routines and experiences of affected populations	Interviews; focus groups; review of secondary sources
Saha (2015)	Sociology	Preparedness and mitigation	Bangladesh	–	Field observation	S: Assessing vulnerability to disaster risks O: developing a conceptual framework for disaster risk reduction	Focus groups
Sienkiewicz-Małyjurek, Kożuch, and Szczygłowski (2019)	Organization and management	Preparedness and response	Poland	Over a 2-year period	Observing exercises at the fire service headquarters at the provincial level (P)	S: Understanding inter-organizational learning processes in the public safety management system	Focus groups; review of secondary sources (e.g., videos of rescue operations, photos, rules of collaboration)

Study	Field	Country	Duration	Observation	Purpose	Methods
Tanwattana and Toyoda (2018)	Environmental research	Thailand	34 months	Observing a game involving different flooding scenarios	S: Strengthening community-based disaster risk management through gaming simulation O: Understanding players' decisions	Interviews; focus groups; workshops on gaming; review of secondary data
Uddin, Ahmad, and Warnitchai (2018)	Environmental resources and development	Nepal	A few hours daily for 1 month	Observing temporary disaster shelter and visiting affected areas	S: Determining why some affected populations stay in shelters while others do not O: Getting in-depth insights into the lives of those who stay in temporary shelters, and to triangulate data from other methods	Informal interviews; review of secondary sources

Disaster Preparedness

Disaster preparedness research involving observational research has typically been completed in emergency shelters and at the EOCs (Phillips, 1997), as well as in emergency drills or with different groups. Adeola (2009), for instance, conducted observation at emergency shelters to better understand the experiences of those who sought refuge (or not) at the shelters during Hurricane Katrina in 2005. The observation method also allowed the researcher to get a closer view of neighborhoods that "remained as ghost towns" (p. 468). Studies at EOCs typically collect data on those participating in government-driven (e.g., Sienkiewicz-Małyjurek, Kożuch, & Szczygłowski, 2019) or researcher-driven scenario building exercises (Javor, Pearce, Thompson, & Moran, 2014). Some also supplement such data with data from interviews, focus groups, or secondary sources (e.g., videos, photos, rules). Researchers also utilize the observation method in emergency drill contexts (Aros & Gibbons, 2018; Kaji & Lewis, 2008; Lorenz, Schulze, & Voss, 2018; Magnussen et al., 2018).

There are also a few noteworthy studies that are based on observing groups of people, including those who are disaster volunteers or residents of disaster-prone communities. Examples of the former include Atsumi and Goltz's (2014) 15-year ethnographic study on disaster volunteers in Japan and Ganapati's (2009, 2012, 2013b) study of place-based search and rescue teams after the 1999 Marmara Earthquake in Turkey. An example of the latter is Tanwattana and Toyoda's (2018) study that was based on structured observations of those who played a disaster simulation game in flood-prone communities in Thailand.

Disaster Response

Disaster response literature utilizing observation focuses on three major themes. The first theme relates to the experiences of those who are at the emergency shelters (e.g., Adeola, 2009; Uddin, Ahmad, & Warnitchai, 2018) and EOCs (e.g., Maki, 2013; Wachtendorf & Kendra, 2012). Uddin et al. (2018), for example, conducted daily observations in temporary shelters in Kathmandu, Nepal, for about a month to collect in-depth insights into the lives of shelter residents following the 2015 Gorkha earthquake. They triangulated such data with data derived from interviews and other data collected by the government (e.g., daily shelter population count). Another example comes from Wachtendorf and Kendra (2012), who conducted their study at an EOC. Their study was conducted after the 9/11 disaster in New York City and involved 750 hours of observation to understand how organizations respond to changing environments. Besides the EOC, the researchers spent time observing Ground Zero, the Federal Disaster Field Office, incident command posts, staging areas, family assistance centers, and interagency coordination meetings, among others. They supplemented data with primary and secondary documents (e.g., situation reports, after action reports) and subsequent interviews.

The second theme present in the literature is organizational response and inter-organizational collaboration during a response. One of the earlier studies on this theme was Drabek's (1968) study on the Indianapolis Coliseum explosion on October 31, 1963. This study focused on inter-organizational coordination and was based on observation of the environment, coordination, control, and preplanning as well as interviews. A more recent study includes Broby, Lassetter, Williams, and Winters (2018). To help international medical disaster relief agencies provide more effective services, the study involved field observations in Greece and Jordan in the context of the Syrian refugee crisis and the Ebola outbreak. In Broby et al.'s study, the authors observed three refugee camps and conducted interviews with key personnel in these agencies to supplement their observational data.

The third theme relates to the disaster experiences of response teams (e.g., Kroll, Remington, Awasthi, & Ganapati, 2020; Remington & Ganapati, 2017; Stadler, 2006) and of communities (or their parts; McLean et al., 2018; Schmeltz et al., 2013). An example of the former is Stadler (2006) that involved observation to understand the experiences of a Jewish ultra-Orthodox organization's volunteers involved in identifying victims of terror attacks by "collecting, matching, and recomposing pieces of human flesh and blood in the public arena" (p. 837). Additionally, an example of the latter is Schmeltz et al. (2013) which used firsthand observation to understand community responses in a low-lying, low-income, and diverse New York neighborhood affected by Hurricane Sandy in 2012.

Disaster Recovery

Disaster recovery literature that uses observation has similar themes with literature focusing on the response phase. Besides studies on emergency shelters that extend beyond the response to recovery phase summarized above (e.g., Uddin et al., 2018; Adeola, 2009), studies utilize the observation to understand inter-organizational collaboration, experiences of those who help affected populations, and recovery at the community level.

Opdyke, Lepropre, Javernick-Will, and Koschmann (2017) constitute an example of studies on inter-organizational collaboration during recovery. This study employed social network analysis to understand inter-organizational resource collaboration for infrastructure reconstruction in 19 communities in the Philippines after Super Typhoon Haiyan in 2013. It involved observation of organizational meetings and informal gatherings, as well as interviews, surveys, and a review of secondary sources collected within 6 and 12 months after the disaster.

There is also a small but growing body of literature that utilizes observation to understand the experiences of recovery workers. For example, the third author of this chapter conducted studies in Haiti after the 2010 earthquake. One of these studies (Remington & Ganapati, 2017), examines the skills that are required of aid workers involved in recovery. Moreover, Kroll et al. (2020) focused on the negative consequences of doing response and recovery work, including burnout and post-traumatic stress disorder. In both, the authors supplement data from in-depth interviews with a review of secondary sources and field observation conducted at aid agencies' operation bases, offices, and the UN Cluster Meetings organized to ensure coordination in recovery.

Studies also utilize the observation method to understand the recovery experiences of affected communities and their residents. Some of the groups studied include subsistence farmers (Epstein et al., 2018), women (Morrow & Enarson, 1996), children (Fothergill & Peek, 2015), and Muslim Americans (Peek, 2005, 2011). For example, in their seminal study, *Children of Katrina*, Fothergill and Peek (2015) spent 7 years observing and interviewing hundreds of children, their teachers, family members, and others important in their lives at parks, playgrounds, and other public places to understand how children affected by Hurricane Katrina experienced, coped with, and recovered from disasters. In another study, Peek (2005) carried out participant observation of the lives of the Muslim Americans in the United States (e.g., by attending prayers, weddings, and dinners) after 9/11 to verify data from focus groups and interviews on religious identity formation.

Other studies have relied on observation to understand the factors that help or hinder recovery in affected communities. For instance, Bhandari, Okada, and Knottnerus (2011) observed the ritual behaviors of earthquake survivors in Nepal to understand their role in recovery. After conducting participant observation of civic networks that emerged after the 1999 earthquake in Turkey, as well as interviews, a focus group, and a review of secondary sources, Ganapati (2012) noted that social capital helps women's recovery as it is "therapeutic in nature and helps women gain empowerment and avoid the stigma of public assistance" (p. 419). In her follow-up work, Ganapati (2013a) highlighted social capital's role in helping perpetuate gender-based assumptions and putting women in conflict with state authorities in Turkey. Finally, Rahill et al. (2014) and Masud-All-Kamal and Hassan (2018) have also relied on observation to highlight the enabling and hindering aspects of social capital in recovery.

Disaster Mitigation

Mitigation studies examined for this chapter have utilized the observation method at the organizational (Grove, 2013, 2014) and community levels. An example of organizational level studies is Grove's institutional ethnographic work (2013, 2014) with the national-level disaster management agency, in addition to their study of participatory resilience programming in Jamaica. This research involved archival research, policy analysis, and interviews with staff from the agency and its partner agencies, along with participatory methods (e.g., transect walks).

At the community level, researchers have used observation techniques in the context of two themes. The first theme relates to community-based groups and interactions between different groups (e.g., Kontar et al., 2018; Tanwattana, 2018). Tanwattana (2018), for example, focused on the formation of spontaneous organizations in flood-prone urban communities in Thailand. Based on participatory action research, the researcher conducted a 34-month community engagement process, collecting primary data from interviews, surveys, and participant observations (e.g., at public and community meetings, and community organizing initiatives).

The second community theme relates to the physical aspects of disaster risk vulnerability and disaster risk reduction (e.g., Amoako, 2016; Chandra et al., 2017; Chowdhooree & Islam, 2018; Nikuze, Sliuzas, Flacke, & van Maarseveen, 2019). In his work on the politics of flooding, specifically the role of local authorities, Amoako (2016) used field observation to map physical vulnerabilities in informal settlements in Accra, Ghana, and gathered additional evidence from secondary sources, focus group discussions, and interviews.

Reflections on the Use of the Observation Method

Based on our critical reading of sample studies, our reflections on the use of observation methods in emergency management literature relate to six areas.

First, although our review is not a systematic one, it is important to note that we noticed more studies utilizing the method during disaster recovery than other disaster phases. Studies on disaster preparedness seemed to be less in general, particularly in the context of the Global South. Preparedness studies that were conducted on the EOCs and emergency drills, for instance, dealt mainly with countries of the Global North, examples being the United States (Aros & Gibbons, 2018; Kaji & Lewis, 2008), Germany (Lorenz et al., 2018), and Norway (Magnussen et al., 2018). Perhaps this trend could be explained by a lack of established EOCs in the Global South, or access-related challenges (e.g., getting permission to attend training drills). Although we found studies focusing on responses, few gave the impression that the observation took place at the time of response. Most were possibly conducted during the recovery phase but explored issues related to the response phase. Exceptions include Wachtendorf and Kendra (2012), whose authors arrived within 2 days after the 9/11 disaster in the United States, and Maki (2013), whose author was embedded at the EOC in Japan during the recovery phase of the Tohoku-Oki earthquake.

Second, researchers utilize observation in a number of venues. These venues include (1) EOCs (e.g., Javor et al., 2014; Wachtendorf & Kendra, 2012); (2) emergency response drills (e.g., Aros & Gibbons, 2018); (3) organizations involved in emergency management, including agencies similar to FEMA in the United States (e.g., Grove, 2014); and (4) affected communities (e.g., Rahill et al., 2014). Some of these venues involve events or places that are open to the public where researchers spend time, such as parks and playgrounds (e.g., Fothergill & Peek, 2015), public meetings (e.g., Epstein et al., 2018), street protests (e.g., Rahill et al., 2014), and public transportation (e.g., Peek, 2005). Others are semi-private places, such as the offices and gatherings of volunteer teams (e.g., Atsumi & Goltz, 2014; Ganapati, 2012, 2013a, 2013b). Still, others are private worlds that may require researchers to receive permission for access, such as emergency drills (e.g., Aros & Gibbons, 2018) and dinners (e.g., Peek, 2005).

Third, although many scholars do not explain the process of their entry into the field in their writing, some researchers find unique ways to obtain access to study participants, connect with them, and gain their trust. The two examples are Rahill et al. (2014), which also involved one of the authors of this chapter, and Atsumi and Goltz (2014). Rahill's research team attended a voodoo ceremony in Haiti to have better access to Haitian elites who held critical positions in the government at the time. To encourage disaster survivors to share their life histories and help relieve their stresses, Atsumi and Goltz (2014) used the footbath technique, a "non-traditional method of interviewing" (p. 226). This technique involved young students bathing the feet of interviewees in warm water (for 10–15 minutes), which is a sign of respect in Japanese culture. The technique served as a status equalizer "between young urban and well-educated interviewers and older, rural residents who have experienced the trauma of a disaster" (p. 227).

Fourth, we find emergency management studies to be lacking important details on the observation method in general. Few studies, for instance, specified the structured (e.g., Lorenz et al., 2018) versus unstructured (e.g., Budosan & Bruno, 2011) or participant (e.g., Ganapati, 2012, 2013a, 2013b) versus non-participant (e.g., Javor et al., 2014) nature of their observation. Similarly, not many studies explained why they used this method in the first place, how they ensured access to the field, what they observed, what the observation's duration was, or how they recorded and analyzed observation data. There was also little to no discussion on the challenges faced in the field, including ethical ones, or how the researchers' identities might have affected the data collection and analysis process (reflexivity). Lack of details on the method has perhaps to do with space limitations in journal articles. However, some articles dedicate separate sections to each data collection method (e.g., Rahill et al.,

2014) and elaborate on what the method involved. Javor et al.'s (2014) study, for instance, explained in great length what the observation involved, how they analyzed transcriptions and used videos to better capture body language and gestures, and how they kept a journal of notes.

Fifth, similar to what was discussed in Chapter 4, most studies in emergency management conduct observation to triangulate data from other data collection methods (e.g., interviews, focus groups; Peek, 2003) or to better understand different aspects of the disaster context, including the lives and daily routines of affected populations (e.g., Adeola, 2009; Peek, 2003) and response and recovery workers (e.g., Ganapati, 2013b; Remington & Ganapati, 2017; Kroll et al., 2020; Weber & Messias, 2012). Some studies highlight observation's unique potential to understand physical changes in communities, such as the impact of the disaster (e.g., Amoako, 2016; Chandra et al., 2017; Chowdhooree & Islam, 2018; Nikuze et al., 2019; Saha, 2015). Other studies note the method's role in building theories or models. Saha (2015), for example, assessed vulnerability to disaster risk in coastal Bangladesh after tropical Cyclone Aila in 2009 through focus group and field observation. The researcher used data collected from these methods to develop a conceptual framework for disaster risk reduction, depicting the relationships between "root causes, dynamic pressures and unsafe conditions of vulnerability, and various elements at disaster risk" (p. 727). Aros and Gibbons's (2018) study utilized the observation method, in combination with what they call "informal" interviews and review of secondary sources (e.g., FEMA documents, exercise data), to develop an agent-based simulation model of inter-organizational communications during the response coordination.[1] In that sense, the study has implications for engineering education.

Sixth, there is an emerging literature that introduces metrics that could be used while conducting structured observation (Leskens, Brugnach, & Hoekstra, 2019; Savoia, Biddinger, Burstein, & Stoto, 2010). For example, Leskens and colleagues (2019) utilize the observation method to assess group decision-making processes in the context of interactive flood simulation models. They introduce measurable metrics that help monitor and evaluate three aspects of such processes: (1) collaborative knowledge construction processes, (2) the content of knowledge available, and (3) outcomes.

Conclusion and Future Directions

In this chapter, we reviewed the observation method in emergency management research, revealing its under-explained nature in the literature and its under-utilization, specifically in preparedness and response phases. We presented the venues within which researchers have conducted observation with varying levels of access and their unique yet creative and context-specific ways of entering into the field. We also summarized the method's potential for theory and model building and acknowledged newer efforts to introduce metrics to collect systematic observation data.

Current applications of the method carried out in natural settings partly reflect limitations imposed by the on-site conditions (Landahl, Bennett, & Phillips, 2019). For instance, unlike hurricane events, earthquakes have no lead time. Hence, they prohibit researchers from conducting observation in communities vulnerable to earthquakes or at organizations immediately before an event (unless the researcher is embedded in that particular context). Researchers can collect data on such communities and organizations only through other data collection methods (e.g., review of secondary sources, interviews, focus groups). Furthermore, post-impact research relies on gaining access to a particular setting, which may be challenging for the researcher, specifically because of the severity of damage on an area and people of interest (see Mukherji et al., 2014 for details). In some cases, the impacted area may be closed even to the residents, not to mention researchers.

Despite the limitations of disaster contexts, emergency management researchers can take several steps while publishing their observation-based research. While using more than one data collection method, for example, they can dedicate separate sections to each method and elaborate on what each method involved, as in Rahill et al. (2014) and Javor et al. (2014) to give due diligence to each method (including observation!).

Researchers can also spell out their specific reasons for conducting observations along with other important methodological details (e.g., participant/structured nature of observation, roles played, location and duration of observation, and recording and data analysis) in their articles, even if observation is not their primary data collection method. Moreover, they can be more reflective researchers in their writing, "consciously stepping back from action in order to theorize what is taking place, and also stepping up to be an active part of that contextualized action" (Attia & Edge, 2017, p. 33). These steps can help their audience evaluate the credibility and quality of their fieldwork and research.

While researchers are designing their studies, they can think beyond using observation for validating results from other data collection methods and for having a more in-depth understanding of the context (especially physical aspects). Observation can also help build theories and models when properly designed and implemented, which we demonstrated in this chapter. Additionally, researchers can also tap more into their creative side, especially while negotiating and/or renegotiating access in the field, and thinking of culturally appropriate techniques to connect with and gain the trust of the study's population.

Our review of the literature indicates several areas for future research. First, there is a need for more observation studies focusing on preparedness, especially in the Global South, at least on hazards with early-warning mechanisms (e.g., hurricanes). Second, future observation studies can focus more on disaster response as observing processes and changes in the environment and the behavior of people can be especially important in such relatively fast-changing contexts. Furthermore, observation can provide important insights that are difficult to derive from the review of secondary sources alone (as most studies focusing on organizational response do). Third, another possible line of observation research is structured observation in both natural and experimental settings, as we came across more studies that seemed to be using the unstructured approach. The observation technique can be useful in uncovering unconscious and unsystematic data in a given context (Rossman & Rallis, 2016). Structured observations can help researchers collect not only textual but also non-textual data, measure different concepts, and examine links between these concepts (e.g., by statistically testing hypotheses) that could be helpful for quantitative or mixed-methods studies. Finally, researchers can take advantage of new technologies that allow for applying ethnography to virtual and digital settings (Hart, 2017; Tunçalp & Lê, 2014). They could, for instance, conduct observation in online communities, as in the case of Saputro's (2016) work that examined crisis communication of members of a web-based organization formed to respond to the crisis after the 2010 Mt. Merapi eruption in Indonesia. Researchers could also conduct synchronous, experimental studies in Second Life using avatars looking at the risk perception, evacuation, and shelter behavior of vulnerable populations or how vulnerable populations and emergency managers interact with one another.

The virtual world is still waiting to be explored! Robert Park's times have changed. You may not need to get your pants literally dirty after all. You may just get your pants virtually dirty in the world of reality.

Note

1. See Mostafavi and Ganapati (2019) and Davidson and Nozick (2018) for simulation applications in and its further potential for interdisciplinary disaster research.

Further Reading

Becker, H.S., & Geer, B. (1957). Participant observation and interviewing: A comparison. *Human Organization, 16*(3), 28–32.

Gans, H.J. (1982). *The Levitt owners: Ways of life and politics in a new suburban community.* New York: Columbia University Press.

Geertz, C. (1973). Thick description: Toward an interpretive theory of culture. In C. Geertz (Ed.), *The interpretation of cultures: Selected essays* (pp. 3–30). New York: Basic Books.

Gold, R.L. (1957). Roles in sociological field observations. *Social Forces, 36(3),* 217–223.

Horowitz, R. (1986). Remaining an outsider: Membership as a threat to research rapport. *Urban Life, 14*(4), 409–430.

Snow, D.A., Benford, R.D., & Anderson, L. (1986). Fieldwork roles and informational yield: A comparison of alternative settings and roles. *Urban Life, 14*(4), 377–408.

References

Adeola, F.O. (2009). Katrina cataclysm: Does duration of residency and prior experience affect impacts, evacuation, and adaptation behavior among survivors? *Environment and Behavior, 41*(4), 459–489.

Amoako, C. (2016). Brutal presence or convenient absence: The role of the state in the politics of flooding in informal Accra, Ghana. *Geoforum, 77,* 5–16.

Aros, S.K., & Gibbons, D.E. (2018). Exploring communication media options in an inter-organizational disaster response coordination network using agent-based simulation. *European Journal of Operational Research, 269*(2), 451–465.

Atsumi, T., & Goltz, J.D. (2014). Fifteen years of disaster volunteers in Japan: A longitudinal fieldwork assessment of a disaster non-profit organization. *International Journal of Mass Emergencies and Disasters, 32*(1), 220–240.

Attia, M., & Edge, J. (2017). Be(com)ing a reflexive researcher: A developmental approach to research methodology. *Open Review of Educational Research, 4*(1), 33–45.

Baker, L. (2006). Observation: A complex research method. *Library Trends, 55*(1), 171–189.

Bhandari, R.B., Okada, N., & Knottnerus, J.D. (2011). Urban ritual events and coping with disaster risk a case study of Lalitpur, Nepal. *Journal of Applied Social Science, 5*(2), 13–32.

Bonner, A., & Tolhurst, G. (2002). Insider-outsider perspectives of participant observation. *Nurse Researcher, 9*(4), 7–19.

Broby, N., Lassetter, J.H., Williams, M., & Winters, B.A. (2018). Effective international medical disaster relief: A qualitative descriptive study. *Prehospital and Disaster Medicine, 33*(2), 119–126.

Budosan, B., & Bruno, R.F. (2011). Strategy for providing integrated mental health/psychosocial support in post-earthquake Haiti. *Intervention, 9*(3), 225–236.

Chandra, A., Dargusch, P., McNamara, K.E., Caspe, A.M., & Dalabajan, D. (2017). A study of climate-smart farming practices and climate-resiliency field schools in Mindanao, the Philippines. *World Development, 98*, 214–230.

Chowdhooree, I., & Islam, I. (2018). Factors and actors for enhancing community flood resilience. *International Journal of Disaster Resilience in the Built Environment, 9*(2), 153–169.

Creswell, J.W., & Miller, D.L. (2000). Determining validity in qualitative inquiry. *Theory Into Practice, 39*(3), 124–130.

Davidson, R.A., & Nozick, L.K. (2018). Computer simulation and optimization. In H. Rodríguez, W. Donner, & J. Trainor (Eds.), *Handbook of disaster research* (2nd ed., pp. 331–356). Cham, Switzerland: Springer.

Delamont, S. (1975). Participant observation and educational anthropology. *Research Intelligence, 1*(1), 13–21.

Drabek, T.E. (1968). *Disaster in aisle 13: A case study of the Coliseum explosion at the Indiana State Fairgrounds, October 31, 1963 (No. MONO-D-1)*. Ohio State University Columbus Disaster Research Center.

Emerson, R.M., Fretz, R.I., & Shaw, L.L. (2001). Participant observation and fieldnotes. In P. Atkinson, A. Coffey, S. Delamont, J. Lofland, & L. Lofland (Eds.), *Handbook of ethnography* (pp. 352–368). London: Sage.

Emerson, R.M., Fretz, R.I., & Shaw, L.L. (2011). *Writing ethnographic fieldnotes*. Chicago: University of Chicago Press.

Epstein, K., DiCarlo, J., Marsh, R., Adhikari, B., Paudel, D., Ray, I., & Måren, I.E. (2018). Recovery and adaptation after the 2015 Nepal earthquakes. *Ecology and Society, 23*(1). https://doi.org/10.2307/26799051

Fothergill, A. (2003). The stigma of charity: Gender, class, and disaster assistance. *Sociological Quarterly, 44*(4), 659–680.

Fothergill, A., & Peek, L. (2015). *Children of Katrina*. Austin: University of Texas Press. https://doi.org/10.5860/choice.194567

Friedman, D. (2012). How to collect and analyze qualitative data. In A. Mackey & S.M. Gass (Eds.), *Research methods in second language acquisition* (pp. 180–200). Malden, MA: Wiley-Blackwell.

Ganapati, N.E. (2009). Rising from the rubble: Emergence of place-based social capital in Gölcük, Turkey. *International Journal of Mass Emergencies and Disasters, 27*(2), 127–166.

Ganapati, N.E. (2012). In good company: Why social capital matters for women during disaster recovery. *Public Administration Review, 72*(3), 419–427.

Ganapati, N.E. (2013a). Downsides of social capital for women during disaster recovery: Toward a more critical approach. *Administration & Society, 45*(1), 72–96.

Ganapati, N.E. (2013b). Measuring the processes and outcomes of post-disaster housing recovery: Lessons from Gölcük, Turkey. *Natural Hazards, 65*(3), 1783–1799.

Ganapati, N.E., & Ganapati, S. (2008). Enabling participatory planning after disasters: A case study of the World Bank's housing reconstruction in Turkey. *Journal of the American Planning Association, 75*(1), 41–59.

Geertz, C. (1973). *The interpretation of cultures* (Vol. 5019). New York: Basic Books.

Gold, R.L. (1957). Roles in sociological field observations. *Social Forces, 36*(3), 217–223.

Gordon, L. (2019). *Real research: Research methods sociology students can use*. Thousand Oaks, CA: Sage.

Gordon, T., Hynninen, P., Lahelma, E., Metso, T., Palmu, T., & Tolonen, T. (2006). Collective ethnography, joint experiences and individual pathways. *Nordisk Pedagogik, 26*(1), 3–15.

Grove, K.J. (2013). From emergency management to managing emergence: A genealogy of disaster management in Jamaica. *Annals of the Association of American Geographers, 103*(3), 570–588.

Grove, K.J. (2014). Agency, affect, and the immunological politics of disaster resilience. *Environment and Planning D: Society and Space, 32*(2), 240–256.

Hart, T. (2017). Online ethnography. *The International Encyclopedia of Communication Research Methods,* 1–8.

Homan, R. (1980). The ethics of covert methods. *British Journal of Sociology,* 46–59.

Javor, A.J., Pearce, L.D., Thompson, A.J., & Moran, C.B. (2014). Modeling psychosocial decision making in emergency operations centres. *International Journal of Mass Emergencies and Disasters, 32*(3), 484–507.

Kaji, A.H., & Lewis, R.J. (2008). Assessment of the reliability of the Johns Hopkins/agency for healthcare research and quality hospital disaster drill evaluation tool. *Annals of Emergency Medicine, 52*(3), 204–210.

Kontar, Y.Y., Eichelberger, J.C., Gavrilyeva, T.N., Filippova, V.V., Savvinova, A.N., Tananaev, N.I., & Trainor, S.F. (2018). Springtime flood risk reduction in rural Arctic: A comparative study of interior Alaska, United States and Central Yakutia, Russia. *Geosciences, 8,* 90. https://doi.org/10.3390/geosciences8030090

Kroll, A., Remington, C.L., Awasthi, P., & Ganapati, N.E. (2020). Mitigating the negative effects of emotional labor: A study of disaster response and recovery workers after the 2010 Haiti earthquake. *Governance,* 1–20.

Landahl, M.R., Bennett, D.M., & Phillips, B.D. (2019). Disaster research. In P. Leavy (Ed.), *The Oxford handbook of methods for public scholarship.* https://doi.org/10.1093/oxfor dhb/9780190274481.013.35

Laurier, E. (2010). Participant observation. In N. Clifford, M. Cope, T. Gillespie, & S. French (Eds.), *Key methods in geography.* Los Angeles: Sage.

Leskens, J.G., Brugnach, M., & Hoekstra, A. (2019). How do interactive flood simulation models influence decision-making? An observations-based evaluation method. *Water, 11*(11), 2427. https://doi.org/10.3390/w11112427

Lorenz, D.F., Schulze, K., & Voss, M. (2018). Emerging citizen responses to disasters in Germany. Disaster myths as an impediment for a collaboration of unaffiliated responders and professional rescue forces. *Journal of Contingencies and Crisis Management, 26*(3), 358–367.

Mack, N., Woodsong, C., MacQueen, K.M., Guest, G., & Namey, E. (2005). *Qualitative research methods: A data collector's field guide.* Research Triangle Park, NC: Family Health International.

Magnussen, L.I., Carlström, E., Sørensen, J.L., Torgersen, G.E., Hagenes, E.F., & Kristiansen, E. (2018). Learning and usefulness stemming from collaboration in a maritime crisis management exercise in Northern Norway. *Disaster Prevention and Management, 27*(1), 129–140.

Mair, J., Whitford, M., & Mackellar, J. (2013). Participant observation at events: Theory, practice and potential. *International Journal of Event and Festival Management, 4*(1), 56–65.

Maki, N. (2013). Disaster response to the 2011 Tohoku-Oki earthquake: National coordination, a common operational picture, and command and control in local governments. *Earthquake Spectra, 29*(Suppl 1), 369–385.

Marshall, C., & Rossman, G.B. (2014). *Designing qualitative research.* Thousand Oaks, CA: Sage.

Masud-All-Kamal, M., & Hassan, S.M. (2018). The link between social capital and disaster recovery: Evidence from coastal communities in Bangladesh. *Natural Hazards, 93*(3), 1547–1564.

Mayo, E. (1949). Hawthorne and the Western Electric Company. *Public Administration: Concepts and Cases,* 149–158.

McKinney, J.C. (1966). *Constructive typology and social theory.* New York: Appleton-Century-Crofts. https://doi.org/10.2307/2091128

McLean, K.E., Abramowitz, S.A., Ball, J.D., Monger, J., Tehoungue, K., McKune, S.L., . . . Omidian, P.A. (2018). Community-based reports of morbidity, mortality, and health-seeking behaviours in four Monrovia communities during the West African Ebola epidemic. *Global Public Health, 13*(5), 528–544.

Morrison, M.A., Haley, E., Sheehan, K.B., & Taylor, R.E. (2011). *Using qualitative research in advertising: Strategies, techniques, and applications.* Thousand Oaks, CA: Sage.

Morrow, B.H., & Enarson, E. (1996). Hurricane Andrew through women's eyes. *International Journal of Mass Emergencies and Disasters, 14*(1), 5–22.

Mostafavi, A., & Ganapati, N.E. (2019). Toward convergence disaster research: Building integrative theories using simulation. *Risk Analysis.* https://doi.org/10.1111/risa.13303

Mukherji, A., Ganapati, N.E., & Rahill, G. (2014). Expecting the unexpected: Field research in post-disaster settings. *Natural Hazards, 73*(2), 805–828.

Mulhall, A. (2003). In the field: Notes on observation in qualitative research. *Journal of Advanced Nursing, 41*(3), 306–313.

Nikuze, A., Sliuzas, R., Flacke, J., & van Maarseveen, M. (2019). Livelihood impacts of displacement and resettlement on informal households – A case study from Kigali, Rwanda. *Habitat International, 86,* 38–47.

O'Leary, M. (2020). *Classroom observation: A guide to the effective observation of teaching and learning.* New York: Routledge.

Oliver-Smith, A. (1996). Anthropological research on hazards and disasters. *Annual Review of Anthropology, 25*(1), 303–328.

Opdyke, A., Lepropre, F., Javernick-Will, A., & Koschmann, M. (2017). Inter-organizational resource coordination in post-disaster infrastructure recovery. *Construction Management and Economics, 35*(8–9), 514–530.

Palinkas, L.A. (2006). Qualitative approaches to studying the effects of disasters. *Methods for Disaster Mental Health Research,* 158–173.

Paterson, B.L., Bottorff, J.L., & Hewat, R. (2003). Blending observational methods: Possibilities, strategies, and challenges. *International Journal of Qualitative Methods, 2*(1), 29–38.

Peek, L.A. (2003). Reactions and response: Muslim students' experiences on New York City campuses post 9/11. *Journal of Muslim Minority Affairs, 23*(2), 271–283.

Peek, L.A. (2005). Becoming Muslim: The development of a religious identity. *Sociology of Religion, 66*(3), 215–242.

Peek, L.A. (2011). *Behind the backlash: Muslim Americans after 9/11.* Philadelphia: Temple University Press.

Phillippi, J., & Lauderdale, J. (2018). A guide to field notes for qualitative research: Context and conversation. *Qualitative Health Research, 28*(3), 381–388.

Phillips, B.D. (1997). Qualitative methods and disaster research. *International Journal of Mass Emergencies and Disasters, 15*(1), 179–195.

Phillips, B.D. (2014). *Qualitative disaster research: Understanding qualitative research.* Oxford: Oxford University Press.

Quarantelli, E.L. (1997). The disaster research center field studies of organized behavior in the crisis time period of disasters. *International Journal of Mass Emergencies and Disasters, 15*(1), 47–69.

Rahill, G.J., Ganapati, N.E., Clérismé, J.C., & Mukherji, A. (2014). Shelter recovery in urban Haiti after the earthquake: The dual role of social capital. *Disasters, 38*(s1), S73–S93.

Remington, C.L., & Ganapati, N.E. (2017). Recovery worker skills in post-earthquake Haiti: The disconnect between employer and employee perspectives. *Natural Hazards, 87*(3), 1673–1690.

Ritchie, J., Lewis, J., Nicholls, C.M., & Ormston, R. (Eds.). (2013). *Qualitative research practice: A guide for social science students and researchers.* New York: Sage.

Rossman, G.B., & Rallis, S.F. (2016). *An introduction to qualitative research: Learning in the field.* New York: Sage.

Saha, C.K. (2015). Dynamics of disaster-induced risk in southwestern coastal Bangladesh: An analysis on Tropical Cyclone Aila 2009. *Natural Hazards, 75*(1), 727–754.

Saputro, K.A. (2016). Information volunteers' strategies in crisis communication. *International Journal of Disaster Resilience in the Built Environment, 7*(1), 63–73.

Savoia, E., Biddinger, P.D., Burstein, J., & Stoto, M.A. (2010). Inter-agency communication and operations capabilities during a hospital functional exercise: Reliability and validity of a measurement tool. *Prehospital and Disaster Medicine, 25*(1), 52–58.

Schmeltz, M.T., González, S.K., Fuentes, L., Kwan, A., Ortega-Williams, A., & Cowan, L.P. (2013). Lessons from Hurricane Sandy: A community response in Brooklyn, New York. *Journal of Urban Health, 90*(5), 799–809.

Sienkiewicz-Małyjurek, K.E., Kożuch, B., & Szczygłowski, J. (2019). Inter-organisational learning in public safety management system. *Disaster Prevention and Management: An International Journal, 28*(2), 286–298.

Stadler, N. (2006). Terror, corpse symbolism, and taboo violation: The "Haredi disaster victim identification team in Israel" (Zaka). *Journal of the Royal Anthropological Institute, 12*(4), 837–858.

Stoller, P. (1989). *The taste of ethnographic things: The senses in anthropology.* Philadelphia: University of Pennsylvania Press.

Tanwattana, P. (2018). Systematizing community-based disaster risk management (CBDRM): Case of urban flood-prone community in Thailand upstream area. *International Journal of Disaster Risk Reduction, 28*, 798–812.

Tanwattana, P., & Toyoda, Y. (2018). Contributions of gaming simulation in building community-based disaster risk management applying Japanese case to flood prone communities in Thailand upstream area. *International Journal of Disaster Risk Reduction, 27*, 199–213.

Tunçalp, D., & Lê, P.L. (2014). (Re) Locating boundaries: A systematic review of online ethnography. *Journal of Organizational Ethnography, 3*(1), 59–79.

Turnock, C., & Gibson, V. (2001). Validity in action research: A discussion on theoretical and practice issues encountered whilst using observation to collect data. *Journal of Advanced Nursing, 36*(3), 471–477.

Uddin, M.S., Ahmad, M.M., & Warnitchai, P. (2018). Surge dynamics of disaster displaced populations in temporary urban shelters: Future challenges and management issues. *Natural Hazards, 94*(1), 201–225.

Wachtendorf, T., & Kendra, J.M. (2012). Reproductive improvisation and the virtues of sameness: The art of reestablishing New York City's emergency operations center. *International Journal of Mass Emergencies and Disasters, 30*(3), 249–274.

Walliman, N. (2017). *Research methods: The basics.* New York: Routledge.

Weber, L., & Messias, D. K. H. (2012). Mississippi front-line recovery work after Hurricane Katrina: An analysis of the intersections of gender, race, and class in advocacy, power relations, and health. *Social Science & Medicine, 74*(11), 1833–1841.

12

Secondary Data and Qualitative Content Analysis in Emergency Management Research

Jerry V. Graves

Introduction

Unobtrusive research methods are valuable tools in the social sciences. Such methods allow researchers to collect data without interfering with human subjects and to analyze phenomena that could not otherwise be personally observed (Philips, 2014; Krippendorff, 2013). Compared to other research methods that involve the direct collection of raw data, which are discussed throughout this book, unobtrusive methods can be less time-consuming, are relatively inexpensive, and allow for easier access to data (Harris, 2001; Hakim, 1982).

Although there are many different approaches to conducting unobtrusive qualitative research, this chapter will specifically focus on the use of secondary data and qualitative content analysis. *Secondary data* are those which have been previously collected by someone other than the researcher for purposes other than the subject research project, and *secondary data analysis* includes the various approaches to further analyze or otherwise repurpose such data (Stallings, 2007; Frankfort-Nachmias & Nachmias, 1996; Hakim, 1982). Additionally, *qualitative content analysis*, a form of secondary data analysis, is a research method in which *social artifacts* (documents, images, art, or any form of text or media) are closely analyzed in a systematic manner for the purpose of uncovering meaning and making valid inferences regarding particular phenomena (Atkinson, 2017; Elo et al., 2014; Krippendorff, 2013; Messinger, 2012). Secondary data and content analysis are effective qualitative research tools throughout the social sciences, including the academic discipline of emergency and disaster management.

Emergency Management

Emergency management has rapidly evolved as a field of practice and an academic discipline since the 20th century. However, its roots can actually be traced back to ancient civilizations (early Egyptian hieroglyphics included references to disasters) and the Bible (Noah shepherded animals into his ark to save them from a flood) (Haddow,

Bullock, & Coppola, 2017). Fast forward a few thousand years, and the evolution of emergency management in the United States coincides with significant events like World War II, 9/11, and Hurricane Katrina (Philips, Neal, & Webb, 2017; Haddow, Bullock, & Coppola, 2017). What made these particular events significant is that they (1) commanded considerable international attention; (2) prompted substantial federal public policy responses; (3) greatly influenced emergency management practices; and (4) began informing related academic research agendas. Contemporary issues in emergency management such as climate change (and the anticipated increase in the frequency and severity of climate-related disasters) and mass shootings are already influencing the practice and study of emergency management in similar fashion. Given the recent developments surrounding COVID-19, it is likely that pandemics will begin to more significantly influence public policy and emergency management practitioners, in addition to researchers going forward.

Moreover, the term 'emergency management' has itself evolved over time. Although there is no standard, universally accepted definition of the term, Haddow et al. (2017) define emergency management as "a discipline that deals with risk and risk avoidance" (p. 2). Philips et al. (2017) provide a more expansive definition that includes "people working to reduce risks, prepare for and respond to emergencies and disasters, and foster post-event recovery" (p. 35). The latter, more comprehensive definition explicitly encompasses what have been widely recognized as the four phases of the emergency management cycle: mitigation, preparedness, response, and recovery (National Governors' Association, 1979).

Risk, Hazards, and Vulnerability

The term "risk" appears in many definitions of emergency management. *Risk* "is a measure of the likelihood that a hazard will manifest into an actual emergency or disaster event and the consequences should that event occur" (Haddow et al., 2017, p. 476). More simply stated, risk "is the probability of an event occurring" (Philips et al., 2017, p. 82). In order to measure risk, emergency management practitioners and researchers must take into account existing *hazards* (those external phenomena, whether natural, technological, anthropogenic, or some combination thereof, that may potentially impact or otherwise disrupt life and/or property) and *vulnerabilities* (those internal characteristics or factors that make impacts to life and/or property more likely to occur, more severe, and more difficult to recover from). The degree to which an event impacts life and property ultimately determines the scope and scale of the required response effort and whether the event rises to the level of an emergency, disaster, or catastrophe.

Emergencies, Disasters, and Catastrophes

Although Sylves in Chapter 17 expands our knowledge of the following terms, for my current purposes an *emergency* is a fairly common event in which negative consequences occur and basic emergency services are required (Haddow et al., 2017; Philips et al., 2017). Examples of such events include traffic accidents and structure fires, both of which typically result in the deployment of local first responders (police, fire, and emergency medical technicians). Since impacts to life and property are usually limited during a common emergency, local first responders are able to effectively manage the incident with minimal outside assistance. Consequently, recovery operations following a common emergency are inherently limited. An event may constitute a *disaster* "when the response requirements in one or more critical areas of assistance are unable to be met" (Haddow et al., 2017, p. 33). Additionally, disasters often cause significant damage to public infrastructure and displace residents and businesses, thereby requiring a more robust set of recovery activities that may include state and/or federal assistance. An event constitutes a *catastrophe* when state and federal capacity have also been exceeded, public infrastructure has been severely damaged, and the daily routines of residents and businesses are significantly disrupted (Philips et al., 2017).

Unobtrusive research methods such as content analysis allow researchers to retroactively utilize a wide range of data to gain a better understanding of pre-event conditions (development practices, level of risk, vulnerability, exposure to hazards, and prior mitigation and preparedness efforts) in impacted communities. In terms of post-event conditions during the dynamic response and recovery phases of emergency management, researchers may have a difficult time gaining entrée into impacted communities, particularly in the immediate aftermath of a significant event. In such instances, unobtrusive research methods provide a means of collecting relevant data from afar, thereby allowing researchers to engage in a meaningful analysis of the ways in which an event was experienced and perceived, identify unmet response and recovery needs, and inform future mitigation and preparedness efforts.

Qualitative Methods and Secondary Data in Emergency and Disaster Research

Disasters (operationalized here to also include catastrophes) are social occurrences that are almost exclusively measured and described in terms of their impacts to life and property. It is therefore impossible to separate the implications of human activities such as public policy, development practices, and prior mitigation and preparedness activities from the occurrence of disasters. For example, a tsunami that makes landfall on a chain of undeveloped islands in the Pacific Ocean and does not cause any impacts to life and property would not be of particular interest to emergency management practitioners and researchers, although the event may still be of interest to natural scientists. However, if that same tsunami made landfall in a heavily populated community in Indonesia, causing severe impacts to life and property (thereby constituting a disaster), the event would garner considerable attention from a broad range of stakeholder groups, including the general public, media, and the emergency management community.

Although disasters attract attention from many stakeholder groups for various reasons, emergency management researchers are primarily interested in examining such occurrences in order to generate knowledge aimed at "reducing the human and financial costs of disasters" (Philips et al., 2017, p. 106). According to Philips et al. (2017), "the goal of disaster research is to generate insights and contribute to a safer, more sustainable future" (p. 106). To this end, it is critical for emergency management researchers to gain an understanding of the context in which disasters occur, how emergency managers and survivors cope with impacts (response and recovery), and the degree to which experienced disasters might inform future pre-disaster emergency management practices (mitigation and preparedness) and other pertinent areas of public policy. The value of qualitative research methods in emergency management is that they allow researchers to produce "rich insights into how people, organizations, and communities face unanticipated events" and behave before, during, and after (Philips, 2014, p. 2).

Selecting a Qualitative Approach

Research topics and questions have a significant bearing on the research method(s) selected and employed in a given study (Altheide & Schneider, 2013, p. 1). As discussed in Chapter 4 of this book, *quantitative* research methods are supposed to be objective in nature and involve the numeric measurement of variables for the purpose of conducting statistical analyses. Such methods allow the researcher to formulate and test hypotheses, statistically examine causality, and present research findings in numeric form. Conversely, *qualitative* research methods are subjective in nature and involve the collection and analysis of various forms of data for the purpose of generating new knowledge and gaining a more nuanced understanding of the subject matter. Qualitative methods allow the researcher a great deal of flexibility in the research design (including the manner in which data are collected and analyzed) and provide the researcher with opportunities to explore, describe, and explain phenomena in great detail (Philips, 2014).

The previously discussed hypothetical tsunami in Indonesia provides a useful illustration of the differences between quantitative and qualitative research methods. A quantitative approach to studying the referenced event might include the measurement and analysis of impacts to life (number of injuries and fatalities) and property (monetary value of property damage). The numeric data generated could be used to compare the impacts of the tsunami to other similar events or to answer research questions regarding the anticipated level of recovery effort and cost. However, such an approach would be less effective in answering research questions regarding the historical, political, and socioeconomic context in which the tsunami occurred or the vulnerabilities and needs of impacted residents (Egner, Schorch, Hitzler, Bergmann, & Wulf, 2012). These types of research questions would be more thoroughly answered by employing a qualitative approach that allowed for a detailed analysis of the processes and lived experiences that occurred before and after the tsunami (Atkinson, 2017; Philips, 2014). While each approach may adequately answer research questions and inform interventions across all four phases of emergency management (i.e., new approaches to mitigation and preparedness in the South Pacific or the deployment of additional response and recovery resources from the United Nations), the qualitative approach would provide the researcher with an opportunity to generate more color and context regarding the social realities surrounding the tsunami (Philips, 2014).

Secondary Data Analysis

Secondary data analysis is any further analysis of data that has been collected by someone other than the researcher for purposes other than the subject research project (Stallings, 2007; Frankfort-Nachmias & Nachmias, 1996; Hakim, 1982). Similarly, when a researcher reanalyzes data from their own previous research, it may be referred to as *auto-data* analysis (Heaton, 2004). *Secondary data sources* stand in contrast to *primary data sources*, which are associated with the direct collection of raw data by researchers for a research project (original research) or the generation of documentation from those who are directly involved in or otherwise have an "inside view" of a particular phenomenon (original documentation; Lippencott Williams and Wilkins, 2009, p. 76). The defining feature of secondary data sources is that they are at least one step removed from the researcher or are otherwise "filtered" (Altheide & Schneider, 2013, p. 7).

Secondary data analysis may be quantitative or qualitative. A common example of quantitative secondary data is that which is generated by the U.S. Census Bureau: these data are collected by the federal government for very specific purposes during regular time intervals, and are often reanalyzed by others for a broad range of research objectives outside of what the U.S. Census Bureau intended when the agency collected the raw data. Qualitative data, such as transcripts generated during interviews or focus groups, field notes, or research diaries may be similarly reanalyzed for new purposes (Heaton, 2008). Ultimately, secondary data analysis provides researchers with an opportunity to analyze, summarize, and draw fresh insights and conclusions regarding phenomena that have previously been examined by others (Lippencott Williams and Wilkins, 2009; Harris, 2001; Hakim, 1982). The purpose of employing secondary data analysis as a research method is to either answer new research questions or generate contextual material in order to explore potential research questions (Jensen, n.d.). It is worth noting that since the data were originally collected by someone else for other purposes, researchers engaged in repurposing secondary data must always carefully consider the materiality of the data to their current work. This limitation is less pronounced when secondary data is used for contextual purposes rather than answering research questions.

Qualitative content analysis may be performed on secondary data in the same manner as other secondary data analysis techniques (Harris, 2001). The unobtrusive nature of this approach allows for easier access to data and reduces instances of bias, distortion, or lack of recall on the part of human subjects (Harris, 2001). Additionally, this approach is generally more affordable when compared to the collection of raw data (Harris, 2001; Hakim, 1982).

Qualitative Content Analysis

Qualitative content analysis is a research method in which social artifacts (documents, images, art, or any form of text or media) are closely analyzed in a systematic manner for the purpose of uncovering meaning and making valid inferences regarding particular phenomena (Atkinson, 2017; Elo et al., 2014; Krippendorff, 2013; Messinger, 2012; Mayring, 2014). Although *quantitative content analysis* includes the use of similar social artifacts, it is focused on counting or measuring the frequency of themes or terms (Atkinson, 2017). However, "merely counting a theme or term, as in quantitative content analysis, is not enough to understand any latent patterns developed within texts" (Atkinson, 2017, p. 84). Qualitative content analysis allows the researcher to explore the context and meaning of social phenomena in a manner that generates new insights, increases understanding, or informs practical action (Krippendorff, 2013, p. 24).

There are several critical advantages to employing content analysis as a qualitative research method. Content analysis is an unobtrusive method that allows for analysis to occur absent the ability to directly observe "phenomena, events, or processes" (Krippendorff, 2013, p. 355; Philips, 2014). This explains why historians value the utility of content analysis as a means of using available social artifacts to make inferences regarding past events (Krippendorff, 2013). The method is also well suited for addressing research questions that are derived from real-world problems. "Content analysts must convert such [real-world] problems into research questions, which they can then attempt to answer through a purposive examination" (Krippendorff, 2013, p. 358) of social artifacts for the purpose of extracting relevance, significance, and meaning (Altheide & Schneider, 2013). Finally, content analysis allows the researcher to interpret and rearticulate the contextual relevance, significance, and meaning of social artifacts through the lens of existing academic literature (Krippendorff, 2013). Researchers interested in the social construction of reality (Atkinson, 2017) and the assignment of *meaning* to social artifacts, as opposed to the counting of data, as in quantitative approaches, purposively "engage in content analysis rather than in some other investigative method" (Krippendorff, 2013, p. 27).

The manner in which social artifacts are selected for content analysis is critical. Since social artifacts exist independent of the researcher and have a multitude of meanings, the researcher not only bears the burden of appropriately selecting and analyzing content but also transforming it into relevant data (Krippendorff, 2013). The contextual meaning and significance of social artifacts to a particular research project depend upon the perspective of the research, and content cannot be transformed into relevant data "without the researcher's 'eye' and question" (Altheide & Schneider, 2013, p. 6). Researchers must therefore think critically about the authenticity, source, and historical context surrounding the social artifacts they are considering during a research project (Philips, 2014). The identification and retrieval of relevant social artifacts, both in terms of the subject matter and research questions, is an important step in conducting content analysis. Technological advances such as the increasing digitization of archival records and the advent of social media and other emerging forms of digital communication (e.g., emails, text messages, blogs) have exponentially increased the availability of social artifacts to researchers. The utility of archived data was discussed in greater detail in the previous section regarding secondary data analysis. The proliferation of archives in all formats provides content analysts with many options in terms of the content they might analyze in pursuit of developing and answering research questions.

Applications in Emergency Management Research

Emergency management is a field of practice and academic discipline that is primarily concerned with the protection of life and property. The first disaster research centers in the United States were established in the 1960s (Philips et al., 2017, p. 27), and academic journals exclusively focused on emergency management and related topics began surfacing in 1975 (Philips, 2014, p. 17). As an academic discipline, emergency management has since evolved to the point where over 150 universities across the United States now offer related degree programs (Philips et al., 2017, p. 10). Qualitative methods, which allow for the production of rich insights and a better understanding of processes that occur over time, have provided emergency management researchers with a number of effective approaches to conducting relevant and impactful research (Philips et al., 2017; Philips, 2014).

Disasters are complex social occurrences that are rarely personally experienced. The emphasis that the emergency management community places on conducting exercises as part of the preparedness phase of emergency management is a reflection of (1) the relative infrequency of disasters and (2) the acknowledgment of emergency management professionals that because of this infrequency, stakeholders must practice disaster response activities in a simulated environment as often as possible (Haddow et al., 2017; Philips et al., 2017). In the rare instance that a significant disaster occurs, access to impacted areas and survivors is often limited for a prolonged period of time, creating a number of unique challenges for emergency management researchers during the response and recovery phases.

As previously discussed, qualitative secondary data analysis may be employed to answer new research questions or to provide context for a new research project that is being explored (Coltart, Henwood, & Shirani, 2013; Heaton, 2008; Jensen, n.d.). Secondary data include those that have already been generated by someone else for some other purpose, including previous studies, reports, or plans. In the field of emergency management, a plethora of secondary data is generated in the academic community as well as the public sector. Since public entities play a unique societal role that often includes constitutional and/or legislative mandates for the preservation of public health, safety, and welfare (and consequently, the implementation of emergency management activities), governmental agencies produce a great deal of data that may be used in secondary data analysis. Whether the data pertain to pre-disaster phenomena (historical context, development practices, hazard mitigation or emergency operations planning efforts, demographic characteristics, vulnerabilities, capacity, or resilience), or post-disaster phenomena (impacts, response performance, or unmet recovery needs), emergency management researchers have ample opportunities to apply secondary data analysis as a means of answering new research questions or developing new research projects in an environment where the collection of primary data is simply not feasible (ACAPS, 2014; World Food Programme, 2009; Seaman & Leather, 2003; World Food Programme, 2003).

Researchers now have unprecedented access to secondary data due to the proliferation of data archives (Mayring, 2014). Data archives (or databases) may be established by academic or public institutions for the purpose of maintaining data in an accessible manner and allowing for *formal data sharing* (Heaton, 2008). What distinguishes formal data sharing from other means of obtaining someone else's primary data is that in formal data sharing, the data have been carefully archived for the explicit purpose of allowing others to access them, meeting "the necessary ethical and legal requirements for [the data] being shared with other researchers, possibly subject to certain requirements being met" (Heaton, 2008). Commonly used formal data sharing platforms in emergency management and throughout the social sciences include online academic journal databases such as EBSCO and JSTOR. Data may be more informally obtained by employing keyword searches through online platforms such as Google.

Box 12.1 illustrates the ways in which formal data archives can be utilized in order to collect secondary data for the purposes of developing contextual material for a study and answering research questions. As previously discussed, one of the advantages of unobtrusive research methods is that they allow for the collection of data regarding phenomena that could not otherwise be personally observed or collected. Formal data archives provide researchers with access to a wide range of secondary data that can be used for various purposes, including conducting content analysis, as described above.

BOX 12.1 UTILIZING DATA ARCHIVES AND PERFORMING CONTENT ANALYSIS TO EXPLORE THE EVOLUTION OF RISK AND VULNERABILITY

In Graves (2012), I posed the following research questions in my study regarding the historical impacts of the Industrial Canal (an artificial navigation canal that had the spatial effect of isolating the neighborhood from the rest of the city) on the Lower Ninth Ward, which was completely devastated during Hurricane Katrina:

(1) How has the presence of the Industrial Canal generated environmental risks and affected social outcomes in the Lower Ninth Ward;

(2) How have vulnerability and exposure to hazards increased risk to the Lower Ninth Ward over time; and

(3) What are the implications of addressing the exacerbation of exposure to natural hazards within the traditional environmental justice framework? (p. 69)

Based on these questions, I selected a case study research design utilizing mostly qualitative data. Content analysis was the primary research method employed and a variety of social artifacts were used in the analysis. Overall, approximately 250 points of data were analyzed during my study, including 42 maps, photos, and other images portraying the geography and population of the Lower Ninth Ward.

To provide an example, in Graves (2012), I explored the history of the Lower Ninth Ward (New Orleans, Louisiana) and its relationship with the Industrial Canal within the context of risk (and consequently, vulnerability and exposure to hazards). The temporal scale of the study (1900–2012) precluded me from directly observing or collecting primary data regarding the many significant historical events that had occurred in the Lower Ninth Ward leading up to Hurricane Katrina, including the construction of the Industrial Canal (the 1920s) and Hurricane Betsy (1965). Additionally, the social processes and general historical context surrounding events related to the canal and disasters such as Betsy and Katrina were central components of the analysis. Collecting archived secondary data was therefore necessary in order to conduct the study.

Table 12.1 includes a list and number of each type of data utilized in Graves (2012). As noted in the table, secondary data sources such as government, university, and non-profit reports and correspondence represented the second most frequently referenced type of data. Local data archives were utilized for the purpose of formally obtaining much of this data.

Data pertaining to the Industrial Canal and Lower Ninth Ward were also retrieved from the *Historic New Orleans Collection*. A number of government documents and correspondence, photographs, maps, and other images pertaining to the Industrial Canal and Lower Ninth Ward, were identified on www.hnoc.org (the official website of the Historic New Orleans Collection) and retrieved in hard copy during multiple visits to the archive. Finally, a great deal of data for this study were retrieved from the *City Archives* located in the Louisiana Division of the New Orleans Public Library. Data such as correspondence between public officials and neighborhood associations, public reports and documents, and other official records pertaining to the Industrial Canal and Lower Ninth Ward were identified on www.nutrias.org (the official website of the New Orleans Public Library) and retrieved in hard copy during multiple visits to the archive.

(Graves, 2012, p. 72)

TABLE 12.1 Sources of Data Collected and Analyzed

Data Type	Number
Newspaper articles	115
Institutional reports and correspondence	50
Maps, photos, and other images	42
Scholarly literature	22
Other articles and web sources	12

Source: Graves (2012).

TABLE 12.2 Coding Scheme

Code	Type
Isolation and distance	A priori
Race and class	A priori
Exposure to hazards	A priori
Neglect and sabotage	A priori
Activism	A priori
Suburban/rural qualities	A priori
Commercial/elite control	Emerging
Appeals to justice and patriotism	Emerging
Boosterism/cause célèbre	Emerging
Industrialization	Emerging

Source: Graves (2012).

While some of the data obtained in the manner described above were used as contextual material, most were used for the purpose of answering the research questions posed in the study. In such instances, the data were subject to the content analysis process. Specific examples of existing data that were collected and analyzed as a means of answering the research questions include neighborhood profiles and planning documents prepared by the City of New Orleans Office of Policy and Planning, and correspondence between citizens (including civic organizations) and various elected officials in New Orleans.

The 42 maps, photos, and other images referenced in the above excerpt were carefully analyzed and coded using the scheme highlighted in Table 12.2. Many of the other approximately 200 points of data were similarly analyzed and coded, and a number of specific themes gradually emerged from the entire body of data. The coding scheme, which included a total of ten a priori and emerging codes, were utilized for the purpose of organizing, analyzing, and identifying themes in the data.

Analysis of Secondary Data

Qualitative content analysis is an effective research method in emergency management because it allows researchers to explore and explain the social context in which disasters occur. Such inquiries may focus on phenomena related to pre-event emergency management activities such as mitigation and preparedness. Additionally, since qualitative content analysis is an unobtrusive method, this approach provides a means of gaining insight into response and recovery activities despite the rare occurrence of disasters and the logistical challenges associated with gaining entrée to impacted areas and disaster survivors following an event. Because the personal experience of disasters is so rare, most knowledge regarding such events is generated via social artifacts like media interpretations, popular culture references, and cultural practices following disasters (Egner et al., 2012; Rodríguez, Díaz, Santos, & Aguirre, 2007; Webb, 2007; Tierney, Bevc, & Kuligowski, 2006; Quarantelli, 1985). The careful examination and interpretation of the social artifacts surrounding a disaster allows for the gradual *emergence* of patterns, themes, and social meaning(s), which the researcher can utilize to draw inferences regarding the context of the event (Altheide & Schneider, 2013).

However, the manner in which disasters are socially constructed has serious implications for impacted communities (Dove & Khan, 1995).

> The post-disaster time period is a contested terrain in which various groups (victims, the media, and public officials) attempt to make sense of the event. In some cases, there is agreement on what happened, and in other cases there is conflict and disagreement.
>
> (Webb, 2007, p. 437)

As a result, how an event is perceived by stakeholders informs not only the recovery process, but also future mitigation and preparedness efforts. "If an event is defined as unforeseeable or beyond human control, it is not likely that corrective measures will be taken to prevent future occurrences" (Webb, 2007, p. 437). Disasters are social phenomena that occur as the result of social processes (political, social, and economic) that have unfolded over time. Such processes tend to unevenly distribute risk in socially structured ways, resulting in a multitude of community, institutional, household, and individual experiences and interpretations of disasters (Alario & Freudenberg, 2010). Theological, cultural, and political philosophies may also influence the manner in which disasters are experienced and interpreted. Qualitative content analysis is an effective means of capturing and examining the various *perspectives* and *voices* surrounding such events (Altheide & Schneider, 2013).

Procedurally, content analysis involves three primary phases: preparation, organization, and reporting of results (Elo et al., 2014). *Preparation* involves the selection of social artifacts that are relevant to the research both in terms of subject matter and context. "Context, or the social situation surrounding the document in question, must be understood to grasp the significance of the document itself"

(Altheide & Schneider, 2013, p. 14). The researcher must also carefully examine the structure (medium, logic, and format) of social artifacts and the points of view, motives, and interests of the people who produced them (Stallings, 2007). *Organization* refers to the development and application of a coding scheme that will be used by the researcher(s) as the content is analyzed and themes in the data emerge. The coding scheme provides the researcher with a logical framework for categorizing, organizing, and interpreting data (Elo et al., 2014). As illustrated in Table 12.2, some codes are established prior to analysis (a priori) and others are established during analysis (emerging). Finally, *reporting* refers to the synthesis of emerging themes from the data and the articulation of how those themes relate to the proposed research question(s).

Table 12.3 illustrates the connection between the coding scheme and emerging themes. Finally, the data was interpreted through the lens of existing academic literature in order to answer the proposed research questions. The study's findings were later organized according to the themes, which ultimately supported the final analysis and conclusions regarding the proposed research questions.

My example illustrates how I employed content analysis as a means of exploring public perceptions (both externally and internally) and the evolution of risk and vulnerability in the Lower Ninth Ward from the beginning of the 20th century leading up to Hurricane Katrina in 2005 and for a brief time period following the event. Since the overarching subject of the study was the evolution of risk, vulnerability, and exposure to hazards surrounding a particular piece of public

TABLE 12.3 Broad Themes

Theme	Code
Isolation and distance	■ Isolation and distance
	■ Neglect and sabotage
	■ Activism
	■ Suburban/rural qualities
	■ Industrialization
Exposure to hazards	■ Exposure to hazards
	■ Neglect and sabotage
	■ Activism
	■ Appeals to justice and patriotism
	■ Boosterism/cause célèbre
Race and class	■ Race and class
	■ Neglect and sabotage
	■ Activism
	■ Commercial/elite control
	■ Boosterism/cause célèbre

Source: Graves (2012).

infrastructure (the Industrial Canal) over the course of more than a century (1900–2012), content analysis was selected as a method because it allowed for a flexible research design and the use of historical data across a wide range of sources and mediums. This approach allowed me to gain a highly nuanced understanding of the ways in which the Lower Ninth Ward changed during the referenced time period, particularly with regard to the dynamic interplay between the social processes and hazard events of all scope and scale that ultimately culminated with the neighborhood becoming the most highly visible example of the many failures that occurred across all four phases of emergency management during Hurricane Katrina.

Conclusion

There is no shortage of relevant content available for analysis in the field of emergency management. Social artifacts may be analyzed for the purpose of (1) gaining a better understanding of how risk and vulnerability evolved in a particular community over time; (2) generating new knowledge regarding how a particular disaster is experienced or perceived by certain demographic groups; (3) exploring public opinion regarding government performance during recovery operations; and (4) many other research questions across all four phases of emergency management. The open-ended nature of content analysis allows for a wide range of social artifacts to be used, including text (newspaper articles, books), images (including maps), works of art, and even audio. Since the mass media plays such a significant role in disseminating information and shaping public opinion regarding emergency management and disasters, the research value of social artifacts produced in print, television, and film cannot be overstated (Egner et al., 2012; Webb, 2007; Tierney et al., 2006; Quarantelli, 1985).

Emergency management is an emerging academic discipline within the social sciences, where there are rich traditions in qualitative research methods. Unobtrusive qualitative research methods are particularly valuable in emergency management, where gaining an understanding of the social processes and historical context surrounding pre-event activities (mitigation and preparedness) is critical and gaining entrée to disaster zones and survivors during post-event activities (response and recovery) may not be possible. As illustrated in the two personal examples provided in this chapter, qualitative approaches to emergency management research allow for flexibility in the research design and facilitate the use of a broad range of data from many sources. Secondary data and content analysis are two closely related unobtrusive research tools that may be effectively employed in emergency management research, particularly when the research questions involve the close examination of processes that have occurred over time or phenomena that could not otherwise be directly observed by the researcher.

Further Readings

Creswell, J. W., & Creswell, J. D. (2018). *Research design: Qualitative, quantitative, and mixed methods approaches* (5th ed.). Thousand Oaks, CA: Sage.

Goodson, I. F., & Anstead, C. J. (2012). Discovering qualitative sources. *Counterpoints, 423*, 9–21.

Hammersley, M. (1997). Qualitative data archiving: Some reflections on its prospects and problems. *Sociology, 31*(1), 131–142.

Hopkins, D.J., & King, G. (2010). A method of automated nonparametric content analysis for social science. *American Journal of Political Science, 54*(1), 229–247.

Yin, R.K. (2016). *Qualitative research from start to finish* (2nd ed.). New York: Guilford Press.

References

ACAPS. (2014). *Secondary data review: Sudden onset natural disasters.* http://www.acaps.org/sites/acaps/files/resources/files/secondary_data_review-sudden_onset_natural_disasters_may_2014.pdf

Alario, M., & Freudenberg, W. (2010). Environmental risks and environmental justice: Or how titanic risks are not so titanic after all. *Sociological Inquiry, 80*(3), 500–512.

Altheide, D.L., & Schneider, C.J. (2013). *Qualitative media analysis* (2nd ed.). Thousand Oaks, CA: Sage.

Atkinson, J.D. (2017). *Journey into social activism: Qualitative approaches.* New York: Fordham University.

Coltart, C., Henwood, K., & Shirani, F. (2013). Qualitative secondary analysis in austere times: Ethical, professional and methodological considerations. *Historical Social Research, 38*(4), 271–292.

Dove, M.R., & Khan, M.H. (1995). Competing constructions of calamity: The April 1991 Bangladesh cyclone. *Population and Environment, 16*, 445–471.

Egner, H., Schorch, M., Hitzler, S., Bergmann, J., & Wulf, V. (2012). Communicating disaster – a case for qualitative approaches to disaster research. *Zeitschrift für Soziologie, 41*(3), 248–255.

Elo, S., Kääriäinen, M., Kanste, O., Pölkki, T., Utriainen, K., & Kyngäs, H. (2014, January–March). Qualitative content analysis: A focus on trustworthiness. *Sage Open*, 1–10. https://sgo.sagepub.com

Frankfort-Nachmias, C., & Nachmias, D. (1996). *Research methods in the social sciences* (5th ed.). London: Arnold.

Graves, J. (2012). Risk, vulnerability, and hazards: The Industrial Canal and the Lower Ninth Ward [Doctoral dissertation]. University of New Orleans Theses and Dissertations. 1557. https://scholarworks.uno.edu/td/1557

Haddow, G.D., Bullock, J.A., & Coppola, D.P. (2017). *Introduction to emergency management* (6th ed.). Cambridge, MA: Elsevier.

Hakim, C. (1982). Secondary analysis and the difference between official and academic research. *Sociology, 16*(1), 12–28.

Harris, H. (2001). Content analysis of secondary data: A study of courage in managerial decision making. *Journal of Business Ethics, 34*(3/4), 191–208.

Heaton, J. (2004). *Reworking qualitative data.* London: Sage.

Heaton, J. (2008). Secondary analysis of qualitative data: An overview. *Historical Social Research, 33*(3), 33–45.

Jensen, J. (n.d.). *Emergency management scholarly research resources.* https://training.fema.gov

Krippendorff, K. (2013). *Content analysis: An introduction to its methodology* (3rd ed.). Thousand Oaks, CA: Sage.

Lippencott Williams and Wilkins. (2009). Primary and secondary sources: Guidelines for authors. *American Journal of Nursing, 109*(4), 76–77.

Mayring, P. (2014). *Qualitative content analysis: Theoretical foundation, basic procedures and software solution.* http://nbn-resolving.de/urn:nbn:de:0168-ssoar-395173

Messinger, A.M. (2012). Teaching content analysis through *Harry Potter. Teaching Sociology, 40*(4), 360–367.

National Governors' Association. (1979). *1978 Emergency Preparedness Project: Final report.* Washington, DC: Defense Civil Preparedness Agency.

Philips, B.D. (2014). *Qualitative disaster research.* New York: Oxford University Press.

Philips, B.D., Neal, D.M., & Webb, G.R. (2017). *Introduction to emergency management* (2nd ed.). Boca Raton, FL: Taylor and Francis Group.

Quarantelli, E.L. (1985). Realities and mythologies in disaster films. *Communications, 11,* 31–44.

Rodríguez, H., Díaz, W., Santos, J.M., & Aguirre, B.E. (2007). Communicating risk and uncertainty: Science, technology, and disasters at the crossroads. In H. Rodríguez, E.L. Quarantelli, & R.R. Dynes (Eds.), *Handbook of disaster research* (pp. 476–488). New York: Springer.

Seaman, J., & Leather, C. (2003, October 28–30). *Emergency needs assessment methodologies. Non-food aid response to food insecurity: How do we identify the most appropriate types of intervention through emergency food security assessments?* Annex A in Report of the Technical Meeting: Key Terms in Emergency Needs Assessment. Rome: Emergency Needs Assessment Unit.

Stallings, R.A. (2007). Methodological issues. In H. Rodríguez, E.L. Quarantelli, & R.R. Dynes (Eds.), *Handbook of disaster research* (pp. 55–82). New York: Springer.

Tierney, K., Bevc, C., & Kuligowski, E. (2006). Metaphors matter: Disaster myths, media frames, and their consequences in Hurricane Katrina. *Annals of the American Academy of Political and Social Science, 604,* 57–81.

Webb, G.R. (2007). The popular culture of disaster: Exploring a new dimension of disaster research. In H. Rodríguez, E.L. Quarantelli, & R.R. Dynes (Eds.), *Handbook of disaster research* (pp. 430–440). New York: Springer.

World Food Programme. (2003). *Key issues in emergency needs assessment.* https://documents.wfp.org/stellent/groups/public/documents/manual_guide_proced/wfp189624.pdf

World Food Programme. (2009). *Comprehensive food security and vulnerability analysis guidelines.* https://documents.wfp.org/stellent/groups/public/documents/manual_guide_proced/wfp203208.pdf?_ga=2.88659163.1177440638.1576420302-866577661.1576420302

Quantitative and Policy Approaches to Studying Disaster and Emergency Management

13

Large Secondary Datasets

Imperative for Addressing Global Public Health Disasters

Njoki Mwarumba

Introduction

To reiterate what was discussed in Chapter 12, disaster managers, public health practitioners, researchers, and institutions independently gather vast amounts of primary data. This data is gathered at an ongoing pace prior to, during, and after public hazard events, including public health outbreaks. This data is inherently multifaceted, being that it is collected from various publics, and also ends up being stored in various formats and locations by any number of local, state, tribal, regional, territorial, national, and international agencies. This data, when available to various researchers, has potential for informing evidence-based practice, policy, and politics, in the ever-critical work of managing disasters including those in the public health realm. Pandemics are an example of quintessential public health disasters, where large secondary data become exponentially important in developing life-saving policies.

When researchers choose to apply large secondary data in their work, they are immediately faced with and need to skillfully navigate challenges on gaining access, curating, and analyzing relevant data. The challenges are to be expected and have successfully been navigated historically and include addressing requisite laws that prohibit sharing of some data, as discussed in Chapter 1. Even when data is sharable, most of it is independently gathered and stored in conditions that may not be immediately functional. During disaster response, gathering and preserving primary data for research purposes is not likely a priority that most practitioners focus on, and this inadvertently has implications for the quality of data gathered by responders. After disasters, the focus shifts to the ever-critical work of recovery, a time when other matters often take primacy over research and data preservation. To navigate this challenge, disaster researchers have sought to ethically gain entrée into responding agencies and locations impacted by disasters, where they can safely embed and gather primary data. The logistical reality of disaster work further poses the challenge of securing access to data without interfering with the work of responders and communities to capture otherwise ephemeral data during a disaster. Achieving this level of entrée during a public health disaster is particularly tenuous, if not entirely impossible. As a result, accessing primary data is not an option majority researchers have, making secondary data the logical next option.

When researchers can access disaster-impacted people, locations, and responders, they apply research methods that are not unique to the field of study but whose context is distinguishably different and more fragile than in other research fields. During public health outbreaks, undertaking research presents an even more complex scenario due to issues of health and safety for both the researcher and participants. Along these lines, specially trained researchers in public health and epidemiologists have been tasked with collecting data. Historically, very few bona fide disaster researchers have engaged in public health primary data collection due to these health and logistical reasons, as well as ethical considerations to neither retraumatize nor interfere with those impacted or working the disaster. Disaster researchers interested in public health events have therefore had to depend on secondary data for research as an intervening opportunity and option.

In this chapter, I discuss the use of secondary quantitative data in the context of public health disasters. Specifically, I address the use of large secondary quantitative datasets in analyzing macro-level constructs and their value for addressing global social vulnerability and determinants of health. I also discuss the availability of various data repositories, extraction, and managing this data. Finally, I discuss some considerations and evolving trends from the ongoing COVID-19 pandemic axis, a public health outbreak that the globe is currently embroiled in, that vividly affords us a live laboratory for successes and failures on ethical gathering, access, availability, analysis, and application of large secondary data.

Public Health Disasters: A Backdrop

Historically, public health outbreaks have remained in the domain of public health professionals and very minimally integrated with emergency management and disaster science. Within extant emergency management literature, however, public health outbreaks can quantifiably and qualitatively be categorized as disasters or catastrophes "observable in time and space, causing physical damage, loss and disruption of routine social functioning" (Fritz, 1961). Whether a public health outbreak evolves into a disaster or catastrophe is contingent upon evident and measurable factors. These factors include the agent itself, in this case emerging and re-emerging pathogens, as well as external factors that facilitate and provide the impetus for pathogen transmission. External factors that disparately impact population health outcomes include sociocultural, economic, and political realities that predispose some to outbreaks worse than others or interfere with access to health care infrastructure. Public health outbreaks can range from routine, locally manageable emergencies, such as re-emerging measles outbreaks, to more threatening novel emergent outbreaks, such as the ongoing COVID-19 pandemic. Quantifiably and qualitatively, management of emerging and re-emerging public health outbreaks triggers some all-hazards-approach type responses yet significantly differ if the outbreak is emergent or novel. A novel outbreak, as is currently being experienced due to the global transmission of SARS-CoV-2 and the impact of COVID-19, demands concerted efforts for convergent response, complex innovative management approaches, and significant sociopolitical and economic shifts.

Public health disasters and catastrophes are certainly not a new human phenomenon. Historical records are replete with infectious diseases (IDs) that shifted the course of humanity by decimating entire civilizations, triggering migration, and fueling wars worldwide. Significant innovations and technological progress have been made over time in response to the threats of IDs, as evidenced in the development of pharmaceutical, therapeutic, and non-pharmaceutical interventions (NPIs). However, this progress, while significant, has not comprehensively addressed these low-probability, high-impact public health events that remain among the leading causes of mortality worldwide to date (Morens, Folkers, & Fauci, 2004).

How these outbreaks emanate is generally articulated, yet knowing with precision when they occur and their progression is a process not as obvious. Human and pathogen characteristics combine to create a uniquely complex reality that limits precise approaches, particularly among unknown emergent events. There are many known and unknown pathogens present and circulating among animals. While various scientists are intently focused on identifying and understanding pathogens, some pathogens are known to evade contemporary technological surveillance and interventions, only to be recognized if and when they cause detectable disease among animals or humans. The consequent diseases are categorized either as emerging or re-emerging depending on whether they have been previously identified or not. The implication is that re-emerging infectious diseases have treatment protocols and therapies and population immunity, while emerging ones do not. When an emerging pathogen is detected in humans and is successfully treated or contained, further transmission and mutation is limited and manageable. However, if the pathogen goes undetected, it has potential for causing a public health outbreak and/or acquiring further antigenic shift, resulting in a new pathogen subtype. This new subtype can in turn become transmissible between humans, creating the possibility of a novel or emerging outbreak, which can scale into an epidemic, a Public Health Emergency of International Concern (PHEIC), or at worst a pandemic. This is the basic path through which the 2019 novel coronavirus-2 (SARS-CoV-2) evolved into the COVID-19 pandemic.

As to human characteristics, containment of novel diseases by identifying the sick and isolating them from those not infected is, according to Kaufmann (2007), one of the most effective strategies for limiting transmission. Containment, when applied together with other NPIs, can significantly decrease transmission and therefore intercept or impede excessive morbidity and mortality. Operationalizing public health interventions calls for comprehensive and cogent approaches among various publics to restrict and control and eventually weaken the outbreak. The complexity with this approach is that there are significant variables that influence adoption, implementation, and enforcement of NPIs at every level. This was the case with the severe acute respiratory syndrome (SARS) coronavirus outbreak of 2002. Early detection and the implementation of NPIs enhanced containment and a fizzling-down of the outbreak. The novel pathogen that could not be contained to mitigate infection and transmission caused the historically notorious Spanish influenza pandemic of 1918, a global catastrophic outbreak that resulted in 50–100 million lives lost (Ghendon, 1994; Taubenberger & Morens, 2006). In 2005, the preeminent world health agency, the World Health Organization (WHO), in concert with other global health organizations such as the Centers for Disease Control and Prevention (CDC), operationalized the International Health Regulations (IHR) program in response to a novel outbreak identified in California. Unable to contain the outbreak, WHO declared a PHEIC due to increased human-to-human transmission, and later the WHO Emergency Committee declared the PHEIC a pandemic. This was a process that triggered enhanced global monitoring, surveillance, and reporting systems; released national stockpiles of personal protective equipment, pharmaceuticals; and generated guidelines for global travel and business, among other interventions. The novel influenza H1N1 outbreak of April 2009 was the century's first pandemic. To visualize the scope of H1N1, cases were reported in over 100 countries and an estimated loss of between 151,700 to 575,400 lives worldwide (Dawood et al., 2012). Middle East Respiratory Syndrome (MERS), first identified in 2012, is an example of a less publicly known novel coronavirus outbreak yet to be fully contained. The outbreak continues to cause severe respiratory illness and some loss of life in over 27 countries. While clinical research on MERS and the quest for a vaccine is ongoing, the implementation of NPIs, pharmaceutical therapies, and enhanced communication are credited with the reduction in new infections globally (Donnelley, Malik, Elkholy, Cauchemez, & Van Kerkoheve, 2019). The Ebola and Zika viruses caused two infectious disease outbreaks in 2014 and 2017, respectively; they each impacted various populations and were declared PHEICs, but neither developed into a pandemic. These examples collectively illuminate the processes and organizations involved in preparing for, responding, mitigating, and recovering from public health outbreaks of various magnitudes. Together they exemplify a more complex framework within which the COVID-19 pandemic evolved.

On December 31, 2019, China reported to WHO, in accordance with IHR, that they had detected novel cases of pneumonia in Wuhan that were neither MERS nor SARS, had sustained human-to-human transmission, and spread throughout the community (Perrett, 2020). By January 30, 2020, the WHO Emergency Committee convened and declared the emerging coronavirus (named 2019-nCoV at the time) outbreak a PHEIC. The novel coronavirus was attributed to zoonotic spread to humans at a Wuhan wet market, and to people in over 25 countries. By this time, 9,826 people had been confirmed as having COVID-19 in 19 countries. Of these, 1,527 had a severe version of the disease, and 213 had lost their lives globally (WHO, 2020a). These figures tell a quantitative, although partial, story that also includes short- and long-term mental, social, and economic components. The economic impact of the disease in China alone, as of January 2020, was estimated at over $60 billion. Yet to be determined is the worldwide implication in lives lost, lives affected, and the financial impact on aviation, health, agricultural sectors, and more. Containment strategies, pharmacological research and development, and NPI implementation as delineated by WHO were recommended globally, and since then have been implemented and enforced with significantly distinct degrees far from the recommended expectation. On March 11, 2020, WHO declared COVID-19 a pandemic. Within a month, the virus had swept across the globe, with nearly 2 million confirmed COVID-19 cases in 185 countries (Johns Hopkins, 2020). At the time of writing this chapter, 8 months into the pandemic, there are 45,942,902 confirmed cases of COVID-19 in 219 countries, and 1,192,644 lives have been confirmed lost (WHO, 2020b). Unfortunately, global trends for loss of life are projected to double to 2,495,789 by February 2021 (IHME, 2020).

The ongoing COVID-19 pandemic offers a calamitous yet practical backdrop for investigating the value, relevance, and application of large secondary datasets generated in a public health disaster. This is particularly salient because public health disasters are inherently global; span myriad sociocultural, economic, and political dimensions; and generate vast, complex data. With increased urbanization, globalization, migration, and aviation travel of greater speed and scope, impending infectious disease outbreaks are projected to proliferate (Morens, Folkers, & Fauci, 2009; Marmot, 2005).

The SARS-CoV-2 virus will not be the last novel virus causing a public health disaster. To address this reality, holistic convergent research, practice, and policy are an imperative. The availability of data, its effective analysis, dissemination of contextualized findings, and implementation of data-based policies and practice has prospects for saving lives immediately during COVID-19 and in future outbreaks. In this chapter, I will discuss the process of using large secondary datasets in this effort. I will also integrate my experience applying large, ex post facto quantitative data to illuminate global vulnerability to pandemics after the 2009 H1N1 pandemic. Additionally, I challenge researchers using large secondary datasets to apply indicators or variable proxy data that authentically reflects diverse lived experiences such as governance, corruption, and human development in addition to typical datasets; for example, those with data on the economy, health, and reported infrastructure.

Large Secondary Datasets

The fundamental difference between secondary and primary data lies in the sourcing process and relative availability and convenience. Vogt (1999) defines secondary data as information collected by primary researchers and availed in databases for use by non-primary researchers in database collections organized, archived, and available for rapid retrieval. The people who typically access secondary data are researchers interested in studying phenomena, developing policy, and advising practice through the analysis of existing data provided by a primary source. Primary researchers and data collection, on the other hand, require that a researcher design and collect data directly in the field through physical or virtual means. The primary researcher is not only responsible for the collection of the data, but most importantly for maintaining and adhering to required ethical considerations and mandates critical for participant protection and data veracity. Secondary researchers use pre-existing secondary data and are required to go through specific approvals determined by the proprietors of data, country of research, and requisite institutional review boards, which are different from primary researchers. As pointed out in Chapter 1, some researchers using secondary data may not be directly obligated by ethical review boards because they are not the ones directly collecting the data from primary sources. Despite this procedural caveat, researchers using secondary data are not precluded from ethical practices.

Centrality of Ethical Considerations

The conversation around ethical handling of data is typically emphasized as an unequivocal requirement in the collection and handling of primary data. As discussed in Chapter 1, the ethical handling and compliance of primary data is facilitated through programs such as the Collaborative Institutional Training Initiative (CITI). Without CITI training and valid certification, institutional organizations do not grant permission for researchers to participate in the collection and analysis of primary data. However, this certification is not typically a requirement when accessing and analyzing secondary data. The exception to this practice occurs when a researcher attempts to secure a dataset that contains various levels of identifying information about respondents, which under these circumstances requires various levels of approval from the institutional review board. In the absence of this requirement, researchers are not absolved from ethical standards. The onus of ethical responsibility to secondary datasets lies with the researcher, especially because of the implications that public health disaster findings have on lives and livelihoods.

The Disaster Research Context and Large Datasets

As earlier stated, disaster research is unique for the context in which it is undertaken. Disaster research is predicated on potential, ongoing, or historical hazard events and can be traumatic to participants, requires researchers to be uniquely cognizant of this reality on participants and on researchers themselves. Stallings (2002) aptly stated that disaster researchers must acknowledge that their research context affects their methods.

Some disaster contexts are less traumatizing than others and minimally impede research. As pointed out by authors of other chapters in this book, collecting primary data among people whose lives and livelihoods have been impacted in disasters can further accentuate their experiences. As such, while it is possible to conduct primary data collection in a disaster setting, as illustrated in other chapters in this book, there are multiple factors that impede such practices. Factors impeding primary research include characteristics that negatively interact with survivors, first responders, and various stakeholders. Further, in some circumstances, the presence of researchers may place survivors or first responder personnel at further risk – a reality that is contradictory to researcher purposes for being there in the first place. In instances where this is the risk, researchers engage in ex post facto studies, which are based on or supplemented by secondary data when available.

Large secondary datasets are typically available online (Vogt, 1999). They originate from local, state, regional, tribal, and national government agencies, non-governmental organizations, private organizations and businesses, think tanks, and research institutions. Some of these datasets are proprietary and protected, making them inaccessible to the general public.

Use of large secondary datasets is becoming increasingly necessary in disaster research. According to Peacock (2002), large secondary datasets "form the backbone for additional efforts at developing indicators of political development, economic inequality, resource depletion and utilization, trade and production flows, and purchasing power" (p. 240). Dynes (1988) and Peacock (2002) articulate the need for conceptualizing the international connectivity of disasters and implementing global disaster reduction approaches. Large secondary datasets are pivotal for facilitating increasing global hazards and hazard impact research. Whether used exclusively or as supplemental to primary data, large secondary datasets are essential to analyzing macro-level convergent systems and their inherent correlations.

Large secondary datasets are also essential for investigating disasters from specific ideological approaches and ecological conceptual models. Examples of two such models are the Pressure and Release (PAR) progression of vulnerability disaster model (Wisner, Blaikie, Cannon, & Davis, 2004) and the social determinants of health (SDoH) model (WHO, 2010). Both models approach and conceptualize disasters and public health outcomes by acknowledging and integrating external factors that indicate vulnerability. Large secondary datasets such as those generated by geographic information systems (GIS) are yet another option for data necessary for addressing disaster phenomenon that spans multiple jurisdictions, countries, regions, or continents (Dash, 2002). Global events include climate-induced disasters, environmental catastrophes, and pandemics. Using large secondary datasets affords most researchers access to data they otherwise may not have the time, resources, or capability to attain at the primary level. By accessing large secondary datasets, researchers have the benefit of leveraging data for the study of multidisciplinary, innovative topics with potential for new meaningful work.

Sources

Multiple international and national organizations are among institutions that gather and directly produce large secondary datasets gathered by their personnel working in the field. This data is oftentimes gathered for specific institutional purposes, offering a practical option for people interested in pursuing specific relevant lines of research (see Box 13.1).

BOX 13.1 SELECTING DATA SOURCES

As a disaster scholar, my interest in social vulnerability to pandemics at a global level led me to access large secondary datasets in an effort to capture external macro forces that are contributing factors to vulnerability. Specifically, I curated and analyzed large secondary datasets to elucidate indicators that amplified vulnerabilities and their correlation to mortality during the 2009 H1N1 pandemic. I selected vulnerability indicators and organized my research using the progression of vulnerability Pressure and Release Model (PAR; Wisner et al., 2004), and the SDoH model (2010). My unit of analysis constituted 193 member states of the United Nations (UN) listed as WHO members in 2009. The macro-level indicators I investigated were represented through large national level datasets on health, education, communication, population, air transport, and governance (Mwarumba, 2017). This necessitated the selection and analysis of large secondary datasets from a variety of international organizations, and it was instructive in beginning to understand how vulnerability may have impacted the number of lives lost during the pandemic.

In order to accomplish this, I intentionally identified and analyzed datasets that most closely corresponded to and contained my selected indicators as follows. WHO and the World Bank (WB) were my sources for three health indicators. The United Nations Educational, Scientific, and Cultural Organization (UNESCO) and WB were my data sources for two education indicators. For the three communications indicators, UNESCO and the International Telecommunication Union (ITU) organization were my sources. Population indicator data for two indicators was sourced from the WB in addition to an indicator for civil air transportation. Finally, data for the two governance indicators was taken from Transparency International's Corruption Perception Index (CPI) and the UN Development Bank's Human Development Index (HDI; Mwarumba, 2017). My choice of governance indicators, human development, and civil transportation was central to my work because of the inherent necessity for understanding dynamics not typically included in the evaluation of pandemic vulnerability.

Box 13.1 illustrates specific data repositories I used for my research on H1N1. These are just a few of the large secondary databases available online in various local, state, tribal, national, international, public, and private institution repositories.

It is incumbent upon researchers interested in curating large datasets to diligently and patiently identify endorsed reliable data. To achieve this, it is necessary to triangulate data resources as a check on which represents the most robust depiction of the phenomenon being studied. For example, a researcher seeking U.S. COVID-19 data disaggregated by race and ethnicity, congregant facility mortality and morbidity, or allocation and expenditure of federal funding to small businesses through the Paycheck Protection Program is are bound to encounter extraordinary inconsistencies and impediments. This is because in various jurisdictions in the United States, racial data transparency has been concealed, congregant facility data has been obscured, and in some instances data outputs have been doctored to display preferred narratives. It is imperative that researchers understand more than what the data reflects to include the all-important sociopolitical and cultural context within which data was originally gathered. Cross checking or "backfilling" data is a method a researcher can use to triangulate data and check its veracity. As an example, census data from various years can be applied to gauge excess loss of life in public health outbreaks. COVID-19 has considerably amplified this reality. Data collection and reporting during the current pandemic has not only been disjointed and marred by political influence, but has resulted in professional public health and public officials bearing the brunt of direct punitive action in institutions of higher learning and local state and federal entities for reporting uncompromised data. As a result, some people have lost their jobs or resigned in protest, institutions have faced backlash for providing data, and others have lost funding. Some institutions and individuals who have experienced this have gone on to establish emergent platforms where they have continued to disseminate salient COVID-19 data. This presents yet another layer of complexity for researchers of COVID-19. It will not only be incumbent on them to understand what the geopolitics were, but also to determine which data resources are "sanctioned" and which are not, and how this will impact their work and probably their careers.

Despite these caveats, researchers can and have made determinations on secondary data alignment to particular study designs. After this determination is successfully made, the next part of the process is analysis.

The Research Process

Historically, the use of large secondary datasets in emergency management research was not common. This usage has evolved significantly since the availability of data supported by new technologies and platforms such as smartphones, social media, and various applications. Leveraging this technology and platforms has facilitated wide-ranging data access and integration as well as enhanced analysis and visualization for optimal decision-making (Wamba et al., 2015; Akter & Wamba, 2019).

Identify Research Interest

It is important that from the onset of a study, a researcher determines their topic, formulates research questions, and identifies variables before selecting the appropriate research methodology and data source. Research interest can be based on a variety of reasons, such as personal interest or experience, or professional, institutional, or funding imperatives. The next step is identifying the type of data and collection method that is most aligned to research objectives. If a determination is made to use large secondary datasets, determining which specific variables and/or indicators from direct secondary or proxy data is central. For example, one of my research questions sought to investigate the following:

> *How well did a nation's gross domestic product, education expenditure, and CPI together predict the number of deaths caused by the 2009 H1N1 flu pandemic?*

The independent variables (predictors) in this research question are national gross domestic product, education expenditure, and CPI. The dependent variable is the number of deaths caused by the 2009 H1N1 flu pandemic. Each of these indicators (and others not stated in this question) were gathered from different data repositories and analyzed for their relationship to H1N1 pandemic mortality. Once a researcher identifies and states the research question, the next step is to find datasets that best encapsulate the variables being studied. When data directly reflecting a selected variable is not available, proxy data may suffice, otherwise a researcher may have to reconsider and abandon specific variable searches in secondary datasets. An example in my work is my interest in overlaying actual corruption data by country on health outcomes during pandemics. The CPI was the closest I could get to capturing this variable in 2009.

Locating Data

There are a large number of secondary data resources that researchers can access to curate specific data. Different sites have guidelines, including some for a fee. To the benefit of researchers, funding agencies and institutions in higher learning are prioritizing the sharing of primary data through various platforms as a central component of good scientific design (Little et al., 2009; Bobrow, 2015; Burton, Banner, Elliot, Knoppers, & Banks, 2017). These practices have lent themselves to enabling new research, minimizing duplication of research and data collection, and stretching available research data and funding further into new frontiers (Bobrow, 2015).

Along these lines, Table 13.1 offers a list of select secondary data repositories that can be used to extract data, including those on COVID-19. These repositories range from international organizations (e.g., WHO) and government and government department data (e.g., Data.gov) to institutions of higher learning (e.g., Harvard Dataverse) and private companies (e.g., Mendeley).

Despite the wide variety of data repositories and potential sets to choose from, the choice of secondary datasets is dependent upon research objectives and resource availability, such as time, finances, and technical ability. In some cases, as I previously mentioned and highlight in Box 13.2, a researcher may out of necessity combine several different datasets to obtain variable data necessary for responding to a research question. From a financial standpoint, most government data is typically free following a basic request such as a Freedom of Information Act request; however, some organizations such as those in the private and non-profit sectors may charge a fee for researchers to join in developing research questions or for access to data. This is a reality that may be prohibitive to researchers without funding.

Some dataset repositories are organized to support very specific searches by topic, chronological demarcation, events, locations, and more. It is therefore important to have an idea what data is central or complementary to research you are doing before you download and/or pay for it. Generally speaking, the key to locating the right data

TABLE 13.1 Sample of Large Secondary Databases and Repositories

Generalist Data Repositories

COVID-19 Forecast Hub Ensemble Model
Data Commons
Figshare Knowledge
GitHub Project
Google Dataset Search Open Science Framework
U.S. spread of COVID-19 maps and analytics (SharedGeo)**Statista*

International Organizations

Center for Research on the Epidemiology of Disasters (CRED)European Centers for Disease Control and Prevention (ECDC)International Social Survey Program (ISSP)NASA Disasters Mapping PortalHumanitarian Data Exchange (HDX) International Emergency Disasters Database (EMDAT)United Nations Office for Disaster Risk Reduction (UNDRR) United Nations Data (UNdata)World Data Center for ClimateNovel coronavirus (COVID-19) outbreak timeline map (HealthMap)**

University Data Sites

Coronavirus COVID-19 global cases**
COVID-19 surveillance dashboard (University of Virginia)**
Harvard DataverseInstitute for Health Metrics and Evaluation (IHME)**

Private/Business Owned Data Sources

Covid19.topos.com**Mendeley (raw data source)
COVID-19 coronavirus tracker (Kaiser Family Foundation)

* Site has free basic option as well as premium and corporate access options for a fee.
** Specific COVID-19 related data sites.

for your study is to ensure that you can match and justify variables of interest with the data or proxy indicators available from a secondary data source.

BOX 13.2 THE NEED TO COMBINE DIFFERENT DATASETS

One of my study variables was communication channels required for pandemic preparedness campaigns and coordination of response activities (Mwarumba, 2017). Because my study reviewed large global datasets from different nation states, levels of economic and technological advancement varied between and within countries. Not only did I need to capture the communication indicator across different countries but also across various media platforms. I categorized communication as traditional and non-traditional as a means of capturing the communication construct across people exposed to various media options. To this end, I identified multiple independent communication indicator datasets, as no single data source encapsulated the intended components. The components included radio and television channel penetration data, defined as a percentage of homes, and global prepaid mobile phone subscriptions per capita as a proxy for actual mobile phone use per country.

Data Veracity

There are also concerns that arise with dataset repositories regarding data quality, access, and security. It is incumbent upon researchers accessing secondary data to check the veracity of the dataset archive, and its collection processes for quality control. Along these lines, there are certification mechanisms online that can check data veracity, sustainability, and trustworthiness before a researcher acquires it. One such mechanism is CoreTrustSeal, a world data system (WDS) certification of the International Science Council, which serves to inform and assure the research community and provide a benchmark for comparing repository strengths and weaknesses (CoreTrustSeal, 2020). This system identifies repositories that meet specific standards with identifiable signs and logos, typically issued for 3 years. The system provides documentation that includes licensure, ethics, data integrity and authenticity, expert guidance, and data quality (Dillo et al., 2019).

Extraction and Cleaning of Data

The data extraction and transfer process requires that a researcher determine the requisite skill set and compatible format. A majority of secondary dataset repositories offer a variety of file formats (with extensions such as *.xls, *.csv, and *.dat) available to the researcher. Once the researcher knows the types of file formats data are stored in, they proceed to use the appropriate tools to further analyze the quantitative or qualitative data from the database.

The liberty to clean secondary data is more limited than with primary data, where the researcher has editing liberties of data cycle cleanliness (Hellerstein, 2008). However, most datasets can be curated directly from the repository website before being transferred for analysis. For example, a researcher can select specific indicators from a large secondary dataset that are relevant to them to download, as opposed to downloading the entire dataset. This is followed by a migration or export to a separate table and then analysis.

An example of this basic application can be found in the EM-DAT data repository. This open access data supports researcher curation by enabling selection from a menu of options ranging from multiple disaster classifications (natural, technological, or complex), location by continent, and year of interest. The output is then generated on a downloadable spreadsheet in as many iterations as desired by the researcher. Another particularly efficient function in large secondary datasets is that as new data is identified, these websites are updated to indicate emerging information. Some datasets, such as those on Mendeley, offer raw data that requires additional cleaning and organization compared to an EM-DAT source that is disaster specific. Researchers need to diligently ensure that secondary datasets align to enable cohesive analysis. Cleaning secondary data is therefore a necessary process, the objective of which is to standardize data by identifying discrepancies and either removing or reorganizing them to achieve a better aligned dataset. Cleaning also functions as a means to identify missing data and enables the aggregation or computing of relevant variables. There are multiple data cleaning strategies that can be applied on raw data to enhance usability, including hiring a trained professional or acquiring and using applicable software.

Conclusion and Future Considerations

Large secondary datasets are pivotal for analyzing macro-level vulnerabilities and global disaster impacts at various levels of analysis. In their usage, researchers should be mindful of drawing inferences, as discussed in Chapter 3. Secondary data also make it possible to customize research indicators to fit research objectives. When used in public health disaster research, these datasets can be useful for developing predictive disaster models pivotal for developing life-saving policy and practice. For example, civil air transport volume and patterns as a variable of public health predictive research are essential for mapping pathogen transmission and the adoption and implementation of public health interventions (Stern & Markel, 2004; Mwarumba, 2017). An important caveat for consideration is that data evolves during public health outbreaks, and researchers need to stay apprised as new information is generated. It is incumbent upon researchers to remain aware of new data and techniques as a novel outbreak unfolds and even after it has officially ended. For example, it is now over 100 years since the Spanish flu pandemic occurred, yet its mortality and morbidity data continue to be adjusted based on new research and forensic findings. Researchers must expect and account for this dynamism. A recommended practice when using large secondary datasets is to ensure that the most recent data adjustments are considered and applied and notification made for possible amendments. Another important consideration when using predictive models that utilize large secondary datasets in public health outbreaks is the imperative to compare data sources and test for veracity. In other words, how close does the model come to real outcomes? In a sense, researchers must step behind the curtain to review and compare predictive model sourcing as this has direct implications for real-time policy and practice. As the COVID-19 pandemic continues, we are inundated by various predictive modeling sources. Popularity of a predictive model should not be the determining factor for adoption.

The role large secondary datasets play in capturing public health outcomes is pivotal for determining intervention measure development and implementation. For example, in their 2020 study, Hsiang et al. (2020) reviewed 1,659 local, regional, and national level COVID-19 NPI policies in China, South Korea, Iran, Italy, France, and the United States. Their goal was to investigate if implementation of NPIs had significant effects on COVID-19 transmission, and how this impacted various populations. Secondary data was used in this study including "epidemiological data, case definition/ testing regimes, and policy data" from the six countries, with data resources drawn from "government public health websites, regional newspaper articles, and crowd-sourced information on Wikipedia" (Hsiang et al., 2020 p. 22). After analysis, the findings of this study indicate that there is significant benefit to implementing policies geared to reducing human contact during the pandemic to limit consequent transmission of the virus.

Large secondary datasets from national and international organizations as well as public and private entities will continue to be what Peacock (2002) calls the "backbone for additional efforts at developing indicators" for capturing the dynamism of disasters and their contexts. These datasets offer opportunities to pursue new lines of research not only for the sake of research but also for the "preservation of cultural and national uniqueness" that distinguishes rather than attempts to homogenize disaster contexts (Øyen, 1990; Peacock, 2002). The Hsiang et al. (2020) study exemplifies what Peacock (2002) and Øyen (1990) refer to. While admitting that there were heterogeneous variables on the timing, intensity, and extent of policy implementation, they report that there was a slowdown of possibly 57–65 million infections in the six countries analyzed. This study and others hold import as a metric for "near misses" during the ongoing first wave of the pandemic and are instructive for the development and implementation of NPIs in anticipation for a protracted pandemic.

The COVID-19 pandemic offers a critical window of opportunity for urgent collaborative and convergent research on global disaster resilience. Development and application of large secondary datasets has progressed significantly in the pandemic, setting the stage for innovative and invigorating research with promise for addressing the confounding aspects of the global threats and health outbreaks.

There remains, however, a tremendous amount of work to be done in gathering, securing, and availing global data vital for addressing dynamic global threats. To start with, data availability still skews heavily toward communities, countries, and regions with the economic, social, and cultural might to gather data. Therefore, the implications are that countries without these capacities may end up with imprecise interpretations of their lived experiences during COVID-19 due to partial data availability or bias from external research agencies and individuals. Another disconcerting trend on data collection and dissemination has become apparent in the United States. Historically perceived as the vanguard for science, scientific rigor, fairly incorruptible institutions, and the rule of law, there have been stunning aspersions cast on these processes and institutions. Data has been politicized and in fact weaponized against historically marginalized communities to limit access to health infrastructure necessary for surviving COVID-19. In some states, statewide and private industry officials have at best obfuscated data collection and reporting, and at worst penalized employees for the same if data was deemed unfavorable to popular political proclivities. Data has been tampered with to represent deceptive outputs, and dissemination has been prohibited or inexplicably curtailed in some instances. In some states, normal data collection techniques and disaggregation along demographic categories such as age, race, and ethnicity have been vetoed. The United States is not alone in this appalling practice. Brazil has mandated a totalitarian approach to erasing and not reporting COVID-19 mortality data (Phillips, 2020). This disconcerting reality poses great concern, particularly for people and communities vulnerable to COVID-19, who are the most and worst affected. The inability to access and analyze data has dire implications for policy development and implementation, which in turn directly affects mortality and morbidity outcomes. For researchers interested in the pursuit of objective, data-based development and implementation of life-saving policies and practice, ethical application of secondary datasets is an imperative.

Further Readings

Afolabi, O. M. (2018). *Public health disaster: A global ethical framework*. Cham, Switzerland: Springer.
Berkman, F. L., Kawachi, I., & Glymour, M. M. (2014). *Social epidemiology*. Oxford: Oxford University Press.
COVID-19 ForecastHub. (2020). *Ensemble model*. https://covid19forecasthub.org/doc/ensemble/
The Humanitarian Data Exchange (2020). *COVID-19 Pandemic data*. http://Data.humdata.org/event/covid-19?q=&ext_page_size=100
Noji, K. E. (Ed.). (1997). *The public health consequences of disasters*. Oxford: Oxford University Press.
University of Colorado, Boulder. (2020). *Converge. Data*. https://converge.colorado.edu/data

References

Akter, S., & Wamba, S. F. (2019). Big data and disaster management: A systematic review and agenda for future research. *Annals of Operations Research, 283*(1–2), 939–959.
Bobrow, M. (2015). Funders must encourage scientists to share. *Nature, 522*, 129. http://www.nature.com/news/funders-must-encourage-scientists-to-share-1.17718

Burton, R.P., Banner, N., Elliot, J.M., Knoppers, M.B., & Banks, J. (2017). Policies and strategies to facilitate secondary use of research data in the health sciences. *International Journal of Epidemiology*, *46*(6), 1729–1733.

Core Trust Seal. (2020). *Core trust seal*. Retrieved November 23, 2020, from www.coretrustseal. org

Dash, N. (2002). The use of geographic information systems in disaster research. In A.R. Stallings (Ed.), *Methods of disaster research* (pp. 320–333). Xlibris Corporation.

Dawood, F.S., Iuliano, A.D., Reed, C., Meltzer, I.M., Shay, K.D., Cheng, P., et al. (2012). First global estimates of 2009 H1N1 pandemic mortality released by CDC-led collaboration. *Lancet Infectious Diseases*. https//doi.org/10.3389/fimmu.2019.00549

Dillo, I., L'Hours, H., Kleemola, M., Crabtree, J., Downs, R.R., et al. (2019). *CoreTrustSeal Trustworthy data repositories requirements 2020–2022*. http://Zenodo.org/record/3638211#. XpPwL1NKhBw

Donnelley, A.C., Malik, R.M., Elkholy, A., Cauchemez, S., & Van Kerkoheve, D.M. (2019). Worldwide reduction in MERS cases and deaths since 2016. *Emerging Infectious Diseases*, *25*(9), 1758–1760.

Dynes, R. (1988). Cross-cultural international research: Sociology and disasters. *International Journal of Mass Emergencies and Disasters*, *6*(2), 101–129.

Fritz, C.E. (1961). Disasters. In K.R. Meton & A.R. Nisbet (Eds.), *Contemporary social problems* (pp. 651–694). New York: Harcourt.

Ghendon, Y. (1994). Introduction to pandemic influenza through history. *European Journal of Epidemiology*, *10*(4), 451–453.

Hellerstein, M.J. (2008). *Quantitative data cleaning for large databases*. United Nations Economic Commission for Europe (UNECE). Retrieved November 23, 2020, from http://db.cs. berkeley.edu/jmh

Hsiang, S., Allen, D., Annan-Phan, S., Bell, K., Bolliger, I., . . . Wu, T. (2020). The effect of large-scale anti-contagion policies on the coronavirus (COVID-19) pandemic. *Nature*, *584*(7820), 262–267.

Institute for Health Metrics and Evaluation (IHME). (2020). *COVID-19 projections*. Retrieved November 23, 2020, from https://covid19.healthdata.org/global?view=total-deaths&tab=trend

Johns Hopkins University Medicine. (2020). *CIVUD-19 dashboard by the Center for Systems Science and Engineering*. Retrieved November 23, 2020, from https://coronavirus.jhu.edu/map.html/

Kaufmann, S. (2007). *The new plagues: Pandemics and poverty in a globalized world*. The Sustainability Project. London: Haus.

Little, J., Higgins, J.P., Ioannidis, J.P., et al. (2009). Strengthening the reporting of genetic association studies (STREGA): An extension of the strengthening the reporting of observational studies in epidemiology (STROBE) statement. *Journal of Clinical Epidemiology*, *33*(7), 581–598.

Marmot, M. (2005). Social determinants of health inequalities. *Lancet*, *365*(9464), 1099–1104.

Morens, D.M., Folkers, G.K., & Fauci, A.S. (2004). The challenge of emerging and re-emerging infectious diseases. *Nature*, *430*(6996), 242–249.

Morens, D.M., Folkers, G.K., & Fauci, A.S. (2009). What is a pandemic? *Journal of Infectious Diseases*, *200*(7), 1018–1021.

Mwarumba, N. (2017). *Global social vulnerability to pandemics: An examination of social determinants of health of H1N1 2009*. (Doctoral dissertation), Oklahoma State University. https://hdl. handle.net/11244/299534

Øyen, E. (1990). The imperfection of comparisons. In E. Øyen (Ed.), *Comparative methodology: Theory and practice in international social research* (pp. 1–18). London: Sage.

Peacock, G.W. (2002). Cross-national and comparative disaster research. In A.R. Stallings (Ed.), *Methods of disaster research* (pp. 235–250). Xlibris Corporation.

Perrett, C. (2020, February 1). *A "highly pathogenic strain" of H5N1 bird flu has been reported in China's Hunan province*. http://www.businessinsider.com/bird-fluchina-coronavirus-pathogenic-strain-of-h5n1-highly-2020-2.

Phillips, D. (2020, June). *Brazil stops releasing Covid-19 death toll and wipes data from official site*. http://www.theguardian.com/world/2020/jun/07/brazil-stops-releasing-covid-19-death-toll-and-wipes-data-from-official-site

Stallings, A.R. (2002). *Methods of disaster research*. Xlibris Corporation.

Stern, A.M., & Markel, H. (2004). International efforts to control infectious diseases, 1851 to the present. *JAMA, 292*(12), 1474–1479.

Taubenberger, J.K., & Morens, D.M. (2006). 1918 influenza: The mother of all pandemics. *Revista Biomedica, 17*(1), 69–79.

Vogt, W.P. (1999). *Dictionary of statistics and methodology: A non-technical guide for the social sciences* (2nd ed.). London: Sage.

Wamba, F.S., Akter, S., Edwards, A., Chopin, G., & Gnanzou, D. (2015). How "big data" can make big impact: Findings from a systematic review and a longitudinal case study. *Journal of Production Economics, 165*, 234–246.

Wisner, B., Blaikie, P., Cannon, T., & Davis, I. (2004). *At risk: Natural hazards, people's vulnerability, and disasters* (2nd ed.). New York: Routledge.

World Health Organization. (2010). *Social determinants of health*. Retrieved November 23, 2020, from www.who.int/teams/social-determinants-of-health

World Health Organization (WHO). (2020a). *Novel coronavirus (2019-nCoV) situation report – 11*. Retrieved November 24, 2020, from www.who.int/docs/default-source/coronaviruse/situation-reports/20200131-sitrep-11-ncov.pdf?sfvrsn=de7c0f7_4

World Health Organization (WHO). (2020b). *Numbers at a glance*. Retrieved January 9, 2020, from www.who.int/emergencies/diseases/novelcoronavirus2019?gclid=EAlalQobChM19qkr8jh7AIVOsDACh1h5ACHEAAYASAAEgKZD_D_BwE

A Brief Introduction to Statistical Modeling for Disaster and Emergency Management Research

Mwarumba Mwavita

Introduction

The use of statistical modeling has increased in recent years in all fields of social science. As indicated in Chapter 13, there has been an explosion of data that has become more accessible to the would-be researcher. In the past, oil has been the most important resource that has pushed economies of many countries. Today, data is the new oil. Technology makes it possible to generate a lot of data. This immense amount of data lends itself to statistical modeling. Thus, researchers need to understand data and how to appropriately use statistical models to answer specific research questions. Prior to discussing the models, I will discuss some statistical concepts that are important to understanding and using statistical models.

First, statistics in generally is broken into two broad categories based on the nature of data. These are parametric and non-parametric. Parametric tests follow certain distribution assumptions (Strunk & Mwavita, 2020) while non-parametric do not. Non-parametric tests do not follow any distribution assumptions, and they are known as distribution-free tests (Siegel & Castellan, 1988). Specifically, distribution-free tests require few, if any, assumptions about the shapes of the underlying population distributions (Siegel & Castellan, 1988). Hence, these tests can be used if the distributions are severely skewed, which does not work with parametric statistics (Siegel & Castellan, 1988). The models I discuss in this chapter are based on data that follow a normal distribution. Thus, I use parametric tests to test hypotheses.

Second, in a normal distribution, data follows a bell-shaped curve. The mean, median, and mode of a normal distribution are equal; the area under the curve equals 1 (100%); approximately 99% of the data lies between 3 standard deviations below and above the mean; approximately 95% of the data lies between 2 standard deviations above and below the mean; approximately 68% of the data lies between 1 standard deviation above and below the mean. The peak of the distribution is the mean, median, and mode of the distribution (Strunk & Mwavita, 2020; Lomax & Hahs-Vaughn, 2012). These properties of the normal distribution form a mathematical curve that provides a model of relative frequency distribution, which is favorably present in social sciences (Shavelson, 1996). In addition, they are important in hypothesis testing since they provide critical values to reject a null hypothesis based on significance levels established by the normal curve. For example, a critical value to reject a two-tailed null hypothesis using an alpha level of .05, the critical value from the normal distribution is ±1.96. This implies if the observed value from the statistics performed on the data is between −1.96 and +1.96, we do not reject the null hypothesis, but if the value is below −1.96 or above +1.96, we reject the null hypothesis and conclude that the parameter estimate is different from zero. Figure 14.1 shows the normal distribution and its properties.

Mean, median, and mode are measures of central tendency of a distribution. More precisely, they are the location statistics for data distribution. Specifically, these measures provide a single value that describes a distribution by identifying the central position within that distribution of the data. In parametric statistics, mean is the most commonly used measure of central tendency.

Third, besides the measures of central tendency, measures of dispersion or spread are very important in understanding and describing the data distribution in parametric statistics. Measures of dispersion for a dataset indicate the average dispersion of each data point from the mean. They assess how well the measure of central tendency (mean) represents the data. The larger the measure of dispersion is, the less representative is the mean; conversely, the smaller the measure of dispersion is, the more representative is the mean for the data. For normal distribution, variance and standard deviation are the commonly used measures of dispersion.

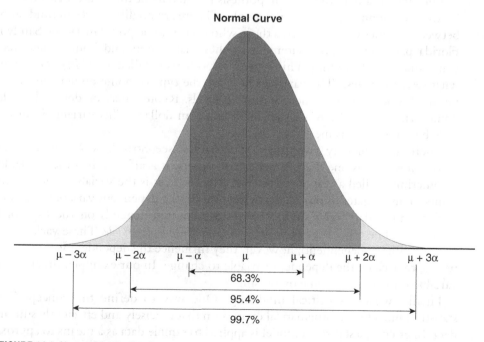

FIGURE 14.1 Normal Distribution Curve

Why Statistics?

So, what is the purpose of statistics? We use statistics to describe and make inferences of data from a sample to some population from which the sample was drawn. In other words, statistics is ideally used in selecting a representative sample from a population as described in Chapter 2. After a sample is selected, we perform analyses on this relatively smaller group, then infer the results we obtain from the sample to the population from which we drew the sample, as described in Chapter 3. Along these lines, the construct or attributes that we measure and assess are known as variables. For example, socioeconomic status, gender, regions hit by disaster, and funds received are just a few of the attributes that we study in the disaster research.

These attributes have certain values, which are called measurement scales. There are four levels of measurement: nominal, ordinal, interval, and ratio. The value or number assigned to a nominal variable is, for identification purposes, a label. For example, a variable *City location* might be represented by Urban = 1; Suburban = 2; and Rural = 3. The numbers serve as labels identifying the type of city. Ordinal scales, on the other hand, order facets of a variable, but there is no equal interval between two consecutive levels. For example, socioeconomic status (SES) can be represented by three levels: High = 3, Medium = 2, and Low = 1; however, we do not conceptually know the actual difference between "High" and "Medium" levels. Interval scales have equal intervals between two consecutive levels, and zero is arbitrary. One example of this is calendar dates. Ratio scales have nominal, ordinal, and interval characteristics, but zero has meaning. Some examples of ratio scales are physical quantities such as weight, height, and time (see Strunk & Mwavita, 2020). The scales of measurement of variables are important because they guide the kind of research questions and statistical models that a researcher can use to answer and test hypotheses.

But, what is a hypothesis? A hypothesis is a statement that illustrates a relationship between or among variables; for example, "There are no differences in funds allocated between families that rent versus those who own a home post–Hurricane Sandy in the Florida panhandle." This statement implies that renters and homeowners received equal amounts of funding. This type of hypothesis is called a *null hypothesis*, which is what researchers test. The variables here are the type of home ownership, which is a nominal scale of measurement with two levels. Renters may be denoted as "1" and homeowners "2." The other variable is funds in dollars. This variable is an interval scale because zero has meaning.

There are generally two types of variables (see Strunk & Mwavita, 2020). A *dependent variable* is one that "depends" on others. It is affected by other variables and is sometimes called a response variable. Moreover, it is the variable that a researcher wants to investigate. In our example hypothesis, the dependent variable is the amount of funds in dollars. The amount of funds allocated depends on the type of home ownership. The other type of variable is an *independent variable*. These variables do not change status (independent); however, they influence the dependent variable. In other words, they cause the dependent variable to change. In our example, the independent variable is the type of home ownership.

Finally, what is statistical modeling? One way to define the concept is that a statistical model is a mathematical expression that precisely and efficiently summarizes data. In essence, a statistical model is applied to sample data as a means to approximate an observed reality. For example, when a researcher examines sample data visually using a scatter plot diagram that contains two continuous variables, they may notice a positive linear trend. We can draw a line of best fit on the scatter plot that estimates the magnitude of strength of the linear relationship. This may lead a researcher to explore a prediction model that approximates the relationship between these two variables. Along these lines, there are a number of statistical models that researchers use to analyze data. However, each model has its own set of assumptions. Moreover, each model's use depends on the nature of the data. Data may be continuous, discrete, or a combination of both. As such, the application of these models depends on what type of questions an investigator wants to answer. All in all, statistical models follow a systematic process: (1) propose a research question and hypotheses; (2) identify the variables and how they are measured; (3) determine the best statistical method/model to use; (4) examine the assumptions; (5) conduct the analyses; (6) present the findings, whether you reject the null or not; and (7) discuss the findings.

Understanding Statistical Modeling

When researchers collect data, they are interested in understanding what the data means; however, data variables can be conceptualized and measured differently. This is why the same data might have different meanings from person to person and between geographic regions and cultures. There can even be different relationships between variables. But despite this potential complication, when we use statistical models there is an assumption that variables are "properly" conceptualized and measured. As such, in a simple model, the data we observe in a population may be expressed in the following way:

Data (observed) = Statistical Model + Error

This expression has two parts. *Data* is the part we observe or the information we collect from our experiments or studies. The second part has two components: statistical model and error. The *statistical model* is the part that provides the best mathematical approximation of the observed data. The *error* is what the statistical model is unable to explain in the data. In other words, error is best understood as follows:

Error = Data (Observed) − Statistical Model

The goal of a statistical model is to explain the data with minimum error. For a model to be "perfect," the error would be equal to zero. In this case, the statistical model would equal the observed data. However, this is typically not possible in reality and in the social sciences. As such, researchers strive to develop a model that approximates the data with minimum error. How small the error should be is based on many factors that are beyond the scope of this chapter. For more information, please refer to Judd, McClelland, and Ryan (2009).

Moving forward, I discuss two types of models generally and then in greater detail. These models are those that examine (1) differences between/among groups on a continuous dependent variable and (2) relationships between/among variables. In the second type of model, I present prediction and probability models. In discussing these models, I provide examples of how disaster researchers can apply them to their specific questions. Overall, I specifically discuss independent *t*-tests, analysis of variance

(ANOVA), multivariate analysis of variance (MANOVA), multiple regression, logistic regression, and multilevel Modeling.

Independent *t*-test

Researchers use independent *t*-tests when they want to examine if mean differences on a continuous outcome differ between two independent treatment groups. For example, if a researcher wanted to examine if there are differences between the amounts of government assistance in dollars provided to male and female households in a county that experienced a hurricane, an independent *t*-test is the appropriate statistical technique. As such, we might follow a process like this:

First, let us define the research question:

> Is there a mean difference in the amount of government assistance awarded to homeowners and the amount given to renters post-Hurricane Michael in 2018?

Now, thinking about the question in more detail, there are some important elements to consider. The independent variable is the type of homeownership. Homeownership is an independent variable because it influences the dependent variable. The dependent variable is the amount in dollars. This variable is continuous, and the independent variable affects its value. Homeownership has two levels in this example: homeowners and renters. This independent variable is nominal, because if we assign a "1" to homeowners, and "2" to renters, the numbers are only labels to identify the type of homeownership.

Second, we now proceed to stating the hypotheses. When we state the hypotheses, we develop statements in terms of population parameters. For our example, since we have two groups in the population of interest – homeowners and renters – we state the null hypothesis in this manner:

> There are no mean differences in the amount of government assistance in dollars awarded to homeowners and the amount given to renters post-Hurricane Michael in 2018 in affected areas of Florida.

However, when we use Greek symbols, which is the typical way to statistically represent statements, the null hypothesis is expressed as follows:

$$H_0: \mu_{HW} = \mu_R \tag{1}$$

In this statistical representation, HW = Homeowners and R = Renters. Similarly, we then state the research hypothesis. In words, we might say that our alternative hypothesis is:

> There are mean differences in the amounts of government assistance in dollars awarded to homeowners versus renters post-Hurricane Michael in 2018 in affected areas of Florida.

Again, using a common statistical depiction, the alternative hypothesis would look like this:

$$H_1: \mu_{HW} \neq \mu_R \tag{2}$$

As in the null hypothesis representation, HW = Homeowners and R = Renters. The alternative hypothesis states that the average amount of funding received by homeowners is different from the average amount received by renters. When we reject the null hypothesis, we accept the alternative hypothesis.

Third, we have to decide the significance level at which we are going to reject or fail to reject the null hypothesis. The researcher sets this significance level before conducting the analysis. In the social sciences, we commonly use a significance level of $\alpha = .05$ or .01. Where one has a relatively large sample and wants to detect a small effect size, we use .10 (Hair, Black, Babin, & Anderson, 2010). Once a significance level is chosen, we know the parameters of making a Type 1 error. By definition, a Type 1 error is the probability of rejecting a true null hypothesis. In other words, this occurs when a researcher states that there is a difference, when in fact there is not (Strunk & Mwavita, 2020; Stevens, 2007). The significance level we choose determines the critical value for whether we reject or fail to reject the null hypothesis on the test statistic. For an independent t-test, the test statistic is a value we obtain from a t-distribution table. To identify the correct table value, we use the degrees of freedom and the level of significance. The degrees of freedom for an independent t-test are found using the following equation:

$$n_1 + n_2 - 2 \qquad [3]$$

In this equation, n_1 is the sample size of group 1 and n_2 is the sample size of group 2. For each significance level and its corresponding degrees of freedom, the t-table provides a value. This table value is referred to as the critical value. If the value we calculate from our data is greater than the critical value, we reject the null and conclude that the means of the dependent variables between the two groups are statistically and significantly different. If the calculated value is less than the critical value, we fail to reject the null and conclude that the means of the two groups are the same.

Fourth, before using any statistical model or technique, we have to know the assumptions underlying the model. After knowing the assumptions, we have to evaluate our data to see whether it meets the assumption of the statistical model. As such, there are three assumptions that must be met when using independent t-tests. The first of these assumptions is normality. Normality refers to whether the dependent variable scores follow a normal distribution for each group. We can evaluate this assumption using the Shapiro--Wilk test. When we use this test, we do not want a statistically significant result. That is, in order to proceed with the independent t-test we want the p value of the Shapiro–Wilk test to be greater than the significance level (Yap & Sim, 2011). For example, if we are using $\alpha = .05$, we then want the p value for Shapiro Wilk's test to be greater than .05 to meet the assumption of normality for the two groups (Strunk & Mwavita, 2020; Stevens, 2007).

The second assumption that must be met is homogeneity of variance. This assumption requires that the population variance is equal for the two groups. We can write the null hypothesis for this assumption in this manner:

$$H_0: \sigma_1^2 = \sigma_2^2 \qquad [4]$$

In order to test this assumption, we use Levene's test to evaluate this assumption (Levene, 1960). Like the normality assumption, we do not want a statistically significant result in order to proceed with the independent t-test. We want the p value to be greater than the significance level to meet the assumption of homogeneity of variance (Keppel & Wickens, 2004)

The third assumption that must be met is independence of observation. This assumption requires that participants in each group do not affect any other participant's score on the dependent variable. That is, each observation provides information about itself only and provides no information about the occurrence of another observation (Keppel & Wickens, 2004; Strunk & Mwavita, 2020). We meet this assumption by randomly assigning participants to each of the groups. In addition to these assumptions, there are some other conditions that must also be met, such as that we have an independent variable with two levels or groups and one continuous dependent variable.

With this in mind, let us return to our example. A disaster researcher wants to investigate whether the amount of funds provided to people after Hurricane Michael differed based on their homeownership status. Specifically, the researcher was interested in finding if there was a mean difference in the amount provided between homeowners and renters for residents of Panama City, Florida. The researcher then went to the city records and obtained the following data in Table 14.1.

Using SPSS, we enter our data into the software, with 1 to indicate that an individual was a renter and 2 to indicate an individual was a Homeowner. To conduct an independent t-test using SPSS, follow the following steps:

1. Open your data in SPSS.

2. Click "Analyze" → Compare means → Independent t-test, then select "Amount" and move it to the Test variable window.

3. Select "Homeownership" to the Grouping variable window and define the groups as "1" and "2."

4. Click "OK," and you get the results of the independent t-test.

Let us now look at the results of the analysis. Table 14.2 shows the descriptive statistics that give you the sample size for each group and the means, standard deviations, and standard errors of the means.

Next follows the independent samples' test, which provides the Levene's and t-test results, depicted in Table 14.3.

TABLE 14.1 Funds Received by Residents

Renters (Amount Received in Dollars)	Homeowner (Amount Received in Dollars)
5,000	1,000
5,000	1,000
6,000	2,000
6,000	3,000
7,000	3,000
8,000	3,000
9,000	4,000

TABLE 14.2 Group Statistics

	Home Ownership	N	M	SD	SE
Award	Homeowner	7	6,571.43	1,511.858	571.429
	Renter	7	2,428.57	1,133.893	428.571

TABLE 14.3 Independent Samples Test

		Levene's Test for Equality of Variances		t-test for Equality of Means							
		F	p	t	df	p (two-tailed)	Mean Difference	Std. Error Difference	95% CI of the Difference		
									LL	UL	
Award	Equal Variances Assumed	.720	.413	5.800	12	.000	4,142.857	714.286	2,586.562	5,699.152	
	Equal Variances not Assumed			5.800	11.128	.000	4,142.857	714.286	2,572.922	5,712.793	

TABLE 14.4 Normality Test

Homeownership	Kolmogorov-Smirnov[a]			Shapiro-Wilk		
	Statistic	df	p	Statistic	df	p
Renters	.219	7	.200[b]	.915	7	.432
Homeowner	.264	7	.149	.887	7	.262

[a] Lilliefors significance correction. [b] Lower bound of the true significance.

Now, based on the SPSS outputs, let us evaluate the assumptions. The first assumption for an independent t-test is that the dependent variable is normally distributed in each of the groups. We visually assess this, using plots of the dependent variable for each group to see the shape of the distribution. Statistically, we use the Shapiro-Wilk test, which states that the distribution of the dependent variable is normally distributed in each group. Now using the following steps, we will conduct the Shapiro-Wilk test in SPSS:

1. Click on "Analyze" → Descriptives → Explore → Select amount and move it to Dependent variable window.

2. Move Homeownership into the Factor list window.

3. Click "Plots" and select "Normality plots with tests.

The results are presented in Table 14.4. Based on the results from Table 14.4, the Shapiro-Wilk test for each group is not statistically significant, suggesting that the distribution of the dependent variable on the two groups ($W_{Renters}(7) = .915$,

$p = .432$; $W_{Homeowner}(7) = .887$, $p = .262$) are normally distributed. As a result, the assumption is met.

To test homogeneity of variance, we use the Levene's test. Based on the output provided in Table 14.3, we see that the equal variance assumption is met since $F = .720$, $p = .413$. That is, the two variances are the same. On the other hand, to evaluate the independence assumption, the fact that participant could be in only one of the two categories (renter or homeowner) and not in both (i.e., an individual is both a renter and a homeowner), then we conclude that the two groups are independent groups. We do not have a homeowner who also was a renter. Ideally, independence is achieved by randomly assigning participants/cases to treatments or groups. In our case, group assignment was predetermined by an individual's home ownership status.

Let us now examine the results. First, we have to revisit our research question: *Is there a mean difference in the amount of government assistance awarded to homeowners and the amount given to renters post-Hurricane Michael in 2018?* Based on the question, our null hypothesis is: *There are no mean differences in the amount of government assistance in dollars awarded to homeowners and the amount given to renters post-Hurricane Michael in 2018 in affected areas of Florida.* Again, we represent the null hypothesis in the following way:

$$H_0: \mu_{HW} = \mu_R \qquad [5]$$

where HW = Homeowners and R = Renters. From Table 14.2, we see that the average amounts awarded in this sample of seven homeowners was $6,571.43 and the average amounts awarded for the seven renters was $2,428.57. What we are investigating is whether the two means are statistically different.

Using our results from Table 14.3, we see that the p value is less than the cutoff alpha value of $p < .05$ ($t(12) = 5.80$, $p < .001$); therefore, the two means are statistically and significantly different. Our decision now is to reject the null hypothesis and conclude that there are significant mean differences between the amount given to homeowners and the amount given to renters. The next step is to describe the pattern of these means. Given that the mean amount awarded in the sample of homeowners was $6,571.43 and the mean amount awarded for the renters was $2,428.57, these results suggest that the homeowners on average tend to receive higher amounts of funding compared to the renters. As a result, we can write up our results in the following manner:

> An independent samples t-test was performed to determine if funds in dollars awarded Hurricane Michael differed between homeowners versus renters in the Florida's panhandle. Homeowners on average received funds that were statistically significant different from renters ($t(12)_8 = -5.80$, $p < .001$). Homeowners' ($M = \$6,571.43$, $SD = \$1,511.86$) funds received was higher than renters ($M = \$2,428.57$, $SD = \$1,133.89$). Among the present sample, homeowners received higher amount than renters.

Analysis of Variance

ANOVA partitions the total variance of the dependent variable that is continuous into two parts. In essence, the total sum of squares (SST) equals the sum of sum of squares between (SSB) plus the sum of squares within (SSW). The formula is given as SST = SSB + SSW. The SSB captures the treatment or grouping effect, while the SSW captures the individual differences; it is known as the error term. ANOVA is appropriate to use when researchers want to examine more than two group mean differences on a continuous dependent variable.

For example, using the previous example, a researcher may want to investigate if there are mean differences in distributed funds post–Hurricane Michael of 2018 based on the race of those affected. The researcher may state the research question in this manner:

> Are there mean differences in the funds awarded to residents affected by Hurricane Michael in 2018 based on race? Specifically, did the affected residents who are White not Hispanic, Hispanic, or African American receive about the same funding on average?

The dependent variable in this example is again the awarded funds in dollars. The independent variable is race. However, this variable has three levels (White not Hispanic, Hispanic, or African American), as opposed to being continuous.

In this situation we can express the model in this form:

$$Y_{ij} = \mu + \alpha_j + \varepsilon_{ij} \tag{6}$$

In this equation, Y_{ij} represents the ith subject amount of funding in a group j, μ is the grand mean for all subjects, α_j represents the treatment effect for the jth treatment/group, and ε_{ij} is the random error for the ith subject in the jth group. Additionally, we can state the hypothesis for this research question in the following way:

Null hypothesis: There are no mean differences in funds awarded based on race.

$$H_0 : \mu_W = \mu_H = \mu_{AA} \tag{7}$$

Alternative hypothesis: At least one of the three means is different from the others.

$$H_1 : \mu_W \neq \mu_H \neq \mu_{AA} \tag{8}$$

Now that we have stated our research question and hypothesis, we need to discuss the assumptions for the ANOVA.

Similar to the independent t-test, the ANOVA has the same three assumptions (normality, homogeneity of variance, and independence of observation), and they are evaluated by the same procedures. However, once we know that these assumptions are met, we can proceed with the ANOVA. So, let us examine the data using ANOVA that are highlighted in Table 14.5.

To perform ANOVA using SPSS, open your data within the program and follow these steps:

1. Click "Analyze" → compare means → One-Way ANOVA.
2. Select funds and move it to the "Dependent" list.
3. Select "Race" and move it to the "Factors" list.
4. Under "Options," select Descriptives, Homogeneity of variance test, and Means plot.

5. Under "Post hoc," select Tukey and then click "continue."

6. Click "OK."

The output that is produced begins with descriptive statistics. Table 14.6 provides the sample sizes, mean standard deviation, standard error of the mean, 95% confidence interval for means, and the minimum and maximum values. However, before we interpret the results, we need to evaluate our three assumptions.

To evaluate normality and following the same process as in the previous example, Shapiro-Wilk's test results indicate that the dependent variable in the three groups followed normal distribution ($W_W(7) = .945$, $p = .686$; W_{Hisp} (70 = .960, $p = .815$; W_{AA} (7) = .826, $p = .074$) since in all three races the test were non-significant. On homogeneity of variance, Levene's statistic shown in Table 14.7 shows that all three variances are about the same, since the p value is greater than .05 and the test is not statistically significant.

Finally, the independence of observation is met because the participants in this study came from independent groups. In other words, respondents identified themselves as one and only one race. Now, all the three assumptions of ANOVA are met.

Since we know that the data meets all three assumptions, we can now perform an ANOVA. Table 14.8 highlights the output of an ANOVA generated in SPSS.

Results from Table 14.8 indicate that there are statistically significant differences among the three means ($F(2, 18) = 4.653$; $p = .024$). This F test is the omnibus test. It

TABLE 14.5 Funds Awarded by Race

White (Not Hispanic)	Hispanic	African American
3,000	2,800	1,500
3,200	1,500	3,200
4,500	1,200	1,850
6,500	2,300	4,500
4,200	1,800	1,400
2,500	2,100	2,100
1,800	1,100	1,300

TABLE 14.6 Descriptive Statistics

	N	M	SD	SE	95% CI LL	95% CI UL	min	max
White	7	3,671.43	1,555.329	587.859	2,232.99	5,109.87	1,800	6,500
Hispanic	7	1,828.57	615.668	232.701	1,259.17	2,397.97	1,100	2,800
African American	7	2,264.29	1,178.528	445.442	1,174.33	3,354.24	1,300	4,500
Total	21	2,588.10	1,380.390	301.226	1,959.75	3,216.44	1,100	6,500

TABLE 14.7 Test of Homogeneity of Variances

Levene Statistic	df1	df2	p
2.066	2	18	.156

TABLE 14.8 ANOVA

	SS	df	MS	F	p
Between Groups	12,987,380.95	2	6,493,690.476	4.653	.024
Within Groups	25,122,142.86	18	1,395,674.603		
Total	38,109,523.81	20			

TABLE 14.9 Post Hoc Tukey Test

(I) Race	(J) Race	Mean Difference (I – J)	SE	p	95% CI	
					LL	UL
White	Hispanic	1,842.857[a]	631.478	.024	231.22	3,454.49
	African American	1,407.143	631.478	.093	−204.49	3,018.78
Hispanic	White	−1,842.857[a]	631.478	.024	−3,454.49	−231.22
	African American	−435.714	631.478	.772	−2,047.35	1,175.92
African American	White	−1,407.143	631.478	.093	−3,018.78	204.49
	Hispanic	435.714	631.478	0.772	−1,175.92	2047.35

[a] The mean difference is significant at the .05 level.

is the overall test that allows the researcher to reject the null hypothesis – in this case, rejecting that the three races received equal funding on average. The F omnibus test does not tell researchers which pairs of group means are different. (Keppel & Wickens, 2004; Strunk & Mwavita, 2020). With a statistically significant F omnibus test, the question researchers ask is, which group means differ? To answer this question, we conduct a post hoc analysis to find the source of the significant differences – in this case, after a significant F test. Post hoc tests compare pairs of means to examine if statistically significant differences are present. In this case, post hoc analysis compares the means of Whites and Hispanics, Whites and African Americans, and African Americans and Hispanics to find out which pairs are statistically significant.

Although there are many post hoc tests that are offered in SPSS, we will use the Tukey test. Tukey is commonly used as it controls the family-wise error rate and makes use of a single value against which all differences are compared (Keppel & Wickens, 2004). The post hoc test results are depicted in Table 14.9, and they indicate that statistically significant differences were observed between White not Hispanic and Hispanic owners.

As a by-product of the ANOVA analysis, we can report the results in the following way:

A researcher was interested in finding out whether there were any differences in funding awarded to families in Florida after Hurricane Michael in 2018. A one-way ANOVA was conducted to determine if funds awarded post-Hurricane Michael in 2018 differed based on homeowner race (African American, Hispanic, or White not Hispanic). There was a significant difference in awarded funds based on race of homeowners ($F(2, 18) = 4.653$, $p < .05$). Post hoc analysis revealed that mean differences in funding awarded differ only between White not Hispanic homeowners and Hispanic homeowners ($p < .05$).

Both independent t-tests and ANOVAs examine differences in group means on a continuous dependent variable in relation to an independent variable that is categorical (nominal), and both have the same three assumptions. However, they do differ in that the independent t-test works when the independent variable has two groups/categories, but ANOVA works when there are two or more groups/categories. For an independent t-test, there does not need to conduct a post hoc analysis after a significant t-test; the significance test shows a difference between the two group means. In other words, you have all the information to make the conclusion. In ANOVA, however, after a significant F test, we follow up with a post hoc test to find where the mean differences are present in the study (Strunk & Mwavita, 2020; Stevens, 2007). For example, if you have significant F test for a comparison of three group means, one cannot tell whether the mean differences are between group 1 and 2, 1 and 3, or 2 and 3. Thus, a post hoc after a significant F test determines which pair's means are significantly different.

Factorial ANOVA

Alternatively, researchers may want to investigate more than one independent variable on a dependent variable. That is, they may want to know if there is a joint effect between two or more independent variables on one dependent variable. Such a design is called factorial ANOVA. It is factorial because there is more than one independent variable. Let us look at an example.

Suppose a researcher wants to find out if race and gender together influence the amount of funding one receives post-Hurricane Michael in 2018. We now have two independent variables: gender with two levels, and race with three levels. We write this ANOVA design as a 2 × 3 ANOVA. The numbers indicate the number of groups or levels for each of the independent variables, respectively. To represent this model, we write a general linear model for a factorial ANOVA, which looks like the following:

$$Y_{ijk} = \mu + \alpha_i + \beta_j + ((\alpha\beta))_{ij} + \varepsilon_{ijk} \qquad [9]$$

where $i = 1, 2, \ldots, i$; $j = 1, 2, \ldots, j$; and $k = 1, 2, \ldots, k$. The value of allocated funds is Y, μ represents the mean, α_i is the contribution of the ith level of a factor A, and β_j is the contribution of the jth level of a factor B. $((\alpha\beta))_{ij}$ is the combined contribution of the ith level of a factor A and the jth level of a factor B. ε_{ijk} represents the contribution of the kth individual, or the random "error." All three assumptions we discussed earlier for the one-way ANOVA apply in factorial ANOVA. However, for this example we will use the data that was collected and highlighted in Table 14.10.

TABLE 14.10 A Numerical Example

Funds	Race	Gender
3,000	White	Male
2,000	White	Female
6,500	White	Male
3,500	White	Female
4,200	White	Male
2,500	White	Female
1,400	White	Male
2,800	Hispanic	Female
1,050	Hispanic	Male
1,200	Hispanic	Male
2,300	Hispanic	Female
1,000	Hispanic	Male
2,100	Hispanic	Female
3,000	Hispanic	Female
1,500	African American	Male
3,200	African American	Female
1,850	African American	Male
4,500	African American	Female
1,400	African American	Male
6,500	African American	Female
1,300	African American	Male

Now to conduct a factorial ANOVA using SPSS, we follow the following process with the data from Table 14.10:

1. Click "Analyze" → General Linear Model → Univariate.
2. Select the dependent variable and random factors.
3. Under Options, select "Descriptives" and "Homogeneity tests."
4. Move the race variable into the plots window.
5. Click continue followed by "OK."

Subsequent to running the test, the first thing we see is the descriptive statistics of the variables as presented in Table 14.11. This table contains the variables' names, their means, standard deviations, and sample sizes.

After the descriptive statistics, an ANOVA summary table should be presented, similar to Table 14.12. Evaluating the ANOVA summary table, we see that the

TABLE 14.11 Descriptive Statistics for Factorial ANOVA

Race	Gender	M	SD	N
White	Male	3,775.00	2,148.449	4
	Female	2,666.67	763.763	3
	Total	3,300.00	1,689.181	7
Hispanic	Male	1,083.33	104.083	3
	Female	2,550.00	420.317	4
	Total	1,921.43	840.564	7
African American	Male	1,512.50	239.357	4
	Female	4,733.33	1,662.328	3
	Total	2,892.86	1,978.305	7
Total	Male	2,218.18	1,720.214	11
	Female	3,240.00	1,366.423	10
	Total	2,704.76	1,610.350	21

TABLE 14.12 Tests of Between-Subjects Effects

Source	Type III SS	df	MS	F	p
Corrected Model	30,600,148.8^a	5	6,120,029.762	4.317	.012
Intercept	15,221,1200.4	1	152,211,200.4	107.371	.000
Race	8,428,710.317	2	4,214,355.159	2.973	.082
Gender	7,320,248.016	1	7,320,248.016	5.164	.038
Race × Gender	16,256,805.56	2	8,128,402.778	5.734	.014
Error	21,264,375.00	15	1,417,625.000		
Total	205,495,000.0	21			
Corrected Total	51,864,523.81	20			

^{a} $R^2 = .590$ (adjusted $R^2 = .453$).

interaction between Race and Gender is statistically significant, $F(2, 15) = 5.734$, $p = .014$. Thus, we are able to reject the null hypothesis and conclude that for this sample, race and gender jointly influenced the amount of funds awarded to the residents of Florida's panhandle post-Hurricane Michael in 2018.

Next, you will see the pattern of mean differences is provided in the pairwise comparisons as in Table 14.13. The table indicates differences between White and Hispanic males ($p = .01$), White and African American males ($p = .017$), and African American and Hispanic females ($p = .03$). In all three comparisons, the mean of White males is higher than Hispanics and African Americans. Moreover, the mean of White females is higher than Hispanic females.

TABLE 14.13 Pairwise Comparisons

Gender	(*I*)Race	(*J*)Race	Mean Difference (*I – J*)	SE	p[a]	95% CI for Difference[a]	
						LL	UL
Male	White	Hispanic	2,691.667[b]	909.367	.010	753.397	4,629.936
		African American	2,262.500[b]	841.910	.017	468.011	4,056.989
	Hispanic	White	−2,691.667[b]	909.367	.010	−4,629.936	−753.397
		African American	−429.167	909.367	.644	−2,367.436	1,509.103
	African American	White	−2,262.500[b]	841.910	.017	−4,056.989	−468.011
		Hispanic	429.167	909.367	.644	−1,509.103	2,367.436
Female	White	Hispanic	116.667	909.367	.900	−1,821.603	2,054.936
		African American	−2,066.667	972.154	.051	−4,138.764	5.430
	Hispanic	White	−116.667	909.367	.900	−2,054.936	1,821.603
		African American	−2,183.33[b]	909.367	.030	−4,121.603	−245.064
	African American	White	2,066.667	972.154	.051	−5.430	4,138.764
		Hispanic	2,183.333[b]	909.367	.030	245.064	4,121.603

Note: Based on estimated marginal means.
[a] Adjustment for multiple comparisons: least significant difference (equivalent to no adjustments). [b] The mean difference is significant at the .05 level.

Additionally, these relationships can be plotted. The plots illustrated in Figure 14.2 shows an intersection of the two lines indicating an interaction effect. We call this interaction disordinal. Disordinal interactions involve crossing of the lines representing the means of the variables. Notice that in Figure 14.2, the two lines do cross. In this case, one should not interpret main effects in the presence of a significant disordinal interaction (Keppel & Wickens, 2004; Strunk & Mwavita, 2020). Whether females received higher funding than males depends on the race. White males received higher funding on average that all the other races, but African American females received higher funding on average than the other races. This is the essence of an interaction effect: results and interpretations of one variable's effect or impact must be qualified in terms of the impact of the second variable. This phenomenon is especially pronounced in the case of the disordinal (Stevens, 2007; Strunk & Mwavita, 2020).

Sometimes, the interactions may not be statistically significant, hence researchers may examine the main effects (the independent variables) if they are statistically significant. If that is the case, we follow the one-way ANOVA procedures of interpreting the results of a statistically significant main effect.

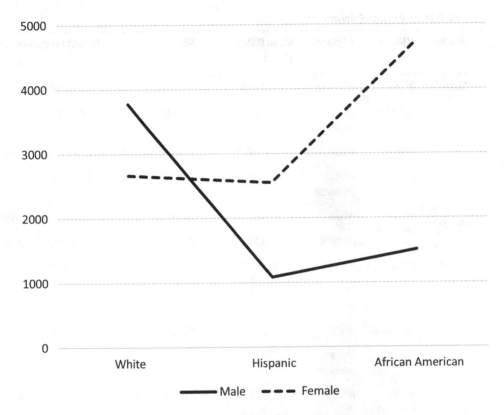

FIGURE 14.2 Estimated Marginal Means of Amount of Funds Awarded, Gender by Race

Multiple Regression

In addition to the previously described tools, multiple regression is a statistical modeling technique that researchers use to explore relationships among variables; specifically, when we want to examine how well a set of variables predict an outcome of interest (Hair, Black, & Badin, 2010). The estimation of the prediction equation in this chapter is the ordinary least square (OLS) regression. This estimation procedure calculates the line of best fit by minimizing the sum of squares residual (the difference between the predicted and actual scores). The dependent and independent variables should be continuous. Similar to the other models that were previously discussed, multiple regression has certain conditions and assumptions that must be met.

First, the dependent variable must be an interval or ratio-level variable. Additionally, the independent variables should be interval or ratio-level variables; however, they can also be dichotomous. The dichotomous independent variables are often nominal categories with numerical codes of 1 and 0. For example, if a predictor variable is type of homeownership categorized as homeowner or renter, we can categorize homeownership as "1" for homeowner and "0" for renter. We term this categorization of 1 and 0 as a dummy variable, with 0 denoting what is not 1.

Second, we must pay attention to high intercorrelations among the predictors. We call these high intercorrelations among independent variables multicollinearity. To ascertain whether there is multicollinearity, we examine the correlation matrix of the predictors and the dependent variable to see the pattern the of intercorrelations. High correlations of

.80 and above between predictors may be a cause for concern. Statistically, a variance inflation factor (VIF) greater than 10 is an indication of the presence of multicollinearity (Pituch & Stevens, 2016). In essence, multicollinearity means that predictors contain the same information. When multicollinearity exists, there are a few different strategies one might use to compensate for this issue; however, the most common way to deal with this situation is to use theory to decide which of the predictors to exclude from the model. Statistically, one may perform a principal component analysis (PCA) to come up with a new component of correlated variables. These new components can then be used as predictors in the multiple regression and are continuous (Pituch & Stevens, 2016).

In addition to these conditions, there several assumptions that must be met for one to use multiple regression. Predictors and the dependent variable should have a linear relationship. We evaluate this assumption by examining the scatter plots of each predictor and the dependent variable for a pattern of linearity. We can also examine the correlation matrix for significant correlations between predictors and the dependent variable. The next assumptions deal with the residuals (difference between predicted and actual scores).

First, the residuals should be normally distributed and have a mean of zero. We evaluate this assumption by examining the distribution of standardized regression residuals for a normal or approximately normal distribution. We can also examine the Q–Q plots to see if the points align on the line, specifically on the edges or end points. Second, the residuals should have a constant variance. To meet this assumption, we examine the plot of standardized predicted values and standardized residuals for a random scatter plot pattern. There should be no defined relationship between the standardized predicted and standardized residuals. Third, the residuals should be independent. The residuals should not have any relationship with themselves or the predictors. We evaluate this assumption by examining the pattern of the scatter plot between the standardized predicted and standardized residuals values for a random pattern. We should not observe any pattern or relationship between the two. A random pattern of the scatter plot indicates that this assumption is met. In addition to these assumptions, and prior to conducting multiple regression, we have to examine our data for outliers, because they affect linear relationships. We examine scatter plots and box plots for outliers. If outliers are present, then researchers remove them.

Now let us apply our knowledge. For example, a researcher wants to examine how a set of variables predicted the number of deaths during the 2009 H1N1 flu pandemic. The unit of analysis in this study is country. We examine data including number of deaths, total television channels, total number of radio channels, percent of education expenditures, and air transit passengers per country. Using this data, we develop the following research question:

> How well do a country's percent of education expenditures and the number of a country's television channels, number of radio channels, and number of transit passengers predict the number reported deaths in that country to the H1N1 flu pandemic of 2009?

Before we perform multiple regression analysis, we have to examine if our data meets the conditions and assumptions for multiple regression. All variables are ratio scale. Also, only 28 countries out of the 168 had data in all of the five variables. In reference to multicollinearity, the pattern of intercorrelations between pairs of predictors does not show high correlations (see Table 14.14)

TABLE 14.14 Correlation Matrix of H1N1 Deaths and Independent Variables

		H1N1 Deaths	Radio Channels	Percen ED Expend	Air Transit Passengers	Tot TV channels
Pearson correlation	H1N1Deaths	1.000	.590	−.162	.745	.692
	RadioChannels	.590	1.000	.135	.319	.603
	PercenEDExpend	−.162	.135	1.000	-.020	−.086
	AirTransitPassengers	.745	.319	−.020	1.000	.244
	TotTVchannels	.692	.603	−.086	.244	1.000
p (one-tailed)	H1N1Deaths	–	.000	.205	.000	.000
	RadioChannels	.000	–	.246	.049	.000
	PercenEDExpend	.205	.246	–	.460	.331
	AirTransitPassengers	.000	.049	.460	–	.105
	TotTVchannels	.000	.000	.331	.105	–
N	H1N1Deaths	28	28	28	28	28
	RadioChannels	28	28	28	28	28
	PercenEDExpend	28	28	28	28	28
	AirTransitPassengers	28	28	28	28	28
	TotTVchannels	28	28	28	28	28

Now, let us examine the multiple regression assumptions for this research question. Linearity of predictors and the criterion was evaluated by the correlation matrix in Table 14.14, which indicates that three of the predictors are statistically significant and related with the criterion. These are the number of radio channels, air transit passengers, and television channels. Percent of education expenditures is not statistically significant and related with the criterion. We see this pattern of relationship with the scatter plots of each predictor and criterion in Figure 14.3.

In reference to the residuals, Figure 14.4 shows a constant variance on the scatter plot, suggesting that no defined relationship between the standardized predicted and standardized residuals; hence, we meet this assumption. On the independence of residuals assumption, the pattern of residuals standardized predicted and standardized residuals in Figure 14.4 depicts a random scatter with no defined pattern of relation meeting the independence of residuals assumption. Finally, the histogram in Figure 14.5 shows that the residuals are approximately normally distributed with a mean of zero, thus meeting the assumptions.

Now that we meet the conditions and assumptions, we can now conduct a multiple regression. The dependent variable is the number of reported deaths due to the 2009 H1N1 flu pandemic. The predictors are the number of radio channels, percent of education expenditure, number of air transit passengers, and number of television channels. The results from performing the analysis give us the descriptive statistics for all our variables (see Table 14.15).

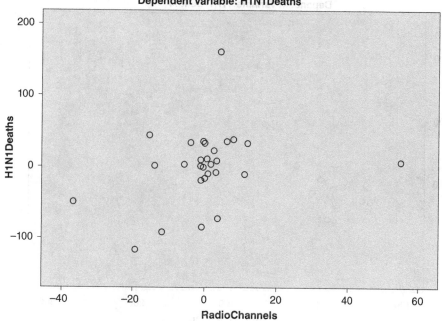

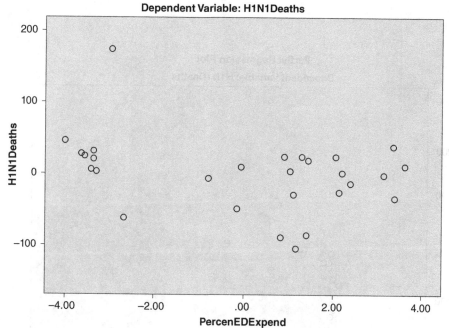

FIGURE 14.3 H1N1 Scatter Plots

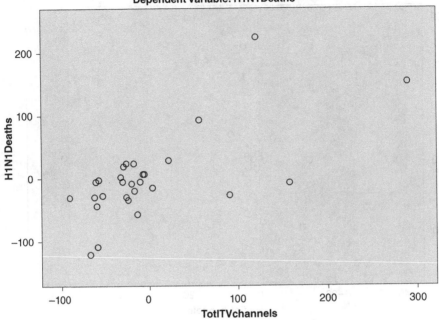

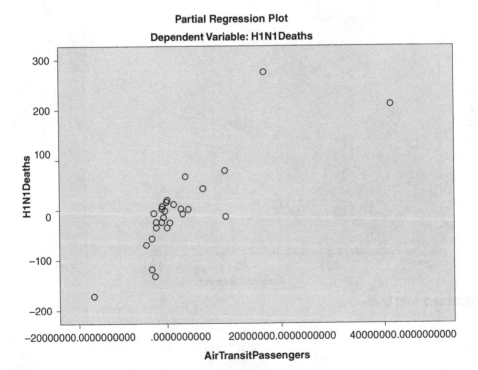

FIGURE 14.3 (Continued)

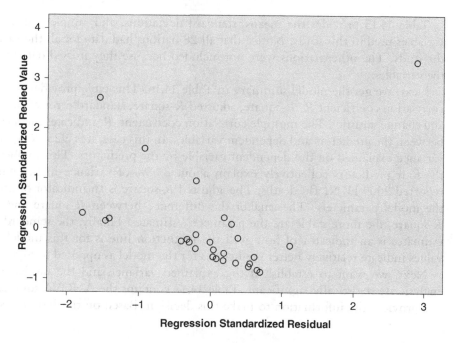

FIGURE 14.4 Scatter Plot of Residuals

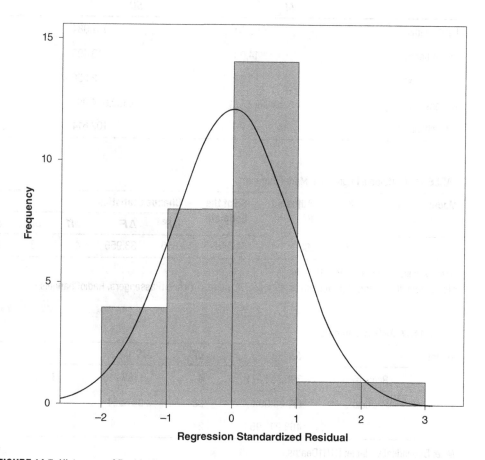

FIGURE 14.5 Histogram of Residuals

Table 14.15 provides the means, standard deviations, and sample sizes for all the variables used in this study. Notice that all 28 nations had data for all the variables in the study. The other nations were not included because they missed data in some of the variables.

Next, we get the model summary in Table 14.16. This table provides the multiple correlation coefficient R, R-square, adjusted R-square, standard error of the estimate and change statistics. The multiple correlation coefficient, R, indicates the relationship between the predictors and dependent variables. In this case, it is .925. R-square is the variance explained on the dependent variable by the predictors. This implies that all the four predictors collectively explain about 85.5% of variance in the number of reported 2009 H1N1 flu deaths. The adjusted R-square is an indicator of how stable the model parameters. The smaller the difference between R-square and adjusted R-square, the more stable are the parameter estimates. Finally, the standard error of estimates is an indicator of how well the prediction line is for this model. Smaller values indicate relatively better predictions for the model as opposed to higher values.

Next, we want to establish if the explained variance and the model from this analysis are statistically significant. Table 14.17 contains the ANOVA summary table and provides the information to make this decision. Based on the F statistics, we see

TABLE 14.15 Descriptive Statistics for Multiple Regression

	M	SD	N
H1N1Deaths	68.54	131.084	28
RadioChannels	14.00	19.408	28
PercenEDExpend	3.5429	2.65657	28
AirTransitPassengers	5,968,263.571	10,689,884.90	28
TotTVchannels	79.96	102.614	28

TABLE 14.16 Multiple Regression Model Summary

Model	R	R^2	Adjusted R^2	SE of the Estimate	Change Statistics				
					ΔR^2	ΔF	df1	df2	Sig. ΔF
1	.925[a]	.855	.830	54.048	.855	33.955	4	23	.00

Note: Dependent variable: H1N1Deaths.
[a] Predictors: (Constant), TotTVchannels, PercenEDExpend, AirTransitPassengers, RadioChannels.

TABLE 14.17 ANOVA Summary

Model		SS	df	MS	F	p
1	Regression	396,754.871	4	99,188.718	33.955	.000[a]
	Residual	67,188.093	23	2,921.221		
	Total	463,942.964	27			

Note: Dependent variable: H1N1Deaths.
[a] Predictors: (Constant), TotTVchannels, PercenEDExpend, AirTransitPassengers, RadioChannels.

TABLE 14.18 Table of Coefficients

Model		Unstandardized Coefficients		Standardized Coefficients	t	p
		B	SE	iβ		
1	(Constant)	−11.032	20.015		−.551	.587
	RadioChannels	1.034	.710	.153	1.456	.159
	PrecenEDExpend	−6.540	4.050	−.133	−1.615	.120
	AirTransitPassengers	7.166E−6	.000	.584	6.953	.000
	TotTVchannels	.569	.130	.445	4.369	.000

that it is statistically significant, $F(4, 23) = 33.955$, $p = .000$. Thus, we determine that R, R-square, and adjusted R-square are statistically significant.

Additionally, if we want to know if each variable is statistically significant, we examine the table of coefficients, as in Table 14.18. This table provides predictors with their unstandardized coefficients, b weights with standard errors of b, standardized coefficients, t, and significance values.

The unstandardized coefficients are in the original scale of each predictor. This table allows us to use the coefficients to produce the prediction model for the data. In this case the prediction model is

$$\text{Predicted H1N1 Deaths} = -11.03 + 1.02 \text{ Radio Channels} - 6.54 \text{ Percent Ed}$$
$$\text{Expenditure} + .00000716 \text{ Air Transit Passengers}$$
$$+ .569 \text{ Tot TV channels}$$

This model equation is statistically significant, $F(4, 23) = 33.955$, $p = .000$, as we indicated previously. For example, from the above equation using the RadioChannels value, for every unit increase in RadioChannels, holding all the other three predictors constant, the predicted reported number of deaths caused by H1N1 flu will be 1.02. The standardized coefficients are in standard deviation units and have a mean of zero. As a result, standardized coefficients do not have constant value. We use standardized coefficients to rank relative importance of predictors, since these are in the same standard units. The t-value column is the test of significance for an individual predictor. Based on these results, we can now report on our observations in the following way:

Multiple regression was conducted to examine how well a country's number of radio channels, percent of education expenditure, number of air transit passengers, and number of television channels predict the number of reported deaths caused by the 2009 H1N1 flu pandemic. Prior to conducting the multiple regression, data were analyzed for missingness and outliers. In addition, assumptions of linearity, normally distributed residuals, constant variance of residuals, and uncorrelated residuals were checked and met. Further, multicollinearity of predictors was examined and there was no evidence of multicollinearity among the predictors. All four predictors together predicted the number of reported deaths during the 2009 H1N1 flu pandemic, $F(4, 23) = 33.955$, $p < .001$. Of the four predictors, air transit passengers and number of television channels were statistically significant, but number of radio channels and percent of education expenditure were not significant. The model with all four variables together explain 85.5% of the variance in the number of reported deaths caused by the 2009 H1N1 flu pandemic. According to Cohen (1988), this is a large effect. The standardized weights (beta-weights) suggest that air transit passengers contributed most to the number of reported deaths during the 2009 H1N1 flu pandemic, followed by number of air transit passengers.

Conclusion

Multiple regression requires that you have a continuous dependent variable, but you can use both continuous and categorical (nominal) predictors. It is a statistical model that can answer predictions as well as explain the variance of the dependent variable by the predictors.

However, what if a researcher wants to predict a discrete outcome? There are a number of modeling techniques that can be used to model discrete outcomes, such as logistic, probit, and ordered multinomial regression models. For example, logistic regression is used when we want to predict a categorical dependent variable; specifically, a binary or dichotomous categorical dependent variable. The predictors can be both continuous and categorical. Since the dependent variable is dichotomous (it can take one of two possible values), we cannot model a linear relationship. Instead, we can model a probability – the likelihood of an event occurring. This probability ranges between 0 and 1, where zero is absence of the event and 1 the presence of the event (Pampel, 2000).

The purpose of this chapter was to briefly describe different statistical models that can be applied to disaster and emergency management data that you generate yourself or acquire secondhand, as discussed in the previous chapter. Prior to discussing each model, I discussed the basic foundations for statistical modelling. This was followed by detailed description and application of each specific model to disaster research. Moreover, I provided examples of how one might present the results of their statistical models. However, two things should be noted. First, my attempt to describe and discuss statistical modeling in this chapter is by no means comprehensive. There are a number of statistical models that I did not discuss due to space, and you as the researcher should investigate whether other models are more appropriate for your own respective analyses. Second, it should be noted that when you write up your results, you need to acknowledge the general validity of your findings based on the sample from which your data is drawn (see Chapter 2) and the unit of analysis the data is met to describe (see Chapter 3). Nevertheless, this chapter provides foundational concepts and practical steps to conducting statistical modeling.

Further Readings

Azen, R., & Walker, C.M. (2010). *Categorical data analysis for the behavioral and social sciences, published by psychology press.* Taylor & Francis.

Hair, J.F., Jr., Black, W.C., Babin, B.J., & Anderson, R.E. (2010). *Multivariate data analysis: A global perspective* (7th ed.). Upper Saddle River, NJ: Pearson Education.

Meyers, L.S., Gamst, G., & Guarino, A.J. (2013). *Applied multivariate research: Design and interpretation* (2nd ed.). Thousand Oaks, CA: Sage.

Strunk, K.K., & Mwavita, M. (2020). *Design and analysis in educational research: ANOVA designs in SPSS*. New York: Routledge.

References

Cohen, J. (1988). *Statistical power analysis for the behavioral sciences* (2nd ed.). Hillsdale, NJ: Lawrence Erlbaum Associates.

Hair, J.F., Jr., Black, W.C., Babin, B.J., & Anderson, R.E. (2010). *Multivariate data analysis: A global perspective* (7th ed.). Upper Saddle River, NJ: Pearson Education.

Judd, C.M., McClelland, G.H., & Ryan, C.S. (2009). *Data analysis: A model comparison approach to regression, ANOVA, and beyond* (3rd ed.). New York: Routledge.

Keppel, G., & Wickens, T.D. (2004). *Design and analysis: A researcher's handbook* (4th ed.). Upper Saddle River, NJ: Pearson Prentice Hall.

Levene, H. (1960). Robust tests for equality of variances. In I. Olkin (Ed.), *Contributions to probability and statistics: Essays in honor of Harold Hotelling* (pp. 278–292). Palo Alto, CA: Stanford University Press.

Lomax, R.G., & Hahs-Vaughn, D.L. (2012). *Statistical concepts: An introduction* (3rd ed.). New York: Routledge.

Pampel, F.C. (2000). *Logistic regression: A primer*. Thousand Oaks, CA: Sage.

Pituch, K.A., & Stevens, J.P. (2016). *Applied multivariate statistics for the social sciences: Analyses with SAS and IBM's SPSS* (6th ed.). New York: Routledge.

Shavelson, R.J. (1996). *Statistical reasoning for the behavioral sciences* (3rd ed.). Boston: Allyn & Bacon.

Siegel, S., & Castellan, N.J., Jr. (1988). *Nonparametric statistics for the behavioral sciences* (2nd ed.). McGraw-Hill Book Company.

Stevens, J.P. (2007). *Intermediate statistics: A modern approach* (3rd ed.). New York: Routledge.

Strunk, K.K., & Mwavita, M. (2020). *Design and analysis in educational research: ANOVA designs in SPSS*. New York: Routledge.

Yap, B.W., & Sim, C.H. (2011). Comparisons of various types of normality tests. *Journal of Statistical Computation and Simulation, 81*(12), 2141–2155.

15

Social Network Analysis for Disaster Management Research

Timothy Fraser, Courtney Page-Tan, and Daniel P. Aldrich

Introduction

Disaster survivors and scholars alike argue that the presence, dearth, and type of social ties in a community can enable or limit disaster adaptation, response, evacuation, and recovery. After Hurricane Katrina struck New Orleans in 2005, the Vietnamese American community returned and rebuilt more quickly than other damaged areas in the city, relying on the strength of their local co-ethnic and religious neighborhood ties, rather than limited finances or education (Aldrich, 2012). Likewise, after Japan's 2011 earthquake, tsunami, and nuclear disaster, prefectures with greater bridging ties aid and governmental organizations recovered faster (Bisri, 2016a, 2016b; Aldrich, 2019). Increasingly, scholars and policymakers see social networks as playing a key role in disaster evacuation, recovery, and resilience. But what kinds of networks can we examine in disaster studies? What kinds of data do we need, what kinds of questions can we answer about these networks, and what tools might students and scholars of disaster studies use to answer these questions?

This chapter seeks to make social network analysis methods accessible to students and scholars of disaster policy. Using a network of disaster reconstruction committee members from our own research, we demonstrate different techniques for network visualization, analysis, and statistics. First, we introduce readers to the logic and types of networks they may encounter, drawing from recent examples. Second, we lay out a process for analyzing networks, describing centrality measures, visualization, and statistical models. These techniques predominantly use R.[1] These accessible techniques allow us to identify what kinds of social ties affect recovery and how we can leverage these to improve disaster outcomes.

A Brief Introduction to Networks

There are several main kinds of networks in disaster studies. All networks have at least four attributes: *nodes, edges, weights,* and *direction. Nodes* are people, places, or things of interest in a network. *Edges* describe the ties that connect nodes. Certain edges between some pairs might be more important, stronger, or numerous than others. *Weights* are numbers describing the strength of those edges, which could simply be absent or present (0/1), or represent a continuous scale, such as number of communications or evacuees (zero to infinity; Leenders, 2002). *Direction* describes which way the edge flows from node A to node B. Additionally, *directed edges* have direction, either from A to B or B to A, or both, as opposed to *undirected edges,* which have no direction, automatically meaning that A and B are connected in *both* directions (Newman, 2010; Barabasi, 2016).

Networks can be represented in two main ways: *edgelists* and *adjacency matrices* (Easley & Kleinberg, 2010). For example, the 2011 triple disaster in Japan especially damaged three prefectures: Fukushima, Miyagi, and Iwate. We might imagine the evacuation among prefectures to look like the edgelist in Table 15.1.

As depicted in Table 15.1, *edgelists* describe the source and destination of an edge, weighted by a number, in this case the number of evacuees who went from the source (e.g., Fukushima) to the destination (e.g., Tokyo). Edgelists are by default directed, but they do not have to be. By giving an edgelist and a complete list of nodes (even if the edgelist does not contain all nodes), you can produce a network. In contrast, an adjacency matrix contains *all* edges between *all* nodes in the network. Table 15.2 depicts the edgelist in Table 15.1 transformed into an adjacency matrix. Practitioners can use several kinds of software to analyze, visualize, and model networks. Gephi is a freely available tool for descriptive analysis and visualization of networks (Bastian, Heymann, & Jacomy, 2009). In the R coding language, the *sna, igraph,* and *tidygraph* packages cover the same functions. For statistical analysis of networks, the *statnet* package is the primary open source tool today (Handcock et al., 2003).

TABLE 15.1 A Hypothetical Evacuation Edgelist

Source	Destination	Evacuees
Fukushima	Tokyo	100
Fukushima	Miyagi	20
Miyagi	Tokyo	200
Iwate	Miyagi	30
Iwate	Tokyo	50

TABLE 15.2 A Hypothetical Evacuation Adjacency Matrix

Source	Destination			
	Nodes	Tokyo	Fukushima	Miyagi	Iwate
	Tokyo	0	0	0	0
	Fukushima	100	0	20	0
	Miyagi	200	0	0	0
	Iwate	50	0	30	0

Networks in disaster studies generally fall into one of three types: affiliation (Haase, Ertan, & Comfort, 2017; Fraser, Aldrich, Small, & Littlejohn, 2020), mobility (e.g., Windzio, 2018), or infrastructure networks (Kim, 2011; Kim & Chang, 2010; Ongkowijoyo & Doloi, 2016). Below, we briefly introduce examples of each, studies that have examined them, and what questions we might have about them.

Affiliation Networks

In affiliation networks, nodes are people or organizations, with edges describing some kind of affiliation or interaction between those individuals or organizations. The greater the weight of the edge, the more two nodes affiliate with each other. Affiliation can be directed when it describes one-way communication or interaction, but it is often undirected, indicating mutual interaction. Affiliation networks are commonly used to answer questions such as: Which organizations in an emergency response network communicate with each other the most? Which organizations work in the same communities the most? Which people have served in the same organizations together the most? Do organizations interact equally with each other, or are some cut off from the rest of the network? Do some individuals or organizations play vital roles bridging different actors in emergency response?

For example, Andrew, Arlikatti, Seibeneck, Pongponrat, and Jaikampan (2016) used semi-structured interviews to create an affiliation network, reporting interactions during the Great Floods in Thailand in 2011 between government agencies, community groups, faith-based organizations, and private businesses. Using these ties, they found that rural organizations had greater betweenness (defined later in this chapter) than their urban counterparts and, as a result, they delivered better disaster aid than urban areas. Others have similarly found that organizational ties greatly affect community resilience in disaster response and health care response (Haase et al., 2017; Hossain & Guan, 2012). In another case, Metaxa-Kakavouli, Maas, and Aldrich (2018) used Facebook data from users affected by Hurricanes Harvey, Irma, and Maria in 2017 to examine whether people with stronger social networks were more likely to evacuate. Their team used five measures of Facebook friend networks to conceptualize bonding, bridging, and linking social capital (cf. Kyne & Aldrich, 2019). Facebook, among other social media platforms, allows us to interact frequently with especially close friends and neighbors, boosting collective action in neighborhoods via bonding or bridging social ties (Hampton & Wellman, 2003). Examining the aftermath of the 2014 South Napa Earthquake in California, Page-Tan (2017) found that communities with higher indicators of social capital saw greater online community engagement through the neighborhood social network platform Nextdoor. Affiliation networks greatly enhance disaster research by providing testable data on the strength of connections between nodes along with their impact on other networks and policy outcomes.

Mobility Networks

In mobility networks, nodes represent locations while edges represent the number of people moving between these locations. They can also be drawn at the individual level to show a single person's path through a network over time. Mobility networks are always directed. Mobility networks are helpful for understanding evacuation but also long-term displacement, answering which cities people evacuate from and where they go to, as well as how many of them come back in the months and years after a disaster.

For example, Fraser, Aldrich, and Morikawa (2020) created a network describing evacuation between cities after a 2018 earthquake in Hokkaido, Japan. Using this network, we could assess which cities sent and received the most evacuees and whether certain kinds of towns sent or received more. There are many sources of mobility data. The U.S. Internal Revenue Service, for example, keeps track of the number of people (if greater than 10) who moved between any pair of counties in the United States each year.

Infrastructure Networks

In infrastructure networks, nodes tend to be vital facilities and edges tend to be infrastructural lines that convey services from these facilities to other facilities. Electricity grids, for example, can convey power from solar farms to hospitals, while telecommunications networks convey messages among cell towers and users. Transportation networks conduct passengers and vital goods among cities and ports using roads, bridges, seaways, and airways. These networks tend to be directed. These networks can be used to answer questions such as: Which facilities are most central to the functioning of the electrical grid or a telecommunications networks? Do nodes on average have many diverse connections to different power sources, or do they all depend on one power plant, making them vulnerable in the event that that plant goes offline? Is there only one bridge between the mainland and an island? Finally, what is the shortest route from a disaster-struck community to an evacuation center? These last methods, including shortest-route analysis, are described more in depth in Chapter 18 on geographic information systems (GIS).

Network Analysis

Social network analysis includes a broad array of tools for disaster studies. Often, however, researchers lean heavily on qualitative or quantitative analysis of networks. This chapter synthesizes these approaches and demonstrates how readers can find causal trends through mixed-methods analysis of networks.

Figure 15.1 depicts an iterative cycle in which the researcher initially collects data and visualizes and describes the network, then uses network statistics to identify which variables truly matter after controlling for others. With this in mind, the

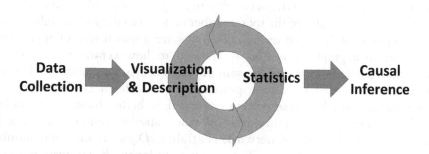

FIGURE 15.1 Causal Inference in Networks

researcher visualizes and describes the network again using the variables found significant in network statistics. Finally, if necessary, the researcher repeats any statistical analyses and concludes whether causal trends were found or not. This cycle is worth noting because it recommends using visualization, a qualitative technique in network analysis, in tandem along with network statistics and quantitative techniques in network analysis to identify causal mechanisms (Yousefi-Nooraie, Marin, & Ross, 2018). This is in the same spirit of nested analysis, which applies both small-*n* and large-*N* analysis strategies to verify a causal process (Lieberman, 2005).

Visualizing without this iterative cycle can be tedious, or worse: it may imply causality where there is none. Visualization is similar to bivariate correlation plots, where it demonstrates to show a relationship between (a) the number of edges and structure of the network and (b) the attributes of nodes in the network, often using color. While early social scientists have found incredible results using bivariate correlation charts (for example, Robert Putnam's study of Italian civic life), the work is arduous (Putnam, 1993). Sometimes it very quickly displays useful, accurate results, but without controlling for other intervening variables, it can be hard to interpret visualizations or determine which node attribute matters more to a network's structure. Instead, we advocate for an iterative cycle that first visualizes networks so that the researcher becomes familiar with the structure of the network, then identifies significant variables with statistical tools, and finally visualizes the network using those significant variables. Below, we introduce visualization and description techniques useful to interpreting disaster networks, followed by statistical tools for analyzing these networks.

Visualization and Description

When analyzing these networks, we can describe these networks using *network centrality measures*, which describe position and structure in networks. These analyses are highly visual. Through visualization, they can help in constructing a narrative describing how different actors relate to one another in the network. Likewise, analysts can also detect *communities* within their network, which interact more with each other than with those outside their community. Centrality measures, community detection, and visualization are all descriptive tools.

Centrality

For example, below we demonstrate a logical flow for describing networks. First, we report the overall structure of the network using edge density and graph centralization scores. *Edge density* is a ratio of the total number of edges to the total number of nodes, with a maximum of 1. *Graph centralization scores* are a useful way of approximating how centralized a graph overall is, as opposed to how central a node is. Graph centralization generates a ratio of the sum of differences among node-level centrality scores compared to their maximum possible sum of differences. These graph-level measures that describe how near or far a graph is from being absolutely centralized in terms of a given network centrality measure, where absolute centralization equals 1.

There are several kinds of network centrality. *Degree* is the total number of edges linked to a node. It describes direct popularity. *Betweenness* is the total number of shortest paths through the network that pass through that node.

Betweenness is a good measure of the diversity of ties in a network, which helps facilitate information flow (Granovetter, 1973; Rogers, 2003). It describes a node's capacity to bridge different groups of people or organizations. *Closeness* is the mean distance of a node from all other nodes. Typically, a high closeness centrality score indicates that an individual or institution is quite connected to a high share of others in the network. Finally, *eigenvector centrality* measures how many other nodes with high degree it is linked to (much like page-rank systems). Each of these measures describes a different kind of centrality (Bonacich, 1987; Bonacich, 2007). Using these measures, we can report which organizations or individuals were most central in our network. Node-level centrality scores can help us compare whether, for example, Person A has higher betweenness than Person B. In contrast, graph-level centralization scores allow us to compare whether a network is more centralized in terms of degree but less centralized in terms of betweenness, for example. These can be useful for comparing different networks, or the same network over time.

Community Detection

Then, we might wonder if some cliques of organizations or people are more densely tied together than with others. To examine this, we use *community detection*. Community detection requires justifying that these cliques are meaningful and not just coincidental groupings. Algorithms usually automatically determine an appropriate number of communities to sort nodes into. If the user uses the algorithm to look for five communities instead of three communities, the network might suddenly tell a different story. We recommend community detection primarily when it helps answer a relevant research question about which groups of nodes associate more with each other than others.

Visualization

Finally, we can visualize our networks. Network visualizations tell a story about disaster related interactions using node size, node color, edge size, edge color, labels, and layout. While the first five are optional, visualization requires the researcher to choose a *layout* for their network. Different layouts highlight different aspects of a network, but each also carry weaknesses. We outline the most relevant layouts for disaster studies in Table 15.3.

First, the Fruchterman–Reingold (FR) layout algorithm positions nodes in a petri-dish shape, spaced according to the weight of their edges. This allows position to reflect connectedness while forcing it into a readable dish shape. For example, we use FR to visualize our disaster committee's layout. However, we might want our visualizations to better reflect the structure of the network. The Yihan Hu layout algorithm creates a branching-tree effect, highlighting nodes that are hubs for other nodes. It is good for displaying connections between disparate parts of the network.

Alternatively, multidimensional scaling (MDS) creates a layout where nodes that are closer together have more or stronger edges between them than nodes that are further apart. While this is generally an excellent idea, strong outliers with many edges can throw off the shape of the network, making it difficult to read. This is why Fruchterman–Reingold's layout is helpful.

TABLE 15.3 Strengths and Weaknesses of Network Layouts

Layout	Shape	Strength	Weakness	Software
Fruchterman–Reingold	Petri dish	Shows highly related nodes while containing the shape of the graph	Unrelated nodes pushed together by petri-dish shape	Igraph, Gephi
Yihan Hu	Hubs and trees	Useful for highlighting indegree, or perhaps betweenness	Does not highlight other traits	Gephi
MDS	Web	Nodes closer to each other have stronger ties	High-degree nodes can stretch the web strangely	Igraph, Gephi
MDS (map)	Map	Displays geographic patterns	Unhelpful if no spatial pattern	Igraph, Gephi
Circle/chord diagram	Circle	Uses order and color around circle to highlight relationship	Unhelpful if no order, and patterns not guaranteed	Igraph, Circlize, Circos, Gephi

However, MDS can also be used with geographic coordinates, creating a map shape of any geographic network. Notably, map layouts should be used sparingly, as they only reveal geographic relationships and hide which nodes are most densely interconnected.

Finally, networks describing flow are ideally visualized using circle layouts or chord diagrams, which describe the flow of people or things between nodes. Chord diagrams arrange nodes around a circle, ordering nodes by degree, betweenness, or another network property, and may color them based on that property or another node attribute. Importantly, color should reflect an attribute that is thought to correlate with the ordering attribute; otherwise, they are difficult to read. Chord diagrams have been frequently used to visualize population movements (Qi, Abel, Muttarak, & Liu, 2017).

For example, Figure 15.2 shows four different layouts visualizing the same social network from our research, which we discuss further in a case study below. This network depicts committees as nodes connected by members who sit on both committees. These committees are disaster reconstruction committees involved in the recovery from Japan's 2011 disaster in the northeast Tōhoku region. We visualize here the relationship between committee connections and the origin of each committee. Committees might be from Iwate or Miyagi Prefectures or run by the Cabinet Office; the Ministry of Land, Transportation, and Infrastructure; or other organizations. These display largely similar patterns – committees from Iwate are generally separate from the rest of the committees. However, the Fruchterman–Reingold layout spaces out nodes well, giving more room to visualize each link in the network, which is why we adopt it below.

In summary, visualizations usually express an argument based on layout, node coloring, and node size. As a result, scholars should always question how and why a network visualization received a given layout.

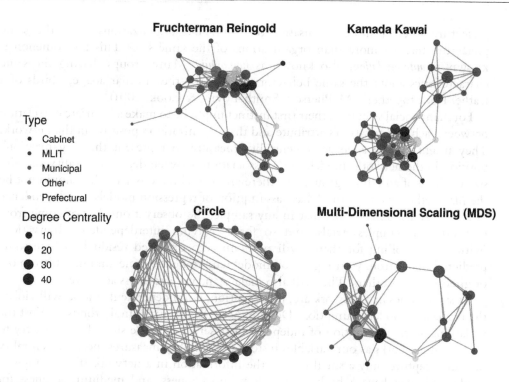

FIGURE 15.2 Multiple Layouts of the Same Network of Disaster Reconstruction Committees

Network Statistics

However, visualizing and describing this network likely poses challenges, because several node attributes might correlate with edges or demonstrate patterns in the network. How should we know which attribute or trend really matters? With good empirical knowledge about the network, we could eliminate some variables, but it still might be hard to know which variable affects the network more. Likewise, one variable's effect might be mediated by another, and visualization provides no easy way of controlling for intervening variables' effects. To bridge this gap, we introduce two statistical tools for making causal arguments about networks. First, *network autocorrelation tests* explain how much network ties affect the likelihood that a node has a given outcome. These produce the network equivalent of a bivariate correlation test's measure of association. Second, *exponential random graph models (ERGM)* explain how much node-level traits affect the likelihood that two nodes share a tie. These produce the network equivalent of a logit model, where the outcome is the presence or absence of a tie between two nodes.

Network Autocorrelation Tests

Social scientists might want to know *how many* of the nodes (e.g., people, institutions, locations) of the same attribute are connected in a network. A number of disaster-related questions fit this approach: Do cities exchange people more after disaster if those cities share more of the same ethnic groups? Do organizations from the same prefecture interact more in disaster recovery? Do organizations from the same prefecture interact more than organizations of the same size? This phenomenon is known as *autocorrelation*, also known as *homophily*. Many groups sharing the same characteristics adopt the same behaviors, known by the familiar adage, "birds of a feather flock together" (McPherson, Smith-Lovin, & Cook, 2001).

For many social scientists, their first instinct might be to make a bivariate correlation between each organization's attribute and that organization's position in the network. They might choose a network centrality measure to represent that organization's position in the network, modeling the association between degree centrality and city size or share of an ethnic group. But there are several reasons why this should not be the *first* method we turn to. A base assumption of regression models is independence of observations. This means that in any sample, the observations do not come from two different samples, trials, and so forth. Having interdependent observations (without controlling for them) will result in autocorrelated residuals, where some predicted values from your regression model tend to be the same amount off from the original values as others. This will also make standard errors less accurate.

As such, nodes in a network are, by definition, not independent, and so will violate the regression model assumption. Despite that, OLS is surprisingly robust against the violations of the assumption of independent observations. We should still first try to use actual networks as our variables instead of centrality measures, because centrality measures capture only a small part of the information in a network. For example, a single node can have a high degree, low betweenness, and medium closeness for centrality measures, yet each captures a very different dynamic about the network. Better instead would be to use an actual matrix (the machine-readable representation of networks) as a predictor or outcome variable in a statistical model.

We recommend that scholars and students use models that include the actual network as a predictor or outcome variable in order to make causal inferences without violating the assumption of independent observations. However, this does become difficult when working with big data. For example, network autocorrelation models are infamously slow. The authors have had trouble running autocorrelation models on networks with more than 1,000 nodes due to memory requirements. Likewise, when dealing with more than 2,000 nodes, exponential random graph models can become quite cumbersome. On ordinary computers, these computations become difficult after only 500 nodes. While some scholars have pioneered new methods for large-N networks for hundreds of thousands of nodes, these models are often not written in R, require considerable expertise with computational methods, or are still in development. In these situations, it might be more appropriate to turn to degree or betweenness as predictors in a model. Using centrality measures as outcome variables is always difficult, because they violate a key assumption of linear regression models: independence of observations. Centrality measures are by definition interdependent, reflecting the relationship between one observation and several others, meaning that these models will usually predict very similar outcomes for interconnected nodes, leading to non-constant variance in regression models. If necessary, these measures should only be used where the centrality measure has a clear empirical meaning, such as in the case of in-migration, net migration, or total migration.

Network autocorrelation tests give us a statistical measure known as Moran's I, which can answer these questions. Moran's I ranges from −1 to 1, where −1 or 1 indicates strong negative or positive autocorrelation. Values from −1 to 0 indicate negative autocorrelation, meaning that if the node attribute is present (if categorical) or higher (if continuous), then those nodes are less likely to have edges among them. Values from 1 to 0 indicate positive autocorrelation, meaning that if the node attribute is present or higher, then those nodes are more likely to have edges among them. Of course, Moran's I, like the Pearson's r from bivariate correlation, does not describe causation. A value closer to 1 or -1 indicates strong autocorrelation, while a value of 0 indicates no autocorrelation – no relationship between that node attribute and edge density. High autocorrelation could also mean that more social ties cause higher node attributes, for example.

In some cases, we might be most interested in predicting how network ties affect a node-level outcome. For example, do organizations that affiliate more with other organizations end up helping a greater number of disaster evacuees? In other words, does the behavior of peers affect the delivery of disaster aid? The ideal way to answer this question is using a network autocorrelation model, where disaster aid is the dependent variable and we use the actual matrix of network ties as a predictor variable. If we were to use the statistical software R, we can use the **nacf()** function in the **sna** R package to get Moran's I between any continuous or categorical variable for a set of nodes and the network connecting those nodes (Leenders, 2002).

What if, however, an intervening variable, not just network ties, might *also* explain that node attribute? We would need a kind of multivariate network model. Linear network autocorrelation models like **lnam()** in the **sna** R package allows us to test the effect of matrices, in addition to node-level predictors, on node-level outcomes. They also allow us to test two kinds of effects of matrices: (1) homophily among the dependent variable (W_1) and (2) homophily among the disturbance of the dependent variable (W_2). Usually, social scientists are looking for W_1, the conventional portrayal of peer effects. In the model effects table, they output an effect named *rho*, which describes positive or negative autocorrelation.

Several issues remain, however. What if you want to test the effect of node traits on network ties, the opposite of a network autocorrelation model? Or, what if you are interested in heterophily – do birds of different feathers flock together? For these, we need *dyadic models*, such as *exponential random graph models* (*ERGMs*).

Exponential Random Graph Models (ERGMs)

ERGMs model the likelihood of an edge appearing between any two nodes, given traits of the sending node, the receiving node, the edge, or the network as a whole. They are a special kind of dyadic logit model, where the unit of analysis is node pairs with edges having the value of 1 and those with no edges having a value of zero. ERGMs have since been extended into count ERGMs (for integers 0, 1, 2, etc.) and generalized ERGMs (GERGMs) (for real numbers such as 0.123 or 456.789). However, these network models require several additional assumptions and careful consideration. Instead, we opt for the simplest and most versatile version, the binary ERGM. For this, the reader takes a weighted network, decides what edge weight counts as an important relationship, and then thresholds the network at that value, keeping all edges that have at least that weight and getting rid of any that do not. Researchers can even compare models for networks' thresholds at different levels.

Many times, we can just use dyadic logit, Poisson, or OLS models, where we simply manipulate the data into dyads and then run the same models, using both the traits of sender and receiver nodes as predictors. If the network is undirected, then just the total or difference between both would suffice. We would use dyadic regression models if we think that nodes are interdependent, where two nodes are related because at least one additional node is related to one of those nodes. These network structures might affect the likelihood of edge formation. For these we need ERGMs. This is because ERGMs can include a *network statistic* for each kind of network structure whose effect on edge formation we want to model. A network statistic is a count of how many times in the network a certain kind of structure occurs. For example, reciprocity (mutual), popularity (k-stars) and concurrency (concurrent), triads (ctriad), and brokerage (transitive) are all concepts in a network that can be included in the model using the terms in parentheses.[2]

For example, if "triadic" relationships between three nodes occur frequently, we can include the propensity to form triads in the model, thus getting a more accurate estimate of the effect of a node-level trait on edge formation. There are nearly a dozen network statistics to choose from that represent this, including *triangle*, which counts the number of triads in your network. Notably, running ERGMs will result in errors when the network structure tested in the model is not present in the network, so network statistics should be used sparingly.

Also useful are terms such as node match, which tests how likely a network is to have edges going between nodes of the same category (e.g., the same prefecture.) This can even be broken down into specific category effects. This allows us to test homophily based on a node characteristic. Similarly, **nodemix** assesses heterophily by category, testing how likely a network is to have edges going between nodes of different categories (e.g., between different prefecture).

Finally, a common way to assess the effect of density and clustering on a network is edgewise pairs (**esp**). This counts the number of times that if A and B are connected and B is connected to C, that C is connected to A. Geometrically weighted edgewise shared partners (**gwesp**) weights these counts by the weight of these edges. Dozens of other network statistics can be included in the model, but the best model is the simplest. As Krivitsky et al. (2012) explain, ERGMs produce a model with which we can simulate a new network. When we compare the mean values of traits in the simulated network with the traits of the original network, a good simulation's mean values should fit within the box plots of the original. Importantly, the simulated network and original should have similar frequencies of basic network structure such as degree or number of edgewise shared partners. If this is not the case, generally, the model fit can be improved by adding another network statistic.

Causal Inference in Networks

Finally, using these network statistical models, we can more confidently identify variables that significantly relate to network structure. After identifying significant variables, we can identify a narrative about what affects relationships in this network and why. Do node traits matter, or is the network predisposed to feature certain network structures? Use those significant variables in a new network visualization, using color and size to convey the association. In these cases, it can be helpful to display only the names that you need to, so as not to overwhelm the reader with too much information. This cycle of description and statistical modeling can be repeated as many times as necessary until the central question is fully answered.

Case Study: Disaster Recovery Committee Networks

To demonstrate these tools, we draw from our working paper on an affiliation network of disaster reconstruction committees across Japan's Tōhoku region (Fraser,

Aldrich, Small, & Littlejohn, 2020). Ever since a 9.0 magnitude earthquake, 60-foot set of tsunami, and nuclear disaster struck Tōhoku in 2011, policymakers and experts have banded together in dozens of reconstruction committees, creating and implementing plans for reconstruction and recovery. Some experts served on multiple committees, sharing influential best practices and spurring recovery in multiple locations. For our study, we wanted to know which committees were most likely to share members and whether any patterns among membership and committee traits could be seen. Tips from local residents during fieldwork had led us to hypothesize that these committees might share a few key members who were dramatically shaping the recovery process in the Tōhoku region.

First, we created an edgelist counting for each committee pair, how many members they shared in common. We analyzed 39 committees, creating 127 distinct committee pairs, which served as our edges. This produced an undirected, weighted co-affiliation network. We visualized this network using Fruchterman–Reingold's force-directed layout to arrange, in a contained space, the most related committees as closest to one another. This network is visualized in Figure 15.3, depicting a dense cluster of Miyagi and national committees and a loosely linked cluster of Iwate committees. However, at this stage, all we could determine was that some committees were densely connected

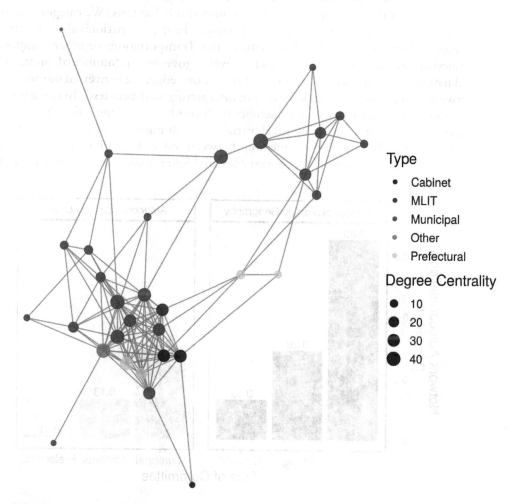

FIGURE 15.3 Do Disaster Recovery Committees of the Same Type Share More Members?

to each other, and committees in a second set of committees were slightly connected to each other. But, what was different about these two sections of the network?

First, we described the network using descriptive measures. The network was somewhat centralized in terms of degree, with a score of 0.34 out of 1. However, this network had high bridging capacity, with a betweenness centralization score of 0.45. Our visualization indicated as much, since several different clusters are jointly linked. But which committees were most interconnected? For this, we turned to degree centrality. The following three committees were connected to the most different committees: These included a nationwide committee, *3.11 Shinsai Densho-Kenkyu-kai* (32 external memberships), the Miyagi Prefecture–based *Watari-cho Shinsai Fukko Kaigi* (32 memberships), and the Miyagi Prefecture–based *Ishinomaki Fukkō Kaigi Vision Kondankai* (30 memberships). The committee with the highest betweenness, indicating ideal position for spreading information, was the Ministry of Land, Infrastructure, and Transportation's reconstruction committee (70). The committee with the second highest betweenness was Miyagi Prefecture's Miyako City reconstruction committee (70) followed by Watari Town's committee again (60). It appears that highly connected committees formed in Miyagi Prefecture and nationwide, but not in Iwate Prefecture.

However, snapshots of single committees do not provide robust evidence for inference. We remain unsure if nationwide or Miyagi-based committees were more connected. For this, we turned to network autocorrelation tests. We categorized each of our 39 committees by geography (Miyagi, Iwate, or nationwide, meaning a Cabinet; Ministry of Land, Infrastructure, and Transportation; or other committee formed in Japan's capital of Tokyo), and by level of government (municipal, prefectural, and national). Then, using a threshold of at least one edge, we converted our weighted network into a binary network for ease in interpreting statistical tests. In this network, if a committee shared at least one member with another committee, they had an edge weight of 1. Using our categorical variables as dummy variables, we calculated Moran's I to describe autocorrelation between edge formation and committee categories, which compare across variables in Figure 15.4. This figure shows that

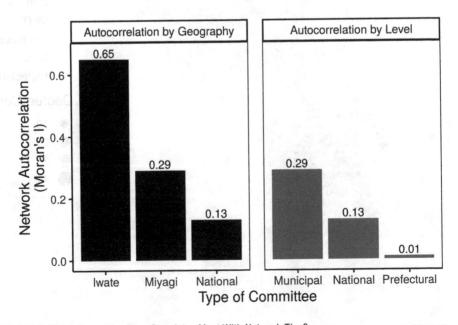

FIGURE 15.4 Which Committee Type Correlates Most With Network Ties?

committees based in Iwate were more interconnected than committees in Miyagi, or nationwide committees; the right panel shows that municipal committees were more interconnected than national or prefectural committees.

We learned this from Moran's I. The resulting values for Moran's I were positive for each test, indicating that committees are more likely to share members if they share the same type or locale. In particular, Iwate committees co-affiliate much more than Miyagi or nationwide committees, and municipal committees co-affiliate much more than national or prefectural committees. Interestingly, prefectural committees co-affiliate less than national committees. This hints that some prefectural committees may be more isolated, not sharing information or members with others as regularly.

However, what if we could see with much higher detail which place pairs and type pairs boost or limit co-membership, while controlling for particular structures in the network? For this, we turn to exponential random graph models. First, we created a simple initial model to test homophily by level (e.g., municipal) and by place (e.g., Miyagi). For example, Miyagi–Miyagi or Municipal–Municipal matches would each receive a positive or negative log-odds coefficient. If positive, this indicates that co-membership is *more likely* to occur among such pairs. If negative, it indicates that co-membership is *less likely* to occur. Finally, we also controlled for the base likelihood that committees from specific places might co-affiliate more than others. Results for this model can be seen in Table 15.4.

TABLE 15.4 Exponential Random Graph Model Results

Log Odds of Membership in Multiple Committees

	Dependent Variable (0/1)
Edges	−5.32***
	(0.71)
0 Edgewise-shared partners	−1.58***
	(0.42)
2 Edgewise-shared partners	−0.70**
	(0.24)
Miyagi	1.71***
	(0.49)
Nationwide	2.68
	(0.44)
Homophily–municipal	0.01
	(0.28)
Homophily–prefectural	2.03†
	(1.06)
Homophily–Iwate	4.25***
	(0.70)
Homophily–Miyagi	0.58
	(0.59)

TABLE 15.4 (Continued)

	Dependent Variable (0/1)
Nodes (committees)	39
Edges	127
AIC	535.75
BIC	577.23
Log likelihood	−258.88

*** $p < .001$. ** $p < .01$. * $p < .05$. † $p < .10$.

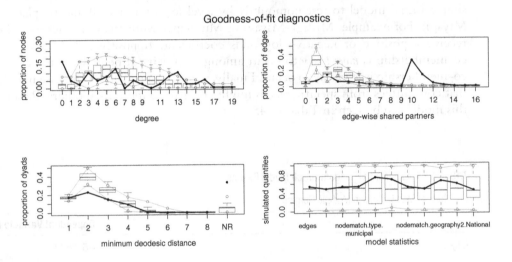

FIGURE 15.5 Exploring Goodness of Fit Plots for ERGMs

When we evaluated the goodness of fit of this model, the network simulated by the model largely matched the traits of the original network, but some traits, namely the number of edgewise shared partners varied. We counted the number of these network structures using the **ergm** package, and our network has many more sets of 0, 2, 10, and 11 edgewise shared partners than the model suggests. As a result, we added as many of these structures as possible to the model as network statistics. Unfortunately, the model could only take 0 and 2, which means it still exaggerates the density of the network. Figure 15.5 compares the model's simulated values as a black line versus the box plots of the original network. Ideally, the black line should fall within the box plots. This ERGM has room for improvement. However, it also supports the same general results indicated by our network autocorrelation tests even after controlling for each type of homophily. Committees from Iwate share members far more with each other than with those from other regions. Committees from Miyagi are much more likely to share members with nationwide groups.

To better represent these findings, we return to our network visualization using the Fruchterman–Reingold layout. This time, we can visualize the network, using size to display the number of external memberships for each committees using degree, and coloring committees using their geography. The result depicts a compelling argument that Miyagi (red) committees co-affiliate with other groups much more than Iwate (blue) committees. This might explain, for example, why Miyagi has recovered faster with novel planning than Iwate. This visualization is driven both by descriptive and inferential statistics. If we want to explore further what network structure or effects we must control for to even out our ERGM model fit, we could repeat the description-statistics cycle to identify what other factors might affect co-affiliation. In this way, we can become even more certain of how regional differences shape post-disaster collaboration.

Conclusion

As illustrated in our example, network analysis can be a powerful tool for analyzing all phases of the disaster cycle, including evacuation, response, and recovery. The case of joint membership in disaster reconstruction planning committees in Japan demonstrates how even using simple categorical variables, we can make powerful inferences about what explains recovery and resilience. This glimpse into visualization layouts, network centrality and centralization measures, network autocorrelation, and network statistics provides a logical process of analysis for students or scholars approaching network data related to disasters.

While some aspects of network statistics can be intimidating for new users, these tools are relatively straightforward, involving counting edges or network structures and building on frequently used statistical models. Visualization, centrality, and autocorrelation can be examined in Gephi, the field's most accessible point-and-click software, with no coding necessary. ERGMs can be run in R or through the *statnet* Web app, an accessible point-and-click software which runs in a browser window. Meanwhile, numerous accessible tutorials have been created recently to prepare social scientists for network data in R. We have indicated several in the references below.

Thanks to these tools, we can ask questions about disasters at scales never thought possible let before. Facebook or other geolocated data can let us examine complete networks of evacuation movement. Data online can let us compare the interactions of disaster response organizations. Network methods allow to answer several important questions: Do disaster relief agencies serve survivors better if they have more diverse ties to other agencies, or if they are well positioned in the network? Do decentralized, polycentric networks of disaster response governance seen in NGO work lead to better response and recovery outcomes than the chain-of-command networks often seen in federal bureaucracy or military operations? Do cities that receive more aid for disaster response see fewer people leave? Are some cities predisposed to receiving evacuees, and why? Do people leapfrog straight to major cities using airports and public transportation after disaster, or do they move to nearby cities? Each of these questions presents an important agenda for disaster research. By using visualizing and modeling networks of disaster data, we can more clearly see how social, political, and physical relationships shape disaster outcomes and design policy to support the relationships and organizations that empower response and recovery.

Notes

1. The code for our analyses will be available on the Harvard Dataverse at the following link: https://doi.org/10.7910/DVN/8XMGVC.
2. Kim et al. (2016) present an excellent description of relevant ERGM terms.

Further Reading

Fraser, T., Aldrich, D.P., Small, A., & Littlejohn, A. (2020). *In the hands of a few: Disaster recovery committee networks*. Northeastern University Global Resilience Institute Working Paper. https://doi.org/10.2139/ssrn.3544373

Gu, Z. (2014). *Circlize* implements and enhances circular visualization in R. *Bioinformatics*. https://doi.org/10.1093/bioinformatics/btu393

Jones, E.C., & Faas, A.J. (Eds.). (2016). *Social network analysis of disaster response, recovery, and adaptation*. Elsevier.

Kolaczyk, E.D., & Csardi, G. (2014). *Statistical analysis of network data with R*. Springer.

Robins, G., Lewis, J.M., & Wang, P. (2012). Statistical network analysis for analyzing policy networks. *Policy Studies Journal, 40*(3), 375–401.

Windzio, M. (2018). The network of global migration 1990–2013. Using ERGMs to test theories of migration between countries. *Social Networks, 53*, 20–29.

References

Aldrich, D.P. (2012). *Building resilience: Social capital in post-disaster recovery*. Chicago: University of Chicago Press.

Aldrich, D.P. (2019). *Black wave: How networks and governance shaped Japan's 3/11 disasters*. Chicago: University of Chicago Press.

Andrew, S., Arlikatti, S., Seibeneck, L., Pongponrat, K., & Jaikampan, K. (2016). Sources of organisational resiliency during the Thailand floods of 2011: A test of the bonding and bridging hypotheses. *Disasters, 40*(1), 65–84.

Barabasi, A.L. (2016). *Network science*. Cambridge: Cambridge University Press.

Bastian, M., Heymann, S., & Jacomy, M. (2009). *Gephi: An open source software for exploring and manipulating networks*. 3rd International AAAI Conference on Weblogs and Social Media, AAAI, San Jose, CA, 361–362.

Bisri, M.B.F. (2016a). Comparative study on inter-organizational cooperation in disaster situations and impact on humanitarian aid operations. *Journal of International Humanitarian Action, 1*(8), 1–14.

Bisri, M.B.F. (2016b). Observing partnership innovation through inter-organizational network analysis on emergency response of the Great East Japan earthquake and tsunami 2011. *Japan Social Innovation Journal, 6*(1), 27–48.

Bonacich, P. (1987). Power and centrality: A family of measures. *American Journal of Sociology, 92*(5), 1170–1182.

Bonacich, P. (2007). Some unique properties of eigenvector centrality. *Social Networks, 29*(4), 555–564.

Easley, D., & Kleinberg, J. (2010). *Networks, crowds, and markets: Reasoning about a highly connected world*. Cambridge: Cambridge University Press.

Fraser, T., Aldrich, D.P., & Morikawa, L. (2020). *Do all roads lead to Sapporo? A social network analysis of evacuation*. Northeastern University Global Resilience Institute Working Paper.

Fraser, T., Aldrich, D.P., Small, A., & Littlejohn, A. (2020). *In the hands of a few: Disaster recovery committee networks*. Northeastern University Global Resilience Institute Working Paper. https://doi.org/10.2139/ssrn.3544373

Granovetter, M.S. (1973). The strength of weak ties. *American Journal of Sociology, 78*(6), 1360–1380.

Haase, T.W., Ertan, G., & Comfort, L. (2017). The roots of community resilience: A comparative analysis of structural change in four gulf coast hurricane response networks. *Homeland Security Affairs, 13*(9), 1–26.

Hampton, K., & Wellman, B. (2003). Neighboring in Netville: How the internet supports community and social capital in a wired suburb. *City and Community, 2*(4), 277, 311.

Handcock, M.S., Hunter, D.R., Butts, C.T., Goodreau, S.M., & Morris, M. (2003). *Statnet: Software tools for the statistical modeling of network data*. http://statnetproject.org

Hossain, L., & Guan, D. C. K. (2012). Modelling coordination in hospital emergency departments through social network analysis. *Disasters, 36*(2), 338–364.

Kim, S.G. (2011). Social network analysis (SNA) and industrial engineering. *Industrial Engineering Magazine, 18*(1), 24–32.

Kim, S.H., & Chang, R.S. (2010). The study on the research trend of social network analysis and its applicability to information science. *Journal of the Korean Society for Information Management, 27*(4), 71–87.

Kim, N., Wilburne, D., Petrović, S., & Rinaldo, A. (2016). *On the geometry and extremal properties of the edge-degeneracy model*. https://arxiv.org/pdf/1602.00180.pdf

Krivitsky, P.N. (2012). Exponential-family random graph models for valued networks. *Electronic Journal of Statistics, 6*, 1100–1028.

Kyne, D., & Aldrich, D.P. (2019). Capturing bonding, bridging, and linking social capital through publicly available data. *Risk, Hazards and Crisis in Public Policy*. https://onlinelibrary.wiley.com/doi/pdf/10.1002/rhc3.12183

Leenders, R. T. A. J. (2002). Modeling social influence through network autocorrelation: Constructing the weight matrix. *Social Networks, 24*(1), 21–47. https://doi.org/10.1016/s0378-8733(01)00049-1

Lieberman, E. (2005). Nested analysis as a mixed-method strategy for comparative research. *American Political Science Review, 99*(3), 435–452.

Metaxa-Kakavouli, D., Maas, P., & Aldrich, D.P. (2018). How social ties influence hurricane evacuation behavior. *Proceedings of the ACM on Human-Computer Interaction, 2*(122).

McPherson, M., Smith-Lovin, L., & Cook, J.M. (2001). Birds of a feather: Homophily in social networks. *Annual Review of Sociology, 27*(1), 415–444.

Newman, M.E. (2010). *Networks: An introduction*. Oxford: Oxford University Press.

Ongkowijoyo, C., & Doloi, H. (2016). Determining critical infrastructure risks using social network analysis. *International Journal of Disaster Resilience in the Built Environment, 8*(1), 5–26.

Page-Tan, C. (2017). *Estimating effects of social capital on online social engagement: The 2014 Napa Valley earthquake*. Conference: Midwest Political Science Association Annual Conference in Chicago IL.

Putnam, R. (1993). *Making democracy work: Civic traditions in modern Italy*. Princeton, NJ: Princeton University Press.

Qi, W., Abel, G.J., Muttarak, R., & Liu, S. (2017). Circular visualization of China's internal migration flows 2010–2015. *Environment and Planning A, 49*(11), 2432–2436.

Rogers, E.M. (2003). *Diffusion of innovations* (5th ed.). New York: Simon & Schuster.

Yousefi-Nooraie, R., Marin, A., & Ross, L.E. (2018). Social network analysis: An example of fusion between quantitative and qualitative methods. *Journal of Mixed Methods Research, 14*(1), 110–124.

16

Quasi-experimental Research in the Wild

Walking the Line Between Quantitative and Qualitative[1]

DeeDee M. Bennett Gayle, Salimah LaForce, and Maureen Linden

Introduction

In contrast to the other methodological approaches discussed in this book, an experimental design is an empirical study that examines causal impacts using specific interventions. Traditional experimental designs include randomized control and intervention groups to make every effort to limit the influence of confounding variables. As such the samples are often quite homogenous. A fundamental limitation of true experiments is the applicability of the findings to the real world and populations with characteristics different from the sample.

Conversely, quasi-experimental designs often do not randomly assign subjects to an intervention or control. These designs may be preferential when the goal is to generalize the study findings to a large and highly variable population. Quasi-experimental designs are appropriate in emergency and disaster research because emergency practices must be responsive to people that are diverse with respect to race/ethnicity, age, ability, and other demographic characteristics. Although quasi-experimental designs center primarily on quantitative data, they can also capture qualitative data, which is essential for applied research involving human behavior. Despite these benefits, few studies have used experimental or quasi-experimental methodologies in disaster or emergency management research.

In response, this chapter summarizes the history of experimental designs. It describes how to conduct quasi-experimental studies, when these studies may offer a unique perspective, and why experimental or quasi-experimental designs may be useful in disaster management. Two examples of quasi-experimental studies are provided in this chapter, each testing the components of the Wireless Emergency Alert (WEA) system with human subjects. As various wireless communications services become useful for preparedness, response, recovery, and mitigation efforts, quasi-experimental designs may increasingly become a standard for investigating their efficacy in addition to other emergency/disaster systems.

What Is Experimental Research?

Experimental research methodologies are used when one wants to identify if there is a causal relationship between variables. To establish causality, one must be able to rule out other explanations or confounding variables. This is done by controlling for potential confounders by having a comparison group(s). To be considered a *true* experiment, the research design must include at least one control group and one intervention group, randomly assign research participants to one of the two groups, and, typically, collect data both before and after the intervention (Gribbons & Herman, 1996; Greeno, 2001; Campbell & Stanley, 2015). In some cases, a post-test-only design is preferable, especially when the research team is concerned about pretest effects. In a post-test-only design, the intervention is given first, and then a post-test is administered. Mean score differences on the post-test are attributed to the intervention. One might prefer this design when weighing the potential impact of the pretest on post-test scores. For example, if seeking to measure the efficacy of a training, collecting pretest data allows for a preview of the content of the training and rehearsal of the testing instrument, thereby potentially affecting post-test scores to some degree. Further, pretest effects, also referred to as interaction effects or reactivity, can introduce bias by priming the subjects for the intervention, causing them to be more attentive to specific details revealed as important in the pretest. However, confounding variables pose a greater threat when selecting a post-test-only design and should be addressed when defining the study's inclusion and exclusion criteria and via post hoc analyses.

Table 16.1 shows examples of experimental designs. The interventions may come in a multitude of forms depending on the goal of the study. Interventions may be educational in nature, such as a training; biological, such as a clinical trial for a new medication; methodological, such as comparing online instruction to the traditional classroom instruction; policy oriented, when wanting to determine the effects of a policy change; or behavioral, when one is interested in how an activity (e.g., volunteering) effects an outcome (e.g., community resilience).

Origins and Evolution: A Brief History of Experimental Research

Experimentation grew from the notion that philosophical, and later, psychological concepts required a method by which veracity could be determined through tests. It was a departure from the metaphysical, sometimes mystical doctrines of the early 20th century and prior, that had been used to explain experience (Creath, 2011). Some would argue that the scientific method was born from the logical empiricism movement, while others attribute it to psychological science's dogged determination to "see," measure, and understand the internal states of humans. Experimental psychologist Wilhelm Wundt is credited with establishing modern psychological science through empirical research. Before his work, the modal view was that only sensation and perception could be empirically evaluated, not the hidden processes by which they happen (Hunt, 2007). In efforts to observe the so-called unobservable, Wundt studied and educated others on quantitative methods for investigating mental

TABLE 16.1 Experimental Research Designs

Pretest–Post-test (used to measure intervention effects)

Random Assignment	Pretest	Intervention	Post-test
Group A	Yes	Yes	Yes
Group B	Yes	No	Yes

Post-test only (used to measure intervention effects while controlling for pretest effects)

	Pretest	Intervention	Post-test
Group A	No	Yes	Yes
Group B	No	No	Yes

Solomon Four Group (used to measure intervention and pretest effects)

	Pretest	Intervention	Post-test
Group A	Yes	Yes	Yes
Group B	Yes	No	Yes
Group C	No	Yes	Yes
Group D	No	No	Yes

Within subjects (used to measure effects of different, but related interventions)

		Participants are randomly assigned to receive either *x* or *y* intervention.	
	Group	Intervention $_x$	Yes
		Intervention $_y$	Yes

processes. Wundtian methods for studying reaction time and association time, using the scientific method and controlling variables, are still in use today, albeit with more advanced measuring tools. In fact, this chapter discusses research that measured the reaction time of research participants to emergency notification signals to determine optimal signal strengths that provoke recognition and reaction (see Box 16.1).

Conventional disciplines that answer research questions using the experimental method include the social and health sciences. As discussed in Chapter 1 of this book, when studying the effects of established and novel interventions, there is an ethical requirement to show that procedures and interventions are efficacious and ethical before implementing them. Beyond ethical considerations, the medical industry embraced experimental methods, specifically randomized control trials (RCTs), because they facilitated cost containment. Also, medically related professional associations, such as the American Psychological Association, National Alliance for the Mentally Ill, the National Association of Social Workers, and the American Speech-Language-Hearing Association endorsed the use of empirically supported interventions because of the academic rigor they imbued on their professions. Experimental methods are valuable to the study of human response to disasters for the same reasons they are prized in health sciences. Empirically supported emergency response efforts can save time, resources, and lives. In 2018, there were 530 deaths and 1,378 injuries associated with weather events (e.g., extreme heat, tornadoes, mudslides) in the United States (National Weather Service, 2019). Evidence-based emergency management practices could decrease the impacts by expanding what is

BOX 16.1 CONTROLLED "AIRPORT" STUDY

Research Question: Within the warning process, how quickly are Wireless Emergency Alerts received by people with sensory-based disabilities in normal settings?

Hypothesis: Mobile phone alerts (sound, light, vibration) impact warning message receipt.

Design: Quasi-experimental design (concurrent mixed-methods design).

Setting: In this design, participants with disabilities were placed in a controlled location to simulate the airport experience, specifically Hartsfield–Jackson Atlanta International Airport. The room contained similar noise and visual distractors present at the airport and were asked to simply check their prototype phones when the Wireless Emergency Alert sound, vibration, or light occurred. The design was intended to test part of the warning process in which individuals must be able to hear and identify the warning before deciding on whether to heed the actual message.

Participants: Thirty-six people with disabilities (blind, low vision, Deaf, and hard of hearing).

Pre-test: Demographics questionnaire and mobile phone survey.

Interventions: Randomly sent WEA message alerts through the prototype using (1) colored light sequences, (2) three different vibration cadences, and (3) three different tone cadences.

Post-test: Interview.

Data collection: Demographic data of the participants, direct observations of the participant–prototype interaction, and collection of quantitative data from the participant.

Results:

Aggregate Response Times (All Participants)

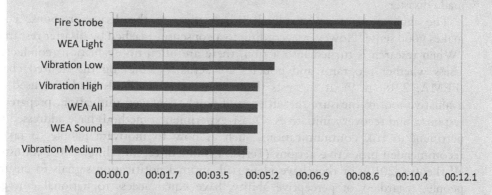

For participants who were Deaf, the top three quickest response times were to the low and medium vibrations, 4.5 and 4.9 seconds, respectively, then the WEA light cadence at 5.1 seconds. The signals that received the slowest response times were the Fire Strobe (10.6 seconds), the WEA sound (6.6 seconds), and WEA All (5.9 seconds).

Participants that were hard of hearing had the quickest response time to the WEA Light cadence; then the high, medium, and low vibrations; then the WEA sound, WEA All; and lastly the Fire Strobe signal. At 16.9 seconds, they had the slowest response time to the Fire Strobe. The WEA All signal response time was 5.1 seconds and the WEA sound and WEA low vibration responses were equal at 4.5 seconds.

Participants who were blind responded most quickly to the vibration signals. They responded equally as fast (3.5 seconds) to both the low and medium vibration strengths. Then the high vibration strength (3.6 seconds), WEA All (4.2 seconds), and lastly the WEA sound (4.8 seconds).

Participants who had low vision responded most quickly to the WEA sound and WEA All signals (both 4.5 seconds), then the high vibration at 5.1 seconds, medium vibration (5.3 seconds), and low vibration (5.4 seconds). Last for this group was the WEA Light at 7.3 seconds and the Fire Strobe (8.5 seconds).

Findings: The timing for message recognition by people with sensory disabilities differs based on disability type and notification mode (i.e., light, vibration, and sound). Vibration strength *is* a factor in response time to WEA messages, but results indicate that stronger is not always better. The data suggest that for people with hearing loss, the inclusion of the WEA light signal would increase their ability to notice incoming WEA messages.

Source: Presti, P., LaForce, S., Mitchell, H., Linden, M., Bennett, D., & Touzet, C. (2015). Optimizing Ability of Message Receipt by People with Disabilities: Prototype Findings Report/Vibration Scale Final Report.). Department of Homeland Security Science and Technology Directorate. Washington, D.C. Available at http://bit.ly/OptimizingNotificationSignals
   * Some the participants that identified as being Deaf used hearing aids which accounts for their ability respond to the WEA sound attention signal.
   Note: The research in this report is supported by DHS S&T under contract #HSHQDC-14-B0004. The opinions contained herein are those of the contractor and do not necessarily reflect those of DHS S&T.

known about human behavior before, after, or in the wake of a natural or human-made disaster.

The application of empirically based practices to the disaster response context makes good sense. However, according to a consensus reached by disaster researchers, "When research is turned into action, there are often no evaluations conducted to assess whether programs and policies are actually achieving the desired change" (FEMA, 2018, p. 9). It suggests that experimental methods could be used as an evaluative tool to measure the efficacy of newly deployed mitigation, preparedness, response, and recovery initiatives. Quasi-experimental methods have addressed issues pertinent to risk communications, such as how to motivate people to take the recommended protective actions (Terpstra, Lindell, & Gutteling, 2009; Johnston & Warkentin, 2010), or they have identified optimal notification signals to ensure all people, regardless of perceptive ability, have equal access to national emergency alerting systems (Presti et al., 2015) (see Box 16.2). When applied to the field, the findings from experimental studies serve to edify emergency management actions and can remove uncertainty about the general effect they can anticipate.

Experimental methods are also used to find support for, challenge, and develop theories. Comiskey (2018) asserts that the field of disaster management is a discipline that currently lacks a theoretical foundation. The concept of disaster resilience, for example, is often misconstrued with other types of resilience. As it stands now, there are several different models and approaches (Kendra, Clay, & Gill, 2019; Abramson et al., 2015; DFID, 1999), though it is difficult to parse the exact nature of disaster resilience from general resilience. An assertion often taken for granted is that the higher the levels of individual preparedness and community resilience, the lesser the demand would be placed on emergency responders and, concomitantly, the more

BOX 16.2 A QUASI-EXPERIMENTAL DESIGN

Research Question:

Does the addition of hazard symbology and an ASL interpreted version of the WEA text message improve WEA message comprehension for people who primarily communicate using American Sign Language (ASL)?

Hypothesis:

If hazard symbology and ASL interpretations were added to the standard WEA text message, there would be an improved understanding of the content of the message by people who primarily communicate using ASL.

Design: Quasi-experimental, within-subjects design.

Participants: Twenty-two participants, Deaf, whose primary language is ASL.

Interventions: Three randomly presented test messages: (a) text only (control condition), (b) text and symbology intervention, or (c) text, symbology, and ASL video intervention.

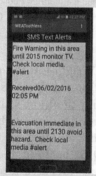   

Data collection:

Direct observation was used to note how participants interacted with the prototype system. To gauge how well the messages were understood; after receipt of each message, the participants were asked:

1. What did the message say?
2. What would you do if you received this message in an actual emergency?

Results:

Some of the symbols helped with message comprehension. However, they understood what was happening but not what action to take. Only 10% understood the entire text-only message.

- Unknown symbols: Civil Emergency, Evacuation Immediate, Hazardous Materials.
- Understood symbols: Flood Warning, Hurricane Warning, and Tornado Warning.
- Partially understood symbols:
- Winter Storm: 40%
- Flash Flood: 40%
- Fire Alert: 50%
- Shelter in Place: 60%

The ASL video intervention was understood by all subjects. However, several participants did not pay attention to the entire video, causing them to miss protective action instructions.

Findings:

Partial support for the research hypothesis was found. While all participants understood the ASL video intervention better than the control text message, only three of the symbols positively impacted comprehension. While some of the symbology added to the comprehension of event type, they did not improve the understanding of what action to take.

Note: This research was conducted under a grant from the National Institute on Disability, Independent Living, and Rehabilitation Research (NIDILRR grant #90RE5007–01–00). NIDILRR is a center within the Administration for Community Living (ACL), Department of Health and Human Services (HHS).

Source: LaForce, S., Linden, M., Mitchell, H. (2016). Wireless Emergency Alerts (WEA) Access: Optimizing Message Content for People that are Deaf [Invited presentation]. Annual Integrated Public Alert & Warning System, Office of Disability Integration, and Coordination Roundtable. Washington, D.C.

resources available to respond to those most in jeopardy. But Wright (2016) indicates that external factors impact not only the ability of one to prepare but also their intention to do so. Such factors are often socioeconomic, with the most vulnerable having delayed recovery and being the least prepared: "proliferation of different challenges facing people in their everyday lives can act to limit people's capacity or inclination to engage with potential futures" (Wright, 2016, p. 159). However, identifying and detailing the causal factors that constrain preparedness could conceivably be deciphered using an experimental research design that controls for socioeconomic status and other confounding variables defined in the literature, such as age and gender (Murphy, Cody, Frank, Glik, & Ang, 2009), disability status (Smith & Notaro, 2009) race/ethnicity (Eisenman et al., 2006), and prior disaster experiences (Hong, Kim, & Xiong, 2019).

Experimental Design in Disaster and Emergency Management Research

Experimental design in disaster and emergency management research is rare, but it has been performed (Norris, 2006; Presti et al., 2015; Greer, Wu, & Murphy, 2018). Researching disasters, however, presents a significant challenge to performing *true* experimental designs. Some designs are impractical, impossible, or unethical to perform. For example, testing how people react under certain stressful conditions, where an artificial stressor is used as an intervention (to simulate a disaster) and randomly assigned to participants, may not be practical or ethical to consider. Occasionally, however, research opportunities may align with the actual impacts of a disaster (Greer et al., 2018; Johnston, Bebbington Chin-Diew Lai, Houghton, & Paton, 1999; Vu & VanLandingham, 2012). For example, as Greer et al. (2018) were surveying risk perceptions of earthquakes in Oklahoma, one of the largest earthquakes in the area occurred. They continued with their survey and ended with a pre-test and a post-test on risk perception for their student respondents. Johnston et al. (1999) surveyed communities on volcanic eruptions in New Zealand in March 1995, and then around September of 1995, a volcano erupted in the region where they conducted research. The team returned to the communities and administered a post-test interview, using the actual volcanic activity as the intervention. As a control group, Johnston and colleagues surveyed a neighboring community pre- and post-eruption that was not impacted by the volcano. Additionally, Vu and VanLandingham (2012), similarly, had an ongoing survey of Vietnamese residents in New Orleans to assess health measures in 2005 before Hurricane Katrina. Nearly a year after Hurricane Katrina, the research team was able to locate the majority of the initial survey respondents to conduct a post-test. However, in the last example, Vu and colleagues used a modified or quasi-research design. In each of these cases, the researchers chose an investigative study that was later the location of an actual disaster. The unforeseen disaster became the "intervention" for their experimental research design (modified or not).

Other experimental designs intend to test other concerns related to disasters without requiring a real-life incident to occur. For example, Farra, Miller, Timm, and Schafer (2013) conducted an experimental design using data from a 3D environment created in Second Life to investigate disaster-related training simulations. Similarly, the study discussed in Box 16.1 utilized a simulated airport environment to test warning message receipt for people with sensory-based disabilities. While purposefully designed, due to the structure, these studies are often considered quasi-experimental.

Experimental Versus Quasi-experimental Designs

Quasi-experimental research, whether qualitative or quantitative, is the most prevalent research design in the social sciences (Reio, 2016) or in any applied science discipline (Coles, Zhang, & Zhuang, 2016; North & Norris, 2006). North and Norris (2006) detail the goal of disaster research as describing, explaining, and predicting individuals' thoughts, feelings, and actions. Goals such as these can be challenging to attain in disaster scenarios when using *true* experimental methods.

Quasi-experimental research can be distinguished from a *true* experiment in multiple ways. For one, in experimental studies, measures are often taken both before and after an intervention. Quasi-experimental research designs may only take one measurement, especially if the precondition or baseline has been established in the literature. For example, prior studies have shown that minority populations, such as people with a native language other than English and people with sensory disabilities, do not receive emergency messages in accessible formats (Bennett & LaForce, 2019; LaForce, Bennett, Linden, Touzet, & Mitchell, 2016). As detailed in Box 16.2 that used a quasi-experimental design, having already observed inaccessibility as the precondition (i.e., ex post facto), data was only collected *after* participants had been exposed to the experimental, accessible intervention. To validate the post-intervention results, researchers also collected qualitative data from participants to query them on their perceptions and experiences with the intervention, and to determine the difference, if any, from the status quo (i.e., precondition).

Second, experimental designs require randomization of research subjects into either an intervention group or a control group. Quasi-experimental designs may not include a classic control group or a random selection of research subjects. For example, suppose researchers are interested in the impact of a new policy or law. In that case, the control condition is the time before the new policy was implemented, and the experimental condition is after. In the disaster and risk reduction context, an emergency manager may wonder if a newly implemented scheduling practice for first responders in her jurisdiction has had the intended impact of reducing the quitting rate. To investigate this research question, data collected on quitting rates before the new scheduling practices were implemented could be compared to data collected after. If there is a measurable difference, say a statistically significant reduction in quitting rates, then the emergency manager could attribute that change to the new scheduling practice. However, because other variables were not controlled for, such as those who quit for reasons unrelated to scheduling, the only claim that could be made is that there is a relationship between the new practice and quitting rates. Still, the assertion that the new practice *caused* fewer first responders to quit would not be an accurate statement. As discussed earlier, causality can only be established in experimental research where variables are controlled to eliminate confounding and mediating variables, and all other reasons for why the variables are associated can be explained away (Warner, 2013). However, finding a cause is not always the endgame. In many cases, the correlation will suffice, especially so in applied research, when a strong relationship between the variables can be quantified.

The selection of a research method involves balancing three assumptions: context, causal inference, and generalization (Coursey, 1989). Experimental research emphasizes the causal inference over generalization and contextual needs. Surveys focus on generalizability, while phenomenological research emphasizes contextual factors. As a result, the selection of quasi-experimental design and the methodology with which it is applied depends upon the purpose of the experiment at hand. Other considerations for the research design include available resources and the availability of the population to be studied. Because disaster services, including emergency communications, are provided to a population of people with broad characteristics in a variety of environments, the data generated about disaster and emergency communications best practices must reflect contextual considerations and be generalizable to a heterogeneous population.

Sampling Considerations

A common criticism of experimental research is that it is too constrained and sterile for the results to be generalizable to the real world. What happens under the controlled conditions of an experimental study may not extrapolate to the wildly varying in vivo conditions. In an experiment, one way to control for confounding variables is to recruit a homogenous study sample, which is in stark contrast to typical social science sampling discussed in Chapter 2. To control for the effects of educational attainment, race, gender, and so on, experimental research designs often result in study groups that share the same demographic profile. Suppose the experiment is an efficacy study for an intervention. In that case, the response to which could vary based on gender or socioeconomic status (SES), then the sample should comprise a single gender and SES. To determine if the results are the same for other populations, the experiment can be repeated using the same procedures on a new sample. However, study repetition is time-consuming and expensive. Emergency managers and disaster researchers often need rapid results that can be quickly applied in their jurisdictions. Further, budget constraints may impact the ability to conduct repeated experiments. Under these conditions, a quasi-experimental study may be more appropriate, as it allows for heterogeneous samples that are more representative of the population. To address the impact of the diversity within the sample on the study's internal validity, post hoc analyses can identify if there are statistically significant differences based on demographic characteristics.

Generalizability of study results to broader populations is the ultimate goal of applied research (Cheng, Dimoka, & Pavlou, 2016), and the sampling method most likely to render that result is probability sampling. Probability sampling means that every individual in the sample frame, or population of interest, has the opportunity to participate in the study. For example, suppose a local emergency manager wanted to investigate disaster risk perception among students at the University of XYZ so they could design appropriate disaster risk messaging. In that case, they could either recruit from the entire student body or randomly select a sample from the total population. So long as the size of the sample had the necessary statistical power, the results of the study, *in theory*, could then be generalized to all students at the University of XYZ. So why the caveat? The process of randomization rules out certain sampling biases, but not all. A possible threat to external validity is self-selection bias. The individuals who choose to participate in the study may differ from those who refuse or do not reply.

In disaster research, the population of interest is often not neatly contained and easily reachable, such as in the university campus example. If one wants to study people who experienced Hurricane Katrina, for example, they would be faced with capturing a widely dispersed population due to the percentage of evacuees that were displaced. Considering displacement, the researcher might determine to only study those evacuees that currently reside in the states impacted. If that sample frame were used, the resulting sample would likely be skewed based on age, race, and income, as young adults, African Americans, and those with low income were found to be the least likely to return to their residence or their county (Groen & Polivka, 2008). In such a case, convenience sampling could be utilized. The advantage of convenience sampling is that one can recruit readily available participants that meet the inclusion criteria, and the endeavor is less costly in both time/effort and money (Suri, 2011). The tradeoff is that when a convenience sample is used, it may not be representative, limiting the applicability of the study results to the study participants and those similar to the study participants (see also Chapter 2).

For example, a convenience sample could result in a sample with relatively equal distributions across the demographic characteristics. That result is not likely to be found in the broader population, as demographic characteristics are not equally dispersed in the actual population of interest for the study. In such a case, the achievement of a diverse sample would not have been purposive but accidental. Convenience (or accidental) sampling is considered the least rigorous sampling method (Suri, 2011) and not associated with experimental research design. However, in disaster research, particularly when studying hard-to-reach populations, convenience sampling may be the best option. Once recruitment is complete, researchers may choose to randomly assign participants to either a control or intervention group. This post-recruitment randomization mitigates some of the sampling bias inserted due to the convenience sampling method.

Other sampling techniques fall in the range between probability sampling and convenience sampling. The following is a brief description of a few sampling strategies, but for a more thorough discussion of them and a host of others, refer to this chapter's Further Readings section in addition to various sections in Chapter 2 of this book.

- *Stratified random sampling* is used when one wants to ensure specific subgroups are well represented in the sample, particularly if they are a minority in the general population and simple or systematic random sampling would likely result in a meager number of participants from the minority group.

- *Cluster random sampling* is used when the unit of analysis is cities, counties, universities, libraries, and the like that are numerous and widespread geographically. The research method requires traveling to the locations to collect data.
- *Purposive sampling* is often used in qualitative studies to compare perspectives of different groups and identify central themes within and across the groups; it is not meant to be a representative sample of the population. It can also be applied in a quasi-experimental design when the desire is to understand if an intervention has differential effects based on group belongingness.
- *Snowball sampling* is used to recruit hard-to-reach or hidden populations, which often comprise people who have been stigmatized, marginalized, or are otherwise vulnerable (e.g., people with mental illness, immigrants, transient populations). As the name suggests, snowball sampling relies on recommendations from participants to grow the sample. Sampling continues as the research progresses (Trochim, 2020).

Types of Data Collected

Research involving human subjects is often couched as qualitative, quantitative, or mixed methods. However, experimental designs can incorporate any one of these methods in disaster research (see Figure 16.1). Experimental designs may collect data through interviews, questionnaires, observations, analysis of documents, and through obtrusive or unobtrusive means (de Vaus, 2001). With experimental designs, there is typically a pre-test, an intervention, and then a post-test. A typical qualitative design may involve an interview before and after, with observations during the intervention.

Conversely, a quantitative study may involve a survey before and after, with numerical data collected via the questionnaires, as well as during the intervention. A mixed-methods design, however, would include a combination of a sequential or concurrent collection of both quantitative and qualitative data before, during, and after the intervention. However, as with any study in which data is collected, it is determined by the questions the investigator seeks to answer.

Because the research goal is to measure change, the data is typically quantitative in both experimental and quasi-experimental designs. Among the relatively limited disaster-specific studies using an experimental design, most are quantitative, and nearly all of them measure risk perception (Table 16.2). In at least three studies, the experimental design happened by chance (Greer et al., 2018; Johnston et al., 1999; Vu &

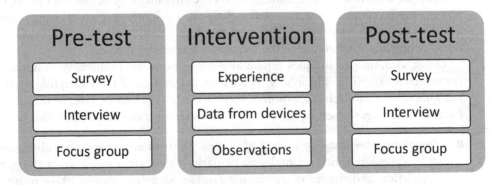

FIGURE 16.1 General Methods Used in Experimental Design During Pre-test, Intervention, and Post-test

VanLandingham, 2012). Instead, a natural disaster occurred during or directly following the data collection phase of their study. Fortuitously, in each case, the researchers seized the opportunity to collect additional data to form an ad-hoc experimental design. The data collection before the incident was transformed into the pretest, while the data collected after the event shifted to the posttest. The disaster became the intervention. In the other studies, the quasi-experiments were purposefully designed to test human behavior during preparedness or planning efforts with a simulated intervention (Nakayachi, 2018; Mulilis, Duval, & Lippa, 1990; Farra et al., 2013).

Pre-tests and Post-tests

Within experimental designs, investigators can employ a variety of research methods. Some examples of pretests include the use of surveys or interviews. The surveys may be used to collect demographic data on participants or to provide a baseline for what participants understand before the intervention. Surveys can provide some quantitative data for statistical analysis later. In our controlled "airport" study highlighted in Box 16.1, investigators used an intake survey to assess individual awareness of Wireless Emergency Alerts and the notification signals used to alert them of an incoming message. Additionally, information was collected to learn how each participant typically received disaster warnings.

In a qualitative design, investigators may choose to hold interviews or focus groups during pre- or post-test phases. Qualitative interview designs allow researchers to deeply explore themes and concepts participants understand or through which they have lived. This research design can be essential when trying to determine (or theorize) human behavior or decision-making during disasters. The post-test can also be used to debrief participants on the experiment. If using deception as part of the intervention, it is an ethical imperative that participants be told during a debriefing the reasons behind the deceit. Key questions to consider during post-test/debriefing include:

1. Did the participants understand the study or directions?

2. Did the participants feel any psychological stress or discomfort?

3. How did the participants feel about the experiment?

4. If using deception, did the participants believe the cover story?

5. Did the participants feel they would have behaved differently if this was not an experiment?

These questions, though not exhaustive, help the investigator to determine potential limitations and participant understanding of the research conducted and the experiment instructions.

Intervention

Intervention is a generally vague term to describe the stage at which the independent variable is introduced to, manipulated for, or collected from participants. The intervention phase of the research may include qualitative, quantitative, or both types

TABLE 16.2 Quasi-experimental Disaster Research

Quasi-experimental Research

Research Topic	Design	Convenience Sample	Pre-test	Intervention	Convenience Sample	Post-test	Follow-up Post-test
Risk perception for earthquakes	Non-longitudinal/different samples	Greer et al. (2018) Group A	Yes	Disaster event	Group B	Yes	No
Mental health after Hurricane Katrina	Longitudinal/within group	Vu and VanLandingham (2012) Group A	Yes	Disaster event	Group A	Yes	Yes
Risk perception in Japan	Non-longitudinal/between groups	Nakayachi (2018) Group A	Yes	Experimental condition	Original sample randomly assigned to control or experiment	Yes	No
				Control condition	Group B	Yes	No
					Group C	Yes	No
Risk perception of warnings	Non-longitudinal/between groups / geographically distinct groups	Johnston et al. (1999) Group A	Yes	Disaster event	Group A	Yes	No
		Group B	Yes		Group B	Yes	No
Wireless Emergency Alerts	Mixed methods/non-longitudinal/between groups	Presti et al. (2015) Group A	Focus groups to inform design of experimental conditions	6 experimental notification signals and 1 control signal	Group A	Reaction times captured during intervention	No
		Group B			Group B		No
		Group C			Group C		No
		Group D			Group D		No

(Continued)

TABLE 16.2 (Continued)

Research Topic	Design	Convenience Sample	Pre-test	Intervention	Convenience Sample	Post-test	Follow-up Post-test
Risk perception	Repeated measures/within group	Mullis et al. (1990)					
		Group A	Yes	Disaster event	Randomly selected from original sample		
					Group B	yes	Yes (repeated every 2 weeks for 2.5 months
	Longitudinal/between groups				Group C	Yes	?
					Group D	Yes	?
Disaster training simulations	Random assignment to group, longitudinal/between groups	Farra et al. (2013)					
		Control group	Yes	Standard web-based training	Control group	Yes	Yes
		Experimental group	Yes	Simulations + web-based training	Experimental group	Yes	Yes

of research methods. While applying the intervention to participants, researchers may observe the effects using qualitative techniques. Researchers may also collect quantitative data directly from devices used by the participants.

This was the case in the controlled "airport" study: investigators wanted to assess the Wireless Emergency Alert signal's accessibility to people with disabilities, where participants were given prototypes of phones (see Box 16.1). Quantitative data were captured in the form of reaction times to the prototype notification signals. Because the researchers anticipated that reaction times to the stimuli would vary based on the participants' mobile phone carry habits (e.g., in purse/backpack, jacket pocket, pants pocket), it was necessary to note these qualitative contextual observations that could help explain the reaction time data.

Before determining which research methods will be used, it is essential to identify the type of research question the study seeks to answer, what type of data is needed, and how the data will be collected and analyzed. Additional key issues to consider include:

1.   Who are the participants? Will there be a control group? Can there be a random assignment?

2.   What is (or where) is the setting for the study?

3.   What interventions need to be employed, and how will they be employed?

4.   What is the timeline for the study?

     a.   Will the intervention take place once?

     b.   Will the intervention take place multiple times within the same time span?

     c.   Will the intervention take place periodically at the same time for multiple days?

Depending on the context of the proposed study, a pure experimental design may not be appropriate. This is especially true in disaster research. While these questions are not exhaustive, they prime the investigator to think about the research design, interventions, and the types of participants needed for the experiment (or quasi-experiment).

Consideration of Contextual Factors

Disaster research must consider the multifaceted impact the environment has on those who are making protective action decisions or experiencing disaster. Demographic factors moderate these impacts, particularly as they relate to the individual's functional abilities and other cultural influences. For example, Brown and Dodman (2014) found that the vulnerability of children in disasters stems from their inexperience and immature reasoning skills, which leads to risky behaviors and the inability to avoid hazardous conditions. Children in urban environments were less susceptible to disasters than those who lived rurally. However, this trend did not hold for children living in urban poverty (Brown & Dodman, 2014). This may be due, in part, to the fact that children's knowledge of disasters, perception of danger in disasters, and response to disasters have been shown to vary significantly with the educational level of each parent (Cvetković & Stanišić, 2015), and education level has been consistently observed to be inversely related to economic status.

The presence of children impacts the behavior of adults experiencing an emergency. Goltz, Russell, and Bourque (1992) surveyed adults who had experienced an earthquake regarding the protective actions they took and found that these actions depended on the individual's environment and who was with them at the time. More than half of those who were at home during the earthquake took cover. Those who were at home with children were twice as likely to take cover than those at home by themselves, while those homes with another adult were 2.5 times less likely to take cover. When in the workplace, less than 40% of individuals took cover, and the presence of other adults did not impact this decision. Further, those at work evacuated the building at nearly twice the rate as those who were at home (Goltz et al., 1992).

The environment and presence of others also impact actions in the immediate aftermath of an earthquake. Interviews conducted in the wake of three separate earthquakes showed that people who were at home were less likely to contact household members than those at work. It is assumed this is because household members were with them. As a result, these individuals were more likely to take more immediate protective actions, such as turning off utilities (Jon et al., 2016).

Finally, environmental cues have been shown to impact protective action decisions. The presence or lack of visual or auditory cues related to an impending disaster have been shown to influence behavior. Gruntfest, Downing, and White (1978) described an incident where people who received a flash flood warning refused to evacuate because there had not been heavy rains in their area and the skies were clear. Shortly afterward, these same people did leave when they received a false message that an upstream dam had failed (Gruntfest et al., 1978). While not true, the second warning was not in conflict with what people could perceive from the environment, so they took protective action. Finally, the actions of others have been shown to encourage protective action decisions. Observing other individuals in the community preparing for an impending disaster reinforces compliance with warnings from emergency management associations or serves as a reminder of protective actions that would be important to take (Lindell & Perry, 2004).

As this research shows, contextual factors and their interactions with each other are important considerations when designing an experiment related to behaviors in a disaster. Experimental research methodologies designed to establish causality must control for potential confounding variables through the use of a comparison group(s). Establishing a *true* control group, in light of the complex interaction between contextual factors, may not be possible or desirable in disaster research. Instead, disaster and emergency communications research must be generalizable to a heterogeneous population. Quasi-experimental designs are more appropriate because practices in these areas must be responsive to people who reflect not only a diverse set of demographic characteristics but also contextual factors, including the presence of other people or children or environmental evidence that supports or contradicts received emergency messaging.

Conclusion

Disasters are not the only form of intervention in experiential designs. Some have been purposefully designed. There may be an increase in these types of studies, beyond risk perception, as the field becomes increasingly applied. Additionally, as we begin to rely more heavily on technology throughout the life cycle of disasters, experimental designs may become more common. Experimental designs may lessen the uncertainty of the effectiveness of novel practices. There is potential for expanding the base of knowledge on what we know about human behavior and the use of technologies in disaster research.

When considering whether to employ experimental or quasi-experimental research designs, one should ponder the trade-offs. For example, classic experiments have high internal validity, whereas quasi-experiments have higher levels of external validity. External validity refers to the generalizability of study results in different populations at different times and under different circumstances (Leedy & Ormrod, 2016). In their seminal work on quasi-experimental methodologies, Campbell and Stanley (1963) recognized limitations in experimental methods while simultaneously detailing the limitations of quasi-experimental studies in attaining both internal and external validity. Internal validity refers to accounting for and ruling out rival explanations for the study results. To claim causality, it is necessary to account for all internal validity factors (history, maturation, test effect, instrumentation, statistical regression, selection, experimental mortality, and selection-maturation interaction). However, several of these factors exist within the actual disaster environment, and controlling for them might lead to incorrect predictions of behaviors in disasters. For example, maturation effects within the participant due to the passage of time include growing more tired, which influences decision-making ability and sensory awareness. These would certainly be of importance in explaining and predicting behavior, and yet challenging to simulate in an experimental environment.

Despite the limitations of the methods, the results of quasi-experimental work can be used to make practice recommendations in applied fields (Reio, 2016), provided that these recommendations are expressed in a manner that does not assert causality. North and Norris (2006) claim that a primary threat to causality in disaster research stems from the lack of suitable comparison data. The availability of pre-disaster (pretest) data is lacking, making one-group studies difficult. However, using separate samples for phases one and two of a study can be designed to attenuate the effects of participant sensitivity to the content of the study (McDermott, 2002). If separate samples are not by design, an ad hoc accounting of all pre-existing differences in an attempt to match subject groups for comparisons is exceedingly difficult (North & Pfefferbaum, 2002). Despite not always having comparative data, quasi-experimental methods provide valuable insight into unknown factors that might influence the reactions of the responders, managers, and victims during and in the aftermath of a disaster. Clear representation of results generated through the use of these methods in disaster research is necessary to avoid inferential claims.

Regardless of whether you determine to do a classic experiment or quasi-experiment, when designing a study that involves human subjects, the research methodology has a direct impact on risks to the participants. The concept of risk level regarding research subjects' participation can be managed by applying the beneficence principle to (a) not harm, and (b) diminish any potential harms while increasing potential benefits (U.S. Department of Health and Human Services, 1979). Data collection methods, the research site, and the format and content of materials used can raise or lower risks. The U.S. Department of Health and Human Services (1979) states that "the manner and context in which information is conveyed is as important as the information itself" (p. 4), particularly so for vulnerable populations. For example, with children, if the content of the research tools (e.g., survey) is not accessible to their age group and developmental capacity to understand and benefit from the intervention, then not only is the research compromised, but the risk of harm is elevated.

Note

1. The research detailed in the vignettes was supported in part by grants from the National Institute on Disability, Independent Living, and Rehabilitation Research's Rehabilitation (H133E1100020) and the U.S. Department of Homeland Security's Science and Technology (S&T) Directorate under (HSHQDC-14-C-B0004). Along with the authors, contributions to the research and development were made by Kay Chiodo, Frank Lucia, Helena Mitchell, Peter Presti, Christina Touzet, Ed Price, and Rich Rarey.

Further Readings

Cresswell, J. (2014). *Research design: Qualitative, quantitative and mixed methods approaches* (4th ed). Thousand Oaks, CA: Sage.

Gonzalez, R. (2009). *Data analysis for experimental design.* New York: Guilford Press.

Kirk, R.E. (2013). *Experimental design: Procedures for behavioral sciences* (4th ed). Thousand Oaks, CA: Sage.

Levy, P.S., & Lemeshow, S. (2013). *Sampling of populations: Methods and applications.* Hoboken, NJ: Wiley.

Reichardt, C. (2019). *Quasi-experimentation: A guide to design and analysis methodology in the social sciences.* New York: Guilford Press.

References

Abramson, D.M., Grattan, L.M., Mayer, B., Colten, C.E., Arosemena, F.A., Bedimo-Rung, A., & Lichtveld, M. (2015). The resilience activation framework: A conceptual model of how access to social resources promotes adaptation and rapid recovery in post-disaster settings. *Journal of Behavioral Health Services and Research, 42*(1), 42–57.

Bennett, D., & LaForce, S. (2019). Text-to-action: Understanding the interaction between accessibility of Wireless Emergency Alerts and behavioral response. In B. Kar & D. Cochran (Eds.), *Risk communication and resilience* (pp. 9–26). New York: Routledge.

Brown, D., & Dodman, D. (2014). *Understanding children's risk and agency in urban areas and their implications for child-centered urban disaster risk reduction in Asia: Insights from Dhaka, Kathmandu, Manila and Jakarta.* London: International Institute for Environment and Development.

Campbell, D.T., & Stanley, J.C. (1963). *Experimental and quasi-experimental designs for research.* Boston: Houghton Mifflin.

Campbell, D.T., & Stanley, J.C. (2015). *Experimental and quasi-experimental designs for research.* Ravenio Books.

Cheng, Z., Dimoka, A., & Pavlou, P.A. (2016). Context may be king, but generalizability is the emperor! *Journal of Information Technology, 31*(3), 257–264. https://doi.org/10.1057/s41265-016-0005-7

Creath, R. (2011). *Logical empiricism.* https://plato.stanford.edu/entries/logical-empiricism/

Coles, J., Zhang, J., & Zhuang, J. (2016). Experiments on partnership and decision making in a disaster environment. *International Journal of Disaster Risk Reduction, 18,* 181–196.

Comiskey, J. (2018). Theory for homeland security. *Journal of Homeland Security Education, 7,* 29–45.

Coursey, D.H. (1989). Using experiments in knowledge utilization research: Strengths, weaknesses and potential applications. *Knowledge, 10*(3), 224–238.

Cvetković, V., & Stanišić, J. (2015). Relationship between demographic and environmental factors and knowledge of secondary school students on natural disasters. *Journal of the Geographical Institute Jovan Cvijic SASA, 65*(3), 323–340.

Department for International Development (DFID). (1999). *Sustainable livelihoods guidance.* http://www.ennonline.net/dfidsustainableliving

de Vaus, D. A. (2001). *Research design in social research*. Thousand Oaks, CA: Sage.

Eisenman, D. P., Wold, C., Fielding, J., Long, A., Setodji, C., Hickey, S., & Gelberg, L. (2006). Differences in individual-level terrorism preparedness in Los Angeles county. *American Journal of Preventive Medicine, 30*(1), 1–6.

Farra, S., Miller, E., Timm, N., & Schafer, J. (2013). Improved training for disasters using 3-D virtual reality simulation. *Western Journal of Nursing Research, 35*(5), 655–671.

FEMA. (2018). *A proposed research agenda for the emergency management higher education community.* https://training.fema.gov/hiedu/docs/latest/2018_fema_research_agenda_final-508%20(march%202018).pdf

Goltz, J. D., Russell, L. A., & Bourque, L. B. (1992). Initial behavioral response to a rapid onset disaster: A case study of the October 1, 1987, Whittier Narrows earthquake. *International Journal of Mass Emergencies and Disasters, 10*(1), 43–69.

Greeno, C. G. (2001). The classic experimental design. *Family Process, 40*(4), 495–499. https://doi.org/10.1111/j.1545-5300.2001.4040100495.x

Greer, A., Wu, C., & Murphy, H. (2018). A serendipitous, quasi-natural experiment: Earthquake risk perceptions and hazard adjustments among college students. *Natural Hazards, 93*(2), 987–1011. https://doi.org/10.1007/s11069-018-3337-5

Gribbons, B., & Herman, J. (1996). True and quasi-experimental designs. *Practical Assessment, Research, and Evaluation, 5*(1), 14.

Groen, J. A., & Polivka, A. E. (2008). Hurricane Katrina evacuees: Who they are, where they are, and how they are faring. *Monthly Labor Review, 131*, 32.

Gruntfest, E., Downing, T., & White, G. (1978). Big Thompson flood exposes need for better flood reaction system. *Civil Engineering, 48*(2), 72–73.

Hong, Y., Kim, J. S., & Xiong, L. (2019). Media exposure and individuals' emergency preparedness behaviors for coping with natural and human-made disasters. *Journal of Environmental Psychology, 63*, 82–91.

Hunt, M. (2007). *The story of psychology*. New York: Anchor Books.

Johnston, A. C., & Warkentin, M. (2010). Fear appeals and information security behaviors: An empirical study. *MIS Quarterly*, 549–566.

Johnston, D. M., Bebbington Chin-Diew Lai, M. S., Houghton, B. F., & Paton, D. (1999). Volcanic hazard perceptions: Comparative shifts in knowledge and risk. *Disaster Prevention and Management: An International Journal, 8*(2), 118–126.

Jon, I., Lindell, M. K., Prater, C. S., Huang, S., Wu, H., Johnston, D. M., . . . Lambie, E. (2016). Behavioral response in the immediate aftermath of shaking: Earthquakes in Christchurch and Wellington, New Zealand, and Hitachi, Japan. *International Journal of Environmental Research and Public Health, 13*, 1137.

Kendra, J., Clay, L., & Gill, K. (2019). Resilience and disasters. In H. Rodríguez, B. Donner, & J. Trainor (Eds.), *The handbook of disaster research* (2nd ed., pp. 87–107). New York: Springer.

LaForce, S., Bennett, D., Linden, M., Touzet, C., & Mitchell, H. (2016). Optimizing accessibility of Wireless Emergency Alerts: 2015 survey findings. *Journal on Technology and Persons with Disabilities, 4*, 42–54.

Leedy, P. D., & Ormrod, J. E. (2016). *Practical research: Planning and design*. Hoboken, NJ: Pearson Education.

Lindell, M. K., & Perry, R. W. (2004). *Communicating environmental risk in multiethnic communities*. Thousand Oaks, CA: Sage.

McDermott, R. (2002). Experimental methods in political science. *Annual Review of Political Science, 5*(1), 31–61. https://doi.org/10.1146/annurev.polisci.5.091001.170657

Mulilis, J. P., Duval, T. S., & Lippa, R. (1990). The effects of a large destructive local earthquake on earthquake preparedness as assessed by an earthquake preparedness scale. *Natural Hazards, 3*(4), 357–371.

Murphy, S. T., Cody, M., Frank, L. B., Glik, D., & Ang, A. (2009). Predictors of emergency preparedness and compliance. *Disaster Med Public Health Prep, 3*(2), 1–10.

Nakayachi, K. (2018). Effects of providing measures against earthquakes: Experimental studies on the perceived risks of disasters and disaster preparedness intentions in Japan. *Natural Hazards*, *90*(3), 1329–1348. https://doi.org/10.1007/s11069-017-3099-5

National Weather Service. (2019). *Summary of natural hazard statistics for 2018 in the United States*. http://www.weather.gov/media/hazstat/sum18.pdf

Norris, F. (2006). Disaster research methods: Past progress and future directions. *Journal of Traumatic Stress, 19*(2), 173–184.

North, C.S., & Norris, F.H. (2006). Choosing research methods to match research goals in studies of disaster or terrorism. In F.H. Norris, S. Galea, M.J. Friedman, & P.J. Watson (Eds.), *Methods for disaster mental health research* (pp. 45–61). New York: Guilford Press.

North, C.S., & Pfefferbaum, B. (2002). Research on the mental health effects of terrorism. *Journal of the American Medical Association, 288*(5), 633–636.

Presti, P., LaForce, S., Mitchell, H., Linden, M., Bennett, D., & Touzet, C. (2015). *Optimizing ability of message receipt by people with disabilities: Prototype findings report/vibration scale final report*. http://www.dhs.gov/publication/wea-optimizing-ability-message-receipt-people-disabilities

Reio, T.G., Jr. (2016). Nonexperimental research: Strengths, weaknesses and issues of precision. *European Journal of Training and Development, 40*(8/9), 676–690.

Smith, D.L., & Notaro, S.J. (2009). Personal emergency preparedness for people with disabilities from the 2006–2007 behavioral risk factor surveillance system. *Disability and Health Journal, 2*(2), 86–94.

Suri, H. (2011). Purposeful sampling in qualitative research synthesis. *Qualitative Research Journal, 11*(2), 63–75.

Terpstra, T., Lindell, M.K., & Gutteling, J.M. (2009). Does communicating (flood) risk affect (flood) risk perceptions? Results of a quasi-experimental study. *Risk Analysis: An International Journal, 29*(8), 1141–1155.

Trochim, W.M.K. (2020). *Sampling. Research methods knowledge base*. https://conjointly.com/kb/sampling-in-research/

U.S. Department of Health and Human Services. (1979). *The Belmont Report*. http://www.hhs.gov/ohrp/regulations-and-policy/belmont-report/read-the-belmont-report/index.html

Vu, L., & VanLandingham, M.J. (2012). Physical and mental health consequences of Katrina on Vietnamese immigrants in New Orleans: A pre-and post-disaster assessment. *Journal of Immigrant and Minority Health, 14*(3), 386–394.

Warner, R.M. (2013). *Applied statistics: From bivariate through multivariate techniques* (2nd ed.). Thousand Oaks, CA: Sage.

Wright, K. (2016). Resilient communities? Experiences of risk and resilience in a time of austerity. *International Journal of Disaster Risk Reduction, 18*, 154–161.

17

Using Historical Institutionalism

FEMA and U.S. Disaster Declarations

Richard Sylves

Introduction

The U.S. Constitution grants the president special powers in times of catastrophic disaster, crisis, and national emergency. Beyond this, enactment of the Federal Disaster Relief Act of 1950 gave current and future presidents the authority to declare major disasters on behalf of the federal government. Presidential power in disaster management was augmented in the Disaster Relief Act of 1974, which provided presidents authority to issue emergency declarations intended to help mobilize and fund federal, state, and local agencies when a disaster was or is imminent or to provide limited types of aid.

Why are presidential declarations worthy of study? What can be learned from the nearly 70-year history of such declarations? America's national government is atop a U.S. system of federalism and intergovernmental relations (Sylves, 2020, pp. 61–63). Canada and Australia, and a few other democratic nations, operate with variants of federalism, but the United States is truly exceptional in how it has devised and operated its national system of emergency management. That system has been configured in such a way that the federal government, at the president's behest, can provide funding and in-kind disaster assistance to state and local governments. When the president has issued a disaster declaration to a state, under terms of that declaration, the federal government can directly provide aid to individuals and households, and can furnish money assistance to state and local governments and certain eligible non-profit and for-profit organizations.

Every declaration embodies a sizable pool of highly useful information and data about the nation's experience with disaster agents of nearly all types. They stand as a long-term record of the nation's disasters and emergencies since 1950. Studied over years and decades, declarations also demonstrate how the official federal definition of "disaster" and "emergency" has changed through time. The increasing number of declarations, the patterns of disaster impact over the nation's political geography, and the demographics of economic development and hazard vulnerability over time is often reflected in disaster declarations broadly. Declarations, despite the interplay of political and administrative factors, embed indicators of climate change and sea level rise. Environmental scientist Keith Smith points to increases in the frequency of wildfires, floods, and severe storms, and perhaps in the elevated frequency and intensity of tornadoes, hurricanes making landfall, and more as indicators (2013, pp. 101, 103).

Declarations are also a repository of human-caused disasters, including acts of terrorism, technological, and industrial failures, and lifeline utility outages. Each president since Truman has affected federal disaster management in some way. Disaster declarations may also be considered a type of national, regional, or local "shock absorber." Disaster declarations are an essential component of disaster response and recovery; plus, they are instruments of preparedness and mitigation ahead of future disasters. "Resilience" is a term now in vogue. In the United States, things that are done or not done under a federal disaster declaration directly affect resilience in future calamities or disaster incidents (Sylves, 2020, p. 71). Declarations have even been used as a tool of federal response in helping states and local governments confront the COVID-19 pandemic that began for the United States in 2020 (FEMA, 2020a).

The president's authority to issue federal disaster declarations came with an implementation arm. However, from 1950 to 1979, federal emergency management was neither fully conceived nor cohesive (Sylves, 2020, pp. 86–99). It was not until 1979 that the Federal Emergency Management Agency (FEMA) came to be. Since its inception, FEMA has evolved into a relatively modest-sized but modular "institution" with a very high public profile. President Carter's executive order, and subsequent congressional enabling legislation, pulled together an assortment of disparate federal offices, bureaus, and divisions to form FEMA. The agency became the "heart, soul, and brain" of federal emergency management. It fused American civil defense and natural disaster preparedness such that civil–military disputes often percolated beneath its bureaucratic surface. However, FEMA is not a research agency, not a science-based or science-driven organization, and not a broad-scale regulatory agency. FEMA is a coordinating body operating "horizontally" across the federal level. It works with, guides, or furnishes mission assignment funding to other federal entities working declared disasters. FEMA is in a "vertical" sense a coordinator through its relationships with state, local, and other subnational entities. FEMA processes and dispenses prodigious sums of federal money on a scale far greater than most Americans appreciate. It also processes state governor requests for presidential declarations of major disaster or emergency (FEMA, 2018b).

When FEMA joined the U.S. Department of Homeland Security (DHS) in 2003, its people learned that FEMA's long-standing links and relationships with U.S. state and local governments were something coveted by many other DHS agencies, especially by those unaccustomed to working with officials of subnational governments. FEMA suffered organizational hardships during its first 3 years in DHS, but the Post-Katrina Emergency Management Reform Act of 2006 mercifully rescued, restored, and reinforced FEMA. That measure also made FEMA a conduit of grants management for a host of DHS organizations not normally associated with emergency management.

This chapter will illustrate how the use of historical institutionalism theory can be used to propose data-backed experiments aimed at factually demonstrating the way in which FEMA has increasingly "institutionalized" since its formation, despite its assimilation into the DHS collective. Specifically, this chapter will demonstrate how, since its formation in 1979, FEMA has become increasingly institutionalized:

1. FEMA has routinized and largely de-politicized disaster declaration request processing over time, which increased its administrative power as a federal agency.

2. FEMA's organizationally self-serving set of low-threshold disaster declaration qualifications for states has invited governors to request more declarations (DR and EM), thus gradually ballooning both the volume and variety of incidents presidents have approved for major disaster declarations.

3. FEMA has greatly expanded its authority and role as an institution by helping and encouraging modern presidents to broaden the range and variety of incidents declared as major disasters and emergencies.

Institutional Theories and a Public Institution

Why institutionalism? An institution is a relatively enduring collection of rules and organized practices, embedded in structures of meaning and resources that do not change much in the face of turnover of individuals. Institutions are more than the idiosyncratic preferences and expectations of the individuals who lead or work in them. They adapt quasi-organically to changing outside circumstances (March & Olsen, 2009). They lawfully establish and refine rules and practices prescribing appropriate behavior of specific actors in specific situations. Institutions are structures of meaning that embed identities, a sense of belonging, advance common purposes, and explain, justify, and legitimate behavioral codes. They are structures of resources that create capabilities for acting by empowering and constraining actors, making them more or less capable of acting according to prescriptive rules of appropriateness (March & Olsen, 2009). Institutions are also reinforced by third parties (i.e., the U.S. Congress, presidents, and the federal judiciary) when they enforce rules and sanction non-compliance.

Here, institutionalism refers to a general approach to the study of political and public administrative institutions. It embodies a set of theoretical ideas and hypotheses about institutional characteristics and their links to political agency, performance, and change. Institutionalism emphasizes the internal nature and social construction of political institutions. Under the general theory, institutions are not merely contracts among self-seeking, calculating individual actors, and they are not simply arenas in which social forces contend. They are collections of structures, rules, and standard operating procedures that have a partly autonomous role in political life. Institutionalism, whether in historical or sociological formats, entails reification, which is attributing physical form or "life" to an abstract concept. In effect, sets of complex social relations appear to be things of substance. Humans are educated and socialized to accept the existence of administrative arrangements as if they were "concrete objects." For example, FEMA is generally perceived by Americans familiar with it as a formal government administrative entity with its own "agency" or power to decide, act, or not act – somewhat like an adult human being. In reality, FEMA is a federal organization operated by its human employees (replaceable over time) under laws, rules, political constraints, and societal norms. Its imagined physicality flows from its organizational actions, its perceived effectiveness or lack thereof, its customs and practices, its power to distribute and manage federal funds allotted to it, its public relations, and its ability to survive in a world of organizational competitors.

Within an institutional perspective, a core assumption is that institutions create elements of order and predictability. They fashion, enable, and constrain political actors as they perform within a logic of appropriate action. Institutions are carriers of identities and roles. Historical institutionalism also considers decisional "outcomes" (Thoenig, 2012). Moreover, another core assumption is that the translation of structures into political action and action into institutional continuity and change are generated by comprehensible and routine processes. These processes produce recurring modes of action (March & Olsen, 2009) and organizational patterns. A challenge for students of institutions is to explain how such processes are stabilized or destabilized, and which factors sustain or interrupt ongoing processes. Institutions are not static. Institutionalization is not an inevitable process, nor is it one directional, monotonic, or irreversible (Weaver & Rockman, 1993). In general, however, because institutions are defended by insiders and validated by outsiders, and because their histories are encoded into rules and routines, their internal structures and rules cannot be changed arbitrarily (March & Olsen, 2009). The changes that do occur are more likely to reflect adaptation to experience in specific case encounters and thus may be both relatively narrow-minded and meandering.

Finally, historical institutionalism posits that outcomes of public policies "do not just reflect the preferences or interests of the strongest social forces. They are also channeled by existing and past arrangements" (Thoenig, 2012, p. 156). In historical institutionalism, "Existing institutions structure the design and content of the decisions themselves" over a period of time. Institutions often function like social systems, producing norms and cognitive references. The analysis that follows will demonstrate how FEMA has evolved as an "institution" and shaped the environment in which it functions.

The Laws and Institutions That Established Presidential Disaster Declarations

Before 1950, the U.S. Congress considered unique relief legislation for each disaster; awkwardness, delay, pork barreling bias, and administrative confusion often resulted (Platt, 1999). By 1950, lawmakers decided that it made more sense to entrust declaration decision-making to the president as an executive responsibility (May, 1985). Presidential authority to address domestic disasters won political support in 1950, in part, because many Americans and their elected lawmakers grew concerned that there was no domestic equivalent of the then post–World War II Marshall Plan, which sent U.S. aid and funding to countries ravaged by world war and famine (Sylves, 2020, p. 319).

A presidential declaration of major disaster or emergency has far-reaching consequences because it opens the door to federal assistance by legitimizing the disaster for affected populations (Schneider, 1995, 2011). The declaration specifies the state and its eligible counties or equivalents (i.e., tribal governments), and delineates exactly who is eligible for federal relief by location. Each declaration is issued to a U.S. state, the District of Columbia, or an eligible American trust territory, commonwealth, or free-association partner. When a declaration identifies counties approved to receive federal disaster assistance, unincorporated jurisdictions within the county will also be eligible for assistance. Incorporated (often chartered) municipalities within a county may receive federal assistance passed through by the state or by the county, depending upon the procedures used in each state.

Some major disaster declarations issued by the president make every county in a state eligible for some form of federal disaster assistance, especially if this is in the respective governor's original request. However, when disaster declarations cover all counties in the state, that state's governor must have either asked for this in her or his original request and/or it must have been agreed to in governor–FEMA negotiations (Sylves, 2020, pp. 252–253).

Under the Stafford Act of 1988 and its predecessor laws, presidents are free, within certain limits, to interpret broadly or narrowly what is declarable as an emergency (Lindsay, 2017a; Sylves, 2014). However, since FEMA began operation, governor requests for major disaster (or emergency) declarations have ordinarily been scrutinized by FEMA's officials before the president renders a decision. On rare occasions, a president can pull a request through to approval even if FEMA recommends a turndown. However, researchers have determined that such actions are extremely uncommon (Sylves & Buzas, 2007). Most request outcomes for major disaster declarations are based on FEMA criteria and thresholds (Lindsay, 2017b). Each president appears to make declaration decisions on a case-by-case basis (U.S. Senate, 1993). However, the case-by-case claim is more myth than reality for a variety of reasons.

Ordinarily, a governor must ask the president to declare a major disaster or emergency before the president can award one. This is because many disaster declarations embody assistance programs requiring a federal/state and local funding match, such that the requesting state must agree to pay its respective matching share during recovery operations. Presidents do not have the legal authority to compel states and their localities to pay their matching shares in the absence of governor (state) approval. However, exceptions apply: federal law empowers the president to declare an emergency when there is a pre-eminent federal responsibility or in the rare event that both a governor and lieutenant governor are unable to ask for one. All governors have the authority to request a declaration. Sometimes a governor may submit an expedited request to the president bypassing the usual FEMA process of submitting the request with damage estimates and other documentation by asking the president directly. That said, the formal administrative process involves an official FEMA recommendation to the president regarding the deservedness of each request. As such, there is a ritualized process that guides, and somewhat constrains, each president that has become increasingly formalized since 1950.

President-invited all-county emergency declarations open to governors are unusual but precedented. In "federal interest" disasters or crises, presidents have in effect pre-approved declaration requests for governors who believe they need them. For example, President George W. Bush's 2006 emergency declaration after Hurricane Katrina invited states outside the damage zone to take advantage of a pre-approved emergency declaration that subsidized respective state and local costs incurred in helping Hurricane Katrina victims who had resettled in their jurisdictions. Likewise, in 2020, President Trump issued an emergency declaration to every state confronting the novel coronavirus pandemic (FEMA, 2020a).

Presidential declarations of major disaster and emergency are intriguing because authority to make the essential decision, by law, legally rests only with the president. Most federal laws require implementation decisions by legions of government officials, many of whom operate some distance from the president (Anderson, 1997). Admittedly, once the president issues a declaration, federal agency and program officials, in concert with their state and local counterparts, undertake an assortment of implementing decisions. Yet the president's approval or denial decision is often highly consequential for the requesting state and its localities (May & Williams, 1986; Sylves, 2006). Yet, as will be shown, it is also true that governor requests since

1950 have escalated dramatically over the years. Consequently, the president often does not have the time to personally ponder the details of each request. Hence, FEMA's role in the process as an institution has, in federal parlance, been greatly "enhanced" since 1979. FEMA's White House Package, the formal portfolio containing a requesting governor's official documents, includes the FEMA director's or administrator's recommendation to either approve or turn down the request (Sylves, 2020, pp. 148, 214).

Every presidential declaration contains an initial statement about the kinds of program assistance people or subnational governments may be eligible to request. This is crucial because it determines whether disaster victims will receive direct cash grants, housing supplements, emergency medical care, disaster unemployment assistance, and so forth. It also specifies whether or not state and local governments are eligible to receive federal disaster assistance to replace or repair public facilities and other infrastructure. Certain non-profit organizations may also qualify for federal disaster aid of various types. Moreover, public and privately owned utilities – electric power, natural gas distributors, communications, water purveyors, wastewater treatment services, certain transportation providers, and so forth – may also receive federal assistance to cover repair or replacement of their disaster damaged infrastructure and equipment (Sylves, 2020, p. 135).

A presidential declaration is vital to those directly affected by the disaster or emergency. It confers on them an "official" victim status needed to qualify for federal aid. Under FEMA's Individuals and Households Program (IHP) and the U.S. Small Business Administration's (SBA) Economic Injury Disaster Loans, people and businesses may apply and qualify for various forms of federal disaster assistance under a declaration. Application is usually made directly to FEMA or SBA (disaster loans); however, some categories of IHP may entail application through a state or tribal government. Most declarations also make aid available through FEMA's Public Assistance Program (PA), which provides government-to-government disaster relief to subsidize much of the cost of repairing, rebuilding, or replacing damaged government, utility, or essential infrastructure. Additionally, the Stafford Act of 1988 authorized presidential declarations of major disasters to include hazard mitigation (HM) funding calculated as a percentage of total FEMA IHP and PA program payouts to the state under the declaration (Sylves, 2020, p. 135).

To the public, including businesspeople, a declaration signifies that a serious event has occurred, requiring the attention and resources of the federal government. The symbolism and content of the presidential declaration, as well as news media coverage, structures popular perceptions about the nature and scope of the disaster. Indirectly, a presidential declaration may also encourage private charitable contributions from people and businesses. It may also help to mobilize more responders and volunteers to serve in the response and recovery phases of the incident. Declarations also spotlight the work of FEMA. As a result, how FEMA responds to declared disasters often has organizational "life and death" consequences for the agency.

Broadening the Definition of Disaster for Political and Institutional Gain

Under economist William A. Niskanen Jr.'s libertarian perspective, some might posit that FEMA has generated demand for the very resources and services it supplies. By setting low qualifying thresholds for states and counties, advising the president to generously issue declarations, encouraging federal lawmakers to fund disaster dedicated budgets, and by promoting state and local emergency management capacity honed to seek federal disaster declarations, FEMA is conforming to Niskanen's theory of bureau behavior (Niskanen, 2017).

Along these lines, some declarations have little or nothing to do with natural hazards or disasters and nothing to do with terrorism. In some cases, a problem is sufficiently anomalous that a president is not guided by existing law, policy, or precedent yet feels compelled to act, and a presidential declaration of major disaster or emergency is an available action tool. Presidents and Congress, often with FEMA guidance and state and local input, influence disaster policy in general ways and in precedent-setting changes in their so-called unique case decision-making. Occasionally, a new type of disaster agent wins a presidential declaration. It then stands as a new precedent open to state governors, redounding to FEMA's long-term institutional benefit.

Specifically, FEMA leaders have long found it beneficial to claim "every disaster is unique," when in fact many types of disasters are repeated in different (or the same) forms and locations, with varying degrees of intensity, and sometimes year after year. The claim of "uniqueness" is fodder to satisfy desperate lawmakers whose home districts and states suffer disaster losses. Uniqueness also encourages FEMA as an institution to largely ignore history and repeating patterns of incidents, blunted only by FEMA's modest structural mitigation and community preparedness activities. The post-2002 DHS-FEMA has, for nearly 20 years, invested massive effort in devising huge, complex, and expensive plans to prepare the nation for terrorist attack and subsequent response to the envisioned incidents. Yet, DHS/FEMA planning for more predictable natural, and non-terror, human-caused disasters is often relegated to a subset of terrorism planning. Consequently, the cry of uniqueness and the vast sums of federal money dedicated to homeland terrorism have helped grow DHS-FEMA as an institution but has also diluted and distorted its original disaster management mission (Sylves, 2020, pp. 158–159).

Federal Disaster Relief Law and Declaration Authority

The Federal Disaster Relief Act of 1950 (DRA; Public Law 81–875) specified that federal resources could be used to supplement the efforts of others in the event of a disaster. The new law made federal disaster assistance more accessible since it no longer required specific congressional legislation to address each new disaster but instead empowered the president to decide when federal disaster assistance was justified. However, federal assistance was intended to supplement, not replace, state and local disaster management efforts. It was also directed to facilitating some disaster response and recovery efforts, more than to advance disaster preparedness and mitigation efforts. The DRA of 1950 provided "an orderly and continuing means of assistance by the federal government to states and local governments in carrying out their responsibilities to alleviate suffering and damage resulting from major disasters" (U.S. Code of Federal Regulations, Title 44, 200.3; see also U.S. Code of Federal Regulations, Title 44, 208.2, 2020a). The Stafford Act of 1988 reaffirms much of the DRA of 1950 original definition:

Major disaster means any natural catastrophe (including any hurricane, tornado, storm, high water, wind-driven water, tidal wave, tsunami, earthquake, volcanic eruption, landslide, mudslide, snowstorm or drought), or regardless of cause, any fire, flood, or explosion in any part of the United States that in the determination of the President, causes damage of sufficient severity and magnitude to warrant major disaster assistance under the Stafford Act to supplement the efforts and available resources of the States, Local Governments (later Native American Tribal Governments), and disaster relief organizations in alleviating the damage, loss, hardship, or suffering thereby.

(U.S. Code of Federal Regulations, Title 44, 208.2, 2020a)

Congress built on the 1950 act by passing a series of laws in the 1970s that expanded the scope of federal government responsibility in disasters. For example, the Disaster Relief Act of 1974 (Public Law 93–288) created a program that provided direct assistance to individuals and families following a disaster (Sylves, 2020, p. 97). The act also gave the president the power to declare an emergency as well, whereas previously only a major disaster could be declared. The 1974 law's "emergency" language was superseded by the Stafford Act of 1988, which conveyed broader authority to the president:

Emergency: Any occasion or instance for which, in the determination of the president, federal assistance is needed to supplement state and local efforts and capabilities to save lives and to protect property and public health and safety, or to lessen or avert the threat of catastrophe in any part of the United States.

(U.S. Code of Federal Regulations, Title 44, 206.35, 2020b)

Generally, an emergency is often of less magnitude and scope than a major disaster. However, the president may issue an emergency declaration to address an ongoing event that may later be declared a major disaster.

The DRA of 1974 also called on the president to:

- Establish a program of disaster preparedness using the services of all appropriate federal agencies;
- Make grants for the development of plans and programs for disaster preparedness and prevention;
- Declare a major disaster at the request of a governor (reaffirming the DRA of 1950);
- Make contributions to state or local governments to help repair or reconstruct public facilities;
- Make grants to help repair or reconstruct non-profit educational, utility, emergency, and medical and custodial care facilities;
- Purchase or lease temporary housing, and provide temporary mortgage or rent payment assistance;
- Provide assistance to people unemployed as a result of the disaster;
- Provide additional relief, including food coupons and commodities, relocation assistance, legal services, and crisis counseling;
- Make grants to a state in order for the state to provide grants to individuals and families if assistance otherwise provided by the act is inadequate; and
- Make loans to local governments suffering a substantial loss of tax and other revenues (National Low Income Coalition, 2014).

Additionally, the Robert T. Stafford Disaster Relief and Emergency Assistance Act of 1988 (Public Law 100–707), approved under President Reagan (Lindsay, 2017b), significantly updated and revamped the DRA of 1950 in other ways. Stafford broadened the president's authority to issue major disaster declarations and added new or improved types of federal disaster assistance:

■ General federal assistance for technical and advisory aid and support to state and local governments to facilitate the distribution of consumable supplies;

■ Essential assistance from federal agencies to distribute aid to victims through state and local governments and voluntary organizations, perform lifesaving and property-saving assistance, clear debris, and use resources of the U.S. Department of Defense before a major disaster or emergency declaration is issued;

■ Hazard mitigation grants to reduce risks and damages that might occur in future disasters;

■ Federal facilities repair and reconstruction; and

■ Repair, restoration, and replacement of damaged facilities owned by state and local governments, as well as private non-profit facilities that provide essential services or commodities (Lindsay, 2017b; FEMA, 2017a).

The Stafford Act also tasked the federal government, most particularly FEMA, with these obligations:

■ Revising and broadening the scope of existing disaster relief programs;

■ Encouraging the development of comprehensive disaster preparedness and assistance plans, programs, capabilities, and organizations by the states and by local governments;

■ Achieving greater coordination and responsiveness of disaster preparedness and relief programs;

■ Encouraging individuals, states, and local governments to protect themselves by obtaining insurance coverage to supplement or replace governmental assistance;

■ Encouraging hazard mitigation measures to reduce losses from disasters, including development of land-use and construction regulations; and

■ Providing federal assistance programs for both public and private losses sustained in disasters (FEMA, 2007).

The Stafford Act furnishes federal post-disaster relief assistance under fixed dollar limits and means-testing of relief for applicants, under FEMA's Individuals and Households Program. Stafford also maintained federal to state and local government assistance: FEMA's Public Assistance Program. In addition, the legal indistinctiveness of the federal definition of emergency has allowed presidents, often guided or encouraged by FEMA officials, to add new categories of emergency. Unclear eligibility for federal disaster assistance programs and vagueness of criteria pose serious problems for applicants but offer opportunities for FEMA officials to expand the agency's jurisdiction.

The Sandy Recovery Improvement Act of 2013 (P.L. 113–2) "authorizes the chief executive of a tribal government to directly request major disaster or emergency declarations from the President, much as a governor can do for a state" (Brown, McCarthy, & Liu, 2013). Under the Stafford Act, "tribes were dependent on a request being made by the governor of the state in which their territory is located" (Brown et al., 2013). Tribal government leaders maintained that this requirement undermined tribal independence and sovereignty keeping them from obtaining needed assistance. Moreover, some tribal lands overlap state borders. The Sandy Recovery Act of 2013 made tribal governments the equivalents of state governments. Governors are still free to add major disaster or emergency impacted tribal lands (as local governments) in their respective state requests for presidential declarations. The benefit for tribal governments is that in the past it has been difficult for many state emergency management officials to assess disaster damage on tribal lands owing to language and cultural differences as well as to the physical isolation of many tribal areas and reservations. The new law includes a section that allows the president to waive the non-federal contribution or to adjust the cost share to a more generous match for tribal governments under the FEMA Public Assistance program (Brown et al., 2013). All of these provisions expanded the pool of potential disaster declaration requestors, again investing DHS-FEMA with more authority, potentially larger budgets, and broadened responsibly.

The "Process" Followed in Requesting Presidential Declarations

Again, the Stafford Act (§ 401) requires that "all requests for a declaration by the President that a major disaster exists shall be made by the Governor of the affected State." State equivalents include the District of Columbia, Puerto Rico, the Virgin Islands, Guam, American Samoa, and the Commonwealth of the Northern Mariana Islands. The Marshall Islands and the Federated States of Micronesia are also eligible to request a declaration and receive assistance. Only governors, or, in the absence of the governor, the lieutenant governor, can request presidential declarations of major disaster or emergency. Sub-state executives (e.g., mayors, county executives, city managers) seeking presidential declarations must ask for them through their governor and appropriate state offices. Legislators at any level can lobby the president to confer declarations, but all legislators are outside the official request process.

In Figure 17.1, the Texas Department of Public Safety, Division of Emergency Management charts the general pathway followed in the declaration process; the process may slightly vary within other states.

The governor's request is made through the state's respective regional FEMA office. FEMA's ten regions are co-incident with the standard 10 federal regional model used by many federal entities. State and federal officials conduct a preliminary damage assessment (PDA) to estimate the extent of the disaster and its impact on individuals and public facilities. This information is included in the governor's request to show that the disaster is of such severity and magnitude that effective response is beyond the capabilities of their state and respective local governments and that federal assistance is necessary (DHS-OIG, 2012). Normally, the PDA is completed prior to the submission of the governor's request; however, when an obviously severe or catastrophic event occurs, the governor's request may be submitted prior to the PDA. Nonetheless, the governor must still make the request.

Based on the governor's request, the president may declare that a major disaster or emergency exists, activating an array of federal programs to assist in response and recovery. Not all programs are activated for every disaster. Though seemingly a presidential duty, FEMA fundamentally decides which programs are activated for each incident based on the needs identified in the damage assessment and in related information (DHS-OIG, 2012). Here again, FEMA's role in disaster management consistently grows over time. Some declarations will provide only Individual Assistance or only Public Assistance. Since 1988, FEMA hazard mitigation funding has also been made available to states, and their respective localities, with most of this

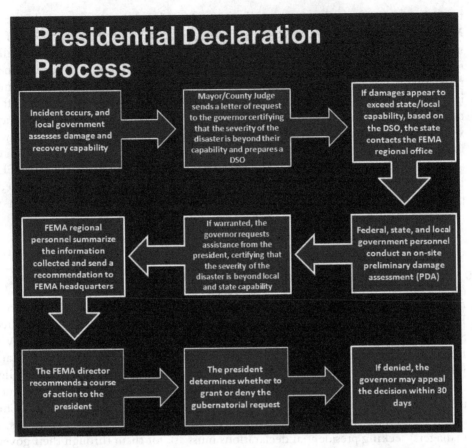

FIGURE 17.1 The Presidential Declaration Process. In the chart, a DSO is a Disaster Summary Outline, a document that local organizations need to submit under the Texas declarations process.
Source: Texas DPS (2015, as cited in Sylves, 2020, p. 141).

modest funding devoted to pre-approved mitigation projects submitted by the recipient state. Consequently, FEMA has staked out duties through every category of the conventional disaster model: mitigation, preparedness, response, and recovery.

Governors almost always consult their respective state emergency management officials before requesting a presidential declaration. The governor may authorize a state-level PDA if state officials are not already assessing damage. Sometimes, if the disaster appears to be beyond state and local response capacity, the governor can ask FEMA to join state and local personnel in conducting a PDA. Due to the vagueness of the criteria FEMA officials use to judge governor requests to the president, plus each governor's keen awareness that under federal law the president can disregard any FEMA recommendation to deny a major disaster request which fails to meet the agency's criteria, governors must contemplate whether to request presidential declarations in an uncertain environment. They can consider previous presidential approvals and turndowns as precedents. They can plead for elevated "need" owing to other disasters the state may have suffered recently. They can gauge the degree of newsworthiness their state's calamity has drawn. However, should their request for a presidential declaration be denied, there is very little "downside" for any governor. They are more likely to suffer criticism if they failed to ask for a declaration, no matter how marginal their case (Sylves, 2014, pp. 44–47; see also McCarthy, 2007).

Governors, in requesting emergency declarations (EMs), only have to demonstrate that federal assistance is needed to save lives, protect property and public health, or lessen or avert the threat of catastrophe. This is a much lower bar to clear than when a governor seeks a major declaration (DR). As such, governors appreciate presidential declarations of emergency because they supply federal funds and other assistance quickly, and often furnish help when the full scope of the emergency or disaster is either not yet understood or is still unfolding. However, the range of assistance provided under emergency declarations is much more limited and much less generous than under major disaster declarations.

The Federal Emergency Management Agency Director/Administrator

Pre-FEMA (1950–1979) agencies, the independent agency FEMA (1979–2003), and the DHS-FEMA (2003–present) deserve attention. The FEMA director/administrator is a politically appointed official who is likely to be personally selected by the president. Various FEMA directors, administrators, or undersecretaries serving through the years have helped shape the agency; impacted the morale of rank-and-file federal disaster workers; built up trained and experienced cadres of federal coordinating officers; advanced the practice and study of emergency management; and represented their respective agency before the president, Congress, and the American public.

Table 17.1 lists appointed and Senate-confirmed FEMA directors (1979–2003) or DHS-FEMA administrators/undersecretaries (2003–present). The table does not

TABLE 17.1 FEMA Directors and Administrators, 1979–2020, With Appointing President

FEMA Directors/Administrators and Period in Office	Federal Organization	Appointing President
John Macy, August 1979 to January 1981*	FEMA	James E. Carter
Louis O. Giuffrida, May 1981 to September 1985	FEMA	Ronald R. Reagan
Julius W. Becton Jr., November 1985 to June 1989	FEMA	Ronald R. Reagan
Wallace E. Stickney, August 1990 to January 1993	FEMA	George H.W. Bush
James L. Witt, April 1993 to January 2001	FEMA	William J. Clinton
Joseph M. Allbaugh, February 2001 to March 2003	FEMA	George W. Bush
Michael D. Brown, March 2003 to September 2005	DHS-FEMA	George W. Bush
R. David Paulison, September 2005 to January 2009	DHS-FEMA	George W. Bush
Nancy Ward (acting), January 2009 to May 2009**	DHS-FEMA	Barack H. Obama
W. Craig Fugate, May 2009 to January 2017	DHS-FEMA	Barack H. Obama
Robert Fenton (acting), January 2017 to June 2017**	DHS-FEMA	Donald J. Trump
W. Brock Long, June 2017 to March 2019	DHS-FEMA	Donald J. Trump
Peter T. Gaynor, March 2019 and confirmed January 2020**	DHS-FEMA	Donald J. Trump

Note: * Does not include acting directors/administrators before 2009. ** Includes acting directors/administrators as of 2009.

Source: Sylves (2020, p. 143)

include the names and terms of "acting FEMA" heads who were temporary appointees before 2009, but it does include those after 2009. Most FEMA directors or administrators were experienced emergency management professionals of some type before their nomination and Senate confirmation. From Table 17.1, Macy, Witt, Paulison, Ward (acting), Fugate, Fenton (acting), Long, and Gaynor all had pre-appointment emergency management experience. A few FEMA directors had military careers but no emergency management experience: Giuffrida and Becton. Others were largely political patronage appointees with no emergency management expertise: Stickney, Allbaugh, and Brown. Several FEMA leaders have vigorously advanced presidentially approved reforms within the agency, Witt foremost. Macy deserves credit for standing up the agency in a professional and non-partisan manner. Paulison and Fugate, though each served very different presidents, steered FEMA back to cohesiveness, reputability, and professional competence (after Hurricane Katrina) but under the constraints of the U.S. Department of Homeland Security.

The head of FEMA is in effect the chief executive officer of the agency, although some who have been appointed to the post have been satisfied in delegating day-to-day management to the deputy administrator. Under the Post-Katrina Emergency Management Reform Act of 2006 (P.L. 109–295) (PKEMRA), the FEMA administrator has been given a more direct line of access to the president, albeit with expected consultation of the DHS Secretary, during periods of disaster response and when carrying out his or her responsibility to help in the processing of emergency and major disaster declaration requests submitted by governors. PKEMRA pulled parts of FEMA that had been shunted into other areas of DHS back into the agency. The authority of the FEMA administrator was reinvigorated, though accountability to overhead DHS officials continued.

Secretary, Department of Homeland Security

DHS is a behemoth. Under the Homeland Security Act of 2002, the Cabinet-level department absorbed many federal entities, including FEMA. Its ever-growing federal workforce stood at 190,000 at its start but is rapidly approaching a quarter million (DHS, 2017, 2020a). The DHS secretary and deputy secretary are managerial supervisors of the FEMA administrator. The DHS secretary has authority to consult with the FEMA administrator and may be shown the White House Package containing a governor's declaration request and other information compiled by FEMA, the respective state, and its localities.

Today, when health and safety is threatened, and a disaster is imminent but not yet declared, the secretary of the DHS may position or "surge" department employees and supplies before an event. DHS monitors the status of the circumstances, communicates with state emergency officials on potential assistance requirements, deploys teams and resources to maximize the speed and effectiveness of the anticipated federal response, and, when necessary, performs preparedness and PDA activities (DHS, 2020b; Bea, 2020). In the aftermath of a succession of great disasters, when FEMA's workforce is hugely challenged, DHS may turn to its Surge Capacity Force. The Surge Capacity Force is made up of volunteer federal employees from within DHS outside of FEMA and from almost every federal department or agency that sends volunteers. In 2017, after Hurricanes Harvey, Irma, and Maria inflicted great damage and hardship, then Acting Secretary of Homeland Security Elaine Duke activated the Surge Capacity Force deploying its federal volunteers to support disaster survivors in Texas, Florida, Puerto Rico, and the U.S. Virgin Islands (DHS, 2020b). The Surge Capacity Force has also helped build a positive public image for both DHS and FEMA.

Path and Content of Governor Requests and FEMA's Criteria of Qualification

Typically, the route of a governor's request starts with the respective state's FEMA Region director, who receives the request, reviews it, and sends a recommendation to FEMA headquarters in Washington. There, a declaration processing unit prepares documents pertaining to the request, and the head of FEMA, after compiling information for the president about the event and, often, consulting with the governor who has requested the declaration, adds a memorandum recommending to the president a course of action: approve or reject. All the information FEMA sends to the president, including the director's recommendation, is protected by rules of executive privilege and therefore unavailable for public scrutiny. The president is neither bound by FEMA's recommendation nor obligated to follow the agency's declaration criteria. The president alone determines whether to approve or reject every governor's request. However, there is little evidence that recent or past presidents have ignored FEMA's state declaration criteria.

In truth, many states with intermediate to low populations have found FEMA's declaration criteria easy to meet, as it is based on state per capita disaster losses compared against a FEMA preset state per capita loss threshold. It is high population states that must generate very large losses to exceed the threshold (Sylves, 2020, p. 43). Moreover, some common factors FEMA officials consider before they make their recommendation are:

- The number of homes destroyed or sustaining major damage;
- The extent to which damage is concentrated or dispersed;
- The estimated cost of repairing the damage;
- The demographics of the affected area; and
- State and local governments' response and recovery capabilities.

Overall, the Stafford Act does not prescribe exact criteria to guide FEMA recommendations or the president's decision. As a prerequisite to federal disaster assistance, a governor must take "appropriate action" and provide information on the nature and amount of state and local resources committed to alleviating the disaster's impacts. Other relevant considerations include the following:[1]

- The demographics of the affected areas with regard to income levels, unemployment, concentrations of senior citizens, and the like;
- The degree to which insurance covers the damage;
- The degree to which people in the disaster area have been "traumatized";
- The amount of disaster-related unemployment the event has produced;
- The amount of assistance available from other federal agencies, such as the SBA and its disaster loans to homeowners and businesses;
- The extent to which state and local governments are capable of dealing with the disaster on their own;
- The amount of disaster assistance coming from volunteer organizations and the adequacy of that assistance given the magnitude of the disaster;

- The amount of rental housing available for emergency occupancy;
- The nature and degree of health and safety problems posed by the disaster and its effects; and
- The extent of damage to essential service facilities, such as utilities and medical, police, and fire services (Sylves, 2020, pp. 144–145).

Finally, FEMA also evaluates the impacts of a disaster at the county, local government, and tribal levels. Along these lines, FEMA personnel consider:

- Whether critical facilities are involved;
- How much insurance coverage is in force that could provide affected parties reimbursement for various losses;
- The degree of hazard mitigation a state or local government has undertaken prior to the disaster;
- Recent disaster history of the respective state and its localities; and
- The availability of federal assistance aside from that to be provided by a presidential declaration.

Factors that reduce the chances that a governor's request for a presidential declaration of major disaster or emergency will be approved are several. Obviously, major infrastructure loss and widespread or intense human suffering advances deservedness, whereas ample insurance coverage that helps alleviate loss and advance recovery diminishes worthiness. Presumably, when it can be shown that the requesting government(s) failed to take reasonable steps to prevent a minor incident from occurring, deservedness goes down.

Sometimes other federal agencies besides FEMA host disaster programs that may sufficiently address the needs of the disaster in question, such that a presidential declaration of major disaster or emergency is unnecessary. Governors contemplating or formally in the process of filing requests for presidential declarations may be dissuaded from doing so by FEMA or White House officials. They may be advised that given the nature of their problem, other federal programs may provide help that is better suited to assist them (Sylves, 2014). For example, when the I-35W highway bridge collapsed incredibly in Minneapolis in August 2007, the Minnesota governor was advised that a presidential disaster declaration was unnecessary because the U.S. Department of Transportation, aided by the U.S. Army Corps of Engineers, the FBI, and other federal agencies, would make help and resources available such that a presidential disaster declaration was duplicative and so unwarranted (Cook, 2009).

When a governor seeks a presidential declaration for an incident that does not conform to standard eligibility requirements, FEMA may recommend to the president that the governor's request be denied. Presidents regularly turn down gubernatorial requests for major disasters or emergencies (Sylves, 2014). However, in rare cases, presidents approve requests for major disaster declarations when damage in the state is relatively light and the state may have been able to recover from the event without federal assistance (Sylves, 1996, pp. 33, 43; Miskel, 2008).

FEMA considers how the assessment of a state's capability compares with the costs imposed by the disaster. Each governor requesting a declaration is expected to demonstrate to FEMA and the president that the state is "unable to adequately respond to the disaster or emergency," of whatever nature, and that federal assistance is therefore needed. The "unable to adequately respond" condition is often highly controversial. Some governors claim that state budget limitations make it impossible for them to "adequately respond." Some offer that they do not have reserve funds sufficient to pay for the costs of the response.

Some governors have explained that their state has no disaster relief programs in law to match FEMA's, and so in the absence of a presidential declaration, many victims will be without government assistance. FEMA officials, and the president, may find it difficult to determine whether a state is "unable to adequately respond," drawing on their own state and local resources. It is possible that DHS-FEMA officials advising the president on whether to approve or reject a governor's request for a declaration of major disaster, may inform the president that the requesting state has not established state-funded disaster relief programs that parallel FEMA's programs when it could have. Weighing the merit of a request is often complicated by media coverage of the event, political pressures imposed on both FEMA officials and the president by legislators and other officials in the damage zone, and the difficulty of actually measuring state (and local) disaster response and recovery capacity.

Congress, FEMA, and the Record of Approvals and Turndowns Over Time

The U.S. Congress as an institution, and congressional lawmakers themselves, enter into the realm of disaster management in countless ways. When a disaster or emergency is threatened or is imminent, lawmakers representing jurisdictions in the threatened zone often press the president to mobilize federal help or issue a declaration of emergency. Some researchers have discovered in presidential library documents evidence that presidents considering a disaster declaration request submitted by a governor receive, as a matter of routine, a list of the names of the lawmakers whose districts are affected by a disaster event (Daniels & Clark-Daniels, 2000).

Senators and representatives often petition the president as an entire state delegation to confer a declaration. Moreover, lawmakers frequently contact the White House and FEMA about matters of disaster or emergency. Sometimes individual legislators seek audiences with the president or with White House staff to press for federal help. Some call FEMA officials to House or Senate hearings, particularly when new legislation is in the works, when oversight is conducted, or when investigations are underway.

FEMA has many overseers within Congress. Before FEMA was folded into the DHS, it had a wide variety of House and Senate committees and subcommittees with jurisdiction over its programs in whole or in part. Since FEMA entered the DHS, Congress has reorganized these committees such that there is now a House Committee on Homeland Security. Moreover, the former Senate Governmental Affairs Committee elected to expand its title to become the Committee on Homeland Security and Governmental Affairs. However, many of the federal agencies folded into DHS retain their traditional jurisdiction and so retain their original House and Senate committee and subcommittee overseers, the majority of which are not also members of the House or Senate homeland security committees. This significantly complicates management of DHS units and risks muddled congressional oversight (Mycoff, 2007, pp. 16–30).

On top of this, some researchers allege that presidential and congressional political considerations affect "the rate of disaster declaration" conferral and the allocation of FEMA disaster expenditures across states (Garrett & Sobel, 2003, pp. 496–509). A few researchers have shown that states electorally essential to the president have relatively higher rates of disaster declaration request approvals than other states. They have also claimed that federal disaster relief expenditures are relatively larger in states having congressional representation on FEMA oversight committees than in states unrepresented on FEMA oversight committees. Remarkably, one pair of political economists posited a congressional dominance model, which posits that nearly half of all disaster relief is motivated politically rather than by need (Garrett & Sobel, 2003, pp. 496–509). The same researchers assert that there is a possibility that political influence may affect the outcome of gubernatorial requests for presidential disaster declarations at two distinct stages: during the initial decision whether to declare a disaster and in the decision of how much money to allocate for the disaster (Garrett & Sobel, 2003, p. i). Here they assume that bureaus, like FEMA, follow congressional preferences and that the responsible congressional committees, FEMA's jurisdictional overseers, make sure that they do so. Here legislators are assumed to behave as wealth maximizers seeking to direct federal resources to their home states or districts (Reeves, 2009, pp. 1–10).

There are other researchers who insist that differences in major disaster declaration approval rates between presidential and non-presidential election years is slight and statistically insignificant. Sylves and Buzas quantitatively calculate that approval rates for major disaster (DR) and emergency (EM) requests only show slight upturns in the months before an incumbent president seeks re-election, and then only in battleground states of relatively high electoral vote value (2007, pp. 3–15). Lindsay shows that from 1974 to 2016, turndowns in non-presidential election years average 16.0 per year, which is an average of 25.3% of all DR and EM requests. In the same interval, for presidential election years, Lindsay shows that turndowns drop to 14.5 per year for all DR and EM requests in the interval (2017b). These small differences may not be significant enough for one to draw political inferences. Whenever the president–governor nexus is considered, one must keep in mind that governors have their own motives, just as presidents do. It may well be that governors of battleground states in presidential election years when an incumbent president seeks re-election, exploit these circumstances by asking presidents to approve declarations for incidents on the cusp of approvability.

However, the political geography of declaration issuance demonstrates that the alleged FEMA effort to "reward legislators" (Reeve's congressional dominance model) who serve on the agency's authorizations or appropriations oversight committees is both far-fetched and arguable. This is because the ultimate decision to approve or reject a governor's request for a declaration is made by the president, not by FEMA officials. In effect, FEMA officials can guide and advise in matters of presidential declaration decision-making, but the ultimate decision resides with the president. To prove Reeve's claim of FEMA legislative bias, one must demonstrate with statistically significant confidence that requests "turned down" can be directly attributed to a bias against lawmakers (and their respective states and districts) by FEMA officials discriminating on the basis of committee membership. Given the ongoing decline in turndowns and the immense political risks FEMA officials would be taking by this behavior, one is hard-pressed to find evidence of Reeve's allegation. It is also difficult to prove this because the FEMA director's memorandum to the president is a matter of executive privilege and so is not open to public scrutiny.

In theory, presidents, on their own, may use their declaration discretion to reward or punish states that are the political homes of key legislators and/or to advance electoral strategies beneficial to themselves. Many suspect that presidents favor their fellow party members on Capitol Hill. Moreover, presidents might be expected to help political actors they judge to be important (Sylves & Buzas, 2007). The president could use his declaration power to punish or reward governors themselves. He may also want to "simply tarnish the image of opposing party governors or legislators in hopes thus undermining their reelection chances" (Garrett & Sobel, 2003, p. 4). However, these claims are mere speculation. Any president's personal or political biases are likely to be evident in how a president, and the White House, choose to use publicity, photo opportunities, and public relations in their dealings with elected officials from states and districts impacted by the event. It is not likely to be evident in their decision to approve or reject a governor's declaration request. Those who are fixated on approvals and turndowns as a function of FEMA's Public Assistance per capita threshold criterion tend to overlook the strong possibility that presidents may make judgments of deservedness based on their perception the human suffering (the number of deaths and injuries, no-notice or high speed of onset tragedies, characteristics of victims, intensity of news coverage, national implications of the incident, etc.) caused by the disaster or emergency.

Table 17.2 shows that a total of 789 turndowns (TDs) for major disasters and 131 TDs for emergencies were issued between May 1953 and August 2017. For all 12 presidents, Eisenhower to Trump, there was a 1 in 4 chance of a turndown of a governor request for a major disaster declaration, whereas there was only a slightly less than a 1 in 4 chance of turndown for a governor request for an emergency declaration. Table 17.2 reveals that pre-FEMA presidents Eisenhower, Kennedy, Johnson, Nixon, and Ford had, by modern standards, high rates of turndown on major disaster requests. Johnson rejected 53% and Nixon 53%. Eisenhower (34%), Kennedy (30%), and Ford (32%) as a group rejected about 3, or slightly more, requests of every 10 requests they received. Oddly, Carter, the president who championed FEMA's creation, rejected 45% of all the governor requests for major disaster declarations received. It may be that governors in the Carter years needed time to become accustomed to FEMA's evolving procedures. Curiously, Carter was tough on requests for major disasters but more generous in approving requests for emergencies (39% TD).

TABLE 17.2 Presidential Approvals and Turndowns of Governor Requests for Disaster Declarations, May 1953 Through December 2017

President	Time Span	Approvals			Turndowns			Turndown Percentage		
		Major[a]	Emerg[b]	Total	Major[c]	Emerg[d]	Total	Major	Emerg	Total
Eisenhower	5/2/53–1/21/61	106	0	106	55	0	55	34	0	34
Kennedy	1/21/61–11/20/63	52	0	52	22	0	22	30	0	30
Johnson	11/23/63–1/21/69	93	0	93	49	0	49	53	0	53
Nixon	1/21/69–8/5/74	195	1	196	102	15	117	52	94	37
Ford	8/5/74–1/21/77	76	23	99	35	7	42	32	23	30
Carter	1/21/77–1/21/81	112	59	171	91	37	128	45	39	43
Reagan	1/21/81–1/21/89	184	9	193	96	16	112	34	64	37

(Continued)

TABLE 17.2 (Continued)

President	Time Span	Approvals			Turndowns			Turndown Percentage		
		Major[a]	Emerg[b]	Total	Major[c]	Emerg[d]	Total	Major	Emerg	Total
G.H.W. Bush	1/21/89–1/21/93	158	2	160	43	3	46	21	60	22
Clinton	1/21/93–1/21/01	380	68	448	103	13	116	21	16	21
G.W. Bush	1/21/01–1/21/09	458	140	598	89	28	117	16.3	16.6	16.4
Obama	1/21/09–1/20/17	476	79	555	96	12	108	16.7	13.1	16.2
Trump	1/20/17–11/20/17	54	15	69	8	N/A	N/A	N/A	N/A	N/A
Total		2344	396	2740	789	131	920	25.2	24.9	27.4

Note: Date of declaration checked for each administration to the day. Remember, turndown percentage is the number of turndowns as a percentage of total requests for the respective category, such that turndown requests and approval requests are summed in the calculation denominator.

[a] Represents approved presidential declarations of major disasters, which began in 1953. [b] Represents approved presidential declarations of emergencies. Emergency declarations began in 1974 [c] Represents president's turndown of a governor's request for a presidential declaration of major disaster. There is about a four-month turndown gap in the data for Obama years, and for Trump, turndown data were only available for his first 7 months in office – and this was for major disaster turndowns only. Little information about possible Trump turndowns of emergency requests has been made available to this author. [d] Represents president's turndown of a governor's request for a presidential declaration of emergency.

Sources: (a) and (b) FEMA, Declaration Information System (DARIS), June 1997, and Federal Emergency Management Information System (FEMIS), December 2001, Department of Homeland Security, Emergency Preparedness and Response Directorate; FEMA, DFSR Obligations Summary – Grouped by Event and Year, Reporting Cycle through January 2013, Automated DFSR Report Export to Excel, database compiled by Bruce Friedman, Manager CFO-FST; (c) and (d) DHS Justification of Estimates fiscal year 04, March 2003; 9/11/01–9/22/05 turndown data: Sen. Thomas R. Carper, D-DE, to author. FEMA, Turndowns of Major Disaster and Emergency Governor Requests through December 2011, compiled by Dean Webster, February 14, 2012 (as cited in Sylves, 2020, p. 171).

Conversely, Reagan went easier on major requests, with a 34% TD rate, but was extremely tough on emergency requests, denying 64%. However, a "sea change" occurred in turndowns after 1988. Presidents from George H. W. Bush to Trump, as a group, turn down only about 1 in 5 requests for majors, with George W. Bush and Obama at very low rates of turndown (16.3% TD and 16.7% TD, respectively). Though the Trump turndown data is largely unavailable, what little is public shows that President Trump's turndown totals and percentages of requests parallel those of President Obama.

Figure 17.2 helps to portray the drop-off in turndown rates, major disaster, and emergency requests combined. Recall, "emergency declarations" were only made available to the president in 1974. Here again, there is a clear long-term trend in declining percentages of turndowns. Presidents George H. W. Bush, Clinton, George W. Bush, and Obama all have lower rates of turndown than the seven presidents that preceded them. Johnson, Nixon, Carter, and Reagan show higher turndown rates

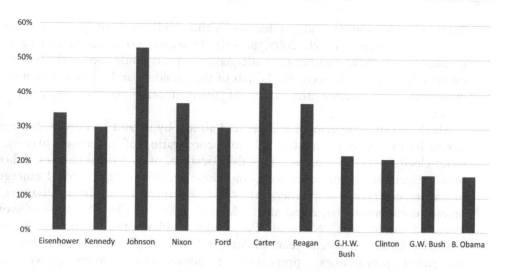

FIGURE 17.2 Turndowns as a Percentage of Total DR and EM Requests: Eisenhower to Obama
Source: Chart composed by author from Table 17.2.

than any of the other presidents who served between 1953 and 2016. When numbers of major disaster declarations are considered for full two-term presidents, Eisenhower shows 106, Reagan has 184, Clinton 380, George W. Bush 458, and Obama 476. As of July 10, 2020, President Trump had approved some 263 major disaster declarations requests since his inauguration in January 2017. This pace of disaster request (DR) issuance exceeds the DR approval pace for all previous one-term presidents. President Obama's 8-year DR approval total stands at 476, so simply dividing it in half yields 238 DRs. Trump, who was more than six months away from the end of his original term of office on July 10, 2020, had already approved 25 more DRs than Obama did, if Obama's 8-year total is divided by two. Over his two terms, Obama approved more DRs than any president to date. These figures show a very substantial rate of increase even given the time span considered. Another way to consider change over time is that from May 1953 to January 1993 – a span of just under 40 years – a total of 976 major declarations were issued. From January 1993 to November 2017 – a little less than 25 years – 1,368 majors were approved.

For example, President Trump, in office only some six months, had to confront three successive massively destructive hurricanes: Harvey in the greater Houston area of Texas, Irma along a south to north line of peninsular Florida, and Maria, which carved a path of mass destruction across the heart of the Island of Puerto Rico and seriously impacted the U.S. Virgin Islands. Most extraordinary for the Trump administration was the outbreak of the novel coronavirus, a disease estimated to be at least 10 times worse than common and anticipated seasonal viruses. Dubbed COVID-19, the rapidly spreading disease, communicable even from those who have it but show no symptoms, required many state governors to impose lockdowns under which those in non-essential occupations were required to self-isolate in their homes. At this writing, well over 500,000 Americans have so far died in the pandemic, with fatalities in every state.

There is a tendency among policymakers to be influenced by, if not fixated upon, the last most memorable disaster or catastrophe. Certain disasters or catastrophes not only stress the nation's disaster management system but also force massive reforms that produce a new normal in the domain of disaster policy and homeland security (Kettl,

2014). FEMA, whether independent or within DHS, is fairly good at managing "routine" disasters (Miskel, 2008, p. 141). However, no single federal agency is invested with sufficient authority to adequately or proficiently cope with an expansive catastrophe or crisis. It becomes the job of the president and administration staff to orchestrate and oversee the work of many federal agencies in catastrophic circumstances.

Much of this management is delegated almost by default to FEMA. Such work has to be carried out with the help and cooperation of governors, mayors, and other elected executives as well as with officials of other federal entities. A host of other players are involved as well, and these include state and local emergency managers, emergency responders, non-profit organizations active in disasters, and private corporations large and small (Miskel, 2008, p. 23). This type of work is expected under the National Preparedness Plan, the National Response Framework, and in recent years under the "five suites" of national frameworks: mitigation, preparedness, prevention, response, and recovery (Sylves, 2020, pp. 286–288).

Finally, the process and criteria of disaster declaration has allowed each president considerable discretion to address a wide range of events and circumstances. Beyond the annual statewide and county per capita damage thresholds set by FEMA to advise the president, governors and their state disaster officials have little to guide them in estimating whether to go ahead with a request for presidential declaration of major disaster or emergency. They have little basis for concluding in advance whether their petition for a presidential declaration will be approved or denied.

However, regarding FEMA public assistance, as long as a governor or other state officials know that the state and its localities can afford to shoulder the 25% share of the 75/25 federal aid formula contained in a presidential disaster declaration, they have an incentive to request a federal declaration. The system tempts governors and local authorities to "cry poor" in petitioning for federal help through underestimating their own ability to address and recover from the disaster.

Those who argue for reducing presidential discretion in the review of governors' requests for disaster declarations often point to the disaster declaration systems used by Canada and Australia. Canadian provinces and Australian states and territories rely less upon federal assistance during disasters than do U.S. states. In Canada and Australia (nations with federal systems), "there is no requirement for an explicit disaster declaration" by the prime minister and "the decision to authorize federal reimbursement is essentially automatic" (Miskel, 2008, pp. 114–117). Canadian provinces and Australian states and territories must pay out sums in disaster relief that exceed certain deductible levels before they qualify for their respective nation's federal assistance. It should be noted that the provinces, states, and some territories of these two nations are expected to shoulder the brunt of disaster management and relief duties, in service to their local governments (Miskel, 2008, pp. 114–117).

The "Programs" of Federal Emergency Management

Once the president approves a disaster declaration or emergency request there are two broad programs for which victims, organizations, and governments may become eligible: Public Assistance (PA) and the Individual and Households Programs (IHP).

FEMA's Public Assistance Program

The Public Assistance Program of FEMA provides grants to state and local governments and certain non-profit entities to help them in their response to, and recovery from, disasters (FEMA Public Assistance Fact Sheet, 2019). PA provides 75% of the funding for debris removal, emergency protective measures, and permanent restoration of infrastructure. Eligible PA applicants include state governments, local governments, and any other political subdivision of the state; Native American tribes; and Alaska Native villages.

FEMA may also add counties to an already in-force presidential disaster declaration without the need for presidential pre-approval. In such cases, if any county is to be added to an in-force major disaster declaration, the county's disaster per capita loss figure should meet or exceed the FEMA county per capita loss threshold. When this happens, FEMA "recommends that the president" issue an approval designating the county as eligible for assistance; this is a pro forma action such that the president need not be involved (Sylves, 2020, p. 147).

Certain private non-profit organizations may also receive assistance. Eligible private non-profits include educational, utility, emergency, medical, temporary or permanent custodial care facilities (including those for the aged and disabled), irrigation, museums, zoos, community centers, libraries, homeless shelters, senior centers, rehabilitation, shelter workshops and health and safety services, and other private non-profit facilities, including houses of worship, that provide essential services of a governmental or quasi-governmental nature to the general public. It also extends to public-serving horticultural institutions as well as sports and recreational stadiums and other types of facilities. FEMA's PA Program process is depicted in the diagram of Figure 17.3.

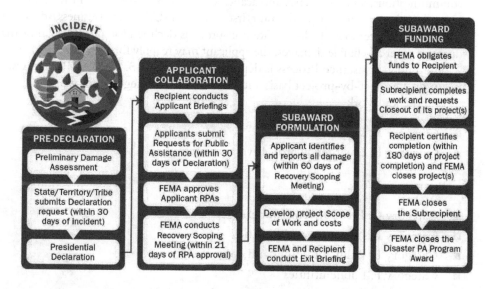

FIGURE 17.3 Process After a Presidential Disaster Declaration Is Conferred That Includes Public Assistance Program Help to State and Local Governments and Eligible Organizations
Source: FEMA (2019).

FEMA examines the estimated cost of the assistance, using such factors as per capita damage totals of the requesting state. In federal fiscal year 2018, FEMA, under its Public Assistance program, used a figure of $1.46 per capita damage costs as an indicator that the disaster is of sufficient magnitude to warrant federal assistance. (FEMA, 2017b). This figure is adjusted annually based on changes in the Consumer Price Index. So, for example, in 2018, a state with a 2010 U.S. Census population of about 1 million (Montana or Rhode Island, for example) has to demonstrate that it has experienced damage costs (not covered by insurance) that meet or exceed $1,460,000 to crack FEMA's threshold of qualification. Remember, as ever, presidents are not bound by FEMA's criteria when they consider governor requests for major disaster declarations. Moreover, these must be eligible damages to public infrastructure and facilities, including public or privately owned utilities and eligible non-profit organizations. As stated, by law FEMA assistance cannot duplicate or replace what is covered by private insurance and all private insurance claims are supposed to be settled before FEMA cash assistance is dispensed.

Under a Trump administration initiative, as of January 2, 2018, FEMA now provides public assistance to "Houses of Worship," on grounds that they are community centers (FEMA, 2018a). Community centers have long been eligible for public assistance. Churches, synagogues, mosques, and other houses of worship before this change were only eligible for assistance to cover the costs they incurred in operating disaster shelters or relief sites on their grounds. The Trump policy change that opened Houses of Worship (HOWs) for public assistance program coverage was applied retroactively; HOWs could apply for PA if they sustained damage in an area covered by a federal disaster declaration after August 23, 2017 (FEMA, 2018a). This backdating allowed HOWs damaged by 2017's Hurricanes Harvey, Irma, and Maria, or from other declared disasters after that date, to apply for FEMA PA.

Private non-profits that provide "critical services" (power, water [including water provided by an irrigation organization or facility], sewer, wastewater treatment, communications, and emergency medical care) may apply directly to FEMA for a disaster grant. All other private non-profits must first apply to the U.S. Small Business Administration (SBA) for a disaster loan. If the private non-profit is declined for an SBA loan or the loan does not cover all eligible damages, the applicant may reapply for FEMA assistance.

The Public Assistance Process is depicted in Figure 17.3. FEMA's Public Assistance is run on a project-by-project basis and covers certain categories of work:

Emergency Work

- Category A: Debris removal
- Category B: Emergency protective measures

Permanent Work

- Category C: Road systems and bridges
- Category D: Water control facilities
- Category E: Public buildings and contents
- Category F: Public utilities
- Category G: Parks, recreational, and other items

This bulleted list of categories may appear to be mundane, but for many local government officials confronting a disaster response and recovery, these categories open a path to highly generous federal funding, even when such funds come with a state and local cost share, as they normally do. In many disasters, including floods, hurricanes, earthquakes, tornadoes, and severe storms, "debris removal" tops out as a government expense category. Repairing or restoring roads, bridges, water and wastewater systems, lifeline service utilities, public buildings and offices, and so on can run far into the millions. The FEMA PA program has even covered a variety of state and local COVID-19 pandemic-related costs. Those who closely examine federal "emergency" declarations will discover that FEMA PA is the primary form of post-disaster aid, and that under some emergency declarations, some but not all categories of PA apply.

FEMA's Assistance to Individuals and Households Program

FEMA's Individuals and Households Program provides financial help or direct services and in-kind aid to those who have necessary post-disaster expenses or serious needs they are unable to meet through other means (FEMA, 2013). The program also provides FEMA an additional mechanism through which to exercise its evolving jurisdiction and powers. Section 408 of the Stafford Act (42 U.S.C. 5174) stipulates that FEMA must annually adjust the maximum amount for assistance provided under the Individuals and Households Program (IHP). Under the IHP, eligible individual may apply for Housing Assistance (including temporary housing, repair, replacement, and semi-permanent or permanent housing construction) and Other Needs Assistance (including personal property and other items; FEMA, 2013, 2018c).

FEMA Individual Assistance goes directly to eligible individuals and families who have sustained losses due to declared disasters. Generally, applicants are told the following:

- Homeowners and renters in designated counties who sustained damage to their primary homes, vehicles, and personal property under a declared disaster may apply for disaster assistance.

- Disaster assistance may include grants to help pay for temporary housing to include rental and lodging expense, emergency home repairs, uninsured and underinsured personal property losses, and medical, dental, and funeral expenses caused by the disaster, along with other serious disaster-related expenses.

- Disaster assistance grants are not taxable income and will not affect eligibility for Social Security, Medicaid, medical waiver programs, welfare assistance, Temporary Assistance for Needy Families, food stamps, Supplemental Security Income, or Social Security Disability Insurance.

- Low-interest disaster loans from the SBA may be available for businesses of all sizes (including landlords), private non-profit organizations, and homeowners and renters. Low-interest disaster loans help fund repairs or rebuilding efforts and cover the cost of replacing lost or disaster-damaged real estate and personal property. Economic Injury disaster loans are available to businesses and private non-profits to assist with working capital needs as a direct result of the disaster (FEMA, 2018c).

Housing assistance is a sub-program of IHP. Various expenses left unreimbursed after insurance claims are settled may be eligible for FEMA assistance of some type. FEMA's temporary housing aid provides money successful applicants can use to rent a different place to live or for a temporary housing unit when rental properties are unavailable.

FEMA housing funds also pay for homeowners to repair damage from the disaster, damage that is not covered by insurance. The goal is to repair the home to a safe and functioning condition. FEMA may provide up to the IHP maximum for home repair ($33,300 in 2018 and $34,900 in 2020); then the homeowner may apply for an SBA disaster loan for additional repair assistance. FEMA will not pay to return a home to its condition before the disaster. In rare cases, FEMA may exceed the cap in paying to "replace" a totally demolished home. Semi-permanent or permanent housing is made available by FEMA in very unusual circumstances, in locations specified by FEMA, and where no other type of housing assistance is possible.

FEMA's Other Needs Assistance

The Other Needs Assistance (ONA) FEMA provision of the IHP provides grants for uninsured, disaster-related necessary expenses and serious needs. Assistance includes the following:

- Medical and dental expenses;
- Funeral and burial costs;
- Repair, cleaning, or replacement of:
  - Clothing
  - Household items (room furnishings, appliances)
  - Specialized tools or protective clothing and equipment required for the applicant's job
  - Necessary educational materials (computers, schoolbooks, supplies);
- Cleanup items (wet/dry vacuum, air purifier, dehumidifier) and fuel for primary heat source (heating oil, gas);
- Vehicles in need of repair or replacement due to damage by the disaster, or reimbursement of public transportation or other transportation costs;
- Moving and storage expenses related to the disaster (including storage or the return of property to a pre-disaster home);
- Other necessary expenses or serious needs (e.g., towing or setup or connecting essential utilities for a housing unit not provided by FEMA); and
- The cost of a National Flood Insurance Program (NFIP) group flood insurance policy to meet the flood insurance requirements (FEMA, 2017c).

Conditions and Limitations of Individuals and Households Program Assistance

Federal disaster-related laws and policies embody rules, conditions, evidence, time limits, applicant rights and protections, and appeal rights. For disaster victims who seek FEMA assistance, documentation may be one of FEMA's most detested requirements. Victims are often hard-pressed or unable to supply FEMA with all of the documents the government requires. Sometimes the lack of a single document makes the applicant ineligible for FEMA Individual and Household Assistance. Conversely, by law FEMA must ensure that its payments are substantiated and legitimate. Disasters often tempt some people to commit fraud, deception, or misrepresentation – all at the federal government's expense. After working a disaster, FEMA is regularly investigated by federal auditors, inspectors general, and congressional oversight committees. FEMA overpayments are grist for news media people. Moreover, FEMA is often excoriated when it demands that money it paid out to victims be paid back on grounds that it was inappropriately obtained or awarded by mistake.

Another limitation to this program is that repair and replacement assistance is provided as a one-time payment. Moreover, FEMA temporary housing assistance (or a manufactured housing unit) is provided for an initial period of 1, 2, or 3 months. To be considered for additional assistance, applicants must demonstrate that they have spent any previous FEMA assistance as instructed and must demonstrate their efforts to reestablish permanent housing. The maximum period for IHP assistance is 18 months, provided 3 months at a time (FEMA, 2017c). Sometimes Individual Assistance (IHP and ONA) closeout dates on a declaration are extended, but they eventually reach a termination date beyond which no more applications are accepted. This often requires people to run a gauntlet of application requirements over a relatively compressed time interval – something difficult for victims given their circumstances.

"Funding" Presidential Disaster Declarations

Both FEMA and lawmakers are key players when it comes to furnishing federal money for disaster relief. The president's Disaster Relief Fund (DRF; largely FEMA-managed funding) is the chief repository of spending authority to pay the federal share of disaster costs. The DRF is replenished by "no-year" appropriations monies. *No year* simply means that there is no time limit attached to the spending authority of an appropriation law. The fund carries over unspent budget authority from previous disasters and receives as well an annual congressional appropriation, though that installment is often insufficient to cover federal payouts for declared major disasters and emergencies in some federal fiscal years. The U.S. Congress has the power to approve emergency supplemental appropriations to recapitalize the fund, subject to a presidential signing or a veto override. Congress endeavors to never let the DRF exhaust its spending authority. Even if the fund's budget authority is exhausted, presidents are legally permitted to borrow money from the U.S. Treasury to continue to pay federal expenses for ongoing declared major disasters and emergencies (Bea, 2020, pp. 28–33).

Also, after the 9/11 attacks, Congress changed budgeting rules in the wake of that disaster; the DRF has been regularly replenished and ordinarily adequately funded (Lindsay, email to the author, May 9, 2018). This has worked to FEMA's advantage and it is another reason why the agency has mushroomed in importance.

Federal spending on disaster relief increases each decade by orders of magnitude. The Conservative Center for American Progress, drawing from annual federal departmental disaster spending records concluded that for fiscal years 2011 through 2013 inclusive, a total $136 billion in taxpayer funds, or "an average of nearly $400 per household," had been expended on disaster relief (Weiss & Weidman, 2013). The center article maintains that the federal Office of Management and Budget, as well as Congress, routinely underestimates federal disaster spending and so fails to budget adequate funds in advance of disaster, thus necessitating federal borrowing when budgeted funds are exhausted during a fiscal year (Weiss & Weidman, 2013). Federal disaster spending has, from 2017 through 2020, escalated dramatically.

As mentioned, once the president approves a governor's request for a declaration, it is the job of FEMA, not the president, to officially allocate relief funds to states, counties, and other eligible entities under specified conditions (i.e., damage assessment), laws, and rules – all subject to audit by a variety of government offices, including congressional organizations like the Governmental Accountability Office. FEMA spending on any single disaster is not capped beforehand. However, the president may use some political discretion when considering gubernatorial requests for low-damage, marginal incidents involving relatively modest relief funding.

This means the relationship is an "inverse one." In other words, the lower the federal payouts are for various declarations, the higher the probability that political considerations at the presidential level played a role in a president's approval of a declaration (Miskel, 2008, pp. 118–120). Nonetheless, FEMA and associated federal agencies are not pushing disaster relief money out of planes. People must apply for it, prove eligibility, document their losses, show that their insurance is not duplicating federal disaster relief, and submit to inspection and audit. State and local governments are expected to do even more than that in securing federal funds to repair infrastructure. State and local governments, in the absence of a federal matching cost waiver (rarely conferred), also must shoulder matching costs in rebuilding under disaster declarations.

Conversely, "politically driven, distributive politics" comes into play when governors and local public officials respond to disasters by attempting to exploit and maximize federal support to their jurisdictions, when in fact their jurisdictions have the ability to respond and recover without federal help. Here, state and local taxpayers unfairly gain at the national taxpayer's expense. On top of this, winning this undeserved federal aid helps to meet their political and constituent needs. These officials want to be re-elected and thus they wish to curry favor with their electorate by providing tangible benefits for which they can claim credit (Miskel, 2008, pp. 118–120). Elected local and state officials also attempt to shield their constituents from the costs of disaster response and recovery by funding these costs at the national level, thus diffusing the fiscal burden over the largest possible population and taking advantage of the federal government's easier borrowing powers (Miskel, 2008, p. 14). State and local government officials strive to conform to FEMA's criteria and conditions in order to secure as much federal funding as possible – a form of moral hazard. The more one can do to stack up eligible losses, the greater the probability that FEMA-dispensed aid will flow commensurately.

In the economics of declaration decision-making, there is a two-track dilemma in president–governor relations. In economic parlance, the first track involves the issues of "ability to pay" and "willingness to pay." If a state is judged "able to pay" (afford) the costs of its disaster response and recovery costs, should the governor's request then be denied by the president with concurrence by FEMA? Here, the grounds for a turndown may be that the state (and its disaster-impacted localities) has an ability to recover using its own resources but an unwillingness to pay these costs. However, structural problems may impede a state's ability to pay (e.g., state balanced budget requirements, restrictions on state borrowing, inability to raise taxes sufficiently quickly to pay for disaster costs). States with an inability to pay must be differentiated from those states able to pay but unwilling to do so.

The second track involves human need (beyond dollar costs), governmental compassion, and astute behavior by elected officials who desire a positive political and electoral future. Need-based declaration decisions, ones that meet established rules and proven qualification, are fundamental administrative, rather than political, determinations. Also, to use economic language, in order to prevent disasters from having negative economic spillover effects in other places and to ensure that all state and local governments possess emergency management capability that is at least consistent with a national minimum standard, the federal government can and does promote state and local emergency management through grants dispensed after disasters and between disasters. Federal disaster policy aims to "sustain or restore a community's pre-disaster condition, not to alter the distribution of wealth."

Conclusion

"People look to the President for reassurance, a feeling that things will be all right, that the President will take care of his people" (Barber, 1995, p. 204). This is a crucial management responsibility for presidents. As the nation has come to face increasing numbers, wider varieties, and often relatively larger-scale disasters and emergencies, changes in law seem to have given presidents more latitude in deciding what actually constitutes an emergency. Also, the line between what is and what is not a Stafford Act–type incident is getting blurred. Presidents appear to be issuing declarations for non–Stafford Act incidents and using the Disaster Relief Fund to pay for them. All of this works to the advantage of FEMA, most especially in terms of jurisdiction over the "plumbing" through which so many federal dollars flow.

This chapter explored presidential declarations of major disaster and emergency, and FEMA's accompanying programs, as instruments by which to analyze the institutionalization of FEMA (1979–2003) and DHS-FEMA (2003–present). The chapter considered practices, processes, leaders, programs, presidential power, politics, and public money. The theory engine behind this exercise was historical institutionalism, an approach that allows the introduction of factual findings that may or may not be based on statistical analysis. Federal emergency management in presidential declaration terms is now 70 years on. FEMA's role in building, shaping, and influencing that process began in 1979 and is at this writing a mature 42 years old. FEMA's "life" within the U.S. Department of Homeland Security today stands at nearly 19 years. There has been an ongoing progression in the institutionalization and professionalization of emergency management in the United States, across all levels of government, fueled by FEMA encouragement, U.S. academic interest, and the demands of public servants. However, under another track of institutionalization, FEMA today has morphed into an arm of national security under which both "emergency management" and "homeland security" coexist and overlap. In addition, as organizationally secure as FEMA seems, its long-term health and welfare is tied not to any single president, but rather to its perceived performance in the judgment of the president and lawmakers. If FEMA badly fails a president, especially in a great crisis or catastrophe, it may be subject to dissolution or subjugation.

In sum, according to proposition "a," FEMA has routinized and largely de-politicized disaster declaration request processing over time, which has increased its administrative power as a federal agency.

From 1950 to the present, the U.S. Congress both granted and tolerated ever-wider presidential discretion in deciding what constituted a declarable major disaster or emergency; the system has become more institutionalized and somewhat more political than lawmakers in 1950 ever expected. Also, in presidential judgments about the deservedness of governors' requests, the system tolerates a degree of subjectivity, but partisan bias is blunted by the wide range of elected officials operating as stakeholders in federal disaster management. FEMA does not benefit by promoting partisan politics. However, when serving presidents are open to its counsel, FEMA benefits institutionally, bureaucratically, and professionally. Ironically, the ever-expanding breadth of FEMA's jurisdiction has promoted a range of pillarization (federal–state–local), as more state and local agencies scamper to clone themselves into miniature homeland security and FEMA-like entities so as to better prove need for federal assistance and to advance a vital public interest.

Some presidents have created new categories of disaster type, thus setting precedents governors have been able to exploit in their quest for declarations and federal help. On top of this, the Disaster Relief Fund furnishes presidents a convenient pool of spending authority to pay the federal costs of major disasters and emergencies they choose to declare. Through all of this, FEMA and DHS-FEMA have had a vested institutional interest in broadening the range of disaster agent types that are presidentially declarable. FEMA has become so proficient in grant and contract management that, since the Post-Katrina Emergency Management Reform Act of 2006, it has become the major conduit through which many DHS grants, disaster-related or otherwise, have flowed to state and local governments. The number of interest groups eligible to receive FEMA disaster relief has continued to mushroom since FEMA was formed.

Thus, there is evidence to support proposition "c": FEMA has greatly expanded its authority and role as an institution by helping and encouraging modern presidents to broaden the range and variety of incidents declared as major disasters and emergencies.

There are those who posit that some governors and their state legislatures have created a type of "moral hazard" under which the respective state government intentionally under-funds, or rebuffs calls to establish a state rainy-day fund, so as to better convince FEMA and the president that the state "lacks" the financial resources to recover on its own from some misfortune. Some states forgo creating parallel FEMA disaster assistance programs because their governors and legislators believe they can then better argue "inability to respond and recover" when they request presidential declarations of major disaster. In the words of W. Brock Long, President Trump's first nominated and confirmed FEMA administrator:

> FEMA's ability to provide support in disasters builds on, and is subject to, the capacity of state, territorial, tribal and local governments. This is not a new lesson or challenge, but one that we are constantly reminded of. If the state, territorial, tribal and local governments are well resourced, well trained, and well organized, the effectiveness of FEMA's assistance is great. If, on the other hand, a state, territorial, tribal or local government is not well resourced, well trained, and well organized – either due to ineffective preparations or due to the significance of the disaster itself – FEMA can help, but the response may not be as quick or as effective as we would like it to be.
>
> (Long, 2018)

Tables and figures of this chapter serve to confirm proposition "b": FEMA's organizationally self-serving set of low-threshold disaster declaration qualifications for states has invited governors to request more declarations (DR and EM), thus gradually ballooning both the volume and variety of incidents presidents have approved for major disaster declarations.

In addition, each president's relationship with his or her top federal emergency manager influences how that president handles emerging disaster circumstances and governor requests for federal assistance. Since enactment of the PKEMRA of 2006, a law that required the president to nominate for FEMA administrator only candidates with previous emergency management experience, the agency has been led by a succession of highly experienced emergency managers.

The U.S. disaster declaration process is the "Main Street" of American emergency management. It is made necessary by American federalism; a complex marriage of federal, state, and local interdependencies; and by a quest for endurance, resilience, burden sharing, and human compassion. The system and process of presidential disaster declaration issuance has been profoundly shaped by FEMA's influence as a burgeoning institution. Today the agency has taken on so many duties and responsibilities, and it manages so much federal money, that it may ultimately become overwhelmed and subsequently disassembled. Many should not have been surprised that in early 2020, President Trump turned to FEMA as one of his go-to agencies in his response to COVID-19, using presidential disaster declarations as a response tool. Any future researcher studying U.S. emergency management would be wise to take into account FEMA's ever-expanding role in processing, executing, and funding presidential disaster declarations.

Note

1. Finding data in all, or even most, of these bulleted categories is extremely difficult. Some of this data may appear in a governor's formal request for a major disaster declaration. FEMA has, in recent years, begun posting governor declaration request letters. Visit OpenFEMA at https://www.fema.gov/about/reports-and-data/openfema to find FEMA datasets, program data, etc.

Further Readings

Capoccia, G., & Kelemen, R. D. (2007). The study of critical junctures: Theory, narrative, and counterfactuals in historical institutionalism. *World Politics, 59*(3), 341–369.

Comfort, L. K., Boin, A., & Demchak, C. C. (Eds.). (2010). *Designing resilience: Preparing for extreme events*. Pittsburgh: University of Pittsburgh Press.

Pierson, P. (2011). *Politics in time: History, institutions, and social analysis*. Princeton, NJ: Princeton University Press.

Pierson, P., & Skocpol, T. (2002). Historical institutionalism in contemporary political science. *Political Science: The State of the Discipline, 3*(1), 1–32.

Steinmo, S. (2008). Historical institutionalism. In D. della Porta & M. Keating (Eds.), *Approaches and methodologies in the social sciences: A pluralist perspective* (pp. 118–138). Cambridge: Cambridge University Press.

Sylves, R. T. (2020). *Disaster policy and politics* (3rd ed.). Thousand Oaks, CA: Sage.

References

Anderson, J. E. (1997). Policy implementation. In J. E. Anderson (Ed.), *Public policymaking: An introduction* (3rd ed., pp. 213–270). Boston: Houghton Mifflin.

Barber, J. D. (1995). Presidential character. In K. O'Connor (Ed.), *American government readings and cases* (p. 204). Boston: Allyn & Bacon.

Bea, K. (2020). The formative years: 1950–1978. In C.B. Rubin (Ed.), *Emergency management: The American experience* (3rd ed., pp. 81–111). New York: Routledge.

Brown, J.T., McCarthy, F.X., & Liu, E.C. (2013, March 11). *Analysis of the Sandy Recovery Improvement Act of 2013*. Washington, DC: U.S. Congressional Research Service, 7–5700, R42991.

Cook, A.H. (2009, August). Towards an emergency response report card: Evaluating the response to the I-35W Bridge collapse. *Journal of Homeland Security and Emergency Management, 6*(1).

Daniels, R.S., & Clark-Daniels, C.L. (2000). *Transforming government: The renewal and revitalization of the Federal Emergency Management Agency, 2000 presidential transition series*. Arlington, VA: Pricewaterhouse Coopers Endowment for the Business of Government.

Department of Homeland Security, Office of Inspector General. (2012, May). *Opportunities to improve FEMA's public assistance preliminary damage assessment process, OIG-12–79*. Retrieved July 13, 2020, from www.oig.dhs.gov/assets/Mgmt/2012/OIG_12-79_May12.pdf

Department of Homeland Security (DHS), U.S. (2017, September 17). *About DHS*. Retrieved May 3, 2018, from www.dhs.gov/about-dhs

DHS, U.S. (2020a). *About DHS*. Retrieved July 19, 2020, from www.dhs.gov/about-dhs

DHS, U.S. (2020b). *Surge capacity force*. Retrieved July 13, 2020, from www.dhs.gov/surge-capacity-force#:~:text=Training%20%26%20Technical%20Assistance-,Surge%20Capacity%20Force,response%20to%20a%20catastrophic%20disaster

Federal Emergency Management Agency [FEMA]. (2007). Robert T. Stafford Disaster Relief and Emergency Assistance Act, as amended, and related authorities. *Title I– Findings, Declarations and Definitions, 101*, 1. Retrieved February 4, 2014, from www.fema.gov/pdf/about/stafford_act.pdf

FEMA. (2013, October 3). *Assistance to individuals and households fact sheet*. Retrieved February 5, 2014, from https://www.fema.gov/public-assistance-local-state-tribal-and-non-profit/recovery-directorate/assistance-individuals-and

FEMA. (2017a, May 3). *FEMA hazard mitigation grants: 404 and 406, FS 001*. Retrieved May 6, 2018, from www.fema.gov/news-release/2017/05/03/4309/fema-hazard-mitigation-grants-404-and-406

FEMA. (2017b, October 11). *Public assistance per capita impact indicator and project thresholds*. Retrieved June 7, 2018, from www.fema.gov/public-assistance-indicator-and-project-thresholds

FEMA. (2017c, February 2). *What is FEMA's individual assistance?* Retrieved July 22, 2020, from www.fema.gov/disaster/4294-4297/updates/fact-sheet-what-femas-individual-assistance-program

FEMA. (2018a, January 26). Public assistance: Private non-profit houses of worship. *Fact Sheet*. Retrieved April 30, 2018, from www.fema.gov/media-library-data/1518794956930-8c2ade230f1a98b484895cacf63c1940/PublicAssistancePrivateNonprofitHousesofWorshipFAQ1.pdf

FEMA. (2018b). *The declaration process*. Retrieved May 6, 2018, from www.fema.gov/declaration-process

FEMA. (2018c, January 15). *Understanding individual assistance and public assistance*. Retrieved April 30, 2018, from www.fema.gov/news-release/2018/01/15/understanding-individual-assistance-and-public-assistance

FEMA. (2019c, March 6). *Public assistance program overview*. Retrieved July 22, 2020, from www.fema.gov/media-library/assets/images/177662

FEMA. (2020a, June 8). *COVID-19 disaster declarations*. Retrieved July 19, 2020, from www.fema.gov/coronavirus/disaster-declarations

FEMA. (2020b, April 17). *Public assistance: Local, state, tribal and private non-profit*. Retrieved July 16, 2020, from www.fema.gov/public-assistance-local-state-tribal-and-non-profit

Garrett, T.A., & Sobel, R.S. (2003). The political economy of FEMA disaster payments. *Economic Inquiry, 41*(3), 496–509.

Kettl, D.F. (2014). *System under stress: Homeland security and American politics* (3rd ed.). Washington, DC: CQ Press.

Lindsay, B.R. (2017a, June 2). *Stafford Act assistance and acts of terrorism − Summary.* Washington, DC: U.S. Congressional Research Service. https://fas.org/sgp/crs/homesec/R44801.pdf

Lindsay, B.R. (2017b). *Stafford Act declarations 1953–2016: Trends, analysis, and implications for Congress − R42702.* Washington, DC: Congressional Research Service.

Long, W.B. (2018, April 11). *Written testimony of FEMA administrator brock long for a Senate Committee on Homeland Security and Governmental Affairs hearing.* FEMA: Prioritizing a Culture of Preparedness. Washington, DC: U.S. DHS. Retrieved May 3, 2018, from www.dhs.gov/news/2018/04/11/written-testimony-fema-administrator-senate-committee-homeland-security-and

March, J.G., & Olsen, J.P. (2009). Elaborating the new institutionalism. In S.A. Binder, R.A.W. Rhodes, A. Bert, & B.A. Rockman (Eds.), *The Oxford handbook of political institutions.* Oxford Handbooks Online. Retrieved July 19, 2020, from www.oxfordhandbooks.com/view/10.1093/oxfordhb/9780199548460.001.0001/oxfordhb-9780199548460-e-1

May, P.J. (1985). *Recovering from catastrophes: Federal disaster relief policy and politics.* Westport, CT: Greenwood Press.

May, P.J., & Williams, W. (1986). *Disaster policy implementation: Managing programs under shared governance.* New York: Plenum Press.

McCarthy, F.X. (2007). *FEMA's disaster declaration process: A primer.* Report RL34146. Washington, DC: U.S. Congressional Research Service.

Miskel, J.F. (2008). *Disaster response and homeland security: What works, what doesn't.* Westport, CT: Praeger.

Mycoff, J. (2007). Congress and Katrina: A failure of oversight. *State and Local Government Review, 39*(1), 16–30.

National Low Income Housing Coalition. (2014, September 29). *40 years ago: The Disaster Relief Act of 1974 − Resource library.* Retrieved April 28, 2018, from http://nlihc.org/article/40-years-ago-disaster-relief-act-1974

Niskanen, W., Jr. (2017). *Bureaucracy and representative government.* New York: Routledge.

O'Connor, A., & Williams, T. (2011, April 27). Scores die in storms across south; tornado ravages city. *The New York Times.* Retrieved July 1, 2013, from www.nytimes.com/2011/04/28/us/28storm.html?_r=0

Ohio Emergency Management Agency. (2004). *Final draft national response plan* (pp. 8–9). Columbus: Ohio EMA. Retrieved February 4, 2014, from http://ema.ohio.gov/Documents/NRP_Final_Draft.pdf

Platt, R. (1999). Shouldering the burden: Federal assumption of disaster costs. In R. Platt (Ed.), *Disasters and democracy: The politics of extreme natural events* (pp. 11–46). Washington, DC: Island Press.

Reeves, A. (2009). Political disaster: Unilateral powers, electoral incentives, and presidential disaster declarations. *Journal of Politics, 1*(1), 1–10.

Schneider, S.K. (1995). *Flirting with disaster: Public management in crisis situations.* Armonk, NY: M.E. Sharpe.

Schneider, S.K. (2011). *Dealing with disaster: Public management in crisis situations* (2nd ed.). Armonk, NY: M.E. Sharpe.

Smith, K. (2013). *Environmental hazards: Assessing risk and reducing disaster* (6th ed.). New York: Routledge.

Sylves, R.T. (1996). The politics and budgeting of federal emergency management. In R.T. Sylves & W.L. Waugh Jr. (Eds.), *Disaster management in the U.S. and Canada.* Springfield, IL: Charles C. Thomas.

Sylves, R.T. (2006, March). President Bush and Hurricane Katrina: A presidential leadership study. *Annals of the American Academy of Political and Social Science, 604,* 26–56.

Sylves, R.T. (2014). Presidential declaration of disaster decisions: The case of turndowns. In J.D. Ramsay & L. Kiltz (Eds.), *Critical issues in homeland security: A casebook* (pp. 35–72). Boulder, CO: Westview Press.

Sylves, R.T. (2020). *Disaster policy and politics* (3rd ed.). Thousand Oaks, CA: Sage.

Sylves, R. T., & Buzas, Z. I. (2007). Presidential disaster declaration decisions, 1953–2003: What influences odds of approval? *State and Local Government Review, 39*(1), 3–15.

Thoenig, J. C. (2012). Institutional theories and public institutions: New agendas and appropriateness. In B. G. Peters & J. Pierre (Eds.), *Sage handbook of public administration* (pp. 155–165). Retrieved July 22, 2020, from www.researchgate.net/publication/508 8430_Institutional_Theories_and_Public_Institutions_Traditions_and_Appropriateness

Townsend, F. F. (2006). Chapter six: Transforming national preparedness. In *The federal response to Hurricane Katrina: Lessons learned* (pp. 65–82). Washington, DC: White House. Retrieved July 16, 2020, from http://library.stmarytx.edu/acadlib/edocs/katrinawh.pdf

U.S. Code of Federal Regulations. (2020a). Title 44-Emergency Management and Assistance, 200.3 and § 208.2 Definitions and Terms, 505. From Cornell University, Legal Information Institute. Retrieved from https://www.law.cornell.edu/cfr/text/44/208.2 Accessed July 24, 2020.

U.S. Code of Federal Regulations. (2020b). Title 44: Emergency Management and Assistance, § 206.35 Sub-part B. Requests for Emergency Declarations. Retrieved July 24, 2020, from www.ecfr.gov/cgi-bin/text-idx?SID=f588519a610591d690201d48c037060c&node=44:1.0. 1.4.57&rgn=div5#44:1.0.1.4.57.2.18.5

U.S. Senate, Senate Committee on Governmental Affairs. (1993, May 18). *Hearing on rebuilding FEMA: Preparing for the next disaster.* 103rd Cong., 1st Sess. Washington, DC: U.S. Government Printing Office.

Weaver, R. K., & Rockman, B. A. (1993). *Do institutions matter? Government capabilities in the United States and abroad.* Washington, DC: Brookings.

Weiss, D. J., & Weidman, J. (2013, April 29). *Disastrous spending: Federal disaster-relief expenditures rise amid more extreme weather.* Center for American Progress. Retrieved June 27, 2013, from www.americanprogress.org/issues/green/report/2013/04/29/61633/disastrous-spending-federal-disaster-relief-expenditures-rise-amid-more-extreme-weather

18

Mapping Resilience

GIS Techniques for Disaster Studies

Courtney Page-Tan, Timothy Fraser, and Daniel P. Aldrich

Introduction

Geographic information system (GIS) programs, such as Esri's ArcGIS and qGIS, are arguably among the most powerful tools (Bodenhamer, 2010) available to scholars of natural hazards (Zerger, 2002). GIS and its tools equip users to extract, select, and manipulate complex datasets rooted in geography. Users can overlay datasets, such as FEMA flood maps, with income and poverty data from the U.S. Census to gain additional insights into how many households living in poverty are also vulnerable to flooding events during a disruptive storm surge.

This chapter provides an overview of the GIS methods and techniques commonly employed by researchers of natural hazards. In doing so, each section will provide a brief overview and summary of the tools discussed, common questions that can be addressed by the tools, and examples from researchers who have applied those tools in actual cases of hazards and disasters. This chapter is by no means an exhaustive overview of all the tools at our disposal. Instead, this chapter provides an initial overview of the commonly used spatial tools to familiarize students and researchers on how GIS tools and techniques can be applied to studying natural hazards.

This chapter proceeds in the following order: a brief introduction to raster and vector data and overviews of some of the more popular tools used in conducting an overlay analysis, proximity analysis, surface creation and analysis, spatial statistics, and analyzing patterns in ArcMap (see Table 18.1), the flagship GIS program of Esri's ArcGIS. There are other programs available to users, such as qGIS and sf, leaflet, raster, mapview, and tmap packages in R, open–source alternatives to ArcMap.

Data Types: Raster and Vector Data

Mapped data are available in two data types: vector and raster. Vector data are coordinate based and are features represented in points, lines, and polygons that possess attributes. Points are single points with a latitude and longitude that represent

TABLE 18.1 Methods and Natural Hazards Questions

Technique	Common Questions
Overlay analysis	How many households are within a 100-year floodplain?
	How many householders were flood affected?
	Which communities are vulnerable to snow and flood events?
	Which census tracts place the greatest demand on 911 dispatch call centers?
	How did building design influence levels of damage from tsunami inundation?
	Which geographies are more susceptible to landslides or flooding events?
Proximity analysis	How many households are within 2 miles of an emergency shelter?
	Which emergency shelter is the closest to a community or household?
	Do local shelters have the capacity to serve the needs of the local community in the event of a disaster?
	Can distance from an earthquake epicenter influence the contagion of disease post-disaster?
	Which communities are most isolated from food and shelter centers in the event of a disaster?
Analyzing patterns and spatial analysis	Are vulnerable communities spatially clustered or more geographically dispersed?

a single data point. For example, results from a household survey on post–disaster rebuilding could be displayed as points, where the unique coordinates of each household are visualized on a map, and attributes of the points could include survey results, such as household income, age of home, size of household, number of floors, total home square footage, number of days to rebuild, and the land surveyor who issued an elevation certificate to rebuild. Lines represent edges from one vertex to another. For example, data on streets, footpaths, and sidewalks are commonly mapped as lines. Polygons are a collection of vertices that make a shape. For example, Census Block Groups and Tracts, flood maps, and storm inundation zones are mapped as polygons. Raster data are organized in equally sized cells on a grid and each cell contains location coordinates and attributes. For example, satellite imagery is primarily displayed as raster data.

Overlay Analysis

Before access to GIS software, if a researcher, or more likely a cartographer, had a question that called upon two mapped datasets, the process involved plastic sheets and a light table. For example, to answer the question of which households were located in a 100-year floodplain, a cartographer would begin by creating two maps on separate plastic sheets at the same scale. The first map would include the households in question, and the second map would be the 100-year floodplain. The cartographer would overlay these two maps on a light table and create a new map of the overlaid data. This process, while on its face was simple, yielded valuable information to homeowners, insurance companies, community planners, disaster managers, engineers, and other interested parties.

Today in 2020, overlay analyses continue to yield valuable insights, but in ArcMap the insights are *n*th dimensional and the process is performed with great ease. Researchers can investigate relationships by overlaying two (or more) datasets, each map with attributes that can serve to advance knowledge of factors such as vulnerable communities or resilient infrastructure. Vector overlay methods, such as Spatial Join and Union, and raster overlay tools, such as Zonal Statistics and Weighted Overlay, among others not discussed here, offer tools to combine datasets with precision to target or omit geographies or attributes to generate new maps and models that can offer researchers of natural hazards new and exciting insights.

Vector Overlay Tools: Spatial Join and Union

The Spatial Join tool joins attributes from one feature to another based on a shared spatial relationship. The Spatial Join tools offers researchers a powerful tool to combine points, lines, and polygons to generate new datasets that can accurately model the complex systems that are affected by environmental disturbances. For example, Figure 18.1 is an overlay analysis undertaken with a series of Spatial Joins in a recent study (Page-Tan, Forthcoming a) of how social networks influenced the rate of recovery in the Houston area following Hurricane Harvey in 2017, an overlay method similar to a study that carried out a survey of households affected by Tropical Storm Allison in the Houston metropolitan area in 2001 (Waring et al., 2005). The study mapped points of households with the attribute of the number of days to rebuild in the Greater Houston Area and overlaid hyperlocal social media use on Nextdoor, a hyperlocal social media platform, before, during, and after Hurricane Harvey to understand how levels of hyperlocal social media activity interacted with the rate of rebuilding. Median age, education, income, language (percent of households that

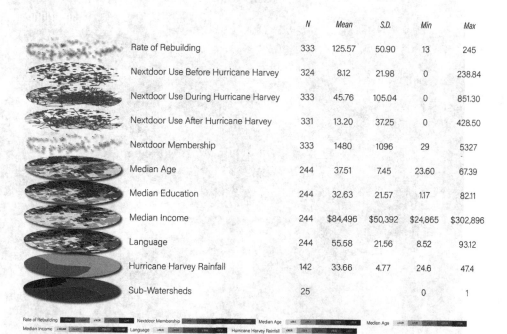

	N	Mean	S.D.	Min	Max
Rate of Rebuilding	333	125.57	50.90	13	245
Nextdoor Use Before Hurricane Harvey	324	8.12	21.98	0	238.84
Nextdoor Use During Hurricane Harvey	333	45.76	105.04	0	851.30
Nextdoor Use After Hurricane Harvey	331	13.20	37.25	0	428.50
Nextdoor Membership	333	1480	1096	29	5327
Median Age	244	37.51	7.45	23.60	67.39
Median Education	244	32.63	21.57	1.17	82.11
Median Income	244	$84,496	$50,392	$24,865	$302,896
Language	244	55.58	21.56	8.52	93.12
Hurricane Harvey Rainfall	142	33.66	4.77	24.6	47.4
Sub-Watersheds	25			0	1

Rate of Rebuilding   Nextdoor Membership   Median Age   Median Age
Median Income   Language   Hurricane Harvey Rainfall
Sub-Watersheds: Bens Branch-Frontal Lake Houston, City of Houston-Buffalo Bayou, Clear Creek-Frontal Galveston Bay, Cole Creek-Whiteoak Bayou, Country Club Bayou-Brays Bayou, Garners Bayou, Halls Bayou, Headwaters Greens Bayou, Hunting Bayou, Jackson Bayou-San Jacinto River, Keegans Bayou-Brays Bayou, Little Whiteoak Bayou-Whiteoak Bayou, Lower Greens Bayou, Lower Sims Bayou, Luce Bayou-Frontal Lake Houston, Middle Greens Bayou, Mustang Bayou, Orange Branch-East Fork San Jacinto River, San Jacinto Dam-Frontal Lake Houston, Seaberg Reservoir-Cedar Bayou, Spring Branch-Buffalo Bayou, Upper Greens Bayou, Upper Sims Bayou, Vince Bayou-Buffalo Bayou, and White Oak Creek-Frontal Lake Houston

FIGURE 18.1 Example of Spatial Join of Polygons and Points

spoke English at home), Hurricane Harvey rainfall, and sub-watersheds were also mapped and spatially joined to the points of the rate of rebuilding to generate a complete model of social, demographic, and environmental drivers of rebuilding in the Houston area following Harvey. The result of this Spatial Join and subsequent statistical analyses found that hyperlocal social media use from all three stages – before, during, and after – expedited the rate of recovery in the Houston area.

Natural hazards researchers have also used spatial joins to explore questions of varying levels of damage to building design from levels of tsunami inundation in the Tōhoku region following the earthquake on March 11, 2011 (Amakuni, Terazono, Yamamoto, & Takahisa, 2012); vulnerability to drought hazards in the Chotanagpur plateau region in Jharkhand, India (Pandey, Pandey, Nathawat, Kumar, & Mahanti, 2012); landslide hazard vulnerability in the Itoshima Area of Japan (Chand, Mitani, Djamaluddin, & Ikemi, 2011); flood-affected residential blocks in the Australian Capital Territory and neighboring Queanbeyan City (Elsergany, Griffin, Tranter, and Alam, 2015); counts of 911 calls in census tracts in Portland, Oregon; and combined vulnerability to snow and flood events (Lee, Lee, & Ham, 2019).

The Union tool joins geometric features and attributes from two vector datasets and creates a new map of the joined features and attributes. This overlay analysis technique is transformative in nature. Unlike the Spatial Join tool, Union combines geometries, in addition to attributes, of two separate maps. Figures 18.2 and 18.3 are from a recent study of walkability in the City of Cambridge, Massachusetts (Page-Tan, Forthcoming a). Figure 18.2 represents mapped polygons of unique land-use

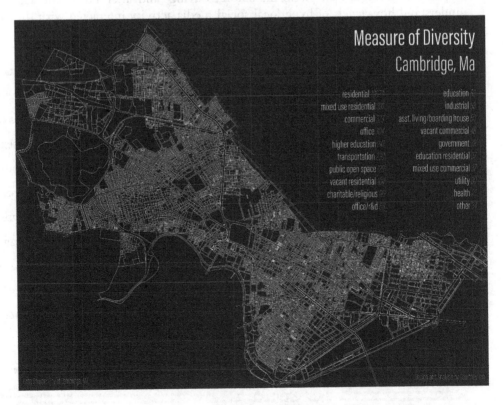

FIGURE 18.2 Mapped Polygons of Unique Land-Use Categories in Cambridge, Massachusetts

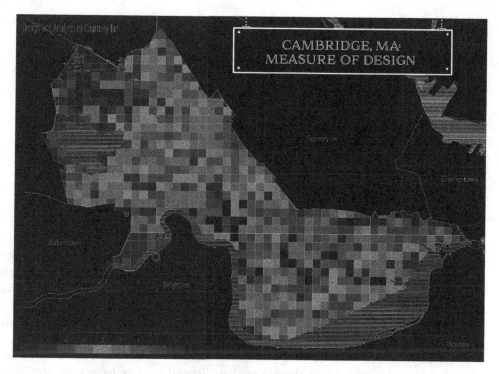

FIGURE 18.3 Combined Land-Use Categories and Fishnet Grid by Union

categories in Cambridge from residential and commercial and from office to education. These unique land-use polygons were joined to a Fishnet grid[1] with the Union tool to calculate an index measure of walkability based on land-use diversity, in addition to destination, design, and density (not featured) based on measures of the built environment (Cervero & Kockelman's, 1997). By performing the Union between these two maps, deciles could then be calculated in each grid cell to compute levels of walkability based on land-use diversity (Figure 18.3), destination, design, and density, to then compute a grand score of walkability.

Researchers of natural hazards have used the Union tool to generate maps that identify susceptibility to landslides in the Yamuna valley in northwest Himalaya in India (Kundu & Patel, 2019); assess risk to livestock in the Valencian Community east of Spain (Gallego, Calafat, Segura, & Quintanilla, 2019); generate flood hazard maps in Beni Mellal, an inland Moroccan city (Werren, Reynard, Lane, & Balin, 2016); and measure drought intensity, duration, frequency, and areal coverage and their variations on different spatial scales of the contiguous United States for the years 2000–2014 (Navaratnam & Padmanabhan, 2017).

Raster Overlay Tools: Zonal Statistics and Weighted Overlay

The Zonal Statistics tool summarizes the values of an attribute in a raster layer by zone from a second raster layer. For example, in a recent study, researchers (Abdi, Kamkar, Shirvani, Teixeira da Silva Jaime, & Buchroithner, 2018) used raster data to determine if environmental, climatic, and anthropogenic factors caused intermittent fires in Golestan, northeast Iran, in late 2010. Environmental factors were derived from a digital elevation model, slope, plan curvature aspect, and forest density. Climatic factors were based on temperature, relative humidity, wind speed, and precipitation. Anthropogenic factors were based on population density, residential distance, paved road distance, dirt road distance, and forest road distance. The mean of these three factors was then calculated across forest regions distributed across the 135 forest fires, which burned a total of 14,550 ha, that occurred between November and December of 2010. Researchers found that environmental and climatic factors often explained the cause and extent of the 2010 rash of forest fires in Golestan. Distance to roads was noted as the only statistically significant anthropogenic cause of the 135 forest fires.

Zonal Statistics have also been used to calculate population potentially exposed to floods in 2007 and 2008 in Algeria, Australia, India, Bangladesh, Zimbabwe, and Kenya (Guha-sapir, Rodriguez-llanes, & Jakubicka, 2011); measure environmental degradation in southern Louisiana following Hurricane Katrina (Chuang, Tarsha, Ahjond, & Roberts, 2019); identify flood inundation areas during the month of August 2017 in Uttar Pradesh, India (Anusha & Bharathi, 2019); and calculate the average Urban Heat Index across Census Blocks in Portland, Oregon, finding that communities with lower levels of formal education and less green space are more vulnerable to flooding and extreme heat hazards (Fahy, Brenneman, Chang, & Shandas, 2019).

The Weighted Overlay tool automates the process of assigning weights to each raster layer before adding them together. Several studies have used the Weighted Overlay tool to measure landslide susceptibility in the northwest Himalayas in Pakistan (Basharat, Shah, & Hameed, 2016); Kodaikanal taluk, South India (Gurugnanam, Bagyaraj, Kumaravel, Vinoth, & Vasudevan, 2012); the Genting Sempah to Bentong Highway in Pahang, Malaysia (Roslee, Mickey, Simon, & Norhisham, 2017); and the Bagh District in the Azad Kashmir region administered by Pakistan (Javed, 2019). Many more have used the Weighted Overlay tool to assess flood hazards across cases in Fogera Woreda in northwest Ethiopia (Gashaw & Legesse, 2011), the Sindh Province in Pakistan (Uddin, Gurung, Giriraj, & Shrestha, 2013), and the areas near the Kabul and Swat Rivers in Charsadda, Pakistan (Bibi, Nawaz, Rahman, & Latif, 2019). This tool allows natural hazards researchers to combine environmental measures and composition, some bearing more weight than others, to determine areas that may be at more risk than others.

Proximity Analysis

Proximity Analysis tools, such as Buffer, Multiple Ring Buffer, Thiessen Polygons, and Euclidean Distance tools offer the computational leverage to answer questions of resource allocation and proximity. For example, if a disaster manager is planning the placement of new emergency shelters, a combination of these tools would identify how many households would be within walkable and drivable distance of these shelters, and among these households, how many are vulnerable to increased risk of flooding from a local river. With these tools, a subset of home addresses can be captured and used to promote the closest emergency center with a mailing, community event, or block party. Disaster planners can assess the local population and whether or not local resources can handle the capacity of community needs in the event of a disaster.

Vector Proximity Analysis Tools: Buffer, Multiple Ring Buffer, and Thiessen Polygons

The Buffer tool creates polygons around a vector input feature to a specified distance. The input feature could be a point, line, or polygon. For example, to understand how many households are within 3 miles of tornado shelter, a 3-mile buffer can be drawn around a tornado shelter and the Summarize Within tool can calculate addresses within the drawn buffer. Addresses within the buffer could also be marked for further preparedness campaigns. In a recent study of walkability in Cambridge, Massachusetts (Page-Tan, Forthcoming a), half-mile buffers – considered a walkable distance in the United States – were drawn around 149 survey respondents to determine measures of household density, walkable destinations, land-use diversity, and built design. Figure 18.4 displays the mapped results of a single survey respondent located at the cross-street of Douglass Street and Massachusetts Avenue in downtown Cambridge. These measures were subsequently joined with the Spatial Join tool to determine how these four factors affected engagement in community programs and activities.

Natural hazards researchers have used buffers to map flood hazard zones in the Yasooj region, Iran (Rahmati, Zeinivand, & Besharat, 2015); track the flow of debris during flood events (Kim, Chung, Kim, & Kim, 2016); determine susceptibility to flooding (Tehrany, Pradhan, & Jebur, 2014; Ojigi, Abdulkadir, & Aderoju, 2013); and assess locations for emergency shelters in the event of a disaster (Chen, Zhai, Ren, Shi, & Zhang, 2018). For example, in a research study (Chen et al., 2018) assessing the suitability of emergency shelters in Guangzhou, China, researchers drew buffers around candidate outdoor and indoor shelters, including green spaces, city squares, school playgrounds, gymnasiums, educational institutions, and community centers, to determine nearness and exposure to key factors. Factors include (1) sea level height in tsunami, tide level in storm surge, and flood level; (2) geological environment;

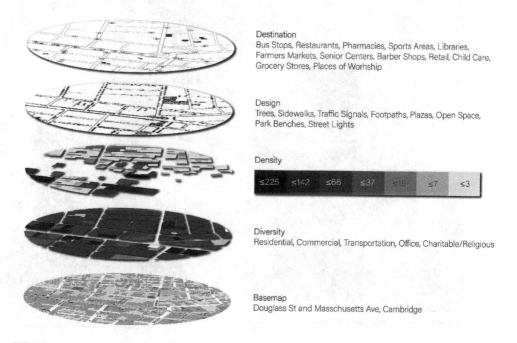

Destination
Bus Stops, Restaurants, Pharmacies, Sports Areas, Libraries, Farmers Markets, Senior Centers, Barber Shops, Retail, Child Care, Grocery Stores, Places of Worhship

Design
Trees, Sidewalks, Traffic Signals, Footpaths, Plazas, Open Space, Park Benches, Street Lights

Density
| ≤225 | ≤142 | ≤66 | ≤37 | ≤15 | ≤7 | ≤3 |

Diversity
Residential, Commercial, Transportation, Office, Charitable/Religious

Basemap
Douglass St and Masschusetts Ave, Cambridge

FIGURE 18.4 Use of Buffers With Survey Data and Publicly Available Data

(3) distance from gas stations, natural gas fueling stations, high-voltage lines, and power plants; (4) distance from dangerous goods warehouses; (5) distance from high-pressure gas pipelines; (6) terrain slope; (7) distance from waters; (8) terrain elevation; (9) distance from heritage conservation areas; and (10) distance from waste treatment stations.

The Multiple Ring Buffer tool affords researchers the added utility of expanding their question to multiple distances from a central point in a single analysis. Instead of iterating over several values with a single tool, researchers can capture data within interval boundaries, for example, within a quarter-mile, half-mile, mile, and 5-mile radius of a point of interest. In an analysis (Ortiz et al., 2017) of the uptick in Zika cases following a 7.8-magnitude earthquake in Ecuador in 2016, researchers used a Multiple Ring Buffer Analysis to visualize cumulative Zika cases at distances of 50, 100, and 300 miles from the earthquake epicenter. Researchers found that distance to the epicenter was spatially correlated with the rise in the pre-earthquake count of 89 cases compared to 2,103 cases post–earthquake.

The Create Thiessen Polygons tool generates polygons based on the input point features. Each Thiessen polygon contains a single point from the input layer. Thiessen polygons are useful for determining efficient and near spaces based on the geographic distribution of points. For example, during Hurricane Harvey, the Red Cross posted a list of active shelters[2] in the Houston area. For demonstrative purposes in this chapter, shelters were mapped and the Create Thiessen Polygons tool generated proximal zones based on nearness to shelter points, displayed in Figure 18.5. Based on this analysis, households in need of shelter would ideally seek out the shelter nearest to them.

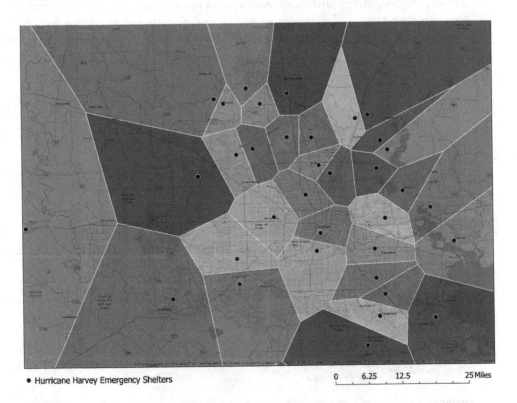

• Hurricane Harvey Emergency Shelters

0   6.25   12.5   25 Miles

FIGURE 18.5 Emergency Shelter Proximal Zones Based on Thiessen Polygons

Natural hazards researchers have used the Create Thiessen Polygons tool to compute average rainfall polygons within proximal zones of rain gauges (Nhamo, Mabhaudhi, & Modi, 2019; Pawestri, Sujono, & Istiarto, 2016), assess the impact of extreme landslide in Brazil (Netto et al., 2013), and assess the capacity and placement of emergency shelters (Masuya, Dewan, & Corner, 2015). For example, researchers (Masuya et al., 2015) found that the spatial distribution of shelters in the Dhaka Metropolitan Development Plan zone and Dhaka megacity in Bangladesh were not ideally or optimally placed and situated in community to serve flood-vulnerable populations. Instead, 63% of potential flood shelters were located more than 1 kilometer away from the nearest vulnerable homes. Their analysis also revealed that 1,098 of the 5,537 of potential flood shelters did not have sufficient capacity to serve local community members.

Raster Proximity Analysis Tool: Euclidean Distance

The Euclidean Distance tool allows for vector and raster data inputs. The Euclidean Distance tool calculates the distance of each cell to the nearest point of interest. For example, to generate a raster grid of nearness to Hurricane Harvey emergency shelters, the Euclidean Distance tool would calculate the nearness for each grid cell to the closest shelter. In a recent study, researchers used the Euclidean Distance Tool to generate flood hazard maps that considered the nearness to the maximum flood extent area and the river centerline of the Poisar River basin in Mumbai, India (Zope, Eldho, & Jothiprakash, 2017). In another study exploring the adaptive capacity of coastal areas affected by tsunamis, researchers (Villagra, Herrmann, Quintana, & Sepúlveda, 2017) proposed a model of measuring nearness to key resources across coastal communities. They measured the Euclidean distances between villages and sources of food and shelter, evacuation routes, and open and built infrastructure, and subsequently conducted analyses on the maps that reflected nearness to their physical, environmental, and social indicators of resilience.

Interpolation Tools

The Interpolation tools create a continuous surface based on available point data that are geographically dispersed but frequently limited. By interpolating a continuous surface, natural hazards researchers can join data from complex systems to data that may otherwise be sparse. There are several interpolation techniques, such as inverse distance weighted (IDW), Empirical Bayesian kriging (EBK), Natural Neighbor, Spline, Spline with Natural Barriers, Topo to Raster, and Trend. Based on the parameters of a study and research question, researchers must determine which is the best fit that most accurately models the data to be interpolated. Researches have used IDW to interpolate rainfall trends in Southern Africa between 1960 to 2007 (Nhamo et al., 2019), rainfall measurements from the meteorological stations located in the vicinity of the Peneus River basin in western Greece (Skilodimou, Bathrellos, Chousianitis, Youssef, & Pradhan, 2019), characteristics of terrain surface in Brisbane City, Queensland, Australia following the January 2011 flood (Espada, Apan, & McDougall, 2017), and Hurricane Harvey rainfall measures from rain gauges in the Houston area, visualized in Figure 18.6 (Page-Tan, Forthcoming b).

For example, to control for storm inundation in the study of hyperlocal social media use and the rate of recovery in the Houston area following Hurricane Harvey,

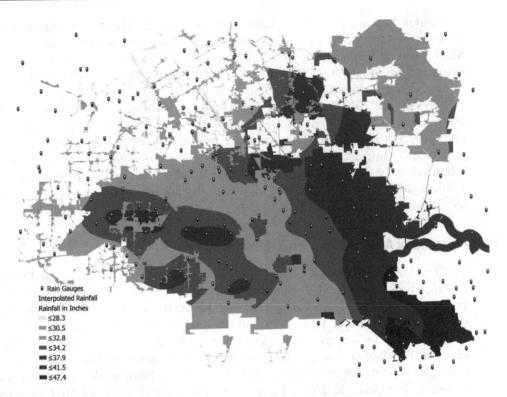

Rain Gauges
Interpolated Rainfall
Rainfall in Inches
- ≤28.3
- ≤30.5
- ≤32.8
- ≤34.2
- ≤37.9
- ≤41.5
- ≤47.4

FIGURE 18.6 Example of Interpolated Point Data Clipped to Houston City Limits

rain gauge data were interpolated to create a continuous surface of measured rainfall that could then be joined with the key independent and dependent variables. Figure 18.6 demonstrates how rainfall measurements from 137 rain gauges managed by the Houston Floodplain Management Office could be interpolated with the EBK technique, and vector contours subsequently generated from this kriging method.

Overview of Analyzing Patterns and Spatial Statistics

Researchers gain much of their insight into phenomena and empirical puzzles by analyzing patterns and trends. Patterns can signal to natural hazards researchers if environmental degradation is getting better or worse over time for coastal communities, or perhaps if the spatial patterns we are seeing in coastal flooding is random or statistically significant. These patterns provide valuable insight to disaster managers and community and environmental planners who are faced with addressing serious issues of climate and environmental changes, but with scarce resources.

Analyzing Patterns and Spatial Statistics tools, such as Spatial Autocorrelation, the Hot Spot Analysis tool, and Exploratory and OLS Regression are powerful tools of inferential statistics in ArcGIS. Researchers of natural hazards can test for spatial randomness or gain insight into spatially significant relationships with mapped data. Spatial Autocorrelation uses the Global Moran's I statistic to measure spatial autocorrelation between feature locations and attributes. More specifically, the tool simultaneously tests for correlations between locations and attributes. The tool evaluates if patterns are random, clustered, or dispersed and calculates a Global

Moran's I value that reports the p value and the z-score to test for significance. Researchers have used Spatial Autocorrelation to identify spatial variations in social vulnerability in flood-prone areas in Louisiana (Lotfata & Ambinakudige, 2019); earthquake disaster probability, subjective resilience, and governmental preparedness in Tainan City, Taiwan (Chang, Chen, & Cheng, 2018); measures of sentiment from geotagged tweets on Twitter during the Napa Valley earthquake and levels of earthquake intensity (Wang & Taylor, 2018); and social vulnerability and geography in Nepal (Aksha, Juran, Resler, & Zhang, 2018).

For example, a recent study (Aksha et al., 2018) mapped Social Vulnerability Index (SoVI)[3] scores in Nepal village to determine if SoVI scores were clustered across space, which in turn has implications that limit a community's ability to draw on neighboring villages for assistance. Researchers used the results from the analysis to classify villages into four SoVI typologies: (1) villages with high SoVI scores surrounded by villages with high SoVI scores; (2) villages with low SoVI scores surrounded by villages with low SoVI scores; (3) villages with high SoVI scores surrounded by villages with low SoVI scores; and (4) villages with low SoVI scores surrounded by villages with high SoVI scores. Results of the Global Moran's I statistic confirmed positive spatial autocorrelation with a coefficient of 0.41 and p value of 0.001 that these four typologies were often clustered together. For example, villages with high SoVI scores surrounded by villages with similarly high SoVI scores were identified in the western Hill and Mountain regions in Nepal and some small isolated pockets of the eastern Tarai region. Clusters of villages with low SoVI scores surrounded by like villages were identified in the eastern and central parts of the Hill and Mountain regions.

The Hot Spot Analysis tool groups features based on their attributes, with the option of imposing spatial or temporal constraints on the model. This Grouping Analysis tool performs calculations to identify statistically significant "hot" and "cold" spots using the Getis-Ord Gi★ statistic. In a study of community resilience to the 2015 Boston Snow Storms (Aldrich & Page-Tan, Forthcoming), researchers used the Hot Spot Analysis tool to identify hot, cold, and neutral spots of social capital to identify communities in cold spots that were likely vulnerable to the continuous subzero temperatures and record-setting snow accumulation that paralyzed the transportation network in the Greater Boston Metro Area. Social capital measures were developed from data on civic participation and engagement from Esri Business Analyst and mapped by Census Block Groups. In Figure 18.7, we see that there are clear patterns of hot and cold spots of social capital in the Boston area. The figure also displays results from a community resilience survey carried out in Dorchester and Mattapan, predominantly minority communities that are historically underrepresented and underserved in the Boston area.

Researchers have also used the Hot Spot Analysis tool to identify the availability and geographic clustering of rainwater harvesting systems in Xochimilco outside of Mexico City (Aldrich & Page-Tan, 2020); to identify concentrations of 911 calls to determine how resources could be better allocated to serve high-demand areas in the Portland Oregon Metropolitan Area (Cramer, Brown, & Hu, 2012); trends in measures of growth and resilience from 1971 to 2011 in Austrian municipalities (Kinga & Gernot, 2019); clustering of school closures following Hurricane Ike (Esnard, Lai, Wyczalkowski, Malmin, & Shah, 2018); and clustering of crowdsourced photographs of disaster debris to predict debris flow (Chu & Chen, 2018).

Finally, ArcGIS offers powerful statistical analysis tools to implement Exploratory and Ordinary Least Squares (OLS) linear regressions to predict and model the outcome

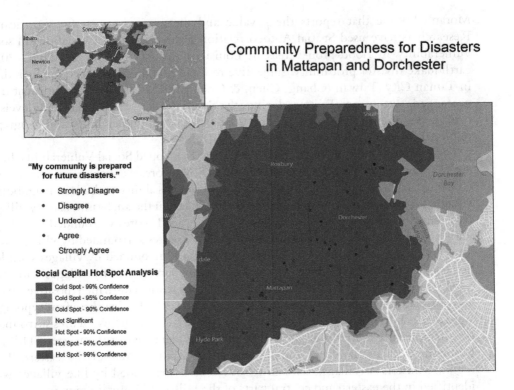

FIGURE 18.7 Example of a Hot Spot Analysis of Social Capital With Community Resilience Survey Responses

of a dependent variable based on explanatory variables. The Exploratory Regression tool runs all possible combinations of independent and dependent variables modeled in ArcGIS; however, aside from identifying trends, researchers should exercise caution with this tool in general. The OLS Regression tool is better suited to test hypotheses grounded in theory to explore relevant phenomena with predetermined models consisting of an outcome variable and explanatory variables. The output of the OLS Regression tool is similar to executing an OLS regression in a statistical package, such as STATA, SPSS, or R, and by exporting the data with the Table to Excel tool, the same data could be read into any statistical package that can read in an Excel table and the results of the OLS would be the same. The added advantage of exporting the data from ArcGIS after a series of joins, unions, buffers, and similar analysis is that some statistical packages are better suited for running more advanced statistical models on data that may not adhere to the assumptions of an OLS model.

Conclusion

GIS is a powerful technical and visual tool for natural hazards researchers and is fundamental to disaster risk reduction (Zerger & Smith, 2003). It allows us to identify vulnerable communities with a series of techniques and tools to aid federal, state, and local disaster managers and decision-makers in allocating and pre-positioning resources to best serve communities that are the greatest risk. Mapped data and subsequent analyses can reduce the loss of life and livelihood if planners can invest in resilience-building education campaigns and activities in communities identified as at-risk before a catastrophic event (Morrow, 1999; Aldrich, 2019). With the tools and techniques of GIS, paired with local knowledge of risk (Tran, Shaw, Chantry, & Norton, 2009), natural hazards researchers can gain new insights into the drivers of resilience and the underlying causes of vulnerability. Finally, GIS can be paired with a variety of other methods discussed throughout this book to provide more holistic and insightful understandings of social phenomena related to a whole host of natural and human induced disasters.

Notes

1. See Esri's How Create Fishnet works: https://pro.arcgis.com/en/pro-app/tool-reference/data-management/how-create-fishnet-works.htm
2. See *Latest Shelter List and Live Map for the Houston Area* at www.houstonpublicmedia.org/articles/news/2017/09/01/234616/shelter-list-friday/
3. The Social Vulnerability Index (SoVI) was initially developed by Cutter et al. See Cutter, S.L., Boruff, B.J., & Shirley, W.L. (2003). Social vulnerability to environmental hazards. *Social Science Quarterly, 84*(2), 242–261. https://doi.org/10.1111/1540-6237.8402002. For an alternative framework focused around social capital (rather than vulnerability) see Kyne, D., & Aldrich, D.P. (2020). Capturing bonding, bridging, and linking social capital through publicly available data. *Risk, Hazards, and Crises in Public Policy, 11*(1), 61–86.

Further Reading

Abdalla, R. (2016). Evaluation of spatial analysis application for urban emergency management. *SpringerPlus, 5*(1), 1–10.

Goodchild, M. F. (2006). GIS and disasters: Planning for catastrophe. *Computers, Environment and Urban Systems, 30*(3), 227–229.

Mukhopadhyay, B., & Bhattacherjee, B. (2015). Use of information technology in emergency and disaster management. *American Journal of Environmental Protection, 4*(2), 101–104.

References

Abdi, O., Kamkar, B., Shirvani, Z., Teixeira da Silva Jaime, A., & Buchroithner, M.F. (2018). Spatial-statistical analysis of factors determining forest fires: A case study from Golestan, Northeast Iran. *Geomatics, Natural Hazards and Risk, 9*(1). https://doi.org/10.1080/19475705.2016.1206629

Aksha, S.K., Juran, L., Resler, L.M., & Zhang, Y. (2018). An analysis of social vulnerability to natural hazards in Nepal using a modified social vulnerability index. *International Journal of Disaster Risk Science, 10*(1), 103–116. https://doi.org/10.1007/s13753-018-0192-7

Aldrich, D. P. (2019). *Black wave: How networks and governance shaped Japan's 3/11 disasters.* Chicago: University of Chicago Press.

Aldrich, D. P., & Page-Tan, C. (2020). Oasis of resilience? An empirical investigation of rainwater harvesting systems in high poverty, peripheral communities. *Economics of Disasters and Climate Change, 4*, 129–144.

Aldrich, D.P., & Page-Tan, C. (forthcoming). *The strength of bonding social capital is the 2015* Boston snow storms.

Amakuni, K., Terazono, N., Yamamoto, T., & Takahisa, E. (2012). *Basic analysis on building damages by tsunami due to the 2011 Great East Japan earthquake disaster using GIS.* Proceedings of the 15th World Conference on Earthquake Engineering, Lisbon, Portugal.

Anusha, N., & Bharathi, B. (2019). Flood detection and flood mapping using multi-temporal synthetic aperture radar and optical data. *Egyptian Journal of Remote Sensing and Space Science.* https://doi.org/10.1016/j.ejrs.2019.01.001

Basharat, M., Shah, H.R., & Hameed, N. (2016). Landslide susceptibility mapping using GIS and weighted overlay method: A case study from NW Himalayas, Pakistan. *Arabian Journal of Geosciences, 9*(4), 292. https://doi.org/10.1007/s12517-016-2308-y

Bibi, T., Nawaz, F., Abdul Rahman, A., & Latif, A. (2019). Flood hazard assessment using participatory approach and weighted overlay methods. *International Archives of the Photogrammetry, Remote Sensing & Spatial Information Sciences.* https://noa.gwlb.de/servlets/MCRFileNodeServlet/cop_derivate_00040784/isprs-archives-XLII-4-W16-153-2019.pdf

Bodenhamer, D.J. (2010). The potential of spatial humanities. In T.M. Harris, J. Corrigan, & D.J. Bodenhamer (Eds.), *The spatial humanities: GIS and the future of humanities scholarship.* Bloomington: Indiana University Press.

Cervero, R., & Kockelman, K. (1997). Travel demand and the 3Ds: Density, diversity, and design. *Transportation Research Part D: Transport and Environment, 2*(3), 199–219.

Chand, J. B., Mitani, Y., Djamaluddin, I., & Ikemi, H. (2011). An integrated methodology for assessment of landslide hazard around residence zones in Itoshima Area of Japan. *Memoirs of the Faculty of Engineering, Kyushu University, 71*(2), 31–45.

Chang, H., Chen, T., & Cheng, H. (2018). Comparing the spatial patterns of earthquake disaster probability and individual risk perception: A case study of Yongkang Township in Tainan, Taiwan. *Natural Hazards, 93*(3), 1589–1610. https://doi.org/10.1007/s11069-018-3369-x

Chen, W., Zhai, G., Ren, C., Shi, Y., & Zhang, J. (2018). Urban resources selection and allocation for emergency shelters: In a Multi-hazard environment. *International Journal of Environmental Research and Public Health, 15*(6), 1261. https://doi.org/10.3390/ijerph15061261

Chu, H.-J., & Chen, Y.C. (2018). Crowdsourcing photograph locations for debris flow hot spot mapping. *Natural Hazards, 90*(3), 1259–1276. https://doi.org/10.1007/s11069-017-3098-6

Chuang, W.-C., Tarsha, E., Ahjond, G., & Roberts, C. (2019). Impact of Hurricane Katrina on the coastal systems of Southern Louisiana. *Frontiers in Environmental Science.* https://doi.org/10.3389/fenvs.2019.00068

Cramer, D., Brown, A.A., & Hu, G. (2012). Predicting 911 calls using spatial analysis. In *Software engineering research, management and applications 2011* (pp. 15–26). Springer.

Elsergany, A. T., Griffin, A.L., Tranter, P., & Alam, S. (2015). *Development of a geographic information system for riverine flood disaster evacuation in Canberra.* Australia: Trip Generation and Distribution Modelling. ISCRAM.

Esnard, A., Lai, B.S., Wyczalkowski, C., Malmin, N., & Shah, H. (2018). School vulnerability to disaster examination of school closure demographic exposure factors in Hurricane Ike's wind swath. *Natural Hazards, 90*(2).

Espada, R., Apan, A., & McDougall, K. (2017). Vulnerability assessment of urban community and critical infrastructures for integrated flood risk management and climate adaptation strategies. *International Journal of Disaster Resilience in the Built Environment, 8*(4), 375–411. https://doi.org/10.1108/IJDRBE-03-2015-0010

Fahy, B., Brenneman, E., Chang, H., & Shandas, V. (2019). Spatial analysis of urban flooding and extreme heat hazard potential in Portland, OR. *International Journal of Disaster Risk Reduction, 39*, 101117. https://doi.org/10.1016/j.ijdrr.2019.101117

Gallego, A., Calafat, C., Segura, M., & Quintanilla, I. (2019). Land planning and risk assessment for livestock production based on an outranking approach and GIS. *Land Use Policy, 83*, 606–621. https://doi.org/10.1016/j.landusepol.2018.10.021

Gashaw, W., & Legesse, D. (2011). Flood hazard and risk assessment using GIS and remote sensing in Fogera Woreda, Northwest Ethiopia. In *Nile river basin* (pp. 179–206). Springer.

Guha-sapir, D., Rodriguez-llanes, J.M., & Jakubicka, T. (2011). Using disaster footprints, population databases and GIS to overcome persistent problems for human impact assessment in flood events. *Natural Hazards, 58*(3), 845–852. https://doi.org/10.1007/s11069-011-9775-y

Gurugnanam, B., Bagyaraj, M., Kumaravel, S., Vinoth, M., & Vasudevan, S. (2012). GIS based weighted overlay analysis in landslide hazard zonation for decision makers using spatial query builder in parts of Kodaikanal taluk, South India. *Journal of Geomatics*, 6(1), 49.

Javed, S. (2019). Landslide hazard mapping of Bagh district in Azad Kashmir. *International Journal of Economic and Environmental Geology*, 47–50.

Kim, H.-S., Chung, C. K., Kim, S. R., & Kim, K. S. (2016). A GIS-based framework for real-time debris-flow hazard assessment for expressways in Korea. *International Journal of Disaster Risk Science*, 7(3), 293–311. https://doi.org/10.1007/s13753-016-0096-3

Kinga, H., & Gernot, S. (2019). How resilient is growth? resilience assessment of Austrian municipalities on the basis of census data from 1971 to 2011. *Sustainability*, 11(6), 1818. https://doi.org/10.3390/su11061818

Kundu, V., & Patel, R. C. (2019). Susceptibility status of landslides in Yamuna Valley, Uttarakhand, NW-Himalaya, India. *Himalayan Geology*, 40(1), 30–49.

Kyne, D., & Aldrich, D. P. (2020). Capturing bonding, bridging, and linking social capital through publicly available data. *Risk, Hazards & Crisis in Public Policy*, 11(1), 61–86.

Lee, I., Lee, J., & Ham, S. (2019). A study on storm and flood insurance management mapping: Case study of Incheon metropolitan city. *ISPRS International Journal of Geo-Information*, 8(11), 485.

Lotfata, A., & Ambinakudige, S. (2019). Natural disaster and vulnerability: An analysis of the 2016 flooding in Louisiana. *Southeastern Geographer*, 59(2), 130–151. https://doi.org/10.1353/sgo.2019.0012

Masuya, A., Dewan, A., & Corner, R. J. (2015). Population evacuation: Evaluating spatial distribution of flood shelters and vulnerable residential units in Dhaka with geographic information systems. *Natural Hazards*, 78(3), 1859–1882. https://doi.org/10.1007/s11069-015-1802-y

Morrow, B. H. (1999). Identifying and mapping community vulnerability. *Disasters*, 23(1), 1. https://doi.org/10.1111/1467-7717.00102

Navaratnam, L., & Padmanabhan, G. (2017). Drought occurrences and their characteristics across selected spatial scales in the contiguous United States. *Geosciences*, 7(3), 59. https://doi.org/10.3390/geosciences7030059

Netto, A. L. C., Mululo Sato, A., de Souza Avelar, A., Vianna, L. G. G., Araújo, I. S., Ferreira, D. L. C., Lima, P. H., Silva, A. P. A., & Silva, R. P. (2013, January). 2011: The extreme landslide disaster in Brazil. In C. Margottini, P. Canuti, & K. Sassa (Eds.), *Landslide science and practice: Volume 6: Risk assessment, management and mitigation* (pp. 377–384). Berlin, Heidelberg: Springer Berlin Heidelberg.

Nhamo, L., Mabhaudhi, T., & Modi, A. T. (2019). Preparedness or repeated short-term relief aid? Building drought resilience through early warning in southern Africa. *Water S.A.*, 45(1), 75–85. https://doi.org/10.4314/wsa.v45i1.09

Ojigi, M. L., Abdulkadir, F. I., & Aderoju, M. O. (2013). *Geospatial mapping and analysis of the 2012 flood disaster in central parts of Nigeria*. 8th National GIS Symposium. Dammam. Saudi Arabia.

Ortiz, M. R., Le, N. K., Sharma, V., Hoare, I., Quizhpe, E., Teran, E., Naik, E., Salihu, H. M., & Izurieta, R. (2017). Post-earthquake Zika virus surge: Disaster and public health threat amid climatic conduciveness. *Scientific Reports*, 7(1), 15408.

Pandey, S., Pandey, A. C., Nathawat, M. S., Kumar, M., & Mahanti, N. C. (2012). Drought hazard assessment using geoinformatics over parts of Chotanagpur plateau region, Jharkhand, India. *Natural hazards*, 63(2), 279–303.

Page-Tan, C. (forthcoming a). *Building hyperlocal ties: The role of the local built environment in building hyperlocal bridging social capital*. Cambridge, MA.

Page-Tan, C. (forthcoming b). *A new era of disaster response: How social media is fueling post-disaster rebuilding*.

Pawestri, M. T., Sujono, J., & Istiarto, I. (2016). Flood hazard mapping of Bogowonto River in Purworejo Regency, Central Java. *Journal of the Civil Engineering Forum*, 2(3), 129–140.

Rahmati, O., Zeinivand, H., & Besharat, M. (2015). Flood hazard zoning in Yasooj region, Iran, using GIS and multi-criteria decision analysis. *Geomatics, Natural Hazards and Risk*, 7(3), 1000–1017. https://doi.org/10.1080/19475705.2015.1045043

Roslee, R., Mickey, A. C., Simon, N., & Norhisham, M. N. (2017). Landslide susceptibility analysis (LSA) using weighted overlay method (WOM) along the Genting Sempah to Bentong Highway, Pahang. *Malaysian Journal of Geosciences (MJG)*, *1*(2), 13–19.

Skilodimou, H. D., Bathrellos, G. D., Chousianitis, K., Youssef, A. M., & Pradhan, B. (2019). Multi-hazard assessment modeling via multi-criteria analysis and GIS: A case study. *Environmental Earth Sciences*, *78*(2), 47. https://doi.org/10.1007/s12665-018-8003-4

Tehrany, M. S., Pradhan, B., & Jebur, M. N. (2014). Flood susceptibility mapping using a novel ensemble weights-of-evidence and support vector machine models in GIS. *Journal of Hydrology*, *512*(C), 332–343. https://doi.org/10.1016/j.jhydrol.2014.03.008

Tran, P., Shaw, R., Chantry, G., & Norton, J. (2009). GIS and local knowledge in disaster management: A case study of flood risk mapping in Viet Nam. *Disasters*, *33*(1), 152–169. https://doi.org/10.1111/j.1467-7717.2008.01067.x

Uddin, Kabir, D. R. G., Giriraj, A., & Shrestha, B. (2013. Application of remote sensing and GIS for flood hazard management: A case study from Sindh Province, Pakistan. *American Journal of Geographic Information System*, *2*(1), 1–5.

Villagra, P., Herrmann, M. G., Quintana, C., & Sepúlveda, R. D. (2017). Community resilience to tsunamis along the Southeastern Pacific: A multivariate approach incorporating physical, environmental, and social indicators. *Natural Hazards*, *88*(2), 1087–1111. https://doi.org/10.1007/s11069-017-2908-1

Wang, Y., & Taylor, J. (2018). Coupling sentiment and human mobility in natural disasters: A Twitter-based study of the 2014 South Napa Earthquake. *Journal of the International Society for the Prevention and Mitigation of Natural Hazards*, *92*(2), 907–925. https://doi.org/10.1007/s11069-018-3231-1

Waring, S., Zakos-Feliberti, A., Wood, R., Stone, M., Padgett, P., & Arafat, R. (2005). The utility of geographic information systems (GIS) in rapid epidemiological assessments following weather-related disasters: Methodological issues based on the tropical Storm Allison experience. *International Journal of Hygiene and Environmental Health*, *208*(1), 109–116. https://doi.org/10.1016/j.ijheh.2005.01.020

Werren, G., Reynard, E., Lane, S. N., & Balin, D. (2016). Flood hazard assessment and mapping in semi-arid piedmont areas: A case study in Beni Mellal, Morocco. *Natural Hazards*, *81*(1), 481–511. https://doi.org/10.1007/s11069-015-2092-0

Zerger, A. (2002). Examining GIS decision utility for natural hazard risk modelling. *Environmental Modelling and Software*, *17*(3), 287–294.

Zerger, A., & Smith, D. I. (2003). Impediments to using GIS for real-time disaster decision support. *Computers, Environment and Urban Systems*, *27*(2), 123–141.

Zope, P. E., Eldho, T. I., & Jothiprakash, V. (2017). Hydrological impacts of land use-land cover change and detention basins on urban flood hazard: A case study of Poisar River basin, Mumbai, India. *Natural Hazards*, *87*(3), 1267–1283. https://doi.org/10.1007/s11069-017-2816-4

Understanding Disasters

Questions Should Drive Methods and Other Interdisciplinary Lessons

Virgil Henry Storr and Stefanie Haeffele

Introduction

Shortly after Hurricane Katrina destroyed so many lives and damaged so much property throughout the Gulf Coast, our colleague Peter J. Boettke launched a multi-year study to understand how the affected communities bounced back, if they did, or what prevented recovery if communities failed to do so.[1] What Boettke understood then, and what all disaster studies scholars quickly come to appreciate – which is also reflected in many chapters of this book – is that understanding disasters requires relying on theories from multiple disciplines and deploying multiple empirical strategies. The team of researchers Boettke put together thus utilized qualitative and quantitative methods and relied on concepts from economics, sociology, political science, and urban studies. While no individual study needs to be an interdisciplinary effort utilizing mixed methods, disaster studies as a field must be multidisciplinary and multi-method. Using research on the role of social capital and social entrepreneurship in promoting disaster recovery, this chapter explores the importance of disaster studies relying on multiple disciplines and empirical techniques.

Disasters are complex phenomena. The interplay of natural and man-made factors makes it difficult to anticipate exactly which individuals and how communities will be impacted by disasters and to discern the full range of economic, social, and political effects of disasters. As such, understanding disasters is a challenge. Because disasters can affect the economic, political, social, and cultural components of daily life, efforts to prepare for, respond to, and recover from disasters are not conducted in a vacuum. For instance, individuals, organizations, communities, and governments must figure out exactly what to spend their time and resources on as they try to prevent, mitigate, and respond to the negative impact of potential disasters. Similarly, disaster recovery can be difficult. Individuals and their families may be dispersed and must deal with not only the physical but emotional and mental impacts of surviving disasters. Businesses may be damaged or closed for an extended period of time, leaving both employers and employees uncertain about their futures. Even if businesses reopen, it is uncertain that customers will return and demand the same goods and services as before. Likewise, churches need parishioners and pastors and schools need students and teachers to return to normalcy. But there will be no students if parents do not rebuild their homes, return to their jobs, and further re-establish their lives.

Indeed, disaster recovery represents a collective action problem (Storr, Haeffele-Balch, & Grube, 2015). When faced with the challenge of deciding to return and rebuild after a disaster, citizens, entrepreneurs, community leaders, and political officials alike face uncertainty. The costs of rebuilding are considerable, yet the benefits are unclear and dependent on others returning as well. In the post-disaster context, when people are dispersed, communication networks disrupted, and damage widespread, the knowledge needed to assess the situation and make decisions based on the expectations of others is hampered. Given these real challenges, it is rational for people to wait for others before deciding whether to recover or start over somewhere new. Yet, communities engage in recovery all the time. Disaster studies must understand how recovery occurs despite how difficult it often is.

Further, disasters such as hurricanes are powerful natural phenomena that may be exacerbated by man-made issues like the human impact on the climate and neglected infrastructure. For instance, it was not just Hurricane Katrina's Category 5–strength rains and winds that devastated New Orleans, Louisiana, in 2005, but the failure of levees to hold back rising water that flooded the city. It can be difficult to fully disentangle the harms caused by nature from those caused by human error, even though such complications may have implications for which parties should fund reconstruction or if compensation is owed to harmed residents. Despite how difficult it is to isolate the causes of disasters and to identify how human factors are exacerbating the levels of disaster damage, disaster studies must sort out these factors and inform strategies for mitigating the effects of disasters.

Arguably, understanding how disasters affect individuals and communities, how vulnerable individuals and communities prepare for disasters, and how disaster survivors and affected communities recover from disasters is more critical now than ever. Disasters are increasingly affecting individuals and societies across the globe. In an ever-connected world facing global issues like climate change, disasters have increased in frequency and result in higher damage costs. Additionally, population growth has increased the number of people affected by disasters, and increased and improved reporting practices have made us more aware of the impact of recent disasters (Strömberg, 2007). According to the Centre for Research on the Epidemiology of Disaster (CRED), the number of disasters worldwide went from 24 in 1950 to 296 in 1990 and to 528 in 2000.[2] In the past decade, the average number of disasters was 354 per year, resulting in an average of 68,273 fatalities, 210 million people impacted, and $141 billion in damages (Below & Wallemacq, 2018, p. 2). While 2017 saw fewer disasters (335) and fatalities (9,697) than average, it also saw increased costs of $335 billion (Below & Wallemacq, 2018, p. 2).[3]

While wealthier and more developed nations incur higher costs for rebuilding and repairing damaged infrastructure, buildings, and goods, they also face fewer fatalities due to better institutions and infrastructure (Kahn, 2005). However, marginalized populations within societies – such as minority and low-income households – are often adversely impacted by disasters due to a lack of resources and social and political support needed for recovery (see Fothergill, 1996; Norris, Perilla, Riad, Kaniasty, & Lavizzo, 1999; Blanchard-Boehm, 1998; Peacock, 2003; Phillips, Metz, & Nieves, 2005; Fothergill & Peek, 2004; Rivera & Miller, 2010; Thomas, Phillips, Lovekamp,

& Fothergill, 2013). How particular individuals and groups are affected by disaster may vary from the overarching trends.

As pointed out in the introduction of this book, due to the increased frequency and scale of recent disasters, efforts to understand disasters are not only more urgent now than ever, but they must pursue mixed methods if they are to yield insight on the key questions in this area. What are the challenges and barriers to recovering from disasters? When is it beneficial for survivors to move and start anew elsewhere? What individuals, activities, and organizations are critical for recovery? What makes resilient communities? What is the role of individuals, communities, and governments in leading, funding, or discouraging rebuilding? These questions are inherently interdisciplinary and require investigations on the ground and an appreciation of the contextual rules, norms, and institutions that guide action (see also Dahlberg, Rubin, & Vendelø, 2015). They require micro- and macro-level analysis to understand how individuals, groups, and governments act after disasters, the patterns of successful and unsuccessful recovery, and the need for reform that better enables resilience.

As a consequence, the field of disaster studies crosses disciplines and methods and includes academics and practitioners. Sociologists, political scientists, and economists join public administration, emergency management, and meteorology to conduct fieldwork, surveys, statistical analysis, and formal modeling. Conferences are held within and across disciplines. Research is combined with practice, resulting in lessons learned and suggestions for reform. As pointed out in Chapter 5, in many ways, the field of disaster studies is a ripe example of an interdisciplinary and mixed-methods approach. Yet, like much of academia, individual scholars often stay within their disciplinary silos and attached to particular methods. For example, the 2019 Natural Hazards Workshop featured several sessions on collaboration that discussed the benefits and challenges of conducting truly collaborative projects.

Amy R. Poteete, Marco A. Janssen, and Elinor Ostrom (2010) saw a similar trend in the field of natural resource management and common pool resources, and in their book they discuss the potential and challenges of mixed methods and collaboration between scholars pursuing different methods. In this chapter, we utilize their framework to argue that disaster studies benefit from mixed methods and collaboration. The questions central to understanding disasters and how communities recover from them drives the need for a variety of methods, formal to informal and quantitative to qualitative.

The chapter proceeds as follows. The next section summarizes the position of Poteete et al. (2010) and applies their approach to disaster studies. We then specifically discuss qualitative and quantitative research methods, highlighting key research that engage these methods and offering lessons from our personal experiences using these methods. Finally, we conclude with a discussion of the benefits of marrying qualitative and quantitative methods in disaster studies and the areas of future research.

An Interdisciplinary and Multiple-method Approach

Poteete et al. (2010) reflect on their own experiences as scholars from different disciplines who conduct collaborative research on natural resource management and common pool resources. They assess the evolution of the literature as well as the methodological debates and career incentives within academia, which tend to favor specialized research by a single author.

The various strengths and weaknesses of methods have been heavily debated within academia. Also, the use of poor research practices has been heavily criticized, as they should be. As a result, however, "Critics sometimes conflate methodological practice with the method itself, arguing that examples of poor application discredit the method," and "others fail to appreciate that research goals are varied and require diverse methods" (Poteete et al., 2010, p. 4). Scholars may, for example, dismiss case studies and interviews because of their small sample sizes that weaken their ability to lead to general assessments and predictions, whereas others may dismiss big data analysis for its inability to tease out the nuances of local context. Still, others see embracing mixed methods as the way around the weaknesses of any given methodological approach (see Chapter 5). "To overcome the limits of any one method, one needs to draw on multiple methods," Poteete et al. (2010, p. 5) summarize, "rigorous research that combines complementary methods will be superior to research that relies on any single method" (see Tarrow, 2004; Lieberman, 2005; Gray, Williamson, Karp, & Dalphin, 2007). Poteete et al. (2010) follow in this tradition while also discussing the challenges and practical suitability of a multiple-method approach.

Their emphasis is an inherently practical one. Many of the important questions worthy of academic research are complex, contextual, and lack readily available data. As they note:

> We are particularly concerned with research on topics for which data are scarce, difficult to collect, and not readily comparable. These conditions affect research on a wide variety of topics, including those concerned with informal institutions, subnational organizations, and nonelite populations.
>
> (Poteete et al., 2010, p. 5)

In these scenarios, researchers often need to obtain contextual knowledge through fieldwork and collect their own data in order to understand the phenomena. While scholars should not dismiss these questions for ones that have more accessible data, they also cannot deny the challenges faced by undertaking this sort of research. Poteete et al. (2010) state:

> As many others have argued, scholars *should* start with a research question and then select methods that match their research goals and their ontological assumptions about causality. Mismatches between ideal and actual methodological practices occur however. . . . Practical considerations often make it difficult-to-impossible to implement the ideal research design, even when scholars are very aware of what they should do.
>
> (p. xxii–xxiii)

Questions, they argue, should drive methods. Methods should not drive questions.

A particular challenge to using multiple empirical strategies is the costs of learning and becoming proficient in any given method. Quantitative methods require substantial technical expertise and qualitative methods require extensive time on the ground, observing and understanding the cultural and local contexts, and skills specific to recording, coding, and analyzing data. Thus, most scholars specialize. In the face of such challenges, Poteete et al. (2010) see collaboration as a way of dealing with non-ideal conditions and incorporating multiple methods: "Collaboration offers a potential solution. Scholars with strengths in complementary methods can work together with increased confidence that each method is applied rigorously" (p. 17).

According to Poteete et al. (2010), mixed methods and collaboration have led to empirical and theoretical advancement in the study of commons. Multiple methods were crucial in observing how groups manage natural resources (through fieldwork), highlighting the importance of communication and trust in community-driven action (through experiments), and overturning theories that predicted the persistent overuse of common resources (through formal modeling and agent-based modeling). As Poteete et al. (2010) summarize:

> Research based on field studies, laboratory and field experiments, game theory, and agent-based models has conclusively demonstrated that it is *possible* for individuals to act collectively to manage shared natural resources on a sustainable basis. . . . In response to these findings, theory related to collective action and the commons has evolved considerably. . . . The earlier conventional theory is no longer viewed as the only relevant theory for understanding the commons.
>
> (p. 215)

These results occurred because scholars undertook complex questions, collected their own data, and provided alternative theories that better reflected cooperation in the real world.

The lessons learned from the study of common pool resources and the multiple-method approach advanced by Poteete et al. (2010) are incredibly relevant to disaster studies. As mentioned above, disaster recovery is a collective action problem, like that of managing commonly shared resources (Storr et al., 2015). Disaster survivors must be able to assess the costs and benefits of recovery individually, yet their decisions are linked to the actions of others. If no one else returns and rebuilds, there will not be a community worth living in. If others also return, not only do the benefits of returning increase but the costs of returning might decrease, since others are able to provide resources, share information, and support one another and their endeavors. Also, the probability that additional displaced disaster survivors will return and rebuild increases as more and more community members signal a commitment to recovery. Yet, when people are dispersed and damage is extensive, uncertainty around who will return and when, and how the community may change, is pervasive. It is rational that people would wait and see if others return before committing to recovery themselves. Understanding the specific epistemic challenges that disaster survivors must overcome arguably requires fieldwork and other qualitative empirical strategies. And, understanding how these epistemic challenges have impacted recovery rates and whether or not other factors are driving or limiting recovery arguably requires quantitative empirical strategies.

Individuals, groups, and governments also face additional epistemic limitations. A successful recovery requires that actors (1) access information about the damage on the ground and the resources needed and available for recovery, (2) prioritize and implement response and recovery activities, and (3) adapt to changing circumstances (Sobel & Leeson, 2007; Chamlee-Wright, 2010; Storr et al., 2015). In the post-disaster context, this task becomes more challenging as networks, business supply chains, and public services may be disrupted or destroyed. In such a scenario, the government may be able to act as a leader in recovery, coordinating efforts and utilizing economies of scale of resources and activities (see Pipa, 2006; Tierney, 2007; Springer, 2009; Fakhruddin & Chivakidakarn, 2014; Coppola, 2015).

However, government efforts are not always effective. Governments, particularly centralized federal and state governments that are further removed from the disaster, have difficultly assessing needs, distributing goods and services to those who need it most, and adjusting course when needed (Sobel & Leeson, 2007; Chamlee-Wright, 2010; Storr et al., 2015). State and local governments also face challenges, such as when attempting to develop comprehensive plans that often fail to receive adequate community buy-in and face backlash from residents, resulting in the need to revise or forgo plans after months or even years of effort (see Nelson, Ehrenfeucht, & Laska, 2007; Chamlee-Wright, 2010; Olshansky & Johnson, 2010; Storr et al., 2015). Politics, such as concerns over re-election and partisanship, can also impact disaster recovery performance (Sobel & Leeson, 2006; Schmidtlein, Finch, & Cutter, 2008; Salkowe & Chakraborty, 2009; Reeves, 2011; Husted & Nickerson, 2014). While particular aspects of the limits that disaster survivors and interested parties must overcome in order to spur recovery can be identified and highlighted in individual studies using single methods, understanding these dynamics in any single disaster requires multiple empirical strategies.

Like with common pool resources, scholars have documented how communities have been able to recover through bottom-up efforts. Specifically, a large number of studies now have pointed to the importance of social capital and social networks in allowing disaster survivors to utilize skills dispersed across the community, coordinate recovery, share information, make adjustments, and learn from their experiences (see Bolin & Stanford, 1998; Hurlbert, Haines, & Beggs, 2000; Hurlbert, Beggs, & Haines, 2001; Nakagawa & Shaw, 2004; Shaw & Goda, 2004; Paton, 2007; Chamlee-Wright, 2010; Hawkins & Maurer, 2010; Aldrich, 2012a; Burton, 2014; Storr et al., 2015; Storr, Haeffele-Balch, & Grube, 2017; Rivera, 2017, 2018). A growing number of studies have also pointed to the importance of social entrepreneurs in driving recovery (Kaufman, Avgar, & Mirsky, 2007; Chamlee-Wright, 2010; Chamlee-Wright & Storr, 2010a, 2011b; Aldrich, 2012a, 2012b; Storr et al., 2015, 2017; Carlton & Mills, 2017). These studies have been qualitive and quantitative, have relied on archival and contemporary, official and unofficial, existing and developed data sources, and have proceeded both independently and in a collaborative fashion.

As illustrated throughout this book, the disaster studies literature has challenged previous theoretical stances and shows the creative use of multiple methods and novel data collection. Disaster studies necessarily focuses on situations that deal with informal institutions, local governments, and non-elite populations – the types of topics that Poteete et al. (2010) are concerned with for their scarce and difficult data. Indeed, recovery is impacted by formal institutions (such as government and the rule of law) and informal institutions (such as culture and norms) at the community, state, and national levels. Moreover, disasters affect all members of society, ranging from children and the poor to business owners and politicians. And unfortunately, certain individuals and groups are better positioned to recover than others. The remainder of this chapter looks at the use of qualitative and quantitative methods in disaster studies, focusing on our experiences using these methods and highlighting some of the key advances using these methods in the literature. The ability of disaster studies to continue to make headway in our understanding of these difficult problems is the continued openness of the field to multiple empirical strategies and the continued willingness of scholars in the field to pursue mixed methods and collaborations between practitioners of multiple empirical strategies as their questions demand.

Qualitative Methods Advance Understanding

Qualitative methods help advance our understanding of *how* communities respond to and recover from disasters. Going into the archives to locate details on past disasters and going into the field to observe and to conduct interviews and surveys on recent disasters allows for scholars to better understand the local context, norms, and culture, the specific challenges and capabilities, and how individuals and groups act within the community. In other words, these methods offer thick descriptions of disaster recovery (Ryle, 1971; Boettke, Haeffele-Balch, & Storr, 2016). In Box 19.1, we reflect on our humbling and inspiring experiences in the field talking to and learning from disaster survivors.

Emily Chamlee-Wright (2010, pp. 27–30) uses an analogy of a puzzle to explain the benefits of going into the field and going after thick descriptions. We can think of studying social interaction as putting together a puzzle. Scholars can observe the pieces from above, examining each individual component as well as the overall picture. Social interaction is impacted by external shocks like disasters, just like a puzzle on a table that falls to the floor when the table is bumped. But rather than a simple puzzle with a clear picture to work from, real-life social interaction is a puzzle with a large number of small pieces, with some pieces missing, some extra pieces from other puzzles thrown into the mix, and no clear blueprint. Rather than being two-dimensional, this puzzle is three-dimensional, and the pieces are able to move and adapt on their own. And, rather than being a puzzle that can fit on a kitchen table, it is much larger and cannot be fully seen from above. Instead, scholars must be able to climb into the puzzle, walk around, and talk to the pieces in order to get a better sense of what is going on. To really understand *how* social interaction takes place, scholars may need to get on the ground rather than just take an aerial-view approach to studying human interaction (Chamlee-Wright, 2010).

Further, Chamlee-Wright argues that scholars should not just get on the ground to observe and survey residents to collect information from participants that they do not have access to otherwise, but also to conduct in-depth interviews. As she states, "Interviews help us get at not only the information that subjects possess that the researchers do not, but interviews also provide access to that interior life that frames problems in particular ways" (Chamlee-Wright, 2010, p. 30). This interior view gets at the mental models that individuals and groups utilize to motivate their activities and overcome challenges. Further, interviews allow for scholars to learn about creative situations and discover new insights that they could not have anticipated without talking to participants (Chamlee-Wright, 2010). This is helpful for understanding the situation and being able to identify the next steps in a research program. While providing useful insights into the disaster recovery process, as Poteete et al. (2010) put it, "qualitative field-based research is [also] necessary to simply identify relevant cases for analysis" (p. 24) and provide a foundation for future research.

BOX 19.1 FIELDWORK AS SCHOLARS AND AS HUMANS

As Poteete et al. (2010) note when talking about the skills needed to conduct qualitative work, "Many of these techniques require a substantial period of fieldwork, keen observation skills, thorough record keeping, and a high degree of self-awareness and ethical management of social relations" (p. 16). In other words, when conducting interviews in the disaster context, we need to remember that we and the survivors being interviewed are human, have emotions, and should be treated with professionalism and kindness. We need to find the balance of making sure our questions are answered, keeping a professional distance, and making sure interviewees feel safe and comfortable. Because of this, conducting such interviews takes its toll while in the field. In our experience, this is another area where collaboration matters. An interview team that is cognizant of the challenges in conducting fieldwork and works together to fulfill the roles of researcher, observer, and fellow human will be better able to navigate the logistical, analytical, and emotional demands of the method.

Conducting interviews with disaster survivors is a humbling experience. Our interview instrument asks disaster survivors about what their communities and lives were like before the disaster, their disaster stories, and the details of their recovery efforts. Survivors recall what can be one of the most challenging times in their lives, a time when they may have evacuated and were separated from family and friends, or a time when they waited out the storm and needed to help rescue neighbors or be rescued themselves. In retelling their stories, we ask them to relive the fear, injury, and loss of loved ones and belongings. We also ask them to relive the strength, determination, and persistence that enabled them to return and rebuild their communities or to start fresh somewhere new. We learn about the people and organizations that helped them get access to resources, information, and goods and services, and that provided emotional support during the difficult times. We learn about the people and organizations that hampered recovery, who had to be persuaded or ignored or challenged. And, we learn about their hopes and dreams for the future of their communities. We also learn about ourselves. In some interviews, the horrors being described and the story of triumph are so moving that we have been overwhelmed by tears. In some interviews, the descriptions of the heroic action of some figure has been so awe-inspiring or the failures of some institution have been so maddening that even a veneer of impartiality is impossible to maintain.

We will forever be grateful for the hundreds of disaster survivors who shared their stories with us as well as our colleagues and graduate students who have been with us in the field. We have undoubtedly grown as scholars and humans by being a part of the interview process.

The scholars at the Mercatus Center at George Mason University, led by our colleague Peter J. Boettke, have embraced this view of studying disaster recovery and engaged in fieldwork after Hurricanes Katrina and Sandy. The project began as a 5-year study that looked at the economic, political, and social factors of the rebuilding and recovery efforts following Hurricane Katrina. The hurricane hit the Gulf Coast region in August 2005, with New Orleans, Louisiana, suffering the worst damage. Eighty percent of the city flooded, 70% of the housing units were damaged or destroyed, and approximately 600,000 residents were still displaced a month after the storm.[4] Scholars and graduate students interviewed hundreds of disaster survivors. Specifically, there were over 300 interviews conducted in the greater New Orleans area and over 50 interviews conducted in Houston, Texas, with survivors who had chosen not to return to New Orleans. Later, a smaller research team conducted 16 interviews in Bayswater, a neighborhood on the Rockaway Peninsula in Queens, New York, following Hurricane Sandy. Hurricane Sandy, which devasted the northeast coast of the United States in 2012, caused 73 deaths in the United States, damaged or destroyed over 37,000 primary residences, and resulted in $60 billion in damages.[5]

These two storms devasted communities from distinct parts of the country. Recovery was uneven and survivors faced unique challenges in different neighborhoods across the impacted areas. Yet, scholars have found similar patterns, challenges, and capabilities in both scenarios. A key conclusion of these studies is the importance of social capital (Chamlee-Wright & Storr, 2009, 2010a, 2011b; Chamlee-Wright, 2010; Storr & Haeffele-Balch, 2012; Storr et al., 2015, 2017). Our fieldwork has shown that communities can utilize their social ties, local expertise, and ingenuity to rebound from disaster. For instance, Chamlee-Wright and Storr (2009) finds that the members of the Mary Queen of Vietnam (MQVN) Catholic Church in New Orleans East leveraged the unique bundle of club goods that they had access to through the church to rebuild their community. Similarly, Chamlee-Wright and Storr (2011a) show that social capital in the form of collective narratives is critical in motivating disaster survivors to rebuild and inspiring particular recovery strategies. Specifically, within St. Bernard Parish there was a collective narrative that theirs was a close-knit, family-oriented community comprised of hard workers, which led them to adopt a strategy that emphasized self-reliance after Hurricane Katrina devasted their community. Likewise, Storr and Haeffele-Balch (2012) find that even diverse, loosely connected communities like Broadmoor in New Orleans can find strategies to work together to bring about post-disaster recovery. And, finally, Storr et al. (2015) highlight the various ways that social entrepreneurs like church leaders, heads of community organizations, and others facilitated disaster recovery. Taken together, these studies show social capital, social entrepreneurs, and social enterprises as being key areas of focus for disaster studies.

Quantitative Strategies Advance Understanding

Quantitative methods help answer the *what* questions and assess trends associated with disaster studies. Quantitative empirical strategies offer insights into questions concerning which communities are likely to recovery, whether communities with different demographic makeups are likely to be more vulnerable or resilient in the wake of disasters, and what factors, resources, and non-profit and public aid programs matter most for disaster recovery (see Bolin, 1986; Norris, Perilla, Riad, Kaniasty, & Lavizzo, 1999; Peacock, 2003; Sobel & Leeson, 2006, 2007; Cutter & Finch, 2008; Flanagan, Gregory, Hallisey, Heitgerd, & Lewis, 2011; Khunwishit & McEntire, 2012; Grube, Fike, & Storr, 2018). In Box 19.2, we summarize our experiences incorporating mixed methods into our research and the insights we have gained from quantitative strategies for studying disaster recovery.

Again, think of the puzzle that Chamlee-Wright (2010) invites us to consider. There are alternatives, she notes, to stepping into the complex puzzle that is society and trying to understand it from the inside out using qualitative strategies. Scholars could, for instance, build a model that tries to highlight how the key pieces of the puzzle interact. This might reveal some key factor or factors and be useful in thinking through the dynamics of the phenomenon in question. Conceiving of disaster recovery as a collective action problem, for instance, is a useful frame for understanding why disaster recovery is a challenge but also for how community members might overcome that challenge. In Chamlee-Wright and Storr (2009) and Storr et al. (2015), for instance, a simple game tree is used to highlight the nature of the collective action problem that community members face after a disaster. That social capital can be an important resource post-recovery (Chamlee-Wright & Storr, 2009, 2011a, 2011b; Storr & Haeffele-Balch, 2012; Storr et al., 2015, 2017), and even that the social capital structure can be altered during the recovery process (Storr et al., 2015, 2017), are insights that were clarified with the aid of this simple game theoretic model.

Another strategy for understanding the puzzle might be to "try to carve off a chunk of the puzzle and study it in the lab" (Chamlee-Wright, 2010, p. 28). These social scientific experiments might allow scholars to figure out how the puzzle pieces respond to different stimuli or which strategies are likely to be the most effective in promoting the phenomenon of disaster recovery. This is, arguably, a somewhat underexplored area within disaster studies. That said, Cassar, Healy, and von Kessler (2017) find that disasters can have a long-term impact on risk aversion as well as on prosocial behavior. Similarly, Segal, Jong, and Halberstadt (2018) explore the prosocial attitudes and behavior of subjects who were primed to recall their experiences with a recent disaster. Admittedly, our own efforts along these lines are somewhat nascent, although Storr is working with Alessandro Del Ponte on the spending and saving decisions of disaster survivors in the face of natural disasters, and with Ginny Seung Choi on the effectiveness of different strategies in overcoming the epistemic challenges that plague post-disaster contexts.

BOX 19.2 EMBRACING MIXED METHODS AND COLLABORATION

While our point of introduction into disaster studies was through conducting interviews and extensive case studies of community recovery after Hurricane Katrina, we have ventured into other methods as our research has progressed. First, quantitative analysis allows for a different type of analysis and understanding. Utilizing available data to study broad trends in damage sustained and assistance provided across demographics can underscore lessons learned through fieldwork. For instance, Grube et al. (2018) find that residents who did not have a high school education or who were foreign-born had a harder time receiving FEMA assistance after Hurricane Sandy. This result tracked with lessons from the field, that individuals and groups struggle to get assistance and navigate the system when they lack social capital in lobbying for aid and when they think government is capable of providing aid but will not choose to help their community (Chamlee-Wright & Storr, 2010b, 2011b).

Second, since fieldwork is a time-extensive process, utilizing survey methods have allowed us to ask some of the same questions without having to dedicate as much time in the field. While this is not ideal, it does allow for us to continue to study different disasters and engage in comparative and meta-analysis to distill patterns of recovery across disasters, time, geographic locations, and cultures. As Poteete et al. (2010) admit, "Practical considerations often make it difficult-to-impossible to implement the ideal research design, even when scholars are very aware of what they should do" (p. xxiii). While scholars should strive to have questions drive method, they also should consider the feasible methods for various stages of their research program.

And third, by delving into experimental studies, we are able to explore what we have seen in the field and advance theory that better reflects real-world behavior. With each venture into new methods, we have collaborated with colleagues trained in these methods. Yet, we do not just see collaboration as the way into a multiple-method approach but as an important aspect of any research project. Co-authors, even when trained in the same discipline and methods, bring their unique backgrounds, experiences, and viewpoints to the project. The teams we have worked with have made the process of conducting research more enjoyable, credible, and valuable.

Another strategy that scholars might adopt to understand the dynamics of the puzzle is what Chamlee-Wright (2010) calls the "aerial view." As she explains, empirical strategies that utilize the aerial view "can be a very useful perspective. It helps us to compare, at least in broad terms, the shape and size of our puzzle to other puzzles, and we can compare the aerial views over time" (Chamlee-Wright, 2010, p. 28). A growing body of research has used quantitative strategies (i.e., the aerial view) to highlight the importance of social capital broadly defined and the resources from information to financial resources that individuals can access as a result of their social networks to bring about recovery (see Minamoto, 2010; Aldrich, 2011, 2012a; Islam & Walkerden, 2014; Rivera, 2018). Our quantitative work in this area has built off of our qualitative work, which serves as our foundation for future research as Poteete et al. (2010) recommends. For instance, Chamlee-Wright and Storr (2010a), Storr and Haeffele-Balch (2012), and Storr et al. (2015) have focused on the role of social entrepreneurs in promoting disaster response, highlighting the critical role of social entrepreneurs in providing necessary goods and services, coordinating recovery efforts, and repairing and replacing damaged social networks. Rayamajhee, Storr, and Bohara (2019) look at how the Namuna village project in Giranchaur, Nepal – supported by the Dhurmus Suntali Foundation and led by two Nepali social entrepreneurs – promoted volunteerism, community engagement, and active citizenship following the earthquake in 2015. Similarly, Chamlee-Wright (2010), Chamlee-Wright and Storr (2011b), and Chamlee-Wright, Haeffele-Balch, and Storr (2017) documented the challenges that community members faced as they tried to negotiate the federal bureaucracy in order to obtain resources for recovery. Motivated by this insight, Grube et al. (2018) find those without high school diplomas and those who were foreign-born – arguably the most disadvantaged – were least likely to receive federal aid. In concert with the qualitative studies in this area, these quantitative studies help to offer a fuller image of disaster recovery.

Conclusion

Disaster studies examines complex social interaction. The field focuses on how communities and governments respond to and rebound after disasters hit as well as how to learn from past disasters, mitigate against future disasters, and foster resilience. As illustrated throughout this entire volume, scholars study how individuals, groups, and organizations find ways to return to normalcy after facing major devastations. Scholars from a variety of disciplines and using a variety of methods look at the *what* and *how* after disasters. Quantitative and qualitative methods have been crucial to these efforts.

Like Poteete et al. (2010), we believe that all methods have their place in social science, and especially within disaster studies. The field, if it is to remain vibrant, must embrace multiple disciplines and multiple methods. Quantitative and qualitative methods provide data and insight into how real-world disaster recovery takes place and the challenges and capabilities of community-based and government responses, and impact theories of disaster recovery and social interaction more generally.

As also pointed out in Chapter 16, one method that should arguably be embraced more is experiments that further examine the hypotheses and results discovered in the field. Poteete et al. (2010, p. 142) argue that "the main goal of experiments is to test well-defined hypotheses under controlled conditions or to study the effects of variables for which theory may be less explicit." Further, "Experimental studies regularly contradict expectations from formal models based on behavioral assumptions of individual utility maximization of material returns. The inconsistency between formal theory and experimental evidence accelerated the search for alternative behavioral models that can explain observed experiments results" (Poteete et al., 2010, p. 141).

Where the theory of collective action predicts that disaster survivors will take a "wait and see" approach to recovery, going into the field has shown how communities recover after every disaster (Chamlee-Wright & Storr, 2009; Storr et al., 2015). Local entrepreneurs signal to others in their community that recovery is desired by others (Storr et al., 2015). While government can provide resources and coordinate recovery, they also suffer from challenges that can slow or hamper recovery. Experimental studies can, for example, explore individuals' likelihood to pursue recovery when conventional theories suggest they will wait, explore the role of collective narrative in motivating decision-making, and the role of social ties in solving collective action problems.

As previously pointed out throughout this volume, embracing multiple methods, while crucial to advancing the field, can be challenging for any given scholar. However, collaboration provides for a way to engage multiple empirical strategies without compromising quality or stretching skill sets. By collaborating with colleagues that specialize in quantitative or experimental methods, we have been able to expand our research and further explore the results we discovered in the field. Like Poteete et al. (2010), we recommend other scholars engage in collaboration as well.

Notes

1. See more on the project here: www.communityrevival.us/blog.
2. Available online at www.emdat.be.
3. Research using CRED data has seen a similar increase in man-made disasters along with a trend of reduced fatalities (Coleman, 2006).
4. This data is from the Data Center (formerly the Greater New Orleans Community Data Center), available online at www.datacenterresearch.org/data-resources/katrina/facts-for-impact/.
5. These figures are available online at www.fema.gov/sandy-recovery-office and www.fema.gov/news-release/2013/10/25/year-after-hurricane-sandy-new-jersey-recovery-numbers.

Further Readings

Aligica, P.D., Boettke, P.J., & Tarko, V. (2019). *Public governance and the classical-liberal perspective: Political economy foundations.* New York: Oxford University Press.

Coyne, C.J. (2013). *Doing bad by doing good: Why humanitarian action fails.* Stanford, CA: Stanford University Press.

Lavoie, D., & Chamlee-Wright, E. (2000). *Culture and enterprise: The development, representation and morality of business.* New York: Routledge.

Mill, J.S. ([1848] 1885). *Principles of political economy.* New York: D. Appleton.

Ostrom, E. (1990). *Governing the commons: The evolution of institutions for collective action.* Cambridge: Cambridge University Press.

Storr, N.M., Chamlee-Wright, E., & Storr, V.H. (2015). *How we came back: Voices from post-Katrina New Orleans.* Arlington, VA: Mercatus Center at George Mason University.

Storr, V.H. (2012). *Understanding the culture of markets.* New York: Routledge.

References

Aldrich, D. P. (2011). The power of people: Social capital's role in recovery from the 1995 Kobe earthquake. *Natural Hazards, 56*(3), 595–611.

Aldrich, D. P. (2012a). *Building resilience social capital in post-disaster recovery.* Chicago: University of Chicago Press.

Aldrich, D. P. (2012b). Social, not physical, infrastructure: The critical role of civil society after the 1923 Tokyo earthquake. *Disasters, 36*(3), 398–419.

Below, R., & Wallemacq, P. (2018). *Annual disaster statistical review 2017.* Brussels, Belgium: Centre for Research on Epidemiology of Disasters (CRED). http:// www.emdat.be/ annual-disaster-statistical-review-2017

Blanchard-Boehm, R. D. (1998). Understanding public response to increased risk from natural hazards: Application of the hazards risk communication framework. *International Journal of Mass Emergencies and Disasters, 16*(3), 247–278.

Boettke, P. J., Haeffele-Balch, S., & Storr, V. H. (Eds.). (2016). *Mainline economics: Six Nobel lectures in the tradition of Adam Smith.* Arlington, VA: Mercatus Center at George Mason University.

Bolin, R. C. (1986). Disaster impact and recovery: A comparison of black and white victims. *International Journal of Mass Emergencies and Disasters, 4*(1), 35–50.

Bolin, R. C., & Stanford, L. (1998). The Northridge earthquake: Community-based approaches to unmet recovery needs. *Disasters, 22*(1), 21–38.

Burton, C. G. (2014). A validation of metrics for community resilience to natural hazards and disasters using the recovery from Hurricane Katrina as a case study. *Annals of the Association of American Geographers, 105*(1), 67–86.

Carlton, S., & Mills, C. E. (2017). The student volunteer army: A "repeat emergent" emergency response organisation. *Disasters, 41*(4), 764–787.

Cassar, A., Healy, A., & von Kessler, C. (2017). Trust, risk, and time preferences after a natural disaster: Experimental evidence from Thailand. *World Development, 94*, 90–105.

Chamlee-Wright, E. (2010). *The cultural and political economy of recovery.* New York: Routledge.

Chamlee-Wright, E., Haeffele-Balch, S., & Storr, V. H. (2017). Local recovery: How robust community rebound necessarily comes from the bottom up. In A. Lepore (Ed.), *The future of disaster management in the us: Rethinking legislation, policy, and finance.* New York: Routledge.

Chamlee-Wright, E., & Storr, V. H. (2009). Club goods and post-disaster community return. *Rationality and Society, 21*(4), 429–458.

Chamlee-Wright, E., & Storr, V. H. (2010a). The role of social entrepreneurship in post-Katrina recovery. *International Journal of Innovation and Regional Development, 2*(1/2), 149–164.

Chamlee-Wright, E., & Storr, V. H. (2010b). Expectations of government's response to disaster. *Public Choice, 144*(1–2), 253–274.

Chamlee-Wright, E., & Storr, V. H. (2011a). Social capital as collective narratives and post-disaster community recovery. *Sociological Review, 59*(2), 266–282.

Chamlee-Wright, E., & Storr, V. H. (2011b). Social capital, lobbying and community-based interest groups. *Public Choice, 149*, 167–185.

Coleman, L. (2006). Frequency of man-made disasters in the 20th century. *Journal of Contingencies and Crisis Management, 14*(1), 3–11.

Coppola, D. (2015). *Introduction to international disaster management.* Oxford: Elsevier.

Cutter, S. L., & Finch, C. (2008). Temporal and spatial changes in social vulnerability to natural hazards. *Proceedings of the National Academy of Sciences of the United States of America (PNAS), 105*(7), 2301–2306.

Dahlberg, R., Rubin, O., & Vendelø, M. T. (2015). *Disaster research: Multidisciplinary and international perspectives.* London: Routledge.

Fakhruddin, S. H. M., & Chivakidakarn, Y. (2014). A case study for early warning and disaster management in Thailand. *International Journal of Disaster Risk Reduction, 9*, 159–180.

Flanagan, B. E., Gregory, E. W., Hallisey, E. J., Heitgerd, J. L., & Lewis, B. (2011). A social vulnerability index for disaster management. *Journal of Homeland Security and Emergency Management, 8*(1), Article 3.

Fothergill, A. (1996). Gender, risk, and disaster. *International Journal of Mass Emergencies and Disasters*, *14*(1), 33–56.

Fothergill, A., & Peek, L. (2004). Poverty and disasters in the United States: A review of recent sociological findings. *Natural Hazards*, *32*(1), 89–110.

Gray, P., Williamson, J., Karp, D., & Dalphin, J. (2007). *The research imagination: An introduction to qualitative and quantitative methods.* New York: Cambridge University Press.

Grube, L.E., Fike, R., & Storr, V.H. (2018). Navigating disaster: An empirical study of federal assistance following Hurricane Sandy. *Eastern Economic Journal*, *44*(4), 576–593.

Hawkins, R.L., & Maurer, K. (2010). Bonding, bridging and linking: How social capital operated in New Orleans following Hurricane Katrina. *British Journal of Social Work*, *40*(6), 1777–1793.

Hurlbert, J., Beggs, J., & Haines, V. (2001). Social capital in extreme environments. In N. Lin, K. Cook, & R. Burt (Eds.), *Social capital: Theory and research.* New York: Aldine De Gruyter.

Hurlbert, J., Haines, V., & Beggs, J. (2000). Core networks and tie activation: What kinds of routine networks allocate resources in nonroutine situations? *American Sociological Review*, *65*(4), 598–618.

Husted, T., & Nickerson, D. (2014). Political economy of presidential disaster declarations and federal disaster assistance. *Public Finance Review*, *42*(1), 35–57.

Islam, R., & Walkerden, G. (2014). How bonding and bridging networks contribute to disaster resilience and recovery on the Bangladeshi coast. *International Journal of Disaster Risk Reduction*, *10*, 281–291.

Kahn, M.E. (2005). The death toll from natural disasters: The role of income, geography, and institutions. *Review of Economics and Statistics*, *87*(2), 271–284.

Kaufman, R., Avgar, A., & Mirsky, J. (2007). Social entrepreneurship in crisis situations. *International Journal of Diversity in Organisations, Communities and Nations*, *7*(3), 227–232.

Khunwishit, S., & McEntire, D.A. (2012). Testing social vulnerability theory: A quantitative study of Hurricane Katrina's perceived impact on residents living in FEMA-designated disaster areas. *Journal of Homeland Security and Emergency Management*, *9*(1), Article 13.

Lieberman, E.S. (2005). Nested analysis as a mixed-method strategy for comparative research. *American Political Science Review*, *99*(3), 435–452.

Nakagawa, Y., & Shaw, R. (2004). Social capital: A missing link to disaster recovery. *International Journal of Mass Emergencies and Disasters*, *22*(1), 5–34.

Nelson, M., Ehrenfeucht, R., & Laska, S. (2007). Planning, plans, and people: Professional expertise, local knowledge, and governmental action in post-Hurricane Katrina New Orleans. *Cityscape*, *9*(3), 23–52.

Norris, F.H., Perilla, J.L., Riad, J.K., Kaniasty, K., & Lavizzo, E.A. (1999). Stability and change in stress, resources, and psychological distress following natural disaster: Findings from Hurricane Andrew. *Anxiety, Stress and Coping*, *12*(4), 363–396.

Olshansky, R.B., & Johnson, L. (2010). *Clear as mud: Planning for the rebuilding of New Orleans.* New York: Routledge.

Paton, D. (2007). Preparing for natural hazards: The role of community trust. *Disaster Prevention and Management: An International Journal*, *16*(3), 370–379.

Peacock, W.G. (2003). Hurricane mitigation status and factors influencing mitigation status among Florida's single-family homeowners. *Natural Hazards Review*, *4*(3), 149–158.

Phillips, B.D., Metz, W.C., & Nieves, L.A. (2005). Disaster threat: Preparedness and potential response of the lowest income quartile. *Global Environmental Change Part B: Environmental Hazards*, *6*(3), 123–133.

Pipa, T. (2006). Weathering the storm: The role of local nonprofits in the Hurricane Katrina relief effort. In *Nonprofit sector research fund.* Washington, DC: Aspen Institute.

Poteete, A.R., Janssen, M.A., & Ostrom, E. (2010). *Working together: Collective action, the commons, and multiple methods in practice.* Princeton, NJ: Princeton University Press.

Rayamajhee, V., Storr, V.H., & Bohara, A.K. (2020). Social entrepreneurship, co-production, and post-disaster recovery. *Disasters.* https://doi.org/10.1111/disa.12454

Reeves, A. (2011). Political disaster: Unilateral powers, electoral incentives, and presidential disaster declarations. *Journal of Politics, 73*(4), 1142–1151.

Rivera, J. D. (2017). Accessing disaster recovery resource information: Reliance on social capital in the aftermath of hurricane sandy. In M. Companion & M. Chaiken (Eds.), *Responses to disasters and climate change: Understanding vulnerability and fostering resilience* (pp. 60–70). Boca Raton, FL: CRC Press.

Rivera, J. D. (2018). Reliance on faith-based organizations for tangible assistance in times of disaster: Exploring the influence of bonding social capital. *Sociological Spectrum, 38*(1), 39–50.

Rivera, J. D., & Miller, D. S. (Eds.). (2010). *How ethnically marginalized Americans cope with catastrophic disasters: Studies in suffering and resiliency.* Lewiston, NY: Edwin Mellen Press.

Ryle, G. (1971). *Collected papers, vol. 2, collected essays 1929–1968.* London: Hutchinson.

Salkowe, R. S., & Chakraborty, J. (2009). Federal disaster relief in the U.S.: The role of political partisanship and preference in presidential disaster declarations and turndowns. *Journal of Homeland Security and Emergency Management, 6*(1), Article 28.

Schmidtlein, M. C., Finch, C., & Cutter, S. L. (2008). Disaster declarations and major hazard occurrences in the United States. *Professional Geographer, 60*(1), 1–14.

Segal, K., Jong, J., & Halberstadt, J. (2018). The fusing power of natural disasters: An experimental study. *Self and Identity, 17*(5), 574–586.

Shaw, R., & Goda, K. (2004). From disaster to sustainable civil society: The Kobe experience. *Disasters, 28*(1), 16–40.

Sobel, R. S., & Leeson, P. T. (2006). Government's response to Hurricane Katrina: A public choice analysis. *Public Choice, 127*(1–2), 55–73.

Sobel, R. S., & Leeson, P. T. (2007). The use of knowledge in natural-disaster relief management. *Independent Review, 11*(4), 519–532.

Springer, C. G. (2009). Emergency managers as change agents. *Ideas from an Emerging Field: Teaching Emergency Management in Higher Education, 12*(1), 197–211.

Storr, V. H., & Haeffele-Balch, S. (2012). Post-disaster community recovery in heterogeneous, loosely connected communities. *Review of Social Economy, 70*(3), 295–314.

Storr, V. H., Haeffele-Balch, S., & Grube, L. E. (2015). *Community revival in the wake of disaster: Lessons in local entrepreneurship.* New York: Palgrave Macmillan.

Storr, V. H., Haeffele-Balch, S., & Grube, L. E. (2017). Social capital and social learning after Hurricane Sandy. *Review of Austrian Economics, 30*(4), 447–467.

Strömberg, D. (2007). Natural disasters, economic development, and humanitarian aid. *Journal of Economic Perspectives, 21*(3), 199–222.

Tarrow, S. (2004). Bridging the quantitative-qualitative divide. In H. E. Brady & D. Collier (Eds.), *Rethinking social inquiry: Diverse tools, shared standards* (pp. 171–179). Lanham, MD: Rowman & Littlefield.

Thomas, D. S. K., Phillips, B. D., Lovekamp, W. E., & Fothergill, A. (Eds.). (2013). *Social vulnerability to disasters* (2nd ed.). Boca Raton, FL: CRC Press and Taylor & Francis.

Tierney, K. J. (2007). Testimony on needed emergency management reforms. *Journal of Homeland Security and Emergency Management, 4*(3), 15.

Index